The History of The Decline and Fall of the Roman Empire by Edward Gibbon

Volume II (of VI)

For decades, perhaps centuries, the standard work of reference on Roman History has been courtesy of Edward Gibbon. In its original printing it was a best-seller and a publishing sensation. History was brought to the masses in vivid detail.

Within its massive six volumes Gibbon put into context the entire sweep of this huge and complex Empire. We visit its far-flung regions, its most charismatic characters as we travel through centuries of its existence and its eternal influence on Western and, most probably, World culture.

Considering the times and the resources at his disposal it quite incredible what Gibbon has been able to put together, to distil, to formulate and precisely plot in this most seducing of histories.

Index of Contents
CHAPTER XVI - Conduct Towards the Christians, From Nero To Constantine
CHAPTER XVII - Foundation of Constantinople
CHAPTER XVIII - Character of Constantine And His Sons
CHAPTER XIX - Constantius Sole Emperor
CHAPTER XX - Conversion of Constantine
CHAPTER XXI - Persecution of Heresy, State of The Church
CHAPTER XXII - Julian Declared Emperor
CHAPTER XXIII - Reign of Julian
CHAPTER XXIV - The Retreat And Death Of Julian
CHAPTER XXV - Reigns of Jovian And Valentinian, Division of The Empire
CHAPTER XXVI - Progress of The Huns
Edward Gibbon – A Short Biography
Edward Gibbon – A Concise Bibliography

CHAPTER XVI

CONDUCT TOWARDS THE CHRISTIANS, FROM NERO TO CONSTANTINE

PART I

THE CONDUCT OF THEROMAN GOVERNMENT TOWARDS THE CHRISTIANS, FROM THE REIGN OF NERO TO THAT OF CONSTANTINE [1a]

[Footnote 1a: The sixteenth chapter I cannot help considering as a very ingenious and specious, but very disgraceful extenuation of the cruelties perpetrated by the Roman magistrates against the Christians. It is written in the most contemptibly factious spirit of prejudice against the sufferers; it is unworthy of a philosopher and of humanity. Let the narrative of Cyprian's death be examined. He had to relate the murder of an innocent man of advanced age, and in a station deemed venerable by a considerable body of the provincials of Africa, put to death because he refused to sacrifice to Jupiter. Instead of pointing the *indignation of posterity against such an atrocious act of tyranny, he dwells, with visible art, on the small circumstances of decorum and politeness which attended this murder, and which he relates with as much parade as if they were the most important particulars of the event. Dr. Robertson has been the subject of much blame for his real or supposed lenity towards the Spanish murderers and tyrants in America. That the sixteenth chapter of Mr. G. did not excite the same or greater disapprobation, is a proof of the unphilosophical and indeed fanatical animosity against Christianity, which was so prevalent during the latter part of the eighteenth century—Mackintosh: see Life, i. p. 244, 245.]*

If we seriously consider the purity of the Christian religion, the sanctity of its moral precepts, and the innocent as well as austere lives of the greater number of those who during the first ages embraced the faith of the gospel, we should naturally suppose, that so benevolent a doctrine would have been received with due reverence, even by the unbelieving world; that the learned and the polite, however they may deride the miracles, would have esteemed the virtues, of the new sect; and that the magistrates, instead of persecuting, would have protected an order of men who yielded the most passive obedience to the laws, though they declined the active cares of war and government. If, on the other hand, we recollect the universal toleration of Polytheism, as it was invariably maintained by the faith of the people, the incredulity of philosophers, and the policy of the Roman senate and emperors, we are at a loss to discover what new offence the Christians had committed, what new provocation could exasperate the mild indifference of antiquity, and what new motives could urge the Roman princes, who beheld without concern a thousand forms of religion subsisting in peace under their gentle sway, to inflict a severe punishment on any part of their subjects, who had chosen for themselves a singular but an inoffensive mode of faith and worship.

The religious policy of the ancient world seems to have assumed a more stern and intolerant character, to oppose the progress of Christianity. About fourscore years after the death of Christ, his innocent disciples were punished with death by the sentence of a proconsul of the most amiable and philosophic character, and according to the laws of an emperor distinguished by the wisdom and justice of his general administration. The apologies which were repeatedly addressed to the successors of Trajan are filled with the most pathetic complaints, that the Christians, who obeyed the dictates, and solicited the liberty, of conscience, were alone, among all the subjects of the Roman empire, excluded from the common benefits of their auspicious government. The deaths of a few eminent martyrs have been recorded with care; and from the time that Christianity was invested with the supreme power, the governors of the church have been no less diligently employed in displaying the cruelty, than in imitating the conduct, of their Pagan adversaries. To separate (if it be possible) a few authentic as well as interesting facts from an undigested mass of fiction and error, and to relate, in a clear and rational manner, the causes, the extent, the duration, and the most important circumstances of the persecutions to which the first Christians were exposed, is the design of the present chapter. [1b]

[Footnote 1b: The history of the first age of Christianity is only found in the Acts of the Apostles, and in order to speak of the first persecutions experienced by the Christians, that book should naturally have been consulted; those persecutions, then limited to individuals and to a narrow sphere, interested only the persecuted, and have been related by them alone. Gibbon making the persecutions ascend no higher than Nero, has entirely omitted those which preceded this epoch, and of which St. Luke has preserved the memory. The only way to justify this omission was, to attack the authenticity of the Acts of the Apostles; for, if authentic, they must necessarily be consulted and quoted. Now, antiquity has left very few works of which the authenticity is so well established as that of the Acts of the Apostles. (See Lardner's Cred. of Gospel Hist. part iii.) It is therefore, without sufficient reason, that Gibbon has maintained silence concerning the narrative of St. Luke, and this omission is not without importance—G.]

The sectaries of a persecuted religion, depressed by fear animated with resentment, and perhaps heated by enthusiasm, are seldom in a proper temper of mind calmly to investigate, or candidly to appreciate, the motives of their enemies, which often escape the impartial and discerning view even of those who are placed at a secure distance from the flames of persecution. A reason has been assigned for the conduct of the emperors towards the primitive Christians, which may appear the more specious and probable as it is drawn from the acknowledged genius of Polytheism. It has already been observed, that the religious concord of the world was principally supported by the implicit assent and reverence which the nations of antiquity expressed for their respective traditions and ceremonies. It might therefore be expected, that they would unite with indignation against any sect or people which should separate itself from the communion of mankind, and claiming the exclusive possession of divine knowledge, should disdain every form of worship, except its own, as impious and idolatrous. The rights of toleration were held by mutual indulgence: they were justly forfeited by a refusal of the accustomed tribute. As the payment of this tribute was inflexibly refused by the Jews, and by them alone, the consideration of the treatment which they experienced from the Roman magistrates, will serve to explain how far these speculations are justified by facts, and will lead us to discover the true causes of the persecution of Christianity.

Without repeating what has already been mentioned of the reverence of the Roman princes and governors for the temple of Jerusalem, we shall only observe, that the destruction of the temple and city was accompanied and followed by every circumstance that could exasperate the minds of the conquerors, and authorize religious persecution by the most specious arguments of political justice and the public safety. From the reign of Nero to that of Antoninus Pius, the Jews discovered a fierce impatience of the dominion of Rome, which repeatedly broke out in the most furious massacres and insurrections. Humanity is shocked at the recital of the horrid cruelties which they committed in the cities of Egypt, of Cyprus, and of Cyrene, where they dwelt in treacherous friendship with the unsuspecting natives; [1] and we are tempted to applaud the severe retaliation which was exercised by the arms of the legions against a race of fanatics, whose dire and credulous superstition seemed to render them the implacable enemies not only of the Roman government, but of human kind. [2] The enthusiasm of the Jews was supported by the opinion, that it was unlawful for them to pay taxes to an idolatrous master; and by the flattering promise which they derived from their ancient oracles, that a conquering Messiah would soon arise, destined to break their fetters, and to invest the favorites of heaven with the empire of the earth. It was by announcing himself as their long-expected deliverer, and by calling on all the descendants of Abraham to assert the hope of Israel, that the famous Barchochebas collected a formidable army, with which he resisted during two years the power of the emperor Hadrian. [3]

[Footnote 1: In Cyrene, they massacred 220,000 Greeks; in Cyprus, 240,000; in Egypt, a very great multitude. Many of these unhappy victims were sawn asunder, according to a precedent to which David had given the sanction of his example. The victorious Jews devoured the flesh, licked up the blood, and twisted the entrails like a girdle round their bodies. See Dion Cassius, l. lxviii. p. 1145. Note: Some commentators, among them Reimar, in his notes on Dion Cassius think that the hatred of the Romans against the Jews has led the historian to exaggerate the cruelties committed by the latter. Don. Cass. lxviii. p. 1146—G.]

[Footnote 2: Without repeating the well-known narratives of Josephus, we may learn from Dion, (l. lxix. p. 1162,) that in Hadrian's war 580,000 Jews were cut off by the sword, besides an infinite number which perished by famine, by disease, and by fire.]

[Footnote 3: For the sect of the Zealots, see Basnage, Histoire des Juifs, l. i. c. 17; for the characters of the Messiah, according to the Rabbis, l. v. c. 11, 12, 13; for the actions of Barchochebas, l. vii. c. 12. (Hist. of Jews iii. 115, &c.)—M.]

Notwithstanding these repeated provocations, the resentment of the Roman princes expired after the victory; nor were their apprehensions continued beyond the period of war and danger. By the general indulgence of polytheism, and by the mild temper of Antoninus Pius, the Jews were restored to their ancient privileges, and once more obtained the permission of circumcising their children, with the easy restraint, that they should never confer on any foreign proselyte that distinguishing mark of the Hebrew race. [4] The numerous remains of that people, though they were still excluded from the precincts of Jerusalem, were permitted to form and to maintain considerable establishments both in Italy and in the provinces, to acquire the freedom of Rome, to enjoy municipal honors, and to obtain at the same time an exemption from the burdensome and expensive offices of society. The moderation or the contempt of the Romans gave a legal sanction to the form of ecclesiastical police which was instituted by the vanquished sect. The patriarch, who had fixed his residence at Tiberias, was empowered to appoint his subordinate ministers and apostles, to exercise a domestic jurisdiction, and to receive from his dispersed brethren an annual contribution. [5] New synagogues were frequently erected in the principal cities of the empire; and the sabbaths, the fasts, and the festivals, which were either commanded by the Mosaic law, or enjoined by the traditions of the Rabbis, were celebrated in the most solemn and public manner. [6] Such gentle treatment insensibly assuaged the stern temper of the Jews. Awakened from their dream of prophecy and conquest, they assumed the behavior of peaceable and industrious subjects. Their irreconcilable hatred of mankind, instead of flaming out in acts of blood and violence, evaporated in less dangerous gratifications. They embraced every opportunity of overreaching the idolaters in trade; and they pronounced secret and ambiguous imprecations against the haughty kingdom of Edom. [7]

[Footnote 4: It is to Modestinus, a Roman lawyer (l. vi. regular.) that we are indebted for a distinct knowledge of the Edict of Antoninus. See Casaubon ad Hist. August. p. 27.]

[Footnote 5: See Basnage, Histoire des Juifs, l. iii. c. 2, 3. The office of Patriarch was suppressed by Theodosius the younger.]

[Footnote 6: We need only mention the Purim, or deliverance of the Jews from he rage of Haman, which, till the reign of Theodosius, was celebrated with insolent triumph and riotous intemperance. Basnage, Hist. des Juifs, l. vi. c. 17, l. viii. c. 6.]

[Footnote 7: According to the false Josephus, Tsepho, the grandson of Esau, conducted into Italy the army of Eneas, king of Carthage. Another colony of Idumaeans, flying from the sword of David, took refuge in the dominions of Romulus. For these, or for other reasons of equal weight, the name of Edom was applied by the Jews to the Roman empire. Note: The false Josephus is a romancer of very modern date, though some of these legends are probably more ancient. It may be worth considering whether many of the stories in the Talmud are not history in a figurative disguise, adopted from prudence. The Jews might dare to say many things of Rome, under the significant appellation of Edom, which they feared to utter publicly. Later and more ignorant ages took literally, and perhaps embellished, what was intelligible among the generation to which it was addressed. Hist. of Jews, iii. 131. —The false Josephus has the inauguration of the emperor, with the seven electors and apparently the pope assisting at the coronation! Pref. page xxvi—M.]

Since the Jews, who rejected with abhorrence the deities adored by their sovereign and by their fellow-subjects, enjoyed, however, the free exercise of their unsocial religion, there must have existed some other cause, which exposed the disciples of Christ to those severities from which the posterity of Abraham was exempt. The difference between them is simple and obvious; but, according to the sentiments of antiquity, it was of the highest importance. The Jews were a nation; the Christians were a sect: and if it was natural for every community to respect the sacred institutions of their neighbors, it was incumbent on them to persevere in those of their ancestors. The voice of oracles, the precepts of philosophers, and the authority of the laws, unanimously enforced this national obligation. By their lofty claim of superior sanctity the Jews might provoke the Polytheists to consider them as an odious and impure race. By disdaining the intercourse of other nations, they might deserve their contempt. The laws of Moses might be for the most part frivolous or absurd; yet, since they had been received during many ages by a large society, his followers were justified by the example of mankind; and it was universally acknowledged, that they had a right to practise what it would have been criminal in them to neglect. But this principle, which protected the Jewish synagogue, afforded not any favor or security to the primitive church. By embracing the faith of the gospel, the Christians incurred the supposed guilt of an unnatural and unpardonable offence. They dissolved the sacred ties of custom and education, violated the religious institutions of their country, and presumptuously despised whatever their fathers had believed as true, or had reverenced as sacred. Nor was this apostasy (if we may use the expression) merely of a partial or local kind; since the pious deserter who withdrew himself from the temples of Egypt or Syria, would equally disdain to seek an asylum in those of Athens or Carthage. Every Christian rejected with contempt the superstitions of his family, his city, and his province. The whole body of Christians unanimously refused to hold any communion with the gods of Rome, of the empire, and of mankind. It was in vain that the oppressed believer asserted the inalienable rights of conscience and private judgment. Though his situation might excite the pity, his arguments could never reach the understanding, either of the philosophic or of the believing part of the Pagan world. To their apprehensions, it was no less a matter of surprise, that any individuals should entertain scruples against complying with the established mode of worship, than if they had conceived a sudden abhorrence to the manners, the dress, or the language of their native country. [8] [8a]

[Footnote 8: *From the arguments of Celsus, as they are represented and refuted by Origen, (l. v. p. 247—259,) we may clearly discover the distinction that was made between the Jewish people and the Christian sect. See, in the Dialogue of Minucius Felix, (c. 5, 6,) a fair and not inelegant description of the popular sentiments, with regard to the desertion of the established worship.*]

[Footnote 8a: *In all this there is doubtless much truth; yet does not the more important difference lie on the surface? The Christians made many converts the Jews but few. Had the Jewish been equally a proselyting religion would it not have encountered as violent persecution?—M.*]

The surprise of the Pagans was soon succeeded by resentment; and the most pious of men were exposed to the unjust but dangerous imputation of impiety. Malice and prejudice concurred in representing the Christians as a society of atheists, who, by the most daring attack on the religious constitution of the empire, had merited the severest animadversion of the civil magistrate. They had separated themselves (they gloried in the confession) from every mode of superstition which was received in any part of the globe by the various temper of polytheism: but it was not altogether so evident what deity, or what form of worship, they had substituted to the gods and temples of antiquity. The pure and sublime idea which they entertained of the Supreme Being escaped the gross conception of the Pagan multitude, who were at a loss to discover a spiritual and solitary God, that was neither represented under any corporeal figure or visible symbol, nor was adored with the accustomed pomp of libations and festivals, of altars and sacrifices. [9] The sages of Greece and Rome, who had elevated their minds to the contemplation of the existence and attributes of the First Cause, were induced by reason or by vanity to reserve for themselves and their chosen disciples the privilege of this philosophical devotion. [10] They were far from admitting the prejudices of mankind as the standard of truth, but they considered them as flowing from the original disposition of human nature; and they supposed that any popular mode of faith and worship which presumed to disclaim the assistance of the senses, would, in proportion as it receded from superstition, find itself incapable of restraining the wanderings of the fancy, and the visions of fanaticism. The careless glance which men of wit and learning condescended to cast on the Christian revelation, served only to confirm their hasty opinion, and to persuade them that the principle, which they might have revered, of the Divine Unity, was defaced by the wild enthusiasm, and annihilated by the airy speculations, of the new sectaries. The author of a celebrated dialogue, which has been attributed to Lucian, whilst he affects to treat the mysterious subject of the Trinity in a style of ridicule and contempt, betrays his own ignorance of the weakness of human reason, and of the inscrutable nature of the divine perfections. [11]

[Footnote 9: Cur nullas aras habent? templa nulla? nulla nota simulacra!—Unde autem, vel quis ille, aut ubi, Deus unicus, solitarius, desti tutus? Minucius Felix, c. 10. The Pagan interlocutor goes on to make a distinction in favor of the Jews, who had once a temple, altars, victims, &c.]

[Footnote 10: It is difficult (says Plato) to attain, and dangerous to publish, the knowledge of the true God. See the Theologie des Philosophes, in the Abbe d'Olivet's French translation of Tully de Natura Deorum, tom. i. p. 275.]

[Footnote 11: The author of the Philopatris perpetually treats the Christians as a company of dreaming enthusiasts, &c.; and in one place he manifestly alludes to the vision in which St. Paul was transported to the third heaven. In another place, Triephon, who personates a Christian, after deriding the gods of Paganism, proposes a mysterious oath.]

It might appear less surprising, that the founder of Christianity should not only be revered by his disciples as a sage and a prophet, but that he should be adored as a God. The Polytheists were disposed to adopt every article of faith, which seemed to offer any resemblance, however distant or imperfect, with the popular mythology; and the legends of Bacchus, of Hercules, and of Aesculapius, had, in some measure, prepared their imagination for the appearance of the Son of God under a human form. [12] But they were astonished that the Christians should abandon the temples of those ancient heroes, who, in the infancy of the world, had invented arts, instituted laws, and vanquished the tyrants or monsters who infested the earth, in order to choose for the exclusive object of their religious worship an obscure teacher, who, in a recent age, and among a barbarous people, had fallen a sacrifice either to the malice of his own countrymen, or to the jealousy of the Roman government. The Pagan multitude, reserving their gratitude for temporal benefits alone, rejected the inestimable present of life and immortality, which was offered to mankind by Jesus of Nazareth. His mild constancy in the midst of cruel and voluntary sufferings, his universal benevolence, and the sublime simplicity of his actions and character, were insufficient, in the opinion of those carnal men, to compensate for the want of fame, of empire, and of success; and whilst they refused to acknowledge his stupendous triumph over the powers of darkness and of the grave, they misrepresented, or they insulted, the equivocal birth, wandering life, and ignominious death, of the divine Author of Christianity. [13]

[Footnote 12: According to Justin Martyr, (Apolog. Major, c. 70-85,) the daemon who had gained some imperfect knowledge of the prophecies, purposely contrived this resemblance, which might deter, though by different means, both the people and the philosophers from embracing the faith of Christ.]

[Footnote 13: In the first and second books of Origen, Celsus treats the birth and character of our Savior with the most impious contempt. The orator Libanius praises Porphyry and Julian for confuting the folly of a sect., which styles a dead man of Palestine, God, and the Son of God. Socrates, Hist. Ecclesiast. iii. 23.]

The personal guilt which every Christian had contracted, in thus preferring his private sentiment to the national religion, was aggravated in a very high degree by the number and union of the criminals. It is well known, and has been already observed, that Roman policy viewed with the utmost jealousy and distrust any association among its subjects; and that the privileges of private corporations, though formed for the most harmless or beneficial purposes, were bestowed with a very sparing hand. [14] The religious assemblies of the Christians who had separated themselves from the public worship, appeared of a much less innocent nature; they were illegal in their principle, and in their consequences might become dangerous; nor were the emperors conscious that they violated the laws of justice, when, for the peace of society, they prohibited those secret and sometimes nocturnal meetings. [15] The pious disobedience of the Christians made their conduct, or perhaps their designs, appear in a much more serious and criminal light; and the Roman princes, who might perhaps have suffered themselves to be disarmed by a ready submission, deeming their honor concerned in the execution of their commands, sometimes attempted, by rigorous punishments, to subdue this independent spirit, which boldly acknowledged an authority superior to that of the magistrate. The extent and duration of this spiritual conspiracy seemed to render it everyday more deserving of his animadversion. We have already seen that the active and successful zeal of the Christians had insensibly diffused them through every province and almost every city of the empire. The new converts seemed to renounce their family and country, that they might connect themselves in an indissoluble band of union with a peculiar society, which every where assumed a different character from the rest of mankind. Their gloomy and austere aspect, their abhorrence of the common business and pleasures of life, and their frequent predictions of impending calamities, [16] inspired the Pagans with the apprehension of some danger, which would arise from the new sect, the more alarming as it was the more obscure. "Whatever," says Pliny, "may be the principle of their conduct, their inflexible obstinacy appeared deserving of punishment." [17]

[Footnote 14: The emperor Trajan refused to incorporate a company of 150 firemen, for the use of the city of Nicomedia. He disliked all associations. See Plin. Epist. x. 42, 43.]

[Footnote 15: The proconsul Pliny had published a general edict against unlawful meetings. The prudence of the Christians suspended their Agapae; but it was impossible for them to omit the exercise of public worship.]

[Footnote 16: As the prophecies of the Antichrist, approaching conflagration, &c., provoked those Pagans whom they did not convert, they were mentioned with caution and reserve; and the Montanists were censured for disclosing too freely the dangerous secret. See Mosheim, 413.]

[Footnote 17: Neque enim dubitabam, quodcunque esset quod faterentur, (such are the words of Pliny,) pervicaciam certe et inflexibilem obstinationem lebere puniri.]

The precautions with which the disciples of Christ performed the offices of religion were at first dictated by fear and necessity; but they were continued from choice. By imitating the awful secrecy which reigned in the Eleusinian mysteries, the Christians had flattered themselves that they should render their sacred institutions more respectable in the eyes of the Pagan world. [18] But the event, as it often happens to the operations of subtle policy, deceived their wishes and their expectations. It was concluded, that they only concealed what they would have blushed to disclose. Their mistaken prudence afforded an opportunity for malice to invent, and for suspicious credulity to believe, the horrid tales which described the Christians as the most wicked of human kind, who practised in their dark recesses every abomination that a depraved fancy could suggest, and who solicited the favor of their unknown God by the sacrifice of every moral virtue. There were many who pretended to confess or to relate the ceremonies of this abhorred society. It was asserted, "that a new-born infant, entirely covered over with flour, was presented, like some mystic symbol of initiation, to the knife of the proselyte, who unknowingly inflicted many a secret and mortal wound on the innocent victim of his error; that as soon as the cruel deed was perpetrated, the sectaries drank up the blood, greedily tore asunder the quivering members, and pledged themselves to eternal secrecy, by a mutual consciousness of guilt. It was as confidently affirmed, that this inhuman sacrifice was succeeded by a suitable entertainment, in which intemperance served as a provocative to brutal lust; till, at the appointed moment, the lights were suddenly extinguished, shame was banished, nature was forgotten; and, as accident might direct, the darkness of the night was polluted by the incestuous commerce of sisters and brothers, of sons and of mothers." [19]

[Footnote 18: See Mosheim's Ecclesiastical History, vol. i. p. 101, and Spanheim, Remarques sur les Caesars de Julien, p. 468, &c.]

[Footnote 19: See Justin Martyr, Apolog. i. 35, ii. 14. Athenagoras, in Legation, c. 27. Tertullian, Apolog. c. 7, 8, 9. Minucius Felix, c. 9, 10, 80, 31. The last of these writers relates the accusation in the most elegant and circumstantial manner. The answer of Tertullian is the boldest and most vigorous.]

But the perusal of the ancient apologies was sufficient to remove even the slightest suspicion from the mind of a candid adversary. The Christians, with the intrepid security of innocence, appeal from the voice of rumor to the equity of the magistrates. They acknowledge, that if any proof can be produced of the crimes which calumny has imputed to them, they are worthy of the most severe punishment. They provoke the punishment, and they challenge the proof. At the same time they urge, with equal truth and propriety, that the charge is not less devoid of probability, than it is destitute of evidence; they ask, whether any one can seriously believe that the pure and holy precepts of the gospel, which so frequently restrain the use of the most lawful enjoyments, should inculcate the practice of the most abominable crimes; that a large society should resolve to dishonor itself in the eyes of its own members; and that a great number of persons of either sex, and every age and character, insensible to the fear of death or infamy, should consent to violate those principles which nature and education had imprinted most deeply in their minds. [20] Nothing, it should seem, could weaken the force or destroy the effect of so unanswerable a justification, unless it were the injudicious conduct of the apologists themselves, who betrayed the common cause of religion, to gratify their devout hatred to the domestic enemies of the church. It was sometimes faintly insinuated, and sometimes boldly asserted, that the same bloody sacrifices, and the same incestuous festivals, which were so falsely ascribed to the orthodox believers, were in reality celebrated by the Marcionites, by the Carpocratians, and by several other sects of the Gnostics, who, notwithstanding they might deviate into the paths of heresy, were still actuated by the sentiments of men, and still governed by the precepts of Christianity. [21] Accusations of a similar kind were retorted upon the church by the schismatics who had departed from its communion, [22] and it was confessed on all sides, that the most scandalous licentiousness of manners prevailed among great numbers of those who affected the name of Christians. A Pagan magistrate, who possessed neither leisure nor abilities to discern the almost imperceptible line which divides the orthodox faith from heretical pravity, might easily have imagined that their mutual animosity had extorted the discovery of their common guilt. It was fortunate for the repose, or at least for the reputation, of the first Christians, that the magistrates sometimes proceeded with more temper and moderation than is usually consistent with religious zeal, and that they reported, as the impartial result of their judicial inquiry, that the sectaries, who had deserted the established worship, appeared to them sincere in their professions, and blameless in their manners; however they might incur, by their absurd and excessive superstition, the censure of the laws. [23]

[Footnote 20: In the persecution of Lyons, some Gentile slaves were compelled, by the fear of tortures, to accuse their Christian master. The church of Lyons, writing to their brethren of Asia, treat the horrid charge with proper indignation and contempt. Euseb. Hist. Eccles. v. i.]

[Footnote 21: See Justin Martyr, Apolog. i. 35. Irenaeus adv. Haeres. i. 24. Clemens. Alexandrin. Stromat. l. iii. p. 438. Euseb. iv. 8. It would be tedious and disgusting to relate all that the succeeding writers have imagined, all that Epiphanius has received, and all that Tillemont has copied. M. de Beausobre (Hist. du Manicheisme, l. ix. c. 8, 9) has exposed, with great spirit, the disingenuous arts of Augustin and Pope Leo I.]

[Footnote 22: When Tertullian became a Montanist, he aspersed the morals of the church which he had so resolutely defended. "Sed majoris est Agape, quia per hanc adolescentes tui cum sororibus dormiunt, appendices scilicet gulae lascivia et luxuria." De Jejuniis c. 17. The 85th canon of the council of Illiberis provides against the scandals which too often polluted the vigils of the church, and disgraced the Christian name in the eyes of unbelievers.]

[Footnote 23: Tertullian (Apolog. c. 2) expatiates on the fair and honorable testimony of Pliny, with much reason and some declamation.]

PART II

History, which undertakes to record the transactions of the past, for the instruction of future ages, would ill deserve that honorable office, if she condescended to plead the cause of tyrants, or to justify the maxims of persecution. It must, however, be acknowledged, that the conduct of the emperors who appeared the least favorable to the primitive church, is by no means so criminal as that of modern sovereigns, who have employed the arm of violence and terror against the religious opinions of any part of their subjects. From their reflections, or even from their own feelings, a Charles V. or a Lewis XIV. might have acquired a just knowledge of the rights of conscience, of the obligation of faith, and of the innocence of error. But the princes and magistrates of ancient Rome were strangers to those principles which inspired and authorized the inflexible obstinacy of the Christians in the cause of truth, nor could they themselves discover in their own breasts any motive which would have prompted them to refuse a legal, and as it were a natural, submission to the sacred institutions of their country. The same reason which contributes to alleviate the guilt, must have tended to abate the vigor, of their persecutions. As they were actuated, not by the furious zeal of bigots, but by the temperate policy of legislators, contempt must often have relaxed, and humanity must frequently have suspended, the execution of those laws which they enacted against the humble and obscure followers of Christ. From the general view of their character and motives we might naturally conclude: I. That a considerable time elapsed before they considered the new sectaries as an object deserving of the attention of government. II. That in the conviction of any of their subjects who were accused of so very singular a crime, they proceeded with caution and reluctance. III. That they were moderate in the use of punishments; and, IV. That the afflicted church enjoyed many intervals of peace and tranquility. Notwithstanding the careless indifference which the most copious and the most minute of the Pagan writers have shown to the affairs of the Christians, [24] it may still be in our power to confirm each of these probable suppositions, by the evidence of authentic facts.

[Footnote 24: In the various compilation of the Augustan History, (a part of which was composed under the reign of Constantine,) there are not six lines which relate to the Christians; nor has the diligence of Xiphilin discovered their name in the large history of Dion Cassius. Note: The greater part of the Augustan History is dedicated to Diocletian. This may account for the silence of its authors concerning Christianity. The notices that occur are almost all in the lives composed under the reign of Constantine. It may fairly be concluded, from the language which he had into the mouth of Maecenas, that Dion was an enemy to all innovations in religion. (See Gibbon, infra, note 105.) In fact, when the silence of Pagan historians is noticed, it should be remembered how meagre and mutilated are all the extant histories of the period—M.]

1. By the wise dispensation of Providence, a mysterious veil was cast over the infancy of the church, which, till the faith of the Christians was matured, and their numbers were multiplied, served to protect them not only from the malice but even from the knowledge of the Pagan world. The slow and gradual abolition of the Mosaic ceremonies afforded a safe and innocent disguise to the more early proselytes of the gospel. As they were, for the greater part, of the race of Abraham, they were distinguished by the peculiar mark of circumcision, offered up their devotions in the Temple of Jerusalem till its final destruction, and received both the Law and the Prophets as the genuine inspirations of the Deity. The Gentile converts, who by a spiritual adoption had been associated to the hope of Israel, were likewise confounded under the garb and appearance of Jews, [25] and as the Polytheists paid less regard to articles of faith than to the external worship, the new sect, which carefully concealed, or faintly announced, its future greatness and ambition, was permitted to shelter itself under the general toleration which was granted to an ancient and celebrated people in the Roman empire. It was not long, perhaps, before the Jews themselves, animated with a fiercer zeal and a more jealous faith, perceived the gradual separation of their Nazarene brethren from the doctrine of the synagogue; and they would gladly have extinguished the dangerous heresy in the blood of its adherents. But the decrees of Heaven had already disarmed their malice; and though they might sometimes exert the licentious privilege of sedition, they no longer possessed the administration of criminal justice; nor did they find it easy to infuse into the calm breast of a Roman magistrate the rancor of their own zeal and prejudice. The provincial governors declared themselves ready to listen to any accusation that might affect the public safety; but as soon as they were informed that it was a question not of facts but of words, a dispute relating only to the interpretation of the Jewish laws and prophecies, they deemed it unworthy of the majesty of Rome seriously to discuss the obscure differences which might arise among a barbarous and superstitious people. The innocence of the first Christians was protected by ignorance and contempt; and the tribunal of the Pagan magistrate often proved their most assured refuge against the fury of the synagogue. [26] If indeed we were disposed to adopt the traditions of a too credulous antiquity, we might relate the distant peregrinations, the wonderful achievements, and the various deaths of the twelve apostles: but a more accurate inquiry will induce us to doubt, whether any of those persons who had been witnesses to the miracles of Christ were permitted, beyond the limits of Palestine, to seal with

their blood the truth of their testimony. [27] From the ordinary term of human life, it may very naturally be presumed that most of them were deceased before the discontent of the Jews broke out into that furious war, which was terminated only by the ruin of Jerusalem. During a long period, from the death of Christ to that memorable rebellion, we cannot discover any traces of Roman intolerance, unless they are to be found in the sudden, the transient, but the cruel persecution, which was exercised by Nero against the Christians of the capital, thirty-five years after the former, and only two years before the latter, of those great events. The character of the philosophic historian, to whom we are principally indebted for the knowledge of this singular transaction, would alone be sufficient to recommend it to our most attentive consideration.

[Footnote 25: An obscure passage of Suetonius (in Claud. c. 25) may seem to offer a proof how strangely the Jews and Christians of Rome were confounded with each other.]

[Footnote 26: See, in the xviiith and xxvth chapters of the Acts of the Apostles, the behavior of Gallio, proconsul of Achaia, and of Festus, procurator of Judea.]

[Footnote 27: In the time of Tertullian and Clemens of Alexandria, the glory of martyrdom was confined to St. Peter, St. Paul, and St. James. It was gradually bestowed on the rest of the apostles, by the more recent Greeks, who prudently selected for the theatre of their preaching and sufferings some remote country beyond the limits of the Roman empire. See Mosheim, p. 81; and Tillemont, Memoires Ecclesiastiques, tom. i. part iii.]

In the tenth year of the reign of Nero, the capital of the empire was afflicted by a fire which raged beyond the memory or example of former ages. [28] The monuments of Grecian art and of Roman virtue, the trophies of the Punic and Gallic wars, the most holy temples, and the most splendid palaces, were involved in one common destruction. Of the fourteen regions or quarters into which Rome was divided, four only subsisted entire, three were levelled with the ground, and the remaining seven, which had experienced the fury of the flames, displayed a melancholy prospect of ruin and desolation. The vigilance of government appears not to have neglected any of the precautions which might alleviate the sense of so dreadful a calamity. The Imperial gardens were thrown open to the distressed multitude, temporary buildings were erected for their accommodation, and a plentiful supply of corn and provisions was distributed at a very moderate price. [29] The most generous policy seemed to have dictated the edicts which regulated the disposition of the streets and the construction of private houses; and as it usually happens, in an age of prosperity, the conflagration of Rome, in the course of a few years, produced a new city, more regular and more beautiful than the former. But all the prudence and humanity affected by Nero on this occasion were insufficient to preserve him from the popular suspicion. Every crime might be imputed to the assassin of his wife and mother; nor could the prince who prostituted his person and dignity on the theatre be deemed incapable of the most extravagant folly. The voice of rumor accused the emperor as the incendiary of his own capital; and as the most Incredible stories are the best adapted to the genius of an enraged people, it was gravely reported, and firmly believed, that Nero, enjoying the calamity which he had occasioned, amused himself with singing to his lyre the destruction of ancient Troy. [30] To divert a suspicion, which the power of despotism was unable to suppress, the emperor resolved to substitute in his own place some fictitious criminals. "With this view," continues Tacitus, "he inflicted the most exquisite tortures on those men, who, under the vulgar appellation of Christians, were already branded with deserved infamy. They derived their name and origin from Christ, who in the reign of Tiberius had suffered death by the sentence of the procurator Pontius Pilate. [31] For a while this dire superstition was checked; but it again burst forth; [31a] and not only spread itself over Judaea, the first seat of this mischievous sect, but was even introduced into

Rome, the common asylum which receives and protects whatever is impure, whatever is atrocious. The confessions of those who were seized discovered a great multitude of their accomplices, and they were all convicted, not so much for the crime of setting fire to the city, as for their hatred of human kind. [32] They died in torments, and their torments were imbittered by insult and derision. Some were nailed on crosses; others sewn up in the skins of wild beasts, and exposed to the fury of dogs; others again, smeared over with combustible materials, were used as torches to illuminate the darkness of the night. The gardens of Nero were destined for the melancholy spectacle, which was accompanied with a horse-race and honored with the presence of the emperor, who mingled with the populace in the dress and attitude of a charioteer. The guilt of the Christians deserved indeed the most exemplary punishment, but the public abhorrence was changed into commiseration, from the opinion that those unhappy wretches were sacrificed, not so much to the public welfare, as to the cruelty of a jealous tyrant." [33] Those who survey with a curious eye the revolutions of mankind, may observe, that the gardens and circus of Nero on the Vatican, which were polluted with the blood of the first Christians, have been rendered still more famous by the triumph and by the abuse of the persecuted religion. On the same spot, [34] a temple, which far surpasses the ancient glories of the Capitol, has been since erected by the Christian Pontiffs, who, deriving their claim of universal dominion from an humble fisherman of Galilee, have succeeded to the throne of the Caesars, given laws to the barbarian conquerors of Rome, and extended their spiritual jurisdiction from the coast of the Baltic to the shores of the Pacific Ocean.

[Footnote 28: Tacit. Annal. xv. 38—44. Sueton in Neron. c. 38. Dion Cassius, l. lxii. p. 1014. Orosius, vii. 7.]

[Footnote 29: The price of wheat (probably of the modius,) was reduced as low as terni Nummi; which would be equivalent to about fifteen shillings the English quarter.]

[Footnote 30: We may observe, that the rumor is mentioned by Tacitus with a very becoming distrust and hesitation, whilst it is greedily transcribed by Suetonius, and solemnly confirmed by Dion.]

[Footnote 31: This testimony is alone sufficient to expose the anachronism of the Jews, who place the birth of Christ near a century sooner. (Basnage, Histoire des Juifs, l. v. c. 14, 15.) We may learn from Josephus, (Antiquitat. xviii. 3,) that the procuratorship of Pilate corresponded with the last ten years of Tiberius, A. D. 27—37. As to the particular time of the death of Christ, a very early tradition fixed it to the 25th of March, A. D. 29, under the consulship of the two Gemini. (Tertullian adv. Judaeos, c. 8.) This date, which is adopted by Pagi, Cardinal Norris, and Le Clerc, seems at least as probable as the vulgar aera, which is placed (I know not from what conjectures) four years later.]

[Footnote 31a: This single phrase, Repressa in praesens exitiabilis superstitio rursus erumpebat, proves that the Christians had already attracted the attention of the government; and that Nero was not the first to persecute them. I am surprised that more stress has not been laid on the confirmation which the Acts of the Apostles derive from these words of Tacitus, Repressa in praesens, and rursus erumpebat—G. —I have been unwilling to suppress this note, but surely the expression of Tacitus refers to the expected extirpation of the religion by the death of its founder, Christ—M.]

[Footnote 32: Odio humani generis convicti. These words may either signify the hatred of mankind towards the Christians, or the hatred of the Christians towards mankind. I have preferred the latter sense, as the most agreeable to the style of Tacitus, and to the popular error, of which a precept of the gospel (see Luke xiv. 26) had been, perhaps, the innocent occasion. My interpretation is justified by the authority of Lipsius; of the Italian, the French, and the English translators of Tacitus; of Mosheim, (p. 102,) of Le Clerc, (Historia Ecclesiast. p. 427,) of Dr. Lardner, (Testimonies, vol. i. p. 345,) and of the

Bishop of Gloucester, (Divine Legation, vol. iii. p. 38.) But as the word convicti does not unite very happily with the rest of the sentence, James Gronovius has preferred the reading of conjuncti, which is authorized by the valuable MS. of Florence.]

[Footnote 33: Tacit. Annal xv. 44.]

[Footnote 34: Nardini Roma Antica, p. 487. Donatus de Roma Antiqua, l. iii. p. 449.]

But it would be improper to dismiss this account of Nero's persecution, till we have made some observations that may serve to remove the difficulties with which it is perplexed, and to throw some light on the subsequent history of the church.

1. The most sceptical criticism is obliged to respect the truth of this extraordinary fact, and the integrity of this celebrated passage of Tacitus. The former is confirmed by the diligent and accurate Suetonius, who mentions the punishment which Nero inflicted on the Christians, a sect of men who had embraced a new and criminal superstition. [35] The latter may be proved by the consent of the most ancient manuscripts; by the inimitable character of the style of Tacitus by his reputation, which guarded his text from the interpolations of pious fraud; and by the purport of his narration, which accused the first Christians of the most atrocious crimes, without insinuating that they possessed any miraculous or even magical powers above the rest of mankind. [36] 2. Notwithstanding it is probable that Tacitus was born some years before the fire of Rome, [37] he could derive only from reading and conversation the knowledge of an event which happened during his infancy. Before he gave himself to the public, he calmly waited till his genius had attained its full maturity, and he was more than forty years of age, when a grateful regard for the memory of the virtuous Agricola extorted from him the most early of those historical compositions which will delight and instruct the most distant posterity. After making a trial of his strength in the life of Agricola and the description of Germany, he conceived, and at length executed, a more arduous work; the history of Rome, in thirty books, from the fall of Nero to the accession of Nerva. The administration of Nerva introduced an age of justice and propriety, which Tacitus had destined for the occupation of his old age; [38] but when he took a nearer view of his subject, judging, perhaps, that it was a more honorable or a less invidious office to record the vices of past tyrants, than to celebrate the virtues of a reigning monarch, he chose rather to relate, under the form of annals, the actions of the four immediate successors of Augustus. To collect, to dispose, and to adorn a series of fourscore years, in an immortal work, every sentence of which is pregnant with the deepest observations and the most lively images, was an undertaking sufficient to exercise the genius of Tacitus himself during the greatest part of his life. In the last years of the reign of Trajan, whilst the victorious monarch extended the power of Rome beyond its ancient limits, the historian was describing, in the second and fourth books of his annals, the tyranny of Tiberius; [39] and the emperor Hadrian must have succeeded to the throne, before Tacitus, in the regular prosecution of his work, could relate the fire of the capital, and the cruelty of Nero towards the unfortunate Christians. At the distance of sixty years, it was the duty of the annalist to adopt the narratives of contemporaries; but it was natural for the philosopher to indulge himself in the description of the origin, the progress, and the character of the new sect, not so much according to the knowledge or prejudices of the age of Nero, as according to those of the time of Hadrian. 3 Tacitus very frequently trusts to the curiosity or reflection of his readers to supply those intermediate circumstances and ideas, which, in his extreme conciseness, he has thought proper to suppress. We may therefore presume to imagine some probable cause which could direct the cruelty of Nero against the Christians of Rome, whose obscurity, as well as innocence, should have shielded them from his indignation, and even from his notice. The Jews, who were numerous in the capital, and oppressed in their own country, were a much fitter object for the suspicions of the emperor

and of the people: nor did it seem unlikely that a vanquished nation, who already discovered their abhorrence of the Roman yoke, might have recourse to the most atrocious means of gratifying their implacable revenge. But the Jews possessed very powerful advocates in the palace, and even in the heart of the tyrant; his wife and mistress, the beautiful Poppaea, and a favorite player of the race of Abraham, who had already employed their intercession in behalf of the obnoxious people. [40] In their room it was necessary to offer some other victims, and it might easily be suggested that, although the genuine followers of Moses were innocent of the fire of Rome, there had arisen among them a new and pernicious sect of Galilaeans, which was capable of the most horrid crimes. Under the appellation of Galilaeans, two distinctions of men were confounded, the most opposite to each other in their manners and principles; the disciples who had embraced the faith of Jesus of Nazareth, [41] and the zealots who had followed the standard of Judas the Gaulonite. [42] The former were the friends, the latter were the enemies, of human kind; and the only resemblance between them consisted in the same inflexible constancy, which, in the defence of their cause, rendered them insensible of death and tortures. The followers of Judas, who impelled their countrymen into rebellion, were soon buried under the ruins of Jerusalem; whilst those of Jesus, known by the more celebrated name of Christians, diffused themselves over the Roman empire. How natural was it for Tacitus, in the time of Hadrian, to appropriate to the Christians the guilt and the sufferings, [42a] which he might, with far greater truth and justice, have attributed to a sect whose odious memory was almost extinguished! 4. Whatever opinion may be entertained of this conjecture, (for it is no more than a conjecture,) it is evident that the effect, as well as the cause, of Nero's persecution, was confined to the walls of Rome, [43] [43a] that the religious tenets of the Galilaeans or Christians, were never made a subject of punishment, or even of inquiry; and that, as the idea of their sufferings was for a long time connected with the idea of cruelty and injustice, the moderation of succeeding princes inclined them to spare a sect, oppressed by a tyrant, whose rage had been usually directed against virtue and innocence.

[Footnote 35: Sueton. in Nerone, c. 16. The epithet of malefica, which some sagacious commentators have translated magical, is considered by the more rational Mosheim as only synonymous to the exitiabilis of Tacitus.]

[Footnote 36: The passage concerning Jesus Christ, which was inserted into the text of Josephus, between the time of Origen and that of Eusebius, may furnish an example of no vulgar forgery. The accomplishment of the prophecies, the virtues, miracles, and resurrection of Jesus, are distinctly related. Josephus acknowledges that he was the Messiah, and hesitates whether he should call him a man. If any doubt can still remain concerning this celebrated passage, the reader may examine the pointed objections of Le Fevre, (Havercamp. Joseph. tom. ii. p. 267-273), the labored answers of Daubuz, (p. 187-232, and the masterly reply (Bibliotheque Ancienne et Moderne, tom. vii. p. 237-288) of an anonymous critic, whom I believe to have been the learned Abbe de Longuerue. Note: The modern editor of Eusebius, Heinichen, has adopted, and ably supported, a notion, which had before suggested itself to the editor, that this passage is not altogether a forgery, but interpolated with many additional clauses. Heinichen has endeavored to disengage the original text from the foreign and more recent matter—M.]

[Footnote 37: See the lives of Tacitus by Lipsius and the Abbe de la Bleterie, Dictionnaire de Bayle a l'article Particle Tacite, and Fabricius, Biblioth. Latin tem. Latin. tom. ii. p. 386, edit. Ernest. Ernst.]

[Footnote 38: Principatum Divi Nervae, et imperium Trajani, uberiorem, securioremque materiam senectuti seposui. Tacit. Hist. i.]

[Footnote 39: See Tacit. Annal. ii. 61, iv. 4. Note: The perusal of this passage of Tacitus alone is sufficient, as I have already said, to show that the Christian sect was not so obscure as not already to have been repressed, (repressa,) and that it did not pass for innocent in the eyes of the Romans—G.]

[Footnote 40: The player's name was Aliturus. Through the same channel, Josephus, (de vita sua, c. 2,) about two years before, had obtained the pardon and release of some Jewish priests, who were prisoners at Rome.]

[Footnote 41: The learned Dr. Lardner (Jewish and Heathen Testimonies, vol ii. p. 102, 103) has proved that the name of Galilaeans was a very ancient, and perhaps the primitive appellation of the Christians.]

[Footnote 42: Joseph. Antiquitat. xviii. 1, 2. Tillemont, Ruine des Juifs, p. 742 The sons of Judas were crucified in the time of Claudius. His grandson Eleazar, after Jerusalem was taken, defended a strong fortress with 960 of his most desperate followers. When the battering ram had made a breach, they turned their swords against their wives their children, and at length against their own breasts. They dies to the last man.]

[Footnote 42a: This conjecture is entirely devoid, not merely of verisimilitude, but even of possibility. Tacitus could not be deceived in appropriating to the Christians of Rome the guilt and the sufferings which he might have attributed with far greater truth to the followers of Judas the Gaulonite, for the latter never went to Rome. Their revolt, their attempts, their opinions, their wars, their punishment, had no other theatre but Judaea (Basn. Hist. des. Juifs, t. i. p. 491.) Moreover the name of Christians had long been given in Rome to the disciples of Jesus; and Tacitus affirms too positively, refers too distinctly to its etymology, to allow us to suspect any mistake on his part—G. —M. Guizot's expressions are not in the least too strong against this strange imagination of Gibbon; it may be doubted whether the followers of Judas were known as a sect under the name of Galilaeans—M.]

[Footnote 43: See Dodwell. Paucitat. Mart. l. xiii. The Spanish Inscription in Gruter. p. 238, No. 9, is a manifest and acknowledged forgery contrived by that noted imposter. Cyriacus of Ancona, to flatter the pride and prejudices of the Spaniards. See Ferreras, Histoire D'Espagne, tom. i. p. 192.]

[Footnote 43a: M. Guizot, on the authority of Sulpicius Severus, ii. 37, and of Orosius, viii. 5, inclines to the opinion of those who extend the persecution to the provinces. Mosheim rather leans to that side on this much disputed question, (c. xxxv.) Neander takes the view of Gibbon, which is in general that of the most learned writers. There is indeed no evidence, which I can discover, of its reaching the provinces; and the apparent security, at least as regards his life, with which St. Paul pursued his travels during this period, affords at least a strong inference against a rigid and general inquisition against the Christians in other parts of the empire—M.]

It is somewhat remarkable that the flames of war consumed, almost at the same time, the temple of Jerusalem and the Capitol of Rome; [44] and it appears no less singular, that the tribute which devotion had destined to the former, should have been converted by the power of an assaulting victor to restore and adorn the splendor of the latter. [45] The emperors levied a general capitation tax on the Jewish people; and although the sum assessed on the head of each individual was inconsiderable, the use for which it was designed, and the severity with which it was exacted, were considered as an intolerable grievance. [46] Since the officers of the revenue extended their unjust claim to many persons who were strangers to the blood or religion of the Jews, it was impossible that the Christians, who had so often sheltered themselves under the shade of the synagogue, should now escape this rapacious persecution.

Anxious as they were to avoid the slightest infection of idolatry, their conscience forbade them to contribute to the honor of that daemon who had assumed the character of the Capitoline Jupiter. As a very numerous though declining party among the Christians still adhered to the law of Moses, their efforts to dissemble their Jewish origin were detected by the decisive test of circumcision; [47] nor were the Roman magistrates at leisure to inquire into the difference of their religious tenets. Among the Christians who were brought before the tribunal of the emperor, or, as it seems more probable, before that of the procurator of Judaea, two persons are said to have appeared, distinguished by their extraction, which was more truly noble than that of the greatest monarchs. These were the grandsons of St. Jude the apostle, who himself was the brother of Jesus Christ. [48] Their natural pretensions to the throne of David might perhaps attract the respect of the people, and excite the jealousy of the governor; but the meanness of their garb, and the simplicity of their answers, soon convinced him that they were neither desirous nor capable of disturbing the peace of the Roman empire. They frankly confessed their royal origin, and their near relation to the Messiah; but they disclaimed any temporal views, and professed that his kingdom, which they devoutly expected, was purely of a spiritual and angelic nature. When they were examined concerning their fortune and occupation, they showed their hands, hardened with daily labor, and declared that they derived their whole subsistence from the cultivation of a farm near the village of Cocaba, of the extent of about twenty-four English acres, [49] and of the value of nine thousand drachms, or three hundred pounds sterling. The grandsons of St. Jude were dismissed with compassion and contempt. [50]

[Footnote 44: The Capitol was burnt during the civil war between Vitellius and Vespasian, the 19th of December, A. D. 69. On the 10th of August, A. D. 70, the temple of Jerusalem was destroyed by the hands of the Jews themselves, rather than by those of the Romans.]

[Footnote 45: The new Capitol was dedicated by Domitian. Sueton. in Domitian. c. 5. Plutarch in Poplicola, tom. i. p. 230, edit. Bryant. The gilding alone cost 12,000 talents (above two millions and a half.) It was the opinion of Martial, (l. ix. Epigram 3,) that if the emperor had called in his debts, Jupiter himself, even though he had made a general auction of Olympus, would have been unable to pay two shillings in the pound.]

[Footnote 46: With regard to the tribute, see Dion Cassius, l. lxvi. p. 1082, with Reimarus's notes. Spanheim, de Usu Numismatum, tom. ii. p. 571; and Basnage, Histoire des Juifs, l. vii. c. 2.]

[Footnote 47: Suetonius (in Domitian. c. 12) had seen an old man of ninety publicly examined before the procurator's tribunal. This is what Martial calls, Mentula tributis damnata.]

[Footnote 48: This appellation was at first understood in the most obvious sense, and it was supposed, that the brothers of Jesus were the lawful issue of Joseph and Mary. A devout respect for the virginity of the mother of God suggested to the Gnostics, and afterwards to the orthodox Greeks, the expedient of bestowing a second wife on Joseph. The Latins (from the time of Jerome) improved on that hint, asserted the perpetual celibacy of Joseph, and justified by many similar examples the new interpretation that Jude, as well as Simon and James, who were styled the brothers of Jesus Christ, were only his first cousins. See Tillemont, Mem. Ecclesiat. tom. i. part iii.: and Beausobre, Hist. Critique du Manicheisme, l. ii. c. 2.]

[Footnote 49: Thirty-nine, squares of a hundred feet each, which, if strictly computed, would scarcely amount to nine acres.]

[Footnote 50: Eusebius, iii. 20. The story is taken from Hegesippus.]

But although the obscurity of the house of David might protect them from the suspicions of a tyrant, the present greatness of his own family alarmed the pusillanimous temper of Domitian, which could only be appeased by the blood of those Romans whom he either feared, or hated, or esteemed. Of the two sons of his uncle Flavius Sabinus, [51] the elder was soon convicted of treasonable intentions, and the younger, who bore the name of Flavius Clemens, was indebted for his safety to his want of courage and ability. [52] The emperor for a long time, distinguished so harmless a kinsman by his favor and protection, bestowed on him his own niece Domitilla, adopted the children of that marriage to the hope of the succession, and invested their father with the honors of the consulship.

[Footnote 51: See the death and character of Sabinus in Tacitus, (Hist. iii. 74) Sabinus was the elder brother, and, till the accession of Vespasian, had been considered as the principal support of the Flavium family]

[Footnote 52: Flavium Clementem patruelem suum contemptissimoe inertice.. ex tenuissima suspicione interemit. Sueton. in Domitian. c. 15.]

But he had scarcely finished the term of his annual magistracy, when, on a slight pretence, he was condemned and executed; Domitilla was banished to a desolate island on the coast of Campania; [53] and sentences either of death or of confiscation were pronounced against a great number of who were involved in the same accusation. The guilt imputed to their charge was that of Atheism and Jewish manners; [54] a singular association of ideas, which cannot with any propriety be applied except to the Christians, as they were obscurely and imperfectly viewed by the magistrates and by the writers of that period. On the strength of so probable an interpretation, and too eagerly admitting the suspicions of a tyrant as an evidence of their honorable crime, the church has placed both Clemens and Domitilla among its first martyrs, and has branded the cruelty of Domitian with the name of the second persecution. But this persecution (if it deserves that epithet) was of no long duration. A few months after the death of Clemens, and the banishment of Domitilla, Stephen, a freedman belonging to the latter, who had enjoyed the favor, but who had not surely embraced the faith, of his mistress, [54a] assassinated the emperor in his palace. [55] The memory of Domitian was condemned by the senate; his acts were rescinded; his exiles recalled; and under the gentle administration of Nerva, while the innocent were restored to their rank and fortunes, even the most guilty either obtained pardon or escaped punishment. [56]

[Footnote 53: The Isle of Pandataria, according to Dion. Bruttius Praesens (apud Euseb. iii. 18) banishes her to that of Pontia, which was not far distant from the other. That difference, and a mistake, either of Eusebius or of his transcribers, have given occasion to suppose two Domitillas, the wife and the niece of Clemens. See Tillemont, Memoires Ecclesiastiques, tom. ii. p. 224.]

[Footnote 54: Dion. l. lxvii. p. 1112. If the Bruttius Praesens, from whom it is probable that he collected this account, was the correspondent of Pliny, (Epistol. vii. 3,) we may consider him as a contemporary writer.]

[Footnote 54a: This is an uncandid sarcasm. There is nothing to connect Stephen with the religion of Domitilla. He was a knave detected in the malversation of money—interceptarum pecuniarum reus—M.]

[Footnote 55: Suet. in Domit. c. 17. Philostratus in Vit. Apollon. l. viii.]

[Footnote 56: Dion. l. lxviii. p. 1118. Plin. Epistol. iv. 22.]

II. About ten years afterwards, under the reign of Trajan, the younger Pliny was intrusted by his friend and master with the government of Bithynia and Pontus. He soon found himself at a loss to determine by what rule of justice or of law he should direct his conduct in the execution of an office the most repugnant to his humanity. Pliny had never assisted at any judicial proceedings against the Christians, with whose name alone he seems to be acquainted; and he was totally uninformed with regard to the nature of their guilt, the method of their conviction, and the degree of their punishment. In this perplexity he had recourse to his usual expedient, of submitting to the wisdom of Trajan an impartial, and, in some respects, a favorable account of the new superstition, requesting the emperor, that he would condescend to resolve his doubts, and to instruct his ignorance. [57] The life of Pliny had been employed in the acquisition of learning, and in the business of the world.

Since the age of nineteen he had pleaded with distinction in the tribunals of Rome, [58] filled a place in the senate, had been invested with the honors of the consulship, and had formed very numerous connections with every order of men, both in Italy and in the provinces. From his ignorance therefore we may derive some useful information. We may assure ourselves, that when he accepted the government of Bithynia, there were no general laws or decrees of the senate in force against the Christians; that neither Trajan nor any of his virtuous predecessors, whose edicts were received into the civil and criminal jurisprudence, had publicly declared their intentions concerning the new sect; and that whatever proceedings had been carried on against the Christians, there were none of sufficient weight and authority to establish a precedent for the conduct of a Roman magistrate.

[Footnote 57: Plin. Epistol. x. 97. The learned Mosheim expresses himself (p. 147, 232) with the highest approbation of Pliny's moderate and candid temper. Notwithstanding Dr. Lardner's suspicions (see Jewish and Heathen Testimonies, vol. ii. p. 46,) I am unable to discover any bigotry in his language or proceedings. Note: Yet the humane Pliny put two female attendants, probably deaconesses to the torture, in order to ascertain the real nature of these suspicious meetings: necessarium credidi, ex duabus ancillis, quae ministrae dicebantor quid asset veri et per tormenta quaerere—M.]

[Footnote 58: Plin. Epist. v. 8. He pleaded his first cause A. D. 81; the year after the famous eruptions of Mount Vesuvius, in which his uncle lost his life.]

PART III

The answer of Trajan, to which the Christians of the succeeding age have frequently appealed, discovers as much regard for justice and humanity as could be reconciled with his mistaken notions of religious policy. [59] Instead of displaying the implacable zeal of an inquisitor, anxious to discover the most minute particles of heresy, and exulting in the number of his victims, the emperor expresses much more solicitude to protect the security of the innocent, than to prevent the escape of the guilty. He acknowledged the difficulty of fixing any general plan; but he lays down two salutary rules, which often afforded relief and support to the distressed Christians. Though he directs the magistrates to punish such persons as are legally convicted, he prohibits them, with a very humane inconsistency, from making any inquiries concerning the supposed criminals. Nor was the magistrate allowed to proceed on every kind of information. Anonymous charges the emperor rejects, as too repugnant to the equity of his government; and he strictly requires, for the conviction of those to whom the guilt of Christianity is imputed, the positive evidence of a fair and open accuser. It is likewise probable, that the persons who assumed so invidiuous an office, were obliged to declare the grounds of their suspicions, to specify (both in respect to time and place) the secret assemblies, which their Christian adversary had frequented, and to disclose a great number of circumstances, which were concealed with the most vigilant jealousy from the eye of the profane. If they succeeded in their prosecution, they were exposed to the resentment of a considerable and active party, to the censure of the more liberal portion of mankind, and to the ignominy which, in every age and country, has attended the character of an informer. If, on the contrary, they failed in their proofs, they incurred the severe and perhaps capital penalty, which, according to a law published by the emperor Hadrian, was inflicted on those who falsely attributed to their fellow-citizens the crime of Christianity. The violence of personal or superstitious animosity might sometimes prevail over the most natural apprehensions of disgrace and danger but it cannot surely be imagined, that accusations of so unpromising an appearance were either lightly or frequently undertaken by the Pagan subjects of the Roman empire. [60] [60a]

[Footnote 59: Plin. Epist. x. 98. Tertullian (Apolog. c. 5) considers this rescript as a relaxation of the ancient penal laws, "quas Trajanus exparte frustratus est:" and yet Tertullian, in another part of his Apology, exposes the inconsistency of prohibiting inquiries, and enjoining punishments.]

[Footnote 60: Eusebius (Hist. Ecclesiast. l. iv. c. 9) has preserved the edict of Hadrian. He has likewise (c. 13) given us one still more favorable, under the name of Antoninus; the authenticity of which is not so universally allowed. The second Apology of Justin contains some curious particulars relative to the accusations of Christians. Note: Professor Hegelmayer has proved the authenticity of the edict of Antoninus, in his Comm. Hist. Theol. in Edict. Imp. Antonini. Tubing. 1777, in 4to—G. —Neander doubts its authenticity, (vol. i. p. 152.) In my opinion, the internal evidence is decisive against it—M]

[Footnote 60a: The enactment of this law affords strong presumption, that accusations of the "crime of Christianity," were by no means so uncommon, nor received with so much mistrust and caution by the ruling authorities, as Gibbon would insinuate. —M.]

The expedient which was employed to elude the prudence of the laws, affords a sufficient proof how effectually they disappointed the mischievous designs of private malice or superstitious zeal. In a large and tumultuous assembly, the restraints of fear and shame, so forcible on the minds of individuals, are deprived of the greatest part of their influence. The pious Christian, as he was desirous to obtain, or to escape, the glory of martyrdom, expected, either with impatience or with terror, the stated returns of the public games and festivals. On those occasions the inhabitants of the great cities of the empire were collected in the circus or the theatre, where every circumstance of the place, as well as of the ceremony, contributed to kindle their devotion, and to extinguish their humanity. Whilst the numerous spectators, crowned with garlands, perfumed with incense, purified with the blood of victims, and surrounded with the altars and statues of their tutelar deities, resigned themselves to the enjoyment of pleasures, which they considered as an essential part of their religious worship, they recollected, that the Christians alone abhorred the gods of mankind, and by their absence and melancholy on these solemn festivals, seemed to insult or to lament the public felicity. If the empire had been afflicted by any recent calamity, by a plague, a famine, or an unsuccessful war; if the Tyber had, or if the Nile had not, risen beyond its banks; if the earth had shaken, or if the temperate order of the seasons had been interrupted, the superstitious Pagans were convinced that the crimes and the impiety of the Christians, who were spared by the excessive lenity of the government, had at length provoked the divine justice. It was not among a licentious and exasperated populace, that the forms of legal proceedings could be observed; it was not in an amphitheatre, stained with the blood of wild beasts and gladiators, that the voice of compassion could be heard. The impatient clamors of the multitude denounced the Christians as the enemies of gods and men, doomed them to the severest tortures, and venturing to accuse by name some of the most distinguished of the new sectaries, required with irresistible vehemence that they should be instantly apprehended and cast to the lions. [61] The provincial governors and magistrates who presided in the public spectacles were usually inclined to gratify the inclinations, and to appease the rage, of the people, by the sacrifice of a few obnoxious victims. But the wisdom of the emperors protected the church from the danger of these tumultuous clamors and irregular accusations, which they justly censured as repugnant both to the firmness and to the equity of their administration. The edicts of Hadrian and of Antoninus Pius expressly declared, that the voice of the multitude should never be admitted as legal evidence to convict or to punish those unfortunate persons who had embraced the enthusiasm of the Christians. [62]

[Footnote 61: See Tertullian, (Apolog. c. 40.) The acts of the martyrdom of Polycarp exhibit a lively picture of these tumults, which were usually fomented by the malice of the Jews.]

[Footnote 62: These regulations are inserted in the above mentioned document of Hadrian and Pius. See the apology of Melito, (apud Euseb. l iv 26)]

III. Punishment was not the inevitable consequence of conviction, and the Christians, whose guilt was the most clearly proved by the testimony of witnesses, or even by their voluntary confession, still retained in their own power the alternative of life or death. It was not so much the past offence, as the actual resistance, which excited the indignation of the magistrate. He was persuaded that he offered them an easy pardon, since, if they consented to cast a few grains of incense upon the altar, they were dismissed from the tribunal in safety and with applause. It was esteemed the duty of a humane judge to endeavor to reclaim, rather than to punish, those deluded enthusiasts. Varying his tone according to the age, the sex, or the situation of the prisoners, he frequently condescended to set before their eyes every circumstance which could render life more pleasing, or death more terrible; and to solicit, nay, to entreat, them, that they would show some compassion to themselves, to their families, and to their friends. [63] If threats and persuasions proved ineffectual, he had often recourse to violence; the scourge and the rack were called in to supply the deficiency of argument, and every art of cruelty was employed to subdue such inflexible, and, as it appeared to the Pagans, such criminal, obstinacy. The ancient apologists of Christianity have censured, with equal truth and severity, the irregular conduct of their persecutors who, contrary to every principle of judicial proceeding, admitted the use of torture, in order to obtain, not a confession, but a denial, of the crime which was the object of their inquiry. [64] The monks of succeeding ages, who, in their peaceful solitudes, entertained themselves with diversifying the deaths and sufferings of the primitive martyrs, have frequently invented torments of a much more refined and ingenious nature. In particular, it has pleased them to suppose, that the zeal of the Roman magistrates, disdaining every consideration of moral virtue or public decency, endeavored to seduce those whom they were unable to vanquish, and that by their orders the most brutal violence was offered to those whom they found it impossible to seduce. It is related, that females, who were prepared to despise death, were sometimes condemned to a more severe trial, [64a] and called upon to determine whether they set a higher value on their religion or on their chastity. The youths to whose licentious embraces they were abandoned, received a solemn exhortation from the judge, to exert their most strenuous efforts to maintain the honor of Venus against the impious virgin who refused to burn incense on her altars. Their violence, however, was commonly disappointed, and the seasonable interposition of some miraculous power preserved the chaste spouses of Christ from the dishonor even of an involuntary defeat. We should not indeed neglect to remark, that the more ancient as well as authentic memorials of the church are seldom polluted with these extravagant and indecent fictions. [65]

[Footnote 63: See the rescript of Trajan, and the conduct of Pliny. The most authentic acts of the martyrs abound in these exhortations. Note: Pliny's test was the worship of the gods, offerings to the statue of the emperor, and blaspheming Christ—praeterea maledicerent Christo—M.]

[Footnote 64: In particular, see Tertullian, (Apolog. c. 2, 3,) and Lactantius, (Institut. Divin. v. 9.) Their reasonings are almost the same; but we may discover, that one of these apologists had been a lawyer, and the other a rhetorician.]

[Footnote 64a: The more ancient as well as authentic memorials of the church, relate many examples of the fact, (of these severe trials,) which there is nothing to contradict. Tertullian, among others, says, Nam proxime ad lenonem damnando Christianam, potius quam ad leonem, confessi estis labem pudicitiae apud nos atrociorem omni poena et omni morte reputari, Apol. cap. ult. Eusebius likewise says, "Other virgins, dragged to brothels, have lost their life rather than defile their virtue." Euseb. Hist. Ecc. viii. 14— G. The miraculous interpositions were the offspring of the coarse imaginations of the monks—M.]

[Footnote 65: See two instances of this kind of torture in the Acta Sincere Martyrum, published by Ruinart, p. 160, 399. Jerome, in his Legend of Paul the Hermit, tells a strange story of a young man, who was chained naked on a bed of flowers, and assaulted by a beautiful and wanton courtesan. He quelled the rising temptation by biting off his tongue.]

The total disregard of truth and probability in the representation of these primitive martyrdoms was occasioned by a very natural mistake. The ecclesiastical writers of the fourth or fifth centuries ascribed to the magistrates of Rome the same degree of implacable and unrelenting zeal which filled their own breasts against the heretics or the idolaters of their own times.

It is not improbable that some of those persons who were raised to the dignities of the empire, might have imbibed the prejudices of the populace, and that the cruel disposition of others might occasionally be stimulated by motives of avarice or of personal resentment. [66] But it is certain, and we may appeal to the grateful confessions of the first Christians, that the greatest part of those magistrates who exercised in the provinces the authority of the emperor, or of the senate, and to whose hands alone the jurisdiction of life and death was intrusted, behaved like men of polished manners and liberal education, who respected the rules of justice, and who were conversant with the precepts of philosophy. They frequently declined the odious task of persecution, dismissed the charge with contempt, or suggested to the accused Christian some legal evasion, by which he might elude the severity of the laws. [67] Whenever they were invested with a discretionary power, [68] they used it much less for the oppression, than for the relief and benefit of the afflicted church. They were far from condemning all the Christians who were accused before their tribunal, and very far from punishing with death all those who were convicted of an obstinate adherence to the new superstition. Contenting themselves, for the most part, with the milder chastisements of imprisonment, exile, or slavery in the mines, [69] they left the unhappy victims of their justice some reason to hope, that a prosperous event, the accession, the marriage, or the triumph of an emperor, might speedily restore them, by a general pardon, to their former state. The martyrs, devoted to immediate execution by the Roman magistrates, appear to have been selected from the most opposite extremes. They were either bishops and presbyters, the persons the most distinguished among the Christians by their rank and influence, and whose example might strike terror into the whole sect; [70] or else they were the meanest and most abject among them, particularly those of the servile condition, whose lives were esteemed of little value, and whose sufferings were viewed by the ancients with too careless an indifference. [71] The learned Origen, who, from his experience as well as reading, was intimately acquainted with the history of the Christians, declares, in the most express terms, that the number of martyrs was very inconsiderable. [72] His authority would alone be sufficient to annihilate that formidable army of martyrs, whose relics, drawn for the most part from the catacombs of Rome, have replenished so many churches, [73] and whose marvellous achievements have been the subject of so many volumes of Holy Romance. [74] But the general assertion of Origen may be explained and confirmed by the particular testimony of his friend Dionysius, who, in the immense city of Alexandria, and under the rigorous persecution of Decius, reckons only ten men and seven women who suffered for the profession of the Christian name. [75]

[Footnote 66: The conversion of his wife provoked Claudius Herminianus, governor of Cappadocia, to treat the Christians with uncommon severity. Tertullian ad Scapulam, c. 3.]

[Footnote 67: Tertullian, in his epistle to the governor of Africa, mentions several remarkable instances of lenity and forbearance, which had happened within his knowledge.]

[Footnote 68: Neque enim in universum aliquid quod quasi certam formam habeat, constitui potest; an expression of Trajan, which gave a very great latitude to the governors of provinces. Note: Gibbon altogether forgets that Trajan fully approved of the course pursued by Pliny. That course was, to order all who persevered in their faith to be led to execution: perseverantes duci jussi—M.]

[Footnote 69: In Metalla damnamur, in insulas relegamur. Tertullian, Apolog. c. 12. The mines of Numidia contained nine bishops, with a proportionable number of their clergy and people, to whom Cyprian addressed a pious epistle of praise and comfort. See Cyprian. Epistol. 76, 77.]

[Footnote 70: Though we cannot receive with entire confidence either the epistles, or the acts, of Ignatius, (they may be found in the 2d volume of the Apostolic Fathers,) yet we may quote that bishop of Antioch as one of these exemplary martyrs. He was sent in chains to Rome as a public spectacle, and when he arrived at Troas, he received the pleasing intelligence, that the persecution of Antioch was already at an end. Note: The acts of Ignatius are generally received as authentic, as are seven of his letters. Eusebius and St. Jerome mention them: there are two editions; in one, the letters are longer, and many passages appear to have been interpolated; the other edition is that which contains the real letters of St. Ignatius; such at least is the opinion of the wisest and most enlightened critics. (See Lardner. Cred. of Gospel Hist.) Less, uber dis Religion, v. i. p. 529. Usser. Diss. de Ign. Epist. Pearson, Vindic, Ignatianae. It should be remarked, that it was under the reign of Trajan that the bishop Ignatius was carried from Antioch to Rome, to be exposed to the lions in the amphitheatre, the year of J. C. 107, according to some; of 116, according to others—G.]

[Footnote 71: Among the martyrs of Lyons, (Euseb. l. v. c. 1,) the slave Blandina was distinguished by more exquisite tortures. Of the five martyrs so much celebrated in the acts of Felicitas and Perpetua, two were of a servile, and two others of a very mean, condition.]

[Footnote 72: Origen. advers. Celsum, l. iii. p. 116. His words deserve to be transcribed. Note: The words that follow should be quoted. "God not permitting that all his class of men should be exterminated:" which appears to indicate that Origen thought the number put to death inconsiderable only when compared to the numbers who had survived. Besides this, he is speaking of the state of the religion under

Caracalla, Elagabalus, Alexander Severus, and Philip, who had not persecuted the Christians. It was during the reign of the latter that Origen wrote his books against Celsus—G.]

[Footnote 73: If we recollect that all the Plebeians of Rome were not Christians, and that all the Christians were not saints and martyrs, we may judge with how much safety religious honors can be ascribed to bones or urns, indiscriminately taken from the public burial-place. After ten centuries of a very free and open trade, some suspicions have arisen among the more learned Catholics. They now require as a proof of sanctity and martyrdom, the letters B.M., a vial full of red liquor supposed to be blood, or the figure of a palm-tree. But the two former signs are of little weight, and with regard to the last, it is observed by the critics, 1. That the figure, as it is called, of a palm, is perhaps a cypress, and perhaps only a stop, the flourish of a comma used in the monumental inscriptions. 2. That the palm was the symbol of victory among the Pagans. 3. That among the Christians it served as the emblem, not only of martyrdom, but in general of a joyful resurrection. See the epistle of P. Mabillon, on the worship of unknown saints, and Muratori sopra le Antichita Italiane, Dissertat. lviii.]

[Footnote 74: As a specimen of these legends, we may be satisfied with 10,000 Christian soldiers crucified in one day, either by Trajan or Hadrian on Mount Ararat. See Baronius ad Martyrologium Romanum; Tille mont, Mem. Ecclesiast. tom. ii. part ii. p. 438; and Geddes's Miscellanies, vol. ii. p. 203. The abbreviation of Mil., which may signify either soldiers or thousands, is said to have occasioned some extraordinary mistakes.]

[Footnote 75: Dionysius ap. Euseb l. vi. c. 41 One of the seventeen was likewise accused of robbery. Note: Gibbon ought to have said, was falsely accused of robbery, for so it is in the Greek text. This Christian, named Nemesion, falsely accused of robbery before the centurion, was acquitted of a crime altogether foreign to his character, but he was led before the governor as guilty of being a Christian, and the governor inflicted upon him a double torture. (Euseb. loc. cit.) It must be added, that Saint Dionysius only makes particular mention of the principal martyrs, [this is very doubtful—M.] and that he says, in general, that the fury of the Pagans against the Christians gave to Alexandria the appearance of a city taken by storm. [This refers to plunder and ill usage, not to actual slaughter—M.] Finally it should be observed that Origen wrote before the persecution of the emperor Decius—G.]

During the same period of persecution, the zealous, the eloquent, the ambitious Cyprian governed the church, not only of Carthage, but even of Africa. He possessed every quality which could engage the reverence of the faithful, or provoke the suspicions and resentment of the Pagan magistrates. His character as well as his station seemed to mark out that holy prelate as the most distinguished object of envy and danger. [76] The experience, however, of the life of Cyprian, is sufficient to prove that our fancy has exaggerated the perilous situation of a Christian bishop; and the dangers to which he was exposed were less imminent than those which temporal ambition is always prepared to encounter in the pursuit of honors. Four Roman emperors, with their families, their favorites, and their adherents, perished by the sword in the space of ten years, during which the bishop of Carthage guided by his authority and eloquence the councils of the African church. It was only in the third year of his administration, that he had reason, during a few months, to apprehend the severe edicts of Decius, the vigilance of the magistrate and the clamors of the multitude, who loudly demanded, that Cyprian, the leader of the Christians, should be thrown to the lions. Prudence suggested the necessity of a temporary retreat, and the voice of prudence was obeyed. He withdrew himself into an obscure solitude, from whence he could maintain a constant correspondence with the clergy and people of Carthage; and, concealing himself till the tempest was past, he preserved his life, without relinquishing either his power or his reputation. His extreme caution did not, however, escape the censure of the more rigid Christians, who lamented, or the reproaches of his personal enemies, who insulted, a conduct which they considered as a pusillanimous and criminal desertion of the most sacred duty. [77] The propriety of reserving himself for the future exigencies of the church, the example of several holy bishops, [78] and the divine admonitions, which, as he declares himself, he frequently received in visions and ecstacies, were the reasons alleged in his justification. [79] But his best apology may be found in the cheerful resolution, with which, about eight years afterwards, he suffered death in the cause of religion. The authentic history of his martyrdom has been recorded with unusual candor and impartiality. A short abstract, therefore, of its most important circumstances, will convey the clearest information of the spirit, and of the forms, of the Roman persecutions. [80]

[Footnote 76: The letters of Cyprian exhibit a very curious and original picture both of the man and of the times. See likewise the two lives of Cyprian, composed with equal accuracy, though with very different views; the one by Le Clerc (Bibliotheque Universelle, tom. xii. p. 208-378,) the other by Tillemont, Memoires Ecclesiastiques, tom. iv part i. p. 76-459.]

[Footnote 77: See the polite but severe epistle of the clergy of Rome to the bishop of Carthage. (Cyprian. Epist. 8, 9.) Pontius labors with the greatest care and diligence to justify his master against the general censure.]

[Footnote 78: In particular those of Dionysius of Alexandria, and Gregory Thaumaturgus, of Neo-Caesarea. See Euseb. Hist. Ecclesiast. l. vi. c. 40; and Memoires de Tillemont, tom. iv. part ii. p. 685.]

[Footnote 79: See Cyprian. Epist. 16, and his life by Pontius.]

[Footnote 80: We have an original life of Cyprian by the deacon Pontius, the companion of his exile, and the spectator of his death; and we likewise possess the ancient proconsular acts of his martyrdom. These two relations are consistent with each other, and with probability; and what is somewhat remarkable, they are both unsullied by any miraculous circumstances.]

PART IV

When Valerian was consul for the third, and Gallienus for the fourth time, Paternus, proconsul of Africa, summoned Cyprian to appear in his private council-chamber. He there acquainted him with the Imperial mandate which he had just received, [81] that those who had abandoned the Roman religion should immediately return to the practice of the ceremonies of their ancestors. Cyprian replied without hesitation, that he was a Christian and a bishop, devoted to the worship of the true and only Deity, to whom he offered up his daily supplications for the safety and prosperity of the two emperors, his lawful sovereigns.

With modest confidence he pleaded the privilege of a citizen, in refusing to give any answer to some invidious and indeed illegal questions which the proconsul had proposed. A sentence of banishment was pronounced as the penalty of Cyprian's disobedience; and he was conducted without delay to Curubis, a free and maritime city of Zeugitania, in a pleasant situation, a fertile territory, and at the distance of about forty miles from Carthage. [82] The exiled bishop enjoyed the conveniences of life and the consciousness of virtue. His reputation was diffused over Africa and Italy; an account of his behavior was published for the edification of the Christian world; [83] and his solitude was frequently interrupted by the letters, the visits, and the congratulations of the faithful. On the arrival of a new proconsul in the province the fortune of Cyprian appeared for some time to wear a still more favorable aspect. He was recalled from banishment; and though not yet permitted to return to Carthage, his own gardens in the neighborhood of the capital were assigned for the place of his residence. [84]

[Footnote 81: It should seem that these were circular orders, sent at the same time to all the governors. Dionysius (ap. Euseb. l. vii. c. 11) relates the history of his own banishment from Alexandria almost in the same manner. But as he escaped and survived the persecution, we must account him either more or less fortunate than Cyprian.]

[Footnote 82: See Plin. Hist. Natur. v. 3. Cellarius, Geograph. Antiq. part iii. p. 96. Shaw's Travels, p. 90; and for the adjacent country, (which is terminated by Cape Bona, or the promontory of Mercury,) l'Afrique de Marmol. tom. ii. p. 494. There are the remains of an aqueduct near Curubis, or Curbis, at present altered into Gurbes; and Dr. Shaw read an inscription, which styles that city Colonia Fulvia. The deacon Pontius (in Vit. Cyprian. c. 12) calls it "Apricum et competentem locum, hospitium pro voluntate secretum, et quicquid apponi eis ante promissum est, qui regnum et justitiam Dei quaerunt."]

[Footnote 83: See Cyprian. Epistol. 77, edit. Fell.]

[Footnote 84: Upon his conversion, he had sold those gardens for the benefit of the poor. The indulgence of God (most probably the liberality of some Christian friend) restored them to Cyprian. See Pontius, c. 15.]

At length, exactly one year [85] after Cyprian was first apprehended, Galerius Maximus, proconsul of Africa, received the Imperial warrant for the execution of the Christian teachers. The bishop of Carthage was sensible that he should be singled out for one of the first victims; and the frailty of nature tempted him to withdraw himself, by a secret flight, from the danger and the honor of martyrdom; [85a] but soon recovering that fortitude which his character required, he returned to his gardens, and patiently expected the ministers of death. Two officers of rank, who were intrusted with that commission, placed Cyprian between them in a chariot, and as the proconsul was not then at leisure, they conducted him, not to a prison, but to a private house in Carthage, which belonged to one of them. An elegant supper was provided for the entertainment of the bishop, and his Christian friends were permitted for the last time to enjoy his society, whilst the streets were filled with a multitude of the faithful, anxious and alarmed at the approaching fate of their spiritual father. [86] In the morning he appeared before the tribunal of the proconsul, who, after informing himself of the name and situation of Cyprian, commanded him to offer sacrifice, and pressed him to reflect on the consequences of his disobedience. The refusal of Cyprian was firm and decisive; and the magistrate, when he had taken the opinion of his council, pronounced with some reluctance the sentence of death. It was conceived in the following terms: "That Thascius Cyprianus should be immediately beheaded, as the enemy of the gods of Rome, and as the chief and ringleader of a criminal association, which he had seduced into an impious resistance against the laws of the most holy emperors, Valerian and Gallienus." [87] The manner of his execution was the mildest and least painful that could be inflicted on a person convicted of any capital offence; nor was the use of torture admitted to obtain from the bishop of Carthage either the recantation of his principles or the discovery of his accomplices.

[Footnote 85: When Cyprian, a twelvemonth before, was sent into exile, he dreamt that he should be put to death the next day. The event made it necessary to explain that word, as signifying a year. Pontius, c. 12.]

[Footnote 85a: This was not, as it appears, the motive which induced St. Cyprian to conceal himself for a short time; he was threatened to be carried to Utica; he preferred remaining at Carthage, in order to suffer martyrdom in the midst of his flock, and in order that his death might conduce to the edification of those whom he had guided during life. Such, at least, is his own explanation of his conduct in one of his letters: Cum perlatum ad nos fuisset, fratres carissimi, frumentarios esse missos qui me Uticam per ducerent, consilioque carissimorum persuasum est, ut de hortis interim recederemus, justa interveniente causa, consensi; eo quod congruat episcopum in ea civitate, in qua Ecclesiae dominicae praeest, illie. Dominum confiteri et plebem universam praepositi praesentis confessione clarificari Ep. 83—G]

[Footnote 86: Pontius (c. 15) acknowledges that Cyprian, with whom he supped, passed the night custodia delicata. The bishop exercised a last and very proper act of jurisdiction, by directing that the younger females, who watched in the streets, should be removed from the dangers and temptations of a nocturnal crowd. Act. Preconsularia, c. 2.]

[Footnote 87: See the original sentence in the Acts, c. 4; and in Pontius, c. 17 The latter expresses it in a more rhetorical manner.]

As soon as the sentence was proclaimed, a general cry of "We will die with him," arose at once among the listening multitude of Christians who waited before the palace gates. The generous effusions of their zeal and their affection were neither serviceable to Cyprian nor dangerous to themselves. He was led away under a guard of tribunes and centurions, without resistance and without insult, to the place of his execution, a spacious and level plain near the city, which was already filled with great numbers of spectators. His faithful presbyters and deacons were permitted to accompany their holy bishop. [87a] They assisted him in laying aside his upper garment, spread linen on the ground to catch the precious relics of his blood, and received his orders to bestow five-and-twenty pieces of gold on the executioner. The martyr then covered his face with his hands, and at one blow his head was separated from his body. His corpse remained during some hours exposed to the curiosity of the Gentiles: but in the night it was removed, and transported in a triumphal procession, and with a splendid illumination, to the burial-place of the Christians. The funeral of Cyprian was publicly celebrated without receiving any interruption from the Roman magistrates; and those among the faithful, who had performed the last offices to his person and his memory, were secure from the danger of inquiry or of punishment. It is remarkable, that of so great a multitude of bishops in the province of Africa, Cyprian was the first who was esteemed worthy to obtain the crown of martyrdom. [88]

[Footnote 87a: There is nothing in the life of St. Cyprian, by Pontius, nor in the ancient manuscripts, which can make us suppose that the presbyters and deacons in their clerical character, and known to be such, had the permission to attend their holy bishop. Setting aside all religious considerations, it is impossible not to be surprised at the kind of complaisance with which the historian here insists, in favor of the persecutors, on some mitigating circumstances allowed at the death of a man whose only crime was maintaining his own opinions with frankness and courage—G.]

[Footnote 88: Pontius, c. 19. M. de Tillemont (Memoires, tom. iv. part i. p. 450, note 50) is not pleased with so positive an exclusion of any former martyr of the episcopal rank. Note: M. de. Tillemont, as an honest writer, explains the difficulties which he felt about the text of Pontius, and concludes by distinctly stating, that without doubt there is some mistake, and that Pontius must have meant only Africa Minor or Carthage; for St. Cyprian, in his 58th (69th) letter addressed to Pupianus, speaks expressly of many bishops his colleagues, qui proscripti sunt, vel apprehensi in carcere et catenis fuerunt; aut qui in exilium *relegati, illustri itinere ed Dominum profecti sunt; aut qui quibusdam locis animadversi, coeleses coronas de Domini clarificatione sumpserunt—G.]*

It was in the choice of Cyprian, either to die a martyr, or to live an apostate; but on the choice depended the alternative of honor or infamy. Could we suppose that the bishop of Carthage had employed the profession of the Christian faith only as the instrument of his avarice or ambition, it was still incumbent on him to support the character he had assumed; [89] and if he possessed the smallest degree of manly fortitude, rather to expose himself to the most cruel tortures, than by a single act to exchange the reputation of a whole life, for the abhorrence of his Christian brethren, and the contempt of the Gentile world. But if the zeal of Cyprian was supported by the sincere conviction of the truth of those doctrines which he preached, the crown of martyrdom must have appeared to him as an object of desire rather than of terror. It is not easy to extract any distinct ideas from the vague though eloquent declamations of the Fathers, or to ascertain the degree of immortal glory and happiness which they confidently promised to those who were so fortunate as to shed their blood in the cause of religion. [90] They inculcated with becoming diligence, that the fire of martyrdom supplied every defect and expiated every sin; that while the souls of ordinary Christians were obliged to pass through a slow and painful purification, the triumphant sufferers entered into the immediate fruition of eternal bliss, where, in the society of the patriarchs, the apostles, and the prophets, they reigned with Christ, and acted as his assessors in the universal judgment of mankind. The assurance of a lasting reputation upon earth, a motive so congenial to the vanity of human nature, often served to animate the courage of the martyrs.

The honors which Rome or Athens bestowed on those citizens who had fallen in the cause of their country, were cold and unmeaning demonstrations of respect, when compared with the ardent gratitude and devotion which the primitive church expressed towards the victorious champions of the faith. The annual commemoration of their virtues and sufferings was observed as a sacred ceremony, and at length terminated in religious worship. Among the Christians who had publicly confessed their religious principles, those who (as it very frequently happened) had been dismissed from the tribunal or the prisons of the Pagan magistrates, obtained such honors as were justly due to their imperfect martyrdom and their generous resolution. The most pious females courted the permission of imprinting kisses on the fetters which they had worn, and on the wounds which they had received. Their persons were esteemed holy, their decisions were admitted with deference, and they too often abused, by their spiritual pride and licentious manners, the preeminence which their zeal and intrepidity had acquired. [91] Distinctions like these, whilst they display the exalted merit, betray the inconsiderable number of those who suffered, and of those who died, for the profession of Christianity.

[Footnote 89: Whatever opinion we may entertain of the character or principles of Thomas Becket, we must acknowledge that he suffered death with a constancy not unworthy of the primitive martyrs. See Lord Lyttleton's History of Henry II. vol. ii. p. 592, &c.]

[Footnote 90: See in particular the treatise of Cyprian de Lapsis, p. 87-98, edit. Fell. The learning of Dodwell (Dissertat. Cyprianic. xii. xiii.,) and the ingenuity of Middleton, (Free Inquiry, p. 162, &c.,) have left scarcely any thing to add concerning the merit, the honors, and the motives of the martyrs.]

[Footnote 91: Cyprian. Epistol. 5, 6, 7, 22, 24; and de Unitat. Ecclesiae. The number of pretended martyrs has been very much multiplied, by the custom which was introduced of bestowing that honorable name on confessors. Note: M. Guizot denies that the letters of Cyprian, to which he refers, bear out the statement in the text. I cannot scruple to admit the accuracy of Gibbon's quotation. To take only the fifth letter, we find this passage: Doleo enim quando audio quosdam improbe et insolenter discurrere, et ad

ineptian vel ad discordias vacare, Christi membra et jam Christum confessa per concubitus illicitos inquinari, nec a diaconis aut presbyteris regi posse, sed id agere ut per paucorum pravos et malos mores, multorum et bonorum confessorum gloria honesta maculetur. Gibbon's misrepresentation lies in the ambiguous expression "too often." Were the epistles arranged in a different manner in the edition consulted by M. Guizot?—M.]

The sober discretion of the present age will more readily censure than admire, but can more easily admire than imitate, the fervor of the first Christians, who, according to the lively expressions of Sulpicius Severus, desired martyrdom with more eagerness than his own contemporaries solicited a bishopric. [92] The epistles which Ignatius composed as he was carried in chains through the cities of Asia, breathe sentiments the most repugnant to the ordinary feelings of human nature. He earnestly beseeches the Romans, that when he should be exposed in the amphitheatre, they would not, by their kind but unseasonable intercession, deprive him of the crown of glory; and he declares his resolution to provoke and irritate the wild beasts which might be employed as the instruments of his death. [93] Some stories are related of the courage of martyrs, who actually performed what Ignatius had intended; who exasperated the fury of the lions, pressed the executioner to hasten his office, cheerfully leaped into the fires which were kindled to consume them, and discovered a sensation of joy and pleasure in the midst of the most exquisite tortures. Several examples have been preserved of a zeal impatient of those restraints which the emperors had provided for the security of the church. The Christians sometimes supplied by their voluntary declaration the want of an accuser, rudely disturbed the public service of paganism, [94] and rushing in crowds round the tribunal of the magistrates, called upon them to pronounce and to inflict the sentence of the law. The behavior of the Christians was too remarkable to escape the notice of the ancient philosophers; but they seem to have considered it with much less admiration than astonishment. Incapable of conceiving the motives which sometimes transported the fortitude of believers beyond the bounds of prudence or reason, they treated such an eagerness to die as the strange result of obstinate despair, of stupid insensibility, or of superstitious frenzy. [95] "Unhappy men!" exclaimed the proconsul Antoninus to the Christians of Asia; "unhappy men! if you are thus weary of your lives, is it so difficult for you to find ropes and precipices?" [96] He was extremely cautious (as it is observed by a learned and picus historian) of punishing men who had found no accusers but themselves, the Imperial laws not having made any provision for so unexpected a case: condemning therefore a few as a warning to their brethren, he dismissed the multitude with indignation and contempt. [97] Notwithstanding this real or affected disdain, the intrepid constancy of the faithful was productive of more salutary effects on those minds which nature or grace had disposed for the easy reception of religious truth. On these melancholy occasions, there were many among the Gentiles who pitied, who admired, and who were converted. The generous enthusiasm was communicated from the sufferer to the spectators; and the blood of martyrs, according to a well-known observation, became the seed of the church.

[Footnote 92: Certatim gloriosa in certamina ruebatur; multique avidius tum martyria gloriosis mortibus quaerebantur, quam nunc Episcopatus pravis ambitionibus appetuntur. Sulpicius Severus, l. ii. He might have omitted the word nunc.]

[Footnote 93: See Epist. ad Roman. c. 4, 5, ap. Patres Apostol. tom. ii. p. 27. It suited the purpose of Bishop Pearson (see Vindiciae Ignatianae, part ii. c. 9) to justify, by a profusion of examples and authorities, the sentiments of Ignatius.]

[Footnote 94: The story of Polyeuctes, on which Corneille has founded a very beautiful tragedy, is one of the most celebrated, though not perhaps the most authentic, instances of this excessive zeal. We should observe, that the 60th canon of the council of Illiberis refuses the title of martyrs to those who exposed themselves to death, by publicly destroying the idols.]

[Footnote 95: See Epictetus, l. iv. c. 7, (though there is some doubt whether he alludes to the Christians.) Marcus Antoninus de Rebus suis, l. xi. c. 3 Lucian in Peregrin.]

[Footnote 96: Tertullian ad Scapul. c. 5. The learned are divided between three persons of the same name, who were all proconsuls of Asia. I am inclined to ascribe this story to Antoninus Pius, who was afterwards emperor; and who may have governed Asia under the reign of Trajan.]

[Footnote 97: Mosheim, de Rebus Christ, ante Constantin. p. 235.]

But although devotion had raised, and eloquence continued to inflame, this fever of the mind, it insensibly gave way to the more natural hopes and fears of the human heart, to the love of life, the apprehension of pain, and the horror of dissolution. The more prudent rulers of the church found themselves obliged to restrain the indiscreet ardor of their followers, and to distrust a constancy which too often abandoned them in the hour of trial. [98] As the lives of the faithful became less mortified and austere, they were every day less ambitious of the honors of martyrdom; and the soldiers of Christ, instead of distinguishing themselves by voluntary deeds of heroism, frequently deserted their post, and fled in confusion before the enemy whom it was their duty to resist. There were three methods, however, of escaping the flames of persecution, which were not attended with an equal degree of guilt: first, indeed, was generally allowed to be innocent; the second was of a doubtful, or at least of a venial, nature; but the third implied a direct and criminal apostasy from the Christian faith.

[Footnote 98: See the Epistle of the Church of Smyrna, ap. Euseb. Hist. Eccles. Liv. c. 15 Note: The 15th chapter of the 10th book of the Eccles. History of Eusebius treats principally of the martyrdom of St. Polycarp, and mentions some other martyrs. A single example of weakness is related; it is that of a Phrygian named Quintus, who, appalled at the sight of the wild beasts and the tortures, renounced his faith. This example proves little against the mass of Christians, and this chapter of Eusebius furnished much stronger evidence of their courage than of their timidity—G—This Quintus had, however, rashly and of his own accord appeared before the tribunal; and the church of Smyrna condemn "his indiscreet ardor," coupled as it was with weakness in the hour of trial—M.]

I. A modern inquisitor would hear with surprise, that whenever an information was given to a Roman magistrate of any person within his jurisdiction who had embraced the sect of the Christians, the charge was communicated to the party accused, and that a convenient time was allowed him to settle his domestic concerns, and to prepare an answer to the crime which was imputed to him. [99] If he entertained any doubt of his own constancy, such a delay afforded him the opportunity of preserving his life and honor by flight, of withdrawing himself into some obscure retirement or some distant province, and of patiently expecting the return of peace and security. A measure so consonant to reason was soon authorized by the advice and example of the most holy prelates; and seems to have been censured by few except by the Montanists, who deviated into heresy by their strict and obstinate adherence to the rigor of ancient discipline. [100]

II. The provincial governors, whose zeal was less prevalent than their avarice, had countenanced the practice of selling certificates, (or libels, as they were called,) which attested, that the persons therein mentioned had complied with the laws, and sacrificed to the Roman deities. By producing these false declarations, the opulent and timid Christians were enabled to silence the malice of an informer, and to reconcile in some measure their safety with their religion. A slight penance atoned for this profane dissimulation. [101] [101a]

III. In every persecution there were great numbers of unworthy Christians who publicly disowned or renounced the faith which they had professed; and who confirmed the sincerity of their abjuration, by the legal acts of burning incense or of offering sacrifices. Some of these apostates had yielded on the first menace or exhortation of the magistrate; whilst the patience of others had been subdued by the length and repetition of tortures. The affrighted countenances of some betrayed their inward remorse, while others advanced with confidence and alacrity to the altars of the gods. [102] But the disguise which fear had imposed, subsisted no longer than the present danger. As soon as the severity of the persecution was abated, the doors of the churches were assailed by the returning multitude of penitents who detested their idolatrous submission, and who solicited with equal ardor, but with various success, their readmission into the society of Christians. [103] [103a]

[Footnote 99: In the second apology of Justin, there is a particular and very curious instance of this legal delay. The same indulgence was granted to accused Christians, in the persecution of Decius: and Cyprian (de Lapsis) expressly mentions the "Dies negantibus praestitutus." Note: The examples drawn by the historian from Justin Martyr and Cyprian relate altogether to particular cases, and prove nothing as to the general practice adopted towards the accused; it is evident, on the contrary, from the same apology of St. Justin, that they hardly ever obtained delay. "A man named Lucius, himself a Christian, present at an unjust sentence passed against a Christian by the judge Urbicus, asked him why he thus punished a man who was neither adulterer nor robber, nor guilty of any other crime but that of avowing himself a Christian." Urbicus answered only in these words: "Thou also hast the appearance of being a Christian." "Yes, without doubt," replied Lucius. The judge ordered that he should be put to death on the instant. A third, who came up, was condemned to be beaten with rods. Here, then, are three examples where no delay was granted—[Surely these acts of a single passionate and irritated judge prove the general practice as little as those quoted by Gibbon—M.] There exist a multitude of others, such as those of Ptolemy, Marcellus, &c. Justin expressly charges the judges with ordering the accused to be executed without hearing the cause. The words of St. Cyprian are as particular, and simply say, that he had appointed a day by which the Christians must have renounced their faith; those who had not done it by that time were condemned—G. This confirms the statement in the text—M.]

[Footnote 100: Tertullian considers flight from persecution as an imperfect, but very criminal, apostasy, as an impious attempt to elude the will of God, &c., &c. He has written a treatise on this subject, (see p. 536—544, edit. Rigalt.,) which is filled with the wildest fanaticism and the most incoherent declamation. It is, however, somewhat remarkable, that Tertullian did not suffer martyrdom himself.]

[Footnote 101: The libellatici, who are chiefly known by the writings of Cyprian, are described with the utmost precision, in the copious commentary of Mosheim, p. 483—489.]

[Footnote 101a: The penance was not so slight, for it was exactly the same with that of apostates who had sacrificed to idols; it lasted several years. See Fleun Hist. Ecc. v. ii. p. 171—G.]

[Footnote 102: Plin. Epist. x. 97. Dionysius Alexandrin. ap. Euseb. l. vi. c. 41. Ad prima statim verba minantis inimici maximus fratrum numerus fidem suam prodidit: nec prostratus est persecutionis impetu, sed voluntario lapsu seipsum prostravit. Cyprian. Opera, p. 89. Among these deserters were many priests, and even bishops.]

[Footnote 103: It was on this occasion that Cyprian wrote his treatise De Lapsis, and many of his epistles. The controversy concerning the treatment of penitent apostates, does not occur among the Christians of the preceding century. Shall we ascribe this to the superiority of their faith and courage, or to our less intimate knowledge of their history!]

[Footnote 103a: Pliny says, that the greater part of the Christians persisted in avowing themselves to be so; the reason for his consulting Trajan was the periclitantium numerus. Eusebius (l. vi. c. 41) does not permit us to doubt that the number of those who renounced their faith was infinitely below the number of those who boldly confessed it. The prefect, he says and his assessors present at the council, were alarmed at seeing the crowd of Christians; the judges themselves trembled. Lastly, St. Cyprian informs us, that the greater part of those who had appeared weak brethren in the persecution of Decius, signalized their courage in that of Gallius. Steterunt fortes, et ipso dolore poenitentiae facti ad praelium fortiores Epist. lx. p. 142—G.]

IV. Notwithstanding the general rules established for the conviction and punishment of the Christians, the fate of those sectaries, in an extensive and arbitrary government, must still in a great measure, have depended on their own behavior, the circumstances of the times, and the temper of their supreme as well as subordinate rulers. Zeal might sometimes provoke, and prudence might sometimes avert or assuage, the superstitious fury of the Pagans. A variety of motives might dispose the provincial governors either to enforce or to relax the execution of the laws; and of these motives the most forcible was their regard not only for the public edicts, but for the secret intentions of the emperor, a glance from whose eye was sufficient to kindle or to extinguish the flames of persecution. As often as any occasional severities were exercised in the different parts of the empire, the primitive Christians lamented and perhaps magnified their own sufferings; but the celebrated number of ten persecutions has been determined by the ecclesiastical writers of the fifth century, who possessed a more distinct view of the prosperous or adverse fortunes of the church, from the age of Nero to that of Diocletian. The ingenious parallels of the ten plagues of Egypt, and of the ten horns of the Apocalypse, first suggested this calculation to their minds; and in their application of the faith of prophecy to the truth of history, they were careful to select those reigns which were indeed the most hostile to the Christian cause. [104] But these transient persecutions served only to revive the zeal and to restore the discipline of the faithful; and the moments of extraordinary rigor were compensated by much longer intervals of peace and security. The indifference of some princes, and the indulgence of others, permitted the Christians to enjoy, though not perhaps a legal, yet an actual and public, toleration of their religion.

[Footnote 104: See Mosheim, p. 97. Sulpicius Severus was the first author of this computation; though he seemed desirous of reserving the tenth and greatest persecution for the coming of the Antichrist.]

PART V

The apology of Tertullian contains two very ancient, very singular, but at the same time very suspicious, instances of Imperial clemency; the edicts published by Tiberius, and by Marcus Antoninus, and designed not only to protect the innocence of the Christians, but even to proclaim those stupendous miracles which had attested the truth of their doctrine. The first of these examples is attended with some difficulties which might perplex a sceptical mind. [105] We are required to believe, that Pontius Pilate informed the emperor of the unjust sentence of death which he had pronounced against an innocent, and, as it appeared, a divine, person; and that, without acquiring the merit, he exposed himself to the danger of martyrdom; that Tiberius, who avowed his contempt for all religion, immediately conceived the design of placing the Jewish Messiah among the gods of Rome; that his servile senate ventured to disobey the commands of their master; that Tiberius, instead of resenting their refusal, contented himself with protecting the Christians from the severity of the laws, many years before such laws were enacted, or before the church had assumed any distinct name or existence; and lastly, that the memory of this extraordinary transaction was preserved in the most public and authentic records, which escaped the knowledge of the historians of Greece and Rome, and were only visible to the eyes of an African Christian, who composed his apology one hundred and sixty years after the death of Tiberius. The edict of Marcus Antoninus is supposed to have been the effect of his devotion and gratitude for the miraculous deliverance which he had obtained in the Marcomannic war. The distress of the legions, the seasonable tempest of rain and hail, of thunder and of lightning, and the dismay and defeat of the barbarians, have been celebrated by the eloquence of several Pagan writers. If there were any Christians in that army, it was natural that they should ascribe some merit to the fervent prayers, which, in the moment of danger, they had offered up for their own and the public safety. But we are still assured by monuments of brass and marble, by the Imperial medals, and by the Antonine column, that neither the prince nor the people entertained any sense of this signal obligation, since they unanimously attribute their deliverance to the providence of Jupiter, and to the interposition of Mercury. During the whole course of his reign, Marcus despised the Christians as a philosopher, and punished them as a sovereign. [106] [106a]

[Footnote 105: The testimony given by Pontius Pilate is first mentioned by Justin. The successive improvements which the story acquired (as if has passed through the hands of Tertullian, Eusebius, Epiphanius, Chrysostom, Orosius, Gregory of Tours, and the authors of the several editions of the acts of Pilate) are very fairly stated by Dom Calmet Dissertat. sur l'Ecriture, tom. iii. p. 651, &c.]

[Footnote 106: On this miracle, as it is commonly called, of the thundering legion, see the admirable criticism of Mr. Moyle, in his Works, vol. ii. p. 81—390.]

[Footnote 106a]: Gibbon, with this phrase, and that below, which admits the injustice of Marcus, has dexterously glossed over one of the most remarkable facts in the early Christian history, that the reign of the wisest and most humane of the heathen emperors was the most fatal to the Christians. Most writers have ascribed the persecutions under Marcus to the latent bigotry of his character; Mosheim, to the influence of the philosophic party; but the fact is admitted by all. A late writer (Mr. Waddington, Hist. of the Church, p. 47) has not scrupled to assert, that "this prince polluted every year of a long reign with innocent blood;" but the causes as well as the date of the persecutions authorized or permitted by Marcus are equally uncertain. Of the Asiatic edict recorded by Melito. the date is unknown, nor is it quite clear that it was an Imperial edict. If it was the act under which Polycarp suffered, his martyrdom is placed by Ruinart in the sixth, by Mosheim in the ninth, year of the reign of Marcus. The martyrs of Vienne and Lyons are assigned by Dodwell to the seventh, by most writers to the seventeenth. In fact, the commencement of the persecutions of the Christians appears to synchronize exactly with the period of the breaking out of the Marcomannic war, which seems to have alarmed the whole empire, and the emperor himself, into a paroxysm of returning piety to their gods, of which the Christians were the victims. See Jul, Capit. Script. Hist August. p. 181, edit. 1661. It is remarkable that Tertullian (Apologet. c. v.) distinctly asserts that Verus (M. Aurelius) issued no edicts against the Christians, and almost positively exempts him from the charge of persecution—M. This remarkable synchronism, which explains the persecutions under M Aurelius, is shown at length in Milman's History of Christianity, book ii. v—M. 1845.]

By a singular fatality, the hardships which they had endured under the government of a virtuous prince, immediately ceased on the accession of a tyrant; and as none except themselves had experienced the injustice of Marcus, so they alone were protected by the lenity of Commodus. The celebrated Marcia, the most favored of his concubines, and who at length contrived the murder of her Imperial lover, entertained a singular affection for the oppressed church; and though it was impossible that she could reconcile the practice of vice with the precepts of the gospel, she might hope to atone for the frailties of her sex and profession by declaring herself the patroness of the Christians. [107] Under the gracious protection of Marcia, they passed in safety the thirteen years of a cruel tyranny; and when the empire was established in the house of Severus, they formed a domestic but more honorable connection with the new court. The emperor was persuaded, that in a dangerous sickness, he had derived some benefit, either spiritual or physical, from the holy oil, with which one of his slaves had anointed him. He always treated with peculiar distinction several persons of both sexes who had embraced the new religion. The nurse as well as the preceptor of Caracalla were Christians; [107a] and if that young prince ever betrayed a sentiment of humanity, it was occasioned by an incident, which, however trifling, bore some relation to the cause of Christianity. [108] Under the reign of Severus, the fury of the populace was checked; the rigor of ancient laws was for some time suspended; and the provincial governors were satisfied with receiving an annual present from the churches within their jurisdiction, as the price, or as the reward, of their moderation. [109] The controversy concerning the precise time of the celebration of Easter, armed the bishops of Asia and Italy against each other, and was considered as the most important business of this period of leisure and tranquillity. [110] Nor was the peace of the church interrupted, till the increasing numbers of proselytes seem at length to have attracted the attention, and to have alienated the mind of Severus. With the design of restraining the progress of Christianity, he published an edict, which, though it was designed to affect only the new converts, could not be carried into strict execution, without exposing to danger and punishment the most zealous of their teachers and missionaries. In this mitigated persecution we may still discover the indulgent spirit of Rome and of Polytheism, which so readily admitted every excuse in favor of those who practised the religious ceremonies of their fathers. [111]

[Footnote 107: Dion Cassius, or rather his abbreviator Xiphilin, l. lxxii. p. 1206. Mr. Moyle (p. 266) has explained the condition of the church under the reign of Commodus.]

[Footnote 107a: The Jews and Christians contest the honor of having furnished a nurse is the fratricide son of Severus Caracalla. Hist. of Jews, iii. 158—M.]

[Footnote 108: Compare the life of Caracalla in the Augustan History, with the epistle of Tertullian to Scapula. Dr. Jortin (Remarks on Ecclesiastical History, vol. ii. p. 5, &c.) considers the cure of Severus by the means of holy oil, with a strong desire to convert it into a miracle.]

[Footnote 109: Tertullian de Fuga, c. 13. The present was made during the feast of the Saturnalia; and it is a matter of serious concern to Tertullian, that the faithful should be confounded with the most infamous professions which purchased the connivance of the government.]

[Footnote 110: Euseb. l. v. c. 23, 24. Mosheim, p. 435—447.]

[Footnote 111: Judaeos fieri sub gravi poena vetuit. Idem etiam de Christianis sanxit. Hist. August. p. 70.]

But the laws which Severus had enacted soon expired with the authority of that emperor; and the Christians, after this accidental tempest, enjoyed a calm of thirty-eight years. [112] Till this period they had usually held their assemblies in private houses and sequestered places. They were now permitted to erect and consecrate convenient edifices for the purpose of religious worship; [113] to purchase lands, even at Rome itself, for the use of the community; and to conduct the elections of their ecclesiastical ministers in so public, but at the same time in so exemplary a manner, as to deserve the respectful attention of the Gentiles. [114] This long repose of the church was accompanied with dignity. The reigns of those princes who derived their extraction from the Asiatic provinces, proved the most favorable to the Christians; the eminent persons of the sect, instead of being reduced to implore the protection of a slave or concubine, were admitted into the palace in the honorable characters of priests and philosophers; and their mysterious doctrines, which were already diffused among the people, insensibly attracted the curiosity of their sovereign. When the empress Mammaea passed through Antioch, she expressed a desire of conversing with the celebrated Origen, the fame of whose piety and learning was spread over the East. Origen obeyed so flattering an invitation, and though he could not expect to succeed in the conversion of an artful and ambitious woman, she listened with pleasure to his eloquent exhortations, and honorably dismissed him to his retirement in Palestine. [115] The sentiments of Mammaea were adopted by her son Alexander, and the philosophic devotion of that emperor was marked by a singular but injudicious regard for the Christian religion. In his domestic chapel he placed the statues of Abraham, of Orpheus, of Apollonius, and of Christ, as an honor justly due to those respectable sages who had instructed mankind in the various modes of addressing their homage to the supreme and universal Deity. [116] A purer faith, as well as worship, was openly professed and practised among his household. Bishops, perhaps for the first time, were seen at court; and, after the death of Alexander, when the inhuman Maximin discharged his fury on the favorites and servants of his unfortunate benefactor, a great number of Christians of every rank and of both sexes, were involved in the promiscuous massacre, which, on their account, has improperly received the name of Persecution. [117] [117a]

[Footnote 112: Sulpicius Severus, l. ii. p. 384. This computation (allowing for a single exception) is confirmed by the history of Eusebius, and by the writings of Cyprian.]

[Footnote 113: The antiquity of Christian churches is discussed by Tillemont, (Memoires Ecclesiastiques, tom. iii. part ii. p. 68-72,) and by Mr. Moyle, (vol. i. p. 378-398.) The former refers the first construction of them to the peace of Alexander Severus; the latter, to the peace of Gallienus.]

[Footnote 114: See the Augustan History, p. 130. The emperor Alexander adopted their method of publicly proposing the names of those persons who were candidates for ordination. It is true that the honor of this practice is likewise attributed to the Jews.]

[Footnote 115: Euseb. Hist. Ecclesiast. l. vi. c. 21. Hieronym. de Script. Eccles. c. 54. Mammaea was styled a holy and pious woman, both by the Christians and the Pagans. From the former, therefore, it was impossible that she should deserve that honorable epithet.]

[Footnote 116: See the Augustan History, p. 123. Mosheim (p. 465) seems to refine too much on the domestic religion of Alexander. His design of building a public temple to Christ, (Hist. August. p. 129,) and the objection which was suggested either to him, or in similar circumstances to Hadrian, appear to have no other foundation than an improbable report, invented by the Christians, and credulously adopted by an historian of the age of Constantine.]

[Footnote 117: Euseb. l. vi. c. 28. It may be presumed that the success of the Christians had exasperated the increasing bigotry of the Pagans. Dion Cassius, who composed his history under the former reign, had most probably intended for the use of his master those counsels of persecution, which he ascribes to a better age, and to and to the favorite of Augustus. Concerning this oration of Maecenas, or rather of Dion, I may refer to my own unbiased opinion, (vol. i. c. 1, note 25,) and to the Abbe de la Bleterie (Memoires de l'Academie, tom. xxiv. p. 303 tom xxv. p. 432.) Note: If this be the case, Dion Cassius must have known the Christians they must have been the subject of his particular attention, since the author supposes that he wished his master to profit by these "counsels of persecution." How are we to reconcile this necessary consequence with what Gibbon has said of the ignorance of Dion Cassius even of the name of the Christians? (c. xvi. n. 24.) (Gibbon speaks of Dion's silence, not of his ignorance—M) The supposition in this note is supported by no proof; it is probable that Dion Cassius has often designated the Christians by the name of Jews. See Dion Cassius, l. lxvii. c 14, lxviii. l—G. On this point I should adopt the view of Gibbon rather than that of M Guizot—M]

[Footnote 107a: It is with good reason that this massacre has been called a persecution, for it lasted during the whole reign of Maximin, as may be seen in Eusebius. (l. vi. c. 28.) Rufinus expressly confirms it: Tribus annis a Maximino persecutione commota, in quibus finem et persecutionis fecit et vitas Hist. l. vi. c. 19—G.]

Notwithstanding the cruel disposition of Maximin, the effects of his resentment against the Christians were of a very local and temporary nature, and the pious Origen, who had been proscribed as a devoted victim, was still reserved to convey the truths of the gospel to the ear of monarchs. [118] He addressed several edifying letters to the emperor Philip, to his wife, and to his mother; and as soon as that prince, who was born in the neighborhood of Palestine, had usurped the Imperial sceptre, the Christians acquired a friend and a protector. The public and even partial favor of Philip towards the sectaries of the new religion, and his constant reverence for the ministers of the church, gave some color to the suspicion, which prevailed in his own times, that the emperor himself was become a convert to the faith; [119] and afforded some grounds for a fable which was afterwards invented, that he had been purified by confession and penance from the guilt contracted by the murder of his innocent predecessor. [120] The fall of Philip introduced, with the change of masters, a new system of government, so oppressive to the Christians, that their former condition, ever since the time of Domitian, was represented as a state of perfect freedom and security, if compared with the rigorous treatment which they experienced under the short reign of Decius. [121] The virtues of that prince will scarcely allow us to suspect that he was actuated by a mean resentment against the favorites of his predecessor; and it is more reasonable to believe, that in the prosecution of his general design to restore the purity of Roman manners, he was desirous of delivering the empire from what he condemned as a recent and criminal superstition. The bishops of the most considerable cities were removed by exile or death: the vigilance of the magistrates prevented the clergy of Rome during sixteen months from proceeding to a new election; and it was the opinion of the Christians, that the emperor would more patiently endure a competitor for the purple, than a bishop in the capital. [122] Were it possible to suppose that the penetration of Decius had discovered pride under the disguise of humility, or that he could foresee the temporal dominion which might insensibly arise from the claims of spiritual authority, we might be less surprised, that he should consider the successors of St. Peter, as the most formidable rivals to those of Augustus.

[Footnote 118: Orosius, l. vii. c. 19, mentions Origen as the object of Maximin's resentment; and Firmilianus, a Cappadocian bishop of that age, gives a just and confined idea of this persecution, (apud Cyprian Epist. 75.)]

[Footnote 119: The mention of those princes who were publicly supposed to be Christians, as we find it in an epistle of Dionysius of Alexandria, (ap. Euseb. l. vii. c. 10,) evidently alludes to Philip and his family, and forms a contemporary evidence, that such a report had prevailed; but the Egyptian bishop, who lived at an humble distance from the court of Rome, expresses himself with a becoming diffidence concerning the truth of the fact. The epistles of Origen (which were extant in the time of Eusebius, see l. vi. c. 36) would most probably decide this curious rather than important question.]

[Footnote 120: Euseb. l. vi. c. 34. The story, as is usual, has been embellished by succeeding writers, and is confuted, with much superfluous learning, by Frederick Spanheim, (Opera Varia, tom. ii. p. 400, &c.)]

[Footnote 121: Lactantius, de Mortibus Persecutorum, c. 3, 4. After celebrating the felicity and increase of the church, under a long succession of good princes, he adds, "Extitit post annos plurimos, execrabile animal, Decius, qui vexaret Ecclesiam."]

[Footnote 122: Euseb. l. vi. c. 39. Cyprian. Epistol. 55. The see of Rome remained vacant from the martyrdom of Fabianus, the 20th of January, A. D. 259, till the election of Cornelius, the 4th of June, A. D. 251 Decius had probably left Rome, since he was killed before the end of that year.]

The administration of Valerian was distinguished by a levity and inconstancy ill suited to the gravity of the Roman Censor. In the first part of his reign, he surpassed in clemency those princes who had been suspected of an attachment to the Christian faith. In the last three years and a half, listening to the insinuations of a minister addicted to the superstitions of Egypt, he adopted the maxims, and imitated the severity, of his predecessor Decius. [123] The accession of Gallienus, which increased the calamities of the empire, restored peace to the church; and the Christians obtained the free exercise of their religion by an edict addressed to the bishops, and conceived in such terms as seemed to acknowledge their office and public character. [124] The ancient laws, without being formally repealed, were suffered to sink into oblivion; and (excepting only some hostile intentions which are attributed to the emperor Aurelian [125] the disciples of Christ passed above forty years in a state of prosperity, far more dangerous to their virtue than the severest trials of persecution.

[Footnote 123: Euseb. l. vii. c. 10. Mosheim (p. 548) has very clearly shown that the praefect Macrianus, and the Egyptian Magus, are one and the same person.]

[Footnote 124: Eusebius (l. vii. c. 13) gives us a Greek version of this Latin edict, which seems to have been very concise. By another edict, he directed that the Coemeteria should be restored to the Christians.]

[Footnote 125: Euseb. l. vii. c. 30. Lactantius de M. P. c. 6. Hieronym. in Chron. p. 177. Orosius, l. vii. c. 23. Their language is in general so ambiguous and incorrect, that we are at a loss to determine how far Aurelian had carried his intentions before he was assassinated. Most of the moderns (except Dodwell, Dissertat. Cyprian. vi. 64) have seized the occasion of gaining a few extraordinary martyrs. Note: Dr. Lardner has detailed, with his usual impartiality, all that has come down to us relating to the persecution of Aurelian, and concludes by saying, "Upon more carefully examining the words of Eusebius, and observing the accounts of other authors, learned men have generally, and, as I think, very judiciously, determined, that Aurelian not only intended, but did actually persecute: but his persecution was short, he having died soon after the publication of his edicts." Heathen Test. c. xxxvi—Basmage positively pronounces the same opinion: Non intentatum modo, sed executum quoque brevissimo tempore *mandatum, nobis infixum est in aniasis. Basn. Ann. 275, No. 2 and compare Pagi Ann. 272, Nos. 4, 12, 27—G.]*

The story of Paul of Samosata, who filled the metropolitan see of Antioch, while the East was in the hands of Odenathus and Zenobia, may serve to illustrate the condition and character of the times. The wealth of that prelate was a sufficient evidence of his guilt, since it was neither derived from the inheritance of his fathers, nor acquired by the arts of honest industry. But Paul considered the service of the church as a very lucrative profession. [126] His ecclesiastical jurisdiction was venal and rapacious; he extorted frequent contributions from the most opulent of the faithful, and converted to his own use a considerable part of the public revenue. By his pride and luxury, the Christian religion was rendered odious in the eyes of the Gentiles. His council chamber and his throne, the splendor with which he appeared in public, the suppliant crowd who solicited his attention, the multitude of letters and petitions to which he dictated his answers, and the perpetual hurry of business in which he was involved, were circumstances much better suited to the state of a civil magistrate, [127] than to the humility of a primitive bishop. When he harangued his people from the pulpit, Paul affected the figurative style and the theatrical gestures of an Asiatic sophist, while the cathedral resounded with the loudest and most extravagant acclamations in the praise of his divine eloquence. Against those who resisted his power, or refused to flatter his vanity, the prelate of Antioch was arrogant, rigid, and inexorable; but he relaxed the discipline, and lavished the treasures of the church on his dependent clergy, who were permitted to imitate their master in the gratification of every sensual appetite. For Paul indulged himself very freely in the pleasures of the table, and he had received into the episcopal palace two young and beautiful women as the constant companions of his leisure moments. [128]

[Footnote 126: Paul was better pleased with the title of Ducenarius, than with that of bishop. The Ducenarius was an Imperial procurator, so called from his salary of two hundred Sestertia, or 1600l. a year. (See Salmatius ad Hist. August. p. 124.) Some critics suppose that the bishop of Antioch had actually obtained such an office from Zenobia, while others consider it only as a figurative expression of his pomp and insolence.]

[Footnote 127: Simony was not unknown in those times; and the clergy some times bought what they intended to sell. It appears that the bishopric of Carthage was purchased by a wealthy matron, named Lucilla, for her servant Majorinus. The price was 400 Folles. (Monument. Antiq. ad calcem Optati, p. 263.) Every Follis contained 125 pieces of silver, and the whole sum may be computed at about 2400l.]

[Footnote 128: If we are desirous of extenuating the vices of Paul, we must suspect the assembled bishops of the East of publishing the most malicious calumnies in circular epistles addressed to all the churches of the empire, (ap. Euseb. l. vii. c. 30.)]

Notwithstanding these scandalous vices, if Paul of Samosata had preserved the purity of the orthodox faith, his reign over the capital of Syria would have ended only with his life; and had a seasonable persecution intervened, an effort of courage might perhaps have placed him in the rank of saints and martyrs. [128a]

Some nice and subtle errors, which he imprudently adopted and obstinately maintained, concerning the doctrine of the Trinity, excited the zeal and indignation of the Eastern churches. [129]

From Egypt to the Euxine Sea, the bishops were in arms and in motion. Several councils were held, confutations were published, excommunications were pronounced, ambiguous explanations were by turns accepted and refused, treaties were concluded and violated, and at length Paul of Samosata was degraded from his episcopal character, by the sentence of seventy or eighty bishops, who assembled for that purpose at Antioch, and who, without consulting the rights of the clergy or people, appointed a successor by their own authority. The manifest irregularity of this proceeding increased the numbers of the discontented faction; and as Paul, who was no stranger to the arts of courts, had insinuated himself into the favor of Zenobia, he maintained above four years the possession of the episcopal house and office. [129a] The victory of Aurelian changed the face of the East, and the two contending parties, who applied to each other the epithets of schism and heresy, were either commanded or permitted to plead their cause before the tribunal of the conqueror. This public and very singular trial affords a convincing proof that the existence, the property, the privileges, and the internal policy of the Christians, were acknowledged, if not by the laws, at least by the magistrates, of the empire. As a Pagan and as a soldier, it could scarcely be expected that Aurelian should enter into the discussion, whether the sentiments of Paul or those of his adversaries were most agreeable to the true standard of the orthodox faith. His determination, however, was founded on the general principles of equity and reason. He considered the bishops of Italy as the most impartial and respectable judges among the Christians, and as soon as he was informed that they had unanimously approved the sentence of the council, he acquiesced in their opinion, and immediately gave orders that Paul should be compelled to relinquish the temporal possessions belonging to an office, of which, in the judgment of his brethren, he had been regularly deprived. But while we applaud the justice, we should not overlook the policy, of Aurelian, who was desirous of restoring and cementing the dependence of the provinces on the capital, by every means which could bind the interest or prejudices of any part of his subjects. [130]

[Footnote 128a: It appears, nevertheless, that the vices and immoralities of Paul of Samosata had much weight in the sentence pronounced against him by the bishops. The object of the letter, addressed by the synod to the bishops of Rome and Alexandria, was to inform them of the change in the faith of Paul, the altercations and discussions to which it had given rise, as well as of his morals and the whole of his conduct. Euseb. Hist. Eccl. l. vii c. xxx—G.]

[Footnote 129: His heresy (like those of Noetus and Sabellius, in the same century) tended to confound the mysterious distinction of the divine persons. See Mosheim, p. 702, &c.]

[Footnote 129a: "Her favorite, (Zenobia's,) Paul of Samosata, seems to have entertained some views of attempting a union between Judaism and Christianity; both parties rejected the unnatural alliance." Hist. of Jews, iii. 175, and Jost. Geschichte der Israeliter, iv. 167. The protection of the severe Zenobia is the only circumstance which may raise a doubt of the notorious immorality of Paul—M.]

[Footnote 130: Euseb. Hist. Ecclesiast. l. vii. c. 30. We are entirely indebted to him for the curious story of Paul of Samosata.]

Amidst the frequent revolutions of the empire, the Christians still flourished in peace and prosperity; and notwithstanding a celebrated aera of martyrs has been deduced from the accession of Diocletian, [131] the new system of policy, introduced and maintained by the wisdom of that prince, continued, during more than eighteen years, to breathe the mildest and most liberal spirit of religious toleration. The mind of Diocletian himself was less adapted indeed to speculative inquiries, than to the active labors of war and government. His prudence rendered him averse to any great innovation, and though his temper was not very susceptible of zeal or enthusiasm, he always maintained an habitual regard for the ancient deities of the empire. But the leisure of the two empresses, of his wife Prisca, and of Valeria, his daughter, permitted them to listen with more attention and respect to the truths of Christianity, which in every age has acknowledged its important obligations to female devotion. [132] The principal eunuchs, Lucian [133] and Dorotheus, Gorgonius and Andrew, who attended the person, possessed the favor, and governed the household of Diocletian, protected by their powerful influence the faith which they had embraced. Their example was imitated by many of the most considerable officers of the palace, who, in their respective stations, had the care of the Imperial ornaments, of the robes, of the furniture, of the jewels, and even of the private treasury; and, though it might sometimes be incumbent on them to accompany the emperor when he sacrificed in the temple, [134] they enjoyed, with their wives, their children, and their slaves, the free exercise of the Christian religion. Diocletian and his colleagues frequently conferred the most important offices on those persons who avowed their abhorrence for the worship of the gods, but who had displayed abilities proper for the service of the state. The bishops held an honorable rank in their respective provinces, and were treated with distinction and respect, not only by the people, but by the magistrates themselves. Almost in every city, the ancient churches were found insufficient to contain the increasing multitude of proselytes; and in their place more stately and capacious edifices were erected for the public worship of the faithful. The corruption of manners and principles, so forcibly lamented by Eusebius, [135] may be considered, not only as a consequence, but as a proof, of the liberty which the Christians enjoyed and abused under the reign of Diocletian. Prosperity had relaxed the nerves of discipline. Fraud, envy, and malice prevailed in every congregation. The presbyters aspired to the episcopal office, which every day became an object more worthy of their ambition. The bishops, who contended with each other for ecclesiastical preeminence, appeared by their conduct to claim a secular and tyrannical power in the church; and the lively faith which still distinguished the Christians from the Gentiles, was shown much less in their lives, than in their controversial writings.

[Footnote 131: The Aera of Martyrs, which is still in use among the Copts and the Abyssinians, must be reckoned from the 29th of August, A. D. 284; as the beginning of the Egyptian year was nineteen days earlier than the real accession of Diocletian. See Dissertation Preliminaire a l'Art de verifier les Dates. Note: On the aera of martyrs see the very curious dissertations of Mons Letronne on some recently discovered inscriptions in Egypt and Nubis, p. 102, &c—M.]

[Footnote 132: The expression of Lactantius, (de M. P. c. 15,) "sacrificio pollui coegit," implies their antecedent conversion to the faith, but does not seem to justify the assertion of Mosheim, (p. 912,) that they had been privately baptized.]

[Footnote 133: M. de Tillemont (Memoires Ecclesiastiques, tom. v. part i. p. 11, 12) has quoted from the Spicilegium of Dom Luc d'Archeri a very curious instruction which Bishop Theonas composed for the use of Lucian.]

[Footnote 134: Lactantius, de M. P. c. 10.]

[Footnote 135: Eusebius, Hist. Ecclesiast. l. viii. c. 1. The reader who consults the original will not accuse me of heightening the picture. Eusebius was about sixteen years of age at the accession of the emperor Diocletian.]

Notwithstanding this seeming security, an attentive observer might discern some symptoms that threatened the church with a more violent persecution than any which she had yet endured. The zeal and rapid progress of the Christians awakened the Polytheists from their supine indifference in the cause of those deities, whom custom and education had taught them to revere. The mutual provocations of a religious war, which had already continued above two hundred years, exasperated the animosity of the contending parties. The Pagans were incensed at the rashness of a recent and obscure sect, which presumed to accuse their countrymen of error, and to devote their ancestors to eternal misery. The habits of justifying the popular mythology against the invectives of an implacable enemy, produced in their minds some sentiments of faith and reverence for a system which they had been accustomed to consider with the most careless levity. The supernatural powers assumed by the church inspired at the same time terror and emulation. The followers of the established religion intrenched themselves behind a similar fortification of prodigies; invented new modes of sacrifice, of expiation, and of initiation; [136] attempted to revive the credit of their expiring oracles; [137] and listened with eager credulity to every impostor, who flattered their prejudices by a tale of wonders. [138] Both parties seemed to acknowledge the truth of those miracles which were claimed by their adversaries; and while they were contented with ascribing them to the arts of magic, and to the power of daemons, they mutually concurred in restoring and establishing the reign of superstition. [139] Philosophy, her most dangerous enemy, was now converted into her most useful ally. The groves of the academy, the gardens of Epicurus, and even the portico of the Stoics, were almost deserted, as so many different schools of scepticism or impiety; [140] and many among the Romans were desirous that the writings of Cicero should be condemned and suppressed by the authority of the senate. [141] The prevailing sect of the new Platonicians judged it prudent to connect themselves with the priests, whom perhaps they despised, against the Christians, whom they had reason to fear. These fashionable Philosophers prosecuted the design of extracting allegorical wisdom from the fictions of the Greek poets; instituted mysterious rites of devotion for the use of their chosen disciples; recommended the worship of the ancient gods as the emblems or ministers of the Supreme Deity, and composed against the faith of the gospel many elaborate treatises, [142] which have since been committed to the flames by the prudence of orthodox emperors. [143]

[Footnote 136: We might quote, among a great number of instances, the mysterious worship of Mythras, and the Taurobolia; the latter of which became fashionable in the time of the Antonines, (see a Dissertation of M. de Boze, in the Memoires de l'Academie des Inscriptions, tom. ii. p. 443.) The romance of Apuleius is as full of devotion as of satire. Note: On the extraordinary progress of the Mahriac rites, in the West, see De Guigniaud's translation of Creuzer, vol. i. p. 365, and Note 9, tom. i. part 2, p. 738, &c—M.]

[Footnote 137: The impostor Alexander very strongly recommended the oracle of Trophonius at Mallos, and those of Apollo at Claros and Miletus, (Lucian, tom. ii. p. 236, edit. Reitz.) The last of these, whose singular history would furnish a very curious episode, was consulted by Diocletian before he published his edicts of persecution, (Lactantius, de M. P. c. 11.)]

[Footnote 138: Besides the ancient stories of Pythagoras and Aristeas, the cures performed at the shrine of Aesculapius, and the fables related of Apollonius of Tyana, were frequently opposed to the miracles of Christ; though I agree with Dr. Lardner, (see Testimonies, vol. iii. p. 253, 352,) that when Philostratus composed the life of Apollonius, he had no such intention.]

[Footnote 139: It is seriously to be lamented, that the Christian fathers, by acknowledging the supernatural, or, as they deem it, the infernal part of Paganism, destroy with their own hands the great advantage which we might otherwise derive from the liberal concessions of our adversaries.]

[Footnote 140: Julian (p. 301, edit. Spanheim) expresses a pious joy, that the providence of the gods had extinguished the impious sects, and for the most part destroyed the books of the Pyrrhonians and

Epicuraeans, which had been very numerous, since Epicurus himself composed no less than 300 volumes. See Diogenes Laertius, l. x. c. 26.]

[Footnote 141: Cumque alios audiam mussitare indignanter, et dicere opportere statui per Senatum, aboleantur ut haec scripta, quibus Christiana Religio comprobetur, et vetustatis opprimatur auctoritas. Arnobius adversus Gentes, l. iii. p. 103, 104. He adds very properly, Erroris convincite Ciceronem... nam intercipere scripta, et publicatam velle submergere lectionem, non est Deum defendere sed veritatis testificationem timere.]

[Footnote 142: Lactantius (Divin. Institut. l. v. c. 2, 3) gives a very clear and spirited account of two of these philosophic adversaries of the faith. The large treatise of Porphyry against the Christians consisted of thirty books, and was composed in Sicily about the year 270.]

[Footnote 143: See Socrates, Hist. Ecclesiast. l. i. c. 9, and Codex Justinian. l. i. i. l. s.]

PART VI

Although the policy of Diocletian and the humanity of Constantius inclined them to preserve inviolate the maxims of toleration, it was soon discovered that their two associates, Maximian and Galerius, entertained the most implacable aversion for the name and religion of the Christians. The minds of those princes had never been enlightened by science; education had never softened their temper. They owed their greatness to their swords, and in their most elevated fortune they still retained their superstitious prejudices of soldiers and peasants. In the general administration of the provinces they obeyed the laws which their benefactor had established; but they frequently found occasions of exercising within their camp and palaces a secret persecution, [144] for which the imprudent zeal of the Christians sometimes offered the most specious pretences. A sentence of death was executed upon Maximilianus, an African youth, who had been produced by his own father [144a] before the magistrate as a sufficient and legal recruit, but who obstinately persisted in declaring, that his conscience would not permit him to embrace the profession of a soldier. [145] It could scarcely be expected that any government should suffer the action of Marcellus the Centurion to pass with impunity. On the day of a public festival, that officer threw away his belt, his arms, and the ensigns of his office, and exclaimed with a loud voice, that he would obey none but Jesus Christ the eternal King, and that he renounced forever the use of carnal weapons, and the service of an idolatrous master. The soldiers, as soon as they recovered from their astonishment, secured the person of Marcellus. He was examined in the city of Tingi by the president of that part of Mauritania; and as he was convicted by his own confession, he was condemned and beheaded for the crime of desertion. [146] Examples of such a nature savor much less of religious persecution than of martial or even civil law; but they served to alienate the mind of the emperors, to justify the severity of Galerius, who dismissed a great number of Christian officers from their employments; and to authorize the opinion, that a sect of enthusiastics, which avowed principles so repugnant to the public safety, must either remain useless, or would soon become dangerous, subjects of the empire.

[Footnote 144: Eusebius, l. viii. c. 4, c. 17. He limits the number of military martyrs, by a remarkable expression, of which neither his Latin nor French translator have rendered the energy. Notwithstanding the authority of Eusebius, and the silence of Lactantius, Ambrose, Sulpicius, Orosius, &c., it has been long believed, that the Thebaean legion, consisting of 6000 Christians, suffered martyrdom by the order of

Maximian, in the valley of the Pennine Alps. The story was first published about the middle of the 5th century, by Eucherius, bishop of Lyons, who received it from certain persons, who received it from Isaac, bishop of Geneva, who is said to have received it from Theodore, bishop of Octodurum. The abbey of St. Maurice still subsists, a rich monument of the credulity of Sigismund, king of Burgundy. See an excellent Dissertation in xxxvith volume of the Bibliotheque Raisonnee, p. 427-454.]

[Footnote 144a: M. Guizot criticizes Gibbon's account of this incident. He supposes that Maximilian was not "produced by his father as a recruit," but was obliged to appear by the law, which compelled the sons of soldiers to serve at 21 years old. Was not this a law of Constantine? Neither does this circumstance appear in the acts. His father had clearly expected him to serve, as he had bought him a new dress for the occasion; yet he refused to force the conscience of his son. and when Maximilian was condemned to death, the father returned home in joy, blessing God for having bestowed upon him such a son—M.]

[Footnote 145: See the Acta Sincera, p. 299. The accounts of his martyrdom and that of Marcellus, bear every mark of truth and authenticity.]

[Footnote 146: Acta Sincera, p. 302. Note: M. Guizot here justly observes, that it was the necessity of sacrificing to the gods, which induced Marcellus to act in this manner—M.]

After the success of the Persian war had raised the hopes and the reputation of Galerius, he passed a winter with Diocletian in the palace of Nicomedia; and the fate of Christianity became the object of their secret consultations. [147] The experienced emperor was still inclined to pursue measures of lenity; and though he readily consented to exclude the Christians from holding any employments in the household or the army, he urged in the strongest terms the danger as well as cruelty of shedding the blood of those deluded fanatics. Galerius at length extorted [147a] from him the permission of summoning a council, composed of a few persons the most distinguished in the civil and military departments of the state.

The important question was agitated in their presence, and those ambitious courtiers easily discerned, that it was incumbent on them to second, by their eloquence, the importunate violence of the Caesar. It may be presumed, that they insisted on every topic which might interest the pride, the piety, or the fears, of their sovereign in the destruction of Christianity. Perhaps they represented, that the glorious work of the deliverance of the empire was left imperfect, as long as an independent people was permitted to subsist and multiply in the heart of the provinces. The Christians, (it might specially be alleged,) renouncing the gods and the institutions of Rome, had constituted a distinct republic, which might yet be suppressed before it had acquired any military force; but which was already governed by its own laws and magistrates, was possessed of a public treasure, and was intimately connected in all its parts by the frequent assemblies of the bishops, to whose decrees their numerous and opulent congregations yielded an implicit obedience. Arguments like these may seem to have determined the reluctant mind of Diocletian to embrace a new system of persecution; but though we may suspect, it is not in our power to relate, the secret intrigues of the palace, the private views and resentments, the jealousy of women or eunuchs, and all those trifling but decisive causes which so often influence the fate of empires, and the councils of the wisest monarchs. [148]

[Footnote 147: De M. P. c. 11. Lactantius (or whoever was the author of this little treatise) was, at that time, an inhabitant of Nicomedia; but it seems difficult to conceive how he could acquire so accurate a knowledge of what passed in the Imperial cabinet. Note: Lactantius, who was subsequently chosen by Constantine to educate Crispus, might easily have learned these details from Constantine himself, *already of sufficient age to interest himself in the affairs of the government, and in a position to obtain the best information—G. This assumes the doubtful point of the authorship of the Treatise—M.]*

[Footnote 147a: This permission was not extorted from Diocletian; he took the step of his own accord. Lactantius says, in truth, Nec tamen deflectere potuit (Diocletianus) praecipitis hominis insaniam; placuit ergo amicorum sententiam experiri. (De Mort. Pers. c. 11.) But this measure was in accordance with the artificial character of Diocletian, who wished to have the appearance of doing good by his own impulse and evil by the impulse of others. Nam erat hujus malitiae, cum bonum quid facere decrevisse sine consilio faciebat, ut ipse laudaretur. Cum autem malum. quoniam id reprehendendum sciebat, in consilium multos advocabat, ut alioram culpao adscriberetur quicquid ipse deliquerat. Lact. ib. Eutropius says likewise, Miratus callide fuit, sagax praeterea et admodum subtilis ingenio, et qui severitatem suam aliena invidia vellet explere. Eutrop. ix. c. 26—G—The manner in which the coarse and unfriendly pencil of the author of the Treatise de Mort. Pers. has drawn the character of Diocletian, seems inconsistent with this profound subtilty. Many readers will perhaps agree with Gibbon—M.]

[Footnote 148: The only circumstance which we can discover, is the devotion and jealousy of the mother of Galerius. She is described by Lactantius, as Deorum montium cultrix; mulier admodum superstitiosa. She had a great influence over her son, and was offended by the disregard of some of her Christian servants. Note: This disregard consisted in the Christians fasting and praying instead of participating in the banquets and sacrifices which she celebrated with the Pagans. Dapibus sacrificabat poene quotidie ac vicariis suis epulis exhibebat. Christiani abstinebant, et illa cum gentibus epulante, jejuniis hi et oratiomibus insisteban; hinc concepit odium Lact de Hist. Pers. c. 11—G.]

The pleasure of the emperors was at length signified to the Christians, who, during the course of this melancholy winter, had expected, with anxiety, the result of so many secret consultations. The twenty-third of February, which coincided with the Roman festival of the Terminalia, [149] was appointed (whether from accident or design) to set bounds to the progress of Christianity. At the earliest dawn of day, the Praetorian praefect, [150] accompanied by several generals, tribunes, and officers of the revenue, repaired to the principal church of Nicomedia, which was situated on an eminence in the most populous and beautiful part of the city. The doors were instantly broke open; they rushed into the sanctuary; and as they searched in vain for some visible object of worship, they were obliged to content themselves with committing to the flames the volumes of the holy Scripture. The ministers of Diocletian were followed by a numerous body of guards and pioneers, who marched in order of battle, and were provided with all the instruments used in the destruction of fortified cities. By their incessant labor, a sacred edifice, which towered above the Imperial palace, and had long excited the indignation and envy of the Gentiles, was in a few hours levelled with the ground. [151]

[Footnote 149: The worship and festival of the god Terminus are elegantly illustrated by M. de Boze, Mem. de l'Academie des Inscriptions, tom. i. p. 50.]

[Footnote 150: In our only MS. of Lactantius, we read profectus; but reason, and the authority of all the critics, allow us, instead of that word, which destroys the sense of the passage, to substitute proefectus.]

[Footnote 151: Lactantius, de M. P. c. 12, gives a very lively picture of the destruction of the church.]

The next day the general edict of persecution was published; [152] and though Diocletian, still averse to the effusion of blood, had moderated the fury of Galerius, who proposed, that every one refusing to offer sacrifice should immediately be burnt alive, the penalties inflicted on the obstinacy of the

Christians might be deemed sufficiently rigorous and effectual. It was enacted, that their churches, in all the provinces of the empire, should be demolished to their foundations; and the punishment of death was denounced against all who should presume to hold any secret assemblies for the purpose of religious worship. The philosophers, who now assumed the unworthy office of directing the blind zeal of persecution, had diligently studied the nature and genius of the Christian religion; and as they were not ignorant that the speculative doctrines of the faith were supposed to be contained in the writings of the prophets, of the evangelists, and of the apostles, they most probably suggested the order, that the bishops and presbyters should deliver all their sacred books into the hands of the magistrates; who were commanded, under the severest penalties, to burn them in a public and solemn manner. By the same edict, the property of the church was at once confiscated; and the several parts of which it might consist were either sold to the highest bidder, united to the Imperial domain, bestowed on the cities and corporations, or granted to the solicitations of rapacious courtiers. After taking such effectual measures to abolish the worship, and to dissolve the government of the Christians, it was thought necessary to subject to the most intolerable hardships the condition of those perverse individuals who should still reject the religion of nature, of Rome, and of their ancestors. Persons of a liberal birth were declared incapable of holding any honors or employments; slaves were forever deprived of the hopes of freedom, and the whole body of the people were put out of the protection of the law. The judges were authorized to hear and to determine every action that was brought against a Christian. But the Christians were not permitted to complain of any injury which they themselves had suffered; and thus those unfortunate sectaries were exposed to the severity, while they were excluded from the benefits, of public justice. This new species of martyrdom, so painful and lingering, so obscure and ignominious, was, perhaps, the most proper to weary the constancy of the faithful: nor can it be doubted that the passions and interest of mankind were disposed on this occasion to second the designs of the emperors. But the policy of a well-ordered government must sometimes have interposed in behalf of the oppressed Christians; [152a] nor was it possible for the Roman princes entirely to remove the apprehension of punishment, or to connive at every act of fraud and violence, without exposing their own authority and the rest of their subjects to the most alarming dangers. [153]

[Footnote 152: Mosheim, (p. 922—926,) from man scattered passages of Lactantius and Eusebius, has collected a very just and accurate notion of this edict though he sometimes deviates into conjecture and refinement.]

[Footnote 152a: This wants proof. The edict of Diocletian was executed in all its right during the rest of his reign. Euseb. Hist. Eccl. l viii. c. 13—G.]

[Footnote 153: Many ages afterwards, Edward J. practised, with great success, the same mode of persecution against the clergy of England. See Hume's History of England, vol. ii. p. 300, last 4to edition.]

This edict was scarcely exhibited to the public view, in the most conspicuous place of Nicomedia, before it was torn down by the hands of a Christian, who expressed at the same time, by the bitterest invectives, his contempt as well as abhorrence for such impious and tyrannical governors. His offence, according to the mildest laws, amounted to treason, and deserved death. And if it be true that he was a person of rank and education, those circumstances could serve only to aggravate his guilt. He was burnt, or rather roasted, by a slow fire; and his executioners, zealous to revenge the personal insult which had been offered to the emperors, exhausted every refinement of cruelty, without being able to subdue his patience, or to alter the steady and insulting smile which in his dying agonies he still preserved in his countenance. The Christians, though they confessed that his conduct had not been strictly conformable to the laws of prudence, admired the divine fervor of his zeal; and the excessive commendations which they lavished on the memory of their hero and martyr, contributed to fix a deep impression of terror and hatred in the mind of Diocletian. [154]

[Footnote 154: Lactantius only calls him quidam, et si non recte, magno tamer animo, &c., c. 12. Eusebius (l. viii. c. 5) adorns him with secular honora Neither have condescended to mention his name; but the Greeks celebrate his memory under that of John. See Tillemont, Memones Ecclesiastiques, tom. v. part ii. p. 320.]

His fears were soon alarmed by the view of a danger from which he very narrowly escaped. Within fifteen days the palace of Nicomedia, and even the bed-chamber of Diocletian, were twice in flames; and though both times they were extinguished without any material damage, the singular repetition of the fire was justly considered as an evident proof that it had not been the effect of chance or negligence. The suspicion naturally fell on the Christians; and it was suggested, with some degree of probability, that those desperate fanatics, provoked by their present sufferings, and apprehensive of impending calamities, had entered into a conspiracy with their faithful brethren, the eunuchs of the palace, against the lives of two emperors, whom they detested as the irreconcilable enemies of the church of God.

Jealousy and resentment prevailed in every breast, but especially in that of Diocletian. A great number of persons, distinguished either by the offices which they had filled, or by the favor which they had enjoyed, were thrown into prison. Every mode of torture was put in practice, and the court, as well as city, was polluted with many bloody executions. [155] But as it was found impossible to extort any discovery of this mysterious transaction, it seems incumbent on us either to presume the innocence, or to admire the resolution, of the sufferers. A few days afterwards Galerius hastily withdrew himself from Nicomedia, declaring, that if he delayed his departure from that devoted palace, he should fall a sacrifice to the rage of the Christians.

The ecclesiastical historians, from whom alone we derive a partial and imperfect knowledge of this persecution, are at a loss how to account for the fears and dangers of the emperors. Two of these writers, a prince and a rhetorician, were eye-witnesses of the fire of Nicomedia. The one ascribes it to lightning, and the divine wrath; the other affirms, that it was kindled by the malice of Galerius himself. [156]

[Footnote 155: Lactantius de M. P. c. 13, 14. Potentissimi quondam Eunuchi necati, per quos Palatium et ipse constabat. Eusebius (l. viii. c. 6) mentions the cruel executions of the eunuchs, Gorgonius and Dorotheus, and of Anthimius, bishop of Nicomedia; and both those writers describe, in a vague but tragical manner, the horrid scenes which were acted even in the Imperial presence.]

[Footnote 156: See Lactantius, Eusebius, and Constantine, ad Coetum Sanctorum, c. xxv. Eusebius confesses his ignorance of the cause of this fire. Note: As the history of these times affords us no example of any attempts made by the Christians against their persecutors, we have no reason, not the slightest probability, to attribute to them the fire in the palace; and the authority of Constantine and Lactantius remains to explain it. M. de Tillemont has shown how they can be reconciled. Hist. des Empereurs, Vie de Diocletian, xix—G. Had it been done by a Christian, it would probably have been a fanatic, who would have avowed and gloried in it. Tillemont's supposition that the fire was first caused by lightning, and fed and increased by the malice of Galerius, seems singularly improbable—M.]

As the edict against the Christians was designed for a general law of the whole empire, and as Diocletian and Galerius, though they might not wait for the consent, were assured of the concurrence, of the Western princes, it would appear more consonant to our ideas of policy, that the governors of all the provinces should have received secret instructions to publish, on one and the same day, this declaration of war within their respective departments. It was at least to be expected, that the convenience of the public highways and established posts would have enabled the emperors to transmit their orders with the utmost despatch from the palace of Nicomedia to the extremities of the Roman world; and that they would not have suffered fifty days to elapse, before the edict was published in Syria, and near four months before it was signified to the cities of Africa. [157]

This delay may perhaps be imputed to the cautious temper of Diocletian, who had yielded a reluctant consent to the measures of persecution, and who was desirous of trying the experiment under his more immediate eye, before he gave way to the disorders and discontent which it must inevitably occasion in the distant provinces. At first, indeed, the magistrates were restrained from the effusion of blood; but the use of every other severity was permitted, and even recommended to their zeal; nor could the Christians, though they cheerfully resigned the ornaments of their churches, resolve to interrupt their religious assemblies, or to deliver their sacred books to the flames. The pious obstinacy of Felix, an African bishop, appears to have embarrassed the subordinate ministers of the government. The curator of his city sent him in chains to the proconsul. The proconsul transmitted him to the Praetorian praefect of Italy; and Felix, who disdained even to give an evasive answer, was at length beheaded at Venusia, in Lucania, a place on which the birth of Horace has conferred fame. [158] This precedent, and perhaps some Imperial rescript, which was issued in consequence of it, appeared to authorize the governors of provinces, in punishing with death the refusal of the Christians to deliver up their sacred books. There were undoubtedly many persons who embraced this opportunity of obtaining the crown of martyrdom; but there were likewise too many who purchased an ignominious life, by discovering and betraying the holy Scripture into the hands of infidels. A great number even of bishops and presbyters acquired, by this criminal compliance, the opprobrious epithet of Traditors; and their offence was productive of much present scandal and of much future discord in the African church. [159]

[Footnote 157: Tillemont, Memoires Ecclesiast. tom. v. part i. p. 43.]

[Footnote 158: See the Acta Sincera of Ruinart, p. 353; those of Felix of Thibara, or Tibiur, appear much less corrupted than in the other editions, which afford a lively specimen of legendary license.]

[Footnote 159: See the first book of Optatus of Milevis against the Donatiste, Paris, 1700, edit. Dupin. He lived under the reign of Valens.]

The copies as well as the versions of Scripture, were already so multiplied in the empire, that the most severe inquisition could no longer be attended with any fatal consequences; and even the sacrifice of those volumes, which, in every congregation, were preserved for public use, required the consent of some treacherous and unworthy Christians. But the ruin of the churches was easily effected by the authority of the government, and by the labor of the Pagans. In some provinces, however, the magistrates contented themselves with shutting up the places of religious worship. In others, they more literally complied with the terms of the edict; and after taking away the doors, the benches, and the pulpit, which they burnt as it were in a funeral pile, they completely demolished the remainder of the edifice. [160] It is perhaps to this melancholy occasion that we should apply a very remarkable story, which is related with so many circumstances of variety and improbability, that it serves rather to excite than to satisfy our curiosity. In a small town in Phrygia, of whose names as well as situation we are left ignorant, it should seem that the magistrates and the body of the people had embraced the Christian faith; and as some resistance might be apprehended to the execution of the edict, the governor of the province was supported by a numerous detachment of legionaries. On their approach the citizens threw themselves into the church, with the resolution either of defending by arms that sacred edifice, or of perishing in its ruins. They indignantly rejected the notice and permission which was given them to retire, till the soldiers, provoked by their obstinate refusal, set fire to the building on all sides, and consumed, by this extraordinary kind of martyrdom, a great number of Phrygians, with their wives and children. [161]

[Footnote 160: The ancient monuments, published at the end of Optatus, p. 261, &c. describe, in a very circumstantial manner, the proceedings of the governors in the destruction of churches. They made a minute inventory of the plate, &c., which they found in them. That of the church of Cirta, in Numidia, is still extant. It consisted of two chalices of gold, and six of silver; six urns, one kettle, seven lamps, all likewise of silver; besides a large quantity of brass utensils, and wearing apparel.]

[Footnote 161: Lactantius (Institut. Divin. v. 11) confines the calamity to the conventiculum, with its congregation. Eusebius (viii. 11) extends it to a whole city, and introduces something very like a regular siege. His ancient Latin translator, Rufinus, adds the important circumstance of the permission given to the inhabitants of retiring from thence. As Phrygia reached to the confines of Isauria, it is possible that the restless temper of those independent barbarians may have contributed to this misfortune. Note: Universum populum. Lact. Inst. Div. v. 11—G.]

Some slight disturbances, though they were suppressed almost as soon as excited, in Syria and the frontiers of Armenia, afforded the enemies of the church a very plausible occasion to insinuate, that those troubles had been secretly fomented by the intrigues of the bishops, who had already forgotten their ostentatious professions of passive and unlimited obedience. [162]

The resentment, or the fears, of Diocletian, at length transported him beyond the bounds of moderation, which he had hitherto preserved, and he declared, in a series of cruel edicts, [162a] his intention of abolishing the Christian name. By the first of these edicts, the governors of the provinces were directed to apprehend all persons of the ecclesiastical order; and the prisons, destined for the vilest criminals, were soon filled with a multitude of bishops, presbyters, deacons, readers, and exorcists. By a second edict, the magistrates were commanded to employ every method of severity, which might reclaim them from their odious superstition, and oblige them to return to the established worship of the gods. This rigorous order was extended, by a subsequent edict, to the whole body of Christians, who were exposed to a violent and general persecution. [163]

Instead of those salutary restraints, which had required the direct and solemn testimony of an accuser, it became the duty as well as the interest of the Imperial officers to discover, to pursue, and to torment the most obnoxious among the faithful. Heavy penalties were denounced against all who should presume to save a prescribed sectary from the just indignation of the gods, and of the emperors. Yet, notwithstanding the severity of this law, the virtuous courage of many of the Pagans, in concealing their friends or relations, affords an honorable proof, that the rage of superstition had not extinguished in their minds the sentiments of nature and humanity. [164]

[Footnote 162: Eusebius, l. viii. c. 6. M. de Valois (with some probability) thinks that he has discovered the Syrian rebellion in an oration of Libanius; and that it was a rash attempt of the tribune Eugenius, who with only five hundred men seized Antioch, and might perhaps allure the Christians by the promise of religious toleration. From Eusebius, (l. ix. c. 8,) as well as from Moses of Chorene, (Hist. Armen. l. ii. 77, &c.,) it may be inferred, that Christianity was already introduced into Armenia.]

[Footnote 162a: He had already passed them in his first edict. It does not appear that resentment or fear had any share in the new persecutions: perhaps they originated in superstition, and a specious apparent respect for its ministers. The oracle of Apollo, consulted by Diocletian, gave no answer; and said that just men hindered it from speaking. Constantine, who assisted at the ceremony, affirms, with an oath, that when questioned about these men, the high priest named the Christians. "The Emperor eagerly seized on this answer; and drew against the innocent a sword, destined only to punish the guilty: he instantly issued edicts, written, if I may use the expression, with a poniard; and ordered the judges to employ all their skill to invent new modes of punishment. Euseb. Vit Constant. l. ii c 54."—G.]

[Footnote 163: See Mosheim, p. 938: the text of Eusebius very plainly shows that the governors, whose powers were enlarged, not restrained, by the new laws, could punish with death the most obstinate Christians as an example to their brethren.]

[Footnote 164: Athanasius, p. 833, ap. Tillemont, Mem. Ecclesiast. tom v part i. 90.]

PART VII

Diocletian had no sooner published his edicts against the Christians, than, as if he had been desirous of committing to other hands the work of persecution, he divested himself of the Imperial purple. The character and situation of his colleagues and successors sometimes urged them to enforce and sometimes inclined them to suspend, the execution of these rigorous laws; nor can we acquire a just and distinct idea of this important period of ecclesiastical history, unless we separately consider the state of Christianity, in the different parts of the empire, during the space of ten years, which elapsed between the first edicts of Diocletian and the final peace of the church.

The mild and humane temper of Constantius was averse to the oppression of any part of his subjects. The principal offices of his palace were exercised by Christians. He loved their persons, esteemed their fidelity, and entertained not any dislike to their religious principles. But as long as Constantius remained in the subordinate station of Caesar, it was not in his power openly to reject the edicts of Diocletian, or to disobey the commands of Maximian. His authority contributed, however, to alleviate the sufferings which he pitied and abhorred. He consented with reluctance to the ruin of the churches; but he ventured to protect the Christians themselves from the fury of the populace, and from the rigor of the laws. The provinces of Gaul (under which we may probably include those of Britain) were indebted for the singular tranquillity which they enjoyed, to the gentle interposition of their sovereign. [165] But Datianus, the president or governor of Spain, actuated either by zeal or policy, chose rather to execute the public edicts of the emperors, than to understand the secret intentions of Constantius; and it can scarcely be doubted, that his provincial administration was stained with the blood of a few martyrs. [166]

The elevation of Constantius to the supreme and independent dignity of Augustus, gave a free scope to the exercise of his virtues, and the shortness of his reign did not prevent him from establishing a system of toleration, of which he left the precept and the example to his son Constantine. His fortunate son, from the first moment of his accession, declaring himself the protector of the church, at length deserved the appellation of the first emperor who publicly professed and established the Christian religion. The motives of his conversion, as they may variously be deduced from benevolence, from policy, from conviction, or from remorse, and the progress of the revolution, which, under his powerful influence and that of his sons, rendered Christianity the reigning religion of the Roman empire, will form a very interesting and important chapter in the present volume of this history. At present it may be sufficient to observe, that every victory of Constantine was productive of some relief or benefit to the church.

[Footnote 165: Eusebius, l. viii. c. 13. Lactantius de M. P. c. 15. Dodwell (Dissertat. Cyprian. xi. 75) represents them as inconsistent with each other. But the former evidently speaks of Constantius in the station of Caesar, and the latter of the same prince in the rank of Augustus.]

[Footnote 166: Datianus is mentioned, in Gruter's Inscriptions, as having determined the limits between the territories of Pax Julia, and those of Ebora, both cities in the southern part of Lusitania. If we recollect the neighborhood of those places to Cape St. Vincent, we may suspect that the celebrated deacon and martyr of that name had been inaccurately assigned by Prudentius, &c., to Saragossa, or Valentia. See the pompous history of his sufferings, in the Memoires de Tillemont, tom. v. part ii. p. 58-85. Some critics are of opinion, that the department of Constantius, as Caesar, did not include Spain, which still continued under the immediate jurisdiction of Maximian.]

The provinces of Italy and Africa experienced a short but violent persecution. The rigorous edicts of Diocletian were strictly and cheerfully executed by his associate Maximian, who had long hated the Christians, and who delighted in acts of blood and violence. In the autumn of the first year of the persecution, the two emperors met at Rome to celebrate their triumph; several oppressive laws appear to have issued from their secret consultations, and the diligence of the magistrates was animated by the presence of their sovereigns. After Diocletian had divested himself of the purple, Italy and Africa were administered under the name of Severus, and were exposed, without defence, to the implacable resentment of his master Galerius. Among the martyrs of Rome, Adauctus deserves the notice of posterity. He was of a noble family in Italy, and had raised himself, through the successive honors of the palace, to the important office of treasurer of the private Jemesnes. Adauctus is the more remarkable for being the only person of rank and distinction who appears to have suffered death, during the whole course of this general persecution. [167]

[Footnote 167: Eusebius, l. viii. c. 11. Gruter, Inscrip. p. 1171, No. 18. Rufinus has mistaken the office of Adauctus, as well as the place of his martyrdom. Note: M. Guizot suggests the powerful cunuchs of the palace. Dorotheus, Gorgonius, and Andrew, admitted by Gibbon himself to have been put to death, p. 66.]

The revolt of Maxentius immediately restored peace to the churches of Italy and Africa; and the same tyrant who oppressed every other class of his subjects, showed himself just, humane, and even partial, towards the afflicted Christians. He depended on their gratitude and affection, and very naturally presumed, that the injuries which they had suffered, and the dangers which they still apprehended from his most inveterate enemy, would secure the fidelity of a party already considerable by their numbers and opulence. [168] Even the conduct of Maxentius towards the bishops of Rome and Carthage may be considered as the proof of his toleration, since it is probable that the most orthodox princes would adopt the same measures with regard to their established clergy. Marcellus, the former of these prelates, had thrown the capital into confusion, by the severe penance which he imposed on a great number of Christians, who, during the late persecution, had renounced or dissembled their religion. The rage of faction broke out in frequent and violent seditions; the blood of the faithful was shed by each other's hands, and the exile of Marcellus, whose prudence seems to have been less eminent than his zeal, was found to be the only measure capable of restoring peace to the distracted church of Rome. [169] The behavior of Mensurius, bishop of Carthage, appears to have been still more reprehensible. A deacon of that city had published a libel against the emperor. The offender took refuge in the episcopal palace; and though it was somewhat early to advance any claims of ecclesiastical immunities, the bishop refused to deliver him up to the officers of justice. For this treasonable resistance, Mensurius was summoned to court, and instead of receiving a legal sentence of death or banishment, he was permitted, after a short examination, to return to his diocese. [170] Such was the happy condition of the Christian subjects of Maxentius, that whenever they were desirous of procuring for their own use any bodies of martyrs, they were obliged to purchase them from the most distant provinces of the East. A story is related of Aglae, a Roman lady, descended from a consular family, and possessed of so ample an estate, that it required the management of seventy-three stewards. Among these Boniface was the favorite of his mistress; and as Aglae mixed love with devotion, it is reported that he was admitted to share her bed. Her fortune enabled her to gratify the pious desire of obtaining some sacred relics from the East. She intrusted Boniface with a considerable sum of gold, and a large quantity of aromatics; and her lover, attended by twelve horsemen and three covered chariots, undertook a remote pilgrimage, as far as Tarsus in Cilicia. [171]

[Footnote 168: Eusebius, l. viii. c. 14. But as Maxentius was vanquished by Constantine, it suited the purpose of Lactantius to place his death among those of the persecutors. Note: M. Guizot directly contradicts this statement of Gibbon, and appeals to Eusebius. Maxentius, who assumed the power in Italy, pretended at first to be a Christian, to gain the favor of the Roman people; he ordered his ministers to cease to persecute the Christians, affecting a hypocritical piety, in order to appear more mild than his predecessors; but his actions soon proved that he was very different from what they had at first hoped. The actions of Maxentius were those of a cruel tyrant, but not those of a persecutor: the Christians, like the rest of his subjects, suffered from his vices, but they were not oppressed as a sect. Christian females were exposed to his lusts, as well as to the brutal violence of his colleague Maximian, but they were not selected as Christians—M.]

[Footnote 169: The epitaph of Marcellus is to be found in Gruter, Inscrip. p 1172, No. 3, and it contains all that we know of his history. Marcellinus and Marcellus, whose names follow in the list of popes, are supposed by many critics to be different persons; but the learned Abbe de Longuerue was convinced that they were one and the same. Veridicus rector lapsis quia crimina flere Praedixit miseris, fuit omnibus hostis amarus. Hinc furor, hinc odium; sequitur discordia, lites, Seditio, caedes; solvuntur foedera pacis. Crimen ob alterius, Christum qui in pace negavit Finibus expulsus patriae est feritate Tyranni. Haec breviter Damasus voluit comperta referre: Marcelli populus meritum cognoscere posset—We may observe that Damasus was made Bishop of Rome, A. D. 366.]

[Footnote 170: Optatus contr. Donatist. l. i. c. 17, 18. Note: The words of Optatus are, Profectus (Roman) causam dixit; jussus con reverti Carthaginem; perhaps, in pleading his cause, he exculpated himself, since he received an order to return to Carthage—G.]

[Footnote 171: The Acts of the Passion of St. Boniface, which abound in miracles and declamation, are published by Ruinart, (p. 283—291,) both in Greek and Latin, from the authority of very ancient manuscripts. Note: We are ignorant whether Aglae and Boniface were Christians at the time of their unlawful connection. See Tillemont. Mem, Eccles. Note on the Persecution of Domitian, tom. v. note 82. M. de Tillemont proves also that the history is doubtful—G. —Sir D. Dalrymple (Lord Hailes) calls the story of Aglae and Boniface as of equal authority with our popular histories of Whittington and Hickathrift. Christian Antiquities, ii. 64—M.]

The sanguinary temper of Galerius, the first and principal author of the persecution, was formidable to those Christians whom their misfortunes had placed within the limits of his dominions; and it may fairly be presumed that many persons of a middle rank, who were not confined by the chains either of wealth or of poverty, very frequently deserted their native country, and sought a refuge in the milder climate of the West. [171a] As long as he commanded only the armies and provinces of Illyricum, he could with difficulty either find or make a considerable number of martyrs, in a warlike country, which had entertained the missionaries of the gospel with more coldness and reluctance than any other part of the empire. [172] But when Galerius had obtained the supreme power, and the government of the East, he indulged in their fullest extent his zeal and cruelty, not only in the provinces of Thrace and Asia, which acknowledged his immediate jurisdiction, but in those of Syria, Palestine, and Egypt, where Maximin gratified his own inclination, by yielding a rigorous obedience to the stern commands of his benefactor. [173] The frequent disappointments of his ambitious views, the experience of six years of persecution, and the salutary reflections which a lingering and painful distemper suggested to the mind of Galerius, at length convinced him that the most violent efforts of despotism are insufficient to extirpate a whole people, or to subdue their religious prejudices. Desirous of repairing the mischief that he had occasioned, he published in his own name, and in those of Licinius and Constantine, a general edict, which, after a pompous recital of the Imperial titles, proceeded in the following manner:—

[Footnote 171a: A little after this, Christianity was propagated to the north of the Roman provinces, among the tribes of Germany: a multitude of Christians, forced by the persecutions of the Emperors to take refuge among the Barbarians, were received with kindness. Euseb. de Vit. Constant. ii. 53. Semler Select. cap. H. E. p. 115. The Goths owed their first knowledge of Christianity to a young girl, a prisoner of war; she continued in the midst of them her exercises of piety; she fasted, prayed, and praised God day and night. When she was asked what good would come of so much painful trouble she answered, "It is thus that Christ, the Son of God, is to be honored." Sozomen, ii. c. 6—G.]

[Footnote 172: During the four first centuries, there exist few traces of either bishops or bishoprics in the western Illyricum. It has been thought probable that the primate of Milan extended his jurisdiction over Sirmium, the capital of that great province. See the Geographia Sacra of Charles de St. Paul, p. 68-76, with the observations of Lucas Holstenius.]

[Footnote 173: The viiith book of Eusebius, as well as the supplement concerning the martyrs of Palestine, principally relate to the persecution of Galerius and Maximin. The general lamentations with which Lactantius opens the vth book of his Divine Institutions allude to their cruelty.] "Among the important cares which have occupied our mind for the utility and preservation of the empire, it was our intention to correct and reestablish all things according to the ancient laws and public discipline of the Romans. We were particularly desirous of reclaiming into the way of reason and nature, the deluded Christians who had renounced the religion and ceremonies instituted by their fathers; and presumptuously despising the practice of antiquity, had invented extravagant laws and opinions, according to the dictates of their fancy, and had collected a various society from the different provinces of our empire. The edicts, which we have published to enforce the worship of the gods, having exposed many of the Christians to danger and distress, many having suffered death, and many more, who still persist in their impious folly, being left destitute of any public exercise of religion, we are disposed to extend to those unhappy men the effects of our wonted clemency. We permit them therefore freely to profess their private opinions, and to assemble in their conventicles without fear or molestation, provided always that they preserve a due respect to the established laws and government. By another rescript we shall signify our intentions to the judges and magistrates; and we hope that our indulgence will engage the Christians to offer up their prayers to the Deity whom they adore, for our safety and prosperity for their own, and for that of the republic." [174] It is not usually in the language of edicts and manifestos that we should search for the real character or the secret motives of princes; but as these were the words of a dying emperor, his situation, perhaps, may be admitted as a pledge of his sincerity.

[Footnote 174: Eusebius (l. viii. c. 17) has given us a Greek version, and Lactantius (de M. P. c. 34) the Latin original, of this memorable edict. Neither of these writers seems to recollect how directly it contradicts whatever they have just affirmed of the remorse and repentance of Galerius. Note: But Gibbon has answered this by his just observation, that it is not in the language of edicts and manifestos that we should search for the secre motives of princes—M.]

When Galerius subscribed this edict of toleration, he was well assured that Licinius would readily comply with the inclinations of his friend and benefactor, and that any measures in favor of the Christians would obtain the approbation of Constantine. But the emperor would not venture to insert in the preamble the name of Maximin, whose consent was of the greatest importance, and who succeeded a few days afterwards to the provinces of Asia. In the first six months, however, of his new reign, Maximin affected to adopt the prudent counsels of his predecessor; and though he never condescended to secure the tranquillity of the church by a public edict, Sabinus, his Praetorian praefect, addressed a circular letter to all the governors and magistrates of the provinces, expatiating on the Imperial clemency, acknowledging the invincible obstinacy of the Christians, and directing the officers of justice to cease their ineffectual prosecutions, and to connive at the secret assemblies of those enthusiasts. In consequence of these orders, great numbers of Christians were released from prison, or delivered from the mines. The confessors, singing hymns of triumph, returned into their own countries; and those who had yielded to the violence of the tempest, solicited with tears of repentance their readmission into the bosom of the church. [175]

[Footnote 175: Eusebius, l. ix. c. 1. He inserts the epistle of the praefect.]

But this treacherous calm was of short duration; nor could the Christians of the East place any confidence in the character of their sovereign. Cruelty and superstition were the ruling passions of the soul of Maximin. The former suggested the means, the latter pointed out the objects of persecution. The emperor was devoted to the worship of the gods, to the study of magic, and to the belief of oracles. The prophets or philosophers, whom he revered as the favorites of Heaven, were frequently raised to the government of provinces, and admitted into his most secret councils. They easily convinced him that the Christians had been indebted for their victories to their regular discipline, and that the weakness of polytheism had principally flowed from a want of union and subordination among the ministers of religion. A system of government was therefore instituted, which was evidently copied from the policy of the church. In all the great cities of the empire, the temples were repaired and beautified by the order of Maximin, and the officiating priests of the various deities were subjected to the authority of a superior pontiff destined to oppose the bishop, and to promote the cause of paganism. These pontiffs acknowledged, in their turn, the supreme jurisdiction of the metropolitans or high priests of the province, who acted as the immediate vicegerents of the emperor himself. A white robe was the ensign of their dignity; and these new prelates were carefully selected from the most noble and opulent families. By the influence of the magistrates, and of the sacerdotal order, a great number of dutiful addresses were obtained, particularly from the cities of Nicomedia, Antioch, and Tyre, which artfully represented the well-known intentions of the court as the general sense of the people; solicited the emperor to consult the laws of justice rather than the dictates of his clemency; expressed their abhorrence of the Christians, and humbly prayed that those impious sectaries might at least be excluded from the limits of their respective territories. The answer of Maximin to the address which he obtained from the citizens of Tyre is still extant. He praises their zeal and devotion in terms of the highest satisfaction, descants on the obstinate impiety of the Christians, and betrays, by the readiness with which he consents to their banishment, that he considered himself as receiving, rather than as conferring, an obligation. The priests as well as the magistrates were empowered to enforce the execution of his edicts, which were engraved on tables of brass; and though it was recommended to them to avoid the effusion of blood, the most cruel and ignominious punishments were inflicted on the refractory Christians. [176]

[Footnote 176: See Eusebius, l. viii. c. 14, l. ix. c. 2—8. Lactantius de M. P. c. 36. These writers agree in representing the arts of Maximin; but the former relates the execution of several martyrs, while the latter expressly affirms, occidi servos Dei vetuit. Note: It is easy to reconcile them; it is sufficient to quote the entire text of Lactantius: Nam cum clementiam specie tenus profiteretur, occidi servos Dei vetuit, debilitari jussit. Itaque confessoribus effodiebantur oculi, amputabantur manus, nares vel auriculae desecabantur. Haec ille moliens Constantini litteris deterretur. Dissimulavit ergo, et tamen, si quis inciderit. mari occulte mergebatur. This detail of torments inflicted on the Christians easily reconciles Lactantius and Eusebius. Those who died in consequence of their tortures, those who were plunged into the sea, might well pass for martyrs. The mutilation of the words of Lactantius has alone given rise to the apparent contradiction—G. —Eusebius. ch. vi., relates the public martyrdom of the aged bishop of Emesa, with two others, who were thrown to the wild beasts, the beheading of Peter, bishop of Alexandria, with several others, and the death of Lucian, presbyter of Antioch, who was carried to Numidia, and put to death in prison. The contradiction is direct and undeniable, for although Eusebius may have misplaced the former martyrdoms, it may be doubted whether the authority of Maximin extended to Nicomedia till after the death of Galerius. The last edict of toleration issued by Maximin and published by Eusebius himself, Eccl. Hist. ix. 9. confirms the statement of Lactantius—M.]

The Asiatic Christians had every thing to dread from the severity of a bigoted monarch who prepared his measures of violence with such deliberate policy. But a few months had scarcely elapsed before the edicts published by the two Western emperors obliged Maximin to suspend the prosecution of his designs: the civil war which he so rashly undertook against Licinius employed all his attention; and the defeat and death of Maximin soon delivered the church from the last and most implacable of her enemies. [177]

[Footnote 177: A few days before his death, he published a very ample edict of toleration, in which he imputes all the severities which the Christians suffered to the judges and governors, who had misunderstood his intentions. See the edict of Eusebius, l. ix. c. 10.]

In this general view of the persecution, which was first authorized by the edicts of Diocletian, I have purposely refrained from describing the particular sufferings and deaths of the Christian martyrs. It would have been an easy task, from the history of Eusebius, from the declamations of Lactantius, and from the most ancient acts, to collect a long series of horrid and disgustful pictures, and to fill many pages with racks and scourges, with iron hooks and red-hot beds, and with all the variety of tortures which fire and steel, savage beasts, and more savage executioners, could inflict upon the human body. These melancholy scenes might be enlivened by a crowd of visions and miracles destined either to delay the death, to celebrate the triumph, or to discover the relics of those canonized saints who suffered for the name of Christ. But I cannot determine what I ought to transcribe, till I am satisfied how much I ought to believe. The gravest of the ecclesiastical historians, Eusebius himself, indirectly confesses, that he has related whatever might redound to the glory, and that he has suppressed all that could tend to the disgrace, of religion. [178] Such an acknowledgment will naturally excite a suspicion that a writer who has so openly violated one of the fundamental laws of history, has not paid a very strict regard to the observance of the other; and the suspicion will derive additional credit from the character of Eusebius, [178a] which was less tinctured with credulity, and more practised in the arts of courts, than that of almost any of his contemporaries. On some particular occasions, when the magistrates were exasperated by some personal motives of interest or resentment, the rules of prudence, and perhaps of decency, to overturn the altars, to pour out imprecations against the emperors, or to strike the judge as he sat on his tribunal, it may be presumed, that every mode of torture which cruelty could invent, or constancy could endure, was exhausted on those devoted victims. [179] Two circumstances, however, have been unwarily mentioned, which insinuate that the general treatment of the Christians, who had been apprehended by the officers of justice, was less intolerable than it is usually imagined to have been. 1. The confessors who were condemned to work in the mines were permitted by the humanity or the negligence of their keepers to build chapels, and freely to profess their religion in the midst of those dreary habitations. [180] 2. The bishops were obliged to check and to censure the forward zeal of the Christians, who voluntarily threw themselves into the hands of the magistrates. Some of these were persons oppressed by poverty and debts, who blindly sought to terminate a miserable existence by a glorious death. Others were allured by the hope that a short confinement would expiate the sins of a whole life; and others again were actuated by the less honorable motive of deriving a plentiful subsistence, and perhaps a considerable profit, from the alms which the charity of the faithful bestowed on the prisoners. [181] After the church had triumphed over all her enemies, the interest as well as vanity of the captives prompted them to magnify the merit of their respective sufferings. A convenient distance of time or place gave an ample scope to the progress of fiction; and the frequent instances which might be alleged of holy martyrs, whose wounds had been instantly healed, whose strength had been renewed, and whose lost members had miraculously been restored, were extremely convenient for the purpose of removing every difficulty, and of silencing every objection. The most extravagant legends, as they conduced to the honor of the church, were applauded by the credulous multitude, countenanced by the power of the clergy, and attested by the suspicious evidence of ecclesiastical history.

[Footnote 178: Such is the fair deduction from two remarkable passages in Eusebius, l. viii. c. 2, and de Martyr. Palestin. c. 12. The prudence of the historian has exposed his own character to censure and suspicion. It was well known that he himself had been thrown into prison; and it was suggested that he had purchased his deliverance by some dishonorable compliance. The reproach was urged in his lifetime, and even in his presence, at the council of Tyre. See Tillemont, Memoires Ecclesiastiques, tom. viii. part i. p. 67.]

[Footnote 178a: Historical criticism does not consist in rejecting indiscriminately all the facts which do not agree with a particular system, as Gibbon does in this chapter, in which, except at the last extremity, he will not consent to believe a martyrdom. Authorities are to be weighed, not excluded from examination. Now, the Pagan historians justify in many places the detail which have been transmitted to us by the historians of the church, concerning the tortures endured by the Christians. Celsus reproaches the Christians with holding their assemblies in secret, on account of the fear inspired by their sufferings, "for when you are arrested," he says, "you are dragged to punishment: and, before you are put to death, you have to suffer all kinds of tortures." Origen cont. Cels. l. i. ii. vi. viii. passing. Libanius, the panegyrist of Julian, says, while speaking of the Christians. "Those who followed a corrupt religion were in continual apprehensions; they feared lest Julian should invent tortures still more refined than those to which they had been exposed before, as mutilation, burning alive, &c.; for the emperors had inflicted upon them all these barbarities." Lib. Parent in Julian. ap. Fab. Bib. Graec. No. 9, No. 58, p. 283—G. —This sentence of Gibbon has given rise to several learned dissertation: Moller, de Fide Eusebii Caesar, &c., Havniae, 1813. Danzius, de Eusebio Caes. Hist. Eccl. Scriptore, ejusque tide historica recte aestimanda, &c., Jenae, 1815. Kestner Commentatio de Eusebii Hist. Eccles. conditoris auctoritate et fide, &c. See also Reuterdahl, de Fontibus Historiae Eccles. Eusebianae, Lond. Goth., 1826. Gibbon's inference may appear stronger than the text will warrant, yet it is difficult, after reading the passages, to dismiss all suspicion of partiality from the mind—M.]

[Footnote 179: The ancient, and perhaps authentic, account of the sufferings of Tarachus and his companions, (Acta Sincera Ruinart, p. 419—448,) is filled with strong expressions of resentment and contempt, which could not fail of irritating the magistrate. The behavior of Aedesius to Hierocles, praefect of Egypt, was still more extraordinary. Euseb. de Martyr. Palestin. c. 5. Note: M. Guizot states, that the acts of Tarachus and his companion contain nothing that appears dictated by violent feelings, (sentiment outre.) Nothing can be more painful than the constant attempt of Gibbon throughout this discussion, to find some flaw in the virtue and heroism of the martyrs, some extenuation for the cruelty of the persecutors. But truth must not be sacrificed even to well-grounded moral indignation. Though the language of these martyrs is in great part that of calm de fiance, of noble firmness, yet there are many expressions which betray "resentment and contempt." "Children of Satan, worshippers of Devils," is their common appellation of the heathen. One of them calls the judge another, one curses, and declares that he will curse the Emperors, as pestilential and bloodthirsty tyrants, whom God will soon visit in his wrath. On the other hand, though at first they speak the milder language of persuasion, the cold barbarity of the judges and officers might surely have called forth one sentence of abhorrence from Gibbon. On the first unsatisfactory answer, "Break his jaw," is the order of the judge. They direct and witness the most excruciating tortures; the people, as M. Guizot observers, were so much revolted by the cruelty of Maximus that when the martyrs appeared in the amphitheatre, fear seized on all hearts, and general murmurs against the unjust judge rank through the assembly. It is singular, at least, that Gibbon should have quoted "as probably authentic," acts so much embellished with miracle as these of Tarachus are, particularly towards the end—M. Note: Scarcely were the authorities informed of this, than the president of the province, a man, says Eusebius, harsh and cruel, banished the confessors, some to Cyprus, others to different parts of Palestine, and ordered them to be tormented by being set to the most painful labors. Four of them, whom he required to abjure their faith and refused, were burnt alive. Euseb. de Mart. Palest. c. xiii—G. Two of these were bishops; a fifth, Silvanus, bishop of Gaza, was the last martyr; another, named John was blinded, but used to officiate, and recite from memory long passages of the sacred writings—M.]

[Footnote 180: Euseb. de Martyr. Palestin. c. 13.]

[Footnote 181: Augustin. Collat. Carthagin. Dei, iii. c. 13, ap. Tillanant, Memoires Ecclesiastiques, tom. v. part i. p. 46. The controversy with the Donatists, has reflected some, though perhaps a partial, light on the history of the African church.]

PART VIII

The vague descriptions of exile and imprisonment, of pain and torture, are so easily exaggerated or softened by the pencil of an artful orator, [181a] that we are naturally induced to inquire into a fact of a more distinct and stubborn kind; the number of persons who suffered death in consequence of the edicts published by Diocletian, his associates, and his successors. The recent legendaries record whole armies and cities, which were at once swept away by the undistinguishing rage of persecution. The more ancient writers content themselves with pouring out a liberal effusion of loose and tragical invectives, without condescending to ascertain the precise number of those persons who were permitted to seal with their blood their belief of the gospel. From the history of Eusebius, it may, however, be collected, that only nine bishops were punished with death; and we are assured, by his particular enumeration of the martyrs of Palestine, that no more than ninety-two Christians were entitled to that honorable appellation. [182] [182a] As we are unacquainted with the degree of episcopal zeal and courage which prevailed at that time, it is not in our power to draw any useful inferences from the former of these facts: but the latter may serve to justify a very important and probable conclusion. According to the distribution of Roman provinces, Palestine may be considered as the sixteenth part of the Eastern empire: [183] and since there were some governors, who from a real or affected clemency had preserved their hands unstained with the blood of the faithful, [184] it is reasonable to believe, that the country which had given birth to Christianity, produced at least the sixteenth part of the martyrs who suffered death within the dominions of Galerius and Maximin; the whole might consequently amount to about fifteen hundred, a number which, if it is equally divided between the ten years of the persecution, will allow an annual consumption of one hundred and fifty martyrs. Allotting the same proportion to the provinces of Italy, Africa, and perhaps Spain, where, at the end of two or three years, the rigor of the penal laws was either suspended or abolished, the multitude of Christians in the Roman empire, on whom a capital punishment was inflicted by a judicia, sentence, will be reduced to somewhat less than two thousand persons. Since it cannot be doubted that the Christians were more numerous, and their enemies more exasperated, in the time of Diocletian, than they had ever been in any former persecution, this probable and moderate computation may teach us to estimate the number of primitive saints and martyrs who sacrificed their lives for the important purpose of introducing Christianity into the world.

[Footnote 181a: Perhaps there never was an instance of an author committing so deliberately the fault which he reprobates so strongly in others. What is the dexterous management of the more inartificial historians of Christianity, in exaggerating the numbers of the martyrs, compared to the unfair address with which Gibbon here quietly dismisses from the account all the horrible and excruciating tortures which fell short of death? The reader may refer to the xiith chapter (book viii.) of Eusebius for the description and for the scenes of these tortures—M.]

[Footnote 182: Eusebius de Martyr. Palestin. c. 13. He closes his narration by assuring us that these were the martyrdoms inflicted in Palestine, during the whole course of the persecution. The 9th chapter of his viiith book, which relates to the province of Thebais in Egypt, may seem to contradict our moderate computation; but it will only lead us to admire the artful management of the historian. Choosing for the scene of the most exquisite cruelty the most remote and sequestered country of the Roman empire, he relates that in Thebais from ten to one hundred persons had frequently suffered martyrdom in the same day. But when he proceeds to mention his own journey into Egypt, his language insensibly becomes more cautious and moderate. Instead of a large, but definite number, he speaks of many Christians, and most artfully selects two ambiguous words, which may signify either what he had seen, or what he had heard; either the expectation, or the execution of the punishment. Having thus provided a secure evasion, he commits the equivocal passage to his readers and translators; justly conceiving that their piety would induce them to prefer the most favorable sense. There was perhaps some malice in the remark of Theodorus Metochita, that all who, like Eusebius, had been conversant with the Egyptians, delighted in an obscure and intricate style. (See Valesius ad loc.)]

[Footnote 182a: This calculation is made from the martyrs, of whom Eusebius speaks by name; but he recognizes a much greater number. Thus the ninth and tenth chapters of his work are entitled, "Of Antoninus, Zebinus, Germanus, and other martyrs; of Peter the monk. of Asclepius the Maroionite, and other martyrs." [Are these vague contents of chapters very good authority?—M.] Speaking of those who suffered under Diocletian, he says, "I will only relate the death of one of these, from which, the reader may divine what befell the rest." Hist. Eccl. viii. 6. [This relates only to the martyrs in the royal household—M.] Dodwell had made, before Gibbon, this calculation and these objections; but Ruinart (Act. Mart. Pref p. 27, et seq.) has answered him in a peremptory manner: Nobis constat Eusebium in historia infinitos passim martyres admisisse. quamvis revera paucorum nomina recensuerit. Nec alium Eusebii interpretem quam ipsummet Eusebium proferimus, qui (l. iii. c. 33) ait sub Trajano plurimosa ex fidelibus martyrii certamen subiisse (l. v. init.) sub Antonino et Vero innumerabiles prope martyres per universum orbem enituisse affirmat. (L. vi. c. 1.) Severum persecutionem concitasse refert, in qua per omnes ubique locorum Ecclesias, ab athletis pro pietate certantibus, illustria confecta fuerunt martyria. Sic de Decii, sic de Valeriani, persecutionibus loquitur, quae an Dodwelli faveant conjectionibus judicet aequus lector. Even in the persecutions which Gibbon has represented as much more mild than that of Diocletian, the number of martyrs appears much greater than that to which he limits the martyrs of the latter: and this number is attested by incontestable monuments. I will quote but one example. We find among the letters of St. Cyprian one from Lucianus to Celerinus, written from the depth of a prison, in which Lucianus names seventeen of his brethren dead, some in the quarries, some in the midst of tortures some of starvation in prison. Jussi sumus (he proceeds) secundum prae ceptum imperatoris, fame et siti necari, et reclusi sumus in duabus cellis, ta ut nos afficerent fame et siti et ignis vapore—G.]

[Footnote 183: When Palestine was divided into three, the praefecture of the East contained forty-eight provinces. As the ancient distinctions of nations were long since abolished, the Romans distributed the provinces according to a general proportion of their extent and opulence.]

[Footnote 184: Ut gloriari possint nullam se innocentium poremisse, nam et ipse audivi aloquos gloriantes, quia administratio sua, in hac paris merit incruenta. Lactant. Institur. Divin v. 11.]

We shall conclude this chapter by a melancholy truth, which obtrudes itself on the reluctant mind; that even admitting, without hesitation or inquiry, all that history has recorded, or devotion has feigned, on the subject of martyrdoms, it must still be acknowledged, that the Christians, in the course of their intestine dissensions, have inflicted far greater severities on each other, than they had experienced from the zeal of infidels. During the ages of ignorance which followed the subversion of the Roman empire in the West, the bishops of the Imperial city extended their dominion over the laity as well as clergy of the Latin church. The fabric of superstition which they had erected, and which might long have defied the feeble efforts of reason, was at length assaulted by a crowd of daring fanatics, who from the twelfth to the sixteenth century assumed the popular character of reformers. The church of Rome defended by violence the empire which she had acquired by fraud; a system of peace and benevolence was soon disgraced by proscriptions, war, massacres, and the institution of the holy office. And as the reformers were animated by the love of civil as well as of religious freedom, the Catholic princes connected their own interest with that of the clergy, and enforced by fire and the sword the terrors of spiritual censures. In the Netherlands alone, more than one hundred thousand of the subjects of Charles V. are said to have suffered by the hand of the executioner; and this extraordinary number is attested by Grotius, [185] a man of genius and learning, who preserved his moderation amidst the fury of contending sects, and who composed the annals of his own age and country, at a time when the invention of printing had facilitated the means of intelligence, and increased the danger of detection.

If we are obliged to submit our belief to the authority of Grotius, it must be allowed, that the number of Protestants, who were executed in a single province and a single reign, far exceeded that of the primitive martyrs in the space of three centuries, and of the Roman empire. But if the improbability of the fact itself should prevail over the weight of evidence; if Grotius should be convicted of exaggerating the merit and sufferings of the Reformers; [186] we shall be naturally led to inquire what confidence can be placed in the doubtful and imperfect monuments of ancient credulity; what degree of credit can be assigned to a courtly bishop, and a passionate declaimer, [186a] who, under the protection of Constantine, enjoyed the exclusive privilege of recording the persecutions inflicted on the Christians by the vanquished rivals or disregarded predecessors of their gracious sovereign.

[Footnote 185: Grot. Annal. de Rebus Belgicis, l. i. p. 12, edit. fol.]

[Footnote 186: Fra Paola (Istoria del Concilio Tridentino, l. iii.) reduces the number of the Belgic martyrs to 50,000. In learning and moderation Fra Paola was not inferior to Grotius. The priority of time gives some advantage to the evidence of the former, which he loses, on the other hand, by the distance of Venice from the Netherlands.]

[Footnote 186a: Eusebius and the author of the Treatise de Mortibus Persecutorum. It is deeply to be regretted that the history of this period rest so much on the loose and, it must be admitted, by no means scrupulous authority of Eusebius. Ecclesiastical history is a solemn and melancholy lesson that the best, even the most sacred, cause will eventually the least departure from truth!—M.]

CHAPTER XVII

FOUNDATION OF CONSTANTINOPLE

PART I

FOUNDATION OF CONSTANTINOPLE—POLITICAL SYSTEM CONSTANTINE, AND HIS SUCCESSORS MILITARY DISCIPLINE—THE PALACE—THE FINANCES

The unfortunate Licinius was the last rival who opposed the greatness, and the last captive who adorned the triumph, of Constantine. After a tranquil and prosperous reign, the conquerer bequeathed to his family the inheritance of the Roman empire; a new capital, a new policy, and a new religion; and the innovations which he established have been embraced and consecrated by succeeding generations. The age of the great Constantine and his sons is filled with important events; but the historian must be oppressed by their number and variety, unless he diligently separates from each other the scenes which are connected only by the order of time. He will describe the political institutions that gave strength and stability to the empire, before he proceeds to relate the wars and revolutions which hastened its decline. He will adopt the division unknown to the ancients of civil and ecclesiastical affairs: the victory of the Christians, and their intestine discord, will supply copious and distinct materials both for edification and for scandal.

After the defeat and abdication of Licinius, his victorious rival proceeded to lay the foundations of a city destined to reign in future times, the mistress of the East, and to survive the empire and religion of

Constantine. The motives, whether of pride or of policy, which first induced Diocletian to withdraw himself from the ancient seat of government, had acquired additional weight by the example of his successors, and the habits of forty years. Rome was insensibly confounded with the dependent kingdoms which had once acknowledged her supremacy; and the country of the Caesars was viewed with cold indifference by a martial prince, born in the neighborhood of the Danube, educated in the courts and armies of Asia, and invested with the purple by the legions of Britain. The Italians, who had received Constantine as their deliverer, submissively obeyed the edicts which he sometimes condescended to address to the senate and people of Rome; but they were seldom honored with the presence of their new sovereign. During the vigor of his age, Constantine, according to the various exigencies of peace and war, moved with slow dignity, or with active diligence, along the frontiers of his extensive dominions; and was always prepared to take the field either against a foreign or a domestic enemy. But as he gradually reached the summit of prosperity and the decline of life, he began to meditate the design of fixing in a more permanent station the strength as well as majesty of the throne. In the choice of an advantageous situation, he preferred the confines of Europe and Asia; to curb with a powerful arm the barbarians who dwelt between the Danube and the Tanais; to watch with an eye of jealousy the conduct of the Persian monarch, who indignantly supported the yoke of an ignominious treaty. With these views, Diocletian had selected and embellished the residence of Nicomedia: but the memory of Diocletian was justly abhorred by the protector of the church: and Constantine was not insensible to the ambition of founding a city which might perpetuate the glory of his own name. During the late operations of the war against Licinius, he had sufficient opportunity to contemplate, both as a soldier and as a statesman, the incomparable position of Byzantium; and to observe how strongly it was guarded by nature against a hostile attack, whilst it was accessible on every side to the benefits of commercial intercourse. Many ages before Constantine, one of the most judicious historians of antiquity [1 had described the advantages of a situation, from whence a feeble colony of Greeks derived the command of the sea, and the honors of a flourishing and independent republic. [2]

[Footnote 1: *Polybius, l. iv. p. 423, edit. Casaubon. He observes that the peace of the Byzantines was frequently disturbed, and the extent of their territory contracted, by the inroads of the wild Thracians.*]

[Footnote 2: *The navigator Byzas, who was styled the son of Neptune, founded the city 656 years before the Christian aera. His followers were drawn from Argos and Megara. Byzantium was afterwards rebuild and fortified by the Spartan general Pausanias. See Scaliger Animadvers. ad Euseb. p. 81. Ducange, Constantinopolis, l. i part i. cap 15, 16. With regard to the wars of the Byzantines against Philip, the Gauls, and the kings of Bithynia, we should trust none but the ancient writers who lived before the greatness of the Imperial city had excited a spirit of flattery and fiction.*]

If we survey Byzantium in the extent which it acquired with the august name of Constantinople, the figure of the Imperial city may be represented under that of an unequal triangle. The obtuse point, which advances towards the east and the shores of Asia, meets and repels the waves of the Thracian Bosphorus. The northern side of the city is bounded by the harbor; and the southern is washed by the Propontis, or Sea of Marmara. The basis of the triangle is opposed to the west, and terminates the continent of Europe. But the admirable form and division of the circumjacent land and water cannot, without a more ample explanation, be clearly or sufficiently understood. The winding channel through which the waters of the Euxine flow with a rapid and incessant course towards the Mediterranean, received the appellation of Bosphorus, a name not less celebrated in the history, than in the fables, of antiquity. [3] A crowd of temples and of votive altars, profusely scattered along its steep and woody banks, attested the unskilfulness, the terrors, and the devotion of the Grecian navigators, who, after the example of the Argonauts, explored the dangers of the inhospitable Euxine. On these banks tradition long preserved the memory of the palace of Phineus, infested by the obscene harpies; [4] and of the sylvan reign of Amycus, who defied the son of Leda to the combat of the cestus. [5] The straits of the Bosphorus are terminated by the Cyanean rocks, which, according to the description of the poets, had once floated on the face of the waters; and were destined by the gods to protect the entrance of the Euxine against the eye of profane curiosity. [6] From the Cyanean rocks to the point and harbor of Byzantium, the winding length of the Bosphorus extends about sixteen miles, [7] and its most ordinary breadth may be computed at about one mile and a half. The new castles of Europe and Asia are constructed, on either continent, upon the foundations of two celebrated temples, of Serapis and of Jupiter Urius. The old castles, a work of the Greek emperors, command the narrowest part of the channel in a place where the opposite banks advance within five hundred paces of each other. These fortresses were destroyed and strengthened by Mahomet the Second, when he meditated the siege of Constantinople: [8] but the Turkish conqueror was most probably ignorant, that near two thousand years before his reign, Darius had chosen the same situation to connect the two continents by a bridge of boats. [9] At a small distance from the old castles we discover the little town of Chrysopolis, or Scutari, which may almost be considered as the Asiatic suburb of Constantinople. The Bosphorus, as it begins to open into the Propontis, passes between Byzantium and Chalcedon. The latter of those cities was built by the Greeks, a few years before the former; and the blindness of its founders, who overlooked the superior advantages of the opposite coast, has been stigmatized by a proverbial expression of contempt. [10]

[Footnote 3: The Bosphorus has been very minutely described by Dionysius of Byzantium, who lived in the time of Domitian, (Hudson, Geograph Minor, tom. iii.,) and by Gilles or Gyllius, a French traveller of the XVIth century. Tournefort (Lettre XV.) seems to have used his own eyes, and the learning of Gyllius. Add Von Hammer, Constantinopolis und der Bosphoros, 8vo—M.]

[Footnote 4: There are very few conjectures so happy as that of Le Clere, (Bibliotehque Universelle, tom. i. p. 148,) who supposes that the harpies were only locusts. The Syriac or Phoenician name of those insects, their noisy flight, the stench and devastation which they occasion, and the north wind which drives them into the sea, all contribute to form the striking resemblance.]

[Footnote 5: The residence of Amycus was in Asia, between the old and the new castles, at a place called Laurus Insana. That of Phineus was in Europe, near the village of Mauromole and the Black Sea. See Gyllius de Bosph. l. ii. c. 23. Tournefort, Lettre XV.]

[Footnote 6: The deception was occasioned by several pointed rocks, alternately sovered and abandoned by the waves. At present there are two small islands, one towards either shore; that of Europe is distinguished by the column of Pompey.]

[Footnote 7: The ancients computed one hundred and twenty stadia, or fifteen Roman miles. They measured only from the new castles, but they carried the straits as far as the town of Chalcedon.]

[Footnote 8: Ducas. Hist. c. 34. Leunclavius Hist. Turcica Mussulmanica, l. xv. p. 577. Under the Greek empire these castles were used as state prisons, under the tremendous name of Lethe, or towers of oblivion.]

[Footnote 9: Darius engraved in Greek and Assyrian letters, on two marble columns, the names of his subject nations, and the amazing numbers of his land and sea forces. The Byzantines afterwards transported these columns into the city, and used them for the altars of their tutelar deities. Herodotus, l. iv. c. 87.]

[Footnote 10: Namque arctissimo inter Europam Asiamque divortio Byzantium in extrema Europa posuere Greci, quibus, Pythium Apollinem consulentibus ubi conderent urbem, redditum oraculum est, quaererent sedem oecerum terris adversam. Ea ambage Chalcedonii monstrabantur quod priores illuc advecti, praevisa locorum utilitate pejora legissent Tacit. Annal. xii. 63.]

The harbor of Constantinople, which may be considered as an arm of the Bosphorus, obtained, in a very remote period, the denomination of the Golden Horn. The curve which it describes might be compared to the horn of a stag, or as it should seem, with more propriety, to that of an ox. [11] The epithet of golden was expressive of the riches which every wind wafted from the most distant countries into the secure and capacious port of Constantinople. The River Lycus, formed by the conflux of two little streams, pours into the harbor a perpetual supply of fresh water, which serves to cleanse the bottom, and to invite the periodical shoals of fish to seek their retreat in that convenient recess. As the vicissitudes of tides are scarcely felt in those seas, the constant depth of the harbor allows goods to be landed on the quays without the assistance of boats; and it has been observed, that in many places the largest vessels may rest their prows against the houses, while their sterns are floating in the water. [12] From the mouth of the Lycus to that of the harbor, this arm of the Bosphorus is more than seven miles in length. The entrance is about five hundred yards broad, and a strong chain could be occasionally drawn across it, to guard the port and city from the attack of a hostile navy. [13]

[Footnote 11: Strabo, l. vii. p. 492, [edit. Casaub.] Most of the antlers are now broken off; or, to speak less figuratively, most of the recesses of the harbor are filled up. See Gill. de Bosphoro Thracio, l. i. c. 5.]

[Footnote 12: Procopius de Aedificiis, l. i. c. 5. His description is confirmed by modern travellers. See Thevenot, part i. l. i. c. 15. Tournefort, Lettre XII. Niebuhr, Voyage d'Arabie, p. 22.]

[Footnote 13: See Ducange, C. P. l. i. part i. c. 16, and his Observations sur Villehardouin, p. 289. The chain was drawn from the Acropolis near the modern Kiosk, to the tower of Galata; and was supported at convenient distances by large wooden piles.]

Between the Bosphorus and the Hellespont, the shores of Europe and Asia, receding on either side, enclose the sea of Marmara, which was known to the ancients by the denomination of Propontis. The navigation from the issue of the Bosphorus to the entrance of the Hellespont is about one hundred and twenty miles.

Those who steer their westward course through the middle of the Propontis, may at once descry the high lands of Thrace and Bithynia, and never lose sight of the lofty summit of Mount Olympus, covered with eternal snows. [14] They leave on the left a deep gulf, at the bottom of which Nicomedia was seated, the Imperial residence of Diocletian; and they pass the small islands of Cyzicus and Proconnesus before they cast anchor at Gallipoli; where the sea, which separates Asia from Europe, is again contracted into a narrow channel.

[Footnote 14: Thevenot (Voyages au Levant, part i. l. i. c. 14) contracts the measure to 125 small Greek miles. Belon (Observations, l. ii. c. 1.) gives a good description of the Propontis, but contents himself with the vague expression of one day and one night's sail. When Sandy's (Travels, p. 21) talks of 150 furlongs in length, as well as breadth we can only suppose some mistake of the press in the text of that judicious traveller.]

The geographers who, with the most skilful accuracy, have surveyed the form and extent of the Hellespont, assign about sixty miles for the winding course, and about three miles for the ordinary breadth of those celebrated straits. [15] But the narrowest part of the channel is found to the northward of the old Turkish castles between the cities of Sestus and Abydus. It was here that the adventurous Leander braved the passage of the flood for the possession of his mistress. [16] It was here likewise, in a place where the distance between the opposite banks cannot exceed five hundred paces, that Xerxes imposed a stupendous bridge of boats, for the purpose of transporting into Europe a hundred and seventy myriads of barbarians. [17] A sea contracted within such narrow limits may seem but ill to deserve the singular epithet of broad, which Homer, as well as Orpheus, has frequently bestowed on the Hellespont. [17a] But our ideas of greatness are of a relative nature: the traveller, and especially the poet, who sailed along the Hellespont, who pursued the windings of the stream, and contemplated the rural scenery, which appeared on every side to terminate the prospect, insensibly lost the remembrance of the sea; and his fancy painted those celebrated straits, with all the attributes of a mighty river flowing with a swift current, in the midst of a woody and inland country, and at length, through a wide mouth, discharging itself into the Aegean or Archipelago. [18] Ancient Troy, [19] seated on a an eminence at the foot of Mount Ida, overlooked the mouth of the Hellespont, which scarcely received an accession of waters from the tribute of those immortal rivulets the Simois and Scamander. The Grecian camp had stretched twelve miles along the shore from the Sigaean to the Rhaetean promontory; and the flanks of the army were guarded by the bravest chiefs who fought under the banners of Agamemnon. The first of those promontories was occupied by Achilles with his invincible myrmidons, and the dauntless Ajax pitched his tents on the other. After Ajax had fallen a sacrifice to his disappointed pride, and to the ingratitude of the Greeks, his sepulchre was erected on the ground where he had defended the navy against the rage of Jove and of Hector; and the citizens of the rising town of Rhaeteum celebrated his memory with divine honors. [20] Before Constantine gave a just preference to the situation of Byzantium, he had conceived the design of erecting the seat of empire on this celebrated spot, from whence the Romans derived their fabulous origin. The extensive plain which lies below ancient Troy, towards the Rhaetean promontory and the tomb of Ajax, was first chosen for his new capital; and though the undertaking was soon relinquished the stately remains of unfinished walls and towers attracted the notice of all who sailed through the straits of the Hellespont. [21]

[Footnote 15: See an admirable dissertation of M. d'Anville upon the Hellespont or Dardanelles, in the Memoires tom. xxviii. p. 318—346. Yet even that ingenious geographer is too fond of supposing new, and perhaps imaginary measures, for the purpose of rendering ancient writers as accurate as himself. The stadia employed by Herodotus in the description of the Euxine, the Bosphorus, &c., (l. iv. c. 85,) must undoubtedly be all of the same species; but it seems impossible to reconcile them either with truth or with each other.]

[Footnote 16: The oblique distance between Sestus and Abydus was thirty stadia. The improbable tale of Hero and Leander is exposed by M. Mahudel, but is defended on the authority of poets and medals by M. de la Nauze. See the Academie des Inscriptions, tom. vii. Hist. p. 74. elem. p. 240. Note: The practical illustration of the possibility of Leander's feat by Lord Byron and other English swimmers is too well known to need particularly reference—M.]

[Footnote 17: See the seventh book of Herodotus, who has erected an elegant trophy to his own fame and to that of his country. The review appears to have been made with tolerable accuracy; but the vanity, first of the Persians, and afterwards of the Greeks, was interested to magnify the armament and the victory. I should much doubt whether the invaders have ever outnumbered the men of any country which they attacked.]

[Footnote 17a: Gibbon does not allow greater width between the two nearest points of the shores of the Hellespont than between those of the Bosphorus; yet all the ancient writers speak of the Hellespontic strait as broader than the other: they agree in giving it seven stadia in its narrowest width, (Herod. in Melp. c. 85. Polym. c. 34. Strabo, p. 591. Plin. iv. c. 12.) which make 875 paces. It is singular that Gibbon, who in the fifteenth note of this chapter reproaches d'Anville with being fond of supposing new and perhaps imaginary measures, has here adopted the peculiar measurement which d'Anville has assigned to the stadium. This great geographer believes that the ancients had a stadium of fifty-one toises, and it is that which he applies to the walls of Babylon. Now, seven of these stadia are equal to about 500 paces, 7 stadia = 2142 feet: 500 paces = 2135 feet 5 inches—G. See Rennell, Geog. of Herod. p. 121. Add Ukert, Geographie der Griechen und Romer, v. i. p. 2, 71—M.]

[Footnote 18: See Wood's Observations on Homer, p. 320. I have, with pleasure, selected this remark from an author who in general seems to have disappointed the expectation of the public as a critic, and still more as a traveller. He had visited the banks of the Hellespont; and had read Strabo; he ought to have consulted the Roman itineraries. How was it possible for him to confound Ilium and Alexandria Troas, (Observations, p. 340, 341,) two cities which were sixteen miles distant from each other? Note: Compare Walpole's Memoirs on Turkey, v. i. p. 101. Dr. Clarke adopted Mr. Walpole's interpretation of the salt Hellespont. But the old interpretation is more graphic and Homeric. Clarke's Travels, ii. 70—M.]

[Footnote 19: Demetrius of Scepsis wrote sixty books on thirty lines of Homer's catalogue. The XIIIth Book of Strabo is sufficient for our curiosity.]

[Footnote 20: Strabo, l. xiii. p. 595, [890, edit. Casaub.] The disposition of the ships, which were drawn upon dry land, and the posts of Ajax and Achilles, are very clearly described by Homer. See Iliad, ix. 220.]

[Footnote 21: Zosim. l. ii. [c. 30,] p. 105. Sozomen, l. ii. c. 3. Theophanes, p. 18. Nicephorus Callistus, l. vii. p. 48. Zonaras, tom. ii. l. xiii. p. 6. Zosimus places the new city between Ilium and Alexandria, but this apparent difference may be reconciled by the large extent of its circumference. Before the foundation of Constantinople, Thessalonica is mentioned by Cedrenus, (p. 283,) and Sardica by Zonaras, as the intended capital. They both suppose with very little probability, that the emperor, if he had not been prevented by a prodigy, would have repeated the mistake of the blind Chalcedonians.]

We are at present qualified to view the advantageous position of Constantinople; which appears to have been formed by nature for the centre and capital of a great monarchy. Situated in the forty-first degree of latitude, the Imperial city commanded, from her seven hills, [22] the opposite shores of Europe and Asia; the climate was healthy and temperate, the soil fertile, the harbor secure and capacious; and the approach on the side of the continent was of small extent and easy defence. The Bosphorus and the Hellespont may be considered as the two gates of Constantinople; and the prince who possessed those important passages could always shut them against a naval enemy, and open them to the fleets of commerce. The preservation of the eastern provinces may, in some degree, be ascribed to the policy of Constantine, as the barbarians of the Euxine, who in the preceding age had poured their armaments into the heart of the Mediterranean, soon desisted from the exercise of piracy, and despaired of forcing this insurmountable barrier. When the gates of the Hellespont and Bosphorus were shut, the capital still enjoyed within their spacious enclosure every production which could supply the wants, or gratify the luxury, of its numerous inhabitants. The sea-coasts of Thrace and Bithynia, which languish under the weight of Turkish oppression, still exhibit a rich prospect of vineyards, of gardens, and of plentiful harvests; and the Propontis has ever been renowned for an inexhaustible store of the most exquisite fish, that are taken in their stated seasons, without skill, and almost without labor. [23] But when the passages of the straits were thrown open for trade, they alternately admitted the natural and artificial riches of the north and south, of the Euxine, and of the Mediterranean. Whatever rude commodities were collected in the forests of Germany and Scythia, and far as the sources of the Tanais and the Borysthenes; whatsoever was manufactured by the skill of Europe or Asia; the corn of Egypt, and the gems and spices of the farthest India, were brought by the varying winds into the port of Constantinople, which for many ages attracted the commerce of the ancient world. [24]

[See Basilica Of Constantinople]

[Footnote 22: Pocock's Description of the East, vol. ii. part ii. p. 127. His plan of the seven hills is clear and accurate. That traveller is seldom unsatisfactory.]

[Footnote 23: See Belon, Observations, c. 72—76. Among a variety of different species, the Pelamides, a sort of Thunnies, were the most celebrated. We may learn from Polybius, Strabo, and Tacitus, that the profits of the fishery constituted the principal revenue of Byzantium.]

[Footnote 24: See the eloquent description of Busbequius, epistol. i. p. 64. Est in Europa; habet in conspectu Asiam, Egyptum. Africamque a dextra: quae tametsi contiguae non sunt, maris tamen navigandique commoditate veluti junguntur. A sinistra vero Pontus est Euxinus, &c.]

The prospect of beauty, of safety, and of wealth, united in a single spot, was sufficient to justify the choice of Constantine. But as some decent mixture of prodigy and fable has, in every age, been supposed to reflect a becoming majesty on the origin of great cities, [25] the emperor was desirous of ascribing his resolution, not so much to the uncertain counsels of human policy, as to the infallible and eternal decrees of divine wisdom. In one of his laws he has been careful to instruct posterity, that in obedience to the commands of God, he laid the everlasting foundations of Constantinople: [26] and though he has not condescended to relate in what manner the celestial inspiration was communicated to his mind, the defect of his modest silence has been liberally supplied by the ingenuity of succeeding writers; who describe the nocturnal vision which appeared to the fancy of Constantine, as he slept within the walls of Byzantium. The tutelar genius of the city, a venerable matron sinking under the weight of years and infirmities, was suddenly transformed into a blooming maid, whom his own hands adorned with all the symbols of Imperial greatness. [27] The monarch awoke, interpreted the auspicious omen, and obeyed, without hesitation, the will of Heaven The day which gave birth to a city or colony was celebrated by the Romans with such ceremonies as had been ordained by a generous superstition; [28] and though Constantine might omit some rites which savored too strongly of their Pagan origin, yet he was anxious to leave a deep impression of hope and respect on the minds of the spectators. On foot, with a lance in his hand, the emperor himself led the solemn procession; and directed the line, which was traced as the boundary of the destined capital: till the growing circumference was observed with astonishment by the assistants, who, at length, ventured to observe, that he had already exceeded the most ample measure of a great city. "I shall still advance," replied Constantine, "till He, the invisible guide who marches before me, thinks proper to stop." [29] Without presuming to investigate the nature or motives of this extraordinary conductor, we shall content ourselves with the more humble task of describing the extent and limits of Constantinople. [30]

[Footnote 25: Datur haec venia antiquitati, ut miscendo humana divinis, primordia urbium augustiora faciat. T. Liv. in prooem.]

[Footnote 26: He says in one of his laws, pro commoditate urbis quam aeteras nomine, jubente Deo, donavimus. Cod. Theodos. l. xiii. tit. v. leg. 7.]

[Footnote 27: The Greeks, Theophanes, Cedrenus, and the author of the Alexandrian Chronicle, confine themselves to vague and general expressions. For a more particular account of the vision, we are obliged to have recourse to such Latin writers as William of Malmesbury. See Ducange, C. P. l. i. p. 24, 25.]

[Footnote 28: See Plutarch in Romul. tom. i. p. 49, edit. Bryan. Among other ceremonies, a large hole, which had been dug for that purpose, was filled up with handfuls of earth, which each of the settlers brought from the place of his birth, and thus adopted his new country.]

[Footnote 29: Philostorgius, l. ii. c. 9. This incident, though borrowed from a suspected writer, is characteristic and probable.]

[Footnote 30: See in the Memoires de l'Academie, tom. xxxv p. 747-758, a dissertation of M. d'Anville on the extent of Constantinople. He takes the plan inserted in the Imperium Orientale of Banduri as the most complete; but, by a series of very nice observations, he reduced the extravagant proportion of the scale, and instead of 9500, determines the circumference of the city as consisting of about 7800 French toises.]

In the actual state of the city, the palace and gardens of the Seraglio occupy the eastern promontory, the first of the seven hills, and cover about one hundred and fifty acres of our own measure. The seat of Turkish jealousy and despotism is erected on the foundations of a Grecian republic; but it may be supposed that the Byzantines were tempted by the conveniency of the harbor to extend their habitations on that side beyond the modern limits of the Seraglio. The new walls of Constantine stretched from the port to the Propontis across the enlarged breadth of the triangle, at the distance of fifteen stadia from the ancient fortification; and with the city of Byzantium they enclosed five of the seven hills, which, to the eyes of those who approach Constantinople, appear to rise above each other in beautiful order. [31] About a century after the death of the founder, the new buildings, extending on one side up the harbor, and on the other along the Propontis, already covered the narrow ridge of the sixth, and the broad summit of the seventh hill. The necessity of protecting those suburbs from the incessant inroads of the barbarians engaged the younger Theodosius to surround his capital with an adequate and permanent enclosure of walls. [32] From the eastern promontory to the golden gate, the extreme length of Constantinople was about three Roman miles; [33] the circumference measured between ten and eleven; and the surface might be computed as equal to about two thousand English acres. It is impossible to justify the vain and credulous exaggerations of modern travellers, who have sometimes stretched the limits of Constantinople over the adjacent villages of the European, and even of the Asiatic coast. [34] But the suburbs of Pera and Galata, though situate beyond the harbor, may deserve to be considered as a part of the city; [35] and this addition may perhaps authorize the measure of a Byzantine historian, who assigns sixteen Greek (about fourteen Roman) miles for the circumference of his native city. [36] Such an extent may not seem unworthy of an Imperial residence. Yet Constantinople must yield to Babylon and Thebes, [37] to ancient Rome, to London, and even to Paris. [38]

[Footnote 31: Codinus, Antiquitat. Const. p. 12. He assigns the church of St. Anthony as the boundary on the side of the harbor. It is mentioned in Ducange, l. iv. c. 6; but I have tried, without success, to discover the exact place where it was situated.]

[Footnote 32: The new wall of Theodosius was constructed in the year 413. In 447 it was thrown down by an earthquake, and rebuilt in three months by the diligence of the praefect Cyrus. The suburb of the Blanchernae was first taken into the city in the reign of Heraclius Ducange, Const. l. i. c. 10, 11.]

[Footnote 33: The measurement is expressed in the Notitia by 14,075 feet. It is reasonable to suppose that these were Greek feet, the proportion of which has been ingeniously determined by M. d'Anville. He compares the 180 feet with 78 Hashemite cubits, which in different writers are assigned for the heights of St. Sophia. Each of these cubits was equal to 27 French inches.]

[Footnote 34: The accurate Thevenot (l. i. c. 15) walked in one hour and three quarters round two of the sides of the triangle, from the Kiosk of the Seraglio to the seven towers. D'Anville examines with care, and receives with confidence, this decisive testimony, which gives a circumference of ten or twelve miles. The extravagant computation of Tournefort (Lettre XI) of thirty-tour or thirty miles, without including Scutari, is a strange departure from his usual character.]

[Footnote 35: The sycae, or fig-trees, formed the thirteenth region, and were very much embellished by Justinian. It has since borne the names of Pera and Galata. The etymology of the former is obvious; that of the latter is unknown. See Ducange, Const. l. i. c. 22, and Gyllius de Byzant. l. iv. c. 10.]

[Footnote 36: One hundred and eleven stadia, which may be translated into modern Greek miles each of seven stadia, or 660, sometimes only 600 French toises. See D'Anville, Mesures Itineraires, p. 53.]

[Footnote 37: When the ancient texts, which describe the size of Babylon and Thebes, are settled, the exaggerations reduced, and the measures ascertained, we find that those famous cities filled the great but not incredible circumference of about twenty-five or thirty miles. Compare D'Anville, Mem. de l'Academie, tom. xxviii. p. 235, with his Description de l'Egypte, p. 201, 202.]

[Footnote 38: If we divide Constantinople and Paris into equal squares of 50 French toises, the former contains 850, and the latter 1160, of those divisions.]

PART II

The master of the Roman world, who aspired to erect an eternal monument of the glories of his reign could employ in the prosecution of that great work, the wealth, the labor, and all that yet remained of the genius of obedient millions. Some estimate may be formed of the expense bestowed with Imperial liberality on the foundation of Constantinople, by the allowance of about two millions five hundred thousand pounds for the construction of the walls, the porticos, and the aqueducts. [39] The forests that overshadowed the shores of the Euxine, and the celebrated quarries of white marble in the little island of Proconnesus, supplied an inexhaustible stock of materials, ready to be conveyed, by the convenience of a short water carriage, to the harbor of Byzantium. [40] A multitude of laborers and artificers urged the conclusion of the work with incessant toil: but the impatience of Constantine soon discovered, that, in the decline of the arts, the skill as well as numbers of his architects bore a very unequal proportion to the greatness of his designs. The magistrates of the most distant provinces were therefore directed to institute schools, to appoint professors, and by the hopes of rewards and privileges, to engage in the study and practice of architecture a sufficient number of ingenious youths, who had received a liberal education. [41] The buildings of the new city were executed by such artificers as the reign of Constantine could afford; but they were decorated by the hands of the most celebrated masters of the age of Pericles and Alexander. To revive the genius of Phidias and Lysippus, surpassed indeed the power of a Roman emperor; but the immortal productions which they had bequeathed to posterity were exposed without defence to the rapacious vanity of a despot. By his commands the cities of Greece and Asia were despoiled of their most valuable ornaments. [42] The trophies of memorable wars, the objects of religious veneration, the most finished statues of the gods and heroes, of the sages and poets, of ancient times, contributed to the splendid triumph of Constantinople; and gave occasion to the remark of the historian Cedrenus, [43] who observes, with some enthusiasm, that nothing seemed wanting except the souls of the illustrious men whom these admirable monuments were intended to represent. But it is not in the city of Constantine, nor in the declining period of an empire, when the human mind was depressed by civil and religious slavery, that we should seek for the souls of Homer and of Demosthenes.

[Footnote 39: Six hundred centenaries, or sixty thousand pounds' weight of gold. This sum is taken from Codinus, Antiquit. Const. p. 11; but unless that contemptible author had derived his information from some purer sources, he would probably have been unacquainted with so obsolete a mode of reckoning.]

[Footnote 40: For the forests of the Black Sea, consult Tournefort, Lettre XVI. for the marble quarries of Proconnesus, see Strabo, l. xiii. p. 588, (881, edit. Casaub.) The latter had already furnished the materials of the stately buildings of Cyzicus.]

[Footnote 41: See the Codex Theodos. l. xiii. tit. iv. leg. 1. This law is dated in the year 334, and was addressed to the praefect of Italy, whose jurisdiction extended over Africa. The commentary of Godefroy on the whole title well deserves to be consulted.]

[Footnote 42: Constantinopolis dedicatur poene omnium urbium nuditate. Hieronym. Chron. p. 181. See Codinus, p. 8, 9. The author of the Antiquitat. Const. l. iii. (apud Banduri Imp. Orient. tom. i. p. 41) enumerates Rome, Sicily, Antioch, Athens, and a long list of other cities. The provinces of Greece and Asia Minor may be supposed to have yielded the richest booty.]

[Footnote 43: Hist. Compend. p. 369. He describes the statue, or rather bust, of Homer with a degree of taste which plainly indicates that Cadrenus copied the style of a more fortunate age.]

During the siege of Byzantium, the conqueror had pitched his tent on the commanding eminence of the second hill. To perpetuate the memory of his success, he chose the same advantageous position for the principal Forum; [44] which appears to have been of a circular, or rather elliptical form. The two opposite entrances formed triumphal arches; the porticos, which enclosed it on every side, were filled with statues; and the centre of the Forum was occupied by a lofty column, of which a mutilated fragment is now degraded by the appellation of the burnt pillar. This column was erected on a pedestal of white marble twenty feet high; and was composed of ten pieces of porphyry, each of which measured about ten feet in height, and about thirty-three in circumference. [45] On the summit of the pillar, above one hundred and twenty feet from the ground, stood the colossal statue of Apollo. It was a bronze, had been transported either from Athens or from a town of Phrygia, and was supposed to be the work of Phidias. The artist had represented the god of day, or, as it was afterwards interpreted, the emperor

Constantine himself, with a sceptre in his right hand, the globe of the world in his left, and a crown of rays glittering on his head. [46] The Circus, or Hippodrome, was a stately building about four hundred paces in length, and one hundred in breadth. [47] The space between the two metoe or goals were filled with statues and obelisks; and we may still remark a very singular fragment of antiquity; the bodies of three serpents, twisted into one pillar of brass. Their triple heads had once supported the golden tripod which, after the defeat of Xerxes, was consecrated in the temple of Delphi by the victorious Greeks. [48] The beauty of the Hippodrome has been long since defaced by the rude hands of the Turkish conquerors; [48a] but, under the similar appellation of Atmeidan, it still serves as a place of exercise for their horses. From the throne, whence the emperor viewed the Circensian games, a winding staircase [49] descended to the palace; a magnificent edifice, which scarcely yielded to the residence of Rome itself, and which, together with the dependent courts, gardens, and porticos, covered a considerable extent of ground upon the banks of the Propontis between the Hippodrome and the church of St. Sophia. [50] We might likewise celebrate the baths, which still retained the name of Zeuxippus, after they had been enriched, by the munificence of Constantine, with lofty columns, various marbles, and above threescore statues of bronze. [51] But we should deviate from the design of this history, if we attempted minutely to describe the different buildings or quarters of the city. It may be sufficient to observe, that whatever could adorn the dignity of a great capital, or contribute to the benefit or pleasure of its numerous inhabitants, was contained within the walls of Constantinople. A particular description, composed about a century after its foundation, enumerates a capitol or school of learning, a circus, two theatres, eight public, and one hundred and fifty-three private baths, fifty-two porticos, five granaries, eight aqueducts or reservoirs of water, four spacious halls for the meetings of the senate or courts of justice, fourteen churches, fourteen palaces, and four thousand three hundred and eighty-eight houses, which, for their size or beauty, deserved to be distinguished from the multitude of plebeian inhabitants. [52]

[Footnote 44: Zosim. l. ii. p. 106. Chron. Alexandrin. vel Paschal. p. 284, Ducange, Const. l. i. c. 24. Even the last of those writers seems to confound the Forum of Constantine with the Augusteum, or court of the palace. I am not satisfied whether I have properly distinguished what belongs to the one and the other.]

[Footnote 45: The most tolerable account of this column is given by Pocock. Description of the East, vol. ii. part ii. p. 131. But it is still in many instances perplexed and unsatisfactory.]

[Footnote 46: Ducange, Const. l. i. c. 24, p. 76, and his notes ad Alexiad. p. 382. The statue of Constantine or Apollo was thrown down under the reign of Alexius Comnenus. Note: On this column (says M. von Hammer) Constantine, with singular shamelessness, placed his own statue with the attributes of Apollo and Christ. He substituted the nails of the Passion for the rays of the sun. Such is the direct testimony of the author of the Antiquit. Constantinop. apud Banduri. Constantine was replaced by the "great and religious" Julian, Julian, by Theodosius. A. D. 1412, the key stone was loosened by an earthquake. The statue fell in the reign of Alexius Comnenus, and was replaced by the cross. The Palladium was said to be buried under the pillar. Von Hammer, Constantinopolis und der Bosporos, i. 162—M.]

[Footnote 47: Tournefort (Lettre XII.) computes the Atmeidan at four hundred paces. If he means geometrical paces of five feet each, it was three hundred toises in length, about forty more than the great circus of Rome. See D'Anville, Mesures Itineraires, p. 73.]

[Footnote 48: The guardians of the most holy relics would rejoice if they were able to produce such a chain of evidence as may be alleged on this occasion. See Banduri ad Antiquitat. Const. p. 668. Gyllius de

Byzant. l. ii. c. 13. 1. The original consecration of the tripod and pillar in the temple of Delphi may be proved from Herodotus and Pausanias. 2. The Pagan Zosimus agrees with the three ecclesiastical historians, Eusebius, Socrates, and Sozomen, that the sacred ornaments of the temple of Delphi were removed to Constantinople by the order of Constantine; and among these the serpentine pillar of the Hippodrome is particularly mentioned. 3. All the European travellers who have visited Constantinople, from Buondelmonte to Pocock, describe it in the same place, and almost in the same manner; the differences between them are occasioned only by the injuries which it has sustained from the Turks. Mahomet the Second broke the under jaw of one of the serpents with a stroke of his battle axe Thevenot, l. i. c. 17. Note: See note 75, ch. lxviii. for Dr. Clarke's rejection of Thevenot's authority. Von Hammer, however, repeats the story of Thevenot without questioning its authenticity—M.]

[Footnote 48a: In 1808 the Janizaries revolted against the vizier Mustapha Baisactar, who wished to introduce a new system of military organization, besieged the quarter of the Hippodrome, in which stood the palace of the viziers, and the Hippodrome was consumed in the conflagration—G.]

[Footnote 49: The Latin name Cochlea was adopted by the Greeks, and very frequently occurs in the Byzantine history. Ducange, Const. i. c. l, p. 104.]

[Footnote 50: There are three topographical points which indicate the situation of the palace. 1. The staircase which connected it with the Hippodrome or Atmeidan. 2. A small artificial port on the Propontis, from whence there was an easy ascent, by a flight of marble steps, to the gardens of the palace. 3. The Augusteum was a spacious court, one side of which was occupied by the front of the palace, and another by the church of St. Sophia.]

[Footnote 51: Zeuxippus was an epithet of Jupiter, and the baths were a part of old Byzantium. The difficulty of assigning their true situation has not been felt by Ducange. History seems to connect them with St. Sophia and the palace; but the original plan inserted in Banduri places them on the other side of the city, near the harbor. For their beauties, see Chron. Paschal. p. 285, and Gyllius de Byzant. l. ii. c. 7. Christodorus (see Antiquitat. Const. l. vii.) composed inscriptions in verse for each of the statues. He was a Theban poet in genius as well as in birth:—Baeotum in crasso jurares aere natum. Note: Yet, for his age, the description of the statues of Hecuba and of Homer are by no means without merit. See Antholog. Palat. (edit. Jacobs) i. 37—M.]

[Footnote 52: See the Notitia. Rome only reckoned 1780 large houses, domus; but the word must have had a more dignified signification. No insulae are mentioned at Constantinople. The old capital consisted of 42 streets, the new of 322.]

The populousness of his favored city was the next and most serious object of the attention of its founder. In the dark ages which succeeded the translation of the empire, the remote and the immediate consequences of that memorable event were strangely confounded by the vanity of the Greeks and the credulity of the Latins. [53] It was asserted, and believed, that all the noble families of Rome, the senate, and the equestrian order, with their innumerable attendants, had followed their emperor to the banks of the Propontis; that a spurious race of strangers and plebeians was left to possess the solitude of the ancient capital; and that the lands of Italy, long since converted into gardens, were at once deprived of cultivation and inhabitants. [54] In the course of this history, such exaggerations will be reduced to their just value: yet, since the growth of Constantinople cannot be ascribed to the general increase of mankind and of industry, it must be admitted that this artificial colony was raised at the expense of the ancient cities of the empire. Many opulent senators of Rome, and of the eastern provinces, were probably invited by Constantine to adopt for their country the fortunate spot, which he had chosen for his own residence. The invitations of a master are scarcely to be distinguished from commands; and the liberality of the emperor obtained a ready and cheerful obedience. He bestowed on his favorites the palaces which he had built in the several quarters of the city, assigned them lands and pensions for the support of their dignity, [55] and alienated the demesnes of Pontus and Asia to grant hereditary estates by the easy tenure of maintaining a house in the capital. [56] But these encouragements and obligations soon became superfluous, and were gradually abolished. Wherever the seat of government is fixed, a considerable part of the public revenue will be expended by the prince himself, by his ministers, by the officers of justice, and by the domestics of the palace. The most wealthy of the provincials will be attracted by the powerful motives of interest and duty, of amusement and curiosity. A third and more numerous class of inhabitants will insensibly be formed, of servants, of artificers, and of merchants, who derive their subsistence from their own labor, and from the wants or luxury of the superior ranks. In less than a century, Constantinople disputed with Rome itself the preeminence of riches and numbers. New piles of buildings, crowded together with too little regard to health or convenience, scarcely allowed the intervals of narrow streets for the perpetual throng of men, of horses, and of carriages. The allotted space of ground was insufficient to contain the increasing people; and the additional foundations, which, on either side, were advanced into the sea, might alone have composed a very considerable city. [57]

[Footnote 53: Liutprand, Legatio ad Imp. Nicephornm, p. 153. The modern Greeks have strangely disfigured the antiquities of Constantinople. We might excuse the errors of the Turkish or Arabian writers; but it is somewhat astonishing, that the Greeks, who had access to the authentic materials preserved in their own language, should prefer fiction to truth, and loose tradition to genuine history. In a single page of Codinus we may detect twelve unpardonable mistakes; the reconciliation of Severus and Niger, the marriage of their son and daughter, the siege of Byzantium by the Macedonians, the invasion of the Gauls, which recalled Severus to Rome, the sixty years which elapsed from his death to the foundation of Constantinople, &c.]

[Footnote 54: Montesquieu, Grandeur et Decadence des Romains, c. 17.]

[Footnote 55: Themist. Orat. iii. p. 48, edit. Hardouin. Sozomen, l. ii. c. 3. Zosim. l. ii. p. 107. Anonym. Valesian. p. 715. If we could credit Codinus, (p. 10,) Constantine built houses for the senators on the exact model of their Roman palaces, and gratified them, as well as himself, with the pleasure of an agreeable surprise; but the whole story is full of fictions and inconsistencies.]

[Footnote 56: The law by which the younger Theodosius, in the year 438, abolished this tenure, may be found among the Novellae of that emperor at the end of the Theodosian Code, tom. vi. nov. 12. M. de Tillemont (Hist. des Empereurs, tom. iv. p. 371) has evidently mistaken the nature of these estates. With a grant from the Imperial demesnes, the same condition was accepted as a favor, which would justly have been deemed a hardship, if it had been imposed upon private property.]

[Footnote 57: The passages of Zosimus, of Eunapius, of Sozomen, and of Agathias, which relate to the increase of buildings and inhabitants at Constantinople, are collected and connected by Gyllius de Byzant. l. i. c. 3. Sidonius Apollinaris (in Panegyr. Anthem. 56, p. 279, edit. Sirmond) describes the moles that were pushed forwards into the sea, they consisted of the famous Puzzolan sand, which hardens in the water.]

The frequent and regular distributions of wine and oil, of corn or bread, of money or provisions, had almost exempted the poorest citizens of Rome from the necessity of labor. The magnificence of the first Caesars was in some measure imitated by the founder of Constantinople: [58] but his liberality, however it might excite the applause of the people, has in curred the censure of posterity. A nation of legislators and conquerors might assert their claim to the harvests of Africa, which had been purchased with their blood; and it was artfully contrived by Augustus, that, in the enjoyment of plenty, the Romans should lose the memory of freedom. But the prodigality of Constantine could not be excused by any consideration either of public or private interest; and the annual tribute of corn imposed upon Egypt for the benefit of his new capital, was applied to feed a lazy and insolent populace, at the expense of the husbandmen of an industrious province. [59] [59a] Some other regulations of this emperor are less liable to blame, but they are less deserving of notice. He divided Constantinople into fourteen regions or quarters, [60] dignified the public council with the appellation of senate, [61] communicated to the citizens the privileges of Italy, [62] and bestowed on the rising city the title of Colony, the first and most favored daughter of ancient Rome. The venerable parent still maintained the legal and acknowledged supremacy, which was due to her age, her dignity, and to the remembrance of her former greatness. [63]

[Footnote 58: Sozomen, l. ii. c. 3. Philostorg. l. ii. c. 9. Codin. Antiquitat. Const. p. 8. It appears by Socrates, l. ii. c. 13, that the daily allowance of the city consisted of eight myriads of which we may either translate, with Valesius, by the words modii of corn, or consider us expressive of the number of loaves of bread. Note: At Rome the poorer citizens who received these gratuities were inscribed in a register; they had only a personal right. Constantine attached the right to the houses in his new capital, to engage the lower classes of the people to build their houses with expedition. Codex Therodos. l. xiv—G.]

[Footnote 59: See Cod. Theodos. l. xiii. and xiv., and Cod. Justinian. Edict. xii. tom. ii. p. 648, edit. Genev. See the beautiful complaint of Rome in the poem of Claudian de Bell. Gildonico, ver. 46-64—Cum subiit par Roma mihi, divisaque sumsit Aequales aurora togas; Aegyptia rura In partem cessere novam.]

[Footnote 59a: This was also at the expense of Rome. The emperor ordered that the fleet of Alexandria should transport to Constantinople the grain of Egypt which it carried before to Rome: this grain supplied Rome during four months of the year. Claudian has described with force the famine occasioned by this measure:—

Haec nobis, haec ante dabas; nunc pabula tantum
Roma precor: miserere tuae; pater optime, gentis:
Extremam defende famem. Claud. de Bell. Gildon. v. 34—G.

It was scarcely this measure. Gildo had cut off the African as well as the Egyptian supplies—M.]

[Footnote 60: The regions of Constantinople are mentioned in the code of Justinian, and particularly described in the Notitia of the younger Theodosius; but as the four last of them are not included within the wall of Constantine, it may be doubted whether this division of the city should be referred to the founder.]

[Footnote 61: Senatum constituit secundi ordinis; Claros vocavit. Anonym Valesian. p. 715. The senators of old Rome were styled Clarissimi. See a curious note of Valesius ad Ammian. Marcellin. xxii. 9. From the eleventh epistle of Julian, it should seem that the place of senator was considered as a burden, rather than as an honor; but the Abbe de la Bleterie (Vie de Jovien, tom. ii. p. 371) has shown that this epistle

could not relate to Constantinople. Might we not read, instead of the celebrated name of the obscure but more probable word Bisanthe or Rhoedestus, now Rhodosto, was a small maritime city of Thrace. See Stephan. Byz. de Urbibus, p. 225, and Cellar. Geograph. tom. i. p. 849.]

[Footnote 62: Cod. Theodos. l. xiv. 13. The commentary of Godefroy (tom. v. p. 220) is long, but perplexed; nor indeed is it easy to ascertain in what the Jus Italicum could consist, after the freedom of the city had been communicated to the whole empire. Note: "This right, (the Jus Italicum,) which by most writers is referred with out foundation to the personal condition of the citizens, properly related to the city as a whole, and contained two parts. First, the Roman or quiritarian property in the soil, (commercium,) and its capability of mancipation, usucaption, and vindication; moreover, as an inseparable consequence of this, exemption from land-tax. Then, secondly, a free constitution in the Italian form, with Duumvirs, Quinquennales. and Aediles, and especially with Jurisdiction." Savigny, Geschichte des Rom. Rechts i. p. 51—M.]

[Footnote 63: Julian (Orat. i. p. 8) celebrates Constantinople as not less superior to all other cities than she was inferior to Rome itself. His learned commentator (Spanheim, p. 75, 76) justifies this language by several parallel and contemporary instances. Zosimus, as well as Socrates and Sozomen, flourished after the division of the empire between the two sons of Theodosius, which established a perfect equality between the old and the new capital.]

As Constantine urged the progress of the work with the impatience of a lover, the walls, the porticos, and the principal edifices were completed in a few years, or, according to another account, in a few months; [64] but this extraordinary diligence should excite the less admiration, since many of the buildings were finished in so hasty and imperfect a manner, that under the succeeding reign, they were preserved with difficulty from impending ruin. [65] But while they displayed the vigor and freshness of youth, the founder prepared to celebrate the dedication of his city. [66] The games and largesses which crowned the pomp of this memorable festival may easily be supposed; but there is one circumstance of a more singular and permanent nature, which ought not entirely to be overlooked. As often as the birthday of the city returned, the statute of Constantine, framed by his order, of gilt wood, and bearing in his right hand a small image of the genius of the place, was erected on a triumphal car. The guards, carrying white tapers, and clothed in their richest apparel, accompanied the solemn procession as it moved through the Hippodrome. When it was opposite to the throne of the reigning emperor, he rose from his seat, and with grateful reverence adored the memory of his predecessor. [67] At the festival of the dedication, an edict, engraved on a column of marble, bestowed the title of Second or New Rome on the city of Constantine. [68] But the name of Constantinople [69] has prevailed over that honorable epithet; and after the revolution of fourteen centuries, still perpetuates the fame of its author. [70]

[Footnote 64: Codinus (Antiquitat. p. 8) affirms, that the foundations of Constantinople were laid in the year of the world 5837, (A. D. 329,) on the 26th of September, and that the city was dedicated the 11th of May, 5838, (A. D. 330.) He connects those dates with several characteristic epochs, but they contradict each other; the authority of Codinus is of little weight, and the space which he assigns must appear insufficient. The term of ten years is given us by Julian, (Orat. i. p. 8;) and Spanheim labors to establish the truth of it, (p. 69-75,) by the help of two passages from Themistius, (Orat. iv. p. 58,) and of Philostorgius, (l. ii. c. 9,) which form a period from the year 324 to the year 334. Modern critics are divided concerning this point of chronology and their different sentiments are very accurately described by Tillemont, Hist. des Empereurs, tom. iv. p. 619-625.]

[Footnote 65: Themistius. Orat. iii. p. 47. Zosim. l. ii. p. 108. Constantine himself, in one of his laws, (Cod. Theod. l. xv. tit. i.,) betrays his impatience.]

[Footnote 66: Cedrenus and Zonaras, faithful to the mode of superstition which prevailed in their own times, assure us that Constantinople was consecrated to the virgin Mother of God.]

[Footnote 67: The earliest and most complete account of this extraordinary ceremony may be found in the Alexandrian Chronicle, p. 285. Tillemont, and the other friends of Constantine, who are offended with the air of Paganism which seems unworthy of a Christian prince, had a right to consider it as doubtful, but they were not authorized to omit the mention of it.]

[Footnote 68: Sozomen, l. ii. c. 2. Ducange C. P. l. i. c. 6. Velut ipsius Romae filiam, is the expression of Augustin. de Civitat. Dei, l. v. c. 25.]

[Footnote 69: Eutropius, l. x. c. 8. Julian. Orat. i. p. 8. Ducange C. P. l. i. c. 5. The name of Constantinople is extant on the medals of Constantine.]

[Footnote 70: The lively Fontenelle (Dialogues des Morts, xii.) affects to deride the vanity of human ambition, and seems to triumph in the disappointment of Constantine, whose immortal name is now lost in the vulgar appellation of Istambol, a Turkish corruption of. Yet the original name is still preserved, 1. By the nations of Europe. 2. By the modern Greeks. 3. By the Arabs, whose writings are diffused over the wide extent of their conquests in Asia and Africa. See D'Herbelot, Bibliotheque Orientale, p. 275. 4. By the more learned Turks, and by the emperor himself in his public mandates Cantemir's History of the Othman Empire, p. 51.]

The foundation of a new capital is naturally connected with the establishment of a new form of civil and military administration. The distinct view of the complicated system of policy, introduced by Diocletian, improved by Constantine, and completed by his immediate successors, may not only amuse the fancy by the singular picture of a great empire, but will tend to illustrate the secret and internal causes of its rapid decay. In the pursuit of any remarkable institution, we may be frequently led into the more early or the more recent times of the Roman history; but the proper limits of this inquiry will be included within a period of about one hundred and thirty years, from the accession of Constantine to the publication of the Theodosian code; [71] from which, as well as from the Notitia [71a] of the East and West, [72] we derive the most copious and authentic information of the state of the empire. This variety of objects will suspend, for some time, the course of the narrative; but the interruption will be censured only by those readers who are insensible to the importance of laws and manners, while they peruse, with eager curiosity, the transient intrigues of a court, or the accidental event of a battle.

[Footnote 71: The Theodosian code was promulgated A. D. 438. See the Prolegomena of Godefroy, c. i. p. 185.]

[Footnote 71a: The Notitia Dignitatum Imperii is a description of all the offices in the court and the state, of the legions, &c. It resembles our court almanacs, (Red Books,) with this single difference, that our almanacs name the persons in office, the Notitia only the offices. It is of the time of the emperor Theodosius II., that is to say, of the fifth century, when the empire was divided into the Eastern and Western. It is probable that it was not made for the first time, and that descriptions of the same kind existed before—G.]

[Footnote 72: Pancirolus, in his elaborate Commentary, assigns to the Notitia a date almost similar to that of the Theodosian Code; but his proofs, or rather conjectures, are extremely feeble. I should be rather inclined to place this useful work between the final division of the empire (A. D. 395) and the successful invasion of Gaul by the barbarians, (A. D. 407.) See Histoire des Anciens Peuples de l'Europe, tom. vii. p. 40.]

PART III

The manly pride of the Romans, content with substantial power, had left to the vanity of the East the forms and ceremonies of ostentatious greatness. [73] But when they lost even the semblance of those virtues which were derived from their ancient freedom, the simplicity of Roman manners was insensibly corrupted by the stately affectation of the courts of Asia. The distinctions of personal merit and influence, so conspicuous in a republic, so feeble and obscure under a monarchy, were abolished by the despotism of the emperors; who substituted in their room a severe subordination of rank and office from the titled slaves who were seated on the steps of the throne, to the meanest instruments of arbitrary power. This multitude of abject dependants was interested in the support of the actual government from the dread of a revolution, which might at once confound their hopes and intercept the reward of their services. In this divine hierarchy (for such it is frequently styled) every rank was marked with the most scrupulous exactness, and its dignity was displayed in a variety of trifling and solemn ceremonies, which it was a study to learn, and a sacrilege to neglect. [74] The purity of the Latin language was debased, by adopting, in the intercourse of pride and flattery, a profusion of epithets, which Tully would scarcely have understood, and which Augustus would have rejected with indignation. The principal officers of the empire were saluted, even by the sovereign himself, with the deceitful titles of your Sincerity, your Gravity, your Excellency, your Eminence, your sublime and wonderful Magnitude, your illustrious and magnificent Highness. [75] The codicils or patents of their office were curiously emblazoned with such emblems as were best adapted to explain its nature and high dignity; the image or portrait of the reigning emperors; a triumphal car; the book of mandates placed on a table, covered with a rich carpet, and illuminated by four tapers; the allegorical figures of the provinces which they governed; or the appellations and standards of the troops whom they commanded Some of these official ensigns were really exhibited in their hall of audience; others preceded their pompous march whenever they appeared in public; and every circumstance of their demeanor, their dress, their ornaments, and their train, was calculated to inspire a deep reverence for the representatives of supreme majesty. By a philosophic observer, the system of the Roman government might have been mistaken for a splendid theatre, filled with players of every character and degree, who repeated the language, and imitated the passions, of their original model. [76]

[Footnote 73: Scilicet externae superbiae sueto, non inerat notitia nostri, (perhaps nostroe;) apud quos vis Imperii valet, inania transmittuntur. Tacit. Annal. xv. 31. The gradation from the style of freedom and simplicity, to that of form and servitude, may be traced in the Epistles of Cicero, of Pliny, and of Symmachus.]

[Footnote 74: The emperor Gratian, after confirming a law of precedency published by Valentinian, the father of his Divinity, thus continues: Siquis igitur indebitum sibi locum usurpaverit, nulla se ignoratione defendat; sitque plane sacrilegii reus, qui divina praecepta neglexerit. Cod. Theod. l. vi. tit. v. leg. 2.]

[Footnote 75: Consult the Notitia Dignitatum at the end of the Theodosian code, tom. vi. p. 316. Note: Constantin, qui remplaca le grand Patriciat par une noblesse titree et qui changea avec d'autres institutions la nature de la societe Latine, est le veritable fondateur de la royaute moderne, dans ce quelle conserva de Romain. Chateaubriand, Etud. Histor. Preface, i. 151. Manso, (Leben Constantins des Grossen,) p. 153, &c., has given a lucid view of the dignities and duties of the officers in the Imperial court—M.]

[Footnote 76: Pancirolus ad Notitiam utriusque Imperii, p. 39. But his explanations are obscure, and he does not sufficiently distinguish the painted emblems from the effective ensigns of office.]

All the magistrates of sufficient importance to find a place in the general state of the empire, were accurately divided into three classes. 1. The Illustrious. 2. The Spectabiles, or Respectable. And, 3. the Clarissimi; whom we may translate by the word Honorable. In the times of Roman simplicity, the last-mentioned epithet was used only as a vague expression of deference, till it became at length the peculiar and appropriated title of all who were members of the senate, [77] and consequently of all who, from that venerable body, were selected to govern the provinces. The vanity of those who, from their rank and office, might claim a superior distinction above the rest of the senatorial order, was long afterwards indulged with the new appellation of Respectable; but the title of Illustrious was always reserved to some eminent personages who were obeyed or reverenced by the two subordinate classes. It was communicated only, I. To the consuls and patricians; II. To the Praetorian praefects, with the praefects of Rome and Constantinople; III. To the masters-general of the cavalry and the infantry; and IV. To the seven ministers of the palace, who exercised their sacred functions about the person of the emperor. [78] Among those illustrious magistrates who were esteemed coordinate with each other, the seniority of appointment gave place to the union of dignities. [79] By the expedient of honorary codicils, the emperors, who were fond of multiplying their favors, might sometimes gratify the vanity, though not the ambition, of impatient courtiers. [80]

[Footnote 77: In the Pandects, which may be referred to the reigns of the Antonines, Clarissimus is the ordinary and legal title of a senator.]

[Footnote 78: Pancirol. p. 12-17. I have not taken any notice of the two inferior ranks, Prefectissimus and Egregius, which were given to many persons who were not raised to the senatorial dignity.]

[Footnote 79: Cod. Theodos. l. vi. tit. vi. The rules of precedency are ascertained with the most minute accuracy by the emperors, and illustrated with equal prolixity by their learned interpreter.]

[Footnote 80: Cod. Theodos. l. vi. tit. xxii.]

I. As long as the Roman consuls were the first magistrates of a free state, they derived their right to power from the choice of the people. As long as the emperors condescended to disguise the servitude which they imposed, the consuls were still elected by the real or apparent suffrage of the senate. From the reign of Diocletian, even these vestiges of liberty were abolished, and the successful candidates who were invested with the annual honors of the consulship, affected to deplore the humiliating condition of their predecessors. The Scipios and the Catos had been reduced to solicit the votes of plebeians, to pass through the tedious and expensive forms of a popular election, and to expose their dignity to the shame of a public refusal; while their own happier fate had reserved them for an age and government in which the rewards of virtue were assigned by the unerring wisdom of a gracious sovereign. [81] In the epistles which the emperor addressed to the two consuls elect, it was declared, that they were created by his sole authority. [82] Their names and portraits, engraved on gilt tables of ivory, were dispersed over the empire as presents to the provinces, the cities, the magistrates, the senate, and the people. [83] Their solemn inauguration was performed at the place of the Imperial residence; and during a period of one hundred and twenty years, Rome was constantly deprived of the presence of her ancient magistrates. [84]

[Footnote 81: Ausonius (in Gratiarum Actione) basely expatiates on this unworthy topic, which is managed by Mamertinus (Panegyr. Vet. xi. [x.] 16, 19) with somewhat more freedom and ingenuity.]

[Footnote 82: Cum de Consulibus in annum creandis, solus mecum volutarem.... te Consulem et designavi, et declaravi, et priorem nuncupavi; are some of the expressions employed by the emperor Gratian to his preceptor, the poet Ausonius.]

[Footnote 83:
Immanesque... dentes
Qui secti ferro in tabulas auroque micantes,
Inscripti rutilum coelato
Consule nomen Per proceres et vulgus eant.
—Claud. in ii. Cons. Stilichon. 456.

Montfaucon has represented some of these tablets or dypticks see Supplement a l'Antiquite expliquee, tom. iii. p. 220.]

[Footnote 84:
Consule laetatur post plurima seculo viso
Pallanteus apex: agnoscunt rostra curules
Auditas quondam proavis:
desuetaque cingit Regius auratis
Fora fascibus Ulpia lictor.
—Claud. in vi. Cons. Honorii, 643.

From the reign of Carus to the sixth consulship of Honorius, there was an interval of one hundred and twenty years, during which the emperors were always absent from Rome on the first day of January. See the Chronologie de Tillemonte, tom. iii. iv. and v.]

On the morning of the first of January, the consuls assumed the ensigns of their dignity. Their dress was a robe of purple, embroidered in silk and gold, and sometimes ornamented with costly gems. [85] On this solemn occasion they were attended by the most eminent officers of the state and army, in the habit of senators; and the useless fasces, armed with the once formidable axes, were borne before them by the lictors. [86] The procession moved from the palace [87] to the Forum or principal square of the city; where the consuls ascended their tribunal, and seated themselves in the curule chairs, which were framed after the fashion of ancient times. They immediately exercised an act of jurisdiction, by the manumission of a slave, who was brought before them for that purpose; and the ceremony was intended to represent the celebrated action of the elder Brutus, the author of liberty and of the consulship, when he admitted among his fellow-citizens the faithful Vindex, who had revealed the conspiracy of the Tarquins. [88] The public festival was continued during several days in all the principal cities in Rome, from custom; in Constantinople, from imitation in Carthage, Antioch, and Alexandria, from the love of pleasure, and the superfluity of wealth. [89] In the two capitals of the empire the annual games of the theatre, the circus, and the amphitheatre, [90] cost four thousand pounds of gold, (about) one hundred and sixty thousand pounds sterling: and if so heavy an expense surpassed the faculties or the inclinations of the magistrates themselves, the sum was supplied from the Imperial treasury. [91] As soon as the consuls had discharged these customary duties, they were at liberty to retire into the shade of private life, and to enjoy, during the remainder of the year, the undisturbed contemplation of their own greatness. They no longer presided in the national councils; they no longer executed the resolutions of peace or war. Their abilities (unless they were employed in more effective offices) were of little moment; and their names served only as the legal date of the year in which they had filled the chair of Marius and of Cicero. Yet it was still felt and acknowledged, in the last period of Roman servitude, that this empty name might be compared, and even preferred, to the possession of substantial power. The title of consul was still the most splendid object of ambition, the noblest reward of virtue and loyalty. The emperors themselves, who disdained the faint shadow of the republic, were conscious that they acquired an additional splendor and majesty as often as they assumed the annual honors of the consular dignity. [92]

[Footnote 85: See Claudian in Cons. Prob. et Olybrii, 178, &c.; and in iv. Cons. Honorii, 585, &c.; though in the latter it is not easy to separate the ornaments of the emperor from those of the consul. Ausonius received from the liberality of Gratian a vestis palmata, or robe of state, in which the figure of the emperor Constantius was embroidered.

Cernis et armorum proceres legumque potentes:
Patricios sumunt habitus; et more Gabino
Discolor incedit legio, positisque parumper
Bellorum signis, sequitur vexilla Quirini. Lictori cedunt aquilae, ridetque
togatus Miles, et in mediis effulget curia castris.
—Claud. in iv. Cons. Honorii, 5.
—strictaque procul radiare secures.
—In Cons. Prob. 229]

[Footnote 87: See Valesius ad Ammian. Marcellin. l. xxii. c. 7.]

[Footnote 88:

Auspice mox laeto sonuit clamore tribunal;
Te fastos ineunte quater; solemnia ludit
Omina libertas; deductum Vindice morem
Lex servat, famulusque jugo laxatus herili
Ducitur, et grato remeat securior ictu.
—Claud. in iv Cons. Honorii, 611]

[Footnote 89: Celebrant quidem solemnes istos dies omnes ubique urbes quae sub legibus agunt; et Roma de more, et Constantinopolis de imitatione, et Antiochia pro luxu, et discincta Carthago, et domus fluminis Alexandria, sed Treviri Principis beneficio. Ausonius in Grat. Actione.]

[Footnote 90: Claudian (in Cons. Mall. Theodori, 279-331) describes, in a lively and fanciful manner, the various games of the circus, the theatre, and the amphitheatre, exhibited by the new consul. The sanguinary combats of gladiators had already been prohibited.]

[Footnote 91: Procopius in Hist. Arcana, c. 26.]

[Footnote 92: In Consulatu honos sine labore suscipitur. (Mamertin. in Panegyr. Vet. xi. [x.] 2.) This exalted idea of the consulship is borrowed from an oration (iii. p. 107) pronounced by Julian in the servile court of Constantius. See the Abbe de la Bleterie, (Memoires de l'Academie, tom. xxiv. p. 289,) who delights to pursue the vestiges of the old constitution, and who sometimes finds them in his copious fancy]

The proudest and most perfect separation which can be found in any age or country, between the nobles and the people, is perhaps that of the Patricians and the Plebeians, as it was established in the first age of the Roman republic. Wealth and honors, the offices of the state, and the ceremonies of religion, were almost exclusively possessed by the former who, preserving the purity of their blood with the most insulting jealousy, [93] held their clients in a condition of specious vassalage. But these distinctions, so incompatible with the spirit of a free people, were removed, after a long struggle, by the persevering efforts of the Tribunes. The most active and successful of the Plebeians accumulated wealth, aspired to honors, deserved triumphs, contracted alliances, and, after some generations, assumed the pride of ancient nobility. [94] The Patrician families, on the other hand, whose original number was never recruited till the end of the commonwealth, either failed in the ordinary course of nature, or were extinguished in so many foreign and domestic wars, or, through a want of merit or fortune, insensibly mingled with the mass of the people. [95] Very few remained who could derive their pure and genuine origin from the infancy of the city, or even from that of the republic, when Caesar and Augustus, Claudius and Vespasian, created from the body of the senate a competent number of new Patrician families, in the hope of perpetuating an order, which was still considered as honorable and sacred. [96] But these artificial supplies (in which the reigning house was always included) were rapidly swept away by the rage of tyrants, by frequent revolutions, by the change of manners, and by the intermixture of nations. [97] Little more was left when Constantine ascended the throne, than a vague and imperfect tradition, that the Patricians had once been the first of the Romans. To form a body of nobles, whose influence may restrain, while it secures the authority of the monarch, would have been very inconsistent with the character and policy of Constantine; but had he seriously entertained such a design, it might have exceeded the measure of his power to ratify, by an arbitrary edict, an institution which must expect the sanction of time and of opinion. He revived, indeed, the title of Patricians, but he revived it as a personal, not as an hereditary distinction. They yielded only to the transient superiority of the annual consuls; but they enjoyed the pre-eminence over all the great officers of state, with the most familiar access to the person of the prince. This honorable rank was bestowed on them for life; and as they were usually favorites, and ministers who had grown old in the Imperial court, the true etymology of the word was perverted by ignorance and flattery; and the Patricians of Constantine were reverenced as the adopted Fathers of the emperor and the republic. [98]

[Footnote 93: Intermarriages between the Patricians and Plebeians were prohibited by the laws of the XII Tables; and the uniform operations of human nature may attest that the custom survived the law. See in Livy (iv. 1-6) the pride of family urged by the consul, and the rights of mankind asserted by the tribune Canuleius.]

[Footnote 94: See the animated picture drawn by Sallust, in the Jugurthine war, of the pride of the nobles, and even of the virtuous Metellus, who was unable to brook the idea that the honor of the consulship should be bestowed on the obscure merit of his lieutenant Marius. (c. 64.) Two hundred years before, the race of the Metelli themselves were confounded among the Plebeians of Rome; and from the etymology of their name of Coecilius, there is reason to believe that those haughty nobles derived their origin from a sutler.]

[Footnote 95: In the year of Rome 800, very few remained, not only of the old Patrician families, but even of those which had been created by Caesar and Augustus. (Tacit. Annal. xi. 25.) The family of Scaurus (a branch of the Patrician Aemilii) was degraded so low that his father, who exercised the trade of a charcoal merchant, left him only teu slaves, and somewhat less than three hundred pounds sterling. (Valerius Maximus, l. iv. c. 4, n. 11. Aurel. Victor in Scauro.) The family was saved from oblivion by the merit of the son.]

[Footnote 96: Tacit. Annal. xi. 25. Dion Cassius, l. iii. p. 698. The virtues of Agricola, who was created a Patrician by the emperor Vespasian, reflected honor on that ancient order; but his ancestors had not any claim beyond an Equestrian nobility.]

[Footnote 97: This failure would have been almost impossible if it were true, as Casaubon compels Aurelius Victor to affirm (ad Sueton, in Caesar v. 24. See Hist. August p. 203 and Casaubon Comment., p. 220) that Vespasian created at once a thousand Patrician families. But this extravagant number is too much even for the whole Senatorial order. unless we should include all the Roman knights who were distinguished by the permission of wearing the laticlave.]

[Footnote 98: Zosimus, l. ii. p. 118; and Godefroy ad Cod. Theodos. l. vi. tit. vi.]

II. The fortunes of the Praetorian praefects were essentially different from those of the consuls and Patricians. The latter saw their ancient greatness evaporate in a vain title.

The former, rising by degrees from the most humble condition, were invested with the civil and military administration of the Roman world. From the reign of Severus to that of Diocletian, the guards and the palace, the laws and the finances, the armies and the provinces, were intrusted to their superintending care; and, like the Viziers of the East, they held with one hand the seal, and with the other the standard, of the empire. The ambition of the praefects, always formidable, and sometimes fatal to the masters whom they served, was supported by the strength of the Praetorian bands; but after those haughty troops had been weakened by Diocletian, and finally suppressed by Constantine, the praefects, who survived their fall, were reduced without difficulty to the station of useful and obedient ministers. When they were no longer responsible for the safety of the emperor's person, they resigned the jurisdiction which they had hitherto claimed and exercised over all the departments of the palace. They were deprived by Constantine of all military command, as soon as they had ceased to lead into the field, under their immediate orders, the flower of the Roman troops; and at length, by a singular revolution, the captains of the guards were transformed into the civil magistrates of the provinces. According to the plan of government instituted by Diocletian, the four princes had each their Praetorian praefect; and after the monarchy was once more united in the person of Constantine, he still continued to create the same number of Four Praefects, and intrusted to their care the same provinces which they already administered. 1. The praefect of the East stretched his ample jurisdiction into the three parts of the globe which were subject to the Romans, from the cataracts of the Nile to the banks of the Phasis, and from the mountains of Thrace to the frontiers of Persia. 2. The important provinces of Pannonia, Dacia, Macedonia, and Greece, once acknowledged the authority of the praefect of Illyricum. 3. The power of the praefect of Italy was not confined to the country from whence he derived his title; it extended over the additional territory of Rhaetia as far as the banks of the Danube, over the dependent islands of the Mediterranean, and over that part of the continent of Africa which lies between the confines of Cyrene and those of Tingitania. 4. The praefect of the Gauls comprehended under that plural denomination the kindred provinces of Britain and Spain, and his authority was obeyed from the wall of Antoninus to the foot of Mount Atlas. [99]

[Footnote 99: Zosimus, l. ii. p. 109, 110. If we had not fortunately possessed this satisfactory account of the division of the power and provinces of the Praetorian praefects, we should frequently have been perplexed amidst the copious details of the Code, and the circumstantial minuteness of the Notitia.]

After the Praetorian praefects had been dismissed from all military command, the civil functions which they were ordained to exercise over so many subject nations, were adequate to the ambition and abilities of the most consummate ministers. To their wisdom was committed the supreme administration of justice and of the finances, the two objects which, in a state of peace, comprehend almost all the respective duties of the sovereign and of the people; of the former, to protect the citizens who are obedient to the laws; of the latter, to contribute the share of their property which is required for the expenses of the state. The coin, the highways, the posts, the granaries, the manufactures, whatever could interest the public prosperity, was moderated by the authority of the Praetorian praefects. As the immediate representatives of the Imperial majesty, they were empowered to explain, to enforce, and on some occasions to modify, the general edicts by their discretionary proclamations. They watched over the conduct of the provincial governors, removed the negligent, and inflicted punishments on the guilty. From all the inferior jurisdictions, an appeal in every matter of importance, either civil or criminal, might be brought before the tribunal of the praefect; but his sentence was final and absolute; and the emperors themselves refused to admit any complaints against the judgment or the integrity of a magistrate whom they honored with such unbounded confidence. [100] His appointments were suitable to his dignity; [101] and if avarice was his ruling passion, he enjoyed frequent opportunities of collecting a rich harvest of fees, of presents, and of perquisites. Though the emperors no longer dreaded the ambition of their praefects, they were attentive to counterbalance the power of this great office by the uncertainty and shortness of its duration. [102]

[Footnote 100: See a law of Constantine himself. A praefectis autem praetorio provocare, non sinimus. Cod. Justinian. l. vii. tit. lxii. leg. 19. Charisius, a lawyer of the time of Constantine, (Heinec. Hist. Romani, p. 349,) who admits this law as a fundamental principle of jurisprudence, compares the Praetorian praefects to the masters of the horse of the ancient dictators. Pandect. l. i. tit. xi.]

[Footnote 101: When Justinian, in the exhausted condition of the empire, instituted a Praetorian praefect for Africa, he allowed him a salary of one hundred pounds of gold. Cod. Justinian. l. i. tit. xxvii. leg. i.]

[Footnote 102: For this, and the other dignities of the empire, it may be sufficient to refer to the ample commentaries of Pancirolus and Godefroy, who have diligently collected and accurately digested in their proper order all the legal and historical materials. From those authors, Dr. Howell (History of the World, vol. ii. p. 24-77) has deduced a very distinct abridgment of the state of the Roman empire]

From their superior importance and dignity, Rome and Constantinople were alone excepted from the jurisdiction of the Praetorian praefects. The immense size of the city, and the experience of the tardy, ineffectual operation of the laws, had furnished the policy of Augustus with a specious pretence for introducing a new magistrate, who alone could restrain a servile and turbulent populace by the strong arm of arbitrary power. [103] Valerius Messalla was appointed the first praefect of Rome, that his reputation might countenance so invidious a measure; but, at the end of a few days, that accomplished citizen [104] resigned his office, declaring, with a spirit worthy of the friend of Brutus, that he found himself incapable of exercising a power incompatible with public freedom. [105] As the sense of liberty became less exquisite, the advantages of order were more clearly understood; and the praefect, who seemed to have been designed as a terror only to slaves and vagrants, was permitted to extend his civil and criminal jurisdiction over the equestrian and noble families of Rome. The praetors, annually created as the judges of law and equity, could not long dispute the possession of the Forum with a vigorous and permanent magistrate, who was usually admitted into the confidence of the prince. Their courts were deserted, their number, which had once fluctuated between twelve and eighteen, [106] was gradually reduced to two or three, and their important functions were confined to the expensive obligation [107] of exhibiting games for the amusement of the people. After the office of the Roman consuls had been changed into a vain pageant, which was rarely displayed in the capital, the praefects assumed their vacant place in the senate, and were soon acknowledged as the ordinary presidents of that venerable assembly. They received appeals from the distance of one hundred miles; and it was allowed as a principle of jurisprudence, that all municipal authority was derived from them alone. [108] In the discharge of his laborious employment, the governor of Rome was assisted by fifteen officers, some of whom had been originally his equals, or even his superiors. The principal departments were relative to the command of a numerous watch, established as a safeguard against fires, robberies, and nocturnal disorders; the custody and distribution of the public allowance of corn and provisions; the care of the port, of the aqueducts, of the common sewers, and of the navigation and bed of the Tyber; the inspection of the markets, the theatres, and of the private as well as the public works. Their vigilance insured the three principal objects of a regular police, safety, plenty, and cleanliness; and as a proof of the attention of government to preserve the splendor and ornaments of the capital, a particular inspector was appointed for the statues; the guardian, as it were, of that inanimate people, which, according to the extravagant computation of an old writer, was scarcely inferior in number to the living inhabitants of Rome. About thirty years after the foundation of Constantinople, a similar magistrate was created in that rising metropolis, for the same uses and with the same powers. A perfect equality was established between the dignity of the two municipal, and that of the four Praetorian praefects. [109]

[Footnote 103: Tacit. Annal. vi. 11. Euseb. in Chron. p. 155. Dion Cassius, in the oration of Maecenas, (l. lvii. p. 675,) describes the prerogatives of the praefect of the city as they were established in his own time.]

[Footnote 104: The fame of Messalla has been scarcely equal to his merit. In the earliest youth he was recommended by Cicero to the friendship of Brutus. He followed the standard of the republic till it was broken in the fields of Philippi; he then accepted and deserved the favor of the most moderate of the conquerors; and uniformly asserted his freedom and dignity in the court of Augustus. The triumph of Messalla was justified by the conquest of Aquitain. As an orator, he disputed the palm of eloquence with Cicero himself. Messalla cultivated every muse, and was the patron of every man of genius. He spent his evenings in philosophic conversation with Horace; assumed his place at table between Delia and Tibullus; and amused his leisure by encouraging the poetical talents of young Ovid.]

[Footnote 105: Incivilem esse potestatem contestans, says the translator of Eusebius. Tacitus expresses the same idea in other words; quasi nescius exercendi.]

[Footnote 106: See Lipsius, Excursus D. ad 1 lib. Tacit. Annal.]

[Footnote 107: Heineccii. Element. Juris Civilis secund ordinem Pandect i. p. 70. See, likewise, Spanheim de Usu. Numismatum, tom. ii. dissertat. x. p. 119. In the year 450, Marcian published a law, that three citizens should be annually created Praetors of Constantinople by the choice of the senate, but with their own consent. Cod. Justinian. li. i. tit. xxxix. leg. 2.]

[Footnote 108: Quidquid igitur intra urbem admittitur, ad P. U. videtur pertinere; sed et siquid intra contesimum milliarium. Ulpian in Pandect l. i. tit. xiii. n. 1. He proceeds to enumerate the various offices of the praefect, who, in the code of Justinian, (l. i. tit. xxxix. leg. 3,) is declared to precede and command all city magistrates sine injuria ac detrimento honoris alieni.]

[Footnote 109: Besides our usual guides, we may observe that Felix Cantelorius has written a separate treatise, De Praefecto Urbis; and that many curious details concerning the police of Rome and Constantinople are contained in the fourteenth book of the Theodosian Code.]

PART IV

Those who, in the imperial hierarchy, were distinguished by the title of Respectable, formed an intermediate class between the illustrious praefects, and the honorable magistrates of the provinces. In this class the proconsuls of Asia, Achaia, and Africa, claimed a preeminence, which was yielded to the remembrance of their ancient dignity; and the appeal from their tribunal to that of the praefects was almost the only mark of their dependence. [110] But the civil government of the empire was distributed into thirteen great Dioceses, each of which equalled the just measure of a powerful kingdom. The first of these dioceses was subject to the jurisdiction of the count of the east; and we may convey some idea of the importance and variety of his functions, by observing, that six hundred apparitors, who would be styled at present either secretaries, or clerks, or ushers, or messengers, were employed in his immediate office. [111] The place of Augustal proefect of Egypt was no longer filled by a Roman knight; but the name was retained; and the extraordinary powers which the situation of the country, and the temper of the inhabitants, had once made indispensable, were still continued to the governor. The eleven remaining dioceses, of Asiana, Pontica, and Thrace; of Macedonia, Dacia, and Pannonia, or Western Illyricum; of Italy and Africa; of Gaul, Spain, and Britain; were governed by twelve vicars or vice-proefects, [112] whose name sufficiently explains the nature and dependence of their office. It may be added, that the lieutenant-generals of the Roman armies, the military counts and dukes, who will be hereafter mentioned, were allowed the rank and title of Respectable.

[Footnote 110: Eunapius affirms, that the proconsul of Asia was independent of the praefect; which must, however, be understood with some allowance. the jurisdiction of the vice-praefect he most assuredly disclaimed. Pancirolus, p. 161.]

[Footnote 111: The proconsul of Africa had four hundred apparitors; and they all received large salaries, either from the treasury or the province See Pancirol. p. 26, and Cod. Justinian. l. xii. tit. lvi. lvii.]

[Footnote 112: In Italy there was likewise the Vicar of Rome. It has been much disputed whether his jurisdiction measured one hundred miles from the city, or whether it stretched over the ten thousand provinces of Italy.]

As the spirit of jealousy and ostentation prevailed in the councils of the emperors, they proceeded with anxious diligence to divide the substance and to multiply the titles of power. The vast countries which the Roman conquerors had united under the same simple form of administration, were imperceptibly crumbled into minute fragments; till at length the whole empire was distributed into one hundred and sixteen provinces, each of which supported an expensive and splendid establishment. Of these, three were governed by proconsuls, thirty-seven by consulars, five by correctors, and seventy-one by presidents. The appellations of these magistrates were different; they ranked in successive order, the ensigns of and their situation, from accidental circumstances, might be more or less agreeable or advantageous. But they were all (excepting only the pro-consuls) alike included in the class of honorable persons; and they were alike intrusted, during the pleasure of the prince, and under the authority of the praefects or their deputies, with the administration of justice and the finances in their respective districts. The ponderous volumes of the Codes and Pandects [113] would furnish ample materials for a minute inquiry into the system of provincial government, as in the space of six centuries it was approved by the wisdom of the Roman statesmen and lawyers.

It may be sufficient for the historian to select two singular and salutary provisions, intended to restrain the abuse of authority.

1. For the preservation of peace and order, the governors of the provinces were armed with the sword of justice. They inflicted corporal punishments, and they exercised, in capital offences, the power of life and death. But they were not authorized to indulge the condemned criminal with the choice of his own execution, or to pronounce a sentence of the mildest and most honorable kind of exile. These prerogatives were reserved to the praefects, who alone could impose the heavy fine of fifty pounds of gold: their vicegerents were confined to the trifling weight of a few ounces. [114] This distinction, which seems to grant the larger, while it denies the smaller degree of authority, was founded on a very rational motive. The smaller degree was infinitely more liable to abuse. The passions of a provincial magistrate might frequently provoke him into acts of oppression, which affected only the freedom or the fortunes of the subject; though, from a principle of prudence, perhaps of humanity, he might still be terrified by the guilt of innocent blood. It may likewise be considered, that exile, considerable fines, or the choice of an easy death, relate more particularly to the rich and the noble; and the persons the most exposed to the avarice or resentment of a provincial magistrate, were thus removed from his obscure persecution to the more august and impartial tribunal of the Praetorian praefect. 2. As it was reasonably apprehended that the integrity of the judge might be biased, if his interest was concerned, or his affections were engaged, the strictest regulations were established, to exclude any person, without the special dispensation of the emperor, from the government of the province where he was born; [115] and to prohibit the governor or his son from contracting marriage with a native, or an inhabitant; [116] or from purchasing slaves, lands, or houses, within the extent of his jurisdiction. [117] Notwithstanding these rigorous precautions, the emperor Constantine, after a reign of twenty-five years, still deplores the venal and oppressive administration of justice, and expresses the warmest indignation that the audience of the judge, his despatch of business, his seasonable delays, and his final sentence, were publicly sold, either by himself or by the officers of his court. The continuance, and perhaps the impunity, of these crimes, is attested by the repetition of impotent laws and ineffectual menaces. [118]

[Footnote 113: Among the works of the celebrated Ulpian, there was one in ten books, concerning the office of a proconsul, whose duties in the most essential articles were the same as those of an ordinary governor of a province.]

[Footnote 114: The presidents, or consulars, could impose only two ounces; the vice-praefects, three; the proconsuls, count of the east, and praefect of Egypt, six. See Heineccii Jur. Civil. tom. i. p. 75. Pandect. l. xlviii. tit. xix. n. 8. Cod. Justinian. l. i. tit. liv. leg. 4, 6.]

[Footnote 115: Ut nulli patriae suae administratio sine speciali principis permissu permittatur. Cod. Justinian. l. i. tit. xli. This law was first enacted by the emperor Marcus, after the rebellion of Cassius. (Dion. l. lxxi.) The same regulation is observed in China, with equal strictness, and with equal effect.]

[Footnote 116: Pandect. l. xxiii. tit. ii. n. 38, 57, 63.]

[Footnote 117: In jure continetur, ne quis in administratione constitutus aliquid compararet. Cod. Theod. l. viii. tit. xv. leg. l. This maxim of common law was enforced by a series of edicts (see the remainder of the title) from Constantine to Justin. From this prohibition, which is extended to the meanest officers of the governor, they except only clothes and provisions. The purchase within five years may be recovered; after which on information, it devolves to the treasury.]

[Footnote 118: Cessent rapaces jam nunc officialium manus; cessent, inquam nam si moniti non cessaverint, gladiis praecidentur, &c. Cod. Theod. l. i. tit. vii. leg. l. Zeno enacted that all governors should remain in the province, to answer any accusations, fifty days after the expiration of their power. Cod Justinian. l. ii. tit. xlix. leg. l.]

All the civil magistrates were drawn from the profession of the law. The celebrated Institutes of Justinian are addressed to the youth of his dominions, who had devoted themselves to the study of Roman jurisprudence; and the sovereign condescends to animate their diligence, by the assurance that their skill and ability would in time be rewarded by an adequate share in the government of the republic. [119] The rudiments of this lucrative science were taught in all the considerable cities of the east and west; but the most famous school was that of Berytus, [120] on the coast of Phoenicia; which flourished above three centuries from the time of Alexander Severus, the author perhaps of an institution so advantageous to his native country. After a regular course of education, which lasted five years, the students dispersed themselves through the provinces, in search of fortune and honors; nor could they want an inexhaustible supply of business in a great empire already corrupted by the multiplicity of laws, of arts, and of vices. The court of the Praetorian praefect of the east could alone furnish employment for one hundred and fifty advocates, sixty-four of whom were distinguished by peculiar privileges, and two were annually chosen, with a salary of sixty pounds of gold, to defend the causes of the treasury. The first experiment was made of their judicial talents, by appointing them to act occasionally as assessors to the magistrates; from thence they were often raised to preside in the tribunals before which they had pleaded. They obtained the government of a province; and, by the aid of merit, of reputation, or of favor, they ascended, by successive steps, to the illustrious dignities of the state. [121] In the practice of the bar, these men had considered reason as the instrument of dispute; they interpreted the laws according to the dictates of private interest and the same pernicious habits might still adhere to their characters in the public administration of the state. The honor of a liberal profession has indeed been vindicated by ancient and modern advocates, who have filled the most important stations, with pure integrity and consummate wisdom: but in the decline of Roman jurisprudence, the ordinary promotion of lawyers was pregnant with mischief and disgrace. The noble art, which had once been preserved as the sacred inheritance of the patricians, was fallen into the hands of freedmen and plebeians, [122] who, with cunning rather than with skill, exercised a sordid and pernicious trade. Some of them procured admittance into families for the purpose of fomenting differences, of encouraging suits, and of preparing a harvest of gain for themselves or their brethren. Others, recluse in their chambers, maintained the dignity of legal professors, by furnishing a rich client with subtleties to confound the plainest truths, and with arguments to color the most unjustifiable pretensions. The splendid and popular class was composed of the advocates, who filled the Forum with the sound of their turgid and loquacious rhetoric. Careless of fame and of justice, they are described, for the most part, as ignorant and rapacious guides, who conducted their clients through a maze of expense, of delay, and of disappointment; from whence, after a tedious series of years, they were at length dismissed, when their patience and fortune were almost exhausted. [123]

[Footnote 119: Summa igitur ope, et alacri studio has leges nostras accipite; et vosmetipsos sic eruditos ostendite, ut spes vos pulcherrima foveat; toto legitimo opere perfecto, posse etiam nostram rempublicam in par tibus ejus vobis credendis gubernari. Justinian in proem. Institutionum.]

[Footnote 120: The splendor of the school of Berytus, which preserved in the east the language and jurisprudence of the Romans, may be computed to have lasted from the third to the middle of the sixth century Heinecc. Jur. Rom. Hist. p. 351-356.]

[Footnote 121: As in a former period I have traced the civil and military promotion of Pertinax, I shall here insert the civil honors of Mallius Theodorus. 1. He was distinguished by his eloquence, while he pleaded as an advocate in the court of the Praetorian praefect. 2. He governed one of the provinces of Africa, either as president or consular, and deserved, by his administration, the honor of a brass statue. 3. He was appointed vicar, or vice-praefect, of Macedonia. 4. Quaestor. 5. Count of the sacred largesses. 6. Praetorian praefect of the Gauls; whilst he might yet be represented as a young man. 7. After a retreat, perhaps a disgrace of many years, which Mallius (confounded by some critics with the poet Manilius; see Fabricius Bibliothec. Latin. Edit. Ernest. tom. i.c. 18, p. 501) employed in the study of the Grecian philosophy he was named Praetorian praefect of Italy, in the year 397. 8. While he still exercised that great office, he was created, it the year 399, consul for the West; and his name, on account of the infamy of his colleague, the eunuch Eutropius, often stands alone in the Fasti. 9. In the year 408, Mallius was appointed a second time Praetorian praefect of Italy. Even in the venal panegyric of Claudian, we may discover the merit of Mallius Theodorus, who, by a rare felicity, was the intimate friend, both of Symmachus and of St. Augustin. See Tillemont, Hist. des Emp. tom. v. p. 1110-1114.]

[Footnote 122: Mamertinus in Panegyr. Vet. xi. [x.] 20. Asterius apud Photium, p. 1500.]

[Footnote 123: The curious passage of Ammianus, (l. xxx. c. 4,) in which he paints the manners of contemporary lawyers, affords a strange mixture of sound sense, false rhetoric, and extravagant satire. Godefroy (Prolegom. ad. Cod. Theod. c. i. p. 185) supports the historian by similar complaints and authentic facts. In the fourth century, many camels might have been laden with law-books. Eunapius in Vit. Aedesii, p. 72.]

III. In the system of policy introduced by Augustus, the governors, those at least of the Imperial provinces, were invested with the full powers of the sovereign himself. Ministers of peace and war, the distribution of rewards and punishments depended on them alone, and they successively appeared on their tribunal in the robes of civil magistracy, and in complete armor at the head of the Roman legions. [124] The influence of the revenue, the authority of law, and the command of a military force, concurred to render their power supreme and absolute; and whenever they were tempted to violate their allegiance, the loyal province which they involved in their rebellion was scarcely sensible of any change in its political state. From the time of Commodus to the reign of Constantine, near one hundred governors might be enumerated, who, with various success, erected the standard of revolt; and though the innocent were too often sacrificed, the guilty might be sometimes prevented, by the suspicious cruelty of their master. [125] To secure his throne and the public tranquillity from these formidable servants, Constantine resolved to divide the military from the civil administration, and to establish, as a permanent and professional distinction, a practice which had been adopted only as an occasional expedient. The supreme jurisdiction exercised by the Praetorian praefects over the armies of the empire, was transferred to the two masters-general whom he instituted, the one for the cavalry, the other for the infantry; and though each of these illustrious officers was more peculiarly responsible for the discipline of those troops which were under his immediate inspection, they both indifferently commanded in the field the several bodies, whether of horse or foot, which were united in the same army. [126] Their number was soon doubled by the division of the east and west; and as separate generals of the same rank and title were appointed on the four important frontiers of the Rhine, of the Upper and the Lower Danube, and of the Euphrates, the defence of the Roman empire was at length committed to eight masters-general of the cavalry and infantry. Under their orders, thirty-five military commanders were stationed in the provinces: three in Britain, six in Gaul, one in Spain, one in Italy, five on the Upper, and four on the Lower Danube; in Asia, eight, three in Egypt, and four in Africa. The titles of counts, and dukes, [127] by which they were properly distinguished, have obtained in modern languages so very different a sense, that the use of them may occasion some surprise. But it should be recollected, that the second of those appellations is only a corruption of the Latin word, which was indiscriminately applied to any military chief. All these provincial generals were therefore dukes; but no more than ten among them were dignified with the rank of counts or companions, a title of honor, or rather of favor, which had been recently invented in the court of Constantine. A gold belt was the ensign which distinguished the office of the counts and dukes; and besides their pay, they received a liberal allowance sufficient to maintain one hundred and ninety servants, and one hundred and fifty-eight horses. They were strictly prohibited from interfering in any matter which related to the administration of justice or the revenue; but the command which they exercised over the troops of their department, was independent of the authority of the magistrates. About the same time that Constantine gave a legal sanction to the ecclesiastical order, he instituted in the Roman empire the nice balance of the civil and the military powers. The emulation, and sometimes the discord, which reigned between two professions of opposite interests and incompatible manners, was productive of beneficial and of pernicious consequences. It was seldom to be expected that the general and the civil governor of a province should either conspire for the disturbance, or should unite for the service, of their country. While the one delayed to offer the assistance which the other disdained to solicit, the troops very frequently remained without orders or without supplies; the public safety was betrayed, and the defenceless subjects were left exposed to the fury of the Barbarians. The divided administration which had been formed by Constantine, relaxed the vigor of the state, while it secured the tranquillity of the monarch.

[Footnote 124: See a very splendid example in the life of Agricola, particularly c. 20, 21. The lieutenant of Britain was intrusted with the same powers which Cicero, proconsul of Cilicia, had exercised in the name of the senate and people.]

[Footnote 125: The Abbe Dubos, who has examined with accuracy (see Hist. de la Monarchie Francoise, tom. i. p. 41-100, edit. 1742) the institutions of Augustus and of Constantine, observes, that if Otho had been put to death the day before he executed his conspiracy, Otho would now appear in history as innocent as Corbulo.]

[Footnote 126: Zosimus, l. ii. p. 110. Before the end of the reign of Constantius, the magistri militum were already increased to four. See Velesius ad Ammian. l. xvi. c. 7.]

[Footnote 127: Though the military counts and dukes are frequently mentioned, both in history and the codes, we must have recourse to the Notitia for the exact knowledge of their number and stations. For the institution, rank, privileges, &c., of the counts in general see Cod. Theod. l. vi. tit. xii—xx., with the commentary of Godefroy.]

The memory of Constantine has been deservedly censured for another innovation, which corrupted military discipline and prepared the ruin of the empire. The nineteen years which preceded his final victory over Licinius, had been a period of license and intestine war. The rivals who contended for the possession of the Roman world, had withdrawn the greatest part of their forces from the guard of the general frontier; and the principal cities which formed the boundary of their respective dominions were filled with soldiers, who considered their countrymen as their most implacable enemies. After the use of these internal garrisons had ceased with the civil war, the conqueror wanted either wisdom or firmness to revive the severe discipline of Diocletian, and to suppress a fatal indulgence, which habit had endeared and almost confirmed to the military order. From the reign of Constantine, a popular and even legal distinction was admitted between the Palatines [128] and the Borderers; the troops of the court, as they were improperly styled, and the troops of the frontier. The former, elevated by the superiority of their pay and privileges, were permitted, except in the extraordinary emergencies of war, to occupy their tranquil stations in the heart of the provinces. The most flourishing cities were oppressed by the intolerable weight of quarters. The soldiers insensibly forgot the virtues of their profession, and contracted only the vices of civil life. They were either degraded by the industry of mechanic trades, or enervated by the luxury of baths and theatres. They soon became careless of their martial exercises, curious in their diet and apparel; and while they inspired terror to the subjects of the empire, they trembled at the hostile approach of the Barbarians. [129] The chain of fortifications which Diocletian and his colleagues had extended along the banks of the great rivers, was no longer maintained with the same care, or defended with the same vigilance. The numbers which still remained under the name of the troops of the frontier, might be sufficient for the ordinary defence; but their spirit was degraded by the humiliating reflection, that they who were exposed to the hardships and dangers of a perpetual warfare, were rewarded only with about two thirds of the pay and emoluments which were lavished on the troops of the court. Even the bands or legions that were raised the nearest to the level of those unworthy favorites, were in some measure disgraced by the title of honor which they were allowed to assume. It was in vain that Constantine repeated the most dreadful menaces of fire and sword against the Borderers who should dare desert their colors, to connive at the inroads of the Barbarians, or to participate in the spoil. [130] The mischiefs which flow from injudicious counsels are seldom removed by the application of partial severities; and though succeeding princes labored to restore the strength and numbers of the frontier garrisons, the empire, till the last moment of its dissolution, continued to languish under the mortal wound which had been so rashly or so weakly inflicted by the hand of Constantine.

[Footnote 128: Zosimus, l ii. p. 111. The distinction between the two classes of Roman troops, is very darkly expressed in the historians, the laws, and the Notitia. Consult, however, the copious paratitlon, or abstract, which Godefroy has drawn up of the seventh book, de Re Militari, of the Theodosian Code, l. vii. tit. i. leg. 18, l. viii. tit. i. leg. 10.]

[Footnote 129: Ferox erat In suos miles et rapax, ignavus vero in hostes et fractus. Ammian. l. xxii. c. 4. He observes, that they loved downy beds and houses of marble; and that their cups were heavier than their swords.]

[Footnote 130: Cod. Theod. l. vii. tit. i. leg. 1, tit. xii. leg. i. See Howell's Hist. of the World, vol. ii. p. 19. That learned historian, who is not sufficiently known, labors to justify the character and policy of Constantine.]

The same timid policy, of dividing whatever is united, of reducing whatever is eminent, of dreading every active power, and of expecting that the most feeble will prove the most obedient, seems to pervade the institutions of several princes, and particularly those of Constantine. The martial pride of the legions, whose victorious camps had so often been the scene of rebellion, was nourished by the memory of their past exploits, and the consciousness of their actual strength. As long as they maintained their ancient establishment of six thousand men, they subsisted, under the reign of Diocletian, each of them singly, a visible and important object in the military history of the Roman empire. A few years afterwards, these gigantic bodies were shrunk to a very diminutive size; and when seven legions, with some auxiliaries, defended the city of Amida against the Persians, the total garrison, with the inhabitants of both sexes, and the peasants of the deserted country, did not exceed the number of twenty thousand persons. [131] From this fact, and from similar examples, there is reason to believe, that the constitution of the legionary troops, to which they partly owed their valor and discipline, was dissolved by Constantine; and that the bands of Roman infantry, which still assumed the same names and the same honors, consisted only of one thousand or fifteen hundred men. [132] The conspiracy of so many separate detachments, each of which was awed by the sense of its own weakness, could easily be checked; and the successors of Constantine might indulge their love of ostentation, by issuing their orders to one hundred and thirty-two legions, inscribed on the muster-roll of their numerous armies. The remainder of their troops was distributed into several hundred cohorts of infantry, and squadrons of cavalry. Their arms, and titles, and ensigns, were calculated to inspire terror, and to display the variety of nations who marched under the Imperial standard. And not a vestige was left of that severe simplicity, which, in the ages of freedom and victory, had distinguished the line of battle of a Roman army from the confused host of an Asiatic monarch. [133] A more particular enumeration, drawn from the Notitia, might exercise the diligence of an antiquary; but the historian will content himself with observing, that the number of permanent stations or garrisons established on the frontiers of the empire, amounted to five hundred and eighty-three; and that, under the successors of Constantine, the complete force of the military establishment was computed at six hundred and forty-five thousand soldiers. [134] An effort so prodigious surpassed the wants of a more ancient, and the faculties of a later, period.

[Footnote 131: Ammian. l. xix. c. 2. He observes, (c. 5,) that the desperate sallies of two Gallic legions were like a handful of water thrown on a great conflagration.]

[Footnote 132: Pancirolus ad Notitiam, p. 96. Memoires de l'Academie des Inscriptions, tom. xxv. p. 491.]

[Footnote 133: Romana acies unius prope formae erat et hominum et armorum genere—Regia acies varia magis multis gentibus dissimilitudine armorum auxiliorumque erat. T. Liv. l. xxxvii. c. 39, 40. Flaminius, even before the event, had compared the army of Antiochus to a supper in which the flesh of one vile animal was diversified by the skill of the cooks. See the Life of Flaminius in Plutarch.]

[Footnote 134: Agathias, l. v. p. 157, edit. Louvre.]

In the various states of society, armies are recruited from very different motives. Barbarians are urged by the love of war; the citizens of a free republic may be prompted by a principle of duty; the subjects, or at least the nobles, of a monarchy, are animated by a sentiment of honor; but the timid and luxurious inhabitants of a declining empire must be allured into the service by the hopes of profit, or compelled by the dread of punishment. The resources of the Roman treasury were exhausted by the increase of pay, by the repetition of donatives, and by the invention of new emolument and indulgences, which, in the opinion of the provincial youth might compensate the hardships and dangers of a military life. Yet, although the stature was lowered, [135] although slaves, least by a tacit connivance, were indiscriminately received into the ranks, the insurmountable difficulty of procuring a regular and adequate supply of volunteers, obliged the emperors to adopt more effectual and coercive methods. The lands bestowed on the veterans, as the free reward of their valor were henceforward granted under a condition which contain the first rudiments of the feudal tenures; that their sons, who succeeded to the inheritance, should devote themselves to the profession of arms, as soon as they attained the age of manhood; and their cowardly refusal was punished by the loss of honor, of fortune, or even of life. [136] But as the annual growth of the sons of the veterans bore a very small proportion to the demands of the service, levies of men were frequently required from the provinces, and every proprietor was obliged either to take up arms, or to procure a substitute, or to purchase his exemption by the payment of a heavy fine. The sum of forty-two pieces of gold, to which it was reduced ascertains the exorbitant price of volunteers, and the reluctance with which the government admitted of this alterative. [137] Such was the horror for the profession of a soldier, which had affected the minds of the degenerate Romans, that many of the youth of Italy and the provinces chose to cut off the fingers of their right hand, to escape from being pressed into the service; and this strange expedient was so commonly practised, as to deserve the severe animadversion of the laws, [138] and a peculiar name in the Latin language. [139]

[Footnote 135: Valentinian (Cod. Theodos. l. vii. tit. xiii. leg. 3) fixes the standard at five feet seven inches, about five feet four inches and a half, English measure. It had formerly been five feet ten inches, and in the best corps, six Roman feet. Sed tunc erat amplior multitude se et plures sequebantur militiam armatam. Vegetius de Re Militari l. i. c. v.]

[Footnote 136: See the two titles, De Veteranis and De Filiis Veteranorum, in the seventh book of the Theodosian Code. The age at which their military service was required, varied from twenty-five to sixteen. If the sons of the veterans appeared with a horse, they had a right to serve in the cavalry; two horses gave them some valuable privileges]

[Footnote 137: Cod. Theod. l. vii. tit. xiii. leg. 7. According to the historian Socrates, (see Godefroy ad loc.,) the same emperor Valens sometimes required eighty pieces of gold for a recruit. In the following law it is faintly expressed, that slaves shall not be admitted inter optimas lectissimorum militum turmas.]

[Footnote 138: The person and property of a Roman knight, who had mutilated his two sons, were sold at public auction by order of Augustus. (Sueton. in August. c. 27.) The moderation of that artful usurper proves, that this example of severity was justified by the spirit of the times. Ammianus makes a distinction between the effeminate Italians and the hardy Gauls. (L. xv. c. 12.) Yet only 15 years afterwards, Valentinian, in a law addressed to the praefect of Gaul, is obliged to enact that these cowardly deserters shall be burnt alive. (Cod. Theod. l. vii. tit. xiii. leg. 5.) Their numbers in Illyricum were so considerable, that the province complained of a scarcity of recruits. (Id. leg. 10.)]

[Footnote 139: They were called Murci. Murcidus is found in Plautus and Festus, to denote a lazy and cowardly person, who, according to Arnobius and Augustin, was under the immediate protection of the goddess Murcia. From this particular instance of cowardice, murcare is used as synonymous to mutilare, by the writers of the middle Latinity. See Linder brogius and Valesius ad Ammian. Marcellin, l. xv. c. 12]

PART V

The introduction of Barbarians into the Roman armies became every day more universal, more necessary, and more fatal. The most daring of the Scythians, of the Goths, and of the Germans, who delighted in war, and who found it more profitable to defend than to ravage the provinces, were enrolled, not only in the auxiliaries of their respective nations, but in the legions themselves, and among the most distinguished of the Palatine troops. As they freely mingled with the subjects of the empire, they gradually learned to despise their manners, and to imitate their arts. They abjured the implicit reverence which the pride of Rome had exacted from their ignorance, while they acquired the knowledge and possession of those advantages by which alone she supported her declining greatness. The Barbarian soldiers, who displayed any military talents, were advanced, without exception, to the most important commands; and the names of the tribunes, of the counts and dukes, and of the generals themselves, betray a foreign origin, which they no longer condescended to disguise. They were often intrusted with the conduct of a war against their countrymen; and though most of them preferred the ties of allegiance to those of blood, they did not always avoid the guilt, or at least the suspicion, of holding a treasonable correspondence with the enemy, of inviting his invasion, or of sparing his retreat. The camps and the palace of the son of Constantine were governed by the powerful faction of the Franks, who preserved the strictest connection with each other, and with their country, and who resented every personal affront as a national indignity. [140] When the tyrant Caligula was suspected of an intention to invest a very extraordinary candidate with the consular robes, the sacrilegious profanation would have scarcely excited less astonishment, if, instead of a horse, the noblest chieftain of Germany or Britain had been the object of his choice. The revolution of three centuries had produced so remarkable a change in the prejudices of the people, that, with the public approbation, Constantine showed his successors the example of bestowing the honors of the consulship on the Barbarians, who, by their merit and services, had deserved to be ranked among the first of the Romans. [141] But as these hardy veterans, who had been educated in the ignorance or contempt of the laws, were incapable of exercising any civil offices, the powers of the human mind were contracted by the irreconcilable separation of talents as well as of professions. The accomplished citizens of the Greek and Roman republics, whose characters could adapt themselves to the bar, the senate, the camp, or the schools, had learned to write, to speak, and to act with the same spirit, and with equal abilities.

[Footnote 140: *Malarichus—adhibitis Francis quorum ea tempestate in palatio multitudo florebat, erectius jam loquebatur tumultuabaturque. Ammian. l. xv. c. 5.*]

[Footnote 141: *Barbaros omnium primus, ad usque fasces auxerat et trabeas consulares. Ammian. l. xx. c. 10. Eusebius (in Vit. Constantin. l. iv c.7) and Aurelius Victor seem to confirm the truth of this assertion yet in the thirty-two consular Fasti of the reign of Constantine cannot discover the name of a single Barbarian. I should therefore interpret the liberality of that prince as relative to the ornaments rather than to the office, of the consulship.*]

IV. Besides the magistrates and generals, who at a distance from the court diffused their delegated authority over the provinces and armies, the emperor conferred the rank of Illustrious on seven of his more immediate servants, to whose fidelity he intrusted his safety, or his counsels, or his treasures. 1. The private apartments of the palace were governed by a favorite eunuch, who, in the language of that age, was styled the proepositus, or praefect of the sacred bed-chamber. His duty was to attend the emperor in his hours of state, or in those of amusement, and to perform about his person all those menial services, which can only derive their splendor from the influence of royalty. Under a prince who deserved to reign, the great chamberlain (for such we may call him) was a useful and humble domestic; but an artful domestic, who improves every occasion of unguarded confidence, will insensibly acquire over a feeble mind that ascendant which harsh wisdom and uncomplying virtue can seldom obtain. The degenerate grandsons of Theodosius, who were invisible to their subjects, and contemptible to their enemies, exalted the praefects of their bed-chamber above the heads of all the ministers of the palace; [142] and even his deputy, the first of the splendid train of slaves who waited in the presence, was thought worthy to rank before the respectable proconsuls of Greece or Asia. The jurisdiction of the chamberlain was acknowledged by the counts, or superintendents, who regulated the two important provinces of the magnificence of the wardrobe, and of the luxury of the Imperial table. [143] 2. The principal administration of public affairs was committed to the diligence and abilities of the master of the offices. [144] He was the supreme magistrate of the palace, inspected the discipline of the civil and military schools, and received appeals from all parts of the empire, in the causes which related to that numerous army of privileged persons, who, as the servants of the court, had obtained for themselves and families a right to decline the authority of the ordinary judges. The correspondence between the prince and his subjects was managed by the four scrinia, or offices of this minister of state. The first was appropriated to memorials, the second to epistles, the third to petitions, and the fourth to papers and orders of a miscellaneous kind. Each of these was directed by an inferior master of respectable dignity, and the whole business was despatched by a hundred and forty-eight secretaries, chosen for the most part from the profession of the law, on account of the variety of abstracts of reports and references which frequently occurred in the exercise of their several functions. From a condescension, which in former ages would have been esteemed unworthy the Roman majesty, a particular secretary was allowed for the Greek language; and interpreters were appointed to receive the ambassadors of the Barbarians; but the department of foreign affairs, which constitutes so essential a part of modern policy, seldom diverted the attention of the master of the offices. His mind was more seriously engaged by the general direction of the posts and arsenals of the empire. There were thirty-four cities, fifteen in the East, and nineteen in the West, in which regular companies of workmen were perpetually employed in fabricating defensive armor, offensive weapons of all sorts, and military engines, which were deposited in the arsenals, and occasionally delivered for the service of the troops. 3. In the course of nine centuries, the office of quaestor had experienced a very singular revolution. In the infancy of Rome, two inferior magistrates were annually elected by the people, to relieve the consuls from the invidious management of the public treasure; [145] a similar assistant was granted to every proconsul, and to every praetor, who exercised a military or provincial command; with the extent of conquest, the two quaestors were gradually multiplied to the number of four, of eight, of twenty, and, for a short time, perhaps, of forty; [146] and the noblest citizens ambitiously solicited an office which gave them a seat in the senate, and a just hope of obtaining the honors of the republic. Whilst Augustus affected to maintain the freedom of election, he consented to accept the annual privilege of recommending, or rather indeed of nominating, a certain proportion of candidates; and it was his custom to select one of these distinguished youths, to read his orations or epistles in the assemblies of the senate. [147] The practice of Augustus was imitated by succeeding princes; the occasional commission was established as a permanent office; and the favored quaestor, assuming a new and more illustrious character, alone survived the suppression of his ancient and useless colleagues. [148] As the orations which he composed in the name of the emperor, [149] acquired the force, and, at length, the form, of absolute edicts, he was considered as the representative of the legislative power, the oracle of the council, and the original source of the civil jurisprudence. He was sometimes invited to take his seat in the supreme judicature of the Imperial consistory, with the Praetorian praefects, and the master of the offices; and he was frequently requested to resolve the doubts of inferior judges: but as he was not oppressed with a variety of subordinate business, his leisure and talents were employed to cultivate that dignified style of eloquence, which, in the corruption of taste and language, still preserves the majesty of the Roman laws. [150] In some respects, the office of the Imperial quaestor may be compared with that of a modern chancellor; but the use of a great seal, which seems to have been adopted by the illiterate barbarians, was never introduced to attest the public acts of the emperors. 4. The extraordinary title of count of the sacred largesses was bestowed on the treasurer-general of the revenue, with the intention perhaps of inculcating, that every payment flowed from the voluntary bounty of the monarch. To conceive the almost infinite detail of the annual and daily expense of the civil and military administration in every part of a great empire, would exceed the powers of the most vigorous imagination.

The actual account employed several hundred persons, distributed into eleven different offices, which were artfully contrived to examine and control their respective operations. The multitude of these agents had a natural tendency to increase; and it was more than once thought expedient to dismiss to their native homes the useless supernumeraries, who, deserting their honest labors, had pressed with too much eagerness into the lucrative profession of the finances. [151] Twenty-nine provincial receivers, of whom eighteen were honored with the title of count, corresponded with the treasurer; and he extended his jurisdiction over the mines from whence the precious metals were extracted, over the mints, in which they were converted into the current coin, and over the public treasuries of the most important cities, where they were deposited for the service of the state. The foreign trade of the empire was regulated by this minister, who directed likewise all the linen and woollen manufactures, in which the successive operations of spinning, weaving, and dyeing were executed, chiefly by women of a servile condition, for the use of the palace and army. Twenty-six of these institutions are enumerated in the West, where the arts had been more recently introduced, and a still larger proportion may be allowed for the industrious provinces of the East. [152] 5. Besides the public revenue, which an absolute monarch might levy and expend according to his pleasure, the emperors, in the capacity of opulent citizens, possessed a very extensive property, which was administered by the count or treasurer of the private estate. Some part had perhaps been the ancient demesnes of kings and republics; some accessions might be derived from the families which were successively invested with the purple; but the most considerable portion flowed from the impure source of confiscations and forfeitures. The Imperial estates were scattered through the provinces, from Mauritania to Britain; but the rich and fertile soil of Cappadocia tempted the monarch to acquire in that country his fairest possessions, [153] and either Constantine or his successors embraced the occasion of justifying avarice by religious zeal. They suppressed the rich temple of Comana, where the high priest of the goddess of war supported the dignity of a sovereign prince; and they applied to their private use the consecrated lands, which were inhabited by six thousand subjects or slaves of the deity and her ministers. [154] But these were not the valuable inhabitants: the plains that stretch from the foot of Mount Argaeus to the banks of the Sarus, bred a generous race of horses, renowned above all others in the ancient world for their majestic shape and incomparable swiftness. These sacred animals, destined for the service of the palace and the Imperial games, were protected by the laws from the profanation of a vulgar master. [155] The demesnes of Cappadocia were important enough to require the inspection of a count; [156] officers of an inferior rank were stationed in the other parts of the empire; and the deputies of the private, as well as those of the public, treasurer were maintained in the exercise of their independent functions, and encouraged to control the authority of the provincial magistrates. [157] 6, 7. The chosen bands of cavalry and infantry, which guarded the person of the emperor, were under the immediate command of the two counts of the domestics. The whole number consisted of three thousand five hundred men, divided into seven schools, or troops, of five hundred each; and in the East, this honorable service was almost entirely appropriated to the Armenians. Whenever, on public ceremonies, they were drawn up in the courts and porticos of the palace, their lofty stature, silent order, and splendid arms of silver and gold, displayed a martial pomp not unworthy of the Roman majesty. [158] From the seven schools two companies of horse and foot were selected, of the protectors, whose advantageous station was the hope and reward of the most deserving soldiers. They mounted guard in the interior apartments, and were occasionally despatched into the provinces, to execute with celerity and vigor the orders of their master. [159] The counts of the domestics had succeeded to the office of the Praetorian praefects; like the praefects, they aspired from the service of the palace to the command of armies.

[Footnote 142: Cod. Theod. l. vi. tit. 8.]

[Footnote 143: By a very singular metaphor, borrowed from the military character of the first emperors, the steward of their household was styled the count of their camp, (comes castrensis.) Cassiodorus very seriously represents to him, that his own fame, and that of the empire, must depend on the opinion which foreign ambassadors may conceive of the plenty and magnificence of the royal table. (Variar. l. vi. epistol. 9.)]

[Footnote 144: Gutherius (de Officiis Domus Augustae, l. ii. c. 20, l. iii.) has very accurately explained the functions of the master of the offices, and the constitution of the subordinate scrinia. But he vainly attempts, on the most doubtful authority, to deduce from the time of the Antonines, or even of Nero, the origin of a magistrate who cannot be found in history before the reign of Constantine.]

[Footnote 145: Tacitus (Annal. xi. 22) says, that the first quaestors were elected by the people, sixty-four years after the foundation of the republic; but he is of opinion, that they had, long before that period, been annually appointed by the consuls, and even by the kings. But this obscure point of antiquity is contested by other writers.]

[Footnote 146: Tacitus (Annal. xi. 22) seems to consider twenty as the highest number of quaestors; and Dion (l. xliii. p 374) insinuates, that if the dictator Caesar once created forty, it was only to facilitate the payment of an immense debt of gratitude. Yet the augmentation which he made of praetors subsisted under the succeeding reigns.]

[Footnote 147: Sueton. in August. c. 65, and Torrent. ad loc. Dion. Cas. p. 755.]

[Footnote 148: The youth and inexperience of the quaestors, who entered on that important office in their twenty-fifth year, (Lips. Excurs. ad Tacit. l. iii. D.,) engaged Augustus to remove them from the management of the treasury; and though they were restored by Claudius, they seem to have been finally dismissed by Nero. (Tacit Annal. xiii. 29. Sueton. in Aug. c. 36, in Claud. c. 24. Dion, p. 696, 961, &c. Plin. Epistol. x. 20, et alibi.) In the provinces of the Imperial division, the place of the quaestors was more ably supplied by the procurators, (Dion Cas. p. 707. Tacit. in Vit. Agricol. c. 15;) or, as they were afterwards called, rationales. (Hist. August. p. 130.) But in the provinces of the senate we may still discover a series of quaestors till the reign of Marcus Antoninus. (See the Inscriptions of Gruter, the Epistles of Pliny, and a decisive fact in the Augustan History, p. 64.) From Ulpian we may learn, (Pandect. l. i. tit. 13,) that under the government of the house of Severus, their provincial administration was abolished; and in the subsequent troubles, the annual or triennial elections of quaestors must have naturally ceased.]

[Footnote 149: Cum patris nomine et epistolas ipse dictaret, et edicta conscrib eret, orationesque in senatu recitaret, etiam quaestoris vice. Sueton, in Tit. c. 6. The office must have acquired new dignity, which was occasionally executed by the heir apparent of the empire. Trajan intrusted the same care to Hadrian, his quaestor and cousin. See Dodwell, Praelection. Cambden, x. xi. p. 362-394.]

[Footnote 150: Terris edicta daturus; Supplicibus responsa—Oracula regis Eloquio crevere tuo; nec dignius unquam Majestas meminit sese Romana locutam—Claudian in Consulat. Mall. Theodor. 33. See likewise Symmachus (Epistol. i. 17) and Cassiodorus. (Variar. iv. 5.)]

[Footnote 151: Cod. Theod. l. vi. tit. 30. Cod. Justinian. l. xii. tit. 24.]

[Footnote 152: In the departments of the two counts of the treasury, the eastern part of the Notitia happens to be very defective. It may be observed, that we had a treasury chest in London, and a gyneceum or manufacture at Winchester. But Britain was not thought worthy either of a mint or of an arsenal. Gaul alone possessed three of the former, and eight of the latter.]

[Footnote 153: Cod. Theod. l. vi. tit. xxx. leg. 2, and Godefroy ad loc.]

[Footnote 154: Strabon. Geograph. l. xxii. p. 809, [edit. Casaub.] The other temple of Comana, in Pontus, was a colony from that of Cappadocia, l. xii. p. 835. The President Des Brosses (see his Saluste, tom. ii. p. 21, [edit. Causub.]) conjectures that the deity adored in both Comanas was Beltis, the Venus of the east, the goddess of generation; a very different being indeed from the goddess of war.]

[Footnote 155: Cod. Theod. l. x. tit. vi. de Grege Dominico. Godefroy has collected every circumstance of antiquity relative to the Cappadocian horses. One of the finest breeds, the Palmatian, was the forfeiture of a rebel, whose estate lay about sixteen miles from Tyana, near the great road between Constantinople and Antioch.]

[Footnote 156: Justinian (Novell. 30) subjected the province of the count of Cappadocia to the immediate authority of the favorite eunuch, who presided over the sacred bed-chamber.]

[Footnote 157: Cod. Theod. l. vi. tit. xxx. leg. 4, &c.]

[Footnote 158: Pancirolus, p. 102, 136. The appearance of these military domestics is described in the Latin poem of Corippus, de Laudibus Justin. l. iii. 157-179. p. 419, 420 of the Appendix Hist. Byzantin. Rom. 177.]

[Footnote 159: Ammianus Marcellinus, who served so many years, obtained only the rank of a protector. The first ten among these honorable soldiers were Clarissimi.]

The perpetual intercourse between the court and the provinces was facilitated by the construction of roads and the institution of posts. But these beneficial establishments were accidentally connected with a pernicious and intolerable abuse. Two or three hundred agents or messengers were employed, under the jurisdiction of the master of the offices, to announce the names of the annual consuls, and the edicts or victories of the emperors. They insensibly assumed the license of reporting whatever they could observe of the conduct either of magistrates or of private citizens; and were soon considered as the eyes of the monarch, [160] and the scourge of the people. Under the warm influence of a feeble reign, they multiplied to the incredible number of ten thousand, disdained the mild though frequent admonitions of the laws, and exercised in the profitable management of the posts a rapacious and insolent oppression. These official spies, who regularly corresponded with the palace, were encouraged by favor and reward, anxiously to watch the progress of every treasonable design, from the faint and latent symptoms of disaffection, to the actual preparation of an open revolt. Their careless or criminal violation of truth and justice was covered by the consecrated mask of zeal; and they might securely aim their poisoned arrows at the breast either of the guilty or the innocent, who had provoked their resentment, or refused to purchase their silence. A faithful subject, of Syria perhaps, or of Britain, was exposed to the danger, or at least to the dread, of being dragged in chains to the court of Milan or

Constantinople, to defend his life and fortune against the malicious charge of these privileged informers. The ordinary administration was conducted by those methods which extreme necessity can alone palliate; and the defects of evidence were diligently supplied by the use of torture. [161]

[Footnote 160: Xenophon, Cyropaed. l. viii. Brisson, de Regno Persico, l. i No 190, p. 264. The emperors adopted with pleasure this Persian metaphor.]

[Footnote 161: For the Agentes in Rebus, see Ammian. l. xv. c. 3, l. xvi. c. 5, l. xxii. c. 7, with the curious annotations of Valesius. Cod. Theod. l. vi. tit. xxvii. xxviii. xxix. Among the passages collected in the Commentary of Godefroy, the most remarkable is one from Libanius, in his discourse concerning the death of Julian.]

The deceitful and dangerous experiment of the criminal quaestion, as it is emphatically styled, was admitted, rather than approved, in the jurisprudence of the Romans. They applied this sanguinary mode of examination only to servile bodies, whose sufferings were seldom weighed by those haughty republicans in the scale of justice or humanity; but they would never consent to violate the sacred person of a citizen, till they possessed the clearest evidence of his guilt. [162] The annals of tyranny, from the reign of Tiberius to that of Domitian, circumstantially relate the executions of many innocent victims; but, as long as the faintest remembrance was kept alive of the national freedom and honor, the last hours of a Roman were secured from the danger of ignominions torture. [163] The conduct of the provincial magistrates was not, however, regulated by the practice of the city, or the strict maxims of the civilians. They found the use of torture established not only among the slaves of oriental despotism, but among the Macedonians, who obeyed a limited monarch; among the Rhodians, who flourished by the liberty of commerce; and even among the sage Athenians, who had asserted and adorned the dignity of human kind. [164] The acquiescence of the provincials encouraged their governors to acquire, or perhaps to usurp, a discretionary power of employing the rack, to extort from vagrants or plebeian criminals the confession of their guilt, till they insensibly proceeded to confound the distinction of rank, and to disregard the privileges of Roman citizens. The apprehensions of the subjects urged them to solicit, and the interest of the sovereign engaged him to grant, a variety of special exemptions, which tacitly allowed, and even authorized, the general use of torture. They protected all persons of illustrious or honorable rank, bishops and their presbyters, professors of the liberal arts, soldiers and their families, municipal officers, and their posterity to the third generation, and all children under the age of puberty. [165] But a fatal maxim was introduced into the new jurisprudence of the empire, that in the case of treason, which included every offence that the subtlety of lawyers could derive from a hostile intention towards the prince or republic, [166] all privileges were suspended, and all conditions were reduced to the same ignominious level. As the safety of the emperor was avowedly preferred to every consideration of justice or humanity, the dignity of age and the tenderness of youth were alike exposed to the most cruel tortures; and the terrors of a malicious information, which might select them as the accomplices, or even as the witnesses, perhaps, of an imaginary crime, perpetually hung over the heads of the principal citizens of the Roman world. [167]

[Footnote 162: The Pandects (l. xlviii. tit. xviii.) contain the sentiments of the most celebrated civilians on the subject of torture. They strictly confine it to slaves; and Ulpian himself is ready to acknowledge that Res est fragilis, et periculosa, et quae veritatem fallat.]

[Footnote 163: In the conspiracy of Piso against Nero, Epicharis (libertina mulier) was the only person tortured; the rest were intacti tormentis. It would be superfluous to add a weaker, and it would be difficult to find a stronger, example. Tacit. Annal. xv. 57.]

[Footnote 164: Dicendum... de Institutis Atheniensium, Rhodiorum, doctissimorum hominum, apud quos etiam (id quod acerbissimum est) liberi, civesque torquentur. Cicero, Partit. Orat. c. 34. We may learn from the trial of Philotas the practice of the Macedonians. (Diodor. Sicul. l. xvii. p. 604. Q. Curt. l. vi. c. 11.)]

[Footnote 165: Heineccius (Element. Jur. Civil. part vii. p. 81) has collected these exemptions into one view.]

[Footnote 166: This definition of the sage Ulpian (Pandect. l. xlviii. tit. iv.) seems to have been adapted to the court of Caracalla, rather than to that of Alexander Severus. See the Codes of Theodosius and ad leg. Juliam majestatis.]

[Footnote 167: Arcadius Charisius is the oldest lawyer quoted to justify the universal practice of torture in all cases of treason; but this maxim of tyranny, which is admitted by Ammianus with the most respectful terror, is enforced by several laws of the successors of Constantine. See Cod. Theod. l. ix. tit. xxxv. majestatis crimine omnibus aequa est conditio.]

These evils, however terrible they may appear, were confined to the smaller number of Roman subjects, whose dangerous situation was in some degree compensated by the enjoyment of those advantages, either of nature or of fortune, which exposed them to the jealousy of the monarch. The obscure millions of a great empire have much less to dread from the cruelty than from the avarice of their masters, and their humble happiness is principally affected by the grievance of excessive taxes, which, gently pressing on the wealthy, descend with accelerated weight on the meaner and more indigent classes of society. An ingenious philosopher [168] has calculated the universal measure of the public impositions by the degrees of freedom and servitude; and ventures to assert, that, according to an invariable law of nature, it must always increase with the former, and diminish in a just proportion to the latter. But this reflection, which would tend to alleviate the miseries of despotism, is contradicted at least by the history of the Roman empire; which accuses the same princes of despoiling the senate of its authority, and the provinces of their wealth. Without abolishing all the various customs and duties on merchandises, which are imperceptibly discharged by the apparent choice of the purchaser, the policy of Constantine and his successors preferred a simple and direct mode of taxation, more congenial to the spirit of an arbitrary government. [169]

[Footnote 168: Montesquieu, Esprit des Loix, l. xii. c. 13.]

[Footnote 169: Mr. Hume (Essays, vol. i. p. 389) has seen this importance with some degree of perplexity.]

PART VI

The name and use of the indictions, [170] which serve to ascertain the chronology of the middle ages, were derived from the regular practice of the Roman tributes. [171] The emperor subscribed with his own hand, and in purple ink, the solemn edict, or indiction, which was fixed up in the principal city of each diocese, during two months previous to the first day of September. And by a very easy connection of ideas, the word indiction was transferred to the measure of tribute which it prescribed, and to the annual term which it allowed for the payment. This general estimate of the supplies was proportioned to the real and imaginary wants of the state; but as often as the expense exceeded the revenue, or the revenue fell short of the computation, an additional tax, under the name of superindiction, was imposed on the people, and the most valuable attribute of sovereignty was communicated to the Praetorian praefects, who, on some occasions, were permitted to provide for the unforeseen and extraordinary exigencies of the public service. The execution of these laws (which it would be tedious to pursue in their minute and intricate detail) consisted of two distinct operations: the resolving the general imposition into its constituent parts, which were assessed on the provinces, the cities, and the individuals of the Roman world; and the collecting the separate contributions of the individuals, the cities, and the provinces, till the accumulated sums were poured into the Imperial treasuries. But as the account between the monarch and the subject was perpetually open, and as the renewal of the demand anticipated the perfect discharge of the preceding obligation, the weighty machine of the finances was moved by the same hands round the circle of its yearly revolution. Whatever was honorable or important in the administration of the revenue, was committed to the wisdom of the praefects, and their provincia. representatives; the lucrative functions were claimed by a crowd of subordinate officers, some of whom depended on the treasurer, others on the governor of the province; and who, in the inevitable conflicts of a perplexed jurisdiction, had frequent opportunities of disputing with each other the spoils of the people. The laborious offices, which could be productive only of envy and reproach, of expense and danger, were imposed on the Decurions, who formed the corporations of the cities, and whom the severity of the Imperial laws had condemned to sustain the burdens of civil society. [172] The whole landed property of the empire (without excepting the patrimonial estates of the monarch) was the object of ordinary taxation; and every new purchaser contracted the obligations of the former proprietor. An accurate census, [173] or survey, was the only equitable mode of ascertaining the proportion which every citizen should be obliged to contribute for the public service; and from the well-known period of the indictions, there is reason to believe that this difficult and expensive operation was repeated at the regular distance of fifteen years. The lands were measured by surveyors, who were sent into the provinces; their nature, whether arable or pasture, or vineyards or woods, was distinctly reported; and an estimate was made of their common value from the average produce of five years. The numbers of slaves and of cattle constituted an essential part of the report; an oath was administered to the proprietors, which bound them to disclose the true state of their affairs; and their attempts to prevaricate, or elude the intention of the legislator, were severely watched, and punished as a capital crime, which included the double guilt of treason and sacrilege. [174] A large portion of the tribute was paid in money; and of the current coin of the empire, gold alone could be legally accepted. [175] The remainder of the taxes, according to the proportions determined by the annual indiction, was furnished in a manner still more direct, and still more oppressive. According to the different nature of lands, their real produce in the various articles of wine or oil, corn or barley, wood or iron, was transported by the labor or at the expense of the provincials [175a] to the Imperial magazines, from whence they were occasionally distributed for the use of the court, of the army, and of two capitals, Rome and Constantinople. The commissioners of the revenue were so frequently obliged to make considerable purchases, that they were strictly prohibited from allowing any compensation, or from receiving in money the value of those supplies which were exacted in kind. In the primitive simplicity of small communities, this method may be well adapted to collect the almost voluntary offerings of the people; but it is at once susceptible of the utmost latitude, and of the utmost strictness, which in a corrupt and absolute monarchy must introduce a perpetual contest between the power of oppression and the arts of fraud. [176] The agriculture of the Roman provinces was insensibly ruined, and, in the progress of despotism which tends to disappoint its own purpose, the emperors were obliged to derive some merit from the forgiveness of debts, or the remission of tributes, which their subjects were utterly incapable of paying. According to the new division of Italy, the fertile and happy province of Campania, the scene of the early victories and of the delicious retirements of the citizens of Rome, extended between the sea and the Apennine, from the Tiber to the Silarus. Within sixty years after the death of Constantine, and on the evidence of an actual survey, an exemption was granted in favor of three hundred and thirty thousand English acres of desert and uncultivated land; which amounted to one eighth of the whole surface of the province. As the footsteps of the Barbarians had not yet been seen in Italy, the cause of this amazing desolation, which is recorded in the laws, can be ascribed only to the administration of the Roman emperors. [177]

[Footnote 170: The cycle of indictions, which may be traced as high as the reign of Constantius, or perhaps of his father, Constantine, is still employed by the Papal court; but the commencement of the year has been very reasonably altered to the first of January. See l'Art de Verifier les Dates, p. xi.; and Dictionnaire Raison. de la Diplomatique, tom. ii. p. 25; two accurate treatises, which come from the workshop of the Benedictines. — It does not appear that the establishment of the indiction is to be at tributed to Constantine: it existed before he had been created Augustus at Rome, and the remission granted by him to the city of Autun is the proof. He would not have ventured while only Caesar, and under the necessity of courting popular favor, to establish such an odious impost. Aurelius Victor and Lactantius agree in designating Diocletian as the author of this despotic institution. Aur. Vict. de Caes. c. 39. Lactant. de Mort. Pers. c. 7—G.]

[Footnote 171: The first twenty-eight titles of the eleventh book of the Theodosian Code are filled with the circumstantial regulations on the important subject of tributes; but they suppose a clearer knowledge of fundamental principles than it is at present in our power to attain.]

[Footnote 172: The title concerning the Decurions (l. xii. tit. i.) is the most ample in the whole Theodosian Code; since it contains not less than one hundred and ninety-two distinct laws to ascertain the duties and privileges of that useful order of citizens. Note: The Decurions were charged with assessing, according to the census of property prepared by the tabularii, the payment due from each proprietor. This odious office was authoritatively imposed on the richest citizens of each town; they had no salary, and all their compensation was, to be exempt from certain corporal punishments, in case they should have incurred them. The Decurionate was the ruin of all the rich. Hence they tried every way of avoiding this dangerous honor; they concealed themselves, they entered into military service; but their efforts were unavailing; they were seized, they were compelled to become Decurions, and the dread inspired by this title was termed Impiety—G. —The Decurions were mutually responsible; they were obliged to undertake for pieces of ground abandoned by their owners on account of the pressure of the taxes, and, finally, to make up all deficiencies. Savigny chichte des Rom. Rechts, i. 25—M.]

[Footnote 173: Habemus enim et hominum numerum qui delati sunt, et agrun modum. Eumenius in Panegyr. Vet. viii. 6. See Cod. Theod. l. xiii. tit. x. xi., with Godefroy's Commentary.]

[Footnote 174: Siquis sacrilega vitem falce succiderit, aut feracium ramorum foetus hebetaverit, quo delinet fidem Censuum, et mentiatur callide paupertatis ingenium, mox detectus capitale subibit exitium, et bona ejus in Fisci jura migrabunt. Cod. Theod. l. xiii. tit. xi. leg. 1. Although this law is not without its studied obscurity, it is, however clear enough to prove the minuteness of the inquisition, and the disproportion of the penalty.]

[Footnote 175: The astonishment of Pliny would have ceased. Equidem miror P. R. victis gentibus argentum semper imperitasse non aurum. Hist Natur. xxxiii. 15.]

[Footnote 175a: The proprietors were not charged with the expense of this transport in the provinces situated on the sea-shore or near the great rivers, there were companies of boatmen, and of masters of vessels, who had this commission, and furnished the means of transport at their own expense. In return, they were themselves exempt, altogether, or in part, from the indiction and other imposts. They had certain privileges; particular regulations determined their rights and obligations. (Cod. Theod. l. xiii. tit. v. ix.) The transports by land were made in the same manner, by the intervention of a privileged company called Bastaga; the members were called Bastagarii Cod. Theod. l. viii. tit. v—G.]

[Footnote 176: Some precautions were taken (see Cod. Theod. l. xi. tit. ii. and Cod. Justinian. l. x. tit. xxvii. leg. 1, 2, 3) to restrain the magistrates from the abuse of their authority, either in the exaction or in the purchase of corn: but those who had learning enough to read the orations of Cicero against Verres, (iii. de Frumento,) might instruct themselves in all the various arts of oppression, with regard to the weight, the price, the quality, and the carriage. The avarice of an unlettered governor would supply the ignorance of precept or precedent.]

[Footnote 177: Cod. Theod. l. xi. tit. xxviii. leg. 2, published the 24th of March, A. D. 395, by the emperor Honorius, only two months after the death of his father, Theodosius. He speaks of 528,042 Roman jugera, which I have reduced to the English measure. The jugerum contained 28,800 square Roman feet.]

Either from design or from accident, the mode of assessment seemed to unite the substance of a land tax with the forms of a capitation. [178] The returns which were sent of every province or district, expressed the number of tributary subjects, and the amount of the public impositions. The latter of these sums was divided by the former; and the estimate, that such a province contained so many capita, or heads of tribute; and that each head was rated at such a price, was universally received, not only in the popular, but even in the legal computation. The value of a tributary head must have varied, according to many accidental, or at least fluctuating circumstances; but some knowledge has been preserved of a very curious fact, the more important, since it relates to one of the richest provinces of the Roman empire, and which now flourishes as the most splendid of the European kingdoms. The rapacious ministers of Constantius had exhausted the wealth of Gaul, by exacting twenty-five pieces of gold for the annual tribute of every head. The humane policy of his successor reduced the capitation to seven pieces. [179] A moderate proportion between these opposite extremes of extraordinary oppression and of transient indulgence, may therefore be fixed at sixteen pieces of gold, or about nine pounds sterling, the common standard, perhaps, of the impositions of Gaul. [180] But this calculation, or rather, indeed, the facts from whence it is deduced, cannot fail of suggesting two difficulties to a thinking mind, who will be at once surprised by the equality, and by the enormity, of the capitation. An attempt to explain them may perhaps reflect some light on the interesting subject of the finances of the declining empire.

[Footnote 178: Godefroy (Cod. Theod. tom. vi. p. 116) argues with weight and learning on the subject of the capitation; but while he explains the caput, as a share or measure of property, he too absolutely excludes the idea of a personal assessment.]

[Footnote 179: Quid profuerit (Julianus) anhelantibus extrema penuria Gallis, hinc maxime claret, quod primitus partes eas ingressus, pro capitibusingulis tributi nomine vicenos quinos aureos reperit flagitari; discedens vero septenos tantum numera universa complentes. Ammian. l. xvi. c. 5.]

[Footnote 180: In the calculation of any sum of money under Constantine and his successors, we need only refer to the excellent discourse of Mr. Greaves on the Denarius, for the proof of the following *principles; 1. That the ancient and modern Roman pound, containing 5256 grains of Troy weight, is about one twelfth lighter than the English pound, which is composed of 5760 of the same grains. 2. That the pound of gold, which had once been divided into forty-eight aurei, was at this time coined into seventy-two smaller pieces of the same denomination. 3. That five of these aurei were the legal tender for a pound of silver, and that consequently the pound of gold was exchanged for fourteen pounds eight ounces of silver, according to the Roman, or about thirteen pounds according to the English weight. 4. That the English pound of silver is coined into sixty-two shillings. From these elements we may compute the Roman pound of gold, the usual method of reckoning large sums, at forty pounds sterling, and we may fix the currency of the aureus at somewhat more than eleven shillings. Note: See, likewise, a Dissertation of M. Letronne, "Considerations Generales sur l'Evaluation des Monnaies Grecques et Romaines" Paris, 1817—M.]*

I. It is obvious, that, as long as the immutable constitution of human nature produces and maintains so unequal a division of property, the most numerous part of the community would be deprived of their subsistence, by the equal assessment of a tax from which the sovereign would derive a very trifling revenue. Such indeed might be the theory of the Roman capitation; but in the practice, this unjust equality was no longer felt, as the tribute was collected on the principle of a real, not of a personal imposition. [180a] Several indigent citizens contributed to compose a single head, or share of taxation; while the wealthy provincial, in proportion to his fortune, alone represented several of those imaginary beings. In a poetical request, addressed to one of the last and most deserving of the Roman princes who reigned in Gaul, Sidonius Apollinaris personifies his tribute under the figure of a triple monster, the Geryon of the Grecian fables, and entreats the new Hercules that he would most graciously be pleased to save his life by cutting off three of his heads. [181] The fortune of Sidonius far exceeded the customary wealth of a poet; but if he had pursued the allusion, he might have painted many of the Gallic nobles with the hundred heads of the deadly Hydra, spreading over the face of the country, and devouring the substance of a hundred families. II. The difficulty of allowing an annual sum of about nine pounds sterling, even for the average of the capitation of Gaul, may be rendered more evident by the comparison of the present state of the same country, as it is now governed by the absolute monarch of an industrious, wealthy, and affectionate people. The taxes of France cannot be magnified, either by fear or by flattery, beyond the annual amount of eighteen millions sterling, which ought perhaps to be shared among four and twenty millions of inhabitants. [182] Seven millions of these, in the capacity of fathers, or brothers, or husbands, may discharge the obligations of the remaining multitude of women and children; yet the equal proportion of each tributary subject will scarcely rise above fifty shillings of our money, instead of a proportion almost four times as considerable, which was regularly imposed on their Gallic ancestors. The reason of this difference may be found, not so much in the relative scarcity or plenty of gold and silver, as in the different state of society, in ancient Gaul and in modern France. In a country where personal freedom is the privilege of every subject, the whole mass of taxes, whether they are levied on property or on consumption, may be fairly divided among the whole body of the nation. But the far greater part of the lands of ancient Gaul, as well as of the other provinces of the Roman world, were cultivated by slaves, or by peasants, whose dependent condition was a less rigid servitude. [183] In such a state the poor were maintained at the expense of the masters who enjoyed the fruits of their labor; and as the rolls of tribute were filled only with the names of those citizens who possessed the means of an honorable, or at least of a decent subsistence, the comparative smallness of their numbers explains and justifies the high rate of their capitation. The truth of this assertion may be illustrated by the following example: The Aedui, one of the most powerful and civilized tribes or cities of Gaul, occupied an extent of territory, which now contains about five hundred thousand inhabitants, in the two ecclesiastical dioceses of Autun and Nevers; [184] and with the probable accession of those of Chalons and Macon, [185] the population would amount to eight hundred thousand souls. In the time of

Constantine, the territory of the Aedui afforded no more than twenty-five thousand heads of capitation, of whom seven thousand were discharged by that prince from the intolerable weight of tribute. [186] A just analogy would seem to countenance the opinion of an ingenious historian, [187] that the free and tributary citizens did not surpass the number of half a million; and if, in the ordinary administration of government, their annual payments may be computed at about four millions and a half of our money, it would appear, that although the share of each individual was four times as considerable, a fourth part only of the modern taxes of France was levied on the Imperial province of Gaul. The exactions of Constantius may be calculated at seven millions sterling, which were reduced to two millions by the humanity or the wisdom of Julian.

[Footnote 180a: Two masterly dissertations of M. Savigny, in the Mem. of the Berlin Academy (1822 and 1823) have thrown new light on the taxation system of the Empire. Gibbon, according to M. Savigny, is mistaken in supposing that there was but one kind of capitation tax; there was a land tax, and a capitation tax, strictly so called. The land tax was, in its operation, a proprietor's or landlord's tax. But, besides this, there was a direct capitation tax on all who were not possessed of landed property. This tax dates from the time of the Roman conquests; its amount is not clearly known. Gradual exemptions released different persons and classes from this tax. One edict exempts painters. In Syria, all under twelve or fourteen, or above sixty-five, were exempted; at a later period, all under twenty, and all unmarried females; still later, all under twenty-five, widows and nuns, soldiers, veterani and clerici—whole dioceses, that of Thrace and Illyricum. Under Galerius and Licinius, the plebs urbana became exempt; though this, perhaps, was only an ordinance for the East. By degrees, however, the exemption was extended to all the inhabitants of towns; and as it was strictly capitatio plebeia, from which all possessors were exempted it fell at length altogether on the coloni and agricultural slaves. These were registered in the same cataster (capitastrum) with the land tax. It was paid by the proprietor, who raised it again from his coloni and laborers—M.]

[Footnote 181: Geryones nos esse puta, monstrumque tributum,
Hic capita ut vivam, tu mihi tolle tria.
Sidon. Apollinar. Carm. xiii.

The reputation of Father Sirmond led me to expect more satisfaction than I have found in his note (p. 144) on this remarkable passage. The words, suo vel suorum nomine, betray the perplexity of the commentator.]

[Footnote 182: This assertion, however formidable it may seem, is founded on the original registers of births, deaths, and marriages, collected by public authority, and now deposited in the Controlee General at Paris. The annual average of births throughout the whole kingdom, taken in five years, (from 1770 to 1774, both inclusive,) is 479,649 boys, and 449,269 girls, in all 928,918 children. The province of French Hainault alone furnishes 9906 births; and we are assured, by an actual enumeration of the people, annually repeated from the year 1773 to the year 1776, that upon an average, Hainault contains 257,097 inhabitants. By the rules of fair analogy, we might infer, that the ordinary proportion of annual births to the whole people, is about 1 to 26; and that the kingdom of France contains 24,151,868 persons of both sexes and of every age. If we content ourselves with the more moderate proportion of 1 to 25, the whole population will amount to 23,222,950. From the diligent researches of the French Government, (which are not unworthy of our own imitation,) we may hope to obtain a still greater degree of certainty on this important subject Note: On no subject has so much valuable information been collected since the time of Gibbon, as the statistics of the different countries of Europe but much is still wanting as to our own—M.]

[Footnote 183: Cod. Theod. l. v. tit. ix. x. xi. Cod. Justinian. l. xi. tit. lxiii. Coloni appellantur qui conditionem debent genitali solo, propter agriculturum sub dominio possessorum. Augustin. de Civitate Dei, l. x. c. i.]

[Footnote 184: The ancient jurisdiction of (Augustodunum) Autun in Burgundy, the capital of the Aedui, comprehended the adjacent territory of (Noviodunum) Nevers. See D'Anville, Notice de l'Ancienne Gaule, p. 491. The two dioceses of Autun and Nevers are now composed, the former of 610, and the latter of 160 parishes. The registers of births, taken during eleven years, in 476 parishes of the same province of Burgundy, and multiplied by the moderate proportion of 25, (see Messance Recherches sur la Population, p. 142,) may authorizes us to assign an average number of 656 persons for each parish, which being again multiplied by the 770 parishes of the dioceses of Nevers and Autun, will produce the sum of 505,120 persons for the extent of country which was once possessed by the Aedui.]

[Footnote 185: We might derive an additional supply of 301,750 inhabitants from the dioceses of Chalons (Cabillonum) and of Macon, (Matisco,) since they contain, the one 200, and the other 260 parishes. This accession of territory might be justified by very specious reasons. 1. Chalons and Macon were undoubtedly within the original jurisdiction of the Aedui. (See D'Anville, Notice, p. 187, 443.) 2. In the Notitia of Gaul, they are enumerated not as Civitates, but merely as Castra. 3. They do not appear to have been episcopal seats before the fifth and sixth centuries. Yet there is a passage in Eumenius (Panegyr. Vet. viii. 7) which very forcibly deters me from extending the territory of the Aedui, in the reign of Constantine, along the beautiful banks of the navigable Saone. Note: In this passage of Eumenius, Savigny supposes the original number to have been 32,000: 7000 being discharged, there remained 25,000 liable to the tribute. See Mem. quoted above—M.]

[Footnote 186: Eumenius in Panegyr Vet. viii. 11.]

[Footnote 187: L'Abbe du Bos, Hist. Critique de la M. F. tom. i. p. 121]

But this tax, or capitation, on the proprietors of land, would have suffered a rich and numerous class of free citizens to escape. With the view of sharing that species of wealth which is derived from art or labor, and which exists in money or in merchandise, the emperors imposed a distinct and personal tribute on the trading part of their subjects. [188] Some exemptions, very strictly confined both in time and place, were allowed to the proprietors who disposed of the produce of their own estates. Some indulgence was granted to the profession of the liberal arts: but every other branch of commercial industry was affected by the severity of the law. The honorable merchant of Alexandria, who imported the gems and spices of India for the use of the western world; the usurer, who derived from the interest of money a silent and ignominious profit; the ingenious manufacturer, the diligent mechanic, and even the most obscure retailer of a sequestered village, were obliged to admit the officers of the revenue into the partnership of their gain; and the sovereign of the Roman empire, who tolerated the profession, consented to share the infamous salary, of public prostitutes. [188a] As this general tax upon industry was collected every fourth year, it was styled the Lustral Contribution: and the historian Zosimus [189] laments that the approach of the fatal period was announced by the tears and terrors of the citizens, who were often compelled by the impending scourge to embrace the most abhorred and unnatural methods of procuring the sum at which their property had been assessed. The testimony of Zosimus cannot indeed be justified from the charge of passion and prejudice; but, from the nature of this tribute it seems reasonable to conclude, that it was arbitrary in the distribution, and extremely rigorous in the mode of collecting. The secret wealth of commerce, and the precarious profits of art or labor, are susceptible only of a discretionary valuation, which is seldom disadvantageous to the interest of the treasury; and as the person of the trader supplies the want of a visible and permanent security, the payment of the imposition, which, in the case of a land tax, may be obtained by the seizure of property, can rarely be extorted by any other means than those of corporal punishments. The cruel treatment of the insolvent debtors of the state, is attested, and was perhaps mitigated by a very humane edict of Constantine, who, disclaiming the use of racks and of scourges, allots a spacious and airy prison for the place of their confinement. [190]

[Footnote 188: See Cod. Theod. l. xiii. tit. i. and iv.]

[Footnote 188a: The emperor Theodosius put an end, by a law. to this disgraceful source of revenue. (Godef. ad Cod. Theod. xiii. tit. i. c. 1.) But before he deprived himself of it, he made sure of some way of replacing this deficit. A rich patrician, Florentius, indignant at this legalized licentiousness, had made representations on the subject to the emperor. To induce him to tolerate it no longer, he offered his own property to supply the diminution of the revenue. The emperor had the baseness to accept his offer—G.]

[Footnote 189: Zosimus, l. ii. p. 115. There is probably as much passion and prejudice in the attack of Zosimus, as in the elaborate defence of the memory of Constantine by the zealous Dr. Howell. Hist. of the World, vol. ii. p. 20.]

[Footnote 190: Cod. Theod. l. xi. tit vii. leg. 3.]

These general taxes were imposed and levied by the absolute authority of the monarch; but the occasional offerings of the coronary gold still retained the name and semblance of popular consent. It was an ancient custom that the allies of the republic, who ascribed their safety or deliverance to the success of the Roman arms, and even the cities of Italy, who admired the virtues of their victorious general, adorned the pomp of his triumph by their voluntary gifts of crowns of gold, which after the ceremony were consecrated in the temple of Jupiter, to remain a lasting monument of his glory to future ages. The progress of zeal and flattery soon multiplied the number, and increased the size, of these popular donations; and the triumph of Caesar was enriched with two thousand eight hundred and twenty-two massy crowns, whose weight amounted to twenty thousand four hundred and fourteen pounds of gold. This treasure was immediately melted down by the prudent dictator, who was satisfied that it would be more serviceable to his soldiers than to the gods: his example was imitated by his successors; and the custom was introduced of exchanging these splendid ornaments for the more acceptable present of the current gold coin of the empire. [191] The spontaneous offering was at length exacted as the debt of duty; and instead of being confined to the occasion of a triumph, it was supposed to be granted by the several cities and provinces of the monarchy, as often as the emperor condescended to announce his accession, his consulship, the birth of a son, the creation of a Caesar, a victory over the Barbarians, or any other real or imaginary event which graced the annals of his reign. The peculiar free gift of the senate of Rome was fixed by custom at sixteen hundred pounds of gold, or about sixty-four thousand pounds sterling. The oppressed subjects celebrated their own felicity, that their sovereign should graciously consent to accept this feeble but voluntary testimony of their loyalty and gratitude. [192]

[Footnote 191: See Lipsius de Magnitud. Romana, l. ii. c. 9. The Tarragonese Spain presented the emperor Claudius with a crown of gold of seven, and Gaul with another of nine, hundred pounds weight. I have followed the rational emendation of Lipsius. Note: This custom is of still earlier date, the Romans had borrowed it from Greece. Who is not acquainted with the famous oration of Demosthenes for the golden crown, which his citizens wished to bestow, and Aeschines to deprive him of?—G.]

[Footnote 192: Cod. Theod. l. xii. tit. xiii. The senators were supposed to be exempt from the Aurum Coronarium; but the Auri Oblatio, which was required at their hands, was precisely of the same nature.]

A people elated by pride, or soured by discontent, are seldom qualified to form a just estimate of their actual situation. The subjects of Constantine were incapable of discerning the decline of genius and manly virtue, which so far degraded them below the dignity of their ancestors; but they could feel and lament the rage of tyranny, the relaxation of discipline, and the increase of taxes. The impartial historian, who acknowledges the justice of their complaints, will observe some favorable circumstances which tended to alleviate the misery of their condition. The threatening tempest of Barbarians, which so soon subverted the foundations of Roman greatness, was still repelled, or suspended, on the frontiers. The arts of luxury and literature were cultivated, and the elegant pleasures of society were enjoyed, by the inhabitants of a considerable portion of the globe. The forms, the pomp, and the expense of the civil administration contributed to restrain the irregular license of the soldiers; and although the laws were violated by power, or perverted by subtlety, the sage principles of the Roman jurisprudence preserved a sense of order and equity, unknown to the despotic governments of the East. The rights of mankind might derive some protection from religion and philosophy; and the name of freedom, which could no longer alarm, might sometimes admonish, the successors of Augustus, that they did not reign over a nation of Slaves or Barbarians. [193]

[Footnote 193: The great Theodosius, in his judicious advice to his son, (Claudian in iv. Consulat. Honorii, 214, &c.,) distinguishes the station of a Roman prince from that of a Parthian monarch. Virtue was necessary for the one; birth might suffice for the other.]

CHAPTER XVIII

CHARACTER OF CONSTANTINE AND HIS SONS

PART I

CHARACTER OF CONSTANTINE—GOTHIC WAR—DEATH OF CONSTANTINE—DIVISION OF THE EMPIRE AMONG HIS THREE SONS—PERSIAN WAR—TRAGIC DEATHS OF CONSTANTINE THE YOUNGER AND CONSTANS—USURPATION OF MAGNENTIUS—CIVIL WAR—VICTORY OF CONSTANTIUS

The character of the prince who removed the seat of empire, and introduced such important changes into the civil and religious constitution of his country, has fixed the attention, and divided the opinions, of mankind. By the grateful zeal of the Christians, the deliverer of the church has been decorated with every attribute of a hero, and even of a saint; while the discontent of the vanquished party has compared Constantine to the most abhorred of those tyrants, who, by their vice and weakness, dishonored the Imperial purple. The same passions have in some degree been perpetuated to succeeding generations, and the character of Constantine is considered, even in the present age, as an object either of satire or of panegyric. By the impartial union of those defects which are confessed by his warmest admirers, and of those virtues which are acknowledged by his most-implacable enemies, we might hope to delineate a just portrait of that extraordinary man, which the truth and candor of history should adopt without a blush. [1] But it would soon appear, that the vain attempt to blend such discordant colors, and to reconcile such inconsistent qualities, must produce a figure monstrous rather than human, unless it is viewed in its proper and distinct lights, by a careful separation of the different periods of the reign of Constantine.

[Footnote 1: On ne se trompera point sur Constantin, en croyant tout le mal ru'en dit Eusebe, et tout le bien qu'en dit Zosime. Fleury, Hist. Ecclesiastique, tom. iii. p. 233. Eusebius and Zosimus form indeed the two extremes of flattery and invective. The intermediate shades are expressed by those writers, whose character or situation variously tempered the influence of their religious zeal.]

The person, as well as the mind, of Constantine, had been enriched by nature with her choices endowments. His stature was lofty, his countenance majestic, his deportment graceful; his strength and activity were displayed in every manly exercise, and from his earliest youth, to a very advanced season of life, he preserved the vigor of his constitution by a strict adherence to the domestic virtues of chastity and temperance. He delighted in the social intercourse of familiar conversation; and though he might sometimes indulge his disposition to raillery with less reserve than was required by the severe dignity of his station, the courtesy and liberality of his manners gained the hearts of all who approached him. The sincerity of his friendship has been suspected; yet he showed, on some occasions, that he was not incapable of a warm and lasting attachment. The disadvantage of an illiterate education had not prevented him from forming a just estimate of the value of learning; and the arts and sciences derived some encouragement from the munificent protection of Constantine. In the despatch of business, his diligence was indefatigable; and the active powers of his mind were almost continually exercised in reading, writing, or meditating, in giving audiences to ambassadors, and in examining the complaints of his subjects. Even those who censured the propriety of his measures were compelled to acknowledge, that he possessed magnanimity to conceive, and patience to execute, the most arduous designs, without being checked either by the prejudices of education, or by the clamors of the multitude. In the field, he infused his own intrepid spirit into the troops, whom he conducted with the talents of a consummate general; and to his abilities, rather than to his fortune, we may ascribe the signal victories which he obtained over the foreign and domestic foes of the republic. He loved glory as the reward, perhaps as the motive, of his labors. The boundless ambition, which, from the moment of his accepting the purple at York, appears as the ruling passion of his soul, may be justified by the dangers of his own situation, by the character of his rivals, by the consciousness of superior merit, and by the prospect that his success would enable him to restore peace and order to the distracted empire. In his civil wars against Maxentius and Licinius, he had engaged on his side the inclinations of the people, who compared the undissembled vices of those tyrants with the spirit of wisdom and justice which seemed to direct the general tenor of the administration of Constantine. [2]

[Footnote 2: The virtues of Constantine are collected for the most part from Eutropius and the younger Victor, two sincere pagans, who wrote after the extinction of his family. Even Zosimus, and the Emperor Julian, acknowledge his personal courage and military achievements.]

Had Constantine fallen on the banks of the Tyber, or even in the plains of Hadrianople, such is the character which, with a few exceptions, he might have transmitted to posterity. But the conclusion of his reign (according to the moderate and indeed tender sentence of a writer of the same age) degraded him from the rank which he had acquired among the most deserving of the Roman princes. [3] In the life of Augustus, we behold the tyrant of the republic, converted, almost by imperceptible degrees, into the father of his country, and of human kind. In that of Constantine, we may contemplate a hero, who had so long inspired his subjects with love, and his enemies with terror, degenerating into a cruel and dissolute monarch, corrupted by his fortune, or raised by conquest above the necessity of dissimulation. The general peace which he maintained during the last fourteen years of his reign, was a period of apparent splendor rather than of real prosperity; and the old age of Constantine was disgraced by the opposite yet reconcilable vices of rapaciousness and prodigality. The accumulated treasures found in the palaces of Maxentius and Licinius, were lavishly consumed; the various innovations introduced by the conqueror, were attended with an increasing expense; the cost of his buildings, his court, and his festivals, required an immediate and plentiful supply; and the oppression of the people was the only fund which could support the magnificence of the sovereign. [4] His unworthy favorites, enriched by the boundless liberality of their master, usurped with impunity the privilege of rapine and corruption. [5] A secret but universal decay was felt in every part of the public administration, and the emperor himself, though he still retained the obedience, gradually lost the esteem, of his subjects. The dress and manners, which, towards the decline of life, he chose to affect, served only to degrade him in the eyes of mankind. The Asiatic pomp, which had been adopted by the pride of Diocletian, assumed an air of softness and effeminacy in the person of Constantine. He is represented with false hair of various colors, laboriously arranged by the skilful artists to the times; a diadem of a new and more expensive fashion; a profusion of gems and pearls, of collars and bracelets, and a variegated flowing robe of silk, most curiously embroidered with flowers of gold. In such apparel, scarcely to be excused by the youth and folly of Elagabalus, we are at a loss to discover the wisdom of an aged monarch, and the simplicity of a Roman veteran. [6] A mind thus relaxed by prosperity and indulgence, was incapable of rising to that magnanimity which disdains suspicion, and dares to forgive. The deaths of Maximian and Licinius may perhaps be justified by the maxims of policy, as they are taught in the schools of tyrants; but an impartial narrative of the executions, or rather murders, which sullied the declining age of Constantine, will suggest to our most candid thoughts the idea of a prince who could sacrifice without reluctance the laws of justice, and the feelings of nature, to the dictates either of his passions or of his interest.

[Footnote 3: See Eutropius, x. 6. In primo Imperii tempore optimis principibus, ultimo mediis comparandus. From the ancient Greek version of Poeanius, (edit. Havercamp. p. 697,) I am inclined to suspect that Eutropius had originally written vix mediis; and that the offensive monosyllable was dropped by the wilful inadvertency of transcribers. Aurelius Victor expresses the general opinion by a vulgar and indeed obscure proverb. Trachala decem annis praestantissimds; duodecim sequentibus latro; decem novissimis pupillus ob immouicas profusiones.]

[Footnote 4: Julian, Orat. i. p. 8, in a flattering discourse pronounced before the son of Constantine; and Caesares, p. 336. Zosimus, p. 114, 115. The stately buildings of Constantinople, &c., may be quoted as a lasting and unexceptionable proof of the profuseness of their founder.]

[Footnote 5: The impartial Ammianus deserves all our confidence. Proximorum fauces aperuit primus omnium Constantinus. L. xvi. c. 8. Eusebius himself confesses the abuse, (Vit. Constantin. l. iv. c. 29, 54;) and some of the Imperial laws feebly point out the remedy. See above, p. 146 of this volume.]

[Footnote 6: Julian, in the Caesars, attempts to ridicule his uncle. His suspicious testimony is confirmed, however, by the learned Spanheim, with the authority of medals, (see Commentaire, p. 156, 299, 397, 459.) Eusebius (Orat. c. 5) alleges, that Constantine dressed for the public, not for himself. Were this admitted, the vainest coxcomb could never want an excuse.]

The same fortune which so invariably followed the standard of Constantine, seemed to secure the hopes and comforts of his domestic life. Those among his predecessors who had enjoyed the longest and most prosperous reigns, Augustus Trajan, and Diocletian, had been disappointed of posterity; and the frequent revolutions had never allowed sufficient time for any Imperial family to grow up and multiply under the shade of the purple. But the royalty of the Flavian line, which had been first ennobled by the Gothic Claudius, descended through several generations; and Constantine himself derived from his royal father the hereditary honors which he transmitted to his children. The emperor had been twice married. Minervina, the obscure but lawful object of his youthful attachment, [7] had left him only one son, who was called Crispus. By Fausta, the daughter of Maximian, he had three daughters, and three sons known by the kindred names of Constantine, Constantius, and Constans. The unambitious brothers of the great Constantine, Julius Constantius, Dalmatius, and Hannibalianus, [8] were permitted to enjoy the most honorable rank, and the most affluent fortune, that could be consistent with a private station. The youngest of the three lived without a name, and died without posterity. His two elder brothers obtained in marriage the daughters of wealthy senators, and propagated new branches of the Imperial race. Gallus and Julian afterwards became the most illustrious of the children of Julius Constantius, the Patrician.

The two sons of Dalmatius, who had been decorated with the vain title of Censor, were named Dalmatius and Hannibalianus. The two sisters of the great Constantine, Anastasia and Eutropia, were bestowed on Optatus and Nepotianus, two senators of noble birth and of consular dignity. His third sister, Constantia, was distinguished by her preeminence of greatness and of misery. She remained the widow of the vanquished Licinius; and it was by her entreaties, that an innocent boy, the offspring of their marriage, preserved, for some time, his life, the title of Caesar, and a precarious hope of the succession. Besides the females, and the allies of the Flavian house, ten or twelve males, to whom the language of modern courts would apply the title of princes of the blood, seemed, according to the order of their birth, to be destined either to inherit or to support the throne of Constantine. But in less than thirty years, this numerous and increasing family was reduced to the persons of Constantius and Julian, who alone had survived a series of crimes and calamities, such as the tragic poets have deplored in the devoted lines of Pelops and of Cadmus.

[Footnote 7: Zosimus and Zonaras agree in representing Minervina as the concubine of Constantine; but Ducange has very gallantly rescued her character, by producing a decisive passage from one of the panegyrics: "Ab ipso fine pueritiae te matrimonii legibus dedisti."]

[Footnote 8: Ducange (Familiae Byzantinae, p. 44) bestows on him, after Zosimus, the name of Constantine; a name somewhat unlikely, as it was already occupied by the elder brother. That of Hannibalianus is mentioned in the Paschal Chronicle, and is approved by Tillemont. Hist. des Empereurs, tom. iv. p. 527.]

Crispus, the eldest son of Constantine, and the presumptive heir of the empire, is represented by impartial historians as an amiable and accomplished youth. The care of his education, or at least of his studies, was intrusted to Lactantius, the most eloquent of the Christians; a preceptor admirably qualified to form the taste, and the excite the virtues, of his illustrious disciple. [9] At the age of seventeen, Crispus was invested with the title of Caesar, and the administration of the Gallic provinces, where the inroads of the Germans gave him an early occasion of signalizing his military prowess. In the civil war which broke out soon afterwards, the father and son divided their powers; and this history has already celebrated the valor as well as conduct displayed by the latter, in forcing the straits of the Hellespont, so obstinately defended by the superior fleet of Lacinius. This naval victory contributed to determine the event of the war; and the names of Constantine and of Crispus were united in the joyful acclamations of their eastern subjects; who loudly proclaimed, that the world had been subdued, and was now governed, by an emperor endowed with every virtue; and by his illustrious son, a prince beloved of

Heaven, and the lively image of his father's perfections. The public favor, which seldom accompanies old age, diffused its lustre over the youth of Crispus. He deserved the esteem, and he engaged the affections, of the court, the army, and the people. The experienced merit of a reigning monarch is acknowledged by his subjects with reluctance, and frequently denied with partial and discontented murmurs; while, from the opening virtues of his successor, they fondly conceive the most unbounded hopes of private as well as public felicity. [10]

[Footnote 9: Jerom. in Chron. The poverty of Lactantius may be applied either to the praise of the disinterested philosopher, or to the shame of the unfeeling patron. See Tillemont, Mem. Ecclesiast. tom. vi. part 1. p. 345. Dupin, Bibliotheque Ecclesiast. tom. i. p. 205. Lardner's Credibility of the Gospel History, part ii. vol. vii. p. 66.]

[Footnote 10: Euseb. Hist. Ecclesiast. l. x. c. 9. Eutropius (x. 6) styles him "egregium virum;" and Julian (Orat. i.) very plainly alludes to the exploits of Crispus in the civil war. See Spanheim, Comment. p. 92.]

This dangerous popularity soon excited the attention of Constantine, who, both as a father and as a king, was impatient of an equal. Instead of attempting to secure the allegiance of his son by the generous ties of confidence and gratitude, he resolved to prevent the mischiefs which might be apprehended from dissatisfied ambition. Crispus soon had reason to complain, that while his infant brother Constantius was sent, with the title of Caesar, to reign over his peculiar department of the Gallic provinces, [11] he, a prince of mature years, who had performed such recent and signal services, instead of being raised to the superior rank of Augustus, was confined almost a prisoner to his father's court; and exposed, without power or defence, to every calumny which the malice of his enemies could suggest. Under such painful circumstances, the royal youth might not always be able to compose his behavior, or suppress his discontent; and we may be assured, that he was encompassed by a train of indiscreet or perfidious followers, who assiduously studied to inflame, and who were perhaps instructed to betray, the unguarded warmth of his resentment. An edict of Constantine, published about this time, manifestly indicates his real or affected suspicions, that a secret conspiracy had been formed against his person and government. By all the allurements of honors and rewards, he invites informers of every degree to accuse without exception his magistrates or ministers, his friends or his most intimate favorites, protesting, with a solemn asseveration, that he himself will listen to the charge, that he himself will revenge his injuries; and concluding with a prayer, which discovers some apprehension of danger, that the providence of the Supreme Being may still continue to protect the safety of the emperor and of the empire. [12]

[Footnote 11: Compare Idatius and the Paschal Chronicle, with Ammianus, (l, xiv. c. 5.) The year in which Constantius was created Caesar seems to be more accurately fixed by the two chronologists; but the historian who lived in his court could not be ignorant of the day of the anniversary. For the appointment of the new Caesar to the provinces of Gaul, see Julian, Orat. i. p. 12, Godefroy, Chronol. Legum, p. 26. and Blondel, de Primaute de l'Eglise, p. 1183.]

[Footnote 12: Cod. Theod. l. ix. tit. iv. Godefroy suspected the secret motives of this law. Comment. tom. iii. p. 9.]

The informers, who complied with so liberal an invitation, were sufficiently versed in the arts of courts to select the friends and adherents of Crispus as the guilty persons; nor is there any reason to distrust the veracity of the emperor, who had promised an ample measure of revenge and punishment. The policy of Constantine maintained, however, the same appearances of regard and confidence towards a son, whom he began to consider as his most irreconcilable enemy. Medals were struck with the customary vows for the long and auspicious reign of the young Caesar; [13] and as the people, who were not admitted into the secrets of the palace, still loved his virtues, and respected his dignity, a poet who solicits his recall from exile, adores with equal devotion the majesty of the father and that of the son. [14] The time was now arrived for celebrating the august ceremony of the twentieth year of the reign of Constantine; and the emperor, for that purpose, removed his court from Nicomedia to Rome, where the most splendid preparations had been made for his reception. Every eye, and every tongue, affected to express their sense of the general happiness, and the veil of ceremony and dissimulation was drawn for a while over the darkest designs of revenge and murder. [15] In the midst of the festival, the unfortunate Crispus was apprehended by order of the emperor, who laid aside the tenderness of a father, without assuming the equity of a judge. The examination was short and private; [16] and as it was thought decent to conceal the fate of the young prince from the eyes of the Roman people, he was sent under a strong guard to Pola, in Istria, where, soon afterwards, he was put to death, either by the hand of the executioner, or by the more gentle operations of poison. [17] The Caesar Licinius, a youth of amiable manners, was involved in the ruin of Crispus: [18] and the stern jealousy of Constantine was unmoved by the prayers and tears of his favorite sister, pleading for the life of a son, whose rank was his only crime, and whose loss she did not long survive. The story of these unhappy princes, the nature and evidence of their guilt, the forms of their trial, and the circumstances of their death, were buried in mysterious obscurity; and the courtly bishop, who has celebrated in an elaborate work the virtues and piety of his hero, observes a prudent silence on the subject of these tragic events. [19] Such haughty contempt for the opinion of mankind, whilst it imprints an indelible stain on the memory of Constantine, must remind us of the very different behavior of one of the greatest monarchs of the present age. The Czar Peter, in the full possession of despotic power, submitted to the judgment of Russia, of Europe, and of posterity, the reasons which had compelled him to subscribe the condemnation of a criminal, or at least of a degenerate son. [20]

[Footnote 13: Ducange, Fam. Byzant. p. 28. Tillemont, tom. iv. p. 610.]

[Footnote 14: His name was Porphyrius Optatianus. The date of his panegyric, written, according to the taste of the age, in vile acrostics, is settled by Scaliger ad Euseb. p. 250, Tillemont, tom. iv. p. 607, and Fabricius, Biblioth. Latin, l. iv. c. 1.]

[Footnote 15: Zosim. l. ii. p. 103. Godefroy, Chronol. Legum, p. 28.]

[Footnote 16: The elder Victor, who wrote under the next reign, speaks with becoming caution. "Natu grandior incertum qua causa, patris judicio occidisset." If we consult the succeeding writers, Eutropius, the younger Victor, Orosius, Jerom, Zosimus, Philostorgius, and Gregory of Tours, their knowledge will appear gradually to increase, as their means of information must have diminished—a circumstance which frequently occurs in historical disquisition.]

[Footnote 17: Ammianus (l. xiv. c. 11) uses the general expression of peremptum Codinus (p. 34) beheads the young prince; but Sidonius Apollinaris (Epistol. v. 8,) for the sake perhaps of an antithesis to Fausta's warm bath, chooses to administer a draught of cold poison.]

[Footnote 18: Sororis filium, commodae indolis juvenem. Eutropius, x. 6 May I not be permitted to conjecture that Crispus had married Helena the daughter of the emperor Licinius, and that on the happy delivery of the princess, in the year 322, a general pardon was granted by Constantine? See Ducange, Fam. Byzant. p. 47, and the law (l. ix. tit. xxxvii.) of the Theodosian code, which has so much embarrassed the interpreters. Godefroy, tom. iii. p. 267 Note: This conjecture is very doubtful. The obscurity of the law quoted from the Theodosian code scarcely allows any inference, and there is extant but one meda which can be attributed to a Helena, wife of Crispus.]

[Footnote 19: See the life of Constantine, particularly l. ii. c. 19, 20. Two hundred and fifty years afterwards Evagrius (l. iii. c. 41) deduced from the silence of Eusebius a vain argument against the reality of the fact.]

[Footnote 20: Histoire de Pierre le Grand, par Voltaire, part ii. c. 10.]

The innocence of Crispus was so universally acknowledged, that the modern Greeks, who adore the memory of their founder, are reduced to palliate the guilt of a parricide, which the common feelings of human nature forbade them to justify. They pretend, that as soon as the afflicted father discovered the falsehood of the accusation by which his credulity had been so fatally misled, he published to the world his repentance and remorse; that he mourned forty days, during which he abstained from the use of the bath, and all the ordinary comforts of life; and that, for the lasting instruction of posterity, he erected a golden statue of Crispus, with this memorable inscription: To my son, whom I unjustly condemned. [21] A tale so moral and so interesting would deserve to be supported by less exceptionable authority; but if we consult the more ancient and authentic writers, they will inform us, that the repentance of Constantine was manifested only in acts of blood and revenge; and that he atoned for the murder of an innocent son, by the execution, perhaps, of a guilty wife. They ascribe the misfortunes of Crispus to the arts of his step-mother Fausta, whose implacable hatred, or whose disappointed love, renewed in the palace of Constantine the ancient tragedy of Hippolitus and of Phaedra. [22] Like the daughter of Minos, the daughter of Maximian accused her son-in-law of an incestuous attempt on the chastity of his father's wife; and easily obtained, from the jealousy of the emperor, a sentence of death against a young prince, whom she considered with reason as the most formidable rival of her own children. But Helena, the aged mother of Constantine, lamented and revenged the untimely fate of her grandson Crispus; nor was it long before a real or pretended discovery was made, that Fausta herself entertained a criminal connection with a slave belonging to the Imperial stables. [23] Her condemnation and punishment were the instant consequences of the charge; and the adulteress was suffocated by the steam of a bath, which, for that purpose, had been heated to an extraordinary degree. [24] By some it will perhaps be thought, that the remembrance of a conjugal union of twenty years, and the honor of their common offspring, the destined heirs of the throne, might have softened the obdurate heart of Constantine, and persuaded him to suffer his wife, however guilty she might appear, to expiate her offences in a solitary prison. But it seems a superfluous labor to weigh the propriety, unless we could ascertain the truth, of this singular event, which is attended with some circumstances of doubt and perplexity. Those who have attacked, and those who have defended, the character of Constantine, have alike disregarded two very remarkable passages of two orations pronounced under the succeeding reign. The former celebrates the virtues, the beauty, and the fortune of the empress Fausta, the daughter, wife, sister, and mother of so many princes. [25] The latter asserts, in explicit terms, that the mother of the younger Constantine, who was slain three years after his father's death, survived to weep over the fate of her son. [26] Notwithstanding the positive testimony of several writers of the Pagan as well as of the Christian religion, there may still remain some reason to believe, or at least to suspect, that Fausta escaped the blind and suspicious cruelty of her husband. [26a] The deaths of a son and a nephew, with the execution of a great number of respectable, and perhaps innocent friends, [27] who were involved in their fall, may be sufficient, however, to justify the discontent of the Roman people, and to explain the satirical verses affixed to the palace gate, comparing the splendid and bloody reigns of Constantine and Nero. [28]

[Footnote 21: In order to prove that the statue was erected by Constantine, and afterwards concealed by the malice of the Arians, Codinus very readily creates (p. 34) two witnesses, Hippolitus, and the younger Herodotus, to whose imaginary histories he appeals with unblushing confidence.]

[Footnote 22: Zosimus (l. ii. p. 103) may be considered as our original. The ingenuity of the moderns, assisted by a few hints from the ancients, has illustrated and improved his obscure and imperfect narrative.]

[Footnote 23: Philostorgius, l. ii. c. 4. Zosimus (l. ii. p. 104, 116) imputes to Constantine the death of two wives, of the innocent Fausta, and of an adulteress, who was the mother of his three successors. According to Jerom, three or four years elapsed between the death of Crispus and that of Fausta. The elder Victor is prudently silent.]

[Footnote 24: If Fausta was put to death, it is reasonable to believe that the private apartments of the palace were the scene of her execution. The orator Chrysostom indulges his fancy by exposing the naked desert mountain to be devoured by wild beasts.]

[Footnote 25: Julian. Orat. i. He seems to call her the mother of Crispus. She might assume that title by adoption. At least, she was not considered as his mortal enemy. Julian compares the fortune of Fausta with that of Parysatis, the Persian queen. A Roman would have more naturally recollected the second Agrippina:

Et moi, qui sur le trone ai suivi mes ancetres:
Moi, fille, femme, soeur, et mere de vos maitres.]

[Footnote 26: Monod. in Constantin. Jun. c. 4, ad Calcem Eutrop. edit. Havercamp. The orator styles her the most divine and pious of queens.]

[Footnote 26a: Manso (Leben Constantins, p. 65) treats this inference o: Gibbon, and the authorities to which he appeals, with too much contempt, considering the general scantiness of proof on this curious question—M.]

[Footnote 27: Interfecit numerosos amicos. Eutrop. xx. 6.]

[Footnote 28: Saturni aurea saecula quis requirat? Sunt haec gemmea, sed Neroniana. Sidon. Apollinar. v. 8. —It is somewhat singular that these satirical lines should be attributed, not to an obscure libeller, or a disappointed patriot, but to Ablavius, prime minister and favorite of the emperor. We may now perceive that the imprecations of the Roman people were dictated by humanity, as well as by superstition. Zosim. l. ii. p. 105.]

PART II

By the death of Crispus, the inheritance of the empire seemed to devolve on the three sons of Fausta, who have been already mentioned under the names of Constantine, of Constantius, and of Constans. These young princes were successively invested with the title of Caesar; and the dates of their promotion may be referred to the tenth, the twentieth, and the thirtieth years of the reign of their father. [29] This conduct, though it tended to multiply the future masters of the Roman world, might be excused by the partiality of paternal affection; but it is not so easy to understand the motives of the emperor, when he endangered the safety both of his family and of his people, by the unnecessary elevation of his two nephews, Dalmatius and Hannibalianus. The former was raised, by the title of Caesar, to an equality with his cousins. In favor of the latter, Constantine invented the new and singular appellation of Nobilissimus; [30] to which he annexed the flattering distinction of a robe of purple and gold. But of the whole series of Roman princes in any age of the empire, Hannibalianus alone was distinguished by the title of King; a name which the subjects of Tiberius would have detested, as the profane and cruel insult of capricious tyranny. The use of such a title, even as it appears under the reign of Constantine, is a strange and unconnected fact, which can scarcely be admitted on the joint authority of Imperial medals and contemporary writers. [31] [31a]

[Footnote 29: Euseb. Orat. in Constantin. c. 3. These dates are sufficiently correct to justify the orator.]

[Footnote 30: Zosim. l. ii. p. 117. Under the predecessors of Constantine, No bilissimus was a vague epithet, rather than a legal and determined title.]

[Footnote 31: Adstruunt nummi veteres ac singulares. Spanheim de Usu Numismat. Dissertat. xii. vol. ii. p. 357. Ammianus speaks of this Roman king (l. xiv. c. l, and Valesius ad loc.) The Valesian fragment styles him King of kings; and the Paschal Chronicle acquires the weight of Latin evidence.]

[Footnote 31a: Hannibalianus is always designated in these authors by the title of king. There still exist medals struck to his honor, on which the same title is found, Fl. Hannibaliano Regi. See Eckhel, Doct. Num. t. viii. 204. Armeniam nationesque circum socias habebat, says Aur. Victor, p. 225. The writer means the Lesser Armenia. Though it is not possible to question a fact supported by such respectable authorities, Gibbon considers it inexplicable and incredible. It is a strange abuse of the privilege of doubting, to refuse all belief in a fact of such little importance in itself, and attested thus formally by contemporary authors and public monuments. St. Martin note to Le Beau i. 341—M.]

The whole empire was deeply interested in the education of these five youths, the acknowledged successors of Constantine. The exercise of the body prepared them for the fatigues of war and the duties of active life. Those who occasionally mention the education or talents of Constantius, allow that he excelled in the gymnastic arts of leaping and running that he was a dexterous archer, a skilful horseman, and a master of all the different weapons used in the service either of the cavalry or of the infantry. [32] The same assiduous cultivation was bestowed, though not perhaps with equal success, to improve the minds of the sons and nephews of Constantine. [33] The most celebrated professors of the Christian faith, of the Grecian philosophy, and of the Roman jurisprudence, were invited by the liberality of the emperor, who reserved for himself the important task of instructing the royal youths in the science of government, and the knowledge of mankind. But the genius of Constantine himself had been formed by adversity and experience. In the free intercourse of private life, and amidst the dangers of the court of Galerius, he had learned to command his own passions, to encounter those of his equals, and to depend for his present safety and future greatness on the prudence and firmness of his personal conduct. His destined successors had the misfortune of being born and educated in the imperial purple. Incessantly surrounded with a train of flatterers, they passed their youth in the enjoyment of luxury, and the expectation of a throne; nor would the dignity of their rank permit them to descend from that elevated station from whence the various characters of human nature appear to wear a smooth and uniform aspect. The indulgence of Constantine admitted them, at a very tender age, to share the administration of the empire; and they studied the art of reigning, at the expense of the people intrusted to their care. The younger Constantine was appointed to hold his court in Gaul; and his brother Constantius exchanged that department, the ancient patrimony of their father, for the more opulent, but less martial, countries of the East. Italy, the Western Illyricum, and Africa, were accustomed to revere Constans, the third of his sons, as the representative of the great Constantine. He fixed Dalmatius on the Gothic frontier, to which he annexed the government of Thrace, Macedonia, and Greece. The city of Caesarea was chosen for the residence of Hannibalianus; and the provinces of Pontus, Cappadocia, and the Lesser Armenia, were destined to form the extent of his new kingdom. For each of these princes a suitable establishment was provided. A just proportion of guards, of legions, and of auxiliaries, was allotted for their respective dignity and defence. The ministers and generals, who were placed about their persons, were such as Constantine could trust to assist, and even to control, these youthful sovereigns in the exercise of their delegated power. As they advanced in years and experience, the limits of their authority were insensibly enlarged: but the emperor always reserved for himself the title of Augustus; and while he showed the Caesars to the armies and provinces, he maintained every part of the empire in equal obedience to its supreme head. [34] The tranquillity of the last fourteen years of his reign was scarcely interrupted by the contemptible insurrection of a camel-driver in the Island of Cyprus, [35] or by the active part which the policy of Constantine engaged him to assume in the wars of the Goths and Sarmatians.

[Footnote 32: His dexterity in martial exercises is celebrated by Julian, (Orat. i. p. 11, Orat. ii. p. 53,) and allowed by Ammianus, (l. xxi. c. 16.)]

[Footnote 33: Euseb. in Vit. Constantin. l. iv. c. 51. Julian, Orat. i. p. 11-16, with Spanheim's elaborate Commentary. Libanius, Orat. iii. p. 109. Constantius studied with laudable diligence; but the dulness of his fancy prevented him from succeeding in the art of poetry, or even of rhetoric.]

[Footnote 34: Eusebius, (l. iv. c. 51, 52,) with a design of exalting the authority and glory of Constantine, affirms, that he divided the Roman empire as a private citizen might have divided his patrimony. His distribution of the provinces may be collected from Eutropius, the two Victors and the Valesian fragment.]

[Footnote 35: Calocerus, the obscure leader of this rebellion, or rather tumult, was apprehended and burnt alive in the market-place of Tarsus, by the vigilance of Dalmatius. See the elder Victor, the Chronicle of Jerom, and the doubtful traditions of Theophanes and Cedrenus.]

Among the different branches of the human race, the Sarmatians form a very remarkable shade; as they seem to unite the manners of the Asiatic barbarians with the figure and complexion of the ancient inhabitants of Europe. According to the various accidents of peace and war, of alliance or conquest, the Sarmatians were sometimes confined to the banks of the Tanais, and they sometimes spread themselves over the immense plains which lie between the Vistula and the Volga. [36] The care of their numerous flocks and herds, the pursuit of game, and the exercises of war, or rather of rapine, directed the vagrant motions of the Sarmatians. The movable camps or cities, the ordinary residence of their wives and children, consisted only of large wagons drawn by oxen, and covered in the form of tents. The military strength of the nation was composed of cavalry; and the custom of their warriors, to lead in their hand one or two spare horses, enabled them to advance and to retreat with a rapid diligence, which surprised the security, and eluded the pursuit, of a distant enemy. [37] Their poverty of iron prompted their rude industry to invent a sort of cuirass, which was capable of resisting a sword or javelin, though it was formed only of horses' hoofs, cut into thin and polished slices, carefully laid over each other in the manner of scales or feathers, and strongly sewed upon an under garment of coarse linen. [38] The offensive arms of the Sarmatians were short daggers, long lances, and a weighty bow with a quiver of arrows. They were reduced to the necessity of employing fish-bones for the points of their weapons; but the custom of dipping them in a venomous liquor, that poisoned the wounds which they inflicted, is alone sufficient to prove the most savage manners, since a people impressed with a sense of humanity would have abhorred so cruel a practice, and a nation skilled in the arts of war would have disdained so impotent a resource. [39] Whenever these Barbarians issued from their deserts in quest of prey, their shaggy beards, uncombed locks, the furs with which they were covered from head to foot, and their fierce countenances, which seemed to express the innate cruelty of their minds, inspired the more civilized provincials of Rome with horror and dismay.

[Footnote 36: Cellarius has collected the opinions of the ancients concerning the European and Asiatic Sarmatia; and M. D'Anville has applied them to modern geography with the skill and accuracy which always distinguish that excellent writer.]

[Footnote 37: Ammian. l. xvii. c. 12. The Sarmatian horses were castrated to prevent the mischievous accidents which might happen from the noisy and ungovernable passions of the males.]

[Footnote 38: Pausanius, l. i. p. 50,. edit. Kuhn. That inquisitive traveller had carefully examined a Sarmatian cuirass, which was preserved in the temple of Aesculapius at Athens.]

[Footnote 39: Aspicis et mitti sub adunco toxica ferro, Et telum causas mortis habere duas. Ovid, ex Ponto, l. iv. ep. 7, ver. 7—See in the Recherches sur les Americains, tom. ii. p. 236—271, a very curious dissertation on poisoned darts. The venom was commonly extracted from the vegetable reign: but that employed by the Scythians appears to have been drawn from the viper, and a mixture of human blood.]

The use of poisoned arms, which has been spread over both worlds, never preserved a savage tribe from the arms of a disciplined enemy. The tender Ovid, after a youth spent in the enjoyment of fame and luxury, was condemned to a hopeless exile on the frozen banks of the Danube, where he was exposed, almost without defence, to the fury of these monsters of the desert, with whose stern spirits he feared that his gentle shade might hereafter be confounded. In his pathetic, but sometimes unmanly lamentations, [40] he describes in the most lively colors the dress and manners, the arms and inroads, of the Getae and Sarmatians, who were associated for the purposes of destruction; and from the accounts of history there is some reason to believe that these Sarmatians were the Jazygae, one of the most numerous and warlike tribes of the nation. The allurements of plenty engaged them to seek a permanent establishment on the frontiers of the empire. Soon after the reign of Augustus, they obliged the Dacians, who subsisted by fishing on the banks of the River Teyss or Tibiscus, to retire into the hilly country, and to abandon to the victorious Sarmatians the fertile plains of the Upper Hungary, which are bounded by the course of the Danube and the semicircular enclosure of the Carpathian Mountains. [41] In this advantageous position, they watched or suspended the moment of attack, as they were provoked by injuries or appeased by presents; they gradually acquired the skill of using more dangerous weapons, and although the Sarmatians did not illustrate their name by any memorable exploits, they occasionally assisted their eastern and western neighbors, the Goths and the Germans, with a formidable body of cavalry. They lived under the irregular aristocracy of their chieftains: [42] but after they had received into their bosom the fugitive Vandals, who yielded to the pressure of the Gothic power, they seem to have chosen a king from that nation, and from the illustrious race of the Astingi, who had formerly dwelt on the hores of the northern ocean. [43]

[Footnote 40: The nine books of Poetical Epistles which Ovid composed during the seven first years of his melancholy exile, possess, beside the merit of elegance, a double value. They exhibit a picture of the human mind under very singular circumstances; and they contain many curious observations, which no Roman except Ovid, could have an opportunity of making. Every circumstance which tends to illustrate the history of the Barbarians, has been drawn together by the very accurate Count de Buat. Hist. Ancienne des Peuples de l'Europe, tom. iv. c. xvi. p. 286-317]

[Footnote 41: The Sarmatian Jazygae were settled on the banks of Pathissus or Tibiscus, when Pliny, in the year 79, published his Natural History. See l. iv. c. 25. In the time of Strabo and Ovid, sixty or seventy years before, they appear to have inhabited beyond the Getae, along the coast of the Euxine.]

[Footnote 42: Principes Sarmaturum Jazygum penes quos civitatis regimen plebem quoque et vim equitum, qua sola valent, offerebant. Tacit. Hist. iii. p. 5. This offer was made in the civil war between Vitellino and Vespasian.]

[Footnote 43: This hypothesis of a Vandal king reigning over Sarmatian subjects, seems necessary to reconcile the Goth Jornandes with the Greek and Latin historians of Constantine. It may be observed that Isidore, who lived in Spain under the dominion of the Goths, gives them for enemies, not the Vandals, but the Sarmatians. See his Chronicle in Grotius, p. 709. Note: I have already noticed the confusion which must necessarily arise in history, when names purely geographical, as this of Sarmatia, are taken for historical names belonging to a single nation. We perceive it here; it has forced Gibbon to suppose, without any reason but the necessity of extricating himself from his perplexity, that the Sarmatians had taken a king from among the Vandals; a supposition entirely contrary to the usages of Barbarians Dacia, at this period, was occupied, not by Sarmatians, who have never formed a distinct race, but by Vandals, whom the ancients have often confounded under the general term Sarmatians. See Gatterer's Welt-Geschiehte p. 464—G.]

This motive of enmity must have inflamed the subjects of contention, which perpetually arise on the confines of warlike and independent nations. The Vandal princes were stimulated by fear and revenge; the Gothic kings aspired to extend their dominion from the Euxine to the frontiers of Germany; and the waters of the Maros, a small river which falls into the Teyss, were stained with the blood of the contending Barbarians. After some experience of the superior strength and numbers of their adversaries, the Sarmatians implored the protection of the Roman monarch, who beheld with pleasure the discord of the nations, but who was justly alarmed by the progress of the Gothic arms. As soon as Constantine had declared himself in favor of the weaker party, the haughty Araric, king of the Goths, instead of expecting the attack of the legions, boldly passed the Danube, and spread terror and devastation through the province of Maesia.

To oppose the inroad of this destroying host, the aged emperor took the field in person; but on this occasion either his conduct or his fortune betrayed the glory which he had acquired in so many foreign and domestic wars. He had the mortification of seeing his troops fly before an inconsiderable detachment of the Barbarians, who pursued them to the edge of their fortified camp, and obliged him to consult his safety by a precipitate and ignominious retreat. [43a] The event of a second and more successful action retrieved the honor of the Roman name; and the powers of art and discipline prevailed, after an obstinate contest, over the efforts of irregular valor. The broken army of the Goths abandoned the field of battle, the wasted province, and the passage of the Danube: and although the eldest of the sons of Constantine was permitted to supply the place of his father, the merit of the victory, which diffused universal joy, was ascribed to the auspicious counsels of the emperor himself.

[Footnote 43a: Gibbon states, that Constantine was defeated by the Goths in a first battle. No ancient author mentions such an event. It is, no doubt, a mistake in Gibbon. St Martin, note to Le Beau. i. 324—M.]

He contributed at least to improve this advantage, by his negotiations with the free and warlike people of Chersonesus, [44] whose capital, situate on the western coast of the Tauric or Crimaean peninsula, still retained some vestiges of a Grecian colony, and was governed by a perpetual magistrate, assisted by a council of senators, emphatically styled the Fathers of the City.

The Chersonites were animated against the Goths, by the memory of the wars, which, in the preceding century, they had maintained with unequal forces against the invaders of their country. They were connected with the Romans by the mutual benefits of commerce; as they were supplied from the provinces of Asia with corn and manufactures, which they purchased with their only productions, salt, wax, and hides. Obedient to the requisition of Constantine, they prepared, under the conduct of their magistrate Diogenes, a considerable army, of which the principal strength consisted in cross-bows and military chariots. The speedy march and intrepid attack of the Chersonites, by diverting the attention of the Goths, assisted the operations of the Imperial generals. The Goths, vanquished on every side, were driven into the mountains, where, in the course of a severe campaign, above a hundred thousand were computed to have perished by cold and hunger Peace was at length granted to their humble supplications; the eldest son of Araric was accepted as the most valuable hostage; and Constantine endeavored to convince their chiefs, by a liberal distribution of honors and rewards, how far the friendship of the Romans was preferable to their enmity. In the expressions of his gratitude towards the faithful Chersonites, the emperor was still more magnificent. The pride of the nation was gratified by the splendid and almost royal decorations bestowed on their magistrate and his successors. A perpetual exemption from all duties was stipulated for their vessels which traded to the ports of the Black Sea. A regular subsidy was promised, of iron, corn, oil, and of every supply which could be useful either in peace or war. But it was thought that the Sarmatians were sufficiently rewarded by their deliverance from impending ruin; and the emperor, perhaps with too strict an economy, deducted some part of the expenses of the war from the customary gratifications which were allowed to that turbulent nation.

[Footnote 44: I may stand in need of some apology for having used, without scruple, the authority of Constantine Porphyrogenitus, in all that relates to the wars and negotiations of the Chersonites. I am aware that he was a Greek of the tenth century, and that his accounts of ancient history are frequently confused and fabulous. But on this occasion his narrative is, for the most part, consistent and probable nor is there much difficulty in conceiving that an emperor might have access to some secret archives, which had escaped the diligence of meaner historians. For the situation and history of Chersone, see Peyssonel, des Peuples barbares qui ont habite les Bords du Danube, c. xvi. 84-90. —Gibbon has confounded the inhabitants of the city of Cherson, the ancient Chersonesus, with the people of the Chersonesus Taurica. If he had read with more attention the chapter of Constantius Porphyrogenitus, from which this narrative is derived, he would have seen that the author clearly distinguishes the republic of Cherson from the rest of the Tauric Peninsula, then possessed by the kings of the Cimmerian Bosphorus, and that the city of Cherson alone furnished succors to the Romans. The English historian is also mistaken in saying that the Stephanephoros of the Chersonites was a perpetual magistrate; since it is easy to discover from the great number of Stephanephoroi mentioned by Constantine Porphyrogenitus, that they were annual magistrates, like almost all those which governed the Grecian republics. St. Martin, note to Le Beau i. 326—M.]

Exasperated by this apparent neglect, the Sarmatians soon forgot, with the levity of barbarians, the services which they had so lately received, and the dangers which still threatened their safety. Their inroads on the territory of the empire provoked the indignation of Constantine to leave them to their fate; and he no longer opposed the ambition of Geberic, a renowned warrior, who had recently ascended the Gothic throne. Wisumar, the Vandal king, whilst alone, and unassisted, he defended his dominions with undaunted courage, was vanquished and slain in a decisive battle, which swept away the flower of the Sarmatian youth. [44a] The remainder of the nation embraced the desperate expedient of arming their slaves, a hardy race of hunters and herdsmen, by whose tumultuary aid they revenged their defeat, and expelled the invader from their confines. But they soon discovered that they had exchanged a foreign for a domestic enemy, more dangerous and more implacable. Enraged by their former servitude, elated by their present glory, the slaves, under the name of Limigantes, claimed and usurped the possession of the country which they had saved. Their masters, unable to withstand the ungoverned fury of the populace, preferred the hardships of exile to the tyranny of their servants. Some of the fugitive Sarmatians solicited a less ignominious dependence, under the hostile standard of the Goths. A more numerous band retired beyond the Carpathian Mountains, among the Quadi, their German allies, and were easily admitted to share a superfluous waste of uncultivated land. But the far greater part of the distressed nation turned their eyes towards the fruitful provinces of Rome. Imploring the protection and forgiveness of the emperor, they solemnly promised, as subjects in peace, and as soldiers in war, the most inviolable fidelity to the empire which should graciously receive them into its bosom. According to the maxims adopted by Probus and his successors, the offers of this barbarian colony were eagerly accepted; and a competent portion of lands in the provinces of Pannonia, Thrace, Macedonia, and Italy, were immediately assigned for the habitation and subsistence of three hundred thousand Sarmatians. [45] [45a]

[Footnote 44a: Gibbon supposes that this war took place because Constantine had deducted a part of the customary gratifications, granted by his predecessors to the Sarmatians. Nothing of this kind appears in the authors. We see, on the contrary, that after his victory, and to punish the Sarmatia is for the ravages they had committed, he withheld the sums which it had been the custom to bestow. St. Martin, note to Le Beau, i. 327—M.]

[Footnote 45: The Gothic and Sarmatian wars are related in so broken and imperfect a manner, that I have been obliged to compare the following writers, who mutually supply, correct, and illustrate each other. Those who will take the same trouble, may acquire a right of criticizing my narrative. Ammianus, l. xvii. c. 12. Anonym. Valesian. p. 715. Eutropius, x. 7. Sextus Rufus de Provinciis, c. 26. Julian Orat. i. p. 9, and Spanheim, Comment. p. 94. Hieronym. in Chron. Euseb. in Vit. Constantin. l. iv. c. 6. Socrates, l. i. c. 18. Sozomen, l. i. c. 8. Zosimus, l. ii. p. 108. Jornandes de Reb. Geticis, c. 22. Isidorus in Chron. p. 709; in Hist. Gothorum Grotii. Constantin. Porphyrogenitus de Administrat. Imperii, c. 53, p. 208, edit. Meursii.]

[Footnote 45a: Compare, on this very obscure but remarkable war, Manso, Leben Coa xantlus, p. 195—M.]

By chastising the pride of the Goths, and by accepting the homage of a suppliant nation, Constantine asserted the majesty of the Roman empire; and the ambassadors of Aethiopia, Persia, and the most remote countries of India, congratulated the peace and prosperity of his government. [46] If he reckoned, among the favors of fortune, the death of his eldest son, of his nephew, and perhaps of his wife, he enjoyed an uninterrupted flow of private as well as public felicity, till the thirtieth year of his reign; a period which none of his predecessors, since Augustus, had been permitted to celebrate. Constantine survived that solemn festival about ten months; and at the mature age of sixty-four, after a short illness, he ended his memorable life at the palace of Aquyrion, in the suburbs of Nicomedia, whither he had retired for the benefit of the air, and with the hope of recruiting his exhausted strength by the use of the warm baths. The excessive demonstrations of grief, or at least of mourning, surpassed whatever had been practised on any former occasion. Notwithstanding the claims of the senate and people of ancient Rome, the corpse of the deceased emperor, according to his last request, was transported to the city, which was destined to preserve the name and memory of its founder. The body of Constantine adorned with the vain symbols of greatness, the purple and diadem, was deposited on a golden bed in one of the apartments of the palace, which for that purpose had been splendidly furnished and illuminated. The forms of the court were strictly maintained. Every day, at the appointed hours, the principal officers of the state, the army, and the household, approaching the person of their sovereign with bended knees and a composed countenance, offered their respectful homage as seriously as if he had been still alive. From motives of policy, this theatrical representation was for some time continued; nor could flattery neglect the opportunity of remarking that Constantine alone, by the peculiar indulgence of Heaven, had reigned after his death. [47]

[Footnote 46: Eusebius (in Vit. Const. l. iv. c. 50) remarks three circumstances relative to these Indians. 1. They came from the shores of the eastern ocean; a description which might be applied to the coast of China or Coromandel. 2. They presented shining gems, and unknown animals. 3. They protested their kings had erected statues to represent the supreme majesty of Constantine.]

[Footnote 47: Funus relatum in urbem sui nominis, quod sane P. R. aegerrime tulit. Aurelius Victor. Constantine prepared for himself a stately tomb in the church of the Holy Apostles. Euseb. l. iv. c. 60. The best, and indeed almost the only account of the sickness, death, and funeral of Constantine, is contained in the fourth book of his Life by Eusebius.]

But this reign could subsist only in empty pageantry; and it was soon discovered that the will of the most absolute monarch is seldom obeyed, when his subjects have no longer anything to hope from his favor, or to dread from his resentment. The same ministers and generals, who bowed with such referential awe before the inanimate corpse of their deceased sovereign, were engaged in secret consultations to exclude his two nephews, Dalmatius and Hannibalianus, from the share which he had assigned them in the succession of the empire. We are too imperfectly acquainted with the court of Constantine to form any judgment of the real motives which influenced the leaders of the conspiracy; unless we should suppose that they were actuated by a spirit of jealousy and revenge against the praefect Ablavius, a proud favorite, who had long directed the counsels and abused the confidence of the late emperor. The arguments, by which they solicited the concurrence of the soldiers and people, are of a more obvious nature; and they might with decency, as well as truth, insist on the superior rank of the children of Constantine, the danger of multiplying the number of sovereigns, and the impending mischiefs which threatened the republic, from the discord of so many rival princes, who were not connected by the tender sympathy of fraternal affection. The intrigue was conducted with zeal and secrecy, till a loud and unanimous declaration was procured from the troops, that they would suffer none except the sons of their lamented monarch to reign over the Roman empire. [48] The younger Dalmatius, who was united with his collateral relations by the ties of friendship and interest, is allowed to have inherited a considerable share of the abilities of the great Constantine; but, on this occasion, he does not appear to have concerted any measure for supporting, by arms, the just claims which himself and his royal brother derived from the liberality of their uncle. Astonished and overwhelmed by the tide of popular fury, they seem to have remained, without the power of flight or of resistance, in the hands of their implacable enemies. Their fate was suspended till the arrival of Constantius, the second, and perhaps the most favored, of the sons of Constantine.

[Footnote 48: Eusebius (l. iv. c. 6) terminates his narrative by this loyal declaration of the troops, and avoids all the invidious circumstances of the subsequent massacre.]

[Footnote 49: The character of Dalmatius is advantageously, though concisely drawn by Eutropius. (x. 9.) Dalmatius Ceasar prosperrima indole, neque patrou absimilis, haud multo post oppressus est factione militari. As both Jerom and the Alexandrian Chronicle mention the third year of the Ceasar, which did not commence till the 18th or 24th of September, A. D. 337, it is certain that these military factions continued above four months.]

PART III

The voice of the dying emperor had recommended the care of his funeral to the piety of Constantius; and that prince, by the vicinity of his eastern station, could easily prevent the diligence of his brothers, who resided in their distant government of Italy and Gaul. As soon as he had taken possession of the palace of Constantinople, his first care was to remove the apprehensions of his kinsmen, by a solemn oath which he pledged for their security. His next employment was to find some specious pretence which might release his conscience from the obligation of an imprudent promise. The arts of fraud were made subservient to the designs of cruelty; and a manifest forgery was attested by a person of the most sacred character. From the hands of the Bishop of Nicomedia, Constantius received a fatal scroll, affirmed to be the genuine testament of his father; in which the emperor expressed his suspicions that he had been poisoned by his brothers; and conjured his sons to revenge his death, and to consult their own safety, by the punishment of the guilty. [50] Whatever reasons might have been alleged by these unfortunate princes to defend their life and honor against so incredible an accusation, they were silenced by the furious clamors of the soldiers, who declared themselves, at once, their enemies, their judges, and their executioners. The spirit, and even the forms of legal proceedings were repeatedly violated in a promiscuous massacre; which involved the two uncles of Constantius, seven of his cousins, of whom Dalmatius and Hannibalianus were the most illustrious, the Patrician Optatus, who had married a sister of the late emperor, and the Praefect Ablavius, whose power and riches had inspired him with some hopes of obtaining the purple. If it were necessary to aggravate the horrors of this bloody scene, we might add, that Constantius himself had espoused the daughter of his uncle Julius, and that he had bestowed his sister in marriage on his cousin Hannibalianus. These alliances, which the policy of Constantine, regardless of the public prejudice, [51] had formed between the several branches of the Imperial house, served only to convince mankind, that these princes were as cold to the endearments of conjugal affection, as they were insensible to the ties of consanguinity, and the moving entreaties of youth and innocence. Of so numerous a family, Gallus and Julian alone, the two youngest children of Julius Constantius, were saved from the hands of the assassins, till their rage, satiated with slaughter, had in some measure subsided. The emperor Constantius, who, in the absence of his brothers, was the most obnoxious to guilt and reproach, discovered, on some future occasions, a faint and transient remorse for those cruelties which the perfidious counsels of his ministers, and the irresistible violence of the troops, had extorted from his unexperienced youth. [52]

[Footnote 50: I have related this singular anecdote on the authority of Philostorgius, l. ii. c. 16. But if such a pretext was ever used by Constantius and his adherents, it was laid aside with contempt, as soon as it served their immediate purpose. Athanasius (tom. i. p. 856) mention the oath which Constantius had taken for the security of his kinsmen. —The authority of Philostorgius is so suspicious, as not to be sufficient to establish this fact, which Gibbon has inserted in his history as certain, while in the note he appears to doubt it—G.]

[Footnote 51: Conjugia sobrinarum diu ignorata, tempore addito percrebuisse. Tacit. Annal. xii. 6, and Lipsius ad loc. The repeal of the ancient law, and the practice of five hundred years, were insufficient to eradicate the prejudices of the Romans, who still considered the marriages of cousins-german as a species of imperfect incest. (Augustin de Civitate Dei, xv. 6;) and Julian, whose mind was biased by superstition and resentment, stigmatizes these unnatural alliances between his own cousins with the opprobrious epithet (Orat. vii. p. 228.). The jurisprudence of the canons has since received and enforced this prohibition, without being able to introduce it either into the civil or the common law of Europe. See on the subject of these marriages, Taylor's Civil Law, p. 331. Brouer de Jure Connub. l. ii. c. 12. Hericourt des Loix Ecclesiastiques, part iii. c. 5. Fleury, Institutions du Droit Canonique, tom. i. p. 331. Paris, 1767, and Fra Paolo, Istoria del Concilio Trident, l. viii.]

[Footnote 52: Julian (ad S. P.. Q. Athen. p. 270) charges his cousin Constantius with the whole guilt of a massacre, from which he himself so narrowly escaped. His assertion is confirmed by Athanasius, who, for reasons of a very different nature, was not less an enemy of Constantius, (tom. i. p. 856.) Zosimus joins in the same accusation. But the three abbreviators, Eutropius and the Victors, use very qualifying expressions: "sinente potius quam jubente;" "incertum quo suasore;" "vi militum."]

The massacre of the Flavian race was succeeded by a new division of the provinces; which was ratified in a personal interview of the three brothers. Constantine, the eldest of the Caesars, obtained, with a certain preeminence of rank, the possession of the new capital, which bore his own name and that of his father. Thrace, and the countries of the East, were allotted for the patrimony of Constantius; and Constans was acknowledged as the lawful sovereign of Italy, Africa, and the Western Illyricum. The armies submitted to their hereditary right; and they condescended, after some delay, to accept from the Roman senate the title of Augustus. When they first assumed the reins of government, the eldest of these princes was twenty-one, the second twenty, and the third only seventeen, years of age. [53]

[Footnote 53: Euseb. in Vit. Constantin. l. iv. c. 69. Zosimus, l. ii. p. 117. Idat. in Chron. See two notes of Tillemont, Hist. des Empereurs, tom. iv. p. 1086-1091. The reign of the eldest brother at Constantinople is noticed only in the Alexandrian Chronicle.]

While the martial nations of Europe followed the standards of his brothers, Constantius, at the head of the effeminate troops of Asia, was left to sustain the weight of the Persian war. At the decease of Constantine, the throne of the East was filled by Sapor, son of Hormouz, or Hormisdas, and grandson of Narses, who, after the victory of Galerius, had humbly confessed the superiority of the Roman power. Although Sapor was in the thirtieth year of his long reign, he was still in the vigor of youth, as the date of his accession, by a very strange fatality, had preceded that of his birth. The wife of Hormouz remained pregnant at the time of her husband's death; and the uncertainty of the sex, as well as of the event, excited the ambitious hopes of the princes of the house of Sassan. The apprehensions of civil war were at length removed, by the positive assurance of the Magi, that the widow of Hormouz had conceived, and would safely produce a son. Obedient to the voice of superstition, the Persians prepared, without delay, the ceremony of his coronation.

A royal bed, on which the queen lay in state, was exhibited in the midst of the palace; the diadem was placed on the spot, which might be supposed to conceal the future heir of Artaxerxes, and the prostrate satraps adored the majesty of their invisible and insensible sovereign. [54] If any credit can be given to this marvellous tale, which seems, however, to be countenanced by the manners of the people, and by the extraordinary duration of his reign, we must admire not only the fortune, but the genius, of Sapor. In the soft, sequestered education of a Persian harem, the royal youth could discover the importance of exercising the vigor of his mind and body; and, by his personal merit, deserved a throne, on which he had been seated, while he was yet unconscious of the duties and temptations of absolute power. His minority was exposed to the almost inevitable calamities of domestic discord; his capital was surprised and plundered by Thair, a powerful king of Yemen, or Arabia; and the majesty of the royal family was degraded by the captivity of a princess, the sister of the deceased king. But as soon as Sapor attained the age of manhood, the presumptuous Thair, his nation, and his country, fell beneath the first effort of the young warrior; who used his victory with so judicious a mixture of rigor and clemency, that he obtained from the fears and gratitude of the Arabs the title of Dhoulacnaf, or protector of the nation. [55] [55a]

[Footnote 54: Agathias, who lived in the sixth century, is the author of this story, (l. iv. p. 135, edit. Louvre.) He derived his information from some extracts of the Persian Chronicles, obtained and translated by the interpreter Sergius, during his embassy at that country. The coronation of the mother of Sapor is likewise mentioned by Snikard, (Tarikh. p. 116,) and D'Herbelot (Bibliotheque Orientale, p. 703.) —The author of the Zenut-ul-Tarikh states, that the lady herself affirmed her belief of this from the extraordinary liveliness of the infant, and its lying on the right side. Those who are sage on such subjects must determine what right she had to be positive from these symptoms. Malcolm, Hist. of Persia, i 83—M.]

[Footnote 55: D'Herbelot, Bibliotheque Orientale, p. 764.]

[Footnote 55a: Gibbon, according to Sir J. Malcolm, has greatly mistaken the derivation of this name; it means Zoolaktaf, the Lord of the Shoulders, from his directing the shoulders of his captives to be pierced and then dislocated by a string passed through them. Eastern authors are agreed with respect to the origin of this title. Malcolm, i. 84. Gibbon took his derivation from D'Herbelot, who gives both, the latter on the authority of the Leb. Tarikh—M.]

The ambition of the Persian, to whom his enemies ascribe the virtues of a soldier and a statesman, was animated by the desire of revenging the disgrace of his fathers, and of wresting from the hands of the Romans the five provinces beyond the Tigris. The military fame of Constantine, and the real or apparent strength of his government, suspended the attack; and while the hostile conduct of Sapor provoked the resentment, his artful negotiations amused the patience of the Imperial court. The death of Constantine was the signal of war, [56] and the actual condition of the Syrian and Armenian frontier seemed to encourage the Persians by the prospect of a rich spoil and an easy conquest. The example of the massacres of the palace diffused a spirit of licentiousness and sedition among the troops of the East, who were no longer restrained by their habits of obedience to a veteran commander. By the prudence of Constantius, who, from the interview with his brothers in Pannonia, immediately hastened to the banks of the Euphrates, the legions were gradually restored to a sense of duty and discipline; but the season of anarchy had permitted Sapor to form the siege of Nisibis, and to occupy several of the mo st important fortresses of Mesopotamia. [57] In Armenia, the renowned Tiridates had long enjoyed the peace and glory which he deserved by his valor and fidelity to the cause of Rome. [57a] The firm alliance which he maintained with Constantine was productive of spiritual as well as of temporal benefits; by the conversion of Tiridates, the character of a saint was applied to that of a hero, the Christian faith was preached and established from the Euphrates to the shores of the Caspian, and Armenia was attached to the empire by the double ties of policy and religion. But as many of the Armenian nobles still refused to abandon the plurality of their gods and of their wives, the public tranquillity was disturbed by a discontented faction, which insulted the feeble age of their sovereign, and impatiently expected the hour of his death. He died at length after a reign of fifty-six years, and the fortune of the Armenian monarchy expired with Tiridates. His lawful heir was driven into exile, the Christian priests were either murdered or expelled from their churches, the barbarous tribes of Albania were solicited to descend from their mountains; and two of the most powerful governors, usurping the ensigns or the powers of royalty, implored the assistance of Sapor, and opened the gates of their cities to the Persian garrisons. The Christian party, under the guidance of the Archbishop of Artaxata, the immediate successor of St. Gregory the Illuminator, had recourse to the piety of Constantius. After the troubles had continued about three years, Antiochus, one of the officers of the household, executed with success the Imperial commission of restoring Chosroes, [57b] the son of Tiridates, to the throne of his fathers, of distributing honors and rewards among the faithful servants of the house of Arsaces, and of proclaiming a general amnesty, which was accepted by the greater part of the rebellious satraps. But the Romans derived more honor than advantage from this revolution. Chosroes was a prince of a puny stature and a pusillanimous spirit. Unequal to the fatigues of war, averse to the society of mankind, he withdrew from his capital to a retired palace, which he built on the banks of the River Eleutherus, and in the centre of a shady grove; where he consumed his vacant hours in the rural sports of hunting and hawking. To secure this inglorious ease, he submitted to the conditions of peace which Sapor condescended to impose; the payment of an annual tribute, and the restitution of the fertile province of Atropatene, which the courage of Tiridates, and the victorious arms of Galerius, had annexed to the Armenian monarchy. [58] [58a]

[Footnote 56: Sextus Rufus, (c. 26,) who on this occasion is no contemptible authority, affirms, that the Persians sued in vain for peace, and that Constantine was preparing to march against them: yet the superior weight of the testimony of Eusebius obliges us to admit the preliminaries, if not the ratification, of the treaty. See Tillemont, Hist. des Empereurs, tom. iv. p. 420. —Constantine had endeavored to allay the fury of the prosecutions, which, at the instigation of the Magi and the Jews, Sapor had commenced against the Christians. Euseb Vit. Hist. Theod. i. 25. Sozom. ii. c. 8, 15—M.]

[Footnote 57: Julian. Orat. i. p. 20.]

[Footnote 57a: Tiridates had sustained a war against Maximin. caused by the hatred of the latter against Christianity. Armenia was the first nation which embraced Christianity. About the year 276 it was the religion of the king, the nobles, and the people of Armenia. From St. Martin, Supplement to Le Beau, v. i. p. 78—Compare Preface to History of Vartan by Professor Neumann, p ix—M.]

[Footnote 57b: Chosroes was restored probably by Licinius, between 314 and 319. There was an Antiochus who was praefectus vigilum at Rome, as appears from the Theodosian Code, (l. iii. de inf. his quae sub ty.,) in 326, and from a fragment of the same work published by M. Amedee Peyron, in 319. He may before this have been sent into Armenia. St. M. p. 407. [Is it not more probable that Antiochus was an officer in the service of the Caesar who ruled in the East?—M.] Chosroes was succeeded in the year 322 by his son Diran. Diran was a weak prince, and in the sixteenth year of his reign. A. D. 337. was betrayed into the power of the Persians by the treachery of his chamberlain and the Persian governor of Atropatene or Aderbidjan. He was blinded: his wife and his son Arsaces shared his captivity, but the princes and nobles of Armenia claimed the protection of Rome; and this was the cause of Constantine's declaration of war against the Persians—The king of Persia attempted to make himself master of Armenia; but the brave resistance of the people, the advance of Constantius, and a defeat which his army suffered at Oskha in Armenia, and the failure before Nisibis, forced Shahpour to submit to terms of peace. Varaz-Shahpour, the perfidious governor of Atropatene, was flayed alive; Diran and his son were released from captivity; Diran refused to ascend the throne, and retired to an obscure retreat: his son Arsaces was crowned king of Armenia. Arsaces pursued a vacillating policy between the influence of Rome and Persia, and the war recommenced in the year 345. At least, that was the period of the expedition of Constantius to the East. See St. Martin, additions to Le Beau, i. 442. The Persians have made an extraordinary romance out of the history of Shahpour, who went as a spy to Constantinople, was taken, harnessed like a horse, and carried to witness the devastation of his kingdom. Malcolm. 84—M.]

[Footnote 58: Julian. Orat. i. p. 20, 21. Moses of Chorene, l. ii. c. 89, l. iii. c. 1—9, p. 226—240. The perfect agreement between the vague hints of the contemporary orator, and the circumstantial narrative of the national historian, gives light to the former, and weight to the latter. For the credit of Moses, it may be likewise observed, that the name of Antiochus is found a few years before in a civil office of inferior dignity. See Godefroy, Cod. Theod. tom. vi. p. 350.]

[Footnote 58a: Gibbon has endeavored, in his History, to make use of the information furnished by Moses of Chorene, the only Armenian historian then translated into Latin. Gibbon has not perceived all the chronological difficulties which occur in the narrative of that writer. He has not thought of all the critical discussions which his text ought to undergo before it can be combined with the relations of the western writers. From want of this attention, Gibbon has made the facts which he has drawn from this source more erroneous than they are in the original. This judgment applies to all which the English historian has derived from the Armenian author. I have made the History of Moses a subject of particular attention; and it is with confidence that I offer the results, which I insert here, and which will appear in the course of my notes. In order to form a judgment of the difference which exists between me and Gibbon, I will content myself with remarking, that throughout he has committed an anachronism of thirty years, from whence it follows, that he assigns to the reign of Constantius many events which took place during that of Constantine. He could not, therefore, discern the true connection which exists between the Roman history and that of Armenia, or form a correct notion of the reasons which induced Constantine, at the close of his life, to make war upon the Persians, or of the motives which detained Constantius so long in the East; he does not even mention them. St. Martin, note on Le Beau, i. 406. I have inserted M. St. Martin's observations, but I must add, that the chronology which he proposes, is not generally received by Armenian scholars, not, I believe, by Professor Neumann—M.]

During the long period of the reign of Constantius, the provinces of the East were afflicted by the calamities of the Persian war. [58c] The irregular incursions of the light troops alternately spread terror and devastation beyond the Tigris and beyond the Euphrates, from the gates of Ctesiphon to those of Antioch; and this active service was performed by the Arabs of the desert, who were divided in their interest and affections; some of their independent chiefs being enlisted in the party of Sapor, whilst others had engaged their doubtful fidelity to the emperor. [59] The more grave and important operations of the war were conducted with equal vigor; and the armies of Rome and Persia encountered each other in nine bloody fields, in two of which Constantius himself commanded in person. [60] The event of the day was most commonly adverse to the Romans, but in the battle of Singara, their imprudent valor had almost achieved a signal and decisive victory. The stationary troops of Singara [60a] retired on the approach of Sapor, who passed the Tigris over three bridges, and occupied near the village of Hilleh an advantageous camp, which, by the labor of his numerous pioneers, he surrounded in one day with a deep ditch and a lofty rampart. His formidable host, when it was drawn out in order of battle, covered the banks of the river, the adjacent heights, and the whole extent of a plain of above twelve miles, which separated the two armies. Both were alike impatient to engage; but the Barbarians, after a slight resistance, fled in disorder; unable to resist, or desirous to weary, the strength of the heavy legions, who, fainting with heat and thirst, pursued them across the plain, and cut in pieces a line of cavalry, clothed in complete armor, which had been posted before the gates of the camp to protect their retreat. Constantius, who was hurried along in the pursuit, attempted, without effect, to restrain the ardor of his troops, by representing to them the dangers of the approaching night, and the certainty of completing their success with the return of day. As they depended much more on their own valor than on the experience or the abilities of their chief, they silenced by their clamors his timid remonstrances; and rushing with fury to the charge, filled up the ditch, broke down the rampart, and dispersed themselves through the tents to recruit their exhausted strength, and to enjoy the rich harvest of their labors. But the prudent Sapor had watched the moment of victory. His army, of which the greater part, securely posted on the heights, had been spectators of the action, advanced in silence, and under the shadow of the night; and his Persian archers, guided by the illumination of the camp, poured a shower of arrows on a disarmed and licentious crowd. The sincerity of history [61] declares, that the Romans were vanquished with a dreadful slaughter, and that the flying remnant of the legions was exposed to the most intolerable hardships. Even the tenderness of panegyric, confessing that the glory of the emperor was sullied by the disobedience of his soldiers, chooses to draw a veil over the circumstances of this melancholy retreat. Yet one of those venal orators, so jealous of the fame of Constantius, relates, with amazing coolness, an act of such incredible cruelty, as, in the judgment of posterity, must imprint a far deeper stain on the honor of the Imperial name. The son of Sapor, the heir of his crown, had been made a captive in the Persian camp. The unhappy youth, who might have excited the compassion of the most savage enemy, was scourged, tortured, and publicly executed by the inhuman Romans. [62]

[Footnote 58c: It was during this war that a bold flatterer (whose name is unknown) published the Itineraries of Alexander and Trajan, in order to direct the victorious Constantius in the footsteps of those great conquerors of the East. The former of these has been published for the first time by M. Angelo Mai (Milan, 1817, reprinted at Frankfort, 1818.) It adds so little to our knowledge of Alexander's campaigns, that it only excites our regret that it is not the Itinerary of Trajan, of whose eastern victories we have no distinct record—M]

[Footnote 59: Ammianus (xiv. 4) gives a lively description of the wandering and predatory life of the Saracens, who stretched from the confines of Assyria to the cataracts of the Nile. It appears from the adventures of Malchus, which Jerom has related in so entertaining a manner, that the high road between Beraea and Edessa was infested by these robbers. See Hieronym. tom. i. p. 256.]

[Footnote 60: We shall take from Eutropius the general idea of the war. A Persis enim multa et gravia perpessus, saepe captis, oppidis, obsessis urbibus, caesis exercitibus, nullumque ei contra Saporem prosperum praelium fuit, nisi quod apud Singaram, &c. This honest account is confirmed by the hints of Ammianus, Rufus, and Jerom. The two first orations of Julian, and the third oration of Libanius, exhibit a more flattering picture; but the recantation of both those orators, after the death of Constantius, while it restores us to the possession of the truth, degrades their own character, and that of the emperor. The Commentary of Spanheim on the first oration of Julian is profusely learned. See likewise the judicious observations of Tillemont, Hist. des Empereurs, tom. iv. p. 656.]

[Footnote 60a: Now Sinjar, or the River Claboras—M.]

[Footnote 61: Acerrima nocturna concertatione pugnatum est, nostrorum copiis ngenti strage confossis. Ammian. xviii. 5. See likewise Eutropius, x. 10, and S. Rufus, c. 27. —The Persian historians, or romancers, do not mention the battle of Singara, but make the captive Shahpour escape, defeat, and take prisoner, the Roman emperor. The Roman captives were forced to repair all the ravages they had committed, even to replanting the smallest trees. Malcolm. i. 82—M.]

[Footnote 62: Libanius, Orat. iii. p. 133, with Julian. Orat. i. p. 24, and Spanneism's Commentary, p. 179.]

Whatever advantages might attend the arms of Sapor in the field, though nine repeated victories diffused among the nations the fame of his valor and conduct, he could not hope to succeed in the execution of his designs, while the fortified towns of Mesopotamia, and, above all, the strong and ancient city of Nisibis, remained in the possession of the Romans. In the space of twelve years, Nisibis, which, since the time of Lucullus, had been deservedly esteemed the bulwark of the East, sustained three memorable sieges against the power of Sapor; and the disappointed monarch, after urging his attacks above sixty, eighty, and a hundred days, was thrice repulsed with loss and ignominy. [63] This large and populous city was situate about two days' journey from the Tigris, in the midst of a pleasant and fertile plain at the foot of Mount Masius. A treble enclosure of brick walls was defended by a deep ditch; [64] and the intrepid resistance of Count Lucilianus, and his garrison, was seconded by the desperate courage of the people. The citizens of Nisibis were animated by the exhortations of their bishop, [65] inured to arms by the presence of danger, and convinced of the intentions of Sapor to plant a Persian colony in their room, and to lead them away into distant and barbarous captivity. The event of the two former sieges elated their confidence, and exasperated the haughty spirit of the Great King, who advanced a third time towards Nisibis, at the head of the united forces of Persia and India. The ordinary machines, invented to batter or undermine the walls, were rendered ineffectual by the superior skill of the Romans; and many days had vainly elapsed, when Sapor embraced a resolution worthy of an eastern monarch, who believed that the elements themselves were subject to his power. At the stated season of the melting of the snows in Armenia, the River Mygdonius, which divides the plain and the city of Nisibis, forms, like the Nile, [66] an inundation over the adjacent country. By the labor of the Persians, the course of the river was stopped below the town, and the waters were confined on every side by solid mounds of earth. On this artificial lake, a fleet of armed vessels filled with soldiers, and with engines which discharged stones of five hundred pounds weight, advanced in order of battle, and engaged, almost upon a level, the troops which defended the ramparts. [66a] The irresistible force of the waters was alternately fatal to the contending parties, till at length a portion of the walls, unable to sustain the accumulated pressure, gave way at once, and exposed an ample breach of one hundred and fifty feet. The Persians were instantly driven to the assault, and the fate of Nisibis depended on the event of the day. The heavy-armed cavalry, who led the van of a deep column, were embarrassed in the mud, and great numbers were drowned in the unseen holes which had been filled by the rushing waters. The elephants, made furious by their wounds, increased the disorder, and trampled down thousands of the Persian archers. The Great King, who, from an exalted throne, beheld the misfortunes of his arms, sounded, with reluctant indignation, the signal of the retreat, and suspended for some hours the prosecution of the attack. But the vigilant citizens improved the opportunity of the night; and the return of day discovered a new wall of six feet in height, rising every moment to fill up the interval of the breach. Notwithstanding the disappointment of his hopes, and the loss of more than twenty thousand men, Sapor still pressed the reduction of Nisibis, with an obstinate firmness, which could have yielded only to the necessity of defending the eastern provinces of Persia against a formidable invasion of the Massagetae. [67] Alarmed by this intelligence, he hastily relinquished the siege, and marched with rapid diligence from the banks of the Tigris to those of the Oxus. The danger and difficulties of the Scythian war engaged him soon afterwards to conclude, or at least to observe, a truce with the Roman emperor, which was equally grateful to both princes; as Constantius himself, after the death of his two brothers, was involved, by the revolutions of the West, in a civil contest, which required and seemed to exceed the most vigorous exertion of his undivided strength.

[Footnote 63: See Julian. Orat. i. p. 27, Orat. ii. p. 62, &c., with the Commentary of Spanheim, (p. 188-202,) who illustrates the circumstances, and ascertains the time of the three sieges of Nisibis. Their dates are likewise examined by Tillemont, (Hist. des Empereurs, tom. iv. p. 668, 671, 674.) Something is added from Zosimus, l. iii. p. 151, and the Alexandrine Chronicle, p. 290.]

[Footnote 64: Sallust. Fragment. lxxxiv. edit. Brosses, and Plutarch in Lucull. tom. iii. p. 184. Nisibis is now reduced to one hundred and fifty houses: the marshy lands produce rice, and the fertile meadows, as far as Mosul and the Tigris, are covered with the ruins of towns and allages. See Niebuhr, Voyages, tom. ii. p. 300-309.]

[Footnote 65: The miracles which Theodoret (l. ii. c. 30) ascribes to St. James, Bishop of Edessa, were at least performed in a worthy cause, the defence of his couutry. He appeared on the walls under the figure of the Roman emperor, and sent an army of gnats to sting the trunks of the elephants, and to discomfit the host of the new Sennacherib.]

[Footnote 66: Julian. Orat. i. p. 27. Though Niebuhr (tom. ii. p. 307) allows a very considerable swell to the Mygdonius, over which he saw a bridge of twelve arches: it is difficult, however, to understand this parallel of a trifling rivulet with a mighty river. There are many circumstances obscure, and almost unintelligible, in the description of these stupendous water-works.]

[Footnote 66a: Macdonald Kinnier observes on these floating batteries, "As the elevation of place is considerably above the level of the country in its immediate vicinity, and the Mygdonius is a very insignificant stream, it is difficult to imagine how this work could have been accomplished, even with the wonderful resources which the king must have had at his disposal" Geographical Memoir. p. 262—M.]

[Footnote 67: We are obliged to Zonaras (tom. ii. l. xiii. p. 11) for this invasion of the Massagetae, which is perfectly consistent with the general series of events to which we are darkly led by the broken history of Ammianus.]

After the partition of the empire, three years had scarcely elapsed before the sons of Constantine seemed impatient to convince mankind that they were incapable of contenting themselves with the dominions which they were unqualified to govern. The eldest of those princes soon complained, that he was defrauded of his just proportion of the spoils of their murdered kinsmen; and though he might yield to the superior guilt and merit of Constantius, he exacted from Constans the cession of the African provinces, as an equivalent for the rich countries of Macedonia and Greece, which his brother had acquired by the death of Dalmatius. The want of sincerity, which Constantine experienced in a tedious and fruitless negotiation, exasperated the fierceness of his temper; and he eagerly listened to those favorites, who suggested to him that his honor, as well as his interest, was concerned in the prosecution of the quarrel. At the head of a tumultuary band, suited for rapine rather than for conquest, he suddenly broke onto the dominions of Constans, by the way of the Julian Alps, and the country round Aquileia felt the first effects of his resentment. The measures of Constans, who then resided in Dacia, were directed with more prudence and ability. On the news of his brother's invasion, he detached a select and disciplined body of his Illyrian troops, proposing to follow them in person, with the remainder of his forces. But the conduct of his lieutenants soon terminated the unnatural contest.

By the artful appearances of flight, Constantine was betrayed into an ambuscade, which had been concealed in a wood, where the rash youth, with a few attendants, was surprised, surrounded, and slain. His body, after it had been found in the obscure stream of the Alsa, obtained the honors of an Imperial sepulchre; but his provinces transferred their allegiance to the conqueror, who, refusing to admit his elder brother Constantius to any share in these new acquisitions, maintained the undisputed possession of more than two thirds of the Roman empire. [68]

[Footnote 68: The causes and the events of this civil war are related with much perplexity and contradiction. I have chiefly followed Zonaras and the younger Victor. The monody (ad Calcem Eutrop. edit. Havercamp.) pronounced on the death of Constantine, might have been very instructive; but prudence and false taste engaged the orator to involve himself in vague declamation.]

PART IV

The fate of Constans himself was delayed about ten years longer, and the revenge of his brother's death was reserved for the more ignoble hand of a domestic traitor. The pernicious tendency of the system introduced by Constantine was displayed in the feeble administration of his sons; who, by their vices and weakness, soon lost the esteem and affections of their people. The pride assumed by Constans, from the unmerited success of his arms, was rendered more contemptible by his want of abilities and application. His fond partiality towards some German captives, distinguished only by the charms of youth, was an object of scandal to the people; [69] and Magnentius, an ambitious soldier, who was himself of Barbarian extraction, was encouraged by the public discontent to assert the honor of the Roman name. [70] The chosen bands of Jovians and Herculians, who acknowledged Magnentius as their leader, maintained the most respectable and important station in the Imperial camp. The friendship of Marcellinus, count of the sacred largesses, supplied with a liberal hand the means of seduction. The soldiers were convinced by the most specious arguments, that the republic summoned them to break the bonds of hereditary servitude; and, by the choice of an active and vigilant prince, to reward the same virtues which had raised the ancestors of the degenerate Constans from a private condition to the throne of the world. As soon as the conspiracy was ripe for execution, Marcellinus, under the pretence of celebrating his son's birthday, gave a splendid entertainment to the illustrious and honorable persons of the court of Gaul, which then resided in the city of Autun. The intemperance of the feast was artfully protracted till a very late hour of the night; and the unsuspecting guests were tempted to indulge themselves in a dangerous and guilty freedom of conversation. On a sudden the doors were thrown open, and Magnentius, who had retired for a few moments, returned into the apartment, invested with the diadem and purple. The conspirators instantly saluted him with the titles of Augustus and Emperor. The surprise, the terror, the intoxication, the ambitious hopes, and the mutual ignorance of the rest of the assembly, prompted them to join their voices to the general acclamation. The guards hastened to take the oath of fidelity; the gates of the town were shut; and before the dawn of day, Magnentius became master of the troops and treasure of the palace and city of Autun. By his secrecy and diligence he entertained some hopes of surprising the person of Constans, who was pursuing in the adjacent forest his favorite amusement of hunting, or perhaps some pleasures of a more private and criminal nature. The rapid progress of fame allowed him, however, an instant for flight, though the desertion of his soldiers and subjects deprived him of the power of resistance. Before he could reach a seaport in Spain, where he intended to embark, he was overtaken near Helena, [71] at the foot of the Pyrenees, by a party of light cavalry, whose chief, regardless of the sanctity of a temple, executed his commission by the murder of the son of Constantine. [72]

[Footnote 69: Quarum (gentium) obsides pretio quaesitos pueros venustiore quod cultius habuerat libidine hujusmodi arsisse pro certo habet. Had not the depraved taste of Constans been publicly avowed, the elder Victor, who held a considerable office in his brother's reign, would not have asserted it in such positive terms.]

[Footnote 70: Julian. Orat. i. and ii. Zosim. l. ii. p. 134. Victor in Epitome. There is reason to believe that Magnentius was born in one of those Barbarian colonies which Constantius Chlorus had established in Gaul, (see this History, vol. i. p. 414.) His behavior may remind us of the patriot earl of Leicester, the famous Simon de Montfort, who could persuade the good people of England, that he, a Frenchman by birth had taken arms to deliver them from foreign favorites.]

[Footnote 71: This ancient city had once flourished under the name of Illiberis (Pomponius Mela, ii. 5.) The munificence of Constantine gave it new splendor, and his mother's name. Helena (it is still called Elne) became the seat of a bishop, who long afterwards transferred his residence to Perpignan, the capital of modern Rousillon. See D'Anville. Notice de l'Ancienne Gaule, p. 380. Longuerue, Description de la France, p. 223, and the Marca Hispanica, l. i. c. 2.]

[Footnote 72: Zosimus, l. ii. p. 119, 120. Zonaras, tom. ii. l. xiii. p. 13, and the Abbreviators.]

As soon as the death of Constans had decided this easy but important revolution, the example of the court of Autun was imitated by the provinces of the West. The authority of Magnentius was acknowledged through the whole extent of the two great praefectures of Gaul and Italy; and the usurper prepared, by every act of oppression, to collect a treasure, which might discharge the obligation of an immense donative, and supply the expenses of a civil war. The martial countries of Illyricum, from the Danube to the extremity of Greece, had long obeyed the government of Vetranio, an aged general, beloved for the simplicity of his manners, and who had acquired some reputation by his experience and services in war. [73] Attached by habit, by duty, and by gratitude, to the house of Constantine, he immediately gave the strongest assurances to the only surviving son of his late master, that he would expose, with unshaken fidelity, his person and his troops, to inflict a just revenge on the traitors of Gaul. But the legions of Vetranio were seduced, rather than provoked, by the example of rebellion; their leader soon betrayed a want of firmness, or a want of sincerity; and his ambition derived a specious pretence from the approbation of the princess Constantina. That cruel and aspiring woman, who had obtained from the great Constantine, her father, the rank of Augusta, placed the diadem with her own hands on the head of the Illyrian general; and seemed to expect from his victory the accomplishment of those unbounded hopes, of which she had been disappointed by the death of her husband Hannibalianus. Perhaps it was without the consent of Constantina, that the new emperor formed a necessary, though dishonorable, alliance with the usurper of the West, whose purple was so recently stained with her brother's blood. [74]

[Footnote 73: Eutropius (x. 10) describes Vetranio with more temper, and probably with more truth, than either of the two Victors. Vetranio was born of obscure parents in the wildest parts of Maesia; and so much had his education been neglected, that, after his elevation, he studied the alphabet.]

[Footnote 74: The doubtful, fluctuating conduct of Vetranio is described by Julian in his first oration, and accurately explained by Spanheim, who discusses the situation and behavior of Constantina.]

The intelligence of these important events, which so deeply affected the honor and safety of the Imperial house, recalled the arms of Constantius from the inglorious prosecution of the Persian war. He recommended the care of the East to his lieutenants, and afterwards to his cousin Gallus, whom he raised from a prison to a throne; and marched towards Europe, with a mind agitated by the conflict of hope and fear, of grief and indignation. On his arrival at Heraclea in Thrace, the emperor gave audience to the ambassadors of Magnentius and Vetranio. The first author of the conspiracy Marcellinus, who in some measure had bestowed the purple on his new master, boldly accepted this dangerous commission; and his three colleagues were selected from the illustrious personages of the state and army. These deputies were instructed to soothe the resentment, and to alarm the fears, of Constantius. They were empowered to offer him the friendship and alliance of the western princes, to cement their union by a double marriage; of Constantius with the daughter of Magnentius, and of Magnentius himself with the ambitious Constantina; and to acknowledge in the treaty the preeminence of rank, which might justly be claimed by the emperor of the East. Should pride and mistaken piety urge him to refuse these equitable conditions, the ambassadors were ordered to expatiate on the inevitable ruin which must attend his rashness, if he ventured to provoke the sovereigns of the West to exert their superior strength; and to employ against him that valor, those abilities, and those legions, to which the house of Constantine had been indebted for so many triumphs. Such propositions and such arguments appeared to deserve the most serious attention; the answer of Constantius was deferred till the next day; and as he had reflected on the importance of justifying a civil war in the opinion of the people, he thus addressed his council, who listened with real or affected credulity: "Last night," said he, "after I retired to rest, the shade of the great Constantine, embracing the corpse of my murdered brother, rose before my eyes; his well-known voice awakened me to revenge, forbade me to despair of the republic, and assured me of the success and immortal glory which would crown the justice of my arms." The authority of such a vision, or rather of the prince who alleged it, silenced every doubt, and excluded all negotiation. The ignominious terms of peace were rejected with disdain. One of the ambassadors of the tyrant was dismissed with the haughty answer of Constantius; his colleagues, as unworthy of the privileges of the law of nations, were put in irons; and the contending powers prepared to wage an implacable war. [75]

[Footnote 75: See Peter the Patrician, in the Excerpta Legationem p. 27.]

Such was the conduct, and such perhaps was the duty, of the brother of Constans towards the perfidious usurper of Gaul. The situation and character of Vetranio admitted of milder measures; and the policy of the Eastern emperor was directed to disunite his antagonists, and to separate the forces of Illyricum from the cause of rebellion. It was an easy task to deceive the frankness and simplicity of Vetranio, who, fluctuating some time between the opposite views of honor and interest, displayed to the world the insincerity of his temper, and was insensibly engaged in the snares of an artful negotiation. Constantius acknowledged him as a legitimate and equal colleague in the empire, on condition that he would renounce his disgraceful alliance with Magnentius, and appoint a place of interview on the frontiers of their respective provinces; where they might pledge their friendship by mutual vows of fidelity, and regulate by common consent the future operations of the civil war. In consequence of this agreement, Vetranio advanced to the city of Sardica, [76] at the head of twenty thousand horse, and of a more numerous body of infantry; a power so far superior to the forces of Constantius, that the Illyrian emperor appeared to command the life and fortunes of his rival, who, depending on the success of his private negotiations, had seduced the troops, and undermined the throne, of Vetranio. The chiefs, who had secretly embraced the party of Constantius, prepared in his favor a public spectacle, calculated to discover and inflame the passions of the multitude. [77] The united armies were commanded to assemble in a large plain near the city. In the centre, according to the rules of ancient discipline, a military tribunal, or rather scaffold, was erected, from whence the emperors were accustomed, on solemn and important occasions, to harangue the troops. The well-ordered ranks of Romans and Barbarians, with drawn swords, or with erected spears, the squadrons of cavalry, and the cohorts of infantry, distinguished by the variety of their arms and ensigns, formed an immense circle round the tribunal; and the attentive silence which they preserved was sometimes interrupted by loud bursts of clamor or of applause. In the presence of this formidable assembly, the two emperors were called upon to explain the situation of public affairs: the precedency of rank was yielded to the royal birth of Constantius; and though he was indifferently skilled in the arts of rhetoric, he acquitted himself, under these difficult circumstances, with firmness, dexterity, and eloquence. The first part of his oration seemed to be pointed only against the tyrant of Gaul; but while he tragically lamented the cruel murder of Constans, he insinuated, that none, except a brother, could claim a right to the succession of his brother. He displayed, with some complacency, the glories of his Imperial race; and recalled to the memory of the troops the valor, the triumphs, the liberality of the great Constantine, to whose sons they had engaged their allegiance by an oath of fidelity, which the ingratitude of his most favored servants had tempted them to violate. The officers, who surrounded the tribunal, and were instructed to act their part in this extraordinary scene, confessed the irresistible power of reason and eloquence, by saluting the emperor Constantius as their lawful sovereign. The contagion of loyalty and repentance was communicated from rank to rank; till the plain of Sardica resounded with the universal acclamation of "Away with these upstart usurpers! Long life and victory to the son of Constantine! Under his banners alone we will fight and conquer." The shout of thousands, their menacing gestures, the fierce clashing of their arms, astonished and subdued the courage of Vetranio, who stood, amidst the defection of his followers, in anxious and silent suspense. Instead of embracing the last refuge of generous despair, he tamely submitted to his fate; and taking the diadem from his head, in the view of both armies fell prostrate at the feet of his conqueror. Constantius used his victory with prudence and moderation; and raising from the ground the aged suppliant, whom he affected to style by the endearing name of Father, he gave him his hand to descend from the throne. The city of Prusa was assigned for the exile or retirement of the abdicated monarch, who lived six years in the enjoyment of ease and affluence. He often expressed his grateful sense of the goodness of Constantius, and, with a very amiable simplicity, advised his benefactor to resign the sceptre of the world, and to seek for content (where alone it could be found) in the peaceful obscurity of a private condition. [78]

[Footnote 76: Zonaras, tom. ii. l. xiii. p. 16. The position of Sardica, near the modern city of Sophia, appears better suited to this interview than the situation of either Naissus or Sirmium, where it is placed by Jerom, Socrates, and Sozomen.]

[Footnote 77: See the two first orations of Julian, particularly p. 31; and Zosimus, l. ii. p. 122. The distinct narrative of the historian serves to illustrate the diffuse but vague descriptions of the orator.]

[Footnote 78: The younger Victor assigns to his exile the emphatical appellation of "Voluptarium otium." Socrates (l. ii. c. 28) is the voucher for the correspondence with the emperor, which would seem to prove that Vetranio was indeed, prope ad stultitiam simplicissimus.]

The behavior of Constantius on this memorable occasion was celebrated with some appearance of justice; and his courtiers compared the studied orations which a Pericles or a Demosthenes addressed to the populace of Athens, with the victorious eloquence which had persuaded an armed multitude to desert and depose the object of their partial choice. [79] The approaching contest with Magnentius was of a more serious and bloody kind. The tyrant advanced by rapid marches to encounter Constantius, at the head of a numerous army, composed of Gauls and Spaniards, of Franks and Saxons; of those provincials who supplied the strength of the legions, and of those barbarians who were dreaded as the most formidable enemies of the republic. The fertile plains [80] of the Lower Pannonia, between the Drave, the Save, and the Danube, presented a spacious theatre; and the operations of the civil war were protracted during the summer months by the skill or timidity of the combatants. [81] Constantius had declared his intention of deciding the quarrel in the fields of Cibalis, a name that would animate his troops by the remembrance of the victory, which, on the same auspicious ground, had been obtained by the arms of his father Constantine. Yet by the impregnable fortifications with which the emperor encompassed his camp, he appeared to decline, rather than to invite, a general engagement.

It was the object of Magnentius to tempt or to compel his adversary to relinquish this advantageous position; and he employed, with that view, the various marches, evolutions, and stratagems, which the knowledge of the art of war could suggest to an experienced officer. He carried by assault the important town of Siscia; made an attack on the city of Sirmium, which lay in the rear of the Imperial camp, attempted to force a passage over the Save into the eastern provinces of Illyricum; and cut in pieces a numerous detachment, which he had allured into the narrow passes of Adarne. During the greater part of the summer, the tyrant of Gaul showed himself master of the field. The troops of Constantius were harassed and dispirited; his reputation declined in the eye of the world; and his pride condescended to solicit a treaty of peace, which would have resigned to the assassin of Constans the sovereignty of the provinces beyond the Alps. These offers were enforced by the eloquence of Philip the Imperial ambassador; and the council as well as the army of Magnentius were disposed to accept them. But the haughty usurper, careless of the remonstrances of his friends, gave orders that Philip should be detained as a captive, or, at least, as a hostage; while he despatched an officer to reproach Constantius with the weakness of his reign, and to insult him by the promise of a pardon if he would instantly abdicate the purple. "That he should confide in the justice of his cause, and the protection of an avenging Deity," was the only answer which honor permitted the emperor to return. But he was so sensible of the difficulties of his situation, that he no longer dared to retaliate the indignity which had been offered to his representative. The negotiation of Philip was not, however, ineffectual, since he determined Sylvanus the Frank, a general of merit and reputation, to desert with a considerable body of cavalry, a few days before the battle of Mursa.

[Footnote 79: Eum Constantius..... facundiae vi dejectum Imperio in pri vatum otium removit. Quae gloria post natum Imperium soli proces sit eloquio clementiaque, &c. Aurelius Victor, Julian, and Themistius (Orat. iii. and iv.) adorn this exploit with all the artificial and gaudy coloring of their rhetoric.]

[Footnote 80: Busbequius (p. 112) traversed the Lower Hungary and Sclavonia at a time when they were reduced almost to a desert, by the reciprocal hostilities of the Turks and Christians. Yet he mentions with admiration the unconquerable fertility of the soil; and observes that the height of the grass was sufficient to conceal a loaded wagon from his sight. See likewise Browne's Travels, in Harris's Collection, vol ii. p. 762 &c.]

[Footnote 81: Zosimus gives a very large account of the war, and the negotiation, (l. ii. p. 123-130.) But as he neither shows himself a soldier nor a politician, his narrative must be weighed with attention, and received with caution.]

The city of Mursa, or Essek, celebrated in modern times for a bridge of boats, five miles in length, over the River Drave, and the adjacent morasses, [82] has been always considered as a place of importance in the wars of Hungary. Magnentius, directing his march towards Mursa, set fire to the gates, and, by a sudden assault, had almost scaled the walls of the town. The vigilance of the garrison extinguished the flames; the approach of Constantius left him no time to continue the operations of the siege; and the emperor soon removed the only obstacle that could embarrass his motions, by forcing a body of troops which had taken post in an adjoining amphitheatre. The field of battle round Mursa was a naked and level plain: on this ground the army of Constantius formed, with the Drave on their right; while their left, either from the nature of their disposition, or from the superiority of their cavalry, extended far beyond the right flank of Magnentius. [83] The troops on both sides remained under arms, in anxious expectation, during the greatest part of the morning; and the son of Constantine, after animating his soldiers by an eloquent speech, retired into a church at some distance from the field of battle, and committed to his generals the conduct of this decisive day. [84] They deserved his confidence by the valor and military skill which they exerted. They wisely began the action upon the left; and advancing their whole wing of cavalry in an oblique line, they suddenly wheeled it on the right flank of the enemy, which was unprepared to resist the impetuosity of their charge. But the Romans of the West soon rallied, by the habits of discipline; and the Barbarians of Germany supported the renown of their national bravery. The engagement soon became general; was maintained with various and singular turns of fortune; and scarcely ended with the darkness of the night. The signal victory which Constantius obtained is attributed to the arms of his cavalry. His cuirassiers are described as so many massy statues of steel, glittering with their scaly armor, and breaking with their ponderous lances the firm array of the Gallic legions. As soon as the legions gave way, the lighter and more active squadrons of the second line rode sword in hand into the intervals, and completed the disorder. In the mean while, the huge bodies of the Germans were exposed almost naked to the dexterity of the Oriental archers; and whole troops of those Barbarians were urged by anguish and despair to precipitate themselves into the broad and rapid stream of the Drave. [85] The number of the slain was computed at fifty-four thousand men, and the slaughter of the conquerors was more considerable than that of the vanquished; [86] a circumstance which proves the obstinacy of the contest, and justifies the observation of an ancient writer, that the forces of the empire were consumed in the fatal battle of Mursa, by the loss of a veteran army, sufficient to defend the frontiers, or to add new triumphs to the glory of Rome. [87] Notwithstanding the invectives of a servile orator, there is not the least reason to believe that the tyrant deserted his own standard in the beginning of the engagement. He seems to have displayed the virtues of a general and of a soldier till the day was irrecoverably lost, and his camp in the possession of the enemy. Magnentius then consulted his safety, and throwing away the Imperial ornaments, escaped with some difficulty from the pursuit of the light horse, who incessantly followed his rapid flight from the banks of the Drave to the foot of the Julian Alps. [88]

[Footnote 82: This remarkable bridge, which is flanked with towers, and supported on large wooden piles, was constructed A. D. 1566, by Sultan Soliman, to facilitate the march of his armies into Hungary.]

[Footnote 83: This position, and the subsequent evolutions, are clearly, though concisely, described by Julian, Orat. i. p. 36.]

[Footnote 84: Sulpicius Severus, l. ii. p. 405. The emperor passed the day in prayer with Valens, the Arian bishop of Mursa, who gained his confidence by announcing the success of the battle. M. de Tillemont (Hist. des Empereurs, tom. iv. p. 1110) very properly remarks the silence of Julian with regard to the personal prowess of Constantius in the battle of Mursa. The silence of flattery is sometimes equal to the most positive and authentic evidence.]

[Footnote 85: Julian. Orat. i. p. 36, 37; and Orat. ii. p. 59, 60. Zonaras, tom ii. l. xiii. p. 17. Zosimus, l. ii. p. 130-133. The last of these celebrates the dexterity of the archer Menelaus, who could discharge three *arrows at the same time; an advantage which, according to his apprehension of military affairs, materially contributed to the victory of Constantius.]*

[Footnote 86: According to Zonaras, Constantius, out of 80,000 men, lost 30,000; and Magnentius lost 24,000 out of 36,000. The other articles of this account seem probable and authentic, but the numbers of the tyrant's army must have been mistaken, either by the author or his transcribers. Magnentius had collected the whole force of the West, Romans and Barbarians, into one formidable body, which cannot fairly be estimated at less than 100,000 men. Julian. Orat. i. p. 34, 35.]

[Footnote 87: Ingentes R. I. vires ea dimicatione consumptae sunt, ad quaelibet bella externa idoneae, quae multum triumphorum possent securitatisque conferre. Eutropius, x. 13. The younger Victor expresses himself to the same effect.]

[Footnote 88: On this occasion, we must prefer the unsuspected testimony of Zosimus and Zonaras to the flattering assertions of Julian. The younger Victor paints the character of Magnentius in a singular light: "Sermonis acer, animi tumidi, et immodice timidus; artifex tamen ad occultandam audaciae specie formidinem." Is it most likely that in the battle of Mursa his behavior was governed by nature or by art should incline for the latter.]

The approach of winter supplied the indolence of Constantius with specious reasons for deferring the prosecution of the war till the ensuing spring. Magnentius had fixed his residence in the city of Aquileia, and showed a seeming resolution to dispute the passage of the mountains and morasses which fortified the confines of the Venetian province. The surprisal of a castle in the Alps by the secret march of the Imperialists, could scarcely have determined him to relinquish the possession of Italy, if the inclinations of the people had supported the cause of their tyrant. [89] But the memory of the cruelties exercised by his ministers, after the unsuccessful revolt of Nepotian, had left a deep impression of horror and resentment on the minds of the Romans. That rash youth, the son of the princess Eutropia, and the nephew of Constantine, had seen with indignation the sceptre of the West usurped by a perfidious barbarian. Arming a desperate troop of slaves and gladiators, he overpowered the feeble guard of the domestic tranquillity of Rome, received the homage of the senate, and assuming the title of Augustus, precariously reigned during a tumult of twenty-eight days. The march of some regular forces put an end to his ambitious hopes: the rebellion was extinguished in the blood of Nepotian, of his mother Eutropia, and of his adherents; and the proscription was extended to all who had contracted a fatal alliance with the name and family of Constantine. [90] But as soon as Constantius, after the battle of Mursa, became master of the sea-coast of Dalmatia, a band of noble exiles, who had ventured to equip a fleet in some harbor of the Adriatic, sought protection and revenge in his victorious camp. By their secret intelligence with their countrymen, Rome and the Italian cities were persuaded to display the banners of Constantius on their walls. The grateful veterans, enriched by the liberality of the father, signalized their gratitude and loyalty to the son. The cavalry, the legions, and the auxiliaries of Italy, renewed their oath of allegiance to Constantius; and the usurper, alarmed by the general desertion, was compelled, with the remains of his faithful troops, to retire beyond the Alps into the provinces of Gaul. The detachments, however, which were ordered either to press or to intercept the flight of Magnentius, conducted themselves with the usual imprudence of success; and allowed him, in the plains of Pavia, an opportunity of turning on his pursuers, and of gratifying his despair by the carnage of a useless victory. [91]

[Footnote 89: Julian. Orat. i. p. 38, 39. In that place, however, as well as in Oration ii. p. 97, he insinuates the general disposition of the senate, the people, and the soldiers of Italy, towards the party of the emperor.]

[Footnote 90: The elder Victor describes, in a pathetic manner, the miserable condition of Rome: "Cujus stolidum ingenium adeo P. R. patribusque exitio fuit, uti passim domus, fora, viae, templaque, cruore, cadaveri busque opplerentur bustorum modo." Athanasius (tom. i. p. 677) deplores the fate of several illustrious victims, and Julian (Orat. ii p 58) execrates the cruelty of Marcellinus, the implacable enemy of the house of Constantine.]

[Footnote 91: Zosim. l. ii. p. 133. Victor in Epitome. The panegyrists of Constantius, with their usual candor, forget to mention this accidental defeat.]

The pride of Magnentius was reduced, by repeated misfortunes, to sue, and to sue in vain, for peace. He first despatched a senator, in whose abilities he confided, and afterwards several bishops, whose holy character might obtain a more favorable audience, with the offer of resigning the purple, and the promise of devoting the remainder of his life to the service of the emperor. But Constantius, though he granted fair terms of pardon and reconciliation to all who abandoned the standard of rebellion, [92] avowed his inflexible resolution to inflict a just punishment on the crimes of an assassin, whom he prepared to overwhelm on every side by the effort of his victorious arms. An Imperial fleet acquired the easy possession of Africa and Spain, confirmed the wavering faith of the Moorish nations, and landed a considerable force, which passed the Pyrenees, and advanced towards Lyons, the last and fatal station of Magnentius. [93] The temper of the tyrant, which was never inclined to clemency, was urged by distress to exercise every act of oppression which could extort an immediate supply from the cities of Gaul. [94] Their patience was at length exhausted; and Treves, the seat of Praetorian government, gave the signal of revolt, by shutting her gates against Decentius, who had been raised by his brother to the rank either of Caesar or of Augustus. [95] From Treves, Decentius was obliged to retire to Sens, where he was soon surrounded by an army of Germans, whom the pernicious arts of Constantius had introduced into the civil dissensions of Rome. [96] In the mean time, the Imperial troops forced the passages of the Cottian Alps, and in the bloody combat of Mount Seleucus irrevocably fixed the title of rebels on the party of Magnentius. [97] He was unable to bring another army into the field; the fidelity of his guards was corrupted; and when he appeared in public to animate them by his exhortations, he was saluted with a unanimous shout of "Long live the emperor Constantius!" The tyrant, who perceived that they were preparing to deserve pardon and rewards by the sacrifice of the most obnoxious criminal, prevented their design by falling on his sword; [98] a death more easy and more honorable than he could hope to obtain from the hands of an enemy, whose revenge would have been colored with the specious pretence of justice and fraternal piety. The example of suicide was imitated by Decentius, who strangled himself on the news of his brother's death. The author of the conspiracy, Marcellinus, had long since disappeared in the battle of Mursa, [99] and the public tranquillity was confirmed by the execution of the surviving leaders of a guilty and unsuccessful faction. A severe inquisition was extended over all who, either from choice or from compulsion, had been involved in the cause of rebellion. Paul, surnamed Catena from his superior skill in the judicial exercise of tyranny, [99a] was sent to explore the latent remains of the conspiracy in the remote province of Britain. The honest indignation expressed by Martin, vice-praefect of the island, was interpreted as an evidence of his own guilt; and the governor was urged to the necessity of turning against his breast the sword with which he had been provoked to wound the Imperial minister. The most innocent subjects of the West were exposed to exile and confiscation, to death and torture; and as the timid are always cruel, the mind of Constantius was inaccessible to mercy. [100]

[Footnote 92: Zonaras, tom. ii. l. xiii. p. 17. Julian, in several places of the two orations, expatiates on the clemency of Constantius to the rebels.]

[Footnote 93: Zosim. l. ii. p. 133. Julian. Orat. i. p. 40, ii. p. 74.]

[Footnote 94: Ammian. xv. 6. Zosim. l. ii. p. 123. Julian, who (Orat. i. p. 40) unveighs against the cruel effects of the tyrant's despair, mentions (Orat. i. p. 34) the oppressive edicts which were dictated by his necessities, or by his avarice. His subjects were compelled to purchase the Imperial demesnes; a doubtful and dangerous species of property, which, in case of a revolution, might be imputed to them as a treasonable usurpation.]

[Footnote 95: The medals of Magnentius celebrate the victories of the two Augusti, and of the Caesar. The Caesar was another brother, named Desiderius. See Tillemont, Hist. des Empereurs, tom. iv. p. 757.]

[Footnote 96: Julian. Orat. i. p. 40, ii. p. 74; with Spanheim, p. 263. His Commentary illustrates the transactions of this civil war. Mons Seleuci was a small place in the Cottian Alps, a few miles distant from Vapincum, or Gap, an episcopal city of Dauphine. See D'Anville, Notice de la Gaule, p. 464; and Longuerue, Description de la France, p. 327— The Itinerary of Antoninus (p. 357, ed. Wess.) places Mons Seleucu twenty-four miles from Vapinicum, (Gap,) and twenty-six from Lucus. (le Luc,) on the road to Die, (Dea Vocontiorum.) The situation answers to Mont Saleon, a little place on the right of the small river Buech, which falls into the Durance. Roman antiquities have been found in this place. St. Martin. Note to Le Beau, ii. 47—M.]

[Footnote 97: Zosimus, l. ii. p. 134. Liban. Orat. x. p. 268, 269. The latter most vehemently arraigns this cruel and selfish policy of Constantius.]

[Footnote 98: Julian. Orat. i. p. 40. Zosimus, l. ii. p. 134. Socrates, l. ii. c. 32. Sozomen, l. iv. c. 7. The younger Victor describes his death with some horrid circumstances: Transfosso latere, ut erat vasti corporis, vulnere naribusque et ore cruorem effundens, exspiravit. If we can give credit to Zonaras, the tyrant, before he expired, had the pleasure of murdering, with his own hand, his mother and his brother Desiderius.]

[Footnote 99: Julian (Orat. i. p. 58, 59) seems at a loss to determine, whether he inflicted on himself the punishment of his crimes, whether he was drowned in the Drave, or whether he was carried by the avenging daemons from the field of battle to his destined place of eternal tortures.]

[Footnote 99a: This is scarcely correct, ut erat in complicandis negotiis artifex dirum made ei Catenae inditum est cognomentum. Amm. Mar. loc. cit—M.]

[Footnote 100: Ammian. xiv. 5, xxi. 16.]

CHAPTER XIX

CONSTANTINUS SOLE EMPEROR

PART I

CONSTANTINUS SOLE EMPEROR—ELEVATION AND DEATH OF GALLUS—DANGER AND ELEVATION OF JULIAN—SARMATIAN AND PERSIAN WARS—VICTORIES OF JULIAN IN GAUL

The divided provinces of the empire were again united by the victory of Constantius; but as that feeble prince was destitute of personal merit, either in peace or war; as he feared his generals, and distrusted his ministers; the triumph of his arms served only to establish the reign of the eunuchs over the Roman world. Those unhappy beings, the ancient production of Oriental jealousy and despotism, [1] were introduced into Greece and Rome by the contagion of Asiatic luxury. [2] Their progress was rapid; and the eunuchs, who, in the time of Augustus, had been abhorred, as the monstrous retinue of an Egyptian queen, [3] were gradually admitted into the families of matrons, of senators, and of the emperors themselves. [4] Restrained by the severe edicts of Domitian and Nerva, cherished by the pride of Diocletian, reduced to an humble station by the prudence of Constantine, [6] they multiplied in the palaces of his degenerate sons, and insensibly acquired the knowledge, and at length the direction, of the secret councils of Constantius. The aversion and contempt which mankind had so uniformly entertained for that imperfect species, appears to have degraded their character, and to have rendered them almost as incapable as they were supposed to be, of conceiving any generous sentiment, or of performing any worthy action. [7] But the eunuchs were skilled in the arts of flattery and intrigue; and they alternately governed the mind of Constantius by his fears, his indolence, and his vanity. [8] Whilst he viewed in a deceitful mirror the fair appearance of public prosperity, he supinely permitted them to intercept the complaints of the injured provinces, to accumulate immense treasures by the sale of justice and of honors; to disgrace the most important dignities, by the promotion of those who had purchased at their hands the powers of oppression, [9] and to gratify their resentment against the few independent spirits, who arrogantly refused to solicit the protection of slaves. Of these slaves the most distinguished was the chamberlain Eusebius, who ruled the monarch and the palace with such absolute sway, that Constantius, according to the sarcasm of an impartial historian, possessed some credit with this haughty favorite. [10] By his artful suggestions, the emperor was persuaded to subscribe the condemnation of the unfortunate Gallus, and to add a new crime to the long list of unnatural murders which pollute the honor of the house of Constantine.

[Footnote 1: Ammianus (l. xiv. c. 6) imputes the first practice of castration to the cruel ingenuity of Semiramis, who is supposed to have reigned above nineteen hundred years before Christ. The use of eunuchs is of high antiquity, both in Asia and Egypt. They are mentioned in the law of Moses, Deuteron. xxxiii. 1. See Goguet, Origines des Loix, &c., Part i. l. i. c. 3.]

[Footnote 2: Eunuchum dixti velle te; Quia solae utuntur his reginae—Terent. Eunuch. act i. scene 2. This play is translated from Meander, and the original must have appeared soon after the eastern conquests of Alexander.]

[Footnote 3: Miles.... spadonibus Servire rugosis potest. Horat. Carm. v. 9, and Dacier ad loe. By the word spado, the Romans very forcibly expressed their abhorrence of this mutilated condition. The Greek appellation of eunuchs, which insensibly prevailed, had a milder sound, and a more ambiguous sense.]

[Footnote 4: We need only mention Posides, a freedman and eunuch of Claudius, in whose favor the emperor prostituted some of the most honorable rewards of military valor. See Sueton. in Claudio, c. 28. Posides employed a great part of his wealth in building.

Ut Spado vincebat Capitolia Nostra Posides. Juvenal. Sat. xiv.]

[Footnote 5: *Castrari mares vetuit.* Sueton. in Domitian. c. 7. See Dion Cassius, l. lxvii. p. 1107, l. lxviii. p. 1119.]

[Footnote 6: There is a passage in the Augustan History, p. 137, in which Lampridius, whilst he praises Alexander Severus and Constantine for restraining the tyranny of the eunuchs, deplores the mischiefs which they occasioned in other reigns. *Huc accedit quod eunuchos nec in consiliis nec in ministeriis habuit; qui soli principes perdunt, dum eos more gentium aut regum Persarum volunt vivere; qui a populo etiam amicissimum semovent; qui internuntii sunt, aliud quam respondetur, referentes; claudentes principem suum, et agentes ante omnia ne quid sciat.*]

[Footnote 7: Xenophon (Cyropaedia, l. viii. p. 540) has stated the specious reasons which engaged Cyrus to intrust his person to the guard of eunuchs. He had observed in animals, that although the practice of castration might tame their ungovernable fierceness, it did not diminish their strength or spirit; and he persuaded himself, that those who were separated from the rest of human kind, would be more firmly attached to the person of their benefactor. But a long experience has contradicted the judgment of Cyrus. Some particular instances may occur of eunuchs distinguished by their fidelity, their valor, and their abilities; but if we examine the general history of Persia, India, and China, we shall find that the power of the eunuchs has uniformly marked the decline and fall of every dynasty.]

[Footnote 8: See Ammianus Marcellinus, l. xxi. c. 16, l. xxii. c. 4. The whole tenor of his impartial history serves to justify the invectives of Mamertinus, of Libanius, and of Julian himself, who have insulted the vices of the court of Constantius.]

[Footnote 9: Aurelius Victor censures the negligence of his sovereign in choosing the governors of the provinces, and the generals of the army, and concludes his history with a very bold observation, as it is much more dangerous under a feeble reign to attack the ministers than the master himself. "*Uti verum absolvam brevi, ut Imperatore ipso clarius ita apparitorum plerisque magis atrox nihil.*"]

[Footnote 10: *Apud quem (si vere dici debeat) multum Constantius potuit.* Ammian. l. xviii. c. 4.]

When the two nephews of Constantine, Gallus and Julian, were saved from the fury of the soldiers, the former was about twelve, and the latter about six, years of age; and, as the eldest was thought to be of a sickly constitution, they obtained with the less difficulty a precarious and dependent life, from the affected pity of Constantius, who was sensible that the execution of these helpless orphans would have been esteemed, by all mankind, an act of the most deliberate cruelty. [11] Different cities of Ionia and Bithynia were assigned for the places of their exile and education; but as soon as their growing years excited the jealousy of the emperor, he judged it more prudent to secure those unhappy youths in the strong castle of Macellum, near Caesarea. The treatment which they experienced during a six years' confinement, was partly such as they could hope from a careful guardian, and partly such as they might dread from a suspicious tyrant. [12] Their prison was an ancient palace, the residence of the kings of Cappadocia; the situation was pleasant, the buildings of stately, the enclosure spacious. They pursued their studies, and practised their exercises, under the tuition of the most skilful masters; and the numerous household appointed to attend, or rather to guard, the nephews of Constantine, was not unworthy of the dignity of their birth. But they could not disguise to themselves that they were deprived of fortune, of freedom, and of safety; secluded from the society of all whom they could trust or esteem, and condemned to pass their melancholy hours in the company of slaves devoted to the commands of a tyrant who had already injured them beyond the hope of reconciliation. At length, however, the emergencies of the state compelled the emperor, or rather his eunuchs, to invest Gallus, in the twenty-fifth year of his age, with the title of Caesar, and to cement this political connection by his marriage with the princess Constantina. After a formal interview, in which the two princes mutually engaged their faith never to undertake any thing to the prejudice of each other, they repaired without delay to their respective stations. Constantius continued his march towards the West, and Gallus fixed his residence at Antioch; from whence, with a delegated authority, he administered the five great dioceses of the eastern praefecture. [13] In this fortunate change, the new Caesar was not unmindful of his brother Julian, who obtained the honors of his rank, the appearances of liberty, and the restitution of an ample patrimony. [14]

[Footnote 11: Gregory Nazianzen (Orat. iii. p. 90) reproaches the apostate with his ingratitude towards Mark, bishop of Arethusa, who had contributed to save his life; and we learn, though from a less respectable authority, (Tillemont, Hist. des Empereurs, tom. iv. p. 916,) that Julian was concealed in the sanctuary of a church. Note: Gallus and Julian were not sons of the same mother. Their father, Julius Constantius, had had Gallus by his first wife, named Galla: Julian was the son of Basilina, whom he had espoused in a second marriage. Tillemont. Hist. des Emp. Vie de Constantin. art. 3—G.]

[Footnote 12: The most authentic account of the education and adventures of Julian is contained in the epistle or manifesto which he himself addressed to the senate and people of Athens. Libanius, (Orat. Parentalis,) on the side of the Pagans, and Socrates, (l. iii. c. 1,) on that of the Christians, have preserved several interesting circumstances.]

[Footnote 13: For the promotion of Gallus, see Idatius, Zosimus, and the two Victors. According to Philostorgius, (l. iv. c. 1,) Theophilus, an Arian bishop, was the witness, and, as it were, the guarantee of this solemn engagement. He supported that character with generous firmness; but M. de Tillemont (Hist. des Empereurs, tom. iv. p. 1120) thinks it very improbable that a heretic should have possessed such virtue.]

[Footnote 14: Julian was at first permitted to pursue his studies at Constantinople, but the reputation which he acquired soon excited the jealousy of Constantius; and the young prince was advised to withdraw himself to the less conspicuous scenes of Bithynia and Ionia.]

The writers the most indulgent to the memory of Gallus, and even Julian himself, though he wished to cast a veil over the frailties of his brother, are obliged to confess that the Caesar was incapable of reigning. Transported from a prison to a throne, he possessed neither genius nor application, nor docility to compensate for the want of knowledge and experience. A temper naturally morose and violent, instead of being corrected, was soured by solitude and adversity; the remembrance of what he had endured disposed him to retaliation rather than to sympathy; and the ungoverned sallies of his rage were often fatal to those who approached his person, or were subject to his power. [15] Constantina, his wife, is described, not as a woman, but as one of the infernal furies tormented with an insatiate thirst of human blood. [16] Instead of employing her influence to insinuate the mild counsels of prudence and humanity, she exasperated the fierce passions of her husband; and as she retained the vanity, though she had renounced, the gentleness of her sex, a pearl necklace was esteemed an equivalent price for the murder of an innocent and virtuous nobleman. [17] The cruelty of Gallus was sometimes displayed in the undissembled violence of popular or military executions; and was sometimes disguised by the abuse of law, and the forms of judicial proceedings. The private houses of Antioch, and the places of public resort, were besieged by spies and informers; and the Caesar himself, concealed in a a plebeian habit, very frequently condescended to assume that odious character. Every apartment of the palace was adorned with the instruments of death and torture, and a general consternation was diffused through the capital of Syria. The prince of the East, as if he had been conscious how much he had to fear, and how little he deserved to reign, selected for the objects of his resentment the provincials accused of some imaginary treason, and his own courtiers, whom with more reason he suspected of incensing, by their secret correspondence, the timid and suspicious mind of Constantius. But he forgot that he was depriving himself of his only support, the affection of the people; whilst he furnished the malice of his enemies with the arms of truth, and afforded the emperor the fairest pretence of exacting the forfeit of his purple, and of his life. [18]

[Footnote 15: See Julian. ad S. P. Q. A. p. 271. Jerom. in Chron. Aurelius Victor, Eutropius, x. 14. I shall copy the words of Eutropius, who wrote his abridgment about fifteen years after the death of Gallus, when there was no longer any motive either to flatter or to depreciate his character. "Multis incivilibus gestis Gallus Caesar.... vir natura ferox et ad tyrannidem pronior, si suo jure imperare licuisset."]

[Footnote 16: Megaera quidem mortalis, inflammatrix saevientis assidua, humani cruoris avida, &c. Ammian. Marcellin. l. xiv. c. 1. The sincerity of Ammianus would not suffer him to misrepresent facts or characters, but his love of ambitious ornaments frequently betrayed him into an unnatural vehemence of expression.]

[Footnote 17: His name was Clematius of Alexandria, and his only crime was a refusal to gratify the desires of his mother-in-law; who solicited his death, because she had been disappointed of his love. Ammian. xiv. c. i.]

[Footnote 18: See in Ammianus (l. xiv. c. 1, 7) a very ample detail of the cruelties of Gallus. His brother Julian (p. 272) insinuates, that a secret conspiracy had been formed against him; and Zosimus names (l. ii. p. 135) the persons engaged in it; a minister of considerable rank, and two obscure agents, who were resolved to make their fortune.]

As long as the civil war suspended the fate of the Roman world, Constantius dissembled his knowledge of the weak and cruel administration to which his choice had subjected the East; and the discovery of some assassins, secretly despatched to Antioch by the tyrant of Gaul, was employed to convince the public, that the emperor and the Caesar were united by the same interest, and pursued by the same enemies. [19] But when the victory was decided in favor of Constantius, his dependent colleague became less useful and less formidable. Every circumstance of his conduct was severely and suspiciously examined, and it was privately resolved, either to deprive Gallus of the purple, or at least to remove him from the indolent luxury of Asia to the hardships and dangers of a German war. The death of Theophilus, consular of the province of Syria, who in a time of scarcity had been massacred by the people of Antioch, with the connivance, and almost at the instigation, of Gallus, was justly resented, not only as an act of wanton cruelty, but as a dangerous insult on the supreme majesty of Constantius. Two ministers of illustrious rank, Domitian the Oriental praefect, and Montius, quaestor of the palace, were empowered by a special commission [19a] to visit and reform the state of the East. They were instructed to behave towards Gallus with moderation and respect, and, by the gentlest arts of persuasion, to engage him to comply with the invitation of his brother and colleague. The rashness of the praefect disappointed these prudent measures, and hastened his own ruin, as well as that of his enemy. On his arrival at Antioch, Domitian passed disdainfully before the gates of the palace, and alleging a slight pretence of indisposition, continued several days in sullen retirement, to prepare an inflammatory memorial, which he transmitted to the Imperial court. Yielding at length to the pressing solicitations of

Gallus, the praefect condescended to take his seat in council; but his first step was to signify a concise and haughty mandate, importing that the Caesar should immediately repair to Italy, and threatening that he himself would punish his delay or hesitation, by suspending the usual allowance of his household. The nephew and daughter of Constantine, who could ill brook the insolence of a subject, expressed their resentment by instantly delivering Domitian to the custody of a guard. The quarrel still admitted of some terms of accommodation. They were rendered impracticable by the imprudent behavior of Montius, a statesman whose arts and experience were frequently betrayed by the levity of his disposition. [20] The quaestor reproached Gallus in a haughty language, that a prince who was scarcely authorized to remove a municipal magistrate, should presume to imprison a Praetorian praefect; convoked a meeting of the civil and military officers; and required them, in the name of their sovereign, to defend the person and dignity of his representatives. By this rash declaration of war, the impatient temper of Gallus was provoked to embrace the most desperate counsels. He ordered his guards to stand to their arms, assembled the populace of Antioch, and recommended to their zeal the care of his safety and revenge. His commands were too fatally obeyed. They rudely seized the praefect and the quaestor, and tying their legs together with ropes, they dragged them through the streets of the city, inflicted a thousand insults and a thousand wounds on these unhappy victims, and at last precipitated their mangled and lifeless bodies into the stream of the Orontes. [21]

[Footnote 19: Zonaras, l. xiii. tom. ii. p. 17, 18. The assassins had seduced a great number of legionaries; but their designs were discovered and revealed by an old woman in whose cottage they lodged.]

[Footnote 19a: The commission seems to have been granted to Domitian alone. Montius interfered to support his authority. Amm. Marc. loc. cit—M]

[Footnote 20: In the present text of Ammianus, we read Asper, quidem, sed ad lenitatem propensior; which forms a sentence of contradictory nonsense. With the aid of an old manuscript, Valesius has rectified the first of these corruptions, and we perceive a ray of light in the substitution of the word vafer. If we venture to change lenitatem into lexitatem, this alteration of a single letter will render the whole passage clear and consistent.]

[Footnote 21: Instead of being obliged to collect scattered and imperfect hints from various sources, we now enter into the full stream of the history of Ammianus, and need only refer to the seventh and ninth chapters of his fourteenth book. Philostorgius, however, (l. iii. c. 28) though partial to Gallus, should not be entirely overlooked.]

After such a deed, whatever might have been the designs of Gallus, it was only in a field of battle that he could assert his innocence with any hope of success. But the mind of that prince was formed of an equal mixture of violence and weakness. Instead of assuming the title of Augustus, instead of employing in his defence the troops and treasures of the East, he suffered himself to be deceived by the affected tranquillity of Constantius, who, leaving him the vain pageantry of a court, imperceptibly recalled the veteran legions from the provinces of Asia. But as it still appeared dangerous to arrest Gallus in his capital, the slow and safer arts of dissimulation were practised with success. The frequent and pressing epistles of Constantius were filled with professions of confidence and friendship; exhorting the Caesar to discharge the duties of his high station, to relieve his colleague from a part of the public cares, and to assist the West by his presence, his counsels, and his arms. After so many reciprocal injuries, Gallus had reason to fear and to distrust. But he had neglected the opportunities of flight and of resistance; he was seduced by the flattering assurances of the tribune Scudilo, who, under the semblance of a rough soldier, disguised the most artful insinuation; and he depended on the credit of his wife Constantina, till the unseasonable death of that princess completed the ruin in which he had been involved by her impetuous passions. [22]

[Footnote 22: She had preceded her husband, but died of a fever on the road at a little place in Bithynia, called Coenum Gallicanum.]

PART II

After a long delay, the reluctant Caesar set forwards on his journey to the Imperial court. From Antioch to Hadrianople, he traversed the wide extent of his dominions with a numerous and stately train; and as he labored to conceal his apprehensions from the world, and perhaps from himself, he entertained the people of Constantinople with an exhibition of the games of the circus. The progress of the journey might, however, have warned him of the impending danger. In all the principal cities he was met by ministers of confidence, commissioned to seize the offices of government, to observe his motions, and to prevent the hasty sallies of his despair. The persons despatched to secure the provinces which he left behind, passed him with cold salutations, or affected disdain; and the troops, whose station lay along the public road, were studiously removed on his approach, lest they might be tempted to offer their swords for the service of a civil war. [23] After Gallus had been permitted to repose himself a few days at Hadrianople, he received a mandate, expressed in the most haughty and absolute style, that his splendid retinue should halt in that city, while the Caesar himself, with only ten post-carriages, should hasten to the Imperial residence at Milan.

In this rapid journey, the profound respect which was due to the brother and colleague of Constantius, was insensibly changed into rude familiarity; and Gallus, who discovered in the countenances of the attendants that they already considered themselves as his guards, and might soon be employed as his executioners, began to accuse his fatal rashness, and to recollect, with terror and remorse, the conduct by which he had provoked his fate. The dissimulation which had hitherto been preserved, was laid aside at Petovio, [23a] in Pannonia. He was conducted to a palace in the suburbs, where the general Barbatio, with a select band of soldiers, who could neither be moved by pity, nor corrupted by rewards, expected the arrival of his illustrious victim. In the close of the evening he was arrested, ignominiously stripped of the ensigns of Caesar, and hurried away to Pola, [23b] in Istria, a sequestered prison, which had been so recently polluted with royal blood. The horror which he felt was soon increased by the appearance of his implacable enemy the eunuch Eusebius, who, with the assistance of a notary and a tribune, proceeded to interrogate him concerning the administration of the East. The Caesar sank under the weight of shame and guilt, confessed all the criminal actions and all the treasonable designs with which he was charged; and by imputing them to the advice of his wife, exasperated the indignation of Constantius, who reviewed with partial prejudice the minutes of the examination. The emperor was easily convinced, that his own safety was incompatible with the life of his cousin: the sentence of death was signed, despatched, and executed; and the nephew of Constantine, with his hands tied behind his back, was beheaded in prison like the vilest malefactor. [24] Those who are inclined to palliate the cruelties of Constantius, assert that he soon relented, and endeavored to recall the bloody mandate; but that the second messenger, intrusted with the reprieve, was detained by the eunuchs, who dreaded the unforgiving temper of Gallus, and were desirous of reuniting to their empire the wealthy provinces of the East. [25]

[Footnote 23: The Thebaean legions, which were then quartered at Hadrianople, sent a deputation to Gallus, with a tender of their services. Ammian. l. xiv. c. 11. The Notitia (s. 6, 20, 38, edit. Labb.) mentions three several legions which bore the name of Thebaean. The zeal of M. de Voltaire to destroy a despicable though celebrated legion, has tempted him on the slightest grounds to deny the existence of a Thenaean legion in the Roman armies. See Oeuvres de Voltaire, tom. xv. p. 414, quarto edition.]

[Footnote 23a: Pettau in Styria—M]

[Footnote 23b: Rather to Flanonia. now Fianone, near Pola. St. Martin—M.]

[Footnote 24: See the complete narrative of the journey and death of Gallus in Ammianus, l. xiv. c. 11. Julian complains that his brother was put to death without a trial; attempts to justify, or at least to excuse, the cruel revenge which he had inflicted on his enemies; but seems at last to acknowledge that he might justly have been deprived of the purple.]

[Footnote 25: Philostorgius, l. iv. c. 1. Zonaras, l. xiii. tom. ii. p. 19. But the former was partial towards an Arian monarch, and the latter transcribed, without choice or criticism, whatever he found in the writings of the ancients.]

Besides the reigning emperor, Julian alone survived, of all the numerous posterity of Constantius Chlorus. The misfortune of his royal birth involved him in the disgrace of Gallus. From his retirement in the happy country of Ionia, he was conveyed under a strong guard to the court of Milan; where he languished above seven months, in the continual apprehension of suffering the same ignominious death, which was daily inflicted almost before his eyes, on the friends and adherents of his persecuted family. His looks, his gestures, his silence, were scrutinized with malignant curiosity, and he was perpetually assaulted by enemies whom he had never offended, and by arts to which he was a stranger. [26] But in the school of adversity, Julian insensibly acquired the virtues of firmness and discretion. He defended his honor, as well as his life, against the insnaring subtleties of the eunuchs, who endeavored to extort some declaration of his sentiments; and whilst he cautiously suppressed his grief and resentment, he nobly disdained to flatter the tyrant, by any seeming approbation of his brother's murder. Julian most devoutly ascribes his miraculous deliverance to the protection of the gods, who had exempted his innocence from the sentence of destruction pronounced by their justice against the impious house of Constantine. [27] As the most effectual instrument of their providence, he gratefully acknowledges the steady and generous friendship of the empress Eusebia, [28] a woman of beauty and merit, who, by the ascendant which she had gained over the mind of her husband, counterbalanced, in some measure, the powerful conspiracy of the eunuchs. By the intercession of his patroness, Julian was admitted into the Imperial presence: he pleaded his cause with a decent freedom, he was heard with favor; and, notwithstanding the efforts of his enemies, who urged the danger of sparing an avenger of the blood of Gallus, the milder sentiment of Eusebia prevailed in the council. But the effects of a second interview were dreaded by the eunuchs; and Julian was advised to withdraw for a while into the neighborhood of Milan, till the emperor thought proper to assign the city of Athens for the place of his honorable exile. As he had discovered, from his earliest youth, a propensity, or rather passion, for the language, the manners, the learning, and the religion of the Greeks, he obeyed with pleasure an order so agreeable to his wishes. Far from the tumult of arms, and the treachery of courts, he spent six months under the groves of the academy, in a free intercourse with the philosophers of the age, who studied to cultivate the genius, to encourage the vanity, and to inflame the devotion of their royal pupil. Their labors were not unsuccessful; and Julian inviolably preserved for Athens that tender regard which seldom fails to arise in a liberal mind, from the recollection of the place where it has discovered and exercised its growing powers. The gentleness and affability of manners, which his temper suggested and his situation imposed, insensibly engaged the affections of the strangers, as well as citizens, with whom he conversed. Some of his fellow-students might perhaps examine his behavior with an eye of prejudice and aversion; but Julian established, in the schools of Athens, a general prepossession in favor of his virtues and talents, which was soon diffused over the Roman world. [29]

[Footnote 26: See Ammianus Marcellin. l. xv. c. 1, 3, 8. Julian himself in his epistle to the Athenians, draws a very lively and just picture of his own danger, and of his sentiments. He shows, however, a tendency to exaggerate his sufferings, by insinuating, though in obscure terms, that they lasted above a year; a period which cannot be reconciled with the truth of chronology.]

[Footnote 27: Julian has worked the crimes and misfortunes of the family of Constantine into an allegorical fable, which is happily conceived and agreeably related. It forms the conclusion of the seventh Oration, from whence it has been detached and translated by the Abbe de la Bleterie, Vie de Jovien, tom. ii. p. 385-408.]

[Footnote 28: She was a native of Thessalonica, in Macedonia, of a noble family, and the daughter, as well as sister, of consuls. Her marriage with the emperor may be placed in the year 352. In a divided age, the historians of all parties agree in her praises. See their testimonies collected by Tillemont, Hist. des Empereurs, tom. iv. p. 750-754.]

[Footnote 29: Libanius and Gregory Nazianzen have exhausted the arts as well as the powers of their eloquence, to represent Julian as the first of heroes, or the worst of tyrants. Gregory was his fellow-student at Athens; and the symptoms which he so tragically describes, of the future wickedness of the apostate, amount only to some bodily imperfections, and to some peculiarities in his speech and manner. He protests, however, that he then foresaw and foretold the calamities of the church and state. (Greg. Nazianzen, Orat. iv. p. 121, 122.)]

Whilst his hours were passed in studious retirement, the empress, resolute to achieve the generous design which she had undertaken, was not unmindful of the care of his fortune. The death of the late Caesar had left Constantius invested with the sole command, and oppressed by the accumulated weight, of a mighty empire. Before the wounds of civil discord could be healed, the provinces of Gaul were overwhelmed by a deluge of Barbarians. The Sarmatians no longer respected the barrier of the Danube. The impunity of rapine had increased the boldness and numbers of the wild Isaurians: those robbers descended from their craggy mountains to ravage the adjacent country, and had even presumed, though without success, to besiege the important city of Seleucia, which was defended by a garrison of three Roman legions. Above all, the Persian monarch, elated by victory, again threatened the peace of Asia, and the presence of the emperor was indispensably required, both in the West and in the East. For the first time, Constantius sincerely acknowledged, that his single strength was unequal to such an extent of care and of dominion. [30] Insensible to the voice of flattery, which assured him that his all-powerful virtue, and celestial fortune, would still continue to triumph over every obstacle, he listened with complacency to the advice of Eusebia, which gratified his indolence, without offending his suspicious pride. As she perceived that the remembrance of Gallus dwelt on the emperor's mind, she artfully turned his attention to the opposite characters of the two brothers, which from their infancy had been compared to those of Domitian and of Titus. [31] She accustomed her husband to consider Julian as a youth of a mild, unambitious disposition, whose allegiance and gratitude might be secured by the gift of the purple, and who was qualified to fill with honor a subordinate station, without aspiring to dispute the commands, or to shade the glories, of his sovereign and benefactor. After an obstinate, though secret struggle, the opposition of the favorite eunuchs submitted to the ascendency of the empress; and it was resolved that Julian, after celebrating his nuptials with Helena, sister of Constantius, should be appointed, with the title of Caesar, to reign over the countries beyond the Alps. [32]

[Footnote 30: *Succumbere tot necessitatibus tamque crebris unum se, quod nunquam fecerat, aperte demonstrans.* Ammian. l. xv. c. 8. He then expresses, in their own words, the flattering assurances of the courtiers.]

[Footnote 31: *Tantum a temperatis moribus Juliani differens fratris quantum inter Vespasiani filios fuit, Domitianum et Titum.* Ammian. l. xiv. c. 11. The circumstances and education of the two brothers, were so nearly the same, as to afford a strong example of the innate difference of characters.]

[Footnote 32: Ammianus, l. xv. c. 8. Zosimus, l. iii. p. 137, 138.]

Although the order which recalled him to court was probably accompanied by some intimation of his approaching greatness, he appeals to the people of Athens to witness his tears of undissembled sorrow, when he was reluctantly torn away from his beloved retirement. [33] He trembled for his life, for his fame, and even for his virtue; and his sole confidence was derived from the persuasion, that Minerva inspired all his actions, and that he was protected by an invisible guard of angels, whom for that purpose she had borrowed from the Sun and Moon. He approached, with horror, the palace of Milan; nor could the ingenuous youth conceal his indignation, when he found himself accosted with false and servile respect by the assassins of his family. Eusebia, rejoicing in the success of her benevolent schemes, embraced him with the tenderness of a sister; and endeavored, by the most soothing caresses, to dispel his terrors, and reconcile him to his fortune. But the ceremony of shaving his beard, and his awkward demeanor, when he first exchanged the cloak of a Greek philosopher for the military habit of a Roman prince, amused, during a few days, the levity of the Imperial court. [34]

[Footnote 33: Julian. ad S. P. Q. A. p. 275, 276. Libanius, Orat. x. p. 268. Julian did not yield till the gods had signified their will by repeated visions and omens. His piety then forbade him to resist.]

[Footnote 34: Julian himself relates, (p. 274) with some humor, the circumstances of his own metamorphoses, his downcast looks, and his perplexity at being thus suddenly transported into a new world, where every object appeared strange and hostile.]

The emperors of the age of Constantine no longer deigned to consult with the senate in the choice of a colleague; but they were anxious that their nomination should be ratified by the consent of the army. On this solemn occasion, the guards, with the other troops whose stations were in the neighborhood of Milan, appeared under arms; and Constantius ascended his lofty tribunal, holding by the hand his cousin Julian, who entered the same day into the twenty-fifth year of his age. [35] In a studied speech, conceived and delivered with dignity, the emperor represented the various dangers which threatened the prosperity of the republic, the necessity of naming a Caesar for the administration of the West, and his own intention, if it was agreeable to their wishes, of rewarding with the honors of the purple the promising virtues of the nephew of Constantine. The approbation of the soldiers was testified by a respectful murmur; they gazed on the manly countenance of Julian, and observed with pleasure, that the fire which sparkled in his eyes was tempered by a modest blush, on being thus exposed, for the first time, to the public view of mankind. As soon as the ceremony of his investiture had been performed, Constantius addressed him with the tone of authority which his superior age and station permitted him to assume; and exhorting the new Caesar to deserve, by heroic deeds, that sacred and immortal name, the emperor gave his colleague the strongest assurances of a friendship which should never be impaired by time, nor interrupted by their separation into the most distant climes. As soon as the speech was ended, the troops, as a token of applause, clashed their shields against their knees; [36] while the officers who surrounded the tribunal expressed, with decent reserve, their sense of the merits of the representative of Constantius.

[Footnote 35: See Ammian. Marcellin. l. xv. c. 8. Zosimus, l. iii. p. 139. Aurelius Victor. Victor Junior in Epitom. Eutrop. x. 14.]

[Footnote 36: Militares omnes horrendo fragore scuta genibus illidentes; quod est prosperitatis indicium plenum; nam contra cum hastis clypei feriuntur, irae documentum est et doloris...... Ammianus adds, with a nice distinction, Eumque ut potiori reverentia servaretur, nec supra modum laudabant nec infra quam decebat.]

The two princes returned to the palace in the same chariot; and during the slow procession, Julian repeated to himself a verse of his favorite Homer, which he might equally apply to his fortune and to his fears. [37] The four-and-twenty days which the Caesar spent at Milan after his investiture, and the first months of his Gallic reign, were devoted to a splendid but severe captivity; nor could the acquisition of honor compensate for the loss of freedom. [38] His steps were watched, his correspondence was intercepted; and he was obliged, by prudence, to decline the visits of his most intimate friends. Of his former domestics, four only were permitted to attend him; two pages, his physician, and his librarian; the last of whom was employed in the care of a valuable collection of books, the gift of the empress, who studied the inclinations as well as the interest of her friend. In the room of these faithful servants, a household was formed, such indeed as became the dignity of a Caesar; but it was filled with a crowd of slaves, destitute, and perhaps incapable, of any attachment for their new master, to whom, for the most part, they were either unknown or suspected. His want of experience might require the assistance of a wise council; but the minute instructions which regulated the service of his table, and the distribution of his hours, were adapted to a youth still under the discipline of his preceptors, rather than to the situation of a prince intrusted with the conduct of an important war. If he aspired to deserve the esteem of his subjects, he was checked by the fear of displeasing his sovereign; and even the fruits of his marriage-bed were blasted by the jealous artifices of Eusebia [39] herself, who, on this occasion alone, seems to have been unmindful of the tenderness of her sex, and the generosity of her character. The memory of his father and of his brothers reminded Julian of his own danger, and his apprehensions were increased by the recent and unworthy fate of Sylvanus. In the summer which preceded his own elevation, that general had been chosen to deliver Gaul from the tyranny of the Barbarians; but Sylvanus soon discovered that he had left his most dangerous enemies in the Imperial court. A dexterous informer, countenanced by several of the principal ministers, procured from him some recommendatory letters; and erasing the whole of the contents, except the signature, filled up the vacant parchment with matters of high and treasonable import. By the industry and courage of his friends, the fraud was however detected, and in a great council of the civil and military officers, held in the presence of the emperor himself, the innocence of Sylvanus was publicly acknowledged. But the discovery came too late; the report of the calumny, and the hasty seizure of his estate, had already provoked the indignant chief to the rebellion of which he was so unjustly accused. He assumed the purple at his head-quarters of Cologne, and his active powers appeared to menace Italy with an invasion, and Milan with a siege. In this emergency, Ursicinus, a general of equal rank, regained, by an act of treachery, the favor which he had lost by his eminent services in the East. Exasperated, as he might speciously allege, by the injuries of a similar nature, he hastened with a few followers to join the standard, and to betray the confidence, of his too credulous friend. After a reign of only twenty-eight days, Sylvanus was assassinated: the soldiers who, without any criminal intention, had blindly followed the example of their leader, immediately returned to their allegiance; and the flatterers of Constantius celebrated the wisdom and felicity of the monarch who had extinguished a civil war without the hazard of a battle. [40]

[Footnote 37: The word purple which Homer had used as a vague but common epithet for death, was applied by Julian to express, very aptly, the nature and object of his own apprehensions.]

[Footnote 38: He represents, in the most pathetic terms, (p. 277,) the distress of his new situation. The provision for his table was, however, so elegant and sumptuous, that the young philosopher rejected it with disdain. Quum legeret libellum assidue, quem Constantius ut privignum ad studia mittens manu sua conscripserat, praelicenter disponens quid in convivio Caesaris impendi deberit: Phasianum, et vulvam et sumen exigi vetuit et inferri. Ammian. Marcellin. l. xvi. c. 5.]

[Footnote 39: If we recollect that Constantine, the father of Helena, died above eighteen years before, in a mature old age, it will appear probable, that the daughter, though a virgin, could not be very young at the time of her marriage. She was soon afterwards delivered of a son, who died immediately, quod obstetrix corrupta mercede, mox natum praesecto plusquam convenerat umbilico necavit. She accompanied the emperor and empress in their journey to Rome, and the latter, quaesitum venenum bibere per fraudem illexit, ut quotiescunque concepisset, immaturum abjiceret partum. Ammian. l. xvi. c. 10. Our physicians will determine whether there exists such a poison. For my own part I am inclined to hope that the public malignity imputed the effects of accident as the guilt of Eusebia.]

[Footnote 40: Ammianus (xv. v.) was perfectly well informed of the conduct and fate of Sylvanus. He himself was one of the few followers who attended Ursicinus in his dangerous enterprise.]

The protection of the Rhaetian frontier, and the persecution of the Catholic church, detained Constantius in Italy above eighteen months after the departure of Julian. Before the emperor returned into the East, he indulged his pride and curiosity in a visit to the ancient capital. [41] He proceeded from Milan to Rome along the Aemilian and Flaminian ways, and as soon as he approached within forty miles of the city, the march of a prince who had never vanquished a foreign enemy, assumed the appearance of a triumphal procession. His splendid train was composed of all the ministers of luxury; but in a time of profound peace, he was encompassed by the glittering arms of the numerous squadrons of his guards and cuirassiers. Their streaming banners of silk, embossed with gold, and shaped in the form of dragons, waved round the person of the emperor. Constantius sat alone in a lofty car, resplendent with gold and precious gems; and, except when he bowed his head to pass under the gates of the cities, he affected a stately demeanor of inflexible, and, as it might seem, of insensible gravity. The severe discipline of the Persian youth had been introduced by the eunuchs into the Imperial palace; and such were the habits of patience which they had inculcated, that during a slow and sultry march, he was never seen to move his hand towards his face, or to turn his eyes either to the right or to the left. He was received by the magistrates and senate of Rome; and the emperor surveyed, with attention, the civil honors of the republic, and the consular images of the noble families. The streets were lined with an innumerable multitude. Their repeated acclamations expressed their joy at beholding, after an absence of thirty-two years, the sacred person of their sovereign, and Constantius himself expressed, with some pleasantry, he affected surprise that the human race should thus suddenly be collected on the same spot. The son of Constantine was lodged in the ancient palace of Augustus: he presided in the senate, harangued the people from the tribunal which Cicero had so often ascended, assisted with unusual courtesy at the games of the Circus, and accepted the crowns of gold, as well as the Panegyrics which had been prepared for the ceremony by the deputies of the principal cities. His short visit of thirty days was employed in viewing the monuments of art and power which were scattered over the seven hills and the interjacent valleys. He admired the awful majesty of the Capitol, the vast extent of the baths of Caracalla and Diocletian, the severe simplicity of the Pantheon, the massy greatness of the amphitheatre of Titus, the elegant architecture of the theatre of Pompey and the Temple of Peace, and, above all, the stately structure of the Forum and column of Trajan; acknowledging that the voice of fame, so prone to invent and to magnify, had made an inadequate report of the metropolis of the world. The traveller, who has contemplated the ruins of ancient Rome, may conceive some imperfect idea of the sentiments which they must have inspired when they reared their heads in the splendor of unsullied beauty.

[See The Pantheon: The severe simplicity of the Pantheon]

[Footnote 41: For the particulars of the visit of Constantius to Rome, see Ammianus, l. xvi. c. 10. We have only to add, that Themistius was appointed deputy from Constantinople, and that he composed his fourth oration for his ceremony.]

The satisfaction which Constantius had received from this journey excited him to the generous emulation of bestowing on the Romans some memorial of his own gratitude and munificence. His first idea was to imitate the equestrian and colossal statue which he had seen in the Forum of Trajan; but when he had maturely weighed the difficulties of the execution, [42] he chose rather to embellish the capital by the gift of an Egyptian obelisk. In a remote but polished age, which seems to have preceded the invention of alphabetical writing, a great number of these obelisks had been erected, in the cities of Thebes and Heliopolis, by the ancient sovereigns of Egypt, in a just confidence that the simplicity of their form, and the hardness of their substance, would resist the injuries of time and violence. [43] Several of these extraordinary columns had been transported to Rome by Augustus and his successors, as the most durable monuments of their power and victory; [44] but there remained one obelisk, which, from its size or sanctity, escaped for a long time the rapacious vanity of the conquerors. It was designed by Constantine to adorn his new city; [45] and, after being removed by his order from the pedestal where it stood before the Temple of the Sun at Heliopolis, was floated down the Nile to Alexandria. The death of Constantine suspended the execution of his purpose, and this obelisk was destined by his son to the ancient capital of the empire. A vessel of uncommon strength and capaciousness was provided to convey this enormous weight of granite, at least a hundred and fifteen feet in length, from the banks of the Nile to those of the Tyber. The obelisk of Constantius was landed about three miles from the city, and elevated, by the efforts of art and labor, in the great Circus of Rome. [46] [46a]

[Footnote 42: Hormisdas, a fugitive prince of Persia, observed to the emperor, that if he made such a horse, he must think of preparing a similar stable, (the Forum of Trajan.) Another saying of Hormisdas is recorded, "that one thing only had displeased him, to find that men died at Rome as well as elsewhere." If we adopt this reading of the text of Ammianus, (displicuisse, instead of placuisse,) we may consider it as a reproof of Roman vanity. The contrary sense would be that of a misanthrope.]

[Footnote 43: When Germanicus visited the ancient monuments of Thebes, the eldest of the priests explained to him the meaning of these hiero glyphics. Tacit. Annal. ii. c. 60. But it seems probable, that before the useful invention of an alphabet, these natural or arbitrary signs were the common characters of the Egyptian nation. See Warburton's Divine Legation of Moses, vol. iii. p. 69-243.]

[Footnote 44: See Plin. Hist. Natur. l. xxxvi. c. 14, 15.]

[Footnote 45: Ammian. Marcellin l. xvii. c. 4. He gives us a Greek interpretation of the hieroglyphics, and his commentator Lindenbrogius adds a Latin inscription, which, in twenty verses of the age of Constantius, contain a short history of the obelisk.]

[Footnote 46: See Donat. Roma. Antiqua, l. iii. c. 14, l. iv. c. 12, and the learned, though confused, Dissertation of Bargaeus on Obelisks, inserted in the fourth volume of Graevius's Roman Antiquities, p. 1897- 1936. This dissertation is dedicated to Pope Sixtus V., who erected the obelisk of Constantius in the square before the patriarchal church of at. John Lateran.]

[Footnote 46a: It is doubtful whether the obelisk transported by Constantius to Rome now exists. Even from the text of Ammianus, it is uncertain whether the interpretation of Hermapion refers to the older obelisk, (obelisco incisus est veteri quem videmus in Circo,) raised, as he himself states, in the Circus Maximus, long before, by Augustus, or to the one brought by Constantius. The obelisk in the square before the church of St. John Lateran is ascribed not to Rameses the Great but to Thoutmos II. Champollion, 1. Lettre a M. de Blacas, p. 32—M]

The departure of Constantius from Rome was hastened by the alarming intelligence of the distress and danger of the Illyrian provinces. The distractions of civil war, and the irreparable loss which the Roman legions had sustained in the battle of Mursa, exposed those countries, almost without defence, to the light cavalry of the Barbarians; and particularly to the inroads of the Quadi, a fierce and powerful nation, who seem to have exchanged the institutions of Germany for the arms and military arts of their Sarmatian allies. [47] The garrisons of the frontiers were insufficient to check their progress; and the indolent monarch was at length compelled to assemble, from the extremities of his dominions, the flower of the Palatine troops, to take the field in person, and to employ a whole campaign, with the preceding autumn and the ensuing spring, in the serious prosecution of the war. The emperor passed the Danube on a bridge of boats, cut in pieces all that encountered his march, penetrated into the heart of the country of the Quadi, and severely retaliated the calamities which they had inflicted on the Roman province. The dismayed Barbarians were soon reduced to sue for peace: they offered the restitution of his captive subjects as an atonement for the past, and the noblest hostages as a pledge of their future conduct. The generous courtesy which was shown to the first among their chieftains who implored the clemency of Constantius, encouraged the more timid, or the more obstinate, to imitate their example; and the Imperial camp was crowded with the princes and ambassadors of the most distant tribes, who occupied the plains of the Lesser Poland, and who might have deemed themselves secure behind the lofty ridge of the Carpathian Mountains. While Constantius gave laws to the Barbarians beyond the Danube, he distinguished, with specious compassion, the Sarmatian exiles, who had been expelled from their native country by the rebellion of their slaves, and who formed a very considerable accession to the power of the Quadi. The emperor, embracing a generous but artful system of policy, released the Sarmatians from the bands of this humiliating dependence, and restored them, by a separate treaty, to the dignity of a nation united under the government of a king, the friend and ally of the republic. He declared his resolution of asserting the justice of their cause, and of securing the peace of the provinces by the extirpation, or at least the banishment, of the Limigantes, whose manners were still infected with the vices of their servile origin. The execution of this design was attended with more difficulty than glory. The territory of the Limigantes was protected against the Romans by the Danube, against the hostile Barbarians by the Teyss. The marshy lands which lay between those rivers, and were often covered by their inundations, formed an intricate wilderness, pervious only to the inhabitants, who were acquainted with its secret paths and inaccessible fortresses. On the approach of Constantius, the Limigantes tried the efficacy of prayers, of fraud, and of arms; but he sternly rejected their supplications, defeated their rude stratagems, and repelled with skill and firmness the efforts of their irregular valor. One of their most warlike tribes, established in a small island towards the conflux of the Teyss and the Danube, consented to pass the river with the intention of surprising the emperor during the security of an amicable conference. They soon became the victims of the perfidy which they meditated. Encompassed on every side, trampled down by the cavalry, slaughtered by the swords of the legions, they disdained to ask for mercy; and with an undaunted countenance, still grasped their weapons in the agonies of death. After this victory, a considerable body of Romans was landed on the opposite banks of the Danube; the Taifalae, a Gothic tribe engaged in the service of the empire, invaded the Limigantes on the side of the Teyss; and their former masters, the free Sarmatians, animated by hope and revenge, penetrated through the hilly country, into the heart of their ancient possessions. A general conflagration revealed the huts of the Barbarians, which were seated in the depth of the wilderness; and the soldier fought with confidence on marshy ground, which it was dangerous for him to tread. In this extremity, the bravest of the Limigantes were resolved to die in arms, rather than to yield: but the milder sentiment, enforced by the authority of their elders, at length prevailed; and the suppliant crowd, followed by their wives and children, repaired to the Imperial camp, to learn their fate from the mouth of the conqueror. After celebrating his own clemency, which was still inclined to pardon their repeated crimes, and to spare the remnant of a guilty nation, Constantius assigned for the place of their exile a remote country, where they might enjoy a safe and honorable repose. The Limigantes obeyed with reluctance; but before they could reach, at least before they could occupy, their destined habitations, they returned to the banks of the Danube, exaggerating the hardships of their situation, and requesting, with fervent professions of fidelity, that the emperor would grant them an undisturbed settlement within the limits of the Roman provinces. Instead of consulting his own experience of their incurable perfidy, Constantius listened to his flatterers, who were ready to represent the honor and advantage of accepting a colony of soldiers, at a time when it was much easier to obtain the pecuniary contributions than the military service of the subjects of the empire. The Limigantes were permitted to pass the Danube; and the emperor gave audience to the multitude in a large plain near the modern city of Buda. They surrounded the tribunal, and seemed to hear with respect an oration full of mildness and dignity when one of the Barbarians, casting his shoe into the air, exclaimed with a loud voice, Marha! Marha! [47a] a word of defiance, which was received as a signal of the tumult. They rushed with fury to seize the person of the emperor; his royal throne and golden couch were pillaged by these rude hands; but the faithful defence of his guards, who died at his feet, allowed him a moment to mount a fleet horse, and to escape from the confusion. The disgrace which had been incurred by a treacherous surprise was soon retrieved by the numbers and discipline of the Romans; and the combat was only terminated by the extinction of the name and nation of the Limigantes. The free Sarmatians were reinstated in the possession of their ancient seats; and although Constantius distrusted the levity of their character, he entertained some hopes that a sense of gratitude might influence their future conduct. He had remarked the lofty stature and obsequious demeanor of Zizais, one of the noblest of their chiefs. He conferred on him the title of King; and Zizais proved that he was not unworthy to reign, by a sincere and lasting attachment to the interests of his benefactor, who, after this splendid success, received the name of Sarmaticus from the acclamations of his victorious army. [48]

[Footnote 47: The events of this Quadian and Sarmatian war are related by Ammianus, xvi. 10, xvii. 12, 13, xix. 11]

[Footnote 47a: Reinesius reads Warrha, Warrha, Guerre, War. Wagner note as a mm. Marc xix. II—M.]

[Footnote 48: Genti Sarmatarum magno decori confidens apud eos regem dedit. Aurelius Victor. In a pompous oration pronounced by Constantius himself, he expatiates on his own exploits with much vanity, and some truth]

PART III

While the Roman emperor and the Persian monarch, at the distance of three thousand miles, defended their extreme limits against the Barbarians of the Danube and of the Oxus, their intermediate frontier experienced the vicissitudes of a languid war, and a precarious truce. Two of the eastern ministers of Constantius, the Praetorian praefect Musonian, whose abilities were disgraced by the want of truth and integrity, and Cassian, duke of Mesopotamia, a hardy and veteran soldier, opened a secret negotiation with the satrap Tamsapor. [49] [49a] These overtures of peace, translated into the servile and flattering language of Asia, were transmitted to the camp of the Great King; who resolved to signify, by an ambassador, the terms which he was inclined to grant to the suppliant Romans. Narses, whom he invested with that character, was honorably received in his passage through Antioch and Constantinople: he reached Sirmium after a long journey, and, at his first audience, respectfully unfolded the silken veil which covered the haughty epistle of his sovereign. Sapor, King of Kings, and Brother of the Sun and Moon, (such were the lofty titles affected by Oriental vanity,) expressed his satisfaction that his brother, Constantius Caesar, had been taught wisdom by adversity. As the lawful successor of Darius Hystaspes, Sapor asserted, that the River Strymon, in Macedonia, was the true and ancient boundary of his empire; declaring, however, that as an evidence of his moderation, he would content himself with the provinces of Armenia and Mesopotamia, which had been fraudulently extorted from his ancestors. He alleged, that, without the restitution of these disputed countries, it was impossible to establish any treaty on a solid and permanent basis; and he arrogantly threatened, that if his ambassador returned in vain, he was prepared to take the field in the spring, and to support the justice of his cause by the strength of his invincible arms. Narses, who was endowed with the most polite and amiable manners, endeavored, as far as was consistent with his duty, to soften the harshness of the message. [50] Both the style and substance were maturely weighed in the Imperial council, and he was dismissed with the following answer: "Constantius had a right to disclaim the officiousness of his ministers, who had acted without any specific orders from the throne: he was not, however, averse to an equal and honorable treaty; but it was highly indecent, as well as absurd, to propose to the sole and victorious emperor of the Roman world, the same conditions of peace which he had indignantly rejected at the time when his power was contracted within the narrow limits of the East: the chance of arms was uncertain; and Sapor should recollect, that if the Romans had sometimes been vanquished in battle, they had almost always been successful in the event of the war." A few days after the departure of Narses, three ambassadors were sent to the court of Sapor, who was already returned from the Scythian expedition to his ordinary residence of Ctesiphon. A count, a notary, and a sophist, had been selected for this important commission; and Constantius, who was secretly anxious for the conclusion of the peace, entertained some hopes that the dignity of the first of these ministers, the dexterity of the second, and the rhetoric of the third, [51] would persuade the Persian monarch to abate of the rigor of his demands. But the progress of their negotiation was opposed and defeated by the hostile arts of Antoninus, [52] a Roman subject of Syria, who had fled from oppression, and was admitted into the councils of Sapor, and even to the royal table, where, according to the custom of the Persians, the most important business was frequently discussed. [53] The dexterous fugitive promoted his interest by the same conduct which gratified his revenge. He incessantly urged the ambition of his new master to embrace the favorable opportunity when the bravest of the Palatine troops were employed with the emperor in a distant war on the Danube. He pressed Sapor to invade the exhausted and defenceless provinces of the East, with the numerous armies of Persia, now fortified by the alliance and accession of the fiercest Barbarians. The ambassadors of Rome retired without success, and a second embassy, of a still more honorable rank, was detained in strict confinement, and threatened either with death or exile.

[Footnote 49: Ammian. xvi. 9.]

[Footnote 49a: In Persian, Ten-schah-pour. St. Martin, ii. 177—M.]

[Footnote 50: Ammianus (xvii. 5) transcribes the haughty letter. Themistius (Orat. iv. p. 57, edit. Petav.) takes notice of the silken covering. Idatius and Zonaras mention the journey of the ambassador; and Peter the Patrician (in Excerpt. Legat. p. 58) has informed us of his behavior.]

[Footnote 51: Ammianus, xvii. 5, and Valesius ad loc. The sophist, or philosopher, (in that age these words were almost synonymous,) was Eustathius the Cappadocian, the disciple of Jamblichus, and the friend of St. Basil. Eunapius (in Vit. Aedesii, p. 44-47) fondly attributes to this philosophic ambassador the glory of enchanting the Barbarian king by the persuasive charms of reason and eloquence. See Tillemont, Hist. des Empereurs, tom. iv. p. 828, 1132.]

[Footnote 52: Ammian. xviii. 5, 6, 8. The decent and respectful behavior of Antoninus towards the Roman general, sets him in a very interesting light; and Ammianus himself speaks of the traitor with some compassion and esteem.]

[Footnote 53: This circumstance, as it is noticed by Ammianus, serves to prove the veracity of Herodotus, (l. i. c. 133,) and the permanency of the Persian manners. In every age the Persians have been addicted to intemperance, and the wines of Shiraz have triumphed over the law of Mahomet. Brisson de Regno Pers. l. ii. p. 462-472, and Voyages en Perse, tom, iii. p. 90.]

The military historian, [54] who was himself despatched to observe the army of the Persians, as they were preparing to construct a bridge of boats over the Tigris, beheld from an eminence the plain of Assyria, as far as the edge of the horizon, covered with men, with horses, and with arms. Sapor appeared in the front, conspicuous by the splendor of his purple. On his left hand, the place of honor among the Orientals, Grumbates, king of the Chionites, displayed the stern countenance of an aged and renowned warrior. The monarch had reserved a similar place on his right hand for the king of the Albanians, who led his independent tribes from the shores of the Caspian. [54a] The satraps and generals were distributed according to their several ranks, and the whole army, besides the numerous train of Oriental luxury, consisted of more than one hundred thousand effective men, inured to fatigue, and selected from the bravest nations of Asia. The Roman deserter, who in some measure guided the councils of Sapor, had prudently advised, that, instead of wasting the summer in tedious and difficult sieges, he should march directly to the Euphrates, and press forwards without delay to seize the feeble and wealthy metropolis of Syria. But the Persians were no sooner advanced into the plains of Mesopotamia, than they discovered that every precaution had been used which could retard their progress, or defeat their design. The inhabitants, with their cattle, were secured in places of strength, the green forage throughout the country was set on fire, the fords of the rivers were fortified by sharp stakes; military engines were planted on the opposite banks, and a seasonable swell of the waters of the Euphrates deterred the Barbarians from attempting the ordinary passage of the bridge of Thapsacus. Their skilful guide, changing his plan of operations, then conducted the army by a longer circuit, but through a fertile territory, towards the head of the Euphrates, where the infant river is reduced to a shallow and accessible stream. Sapor overlooked, with prudent disdain, the strength of Nisibis; but as he passed under the walls of Amida, he resolved to try whether the majesty of his presence would not awe the garrison into immediate submission. The sacrilegious insult of a random dart, which glanced against the royal tiara, convinced him of his error; and the indignant monarch listened with impatience to the advice of his ministers, who conjured him not to sacrifice the success of his ambition to the gratification of his resentment. The following day Grumbates advanced towards the gates with a select body of troops, and required the instant surrender of the city, as the only atonement which could be accepted for such an act of rashness and insolence. His proposals were answered by a general discharge, and his only son, a beautiful and valiant youth, was pierced through the heart by a javelin, shot from one of the balistae. The funeral of the prince of the Chionites was celebrated according to the rites of the country; and the grief of his aged father was alleviated by the solemn promise of Sapor, that the guilty city of Amida should serve as a funeral pile to expiate the death, and to perpetuate the memory, of his son.

[Footnote 54: Ammian. lxviii. 6, 7, 8, 10.]

[Footnote 54a: These perhaps were the barbarous tribes who inhabit the northern part of the present Schirwan, the Albania of the ancients. This country, now inhabited by the Lezghis, the terror of the neighboring districts, was then occupied by the same people, called by the ancients Legae, by the Armenians Gheg, or Leg. The latter represent them as constant allies of the Persians in their wars against Armenia and the Empire. A little after this period, a certain Schergir was their king, and it is of him doubtless Ammianus Marcellinus speaks. St. Martin, ii. 285—M.]

The ancient city of Amid or Amida, [55] which sometimes assumes the provincial appellation of Diarbekir, [56] is advantageously situate in a fertile plain, watered by the natural and artificial channels of the Tigris, of which the least inconsiderable stream bends in a semicircular form round the eastern part of the city. The emperor Constantius had recently conferred on Amida the honor of his own name, and the additional fortifications of strong walls and lofty towers. It was provided with an arsenal of military engines, and the ordinary garrison had been reenforced to the amount of seven legions, when the place was invested by the arms of Sapor. [57] His first and most sanguine hopes depended on the success of a general assault. To the several nations which followed his standard, their respective posts were assigned; the south to the Vertae; the north to the Albanians; the east to the Chionites, inflamed with grief and indignation; the west to the Segestans, the bravest of his warriors, who covered their front with a formidable line of Indian elephants. [58] The Persians, on every side, supported their efforts, and animated their courage; and the monarch himself, careless of his rank and safety, displayed, in the prosecution of the siege, the ardor of a youthful soldier. After an obstinate combat, the Barbarians were repulsed; they incessantly returned to the charge; they were again driven back with a dreadful slaughter, and two rebel legions of Gauls, who had been banished into the East, signalized their undisciplined courage by a nocturnal sally into the heart of the Persian camp. In one of the fiercest of these repeated assaults, Amida was betrayed by the treachery of a deserter, who indicated to the Barbarians a secret and neglected staircase, scooped out of the rock that hangs over the stream of the Tigris. Seventy chosen archers of the royal guard ascended in silence to the third story of a lofty tower, which commanded the precipice; they elevated on high the Persian banner, the signal of confidence to the assailants, and of dismay to the besieged; and if this devoted band could have maintained their post a few minutes longer, the reduction of the place might have been purchased by the sacrifice of their lives. After Sapor had tried, without success, the efficacy of force and of stratagem, he had recourse to the slower but more certain operations of a regular siege, in the conduct of which he was instructed by the skill of the Roman deserters. The trenches were opened at a convenient distance, and the troops destined for that service advanced under the portable cover of strong hurdles, to fill up the ditch, and undermine the foundations of the walls. Wooden towers were at the same time constructed, and moved forwards on wheels, till the soldiers, who were provided with every species of missile weapons, could engage almost on level ground with the troops who defended the rampart. Every mode of resistance which art could suggest, or courage could execute, was employed in the defence of Amida, and the works of Sapor were more than once destroyed by the fire of the Romans. But the resources of a besieged city may be exhausted. The Persians repaired their losses, and pushed their approaches; a large preach was made by the battering-ram, and the strength of the garrison, wasted by the sword and by disease, yielded to the fury of the assault. The soldiers, the citizens, their wives, their children, all who had not time to escape through the opposite gate, were involved by the conquerors in a promiscuous massacre.

[Footnote 55: For the description of Amida, see D'Herbelot, Bebliotheque Orientale, p. Bibliotheque Orientale, p. 108. Histoire de Timur Bec, par Cherefeddin Ali, l. iii. c. 41. Ahmed Arabsiades, tom. i. p. 331, c. 43. Voyages de Tavernier, tom. i. p. 301. Voyages d'Otter, tom. ii. p. 273, and Voyages de Niebuhr, tom. ii. p. 324-328. The last of these travellers, a learned and accurate Dane, has given a plan of Amida, which illustrates the operations of the siege.]

[Footnote 56: Diarbekir, which is styled Amid, or Kara Amid, in the public writings of the Turks, contains above 16,000 houses, and is the residence of a pacha with three tails. The epithet of Kara is derived from the blackness of the stone which composes the strong and ancient wall of Amida. —In my Mem. Hist. sur l'Armenie, l. i. p. 166, 173, I conceive that I have proved this city, still called, by the Armenians, Dirkranagerd, the city of Tigranes, to be the same with the famous Tigranocerta, of which the situation was unknown. St. Martin, i. 432. On the siege of Amida, see St. Martin's Notes, ii. 290. Faustus of Byzantium, nearly a contemporary, (Armenian,) states that the Persians, on becoming masters of it, destroyed 40,000 houses though Ammianus describes the city as of no great extent, (civitatis ambitum non nimium amplae.) Besides the ordinary population, and those who took refuge from the country, it contained 20,000 soldiers. St. Martin, ii. 290. This interpretation is extremely doubtful. Wagner (note on Ammianus) considers the whole population to amount only to—M.]

[Footnote 57: The operations of the siege of Amida are very minutely described by Ammianus, (xix. 1-9,) who acted an honorable part in the defence, and escaped with difficulty when the city was stormed by the Persians.]

[Footnote 58: Of these four nations, the Albanians are too well known to require any description. The Segestans [Sacastene. St. Martin.] inhabited a large and level country, which still preserves their name, to the south of Khorasan, and the west of Hindostan. (See Geographia Nubiensis. p. 133, and D'Herbelot, Bibliotheque Orientale, p. 797.) Notwithstanding the boasted victory of Bahram, (vol. i. p. 410,) the Segestans, above fourscore years afterwards, appear as an independent nation, the ally of Persia. We are ignorant of the situation of the Vertae and Chionites, but I am inclined to place them (at least the latter) towards the confines of India and Scythia. See Ammian. —Klaproth considers the real Albanians the same with the ancient Alani, and quotes a passage of the emperor Julian in support of his opinion. They are the Ossetae, now inhabiting part of Caucasus. Tableaux Hist. de l'Asie, p. 179, 180—M. —The Vertae are still unknown. It is possible that the Chionites are the same as the Huns. These people were already known; and we find from Armenian authors that they were making, at this period, incursions into Asia. They were often at war with the Persians. The name was perhaps pronounced differently in the East and in the West, and this prevents us from recognizing it. St. Martin, ii. 177—M.]

But the ruin of Amida was the safety of the Roman provinces.

As soon as the first transports of victory had subsided, Sapor was at leisure to reflect, that to chastise a disobedient city, he had lost the flower of his troops, and the most favorable season for conquest. [59] Thirty thousand of his veterans had fallen under the walls of Amida, during the continuance of a siege, which lasted seventy-three days; and the disappointed monarch returned to his capital with affected triumph and secret mortification. It is more than probable, that the inconstancy of his Barbarian allies was tempted to relinquish a war in which they had encountered such unexpected difficulties; and that the aged king of the Chionites, satiated with revenge, turned away with horror from a scene of action where he had been deprived of the hope of his family and nation. The strength as well as the spirit of the army with which Sapor took the field in the ensuing spring was no longer equal to the unbounded views of his ambition. Instead of aspiring to the conquest of the East, he was obliged to content himself with the reduction of two fortified cities of Mesopotamia, Singara and Bezabde; [60] the one situate in the midst of a sandy desert, the other in a small peninsula, surrounded almost on every side by the deep and rapid stream of the Tigris. Five Roman legions, of the diminutive size to which they had been reduced in the age of Constantine, were made prisoners, and sent into remote captivity on the extreme confines of Persia. After dismantling the walls of Singara, the conqueror abandoned that solitary and sequestered place; but he carefully restored the fortifications of Bezabde, and fixed in that important post a garrison or colony of veterans; amply supplied with every means of defence, and animated by high sentiments of honor and fidelity. Towards the close of the campaign, the arms of Sapor incurred some disgrace by an unsuccessful enterprise against Virtha, or Tecrit, a strong, or, as it was universally esteemed till the age of Tamerlane, an impregnable fortress of the independent Arabs. [61] [61a]

[Footnote 59: Ammianus has marked the chronology of this year by three signs, which do not perfectly coincide with each other, or with the series of the history. 1 The corn was ripe when Sapor invaded Mesopotamia; "Cum jam stipula flaveate turgerent;" a circumstance, which, in the latitude of Aleppo, would naturally refer us to the month of April or May. See Harmer's Observations on Scripture vol. i. p. 41. Shaw's Travels, p. 335, edit 4to. 2. The progress of Sapor was checked by the overflowing of the Euphrates, which generally happens in July and August. Plin. Hist. Nat. v. 21. Viaggi di Pietro della Valle, tom. i. p. 696. 3. When Sapor had taken Amida, after a siege of seventy-three days, the autumn was far advanced. "Autumno praecipiti haedorumque improbo sidere exorto." To reconcile these apparent contradictions, we must allow for some delay in the Persian king, some inaccuracy in the historian, and some disorder in the seasons.]

[Footnote 60: The account of these sieges is given by Ammianus, xx. 6, 7. —The Christian bishop of Bezabde went to the camp of the king of Persia, to persuade him to check the waste of human blood Amm. Mare xx. 7—M.]

[Footnote 61: For the identity of Virtha and Tecrit, see D'Anville, Geographie. For the siege of that castle by Timur Bec or Tamerlane, see Cherefeddin, l. iii. c. 33. The Persian biographer exaggerates the merit and difficulty of this exploit, which delivered the caravans of Bagdad from a formidable gang of robbers.]

[Footnote 61a: St. Martin doubts whether it lay so much to the south. "The word Girtha means in Syriac a castle or fortress, and might be applied to many places."]

The defence of the East against the arms of Sapor required and would have exercised, the abilities of the most consummate general; and it seemed fortunate for the state, that it was the actual province of the brave Ursicinus, who alone deserved the confidence of the soldiers and people. In the hour of danger, [62] Ursicinus was removed from his station by the intrigues of the eunuchs; and the military command of the East was bestowed, by the same influence, on Sabinian, a wealthy and subtle veteran, who had attained the infirmities, without acquiring the experience, of age. By a second order, which issued from the same jealous and inconstant councils, Ursicinus was again despatched to the frontier of Mesopotamia, and condemned to sustain the labors of a war, the honors of which had been transferred to his unworthy rival. Sabinian fixed his indolent station under the walls of Edessa; and while he amused himself with the idle parade of military exercise, and moved to the sound of flutes in the Pyrrhic dance, the public defence was abandoned to the boldness and diligence of the former general of the East. But whenever Ursicinus recommended any vigorous plan of operations; when he proposed, at the head of a light and active army, to wheel round the foot of the mountains, to intercept the convoys of the enemy, to harass the wide extent of the Persian lines, and to relieve the distress of Amida; the timid and envious commander alleged, that he was restrained by his positive orders from endangering the safety of the troops. Amida was at length taken; its bravest defenders, who had escaped the sword of the Barbarians, died in the Roman camp by the hand of the executioner: and Ursicinus himself, after supporting the disgrace of a partial inquiry, was punished for the misconduct of Sabinian by the loss of his military rank. But Constantius soon experienced the truth of the prediction which honest indignation had extorted from his injured lieutenant, that as long as such maxims of government were suffered to prevail, the emperor himself would find it is no easy task to defend his eastern dominions from the invasion of a foreign enemy. When he had subdued or pacified the Barbarians of the Danube, Constantius proceeded by slow marches into the East; and after he had wept over the smoking ruins of Amida, he formed, with a powerful army, the siege of Becabde. The walls were shaken by the reiterated efforts of the most enormous of the battering-rams; the town was reduced to the last extremity; but it was still defended by the patient and intrepid valor of the garrison, till the approach of the rainy season obliged the emperor to raise the siege, and ingloriously to retreat into his winter quarters at Antioch. [63] The pride of Constantius, and the ingenuity of his courtiers, were at a loss to discover any materials for panegyric in the events of the Persian war; while the glory of his cousin Julian, to whose military command he had intrusted the provinces of Gaul, was proclaimed to the world in the simple and concise narrative of his exploits.

[Footnote 62: Ammianus (xviii. 5, 6, xix. 3, xx. 2) represents the merit and disgrace of Ursicinus with that faithful attention which a soldier owed to his general. Some partiality may be suspected, yet the whole account is consistent and probable.]

[Footnote 63: Ammian. xx. 11. Omisso vano incepto, hiematurus Antiochiae redit in Syriam aerumnosam, perpessus et ulcerum sed et atrocia, diuque deflenda. It is thus that James Gronovius has restored an obscure passage; and he thinks that this correction alone would have deserved a new edition of his author: whose sense may now be darkly perceived. I expected some additional light from the recent labors of the learned Ernestus. (Lipsiae, 1773.) Note: The late editor (Wagner) has nothing better to suggest, and le menta with Gibbon, the silence of Ernesti—M.]

In the blind fury of civil discord, Constantius had abandoned to the Barbarians of Germany the countries of Gaul, which still acknowledged the authority of his rival. A numerous swarm of Franks and Alemanni were invited to cross the Rhine by presents and promises, by the hopes of spoil, and by a perpetual grant of all the territories which they should be able to subdue. [64] But the emperor, who for a temporary service had thus imprudently provoked the rapacious spirit of the Barbarians, soon discovered and lamented the difficulty of dismissing these formidable allies, after they had tasted the richness of the Roman soil. Regardless of the nice distinction of loyalty and rebellion, these undisciplined robbers treated as their natural enemies all the subjects of the empire, who possessed any property which they were desirous of acquiring Forty-five flourishing cities, Tongres, Cologne, Treves, Worms, Spires, Strasburgh, &c., besides a far greater number of towns and villages, were pillaged, and for the most part reduced to ashes. The Barbarians of Germany, still faithful to the maxims of their ancestors, abhorred the confinement of walls, to which they applied the odious names of prisons and sepulchres; and fixing their independent habitations on the banks of rivers, the Rhine, the Moselle, and the Meuse, they secured themselves against the danger of a surprise, by a rude and hasty fortification of large trees, which were felled and thrown across the roads. The Alemanni were established in the modern countries of Alsace and Lorraine; the Franks occupied the island of the Batavians, together with an extensive district of Brabant, which was then known by the appellation of Toxandria, [65] and may deserve to be considered as the original seat of their Gallic monarchy. [66] From the sources, to the mouth, of the Rhine, the conquests of the Germans extended above forty miles to the west of that river, over a country peopled by colonies of their own name and nation: and the scene of their devastations was three times more extensive than that of their conquests. At a still greater distance the open towns of Gaul were deserted, and the inhabitants of the fortified cities, who trusted to their strength and vigilance, were obliged to content themselves with such supplies of corn as they could raise on the vacant land within the enclosure of their walls. The diminished legions, destitute of pay and provisions, of arms and discipline, trembled at the approach, and even at the name, of the Barbarians.

[Footnote 64: The ravages of the Germans, and the distress of Gaul, may be collected from Julian himself. Orat. ad S. P. Q. Athen. p. 277. Ammian. xv. ll. Libanius, Orat. x. Zosimus, l. iii. p. 140. Sozomen, l. iii. c. l. (Mamertin. Grat. Art. c. iv.)]

[Footnote 65: Ammianus, xvi. 8. This name seems to be derived from the Toxandri of Pliny, and very frequently occurs in the histories of the middle age. Toxandria was a country of woods and morasses, which extended from the neighborhood of Tongres to the conflux of the Vahal and the Rhine. See Valesius, Notit. Galliar. p. 558.]

[Footnote 66: The paradox of P. Daniel, that the Franks never obtained any permanent settlement on this side of the Rhine before the time of Clovis, is refuted with much learning and good sense by M. Biet, who has proved by a chain of evidence, their uninterrupted possession of Toxandria, one hundred and thirty years before the accession of Clovis. The Dissertation of M. Biet was crowned by the Academy of Soissons, in the year 1736, and seems to have been justly preferred to the discourse of his more celebrated competitor, the Abbe le Boeuf, an antiquarian, whose name was happily expressive of his talents.]

PART IV

Under these melancholy circumstances, an unexperienced youth was appointed to save and to govern the provinces of Gaul, or rather, as he expressed it himself, to exhibit the vain image of Imperial greatness. The retired scholastic education of Julian, in which he had been more conversant with books than with arms, with the dead than with the living, left him in profound ignorance of the practical arts of war and government; and when he awkwardly repeated some military exercise which it was necessary for him to learn, he exclaimed with a sigh, "O Plato, Plato, what a task for a philosopher!" Yet even this speculative philosophy, which men of business are too apt to despise, had filled the mind of Julian with the noblest precepts and the most shining examples; had animated him with the love of virtue, the desire of fame, and the contempt of death. The habits of temperance recommended in the schools, are still more essential in the severe discipline of a camp. The simple wants of nature regulated the measure of his food and sleep. Rejecting with disdain the delicacies provided for his table, he satisfied his appetite with the coarse and common fare which was allotted to the meanest soldiers. During the rigor of a Gallic winter, he never suffered a fire in his bed-chamber; and after a short and interrupted slumber, he frequently rose in the middle of the night from a carpet spread on the floor, to despatch any urgent business, to visit his rounds, or to steal a few moments for the prosecution of his favorite studies. [67] The precepts of eloquence, which he had hitherto practised on fancied topics of declamation, were more usefully applied to excite or to assuage the passions of an armed multitude: and although Julian, from his early habits of conversation and literature, was more familiarly acquainted with the beauties of the Greek language, he had attained a competent knowledge of the Latin tongue. [68] Since Julian was not originally designed for the character of a legislator, or a judge, it is probable that the civil jurisprudence of the Romans had not engaged any considerable share of his attention: but he derived from his philosophic studies an inflexible regard for justice, tempered by a disposition to clemency; the knowledge of the general principles of equity and evidence, and the faculty of patiently investigating the most intricate and tedious questions which could be proposed for his discussion. The measures of policy, and the operations of war, must submit to the various accidents of circumstance and character, and the unpractised student will often be perplexed in the application of the most perfect theory.

But in the acquisition of this important science, Julian was assisted by the active vigor of his own genius, as well as by the wisdom and experience of Sallust, and officer of rank, who soon conceived a sincere attachment for a prince so worthy of his friendship; and whose incorruptible integrity was adorned by the talent of insinuating the harshest truths without wounding the delicacy of a royal ear. [69]

[Footnote 67: The private life of Julian in Gaul, and the severe discipline which he embraced, are displayed by Ammianus, (xvi. 5,) who professes to praise, and by Julian himself, who affects to ridicule, (Misopogon, p. 340,) a conduct, which, in a prince of the house of Constantine, might justly excite the surprise of mankind.]

[Footnote 68: Aderat Latine quoque disserenti sufficiens sermo. Ammianus xvi. 5. But Julian, educated in the schools of Greece, always considered the language of the Romans as a foreign and popular dialect which he might use on necessary occasions.]

[Footnote 69: We are ignorant of the actual office of this excellent minister, whom Julian afterwards created praefect of Gaul. Sallust was speedily recalled by the jealousy of the emperor; and we may still read a sensible but pedantic discourse, (p. 240-252,) in which Julian deplores the loss of so valuable a friend, to whom he acknowledges himself indebted for his reputation. See La Bleterie, Preface a la Vie de Iovien, p. 20.]

Immediately after Julian had received the purple at Milan, he was sent into Gaul with a feeble retinue of three hundred and sixty soldiers. At Vienna, where he passed a painful and anxious winter in the hands of those ministers to whom Constantius had intrusted the direction of his conduct, the Caesar was informed of the siege and deliverance of Autun. That large and ancient city, protected only by a ruined wall and pusillanimous garrison, was saved by the generous resolution of a few veterans, who resumed their arms for the defence of their country. In his march from Autun, through the heart of the Gallic provinces, Julian embraced with ardor the earliest opportunity of signalizing his courage. At the head of a small body of archers and heavy cavalry, he preferred the shorter but the more dangerous of two roads; [69a] and sometimes eluding, and sometimes resisting, the attacks of the Barbarians, who were masters of the field, he arrived with honor and safety at the camp near Rheims, where the Roman troops had been ordered to assemble. The aspect of their young prince revived the drooping spirits of the soldiers, and they marched from Rheims in search of the enemy, with a confidence which had almost proved fatal to them. The Alemanni, familiarized to the knowledge of the country, secretly collected their scattered forces, and seizing the opportunity of a dark and rainy day, poured with unexpected fury on the rear-guard of the Romans. Before the inevitable disorder could be remedied, two legions were destroyed; and Julian was taught by experience that caution and vigilance are the most important lessons of the art of war. In a second and more successful action, he recovered and established his military fame; but as the agility of the Barbarians saved them from the pursuit, his victory was neither bloody nor decisive. He advanced, however, to the banks of the Rhine, surveyed the ruins of Cologne, convinced himself of the difficulties of the war, and retreated on the approach of winter, discontented with the court, with his army, and with his own success. [70] The power of the enemy was yet unbroken; and the Caesar had no sooner separated his troops, and fixed his own quarters at Sens, in the centre of Gaul, than he was surrounded and besieged, by a numerous host of Germans. Reduced, in this extremity, to the resources of his own mind, he displayed a prudent intrepidity, which compensated for all the deficiencies of the place and garrison; and the Barbarians, at the end of thirty days, were obliged to retire with disappointed rage.

[Footnote 69a: Aliis per Arbor—quibusdam per Sedelaucum et Coram in debere firrantibus. Amm. Marc. xvi. 2. I do not know what place can be meant by the mutilated name Arbor. Sedelanus is Saulieu, a small town of the department of the Cote d'Or, six leagues from Autun. Cora answers to the village of Cure, on the river of the same name, between Autun and Nevera 4; Martin, ii. 162—M. —Note: At Brocomages, Brumat, near Strasburgh. St. Martin, ii. 184—M.]

[Footnote 70: Ammianus (xvi. 2, 3) appears much better satisfied with the success of his first campaign than Julian himself; who very fairly owns that he did nothing of consequence, and that he fled before the enemy.]

The conscious pride of Julian, who was indebted only to his sword for this signal deliverance, was imbittered by the reflection, that he was abandoned, betrayed, and perhaps devoted to destruction, by those who were bound to assist him, by every tie of honor and fidelity. Marcellus, master-general of the cavalry in Gaul, interpreting too strictly the jealous orders of the court, beheld with supine indifference the distress of Julian, and had restrained the troops under his command from marching to the relief of Sens. If the Caesar had dissembled in silence so dangerous an insult, his person and authority would have been exposed to the contempt of the world; and if an action so criminal had been suffered to pass with impunity, the emperor would have confirmed the suspicions, which received a very specious color from his past conduct towards the princes of the Flavian family. Marcellus was recalled, and gently dismissed from his office. [71] In his room Severus was appointed general of the cavalry; an experienced soldier, of approved courage and fidelity, who could advise with respect, and execute with zeal; and who submitted, without reluctance to the supreme command which Julian, by the inrerest of his patroness Eusebia, at length obtained over the armies of Gaul. [72] A very judicious plan of operations was adopted for the approaching campaign. Julian himself, at the head of the remains of the veteran bands, and of some new levies which he had been permitted to form, boldly penetrated into the centre of the German cantonments, and carefully reestablished the fortifications of Saverne, in an advantageous post, which would either check the incursions, or intercept the retreat, of the enemy. At the same time, Barbatio, general of the infantry, advanced from Milan with an army of thirty thousand men, and passing the mountains, prepared to throw a bridge over the Rhine, in the neighborhood of Basil. It was reasonable to expect that the Alemanni, pressed on either side by the Roman arms, would soon be forced to evacuate the provinces of Gaul, and to hasten to the defence of their native country. But the hopes of the campaign were defeated by the incapacity, or the envy, or the secret instructions, of Barbatio; who acted as if he had been the enemy of the Caesar, and the secret ally of the Barbarians.

The negligence with which he permitted a troop of pillagers freely to pass, and to return almost before the gates of his camp, may be imputed to his want of abilities; but the treasonable act of burning a number of boats, and a superfluous stock of provisions, which would have been of the most essential service to the army of Gaul, was an evidence of his hostile and criminal intentions. The Germans despised an enemy who appeared destitute either of power or of inclination to offend them; and the ignominious retreat of Barbatio deprived Julian of the expected support; and left him to extricate himself from a hazardous situation, where he could neither remain with safety, nor retire with honor. [73]

[Footnote 71: Ammian. xvi. 7. Libanius speaks rather more advantageously of the military talents of Marcellus, Orat. x. p. 272. And Julian insinuates, that he would not have been so easily recalled, unless he had given other reasons of offence to the court, p. 278.]

[Footnote 72: Severus, non discors, non arrogans, sed longa militiae frugalitate compertus; et eum recta praeeuntem secuturus, ut duetorem morigeran miles. Ammian xvi. 11. Zosimus, l. iii. p. 140.]

[Footnote 73: On the design and failure of the cooperation between Julian and Barbatio, see Ammianus (xvi. 11) and Libanius, (Orat. x. p. 273.) Note: Barbatio seems to have allowed himself to be surprised and defeated—M.]

As soon as they were delivered from the fears of invasion, the Alemanni prepared to chastise the Roman youth, who presumed to dispute the possession of that country, which they claimed as their own by the right of conquest and of treaties. They employed three days, and as many nights, in transporting over the Rhine their military powers. The fierce Chnodomar, shaking the ponderous javelin which he had victoriously wielded against the brother of Magnentius, led the van of the Barbarians, and moderated by his experience the martial ardor which his example inspired. [74] He was followed by six other kings, by ten princes of regal extraction, by a long train of high-spirited nobles, and by thirty-five thousand of the bravest warriors of the tribes of Germany. The confidence derived from the view of their own strength, was increased by the intelligence which they received from a deserter, that the Caesar, with a feeble army of thirteen thousand men, occupied a post about one-and-twenty miles from their camp of Strasburgh. With this inadequate force, Julian resolved to seek and to encounter the Barbarian host; and the chance of a general action was preferred to the tedious and uncertain operation of separately engaging the dispersed parties of the Alemanni. The Romans marched in close order, and in two columns; the cavalry on the right, the infantry on the left; and the day was so far spent when they appeared in sight of the enemy, that Julian was desirous of deferring the battle till the next morning, and of allowing his troops to recruit their exhausted strength by the necessary refreshments of sleep and food. Yielding, however, with some reluctance, to the clamors of the soldiers, and even to the opinion of his council, he exhorted them to justify by their valor the eager impatience, which, in case of a defeat, would be universally branded with the epithets of rashness and presumption. The trumpets sounded, the military shout was heard through the field, and the two armies rushed with equal fury to the charge. The Caesar, who conducted in person his right wing, depended on the dexterity of his archers, and the weight of his cuirassiers. But his ranks were instantly broken by an irregular mixture of light horse and of light infantry, and he had the mortification of beholding the flight of six hundred of his most renowned cuirassiers. [75] The fugitives were stopped and rallied by the presence and authority of Julian, who, careless of his own safety, threw himself before them, and urging every motive of shame and honor, led them back against the victorious enemy. The conflict between the two lines of infantry was obstinate and bloody. The Germans possessed the superiority of strength and stature, the Romans that of discipline and temper; and as the Barbarians, who served under the standard of the empire, united the respective advantages of both parties, their strenuous efforts, guided by a skilful leader, at length determined the event of the day. The Romans lost four tribunes, and two hundred and forty-three soldiers, in this memorable battle of Strasburgh, so glorious to the Caesar, [76] and so salutary to the afflicted provinces of Gaul. Six thousand of the Alemanni were slain in the field, without including those who were drowned in the Rhine, or transfixed with darts while they attempted to swim across the river. [77] Chnodomar himself was surrounded and taken prisoner, with three of his brave companions, who had devoted themselves to follow in life or death the fate of their chieftain. Julian received him with military pomp in the council of his officers; and expressing a generous pity for the fallen state, dissembled his inward contempt for the abject humiliation, of his captive. Instead of exhibiting the vanquished king of the Alemanni, as a grateful spectacle to the cities of Gaul, he respectfully laid at the feet of the emperor this splendid trophy of his victory. Chnodomar experienced an honorable treatment: but the impatient Barbarian could not long survive his defeat, his confinement, and his exile. [78]

[Footnote 74: Ammianus (xvi. 12) describes with his inflated eloquence the figure and character of Chnodomar. Audax et fidens ingenti robore lacertorum, ubi ardor proelii sperabatur immanis, equo spumante sublimior, erectus in jaculum formidandae vastitatis, armorumque nitore conspicuus: antea strenuus et miles, et utilis praeter caeteros ductor... Decentium Caesarem superavit aequo marte congressus.]

[Footnote 75: After the battle, Julian ventured to revive the rigor of ancient discipline, by exposing these fugitives in female apparel to the derision of the whole camp. In the next campaign, these troops nobly retrieved their honor. Zosimus, l. iii. p. 142.]

[Footnote 76: Julian himself (ad S. P. Q. Athen. p. 279) speaks of the battle of Strasburgh with the modesty of conscious merit; Zosimus compares it with the victory of Alexander over Darius; and yet we are at a loss to discover any of those strokes of military genius which fix the attention of ages on the conduct and success of a single day.]

[Footnote 77: Ammianus, xvi. 12. Libanius adds 2000 more to the number of the slain, (Orat. x. p. 274.) But these trifling differences disappear before the 60,000 Barbarians, whom Zosimus has sacrificed to the glory of his hero, (l. iii. p. 141.) We might attribute this extravagant number to the carelessness of transcribers, if this credulous or partial historian had not swelled the army of 35,000 Alemanni to an innumerable multitude of Barbarians,. It is our own fault if this detection does not inspire us with proper distrust on similar occasions.]

[Footnote 78: Ammian. xvi. 12. Libanius, Orat. x. p. 276.]

After Julian had repulsed the Alemanni from the provinces of the Upper Rhine, he turned his arms against the Franks, who were seated nearer to the ocean, on the confines of Gaul and Germany; and who, from their numbers, and still more from their intrepid valor, had ever been esteemed the most formidable of the Barbarians. [79] Although they were strongly actuated by the allurements of rapine, they professed a disinterested love of war; which they considered as the supreme honor and felicity of human nature; and their minds and bodies were so completely hardened by perpetual action, that, according to the lively expression of an orator, the snows of winter were as pleasant to them as the flowers of spring. In the month of December, which followed the battle of Strasburgh, Julian attacked a body of six hundred Franks, who had thrown themselves into two castles on the Meuse. [80] In the midst of that severe season they sustained, with inflexible constancy, a siege of fifty-four days; till at length, exhausted by hunger, and satisfied that the vigilance of the enemy, in breaking the ice of the river, left them no hopes of escape, the Franks consented, for the first time, to dispense with the ancient law which commanded them to conquer or to die. The Caesar immediately sent his captives to the court of Constantius, who, accepting them as a valuable present, [81] rejoiced in the opportunity of adding so many heroes to the choicest troops of his domestic guards. The obstinate resistance of this handful of Franks apprised Julian of the difficulties of the expedition which he meditated for the ensuing spring, against the whole body of the nation. His rapid diligence surprised and astonished the active Barbarians. Ordering his soldiers to provide themselves with biscuit for twenty days, he suddenly pitched his camp near Tongres, while the enemy still supposed him in his winter quarters of Paris, expecting the slow arrival of his convoys from Aquitain. Without allowing the Franks to unite or deliberate, he skilfully spread his legions from Cologne to the ocean; and by the terror, as well as by the success, of his arms, soon reduced the suppliant tribes to implore the clemency, and to obey the commands, of their conqueror. The Chamavians submissively retired to their former habitations beyond the Rhine; but the Salians were permitted to possess their new establishment of Toxandria, as the subjects and auxiliaries of the Roman empire. [82] The treaty was ratified by solemn oaths; and perpetual inspectors were appointed to reside among the Franks, with the authority of enforcing the strict observance of the conditions. An incident is related, interesting enough in itself, and by no means repugnant to the character of Julian, who ingeniously contrived both the plot and the catastrophe of the tragedy. When the Chamavians sued for peace, he required the son of their king, as the only hostage on whom he could rely. A mournful silence, interrupted by tears and groans, declared the sad perplexity of the Barbarians; and their aged chief lamented in pathetic language, that his private loss was now imbittered by a sense of public calamity. While the Chamavians lay prostrate at the foot of his throne, the royal captive, whom they believed to have been slain, unexpectedly appeared before their eyes; and as soon as the tumult of joy was hushed into attention, the Caesar addressed the assembly in the following terms: "Behold the son, the prince, whom you wept. You had lost him by your fault. God and the Romans have restored him to you. I shall still preserve and educate the youth, rather as a monument of my own virtue, than as a pledge of your sincerity. Should you presume to violate the faith which you have sworn, the arms of the republic will avenge the perfidy, not on the innocent, but on the guilty." The Barbarians withdrew from his presence, impressed with the warmest sentiments of gratitude and admiration. [83]

[Footnote 79: Libanius (Orat. iii. p. 137) draws a very lively picture of the manners of the Franks.]

[Footnote 80: Ammianus, xvii. 2. Libanius, Orat. x. p. 278. The Greek orator, by misapprehending a passage of Julian, has been induced to represent the Franks as consisting of a thousand men; and as his head was always full of the Peloponnesian war, he compares them to the Lacedaemonians, who were besieged and taken in the Island of Sphatoria.]

[Footnote 81: Julian. ad S. P. Q. Athen. p. 280. Libanius, Orat. x. p. 278. According to the expression of Libanius, the emperor, which La Bleterie understands (Vie de Julien, p. 118) as an honest confession, and Valesius (ad Ammian. xvii. 2) as a mean evasion, of the truth. Dom Bouquet, (Historiens de France, tom. i. p. 733,) by substituting another word, would suppress both the difficulty and the spirit of this passage.]

[Footnote 82: Ammian. xvii. 8. Zosimus, l. iii. p. 146-150, (his narrative is darkened by a mixture of fable,) and Julian. ad S. P. Q. Athen. p. 280. His expression. This difference of treatment confirms the opinion that the Salian Franks were permitted to retain the settlements in Toxandria. Note: A newly discovered fragment of Eunapius, whom Zosimus probably transcribed, illustrates this transaction. "Julian commanded the Romans to abstain from all hostile measures against the Salians, neither to waste or ravage their own country, for he called every country their own which was surrendered without resistance or toil on the part of the conquerors." Mai, Script. Vez Nov. Collect. ii. 256, and Eunapius in Niebuhr, Byzant. Hist.]

[Footnote 83: This interesting story, which Zosimus has abridged, is related by Eunapius, (in Excerpt. Legationum, p. 15, 16, 17,) with all the amplifications of Grecian rhetoric: but the silence of Libanius, of Ammianus, and of Julian himself, renders the truth of it extremely suspicious.]

It was not enough for Julian to have delivered the provinces of Gaul from the Barbarians of Germany. He aspired to emulate the glory of the first and most illustrious of the emperors; after whose example, he composed his own commentaries of the Gallic war. [84] Caesar has related, with conscious pride, the manner in which he twice passed the Rhine. Julian could boast, that before he assumed the title of Augustus, he had carried the Roman eagles beyond that great river in three successful expeditions. [85] The consternation of the Germans, after the battle of Strasburgh, encouraged him to the first attempt; and the reluctance of the troops soon yielded to the persuasive eloquence of a leader, who shared the fatigues and dangers which he imposed on the meanest of the soldiers. The villages on either side of the Meyn, which were plentifully stored with corn and cattle, felt the ravages of an invading army. The principal houses, constructed with some imitation of Roman elegance, were consumed by the flames; and the Caesar boldly advanced about ten miles, till his progress was stopped by a dark and impenetrable forest, undermined by subterraneous passages, which threatened with secret snares and ambush every step of the assailants. The ground was already covered with snow; and Julian, after repairing an ancient castle which had been erected by Trajan, granted a truce of ten months to the submissive Barbarians. At the expiration of the truce, Julian undertook a second expedition beyond the Rhine, to humble the pride of Surmar and Hortaire, two of the kings of the Alemanni, who had been present at the battle of Strasburgh. They promised to restore all the Roman captives who yet remained alive; and as the Caesar had procured an exact account from the cities and villages of Gaul, of the inhabitants whom they had lost, he detected every attempt to deceive him, with a degree of readiness and accuracy, which almost established the belief of his supernatural knowledge. His third expedition was still more splendid and important than the two former. The Germans had collected their military powers, and moved along the opposite banks of the river, with a design of destroying the bridge, and of preventing the passage of the Romans. But this judicious plan of defence was disconcerted by a skilful diversion. Three hundred light-armed and active soldiers were detached in forty small boats, to fall down the stream in silence, and to land at some distance from the posts of the enemy. They executed their orders with so much boldness and celerity, that they had almost surprised the Barbarian chiefs, who returned in the fearless confidence of intoxication from one of their nocturnal festivals. Without repeating the uniform and disgusting tale of slaughter and devastation, it is sufficient to observe, that Julian dictated his own conditions of peace to six of the haughtiest kings of the Alemanni, three of whom were permitted to view the severe discipline and martial pomp of a Roman camp. Followed by twenty thousand captives, whom he had rescued from the chains of the Barbarians, the Caesar repassed the Rhine, after terminating a war, the success of which has been compared to the ancient glories of the Punic and Cimbric victories.

[Footnote 84: Libanius, the friend of Julian, clearly insinuates (Orat. ix. p. 178) that his hero had composed the history of his Gallic campaigns But Zosimus (l. iii. p, 140) seems to have derived his information only from the Orations and the Epistles of Julian. The discourse which is addressed to the Athenians contains an accurate, though general, account of the war against the Germans.]

[Footnote 85: See Ammian. xvii. 1, 10, xviii. 2, and Zosim. l. iii. p. 144. Julian ad S. P. Q. Athen. p. 280.]

As soon as the valor and conduct of Julian had secured an interval of peace, he applied himself to a work more congenial to his humane and philosophic temper. The cities of Gaul, which had suffered from the inroads of the Barbarians, he diligently repaired; and seven important posts, between Mentz and the mouth of the Rhine, are particularly mentioned, as having been rebuilt and fortified by the order of Julian. [86] The vanquished Germans had submitted to the just but humiliating condition of preparing and conveying the necessary materials. The active zeal of Julian urged the prosecution of the work; and such was the spirit which he had diffused among the troops, that the auxiliaries themselves, waiving their exemption from any duties of fatigue, contended in the most servile labors with the diligence of the Roman soldiers. It was incumbent on the Caesar to provide for the subsistence, as well as for the safety, of the inhabitants and of the garrisons. The desertion of the former, and the mutiny of the latter, must have been the fatal and inevitable consequences of famine. The tillage of the provinces of Gaul had been interrupted by the calamities of war; but the scanty harvests of the continent were supplied, by his paternal care, from the plenty of the adjacent island. Six hundred large barks, framed in the forest of the Ardennes, made several voyages to the coast of Britain; and returning from thence, laden with corn, sailed up the Rhine, and distributed their cargoes to the several towns and fortresses along the banks of the river. [87] The arms of Julian had restored a free and secure navigation, which Constantinius had offered to purchase at the expense of his dignity, and of a tributary present of two thousand pounds of silver. The emperor parsimoniously refused to his soldiers the sums which he granted with a lavish and trembling hand to the Barbarians. The dexterity, as well as the firmness, of Julian was put to a severe trial, when he took the field with a discontented army, which had already served two campaigns, without receiving any regular pay or any extraordinary donative. [88]

[Footnote 86: Ammian. xviii. 2. Libanius, Orat. x. p. 279, 280. Of these seven posts, four are at present towns of some consequence; Bingen, Andernach, Bonn, and Nuyss. The other three, Tricesimae, Quadriburgium, and Castra Herculis, or Heraclea, no longer subsist; but there is room to believe, that on the ground of Quadriburgium the Dutch have constructed the fort of Schenk, a name so offensive to the fastidious delicacy of Boileau. See D'Anville, Notice de l'Ancienne Gaule, p. 183. Boileau, Epitre iv. and the notes. Note: Tricesimae, Kellen, Mannert, quoted by Wagner. Heraclea, Erkeleus in the district of Juliers. St. Martin, ii. 311—M.]

[Footnote 87: We may credit Julian himself, (Orat. ad S. P. Q. Atheniensem, p. 280,) who gives a very particular account of the transaction. Zosimus adds two hundred vessels more, (l. iii. p. 145.) If we compute the 600 corn ships of Julian at only seventy tons each, they were capable of exporting 120,000 quarters, (see Arbuthnot's Weights and Measures, p. 237;) and the country which could bear so large an exportation, must already have attained an improved state of agriculture.]

[Footnote 88: The troops once broke out into a mutiny, immediately before the second passage of the Rhine. Ammian. xvii. 9.]

A tender regard for the peace and happiness of his subjects was the ruling principle which directed, or seemed to direct, the administration of Julian. [89] He devoted the leisure of his winter quarters to the offices of civil government; and affected to assume, with more pleasure, the character of a magistrate than that of a general. Before he took the field, he devolved on the provincial governors most of the public and private causes which had been referred to his tribunal; but, on his return, he carefully revised their proceedings, mitigated the rigor of the law, and pronounced a second judgment on the judges themselves. Superior to the last temptation of virtuous minds, an indiscreet and intemperate zeal for justice, he restrained, with calmness and dignity, the warmth of an advocate, who prosecuted, for extortion, the president of the Narbonnese province. "Who will ever be found guilty," exclaimed the vehement Delphidius, "if it be enough to deny?" "And who," replied Julian, "will ever be innocent, if it be sufficient to affirm?" In the general administration of peace and war, the interest of the sovereign is commonly the same as that of his people; but Constantius would have thought himself deeply injured, if the virtues of Julian had defrauded him of any part of the tribute which he extorted from an oppressed and exhausted country. The prince who was invested with the ensigns of royalty, might sometimes presume to correct the rapacious insolence of his inferior agents, to expose their corrupt arts, and to introduce an equal and easier mode of collection. But the management of the finances was more safely intrusted to Florentius, praetorian praefect of Gaul, an effeminate tyrant, incapable of pity or remorse: and the haughty minister complained of the most decent and gentle opposition, while Julian himself was rather inclined to censure the weakness of his own behavior. The Caesar had rejected, with abhorrence, a mandate for the levy of an extraordinary tax; a new superindiction, which the praefect had offered for his signature; and the faithful picture of the public misery, by which he had been obliged to justify his refusal, offended the court of Constantius. We may enjoy the pleasure of reading the sentiments of Julian, as he expresses them with warmth and freedom in a letter to one of his most intimate friends. After stating his own conduct, he proceeds in the following terms: "Was it possible for the disciple of Plato and Aristotle to act otherwise than I have done? Could I abandon the unhappy subjects intrusted to my care? Was I not called upon to defend them from the repeated injuries of these unfeeling robbers? A tribune who deserts his post is punished with death, and deprived of the honors of burial. With what justice could I pronounce his sentence, if, in the hour of danger, I myself neglected a duty far more sacred and far more important? God has placed me in this elevated post; his providence will guard and support me. Should I be condemned to suffer, I shall derive comfort from the testimony of a pure and upright conscience. Would to Heaven that I still possessed a counsellor like Sallust! If they think proper to send me a successor, I shall submit without reluctance; and had much rather improve the short opportunity of doing good, than enjoy a long and lasting impunity of evil." [90] The precarious and dependent situation of Julian displayed his virtues and concealed his defects. The young hero who supported, in Gaul, the throne of Constantius, was not permitted to reform the vices of the government; but he had courage to alleviate or to pity the distress of the people. Unless he had been able to revive the martial spirit of the Romans, or to introduce the arts of industry and refinement among their savage enemies, he could not entertain any rational hopes of securing the public tranquillity, either by the peace or conquest of Germany. Yet the victories of Julian suspended, for a short time, the inroads of the Barbarians, and delayed the ruin of the Western Empire.

[Footnote 89: Ammian. xvi. 5, xviii. 1. Mamertinus in Panegyr. Vet. xi. 4]

[Footnote 90: Ammian. xvii. 3. Julian. Epistol. xv. edit. Spanheim. Such a conduct almost justifies the encomium of Mamertinus. Ita illi anni spatia divisa sunt, ut aut Barbaros domitet, aut civibus jura restituat, perpetuum professus, aut contra hostem, aut contra vitia, certamen.]

His salutary influence restored the cities of Gaul, which had been so long exposed to the evils of civil discord, Barbarian war, and domestic tyranny; and the spirit of industry was revived with the hopes of enjoyment. Agriculture, manufactures, and commerce, again flourished under the protection of the laws; and the curioe, or civil corporations, were again filled with useful and respectable members: the youth were no longer apprehensive of marriage; and married persons were no longer apprehensive of posterity: the public and private festivals were celebrated with customary pomp; and the frequent and secure intercourse of the provinces displayed the image of national prosperity. [91] A mind like that of Julian must have felt the general happiness of which he was the author; but he viewed, with particular satisfaction and complacency, the city of Paris; the seat of his winter residence, and the object even of his partial affection. [92] That splendid capital, which now embraces an ample territory on either side of the Seine, was originally confined to the small island in the midst of the river, from whence the inhabitants derived a supply of pure and salubrious water. The river bathed the foot of the walls; and the town was accessible only by two wooden bridges. A forest overspread the northern side of the Seine, but on the south, the ground, which now bears the name of the University, was insensibly covered with houses, and adorned with a palace and amphitheatre, baths, an aqueduct, and a field of Mars for the exercise of the Roman troops. The severity of the climate was tempered by the neighborhood of the ocean; and with some precautions, which experience had taught, the vine and fig-tree were successfully cultivated. But in remarkable winters, the Seine was deeply frozen; and the huge pieces of ice that floated down the stream, might be compared, by an Asiatic, to the blocks of white marble which were extracted from the quarries of Phrygia. The licentiousness and corruption of Antioch recalled to the memory of Julian the severe and simple manners of his beloved Lutetia; [93] where the amusements of the theatre were unknown or despised. He indignantly contrasted the effeminate Syrians with the brave and honest simplicity of the Gauls, and almost forgave the intemperance, which was the only stain of the Celtic character. [94] If Julian could now revisit the capital of France, he might converse with men of science and genius, capable of understanding and of instructing a disciple of the Greeks; he might excuse the lively and graceful follies of a nation, whose martial spirit has never been enervated by the indulgence of luxury; and he must applaud the perfection of that inestimable art, which softens and refines and embellishes the intercourse of social life.

[Footnote 91: Libanius, Orat. Parental. in Imp. Julian. c. 38, in Fabricius Bibliothec. Graec. tom. vii. p. 263, 264.]

[Footnote 92: See Julian. in Misopogon, p. 340, 341. The primitive state of Paris is illustrated by Henry Valesius, (ad Ammian. xx. 4,) his brother Hadrian Valesius, or de Valois, and M. D'Anville, (in their respective Notitias of ancient Gaul,) the Abbe de Longuerue, (Description de la France, tom. i. p. 12, 13,) and M. Bonamy, (in the Mem. de l'Aca demie des Inscriptions, tom. xv. p. 656-691.)]

[Footnote 93: Julian, in Misopogon, p. 340. Leuce tia, or Lutetia, was the ancient name of the city, which, according to the fashion of the fourth century, assumed the territorial appellation of Parisii.]

[Footnote 94: Julian in Misopogon, p. 359, 360.]

CHAPTER XX

CONVERSION OF CONSTANTINE

PART I

THE MOTIVES, PROGRESS, AND EFFECTS OF THE CONVERSION OF CONSTANTINE—LEGAL ESTABLISHMENT AND CONSTITUTION OF THE CHRISTIAN OR CATHOLIC CHURCH

The public establishment of Christianity may be considered as one of those important and domestic revolutions which excite the most lively curiosity, and afford the most valuable instruction. The victories and the civil policy of Constantine no longer influence the state of Europe; but a considerable portion of the globe still retains the impression which it received from the conversion of that monarch; and the ecclesiastical institutions of his reign are still connected, by an indissoluble chain, with the opinions, the passions, and the interests of the present generation. In the consideration of a subject which may be examined with impartiality, but cannot be viewed with indifference, a difficulty immediately arises of a very unexpected nature; that of ascertaining the real and precise date of the conversion of Constantine. The eloquent Lactantius, in the midst of his court, seems impatient [1] to proclaim to the world the glorious example of the sovereign of Gaul; who, in the first moments of his reign, acknowledged and adored the majesty of the true and only God. [2] The learned Eusebius has ascribed the faith of Constantine to the miraculous sign which was displayed in the heavens whilst he meditated and prepared the Italian expedition. [3] The historian Zosimus maliciously asserts, that the emperor had imbrued his hands in the blood of his eldest son, before he publicly renounced the gods of Rome and of his ancestors. [4] The perplexity produced by these discordant authorities is derived from the behavior of Constantine himself. According to the strictness of ecclesiastical language, the first of the Christian emperors was unworthy of that name, till the moment of his death; since it was only during his last illness that he received, as a catechumen, the imposition of hands, [5] and was afterwards admitted, by the initiatory rites of baptism, into the number of the faithful. [6] The Christianity of Constantine must be allowed in a much more vague and qualified sense; and the nicest accuracy is required in tracing the slow and almost imperceptible gradations by which the monarch declared himself the protector, and at length the proselyte, of the church. It was an arduous task to eradicate the habits and prejudices of his education, to acknowledge the divine power of Christ, and to understand that the truth of his revelation was incompatible with the worship of the gods. The obstacles which he had probably experienced in his own mind, instructed him to proceed with caution in the momentous change of a national religion; and he insensibly discovered his new opinions, as far as he could enforce them with safety and with effect. During the whole course of his reign, the stream of Christianity flowed with a gentle, though accelerated, motion: but its general direction was sometimes checked, and sometimes diverted, by the accidental circumstances of the times, and by the prudence, or possibly by the caprice, of the monarch. His ministers were permitted to signify the intentions of their master in the various language which was best adapted to their respective principles; [7] and he artfully balanced the hopes and fears of his subjects, by publishing in the same year two edicts; the first of which enjoined the solemn observance of Sunday, [8] and the second directed the regular consultation of the Aruspices. [9] While this important revolution yet remained in suspense, the Christians and the Pagans watched the conduct of their sovereign with the same anxiety, but with very opposite sentiments. The former were prompted by every motive of zeal, as well as vanity, to exaggerate the marks of his favor, and the evidences of his faith. The latter, till their just apprehensions were changed into despair and resentment, attempted to conceal from the world, and from themselves, that the gods of Rome could no longer reckon the emperor in the number of their votaries. The same passions and prejudices have engaged the partial writers of the times to connect the public profession of Christianity with the most glorious or the most ignominious aera of the reign of Constantine.

[Footnote 1: The date of the Divine Institutions of Lactantius has been accurately discussed, difficulties have been started, solutions proposed, and an expedient imagined of two original editions; the former published during the persecution of Diocletian, the latter under that of Licinius. See Dufresnoy, Prefat. p. v. Tillemont, Mem. Ecclesiast. tom. vi. p. 465-470. Lardner's Credibility, part ii. vol. vii. p. 78-86. For my own part, I am almost convinced that Lactantius dedicated his Institutions to the sovereign of Gaul, at a time when Galerius, Maximin, and even Licinius, persecuted the Christians; that is, between the years 306 and 311.]

[Footnote 2: Lactant. Divin. Instit. i. l. vii. 27. The first and most important of these passages is indeed wanting in twenty-eight manuscripts; but it is found in nineteen. If we weigh the comparative value of these manuscripts, one of 900 years old, in the king of France's library may be alleged in its favor; but the *passage is omitted in the correct manuscript of Bologna, which the P. de Montfaucon ascribes to the sixth or seventh century (Diarium Italic. p. 489.) The taste of most of the editors (except Isaeus; see Lactant. edit. Dufresnoy, tom. i. p. 596) has felt the genuine style of Lactantius.]*

[Footnote 3: Euseb. in Vit. Constant. l. i. c. 27-32.]

[Footnote 4: Zosimus, l. ii. p. 104.]

[Footnote 5: That rite was always used in making a catechumen, (see Bingham's Antiquities. l. x. c. i. p. 419. Dom Chardon, Hist. des Sacramens, tom. i. p. 62,) and Constantine received it for the first time (Euseb. in Vit Constant. l. iv. c. 61) immediately before his baptism and death. From the connection of these two facts, Valesius (ad loc. Euseb.) has drawn the conclusion which is reluctantly admitted by Tillemont, (Hist. des Empereurs, tom. iv. p. 628,) and opposed with feeble arguments by Mosheim, (p. 968.)]

[Footnote 6: Euseb. in Vit. Constant. l. iv. c. 61, 62, 63. The legend of Constantine's baptism at Rome, thirteen years before his death, was invented in the eighth century, as a proper motive for his donation. Such has been the gradual progress of knowledge, that a story, of which Cardinal Baronius (Annual Ecclesiast. A. D. 324, No. 43-49) declared himself the unblushing advocate, is now feebly supported, even within the verge of the Vatican. See the Antiquitates Christianae, tom. ii. p. 232; a work published with six approbations at Rome, in the year 1751 by Father Mamachi, a learned Dominican.]

[Footnote 7: The quaestor, or secretary, who composed the law of the Theodosian Code, makes his master say with indifference, "hominibus supradictae religionis," (l. xvi. tit. ii. leg. 1.) The minister of ecclesiastical affairs was allowed a more devout and respectful style, the legal, most holy, and Catholic worship.]

[Footnote 8: Cod. Theodos. l. ii. viii. tit. leg. 1. Cod. Justinian. l. iii. tit. xii. leg. 3. Constantine styles the Lord's day dies solis, a name which could not offend the ears of his pagan subjects.]

[Footnote 9: Cod. Theodos. l. xvi. tit. x. leg. l. Godefroy, in the character of a commentator, endeavors (tom. vi. p. 257) to excuse Constantine; but the more zealous Baronius (Annal. Eccles. A. D. 321, No. 17) censures his profane conduct with truth and asperity.]

Whatever symptoms of Christian piety might transpire in the discourses or actions of Constantine, he persevered till he was near forty years of age in the practice of the established religion; [10] and the same conduct which in the court of Nicomedia might be imputed to his fear, could be ascribed only to the inclination or policy of the sovereign of Gaul. His liberality restored and enriched the temples of the gods; the medals which issued from his Imperial mint are impressed with the figures and attributes of Jupiter and Apollo, of Mars and Hercules; and his filial piety increased the council of Olympus by the solemn apotheosis of his father Constantius. [11] But the devotion of Constantine was more peculiarly directed to the genius of the Sun, the Apollo of Greek and Roman mythology; and he was pleased to be represented with the symbols of the God of Light and Poetry. The unerring shafts of that deity, the brightness of his eyes, his laurel wreath, immortal beauty, and elegant accomplishments, seem to point him out as the patron of a young hero. The altars of Apollo were crowned with the votive offerings of Constantine; and the credulous multitude were taught to believe, that the emperor was permitted to behold with mortal eyes the visible majesty of their tutelar deity; and that, either walking or in a vision, he was blessed with the auspicious omens of a long and victorious reign. The Sun was universally celebrated as the invincible guide and protector of Constantine; and the Pagans might reasonably expect that the insulted god would pursue with unrelenting vengeance the impiety of his ungrateful favorite. [12]

[Footnote 10: Theodoret. (l. i. c. 18) seems to insinuate that Helena gave her son a Christian education; but we may be assured, from the superior authority of Eusebius, (in Vit. Constant. l. iii. c. 47,) that she herself was indebted to Constantine for the knowledge of Christianity.]

[Footnote 11: See the medals of Constantine in Ducange and Banduri. As few cities had retained the privilege of coining, almost all the medals of that age issued from the mint under the sanction of the Imperial authority.]

[Footnote 12: The panegyric of Eumenius, (vii. inter Panegyr. Vet.,) which was pronounced a few months before the Italian war, abounds with the most unexceptionable evidence of the Pagan superstition of Constantine, and of his particular veneration for Apollo, or the Sun; to which Julian alludes.]

As long as Constantine exercised a limited sovereignty over the provinces of Gaul, his Christian subjects were protected by the authority, and perhaps by the laws, of a prince, who wisely left to the gods the care of vindicating their own honor. If we may credit the assertion of Constantine himself, he had been an indignant spectator of the savage cruelties which were inflicted, by the hands of Roman soldiers, on those citizens whose religion was their only crime. [13] In the East and in the West, he had seen the different effects of severity and indulgence; and as the former was rendered still more odious by the example of Galerius, his implacable enemy, the latter was recommended to his imitation by the authority and advice of a dying father. The son of Constantius immediately suspended or repealed the edicts of persecution, and granted the free exercise of their religious ceremonies to all those who had already professed themselves members of the church. They were soon encouraged to depend on the favor as well as on the justice of their sovereign, who had imbibed a secret and sincere reverence for the name of Christ, and for the God of the Christians. [14]

[Footnote 13: Constantin. Orat. ad Sanctos, c. 25. But it might easily be shown, that the Greek translator has improved the sense of the Latin original; and the aged emperor might recollect the persecution of Diocletian with a more lively abhorrence than he had actually felt to the days of his youth and Paganism.]

[Footnote 14: See Euseb. Hist. Eccles. l. viii. 13, l. ix. 9, and in Vit. Const. l. i. c. 16, 17 Lactant. Divin. Institut. i. l. Caecilius de Mort. Persecut. c. 25.]

About five months after the conquest of Italy, the emperor made a solemn and authentic declaration of his sentiments by the celebrated edict of Milan, which restored peace to the Catholic church. In the personal interview of the two western princes, Constantine, by the ascendant of genius and power, obtained the ready concurrence of his colleague, Licinius; the union of their names and authority disarmed the fury of Maximin; and after the death of the tyrant of the East, the edict of Milan was received as a general and fundamental law of the Roman world. [15]

[Footnote 15: Caecilius (de Mort. Persecut. c. 48) has preserved the Latin original; and Eusebius (Hist. Eccles. l. x. c. 5) has given a Greek translation of this perpetual edict, which refers to some provisional regulations.]

The wisdom of the emperors provided for the restitution of all the civil and religious rights of which the Christians had been so unjustly deprived. It was enacted that the places of worship, and public lands, which had been confiscated, should be restored to the church, without dispute, without delay, and without expense; and this severe injunction was accompanied with a gracious promise, that if any of the purchasers had paid a fair and adequate price, they should be indemnified from the Imperial treasury. The salutary regulations which guard the future tranquillity of the faithful are framed on the principles of enlarged and equal toleration; and such an equality must have been interpreted by a recent sect as an advantageous and honorable distinction. The two emperors proclaim to the world, that they have granted a free and absolute power to the Christians, and to all others, of following the religion which each individual thinks proper to prefer, to which he has addicted his mind, and which he may deem the best adapted to his own use. They carefully explain every ambiguous word, remove every exception, and exact from the governors of the provinces a strict obedience to the true and simple meaning of an edict, which was designed to establish and secure, without any limitation, the claims of religious liberty. They condescend to assign two weighty reasons which have induced them to allow this universal toleration: the humane intention of consulting the peace and happiness of their people; and the pious hope, that, by such a conduct, they shall appease and propitiate the Deity, whose seat is in heaven. They gratefully acknowledge the many signal proofs which they have received of the divine favor; and they trust that the same Providence will forever continue to protect the prosperity of the prince and people. From these vague and indefinite expressions of piety, three suppositions may be deduced, of a different, but not of an incompatible nature. The mind of Constantine might fluctuate between the Pagan and the Christian religions. According to the loose and complying notions of Polytheism, he might acknowledge the God of the Christians as one of the many deities who compose the hierarchy of heaven. Or perhaps he might embrace the philosophic and pleasing idea, that, notwithstanding the variety of names, of rites, and of opinions, all the sects, and all the nations of mankind, are united in the worship of the common Father and Creator of the universe. [16]

[Footnote 16: A panegyric of Constantine, pronounced seven or eight months after the edict of Milan, (see Gothofred. Chronolog. Legum, p. 7, and Tillemont, Hist. des Empereurs, tom. iv. p. 246,) uses the following remarkable expression: "Summe rerum sator, cujus tot nomina sant, quot linguas gentium esse voluisti, quem enim te ipse dici velin, scire non possumus." (Panegyr. Vet. ix. 26.) In explaining Constantine's progress in the faith, Mosheim (p. 971, &c.) is ingenious, subtle, prolix.]

But the counsels of princes are more frequently influenced by views of temporal advantage, than by considerations of abstract and speculative truth. The partial and increasing favor of Constantine may naturally be referred to the esteem which he entertained for the moral character of the Christians; and to a persuasion, that the propagation of the gospel would inculcate the practice of private and public virtue. Whatever latitude an absolute monarch may assume in his own conduct, whatever indulgence he may claim for his own passions, it is undoubtedly his interest that all his subjects should respect the natural and civil obligations of society. But the operation of the wisest laws is imperfect and precarious. They seldom inspire virtue, they cannot always restrain vice. Their power is insufficient to prohibit all that they condemn, nor can they always punish the actions which they prohibit. The legislators of antiquity had summoned to their aid the powers of education and of opinion. But every principle which had once maintained the vigor and purity of Rome and Sparta, was long since extinguished in a declining and despotic empire. Philosophy still exercised her temperate sway over the human mind, but the cause of virtue derived very feeble support from the influence of the Pagan superstition. Under these discouraging circumstances, a prudent magistrate might observe with pleasure the progress of a religion which diffused among the people a pure, benevolent, and universal system of ethics, adapted to every duty and every condition of life; recommended as the will and reason of the supreme Deity, and enforced by the sanction of eternal rewards or punishments. The experience of Greek and Roman history could not inform the world how far the system of national manners might be reformed and improved by the precepts of a divine revelation; and Constantine might listen with some confidence to the flattering, and indeed reasonable, assurances of Lactantius. The eloquent apologist seemed firmly to expect, and almost ventured to promise, that the establishment of Christianity would restore the innocence and felicity of the primitive age; that the worship of the true God would extinguish war and dissension among those who mutually considered themselves as the children of a common parent; that every impure desire, every angry or selfish passion, would be restrained by the knowledge of the gospel; and that the magistrates might sheath the sword of justice among a people who would be universally actuated by the sentiments of truth and piety, of equity and moderation, of harmony and universal love. [17]

[Footnote 17: See the elegant description of Lactantius, (Divin Institut. v. 8,) who is much more perspicuous and positive than becomes a discreet prophet.]

The passive and unresisting obedience, which bows under the yoke of authority, or even of oppression, must have appeared, in the eyes of an absolute monarch, the most conspicuous and useful of the evangelic virtues. [18] The primitive Christians derived the institution of civil government, not from the consent of the people, but from the decrees of Heaven. The reigning emperor, though he had usurped the sceptre by treason and murder, immediately assumed the sacred character of vicegerent of the Deity. To the Deity alone he was accountable for the abuse of his power; and his subjects were indissolubly bound, by their oath of fidelity, to a tyrant, who had violated every law of nature and society. The humble Christians were sent into the world as sheep among wolves; and since they were not permitted to employ force even in the defence of their religion, they should be still more criminal if they were tempted to shed the blood of their fellow-creatures in disputing the vain privileges, or the sordid possessions, of this transitory life. Faithful to the doctrine of the apostle, who in the reign of Nero had preached the duty of unconditional submission, the Christians of the three first centuries preserved their conscience pure and innocent of the guilt of secret conspiracy, or open rebellion. While they experienced the rigor of persecution, they were never provoked either to meet their tyrants in the field, or indignantly to withdraw themselves into some remote and sequestered corner of the globe. [19] The Protestants of France, of Germany, and of Britain, who asserted with such intrepid courage their civil and religious freedom, have been insulted by the invidious comparison between the conduct of the primitive and of the reformed Christians. [20] Perhaps, instead of censure, some applause may be due to the superior sense and spirit of our ancestors, who had convinced themselves that religion cannot abolish the unalienable rights of human nature. [21] Perhaps the patience of the primitive church may be ascribed to its weakness, as well as to its virtue.

A sect of unwarlike plebeians, without leaders, without arms, without fortifications, must have encountered inevitable destruction in a rash and fruitless resistance to the master of the Roman legions. But the Christians, when they deprecated the wrath of Diocletian, or solicited the favor of Constantine, could allege, with truth and confidence, that they held the principle of passive obedience, and that, in the space of three centuries, their conduct had always been conformable to their principles. They might add, that the throne of the emperors would be established on a fixed and permanent basis, if all their subjects, embracing the Christian doctrine, should learn to suffer and to obey.

[Footnote 18: The political system of the Christians is explained by Grotius, de Jure Belli et Pacis, l. i. c. 3, 4. Grotius was a republican and an exile, but the mildness of his temper inclined him to support the established powers.]

[Footnote 19: Tertullian. Apolog. c. 32, 34, 35, 36. Tamen nunquam Albiniani, nec Nigriani vel Cassiani inveniri potuerunt Christiani. Ad Scapulam, c. 2. If this assertion be strictly true, it excludes the Christians of that age from all civil and military employments, which would have compelled them to take an active part in the service of their respective governors. See Moyle's Works, vol. ii. p. 349.]

[Footnote 20: See the artful Bossuet, (Hist. des Variations des Eglises Protestantes, tom. iii. p. 210-258.) and the malicious Bayle, (tom ii. p. 820.) I name Bayle, for he was certainly the author of the Avis aux Refugies; consult the Dictionnaire Critique de Chauffepie, tom. i. part ii. p. 145.]

[Footnote 21: Buchanan is the earliest, or at least the most celebrated, of the reformers, who has justified the theory of resistance. See his Dialogue de Jure Regni apud Scotos, tom. ii. p. 28, 30, edit. fol. Rudiman.]

In the general order of Providence, princes and tyrants are considered as the ministers of Heaven, appointed to rule or to chastise the nations of the earth. But sacred history affords many illustrious examples of the more immediate interposition of the Deity in the government of his chosen people. The sceptre and the sword were committed to the hands of Moses, of Joshua, of Gideon, of David, of the Maccabees; the virtues of those heroes were the motive or the effect of the divine favor, the success of their arms was destined to achieve the deliverance or the triumph of the church. If the judges of Israel were occasional and temporary magistrates, the kings of Judah derived from the royal unction of their great ancestor an hereditary and indefeasible right, which could not be forfeited by their own vices, nor recalled by the caprice of their subjects. The same extraordinary providence, which was no longer confined to the Jewish people, might elect Constantine and his family as the protectors of the Christian world; and the devout Lactantius announces, in a prophetic tone, the future glories of his long and universal reign. [22] Galerius and Maximin, Maxentius and Licinius, were the rivals who shared with the favorite of heaven the provinces of the empire. The tragic deaths of Galerius and Maximin soon gratified the resentment, and fulfilled the sanguine expectations, of the Christians. The success of Constantine against Maxentius and Licinius removed the two formidable competitors who still opposed the triumph of the second David, and his cause might seem to claim the peculiar interposition of Providence. The character of the Roman tyrant disgraced the purple and human nature; and though the Christians might enjoy his precarious favor, they were exposed, with the rest of his subjects, to the effects of his wanton and capricious cruelty. The conduct of Licinius soon betrayed the reluctance with which he had consented to the wise and humane regulations of the edict of Milan. The convocation of provincial synods was prohibited in his dominions; his Christian officers were ignominiously dismissed; and if he avoided the guilt, or rather danger, of a general persecution, his partial oppressions were rendered still more odious by the violation of a solemn and voluntary engagement. [23] While the East, according to the lively expression of Eusebius, was involved in the shades of infernal darkness, the auspicious rays of celestial light warmed and illuminated the provinces of the West. The piety of Constantine was admitted as an unexceptionable proof of the justice of his arms; and his use of victory confirmed the opinion of the Christians, that their hero was inspired, and conducted, by the Lord of Hosts. The conquest of Italy produced a general edict of toleration; and as soon as the defeat of Licinius had invested Constantine with the sole dominion of the Roman world, he immediately, by circular letters, exhorted all his subjects to imitate, without delay, the example of their sovereign, and to embrace the divine truth of Christianity. [24]

[Footnote 22: Lactant Divin. Institut. i. l. Eusebius in the course of his history, his life, and his oration, repeatedly inculcates the divine right of Constantine to the empire.]

[Footnote 23: Our imperfect knowledge of the persecution of Licinius is derived from Eusebius, (Hist. l. x. c. 8. Vit. Constantin. l. i. c. 49-56, l. ii. c. 1, 2.) Aurelius Victor mentions his cruelty in general terms.]

[Footnote 24: Euseb. in Vit. Constant. l. ii. c. 24-42 48-60.]

PART II

The assurance that the elevation of Constantine was intimately connected with the designs of Providence, instilled into the minds of the Christians two opinions, which, by very different means, assisted the accomplishment of the prophecy. Their warm and active loyalty exhausted in his favor every resource of human industry; and they confidently expected that their strenuous efforts would be seconded by some divine and miraculous aid. The enemies of Constantine have imputed to interested motives the alliance which he insensibly contracted with the Catholic church, and which apparently contributed to the success of his ambition. In the beginning of the fourth century, the Christians still bore a very inadequate proportion to the inhabitants of the empire; but among a degenerate people, who viewed the change of masters with the indifference of slaves, the spirit and union of a religious party might assist the popular leader, to whose service, from a principle of conscience, they had devoted their lives and fortunes. [25] The example of his father had instructed Constantine to esteem and to reward the merit of the Christians; and in the distribution of public offices, he had the advantage of strengthening his government, by the choice of ministers or generals, in whose fidelity he could repose a just and unreserved confidence. By the influence of these dignified missionaries, the proselytes of the new faith must have multiplied in the court and army; the Barbarians of Germany, who filled the ranks of the legions, were of a careless temper, which acquiesced without resistance in the religion of their commander; and when they passed the Alps, it may fairly be presumed, that a great number of the soldiers had already consecrated their swords to the service of Christ and of Constantine. [26] The habits of mankind and the interests of religion gradually abated the horror of war and bloodshed, which had so long prevailed among the Christians; and in the councils which were assembled under the gracious protection of Constantine, the authority of the bishops was seasonably employed to ratify the obligation of the military oath, and to inflict the penalty of excommunication on those soldiers who threw away their arms during the peace of the church. [27] While Constantine, in his own dominions, increased the number and zeal of his faithful adherents, he could depend on the support of a powerful faction in those provinces which were still possessed or usurped by his rivals. A secret disaffection was diffused among the Christian subjects of Maxentius and Licinius; and the resentment, which the latter did not attempt to conceal, served only to engage them still more deeply in the interest of his competitor. The regular correspondence which connected the bishops of the most distant provinces, enabled them freely to communicate their wishes and their designs, and to transmit without danger any useful intelligence, or any pious contributions, which might promote the service of Constantine, who publicly declared that he had taken up arms for the deliverance of the church. [28]

[Footnote 25: In the beginning of the last century, the Papists of England were only a thirtieth, and the Protestants of France only a fifteenth, part of the respective nations, to whom their spirit and power were a constant object of apprehension. See the relations which Bentivoglio (who was then nuncio at Brussels, and afterwards cardinal) transmitted to the court of Rome, (Relazione, tom. ii. p. 211, 241.) Bentivoglio was curious, well informed, but somewhat partial.]

[Footnote 26: This careless temper of the Germans appears almost uniformly on the history of the conversion of each of the tribes. The legions of Constantine were recruited with Germans, (Zosimus, l. ii. p. 86;) and the court even of his father had been filled with Christians. See the first book of the Life of Constantine, by Eusebius.]

[Footnote 27: De his qui arma projiciunt in pace, placuit eos abstinere a communione. Council. Arelat. Canon. iii. The best critics apply these words to the peace of the church.]

[Footnote 28: Eusebius always considers the second civil war against Licinius as a sort of religious crusade. At the invitation of the tyrant, some Christian officers had resumed their zones; or, in other words, had returned to the military service. Their conduct was afterwards censured by the twelfth canon of the Council of Nice; if this particular application may be received, instead of the lo se and general sense of the Greek interpreters, Balsamor Zonaras, and Alexis Aristenus. See Beveridge, Pandect. Eccles. Graec. tom. i. p. 72, tom. ii. p. 73 Annotation.]

The enthusiasm which inspired the troops, and perhaps the emperor himself, had sharpened their swords while it satisfied their conscience. They marched to battle with the full assurance, that the same God, who had formerly opened a passage to the Israelites through the waters of Jordan, and had thrown down the walls of Jericho at the sound of the trumpets of Joshua, would display his visible majesty and power in the victory of Constantine. The evidence of ecclesiastical history is prepared to affirm, that their expectations were justified by the conspicuous miracle to which the conversion of the first Christian emperor has been almost unanimously ascribed. The real or imaginary cause of so important an event, deserves and demands the attention of posterity; and I shall endeavor to form a just estimate of the famous vision of Constantine, by a distinct consideration of the standard, the dream, and the celestial sign; by separating the historical, the natural, and the marvellous parts of this extraordinary story, which, in the composition of a specious argument, have been artfully confounded in one splendid and brittle mass.

I. An instrument of the tortures which were inflicted only on slaves and strangers, became on object of horror in the eyes of a Roman citizen; and the ideas of guilt, of pain, and of ignominy, were closely united with the idea of the cross. [29] The piety, rather than the humanity, of Constantine soon abolished in his dominions the punishment which the Savior of mankind had condescended to suffer; [30] but the emperor had already learned to despise the prejudices of his education, and of his people, before he could erect in the midst of Rome his own statue, bearing a cross in its right hand; with an inscription which referred the victory of his arms, and the deliverance of Rome, to the virtue of that salutary sign, the true symbol of force and courage. [31] The same symbol sanctified the arms of the soldiers of Constantine; the cross glittered on their helmet, was engraved on their shields, was interwoven into their banners; and the consecrated emblems which adorned the person of the emperor himself, were distinguished only by richer materials and more exquisite workmanship. [32] But the principal standard which displayed the triumph of the cross was styled the Labarum, [33] an obscure, though celebrated name, which has been vainly derived from almost all the languages of the world. It is described [34] as a long pike intersected by a transversal beam. The silken veil, which hung down from the beam, was curiously inwrought with the images of the reigning monarch and his children. The summit of the pike supported a crown of gold which enclosed the mysterious monogram, at once expressive of the figure of the cross, and the initial letters, of the name of Christ. [35] The safety of the labarum was intrusted to fifty guards, of approved valor and fidelity; their station was marked by honors and emoluments; and some fortunate accidents soon introduced an opinion, that as long as the guards of the labarum were engaged in the execution of their office, they were secure and invulnerable amidst the darts of the enemy. In the second civil war, Licinius felt and dreaded the power of this consecrated banner, the sight of which, in the distress of battle, animated the soldiers of Constantine with an invincible enthusiasm, and scattered terror and dismay through the ranks of the adverse legions. [36] The Christian emperors, who respected the example of Constantine, displayed in all their military expeditions the standard of the cross; but when the degenerate successors of Theodosius had ceased to appear in person at the head of their armies, the labarum was deposited as a venerable but useless relic in the palace of Constantinople. [37] Its honors are still preserved on the medals of the Flavian family. Their grateful devotion has placed the monogram of Christ in the midst of the ensigns of Rome. The solemn epithets of, safety of the republic, glory of the army, restoration of public happiness, are equally applied to the religious and military trophies; and there is still extant a medal of the emperor Constantius, where the standard of the labarum is accompanied with these memorable words, By This Sign Thou Shalt Conquer. [38]

[Footnote 29: Nomen ipsum crucis absit non modo a corpore civium Romano rum, sed etiam a cogitatione, oculis, auribus. Cicero pro Raberio, c. 5. The Christian writers, Justin, Minucius Felix, Tertullian, Jerom, and Maximus of Turin, have investigated with tolerable success the figure or likeness of a cross in almost every object of nature or art; in the intersection of the meridian and equator, the human face, a bird flying, a man swimming, a mast and yard, a plough, a standard, &c., &c., &c. See Lipsius de Cruce, l. i. c. 9.]

[Footnote 30: See Aurelius Victor, who considers this law as one of the examples of Constantine's piety. An edict so honorable to Christianity deserved a place in the Theodosian Code, instead of the indirect mention of it, which seems to result from the comparison of the fifth and eighteenth titles of the ninth book.]

[Footnote 31: Eusebius, in Vit. Constantin. l. i. c. 40. This statue, or at least the cross and inscription, may be ascribed with more probability to the second, or even third, visit of Constantine to Rome. Immediately after the defeat of Maxentius, the minds of the senate and people were scarcely ripe for this public monument.]

[Footnote 32: Agnoscas, regina, libens mea signa necesse est; In quibus effigies crucis aut gemmata refulget Aut longis solido ex auro praefertur in hastis. Hoc signo invictus, transmissis Alpibus Ultor Servitium solvit miserabile Constantinus. Christus purpureum gemmanti textus in auro Signabat Labarum, clypeorum insignia Christus Scripserat; ardebat summis crux addita cristis. Prudent. in Symmachum, l. ii. 464, 486.]

[Footnote 33: The derivation and meaning of the word Labarum or Laborum, which is employed by Gregory Nazianzen, Ambrose, Prudentius, &c., still remain totally unknown, in spite of the efforts of the critics, who have ineffectually tortured the Latin, Greek, Spanish, Celtic, Teutonic, Illyric, Armenian, &c., in search of an etymology. See Ducange, in Gloss. Med. et infim. Latinitat. sub voce Labarum, and Godefroy, ad Cod. Theodos. tom. ii. p. 143.]

[Footnote 34: Euseb. in Vit. Constantin. l. i. c. 30, 31. Baronius (Annal. Eccles. A. D. 312, No. 26) has engraved a representation of the Labarum.]

[Footnote 35: Transversa X litera, summo capite circumflexo, Christum in scutis notat. Caecilius de M. P. c. 44, Cuper, (ad M. P. in edit. Lactant. tom. ii. p. 500,) and Baronius (A. D. 312, No. 25) have engraved from ancient monuments several specimens (as thus of these monograms) which became extremely fashionable in the Christian world.]

[Footnote 36: Euseb. in Vit. Constantin. l. ii. c. 7, 8, 9. He introduces the Labarum before the Italian expedition; but his narrative seems to indicate that it was never shown at the head of an army till Constantine above ten years afterwards, declared himself the enemy of Licinius, and the deliverer of the church.]

[Footnote 37: See Cod. Theod. l. vi. tit. xxv. Sozomen, l. i. c. 2. Theophan. Chronograph. p. 11. Theophanes lived towards the end of the eighth century, almost five hundred years after Constantine. The modern Greeks were not inclined to display in the field the standard of the empire and of Christianity; and though they depended on every superstitious hope of defence, the promise of victory would have appeared too bold a fiction.]

[Footnote 38: The Abbe du Voisin, p. 103, &c., alleges several of these medals, and quotes a particular dissertation of a Jesuit the Pere de Grainville, on this subject.]

II. In all occasions of danger and distress, it was the practice of the primitive Christians to fortify their minds and bodies by the sign of the cross, which they used, in all their ecclesiastical rites, in all the daily occurrences of life, as an infallible preservative against every species of spiritual or temporal evil. [39] The authority of the church might alone have had sufficient weight to justify the devotion of Constantine, who in the same prudent and gradual progress acknowledged the truth, and assumed the symbol, of Christianity. But the testimony of a contemporary writer, who in a formal treatise has avenged the cause of religion, bestows on the piety of the emperor a more awful and sublime character. He affirms, with the most perfect confidence, that in the night which preceded the last battle against Maxentius, Constantine was admonished in a dream [39a] to inscribe the shields of his soldiers with the celestial sign of God, the sacred monogram of the name of Christ; that he executed the commands of Heaven, and that his valor and obedience were rewarded by the decisive victory of the Milvian Bridge. Some considerations might perhaps incline a sceptical mind to suspect the judgment or the veracity of the rhetorician, whose pen, either from zeal or interest, was devoted to the cause of the prevailing faction. [40] He appears to have published his deaths of the persecutors at Nicomedia about three years after the Roman victory; but the interval of a thousand miles, and a thousand days, will allow an ample latitude for the invention of declaimers, the credulity of party, and the tacit approbation of the emperor himself who might listen without indignation to a marvellous tale, which exalted his fame, and promoted his designs. In favor of Licinius, who still dissembled his animosity to the Christians, the same author has provided a similar vision, of a form of prayer, which was communicated by an angel, and repeated by the whole army before they engaged the legions of the tyrant Maximin. The frequent repetition of miracles serves to provoke, where it does not subdue, the reason of mankind; [41] but if the dream of Constantine is separately considered, it may be naturally explained either by the policy or the enthusiasm of the emperor. Whilst his anxiety for the approaching day, which must decide the fate of the empire, was suspended by a short and interrupted slumber, the venerable form of Christ, and the well-known symbol of his religion, might forcibly offer themselves to the active fancy of a prince who reverenced the name, and had perhaps secretly implored the power, of the God of the Christians. As readily might a consummate statesman indulge himself in the use of one of those military stratagems, one of those pious frauds, which Philip and Sertorius had employed with such art and effect. [42] The praeternatural origin of dreams was universally admitted by the nations of antiquity, and a considerable part of the Gallic army was already prepared to place their confidence in the salutary sign of the Christian religion. The secret vision of Constantine could be disproved only by the event; and the intrepid hero who had passed the Alps and the Apennine, might view with careless despair the consequences of a defeat under the walls of Rome. The senate and people, exulting in their own deliverance from an odious tyrant, acknowledged that the victory of Constantine surpassed the powers of man, without daring to insinuate that it had been obtained by the protection of the gods. The triumphal arch, which was erected about three years after the event, proclaims, in ambiguous language, that by the greatness of his own mind, and by an instinct or impulse of the Divinity, he had saved and avenged the Roman republic. [43] The Pagan orator, who had seized an earlier opportunity of celebrating the virtues of the conqueror, supposes that he alone enjoyed a secret and intimate commerce with the Supreme Being, who delegated the care of mortals to his subordinate deities; and thus assigns a very plausible reason why the subjects of Constantine should not presume to embrace the new religion of their sovereign. [44]

[Footnote 39: Tertullian de Corona, c. 3. Athanasius, tom. i. p. 101. The learned Jesuit Petavius (Dogmata Theolog. l. xv. c. 9, 10) has collected many similar passages on the virtues of the cross, which in the last age embarrassed our Protestant disputants.]

[Footnote 39a: Manso has observed, that Gibbon ought not to have separated the vision of Constantine from the wonderful apparition in the sky, as the two wonders are closely connected in Eusebius. Manso, Leben Constantine, p. 82—M.]

[Footnote 40: Caecilius de M. P. c. 44. It is certain, that this historical declamation was composed and published while Licinius, sovereign of the East, still preserved the friendship of Constantine and of the Christians. Every reader of taste must perceive that the style is of a very different and inferior character to that of Lactantius; and such indeed is the judgment of Le Clerc and Lardner, (Bibliotheque Ancienne et Moderne, tom. iii. p. 438. Credibility of the Gospel, &c., part ii. vol. vii. p. 94.) Three arguments from the title of the book, and from the names of Donatus and Caecilius, are produced by the advocates for Lactantius. (See the P. Lestocq, tom. ii. p. 46-60.) Each of these proofs is singly weak and defective; but their concurrence has great weight. I have often fluctuated, and shall tamely follow the Colbert Ms. in calling the author (whoever he was) Caecilius.]

[Footnote 41: Caecilius de M. P. c. 46. There seems to be some reason in the observation of M. de Voltaire, (Euvres, tom. xiv. p. 307.) who ascribes to the success of Constantine the superior fame of his Labarum above the angel of Licinius. Yet even this angel is favorably entertained by Pagi, Tillemont, Fleury, &c., who are fond of increasing their stock of miracles.]

[Footnote 42: Besides these well-known examples, Tollius (Preface to Boileau's translation of Longinus) has discovered a vision of Antigonus, who assured his troops that he had seen a pentagon (the symbol of safety) with these words, "In this conquer." But Tollius has most inexcusably omitted to produce his authority, and his own character, literary as well as moral, is not free from reproach. (See Chauffepie, Dictionnaire Critique, tom. iv. p. 460.) Without insisting on the silence of Diodorus Plutarch, Justin, &c., it may be observed that Polyaenus, who in a separate chapter (l. iv. c. 6) has collected nineteen military stratagems of Antigonus, is totally ignorant of this remarkable vision.]

[Footnote 43: Instinctu Divinitatis, mentis magnitudine. The inscription on the triumphal arch of Constantine, which has been copied by Baronius, Gruter, &c., may still be perused by every curious traveller.]

[Footnote 44: Habes profecto aliquid cum illa mente Divina secretum; qua delegata nostra Diis Minoribus cura uni se tibi dignatur ostendere Panegyr. Vet. ix. 2.]

III. The philosopher, who with calm suspicion examines the dreams and omens, the miracles and prodigies, of profane or even of ecclesiastical history, will probably conclude, that if the eyes of the spectators have sometimes been deceived by fraud, the understanding of the readers has much more frequently been insulted by fiction. Every event, or appearance, or accident, which seems to deviate from the ordinary course of nature, has been rashly ascribed to the immediate action of the Deity; and the astonished fancy of the multitude has sometimes given shape and color, language and motion, to the fleeting but uncommon meteors of the air. [45] Nazarius and Eusebius are the two most celebrated orators, who, in studied panegyrics, have labored to exalt the glory of Constantine. Nine years after the Roman victory, Nazarius [46] describes an army of divine warriors, who seemed to fall from the sky: he marks their beauty, their spirit, their gigantic forms, the stream of light which beamed from their celestial armor, their patience in suffering themselves to be heard, as well as seen, by mortals; and their declaration that they were sent, that they flew, to the assistance of the great Constantine. For the truth of this prodigy, the Pagan orator appeals to the whole Gallic nation, in whose presence he was then speaking; and seems to hope that the ancient apparitions [47] would now obtain credit from this recent and public event. The Christian fable of Eusebius, which, in the space of twenty-six years, might arise from the original dream, is cast in a much more correct and elegant mould. In one of the marches of Constantine, he is reported to have seen with his own eyes the luminous trophy of the cross, placed above the meridian sun and inscribed with the following words: By This Conquer. This amazing object in the sky astonished the whole army, as well as the emperor himself, who was yet undetermined in the choice of a religion: but his astonishment was converted into faith by the vision of the ensuing night. Christ appeared before his eyes; and displaying the same celestial sign of the cross, he directed Constantine to frame a similar standard, and to march, with an assurance of victory, against Maxentius and all his enemies. [48] The learned bishop of Caesarea appears to be sensible, that the recent discovery of this marvellous anecdote would excite some surprise and distrust among the most pious of his readers. Yet, instead of ascertaining the precise circumstances of time and place, which always serve to detect falsehood or establish truth; [49] instead of collecting and recording the evidence of so many living witnesses who must have been spectators of this stupendous miracle; [50] Eusebius contents himself with alleging a very singular testimony; that of the deceased Constantine, who, many years after the event, in the freedom of conversation, had related to him this extraordinary incident of his own life, and had attested the truth of it by a solemn oath. The prudence and gratitude of the learned prelate forbade him to suspect the veracity of his victorious master; but he plainly intimates, that in a fact of such a nature, he should have refused his assent to any meaner authority. This motive of credibility could not survive the power of the Flavian family; and the celestial sign, which the Infidels might afterwards deride, [51] was disregarded by the Christians of the age which immediately followed the conversion of Constantine. [52] But the Catholic church, both of the East and of the West, has adopted a prodigy which favors, or seems to favor, the popular worship of the cross. The vision of Constantine maintained an honorable place in the legend of superstition, till the bold and sagacious spirit of criticism presumed to depreciate the triumph, and to arraign the truth, of the first Christian emperor. [53]

[Footnote 45: M. Freret (Memoires de l'Academie des Inscriptions, tom. iv. p. 411-437) explains, by physical causes, many of the prodigies of antiquity; and Fabricius, who is abused by both parties, vainly tries to introduce the celestial cross of Constantine among the solar halos. Bibliothec. Graec. tom. iv. p. 8-29. Note: The great difficulty in resolving it into a natural phenomenon, arises from the inscription; even the most heated or awe-struck imagination would hardly discover distinct and legible letters in a solar halo. But the inscription may have been a later embellishment, or an interpretation of the meaning

which the sign was construed to convey. Compare Heirichen, Excur in locum Eusebii, and the authors quoted.]

[Footnote 46: Nazarius inter Panegyr. Vet. x. 14, 15. It is unnecessary to name the moderns, whose undistinguishing and ravenous appetite has swallowed even the Pagan bait of Nazarius.]

[Footnote 47: The apparitions of Castor and Pollux, particularly to announce the Macedonian victory, are attested by historians and public monuments. See Cicero de Natura Deorum, ii. 2, iii. 5, 6. Florus, ii. 12. Valerius Maximus, l. i. c. 8, No. 1. Yet the most recent of these miracles is omitted, and indirectly denied, by Livy, (xlv. i.)]

[Footnote 48: Eusebius, l. i. c. 28, 29, 30. The silence of the same Eusebius, in his Ecclesiastical History, is deeply felt by those advocates for the miracle who are not absolutely callous.]

[Footnote 49: The narrative of Constantine seems to indicate, that he saw the cross in the sky before he passed the Alps against Maxentius. The scene has been fixed by provincial vanity at Treves, Besancon, &c. See Tillemont, Hist. des Empereurs, tom. iv. p. 573.]

[Footnote 50: The pious Tillemont (Mem. Eccles. tom. vii. p. 1317) rejects with a sigh the useful Acts of Artemius, a veteran and a martyr, who attests as an eye-witness to the vision of Constantine.]

[Footnote 51: Gelasius Cyzic. in Act. Concil. Nicen. l. i. c. 4.]

[Footnote 52: The advocates for the vision are unable to produce a single testimony from the Fathers of the fourth and fifth centuries, who, in their voluminous writings, repeatedly celebrate the triumph of the church and of Constantine. As these venerable men had not any dislike to a miracle, we may suspect, (and the suspicion is confirmed by the ignorance of Jerom,) that they were all unacquainted with the life of Constantine by Eusebius. This tract was recovered by the diligence of those who translated or continued his Ecclesiastical History, and who have represented in various colors the vision of the cross.]

[Footnote 53: Godefroy was the first, who, in the year 1643, (Not ad Philostorgium, l. i. c. 6, p. 16,) expressed any doubt of a miracle which had been supported with equal zeal by Cardinal Baronius, and the Centuriators of Magdeburgh. Since that time, many of the Protestant critics have inclined towards doubt and disbelief. The objections are urged, with great force, by M. Chauffepie, (Dictionnaire Critique, tom. iv. p. 6—11;) and, in the year 1774, a doctor of Sorbonne, the Abbe du Veisin published an apology, which deserves the praise of learning and moderation. Note: The first Excursus of Heinichen (in Vitam Constantini, p. 507) contains a full summary of the opinions and arguments of the later writers who have discussed this interminable subject. As to his conversion, where interest and inclination, state policy, and, if not a sincere conviction of its truth, at least a respect, an esteem, an awe of Christianity, thus coincided, Constantine himself would probably have been unable to trace the actual history of the workings of his own mind, or to assign its real influence to each concurrent motive—M]

The Protestant and philosophic readers of the present age will incline to believe, that in the account of his own conversion, Constantine attested a wilful falsehood by a solemn and deliberate perjury. They may not hesitate to pronounce, that in the choice of a religion, his mind was determined only by a sense of interest; and that (according to the expression of a profane poet) [54] he used the altars of the church as a convenient footstool to the throne of the empire. A conclusion so harsh and so absolute is not, however, warranted by our knowledge of human nature, of Constantine, or of Christianity. In an age of religious fervor, the most artful statesmen are observed to feel some part of the enthusiasm which they inspire, and the most orthodox saints assume the dangerous privilege of defending the cause of truth by the arms of deceit and falsehood.

Personal interest is often the standard of our belief, as well as of our practice; and the same motives of temporal advantage which might influence the public conduct and professions of Constantine, would insensibly dispose his mind to embrace a religion so propitious to his fame and fortunes. His vanity was gratified by the flattering assurance, that he had been chosen by Heaven to reign over the earth; success had justified his divine title to the throne, and that title was founded on the truth of the Christian revelation. As real virtue is sometimes excited by undeserved applause, the specious piety of Constantine, if at first it was only specious, might gradually, by the influence of praise, of habit, and of example, be matured into serious faith and fervent devotion. The bishops and teachers of the new sect, whose dress and manners had not qualified them for the residence of a court, were admitted to the Imperial table; they accompanied the monarch in his expeditions; and the ascendant which one of them, an Egyptian or a Spaniard, [55] acquired over his mind, was imputed by the Pagans to the effect of magic. [56] Lactantius, who has adorned the precepts of the gospel with the eloquence of Cicero, [57] and Eusebius, who has consecrated the learning and philosophy of the Greeks to the service of religion, [58] were both received into the friendship and familiarity of their sovereign; and those able masters of controversy could patiently watch the soft and yielding moments of persuasion, and dexterously apply the arguments which were the best adapted to his character and understanding. Whatever advantages might be derived from the acquisition of an Imperial proselyte, he was distinguished by the splendor of his purple, rather than by the superiority of wisdom, or virtue, from the many thousands of his subjects who had embraced the doctrines of Christianity. Nor can it be deemed incredible, that the mind of an unlettered soldier should have yielded to the weight of evidence, which, in a more enlightened age, has satisfied or subdued the reason of a Grotius, a Pascal, or a Locke. In the midst of the incessant labors of his great office, this soldier employed, or affected to employ, the hours of the night in the diligent study of the Scriptures, and the composition of theological discourses; which he afterwards pronounced in the presence of a numerous and applauding audience. In a very long discourse, which is still extant, the royal preacher expatiates on the various proofs still extant, the royal preacher expatiates on the various proofs of religion; but he dwells with peculiar complacency on the Sibylline verses, [59] and the fourth eclogue of Virgil. [60] Forty years before the birth of Christ, the Mantuan bard, as if inspired by the celestial muse of Isaiah, had celebrated, with all the pomp of oriental metaphor, the return of the Virgin, the fall of the serpent, the approaching birth of a godlike child, the offspring of the great Jupiter, who should expiate the guilt of human kind, and govern the peaceful universe with the virtues of his father; the rise and appearance of a heavenly race, primitive nation throughout the world; and the gradual restoration of the innocence and felicity of the golden age. The poet was perhaps unconscious of the secret sense and object of these sublime predictions, which have been so unworthily applied to the infant son of a consul, or a triumvir; [61] but if a more splendid, and indeed specious interpretation of the fourth eclogue contributed to the conversion of the first Christian emperor, Virgil may deserve to be ranked among the most successful missionaries of the gospel. [62]

[Footnote 54:
Lors Constantin dit ces propres paroles:
J'ai renverse le culte des idoles:
Sur les debris de leurs temples fumans
Au Dieu du Ciel j'ai prodigue l'encens.
Mais tous mes soins pour sa grandeur supreme
N'eurent jamais d'autre objet que moi-meme;

> Les saints autels n'etoient a mes regards
> Qu'un marchepie du trone des Cesars.
> L'ambition, la fureur, les delices
> Etoient mes Dieux, avoient mes sacrifices.
> L'or des Chretiens, leur intrigues, leur sang
> Ont cimente ma fortune et mon rang.

The poem which contains these lines may be read with pleasure, but cannot be named with decency.]

[Footnote 55: This favorite was probably the great Osius, bishop of Cordova, who preferred the pastoral care of the whole church to the government of a particular diocese. His character is magnificently, though concisely, expressed by Athanasius, (tom. i. p. 703.) See Tillemont, Mem. Eccles. tom. vii. p. 524-561. Osius was accused, perhaps unjustly, of retiring from court with a very ample fortune.]

[Footnote 56: See Eusebius (in Vit. Constant. passim) and Zosimus, l. ii. p. 104.]

[Footnote 57: The Christianity of Lactantius was of a moral rather than of a mysterious cast. "Erat paene rudis (says the orthodox Bull) disciplinae Christianae, et in rhetorica melius quam in theologia versatus." Defensio Fidei Nicenae, sect. ii. c. 14.]

[Footnote 58: Fabricius, with his usual diligence, has collected a list of between three and four hundred authors quoted in the Evangelical Preparation of Eusebius. See Bibl. Graec. l. v. c. 4, tom. vi. p. 37-56.]

[Footnote 59: See Constantin. Orat. ad Sanctos, c. 19 20. He chiefly depends on a mysterious acrostic, composed in the sixth age after the Deluge, by the Erythraean Sibyl, and translated by Cicero into Latin. The initial letters of the thirty-four Greek verses form this prophetic sentence: Jesus Christ, Son of God, Savior of the World.]

[Footnote 60: In his paraphrase of Virgil, the emperor has frequently assisted and improved the literal sense of the Latin ext. See Blondel des Sibylles, l. i. c. 14, 15, 16.]

[Footnote 61: The different claims of an elder and younger son of Pollio, of Julia, of Drusus, of Marcellus, are found to be incompatible with chronology, history, and the good sense of Virgil.]

[Footnote 62: See Lowth de Sacra Poesi Hebraeorum Praelect. xxi. p. 289- 293. In the examination of the fourth eclogue, the respectable bishop of London has displayed learning, taste, ingenuity, and a temperate enthusiasm, which exalts his fancy without degrading his judgment.]

PART III

The awful mysteries of the Christian faith and worship were concealed from the eyes of strangers, and even of catechu mens, with an affected secrecy, which served to excite their wonder and curiosity. [63] But the severe rules of discipline which the prudence of the bishops had instituted, were relaxed by the same prudence in favor of an Imperial proselyte, whom it was so important to allure, by every gentle condescension, into the pale of the church; and Constantine was permitted, at least by a tacit dispensation, to enjoy most of the privileges, before he had contracted any of the obligations, of a Christian. Instead of retiring from the congregation, when the voice of the deacon dismissed the profane multitude, he prayed with the faithful, disputed with the bishops, preached on the most sublime and intricate subjects of theology, celebrated with sacred rites the vigil of Easter, and publicly declared himself, not only a partaker, but, in some measure, a priest and hierophant of the Christian mysteries. [64] The pride of Constantine might assume, and his services had deserved, some extraordinary distinction: and ill-timed rigor might have blasted the unripened fruits of his conversion; and if the doors of the church had been strictly closed against a prince who had deserted the altars of the gods, the master of the empire would have been left destitute of any form of religious worship. In his last visit to Rome, he piously disclaimed and insulted the superstition of his ancestors, by refusing to lead the military procession of the equestrian order, and to offer the public vows to the Jupiter of the Capitoline Hill. [65] Many years before his baptism and death, Constantine had proclaimed to the world, that neither his person nor his image should ever more be seen within the walls of an idolatrous temple; while he distributed through the provinces a variety of medals and pictures, which represented the emperor in an humble and suppliant posture of Christian devotion. [66]

[Footnote 63: The distinction between the public and the secret parts of divine service, the missa catechumenorum and the missa fidelium, and the mysterious veil which piety or policy had cast over the latter, are very judiciously explained by Thiers, Exposition du Saint Sacrament, l. i. c. 8- 12, p. 59-91: but as, on this subject, the Papists may reasonably be suspected, a Protestant reader will depend with more confidence on the learned Bingham, Antiquities, l. x. c. 5.]

[Footnote 64: See Eusebius in Vit. Const. l. iv. c. 15-32, and the whole tenor of Constantine's Sermon. The faith and devotion of the emperor has furnished Batonics with a specious argument in favor of his early baptism. Note: Compare Heinichen, Excursus iv. et v., where these questions are examined with candor and acuteness, and with constant reference to the opinions of more modern writers—M.]

[Footnote 65: Zosimus, l. ii. p. 105.]

[Footnote 66: Eusebius in Vit. Constant. l. iv. c. 15, 16.]

The pride of Constantine, who refused the privileges of a catechumen, cannot easily be explained or excused; but the delay of his baptism may be justified by the maxims and the practice of ecclesiastical antiquity. The sacrament of baptism [67] was regularly administered by the bishop himself, with his assistant clergy, in the cathedral church of the diocese, during the fifty days between the solemn festivals of Easter and Pentecost; and this holy term admitted a numerous band of infants and adult persons into the bosom of the church. The discretion of parents often suspended the baptism of their children till they could understand the obligations which they contracted: the severity of ancient bishops exacted from the new converts a novitiate of two or three years; and the catechumens themselves, from different motives of a temporal or a spiritual nature, were seldom impatient to assume the character of perfect and initiated Christians. The sacrament of baptism was supposed to contain a full and absolute expiation of sin; and the soul was instantly restored to its original purity, and entitled to the promise of eternal salvation. Among the proselytes of Christianity, there are many who judged it imprudent to precipitate a salutary rite, which could not be repeated; to throw away an inestimable privilege, which could never be recovered. By the delay of their baptism, they could venture freely to indulge their passions in the enjoyments of this world, while they still retained in their own hands the means of a sure and easy absolution. [68] The sublime theory of the gospel had made a much fainter impression on the heart than on the understanding of Constantine himself. He pursued the great object of his ambition through the dark and bloody paths of war and policy; and, after the victory, he abandoned himself, without moderation, to the abuse of his fortune. Instead of asserting his just superiority above the imperfect heroism and profane philosophy of Trajan and the Antonines, the mature age of Constantine forfeited the reputation which he had acquired in his youth. As he gradually advanced in the knowledge of truth, he proportionally declined in the practice of virtue; and the same year of his reign in which he convened the council of Nice, was polluted by the execution, or rather murder, of his eldest son. This date is alone sufficient to refute the ignorant and malicious suggestions of Zosimus, [69] who affirms, that, after the death of Crispus, the remorse of his father accepted from the ministers of christianity the expiation which he had vainly solicited from the Pagan pontiffs. At the time of the death of Crispus, the emperor could no longer hesitate in the choice of a religion; he could no longer be ignorant that the church was possessed of an infallible remedy, though he chose to defer the application of it till the approach of death had removed the temptation and danger of a relapse. The bishops whom he summoned, in his last illness, to the palace of Nicomedia, were edified by the fervor with which he requested and received the sacrament of baptism, by the solemn protestation that the remainder of his life should be worthy of a disciple of Christ, and by his humble refusal to wear the Imperial purple after he had been clothed in the white garment of a Neophyte. The example and reputation of Constantine seemed to countenance the delay of baptism. [70] Future tyrants were encouraged to believe, that the innocent blood which they might shed in a long reign would instantly be washed away in the waters of regeneration; and the abuse of religion dangerously undermined the foundations of moral virtue.

[Footnote 67: The theory and practice of antiquity, with regard to the sacrament of baptism, have been copiously explained by Dom Chardon, Hist. des Sacremens, tom. i. p. 3-405; Dom Martenne de Ritibus Ecclesiae Antiquis, tom. i.; and by Bingham, in the tenth and eleventh books of his Christian Antiquities. One circumstance may be observed, in which the modern churches have materially departed from the ancient custom. The sacrament of baptism (even when it was administered to infants) was immediately followed by confirmation and the holy communion.]

[Footnote 68: The Fathers, who censured this criminal delay, could not deny the certain and victorious efficacy even of a death-bed baptism. The ingenious rhetoric of Chrysostom could find only three arguments against these prudent Christians. 1. That we should love and pursue virtue for her own sake, and not merely for the reward. 2. That we may be surprised by death without an opportunity of baptism. 3. That although we shall be placed in heaven, we shall only twinkle like little stars, when compared to the suns of righteousness who have run their appointed course with labor, with success, and with glory. Chrysos tom in Epist. ad Hebraeos, Homil. xiii. apud Chardon, Hist. des Sacremens, tom. i. p. 49. I believe that this delay of baptism, though attended with the most pernicious consequences, was never condemned by any general or provincial council, or by any public act or declaration of the church. The zeal of the bishops was easily kindled on much slighter occasion. Note: This passage of Chrysostom, though not in his more forcible manner, is not quite fairly represented. He is stronger in other places, in Act. Hom. xxiii—and Hom. i. Compare, likewise, the sermon of Gregory of Nysea on this subject, and Gregory Nazianzen. After all, to those who believed in the efficacy of baptism, what argument could be more conclusive, than the danger of dying without it? Orat. xl—M.]

[Footnote 69: Zosimus, l. ii. p. 104. For this disingenuous falsehood he has deserved and experienced the harshest treatment from all the ecclesiastical writers, except Cardinal Baronius, (A. D. 324, No. 15-28,) who had occasion to employ the infidel on a particular service against the Arian Eusebius. Note: Heyne, in a valuable note on this passage of Zosimus, has shown decisively that this malicious way of accounting for the conversion of Constantine was not an invention of Zosimus. It appears to have been the current *calumny eagerly adopted and propagated by the exasperated Pagan party. Reitemeter, a later editor of Zosimus, whose notes are retained in the recent edition, in the collection of the Byzantine historians, has a disquisition on the passage, as candid, but not more conclusive than some which have preceded him—M.]*

[Footnote 70: Eusebius, l. iv. c. 61, 62, 63. The bishop of Caesarea supposes the salvation of Constantine with the most perfect confidence.]

The gratitude of the church has exalted the virtues and excused the failings of a generous patron, who seated Christianity on the throne of the Roman world; and the Greeks, who celebrate the festival of the Imperial saint, seldom mention the name of Constantine without adding the title of equal to the Apostles. [71] Such a comparison, if it allude to the character of those divine missionaries, must be imputed to the extravagance of impious flattery. But if the parallel be confined to the extent and number of their evangelic victories the success of Constantine might perhaps equal that of the Apostles themselves. By the edicts of toleration, he removed the temporal disadvantages which had hitherto retarded the progress of Christianity; and its active and numerous ministers received a free permission, a liberal encouragement, to recommend the salutary truths of revelation by every argument which could affect the reason or piety of mankind. The exact balance of the two religions continued but a moment; and the piercing eye of ambition and avarice soon discovered, that the profession of Christianity might contribute to the interest of the present, as well as of a future life. [72] The hopes of wealth and honors, the example of an emperor, his exhortations, his irresistible smiles, diffused conviction among the venal and obsequious crowds which usually fill the apartments of a palace. The cities which signalized a forward zeal by the voluntary destruction of their temples, were distinguished by municipal privileges, and rewarded with popular donatives; and the new capital of the East gloried in the singular advantage that Constantinople was never profaned by the worship of idols. [73] As the lower ranks of society are governed by imitation, the conversion of those who possessed any eminence of birth, of power, or of riches, was soon followed by dependent multitudes. [74] The salvation of the common people was purchased at an easy rate, if it be true that, in one year, twelve thousand men were baptized at Rome, besides a proportionable number of women and children, and that a white garment, with twenty pieces of gold, had been promised by the emperor to every convert. [75] The powerful influence of Constantine was not circumscribed by the narrow limits of his life, or of his dominions. The education which he bestowed on his sons and nephews secured to the empire a race of princes, whose faith was still more lively and sincere, as they imbibed, in their earliest infancy, the spirit, or at least the doctrine, of Christianity. War and commerce had spread the knowledge of the gospel beyond the confines of the Roman provinces; and the Barbarians, who had disdained as humble and proscribed sect, soon learned to esteem a religion which had been so lately embraced by the greatest monarch, and the most civilized nation, of the globe. [76] The Goths and Germans, who enlisted under the standard of Rome, revered the cross which glittered at the head of the legions, and their fierce countrymen received at the same time the lessons of faith and of humanity. The kings of Iberia and Armenia [76a] worshipped the god of their protector; and their subjects, who have invariably preserved the name of Christians, soon formed a sacred and perpetual connection with their Roman brethren. The Christians of Persia were suspected, in time of war, of preferring their religion to their country; but as long as peace subsisted between the two empires, the persecuting spirit of the Magi was effectually restrained by the interposition of Constantine. [77] The rays of the gospel illuminated the coast of India. The colonies of Jews, who had penetrated into Arabia and Ethiopia, [78] opposed the progress of Christianity; but the labor of the missionaries was in some measure facilitated by a previous knowledge of the Mosaic revelation; and Abyssinia still reveres the memory of Frumentius, [78a] who, in the time of Constantine, devoted his life to the conversion of those sequestered regions. Under the reign of his son

Constantius, Theophilus, [79] who was himself of Indian extraction, was invested with the double character of ambassador and bishop. He embarked on the Red Sea with two hundred horses of the purest breed of Cappadocia, which were sent by the emperor to the prince of the Sabaeans, or Homerites. Theophilus was intrusted with many other useful or curious presents, which might raise the admiration, and conciliate the friendship, of the Barbarians; and he successfully employed several years in a pastoral visit to the churches of the torrid zone. [80]

[Footnote 71: See Tillemont, Hist. des Empereurs, tom. iv. p. 429. The Greeks, the Russians, and, in the darker ages, the Latins themselves, have been desirous of placing Constantine in the catalogue of saints.]

[Footnote 72: See the third and fourth books of his life. He was accustomed to say, that whether Christ was preached in pretence, or in truth, he should still rejoice, (l. iii. c. 58.)]

[Footnote 73: M. de Tillemont (Hist. des Empereurs, tom. iv. p. 374, 616) has defended, with strength and spirit, the virgin purity of Constantinople against some malevolent insinuations of the Pagan Zosimus.]

[Footnote 74: The author of the Histoire Politique et Philosophique des deux Indes (tom. i. p. 9) condemns a law of Constantine, which gave freedom to all the slaves who should embrace Christianity. The emperor did indeed publish a law, which restrained the Jews from circumcising, perhaps from keeping, any Christian slave. (See Euseb. in Vit. Constant. l. iv. c. 27, and Cod. Theod. l. xvi. tit. ix., with Godefroy's Commentary, tom. vi. p. 247.) But this imperfect exception related only to the Jews, and the great body of slaves, who were the property of Christian or Pagan masters, could not improve their temporal condition by changing their religion. I am ignorant by what guides the Abbe Raynal was deceived; as the total absence of quotations is the unpardonable blemish of his entertaining history.]

[Footnote 75: See Acta S Silvestri, and Hist. Eccles. Nicephor. Callist. l. vii. c. 34, ap. Baronium Annal. Eccles. A. D. 324, No. 67, 74. Such evidence is contemptible enough; but these circumstances are in themselves so probable, that the learned Dr. Howell (History of the World, vol. iii. p. 14) has not scrupled to adopt them.]

[Footnote 76: The conversion of the Barbarians under the reign of Constantine is celebrated by the ecclesiastical historians. (See Sozomen, l. ii. c. 6, and Theodoret, l. i. c. 23, 24.) But Rufinus, the Latin translator of Eusebius, deserves to be considered as an original authority. His information was curiously collected from one of the companions of the Apostle of Aethiopia, and from Bacurius, an Iberian prince, who was count of the domestics. Father Mamachi has given an ample compilation on the progress of Christianity, in the first and second volumes of his great but imperfect work.]

[Footnote 76a: According to the Georgian chronicles, Iberia (Georgia) was converted by the virgin Nino, who effected an extraordinary cure on the wife of the king Mihran. The temple of the god Aramazt, or Armaz, not far from the capital Mtskitha, was destroyed, and the cross erected in its place. Le Beau, i. 202, with St. Martin's Notes. —St. Martin has likewise clearly shown (St. Martin, Add. to Le Beau, i. 291) Armenia was the first nation w hich embraced Christianity, (Addition to Le Beau, i. 76. and Memoire sur l'Armenie, i. 305.) Gibbon himself suspected this truth—"Instead of maintaining that the conversion of Armenia was not attempted with any degree of success, till the sceptre was in the hands of an orthodox emperor," I ought to have said, that the seeds of the faith were deeply sown during the season of the last and greatest persecution, that many Roman exiles might assist the labors of Gregory, and that the renowned Tiridates, the hero of the East, may dispute with Constantine the honor of being the first sovereign who embraced the Christian religion Vindication]

[Footnote 77: See, in Eusebius, (in Vit. l. iv. c. 9,) the pressing and pathetic epistle of Constantine in favor of his Christian brethren of Persia.]

[Footnote 78: See Basnage, Hist. des Juifs, tom. vii. p. 182, tom. viii. p. 333, tom. ix. p. 810. The curious diligence of this writer pursues the Jewish exiles to the extremities of the globe.]

[Footnote 78a: Abba Salama, or Fremonatus, is mentioned in the Tareek Negushti, chronicle of the kings of Abyssinia. Salt's Travels, vol. ii. p. 464—M.]

[Footnote 79: Theophilus had been given in his infancy as a hostage by his countrymen of the Isle of Diva, and was educated by the Romans in learning and piety. The Maldives, of which Male, or Diva, may be the capital, are a cluster of 1900 or 2000 minute islands in the Indian Ocean. The ancients were imperfectly acquainted with the Maldives; but they are described in the two Mahometan travellers of the ninth century, published by Renaudot, Geograph. Nubiensis, p. 30, 31 D'Herbelot, Bibliotheque Orientale p. 704. Hist. Generale des Voyages, tom. viii. —See the dissertation of M. Letronne on this question. He conceives that Theophilus was born in the island of Dahlak, in the Arabian Gulf. His embassy was to Abyssinia rather than to India. Letronne, Materiaux pour l'Hist. du Christianisme en Egypte Indie, et Abyssinie. Paris, 1832 3d Dissert—M.]

[Footnote 80: Philostorgius, l. iii. c. 4, 5, 6, with Godefroy's learned observations. The historical narrative is soon lost in an inquiry concerning the seat of Paradise, strange monsters, &c.]

The irresistible power of the Roman emperors was displayed in the important and dangerous change of the national religion. The terrors of a military force silenced the faint and unsupported murmurs of the Pagans, and there was reason to expect, that the cheerful submission of the Christian clergy, as well as people, would be the result of conscience and gratitude. It was long since established, as a fundamental maxim of the Roman constitution, that every rank of citizens was alike subject to the laws, and that the care of religion was the right as well as duty of the civil magistrate. Constantine and his successors could not easily persuade themselves that they had forfeited, by their conversion, any branch of the Imperial prerogatives, or that they were incapable of giving laws to a religion which they had protected and embraced. The emperors still continued to exercise a supreme jurisdiction over the ecclesiastical order, and the sixteenth book of the Theodosian code represents, under a variety of titles, the authority which they assumed in the government of the Catholic church. But the distinction of the spiritual and temporal powers, [81] which had never been imposed on the free spirit of Greece and Rome, was introduced and confirmed by the legal establishment of Christianity. The office of supreme pontiff, which, from the time of Numa to that of Augustus, had always been exercised by one of the most eminent of the senators, was at length united to the Imperial dignity. The first magistrate of the state, as often as he was prompted by superstition or policy, performed with his own hands the sacerdotal functions; [82] nor was there any order of priests, either at Rome or in the provinces, who claimed a more sacred character among men, or a more intimate communication with the gods. But in the Christian church, which instructs the service of the altar to a perpetual succession of consecrated ministers, the monarch, whose spiritual rank is less honorable than that of the meanest deacon, was seated below the rails of the sanctuary, and confounded with the rest of the faithful multitude. [83] The emperor might be saluted as the father of his people, but he owed a filial duty and reverence to the fathers of the church; and the same marks of respect, which Constantine had paid to the persons of saints and confessors, were soon exacted by the pride of the episcopal order. [84] A secret conflict between the civil and ecclesiastical jurisdictions embarrassed the operation of the Roman government; and a pious emperor was alarmed by the guilt and danger of touching with a profane hand the ark of the covenant. The separation of men into the two orders of the clergy and of the laity was, indeed, familiar to many nations of antiquity; and the priests of India, of Persia, of Assyria, of Judea, of Aethiopia, of Egypt, and of Gaul, derived from a celestial origin the temporal power and possessions which they had acquired. These venerable institutions had gradually assimilated themselves to the manners and government of their respective countries; [85] but the opposition or contempt of the civil power served to cement the discipline of the primitive church. The Christians had been obliged to elect their own magistrates, to raise and distribute a peculiar revenue, and to regulate the internal policy of their republic by a code of laws, which were ratified by the consent of the people and the practice of three hundred years. When Constantine embraced the faith of the Christians, he seemed to contract a perpetual alliance with a distinct and independent society; and the privileges granted or confirmed by that emperor, or by his successors, were accepted, not as the precarious favors of the court, but as the just and inalienable rights of the ecclesiastical order.

[Footnote 81: See the epistle of Osius, ap. Athanasium, vol. i. p. 840. The public remonstrance which Osius was forced to address to the son, contained the same principles of ecclesiastical and civil government which he had secretly instilled into the mind of the father.]

[Footnote 82: M. de la Bastiel has evidently proved, that Augustus and his successors exercised in person all the sacred functions of pontifex maximus, of high priest, of the Roman empire.]

[Footnote 83: Something of a contrary practice had insensibly prevailed in the church of Constantinople; but the rigid Ambrose commanded Theodosius to retire below the rails, and taught him to know the difference between a king and a priest. See Theodoret, l. v. c. 18.]

[Footnote 84: At the table of the emperor Maximus, Martin, bishop of Tours, received the cup from an attendant, and gave it to the presbyter, his companion, before he allowed the emperor to drink; the empress waited on Martin at table. Sulpicius Severus, in Vit. S Martin, c. 23, and Dialogue ii. 7. Yet it may be doubted, whether these extraordinary compliments were paid to the bishop or the saint. The honors usually granted to the former character may be seen in Bingham's Antiquities, l. ii. c. 9, and Vales ad Theodoret, l. iv. c. 6. See the haughty ceremonial which Leontius, bishop of Tripoli, imposed on the empress. Tillemont, Hist. des Empereurs, tom. iv. p. 754. (Patres Apostol. tom. ii. p. 179.)]

[Footnote 85: Plutarch, in his treatise of Isis and Osiris, informs us that the kings of Egypt, who were not already priests, were initiated, after their election, into the sacerdotal order.]

The Catholic church was administered by the spiritual and legal jurisdiction of eighteen hundred bishops; [86] of whom one thousand were seated in the Greek, and eight hundred in the Latin, provinces of the empire. The extent and boundaries of their respective dioceses had been variously and accidentally decided by the zeal and success of the first missionaries, by the wishes of the people, and by the propagation of the gospel. Episcopal churches were closely planted along the banks of the Nile, on the sea-coast of Africa, in the proconsular Asia, and through the southern provinces of Italy. The bishops of Gaul and Spain, of Thrace and Pontus, reigned over an ample territory, and delegated their rural suffragans to execute the subordinate duties of the pastoral office. [87] A Christian diocese might be spread over a province, or reduced to a village; but all the bishops possessed an equal and indelible character: they all derived the same powers and privileges from the apostles, from the people, and from the laws. While the civil and military professions were separated by the policy of Constantine, a new and perpetual order of ecclesiastical ministers, always respectable, sometimes dangerous, was established in the church and state. The important review of their station and attributes may be distributed under the following heads: I. Popular Election. II. Ordination of the Clergy. III. Property. IV. Civil Jurisdiction. V. Spiritual censures. VI. Exercise of public oratory. VII. Privilege of legislative assemblies.

[Footnote 86: The numbers are not ascertained by any ancient writer or original catalogue; for the partial lists of the eastern churches are comparatively modern. The patient diligence of Charles a Sto Paolo, of Luke Holstentius, and of Bingham, has laboriously investigated all the episcopal sees of the Catholic church, which was almost commensurate with the Roman empire. The ninth book of the Christian antiquities is a very accurate map of ecclesiastical geography.]

[Footnote 87: On the subject of rural bishops, or Chorepiscopi, who voted in tynods, and conferred the minor orders, See Thomassin, Discipline de l'Eglise, tom. i. p. 447, &c., and Chardon, Hist. des Sacremens, tom. v. p. 395, &c. They do not appear till the fourth century; and this equivocal character, which had excited the jealousy of the prelates, was abolished before the end of the tenth, both in the East and the West.]

I. The freedom of election subsisted long after the legal establishment of Christianity; [88] and the subjects of Rome enjoyed in the church the privilege which they had lost in the republic, of choosing the magistrates whom they were bound to obey. As soon as a bishop had closed his eyes, the metropolitan issued a commission to one of his suffragans to administer the vacant see, and prepare, within a limited time, the future election. The right of voting was vested in the inferior clergy, who were best qualified to judge of the merit of the candidates; in the senators or nobles of the city, all those who were distinguished by their rank or property; and finally in the whole body of the people, who, on the appointed day, flocked in multitudes from the most remote parts of the diocese, [89] and sometimes silenced by their tumultuous acclamations, the voice of reason and the laws of discipline. These acclamations might accidentally fix on the head of the most deserving competitor; of some ancient presbyter, some holy monk, or some layman, conspicuous for his zeal and piety. But the episcopal chair was solicited, especially in the great and opulent cities of the empire, as a temporal rather than as a spiritual dignity. The interested views, the selfish and angry passions, the arts of perfidy and dissimulation, the secret corruption, the open and even bloody violence which had formerly disgraced the freedom of election in the commonwealths of Greece and Rome, too often influenced the choice of the successors of the apostles. While one of the candidates boasted the honors of his family, a second allured his judges by the delicacies of a plentiful table, and a third, more guilty than his rivals, offered to share the plunder of the church among the accomplices of his sacrilegious hopes [90] The civil as well as ecclesiastical laws attempted to exclude the populace from this solemn and important transaction. The canons of ancient discipline, by requiring several episcopal qualifications, of age, station, &c., restrained, in some measure, the indiscriminate caprice of the electors. The authority of the provincial bishops, who were assembled in the vacant church to consecrate the choice of the people, was interposed to moderate their passions and to correct their mistakes. The bishops could refuse to ordain an unworthy candidate, and the rage of contending factions sometimes accepted their impartial mediation. The submission, or the resistance, of the clergy and people, on various occasions, afforded different precedents, which were insensibly converted into positive laws and provincial customs; [91] but it was every where admitted, as a fundamental maxim of religious policy, that no bishop could be imposed on an orthodox church, without the consent of its members. The emperors, as the guardians of the public peace, and as the first citizens of Rome and Constantinople, might effectually declare their wishes in the choice of a primate; but those absolute monarchs respected the freedom of ecclesiastical elections; and while they distributed and resumed the honors of the state and army, they allowed eighteen hundred perpetual magistrates to receive their important offices from the free suffrages of the people. [92] It was agreeable to the dictates of justice, that these magistrates should not desert an honorable station from which they could not be removed; but the wisdom of councils endeavored, without much success, to enforce the residence, and to prevent the translation, of bishops. The discipline of the West was indeed less relaxed than that of the East; but the same passions which made those regulations necessary, rendered them ineffectual. The reproaches which angry prelates have so vehemently urged against each other, serve only to expose their common guilt, and their mutual indiscretion.

[Footnote 88: Thomassin (Discipline de l'Eglise, tom, ii. l. ii. c. 1-8, p. 673-721) has copiously treated of the election of bishops during the five first centuries, both in the East and in the West; but he shows a very partial bias in favor of the episcopal aristocracy. Bingham, (l. iv. c. 2) is moderate; and Chardon (Hist. des Sacremens tom. v. p. 108-128) is very clear and concise. Note: This freedom was extremely limited, and soon annihilated; already, from the third century, the deacons were no longer nominated by the members of the community, but by the bishops. Although it appears by the letters of Cyprian, that even in his time, no priest could be elected without the consent of the community. (Ep. 68,) that election was far from being altogether free. The bishop proposed to his parishioners the candidate whom he had chosen, and they were permitted to make such objections as might be suggested by his conduct and morals. (St. Cyprian, Ep. 33.) They lost this last right towards the middle of the fourth century—G]

[Footnote 89: Incredibilis multitudo, non solum ex eo oppido, (Tours,) sed etiam ex vicinis urbibus ad suffragia ferenda convenerat, &c. Sulpicius Severus, in Vit. Martin. c. 7. The council of Laodicea, (canon xiii.) prohibits mobs and tumults; and Justinian confines confined the right of election to the nobility. Novel. cxxiii. l.]

[Footnote 90: The epistles of Sidonius Apollinaris (iv. 25, vii. 5, 9) exhibit some of the scandals of the Gallican church; and Gaul was less polished and less corrupt than the East.]

[Footnote 91: A compromise was sometimes introduced by law or by consent; either the bishops or the people chose one of the three candidates who had been named by the other party.]

[Footnote 92: All the examples quoted by Thomassin (Discipline de l'Eglise, tom. ii. l. iii. c. vi. p. 704-714) appear to be extraordinary acts of power, and even of oppression. The confirmation of the bishop of Alexandria is mentioned by Philostorgius as a more regular proceeding. (Hist Eccles. l. ii. ll.) Note: The statement of Planck is more consistent with history: "From the middle of the fourth century, the bishops of some of the larger churches, particularly those of the Imperial residence, were almost always chosen under the influence of the court, and often directly and immediately nominated by the emperor." Planck, Geschichte der Christlich-kirchlichen Gesellschafteverfassung, verfassung, vol. i p 263—M.]

II. The bishops alone possessed the faculty of spiritual generation: and this extraordinary privilege might compensate, in some degree, for the painful celibacy [93] which was imposed as a virtue, as a duty, and at length as a positive obligation. The religions of antiquity, which established a separate order of priests, dedicated a holy race, a tribe or family, to the perpetual service of the gods. [94] Such institutions were founded for possession, rather than conquest. The children of the priests enjoyed, with proud and indolent security, their sacred inheritance; and the fiery spirit of enthusiasm was abated by the cares, the pleasures, and the endearments of domestic life. But the Christian sanctuary was open to every ambitious candidate, who aspired to its heavenly promises or temporal possessions. This office of priests, like that of soldiers or magistrates, was strenuously exercised by those men, whose temper and abilities had prompted them to embrace the ecclesiastical profession, or who had been selected by a discerning bishop, as the best qualified to promote the glory and interest of the church. The bishops [95] (till the abuse was restrained by the prudence of the laws) might constrain the reluctant, and protect the distressed; and the imposition of hands forever bestowed some of the most valuable privileges of civil society. The whole body of the Catholic clergy, more numerous perhaps than the legions, was exempted [95a] by the emperors from all service, private or public, all municipal offices, and all personal taxes and contributions, which pressed on their fellow- citizens with intolerable weight; and the duties of their holy profession were accepted as a full discharge of their obligations to the republic. [96] Each bishop acquired an absolute and indefeasible right to the perpetual obedience of the clerk whom he ordained: the clergy of each episcopal church, with its dependent parishes, formed a regular and permanent society; and the cathedrals of Constantinople [97] and Carthage [98] maintained their peculiar establishment of five hundred ecclesiastical ministers. Their ranks [99] and numbers were insensibly multiplied by the superstition of the times, which introduced into the church the splendid ceremonies of a Jewish or Pagan temple; and a long train of priests, deacons, sub-deacons, acolythes, exorcists, readers, singers, and doorkeepers, contributed, in their respective stations, to swell the pomp and harmony of religious worship. The clerical name and privileges were extended to many pious fraternities, who devoutly supported the ecclesiastical throne. [100] Six hundred parabolani, or adventurers, visited the sick at Alexandria; eleven hundred copiatoe, or grave-diggers, buried the dead at Constantinople; and the swarms of monks, who arose from the Nile, overspread and darkened the face of the Christian world.

[Footnote 93: The celibacy of the clergy during the first five or six centuries, is a subject of discipline, and indeed of controversy, which has been very diligently examined. See in particular, Thomassin, Discipline de l'Eglise, tom. i. l. ii. c. lx. lxi. p. 886-902, and Bingham's Antiquities, l. iv. c. 5. By each of these learned but partial critics, one half of the truth is produced, and the other is concealed. —Note: Compare Planck, (vol. i. p. 348.) This century, the third, first brought forth the monks, or the spirit of monkery, the celibacy of the clergy. Planck likewise observes, that from the history of Eusebius alone, names of married bishops and presbyters may be adduced by dozens—M.]

[Footnote 94: Diodorus Siculus attests and approves the hereditary succession of the priesthood among the Egyptians, the Chaldeans, and the Indians, (l. i. p. 84, l. ii. p. 142, 153, edit. Wesseling.) The magi are described by Ammianus as a very numerous family: "Per saecula multa ad praesens una eademque prosapia multitudo creata, Deorum cultibus dedicata." (xxiii. 6.) Ausonius celebrates the Stirps Druidarum, (De Professorib. Burdigal. iv.;) but we may infer from the remark of Caesar, (vi. 13,) that in the Celtic hierarchy, some room was left for choice and emulation.]

[Footnote 95: The subject of the vocation, ordination, obedience, &c., of the clergy, is laboriously discussed by Thomassin (Discipline de l'Eglise, tom. ii. p. 1-83) and Bingham, (in the 4th book of his Antiquities, more especially the 4th, 6th, and 7th chapters.) When the brother of St. Jerom was ordained in Cyprus, the deacons forcibly stopped his mouth, lest he should make a solemn protestation, which might invalidate the holy rites.]

[Footnote 95a: This exemption was very much limited. The municipal offices were of two kinds; the one attached to the individual in his character of inhabitant, the other in that of proprietor. Constantine had exempted ecclesiastics from offices of the first description. (Cod. Theod. xvi. t. ii. leg. 1, 2 Eusebius, Hist. Eccles. l. x. c. vii.) They sought, also, to be exempted from those of the second, (munera patrimoniorum.) The rich, to obtain this privilege, obtained subordinate situations among the clergy. Constantine published in 320 an edict, by which he prohibited the more opulent citizens (decuriones and curiales) from embracing the ecclesiastical profession, and the bishops from admitting new ecclesiastics, before a place should be vacant by the death of the occupant, (Godefroy ad Cod. Theod.t. xii. t. i. de Decur.)

Valentinian the First, by a rescript still more general enacted that no rich citizen should obtain a situation in the church, (De Episc 1. lxvii.) He also enacted that ecclesiastics, who wished to be exempt from offices which they were bound to discharge as proprietors, should be obliged to give up their property to their relations. Cod Theodos l. xii t. i. leb. 49—G.]

[Footnote 96: The charter of immunities, which the clergy obtained from the Christian emperors, is contained in the 16th book of the Theodosian code; and is illustrated with tolerable candor by the learned Godefroy, whose mind was balanced by the opposite prejudices of a civilian and a Protestant.]

[Footnote 97: Justinian. Novell. ciii. Sixty presbyters, or priests, one hundred deacons, forty deaconesses, ninety sub-deacons, one hundred and ten readers, twenty-five chanters, and one hundred door-keepers; in all, five hundred and twenty-five. This moderate number was fixed by the emperor to relieve the distress of the church, which had been involved in debt and usury by the expense of a much higher establishment.]

[Footnote 98: Universus clerus ecclesiae Carthaginiensis.... fere quingenti vei amplius; inter quos quamplurima erant lectores infantuli. Victor Vitensis, de Persecut. Vandal. v. 9, p. 78, edit. Ruinart. This remnant of a more prosperous state still subsisted under the oppression of the Vandals.]

[Footnote 99: The number of seven orders has been fixed in the Latin church, exclusive of the episcopal character. But the four inferior ranks, the minor orders, are now reduced to empty and useless titles.]

[Footnote 100: See Cod. Theodos. l. xvi. tit. ii. leg. 42, 43. Godefroy's Commentary, and the Ecclesiastical History of Alexandria, show the danger of these pious institutions, which often disturbed the peace of that turbulent capital.]

PART IV

III. The edict of Milan secured the revenue as well as the peace of the church. [101] The Christians not only recovered the lands and houses of which they had been stripped by the persecuting laws of Diocletian, but they acquired a perfect title to all the possessions which they had hitherto enjoyed by the connivance of the magistrate. As soon as Christianity became the religion of the emperor and the empire, the national clergy might claim a decent and honorable maintenance; and the payment of an annual tax might have delivered the people from the more oppressive tribute, which superstition imposes on her votaries. But as the wants and expenses of the church increased with her prosperity, the ecclesiastical order was still supported and enriched by the voluntary oblations of the faithful. Eight years after the edict of Milan, Constantine granted to all his subjects the free and universal permission of bequeathing their fortunes to the holy Catholic church; [102] and their devout liberality, which during their lives was checked by luxury or avarice, flowed with a profuse stream at the hour of their death. The wealthy Christians were encouraged by the example of their sovereign. An absolute monarch, who is rich without patrimony, may be charitable without merit; and Constantine too easily believed that he should purchase the favor of Heaven, if he maintained the idle at the expense of the industrious; and distributed among the saints the wealth of the republic. The same messenger who carried over to Africa the head of Maxentius, might be intrusted with an epistle to Caecilian, bishop of Carthage. The emperor acquaints him, that the treasurers of the province are directed to pay into his hands the sum of three thousand folles, or eighteen thousand pounds sterling, and to obey his further requisitions for the relief of the churches of Africa, Numidia, and Mauritania. [103] The liberality of Constantine increased in a just proportion to his faith, and to his vices. He assigned in each city a regular allowance of corn, to supply the fund of ecclesiastical charity; and the persons of both sexes who embraced the monastic life became the peculiar favorites of their sovereign. The Christian temples of Antioch, Alexandria, Jerusalem, Constantinople &c., displayed the ostentatious piety of a prince, ambitious in a declining age to equal the perfect labors of antiquity. [104] The form of these religious edifices was simple and oblong; though they might sometimes swell into the shape of a dome, and sometimes branch into the figure of a cross. The timbers were framed for the most part of cedars of Libanus; the roof was covered with tiles, perhaps of gilt brass; and the walls, the columns, the pavement, were encrusted with variegated marbles. The most precious ornaments of gold and silver, of silk and gems, were profusely dedicated to the service of the altar; and this specious magnificence was supported on the solid and perpetual basis of landed property. In the space of two centuries, from the reign of Constantine to that of Justinian, the eighteen hundred churches of the empire were enriched by the frequent and unalienable gifts of the prince and people. An annual income of six hundred pounds sterling may be reasonably assigned to the bishops, who were placed at an equal distance between riches and poverty, [105] but the standard of their wealth insensibly rose with the dignity and opulence of the cities which they governed. An authentic but imperfect [106] rent-roll specifies some houses, shops, gardens, and farms, which belonged to the three Basilicoe of Rome, St. Peter, St. Paul, and St. John Lateran, in the provinces of Italy, Africa, and the East. They produce, besides a reserved rent of oil, linen, paper, aromatics, &c., a clear annual revenue of twenty-two thousand pieces of gold, or twelve thousand pounds sterling. In the age of Constantine and Justinian, the bishops no longer possessed, perhaps they no longer deserved, the unsuspecting confidence of their clergy and people. The ecclesiastical revenues of each diocese were divided into four parts for the respective uses of the bishop himself, of his inferior clergy, of the poor, and of the public worship; and the abuse of this sacred trust was strictly and repeatedly checked. [107] The patrimony of the church was still subject to all the public compositions of the state. [108] The clergy of Rome, Alexandria, Chessaionica, &c., might solicit and obtain some partial exemptions; but the premature attempt of the great council of Rimini, which aspired to universal freedom, was successfully resisted by the son of Constantine. [109]

[Footnote 101: The edict of Milan (de M. P. c. 48) acknowledges, by reciting, that there existed a species of landed property, ad jus corporis eorum, id est, ecclesiarum non hominum singulorum pertinentia. Such a solemn declaration of the supreme magistrate must have been received in all the tribunals as a maxim of civil law.]

[Footnote 102: Habeat unusquisque licentiam sanctissimo Catholicae (ecclesioe) venerabilique concilio, decedens bonorum quod optavit relinquere. Cod. Theodos. l. xvi. tit. ii. leg. 4. This law was published at Rome, A. D. 321, at a time when Constantine might foresee the probability of a rupture with the emperor of the East.]

[Footnote 103: Eusebius, Hist. Eccles. l. x. 6; in Vit. Constantin. l. iv. c. 28. He repeatedly expatiates on the liberality of the Christian hero, which the bishop himself had an opportunity of knowing, and even of lasting.]

[Footnote 104: Eusebius, Hist. Eccles. l. x. c. 2, 3, 4. The bishop of Caesarea who studied and gratified the taste of his master, pronounced in public an elaborate description of the church of Jerusalem, (in Vit Cons. l. vi. c. 46.) It no longer exists, but he has inserted in the life of Constantine (l. iii. c. 36) a short account of the architecture and ornaments. He likewise mentions the church of the Holy Apostles at Constantinople, (l. iv. c. 59.)]

[Footnote 105: See Justinian. Novell. cxxiii. 3. The revenue of the patriarchs, and the most wealthy bishops, is not expressed: the highest annual valuation of a bishopric is stated at thirty, and the lowest at two, pounds of gold; the medium might be taken at sixteen, but these valuations are much below the real value.]

[Footnote 106: See Baronius, (Annal. Eccles. A. D. 324, No. 58, 65, 70, 71.) Every record which comes from the Vatican is justly suspected; yet these rent-rolls have an ancient and authentic color; and it is at least evident, that, if forged, they were forged in a period when farms not kingdoms, were the objects of papal avarice.]

[Footnote 107: See Thomassin, Discipline de l'Eglise, tom. iii. l. ii. c. 13, 14, 15, p. 689-706. The legal division of the ecclesiastical revenue does not appear to have been established in the time of Ambrose and Chrysostom. Simplicius and Gelasius, who were bishops of Rome in the latter part of the fifth century, mention it in their pastoral letters as a general law, which was already confirmed by the custom of Italy.]

[Footnote 108: Ambrose, the most strenuous assertor of ecclesiastical privileges, submits without a murmur to the payment of the land tax. "Si tri butum petit Imperator, non negamus; agri ecclesiae solvunt tributum solvimus quae sunt Caesaris Caesari, et quae sunt Dei Deo; tributum Caesaris est; non negatur." Baronius labors to interpret this tribute as an act of charity rather than of duty, (Annal. Eccles. A. D. 387;) but the words, if not the intentions of Ambrose are more candidly explained by Thomassin, Discipline de l'Eglise, tom. iii. l. i. c. 34. p. 668.]

[Footnote 109: In Ariminense synodo super ecclesiarum et clericorum privilegiis tractatu habito, usque eo dispositio progressa est, ut juqa quae viderentur ad ecclesiam pertinere, a publica functione cessarent inquietudine desistente; quod nostra videtur dudum sanctio repulsisse. Cod. Theod. l. xvi. tit. ii. leg. 15. Had the synod of Rimini carried this point, such practical merit might have atoned for some speculative heresies.]

IV. The Latin clergy, who erected their tribunal on the ruins of the civil and common law, have modestly accepted, as the gift of Constantine, [110] the independent jurisdiction, which was the fruit of time, of accident, and of their own industry. But the liberality of the Christian emperors had actually endowed them with some legal prerogatives, which secured and dignified the sacerdotal character. [111] 1. Under a despotic government, the bishops alone enjoyed and asserted the inestimable privilege of being tried only by their peers; and even in a capital accusation, a synod of their brethren were the sole judges of their guilt or innocence. Such a tribunal, unless it was inflamed by personal resentment or religious discord, might be favorable, or even partial, to the sacerdotal order: but Constantine was satisfied, [112] that secret impunity would be less pernicious than public scandal: and the Nicene council was edited by his public declaration, that if he surprised a bishop in the act of adultery, he should cast his Imperial mantle over the episcopal sinner. 2. The domestic jurisdiction of the bishops was at once a privilege and a restraint of the ecclesiastical order, whose civil causes were decently withdrawn from the cognizance of a secular judge. Their venial offences were not exposed to the shame of a public trial or punishment; and the gentle correction which the tenderness of youth may endure from its parents or instructors, was inflicted by the temperate severity of the bishops. But if the clergy were guilty of any crime which could not be sufficiently expiated by their degradation from an honorable and beneficial profession, the Roman magistrate drew the sword of justice, without any regard to ecclesiastical immunities. 3. The arbitration of the bishops was ratified by a positive law; and the judges were instructed to execute, without appeal or delay, the episcopal decrees, whose validity had hitherto depended on the consent of the parties. The conversion of the magistrates themselves, and of the whole empire, might gradually remove the fears and scruples of the Christians. But they still resorted to the tribunal of the bishops, whose abilities and integrity they esteemed; and the venerable Austin enjoyed the satisfaction of complaining that his spiritual functions were perpetually interrupted by the invidious labor of deciding the claim or the possession of silver and gold, of lands and cattle. 4. The ancient privilege of sanctuary was transferred to the Christian temples, and extended, by the liberal piety of the younger Theodosius, to the precincts of consecrated ground. [113] The fugitive, and even guilty suppliants,were permitted to implore either the justice, or the mercy, of the Deity and his ministers. The rash violence of despotism was suspended by the mild interposition of the church; and the lives or fortunes of the most eminent subjects might be protected by the mediation of the bishop.

[Footnote 110: From Eusebius (in Vit. Constant. l. iv. c. 27) and Sozomen (l. i. c. 9) we are assured that the episcopal jurisdiction was extended and confirmed by Constantine; but the forgery of a famous edict, which was never fairly inserted in the Theodosian Code (see at the end, tom. vi. p. 303,) is demonstrated by Godefroy in the most satisfactory manner. It is strange that M. de Montesquieu, who was a lawyer as well as a philosopher, should allege this edict of Constantine (Esprit des Loix, l. xxix. c. 16) without intimating any suspicion.]

[Footnote 111: The subject of ecclesiastical jurisdiction has been involved in a mist of passion, of prejudice, and of interest. Two of the fairest books which have fallen into my hands, are the Institutes of Canon Law, by the Abbe de Fleury, and the Civil History of Naples, by Giannone. Their moderation was the effect of situation as well as of temper. Fleury was a French ecclesiastic, who respected the authority of the parliaments; Giannone was an Italian lawyer, who dreaded the power of the church. And here let me observe, that as the general propositions which I advance are the result of many particular and imperfect facts, I must either refer the reader to those modern authors who have expressly treated the subject, or swell these notes disproportioned size.]

[Footnote 112: Tillemont has collected from Rufinus, Theodoret, &c., the sentiments and language of Constantine. Mem Eccles tom. iii p. 749, 759.]

[Footnote 113: See Cod. Theod. l. ix. tit. xlv. leg. 4. In the works of Fra Paolo. (tom. iv. p. 192, &c.,) there is an excellent discourse on the origin, claims, abuses, and limits of sanctuaries. He justly observes, that ancient Greece might perhaps contain fifteen or twenty axyla or sanctuaries; a number which at present may be found in Italy within the walls of a single city.]

V. The bishop was the perpetual censor of the morals of his people The discipline of penance was digested into a system of canonical jurisprudence, [114] which accurately defined the duty of private or public confession, the rules of evidence, the degrees of guilt, and the measure of punishment. It was impossible to execute this spiritual censure, if the Christian pontiff, who punished the obscure sins of the multitude, respected the conspicuous vices and destructive crimes of the magistrate: but it was impossible to arraign the conduct of the magistrate, without, controlling the administration of civil government. Some considerations of religion, or loyalty, or fear, protected the sacred persons of the emperors from the zeal or resentment of the bishops; but they boldly censured and excommunicated the subordinate tyrants, who were not invested with the majesty of the purple. St. Athanasius excommunicated one of the ministers of Egypt; and the interdict which he pronounced, of fire and water, was solemnly transmitted to the churches of Cappadocia. [115] Under the reign of the younger Theodosius, the polite and eloquent Synesius, one of the descendants of Hercules, [116] filled the episcopal seat of Ptolemais, near the ruins of ancient Cyrene, [117] and the philosophic bishop supported with dignity the character which he had assumed with reluctance. [118] He vanquished the monster of Libya, the president Andronicus, who abused the authority of a venal office, invented new modes of rapine and torture, and aggravated the guilt of oppression by that of sacrilege. [119] After a fruitless attempt to reclaim the haughty magistrate by mild and religious admonition, Synesius proceeds to inflict the last sentence of ecclesiastical justice, [120] which devotes Andronicus, with his associates and their families, to the abhorrence of earth and heaven. The impenitent sinners, more cruel than Phalaris or Sennacherib, more destructive than war, pestilence, or a cloud of locusts, are deprived of the name and privileges of Christians, of the participation of the sacraments, and of the hope of Paradise. The bishop exhorts the clergy, the magistrates, and the people, to renounce all society with the enemies of Christ; to exclude them from their houses and tables; and to refuse them the common offices of life, and the decent rites of burial. The church of Ptolemais, obscure and contemptible as she may appear, addresses this declaration to all her sister churches of the world; and the profane who reject her decrees, will be involved in the guilt and punishment of Andronicus and his impious followers. These spiritual terrors were enforced by a dexterous application to the Byzantine court; the trembling president implored the mercy of the church; and the descendants of Hercules enjoyed the satisfaction of raising a prostrate tyrant from the ground. [121] Such principles and such examples insensibly prepared the triumph of the Roman pontiffs, who have trampled on the necks of kings.

[Footnote 114: The penitential jurisprudence was continually improved by the canons of the councils. But as many cases were still left to the discretion of the bishops, they occasionally published, after the example of the Roman Praetor, the rules of discipline which they proposed to observe. Among the canonical epistles of the fourth century, those of Basil the Great were the most celebrated. They are inserted in the Pandects of Beveridge, (tom. ii. p. 47-151,) and are translated by Chardon, Hist. des Sacremens, tom. iv. p. 219-277.]

[Footnote 115: Basil, Epistol. xlvii. in Baronius, (Annal. Eccles. A. D. 370. N. 91,) who declares that he purposely relates it, to convince govern that they were not exempt from a sentence of excommunication his opinion, even a royal head is not safe from the thunders of the Vatican; and the cardinal shows himself much more consistent than the lawyers and theologians of the Gallican church.]

[Footnote 116: The long series of his ancestors, as high as Eurysthenes, the first Doric king of Sparta, and the fifth in lineal descent from Hercules, was inscribed in the public registers of Cyrene, a Lacedaemonian colony. (Synes. Epist. lvii. p. 197, edit. Petav.) Such a pure and illustrious pedigree of seventeen hundred years, without adding the royal ancestors of Hercules, cannot be equalled in the history of mankind.]

[Footnote 117: Synesius (de Regno, p. 2) pathetically deplores the fallen and ruined state of Cyrene. Ptolemais, a new city, 82 miles to the westward of Cyrene, assumed the metropolitan honors of the Pentapolis, or Upper Libya, which were afterwards transferred to Sozusa.]

[Footnote 118: Synesius had previously represented his own disqualifications. He loved profane studies and profane sports; he was incapable of supporting a life of celibacy; he disbelieved the resurrection; and he refused to preach fables to the people unless he might be permitted to philosophize at home. Theophilus primate of Egypt, who knew his merit, accepted this extraordinary compromise.]

[Footnote 119: The promotion of Andronicus was illegal; since he was a native of Berenice, in the same province. The instruments of torture are curiously specified; the press that variously pressed on distended the fingers, the feet, the nose, the ears, and the lips of the victims.]

[Footnote 120: The sentence of excommunication is expressed in a rhetorical style. (Synesius, Epist. lviii. p. 201-203.) The method of involving whole families, though somewhat unjust, was improved into national interdicts.]

[Footnote 121: See Synesius, Epist. xlvii. p. 186, 187. Epist. lxxii. p. 218, 219 Epist. lxxxix. p. 230, 231.]

VI. Every popular government has experienced the effects of rude or artificial eloquence. The coldest nature is animated, the firmest reason is moved, by the rapid communication of the prevailing impulse; and each hearer is affected by his own passions, and by those of the surrounding multitude. The ruin of civil liberty had silenced the demagogues of Athens, and the tribunes of Rome; the custom of preaching which seems to constitute a considerable part of Christian devotion, had not been introduced into the temples of antiquity; and the ears of monarchs were never invaded by the harsh sound of popular eloquence, till the pulpits of the empire were filled with sacred orators, who possessed some advantages unknown to their profane predecessors. [122] The arguments and rhetoric of the tribune were instantly opposed with equal arms, by skilful and resolute antagonists; and the cause of truth and reason might derive an accidental support from the conflict of hostile passions. The bishop, or some distinguished presbyter, to whom he cautiously delegated the powers of preaching, harangued, without the danger of interruption or reply, a submissive multitude, whose minds had been prepared and subdued by the awful ceremonies of religion. Such was the strict subordination of the Catholic church, that the same concerted sounds might issue at once from a hundred pulpits of Italy or Egypt, if they were tuned [123] by the master hand of the Roman or Alexandrian primate. The design of this institution was laudable, but the fruits were not always salutary. The preachers recommended the practice of the social duties; but they exalted the perfection of monastic virtue, which is painful to the individual, and useless to mankind. Their charitable exhortations betrayed a secret wish that the clergy might be permitted to manage the wealth of the faithful, for the benefit of the poor. The most sublime representations of the attributes and laws of the Deity were sullied by an idle mixture of metaphysical subleties, puerile rites, and fictitious miracles: and they expatiated, with the most fervent zeal, on the religious merit of hating the adversaries, and obeying the ministers of the church. When the public peace was distracted by heresy and schism, the sacred orators sounded the trumpet of discord, and, perhaps, of sedition. The understandings of their congregations were perplexed by mystery, their passions were inflamed by invectives; and they rushed from the Christian temples of Antioch or Alexandria, prepared either to suffer or to inflict martyrdom. The corruption of taste and language is strongly marked in the vehement declamations of the Latin bishops; but the compositions of Gregory and Chrysostom have been compared with the most splendid models of Attic, or at least of Asiatic, eloquence. [124]

[Footnote 122: See Thomassin (Discipline de l'Eglise, tom. ii. l. iii. c. 83, p. 1761-1770,) and Bingham, (Antiquities, vol. i. l. xiv. c. 4, p. 688- 717.) Preaching was considered as the most important office of the bishop but this function was sometimes intrusted to such presbyters as Chrysoetom and Augustin.]

[Footnote 123: Queen Elizabeth used this expression, and practised this art whenever she wished to prepossess the minds of her people in favor of any extraordinary measure of government. The hostile effects of this music were apprehended by her successor, and severely felt by his son. "When pulpit, drum ecclesiastic," &c. See Heylin's Life of Archbishop Laud, p. 153.]

[Footnote 124: Those modest orators acknowledged, that, as they were destitute of the gift of miracles, they endeavored to acquire the arts of eloquence.]

VII. The representatives of the Christian republic were regularly assembled in the spring and autumn of each year; and these synods diffused the spirit of ecclesiastical discipline and legislation through the hundred and twenty provinces of the Roman world. [125] The archbishop or metropolitan was empowered, by the laws, to summon the suffragan bishops of his province; to revise their conduct, to vindicate their rights, to declare their faith, and to examine the merits of the candidates who were elected by the clergy and people to supply the vacancies of the episcopal college. The primates of Rome, Alexandria, Antioch, Carthage, and afterwards Constantinople, who exercised a more ample jurisdiction, convened the numerous assembly of their dependent bishops. But the convocation of great and extraordinary synods was the prerogative of the emperor alone. Whenever the emergencies of the church required this decisive measure, he despatched a peremptory summons to the bishops, or the deputies of each province, with an order for the use of post-horses, and a competent allowance for the expenses of their journey. At an early period, when Constantine was the protector, rather than the proselyte, of Christianity, he referred the African controversy to the council of Arles; in which the bishops of York of Treves, of Milan, and of Carthage, met as friends and brethren, to debate in their native tongue on the common interest of the Latin or Western church. [126] Eleven years afterwards, a more numerous and celebrated assembly was convened at Nice in Bithynia, to extinguish, by their final sentence, the subtle disputes which had arisen in Egypt on the subject of the Trinity. Three hundred and eighteen bishops obeyed the summons of their indulgent master; the ecclesiastics of every rank, and sect, and denomination, have been computed at two thousand and forty-eight persons; [127] the Greeks appeared in person; and the consent of the Latins was expressed by the legates of the Roman pontiff. The session, which lasted about two months, was frequently honored by the presence of the emperor. Leaving his guards at the door, he seated himself (with the permission of the council) on a low stool in the midst of the hall. Constantine listened with patience, and spoke with modesty: and while he influenced the debates, he humbly professed that he was the minister, not the judge, of the successors of the apostles, who had been established as priests and as gods upon earth. [128] Such profound reverence of an absolute monarch towards a feeble and unarmed assembly of his own subjects, can only be compared to the respect with which the senate had been treated by the Roman princes who adopted the policy of Augustus. Within the space of fifty years, a philosophic spectator of the vicissitudes of human affairs might have contemplated Tacitus in the senate of Rome, and Constantine in the council of Nice. The fathers of the Capitol and those of the church had alike degenerated from the virtues of their founders; but as the bishops were more deeply rooted in the public opinion, they sustained their dignity with more decent pride, and sometimes opposed with a manly spirit the wishes of their sovereign. The progress of time and superstition erased the memory of the weakness, the passion, the ignorance, which disgraced these ecclesiastical synods; and the Catholic world has unanimously submitted [129] to the infallible decrees of the general councils. [130]

[Footnote 125: The council of Nice, in the fourth, fifth, sixth, and seventh canons, has made some fundamental regulations concerning synods, metropolitan, and primates. The Nicene canons have been variously tortured, abused, interpolated, or forged, according to the interest of the clergy. The Suburbicarian churches, assigned (by Rufinus) to the bishop of Rome, have been made the subject of vehement controversy (See Sirmond, Opera, tom. iv. p. 1-238.)]

[Footnote 126: We have only thirty-three or forty-seven episcopal subscriptions: but Addo, a writer indeed of small account, reckons six hundred bishops in the council of Arles. Tillemont, Mem. Eccles. tom. vi. p. 422.]

[Footnote 127: See Tillemont, tom. vi. p. 915, and Beausobre, Hist. du Mani cheisme, tom i p. 529. The name of bishop, which is given by Eusychius to the 2048 ecclesiastics, (Annal. tom. i. p. 440, vers. Pocock,) must be extended far beyond the limits of an orthodox or even episcopal ordination.]

[Footnote 128: See Euseb. in Vit. Constantin. l. iii. c. 6-21. Tillemont, Mem. Ecclesiastiques, tom. vi. p. 669-759.]

[Footnote 129: Sancimus igitur vicem legum obtinere, quae a quatuor Sanctis Coueiliis.... expositae sunt act firmatae. Praedictarum enim quat uor synodorum dogmata sicut sanctas Scripturas et regulas sicut leges observamus. Justinian. Novell. cxxxi. Beveridge (ad Pandect. proleg. p. 2) remarks, that the emperors never made new laws in ecclesiastical matters; and Giannone observes, in a very different spirit, that they gave a legal sanction to the canons of councils. Istoria Civile di Napoli, tom. i. p. 136.]

[Footnote 130: See the article Concile in the Eucyclopedie, tom. iii. p. 668-879, edition de Lucques. The author, M. de docteur Bouchaud, has discussed, according to the principles of the Gallican church, the principal questions which relate to the form and constitution of general, national, and provincial councils. The editors (see Preface, p. xvi.) have reason to be proud of this article. Those who consult their immense compilation, seldom depart so well satisfied.]

CHAPTER XXI

PERSECUTION OF HERESY, STATE OF THE CHURCH

PART I

PERSECUTION OF HERESY—THE SCHISM OF THE DONATISTS—THE ARIAN CONTROVERSY—ATHANASIUS—DISTRACTED STATE OF THE CHURCH AND EMPIRE UNDER CONSTANTINE AND HIS SONS—TOLERATION OF PAGANISM

The grateful applause of the clergy has consecrated the memory of a prince who indulged their passions and promoted their interest. Constantine gave them security, wealth, honors, and revenge; and the support of the orthodox faith was considered as the most sacred and important duty of the civil magistrate. The edict of Milan, the great charter of toleration, had confirmed to each individual of the Roman world the privilege of choosing and professing his own religion. But this inestimable privilege was soon violated; with the knowledge of truth, the emperor imbibed the maxims of persecution; and the sects which dissented from the Catholic church were afflicted and oppressed by the triumph of Christianity. Constantine easily believed that the Heretics, who presumed to dispute his opinions, or to oppose his commands, were guilty of the most absurd and criminal obstinacy; and that a seasonable application of moderate severities might save those unhappy men from the danger of an everlasting condemnation. Not a moment was lost in excluding the ministers and teachers of the separated congregations from any share of the rewards and immunities which the emperor had so liberally bestowed on the orthodox clergy. But as the sectaries might still exist under the cloud of royal disgrace, the conquest of the East was immediately followed by an edict which announced their total destruction. [1] After a preamble filled with passion and reproach, Constantine absolutely prohibits the assemblies of the Heretics, and confiscates their public property to the use either of the revenue or of the Catholic church. The sects against whom the Imperial severity was directed, appear to have been the adherents of Paul of Samosata; the Montanists of Phrygia, who maintained an enthusiastic succession of prophecy; the Novatians, who sternly rejected the temporal efficacy of repentance; the Marcionites and Valentinians, under whose leading banners the various Gnostics of Asia and Egypt had insensibly rallied; and perhaps the Manichaeans, who had recently imported from Persia a more artful composition of Oriental and Christian theology. [2] The design of extirpating the name, or at least of restraining the progress, of these odious Heretics, was prosecuted with vigor and effect. Some of the penal regulations were copied from the edicts of Diocletian; and this method of conversion was applauded by the same bishops who had felt the hand of oppression, and pleaded for the rights of humanity. Two immaterial circumstances may serve, however, to prove that the mind of Constantine was not entirely corrupted by the spirit of zeal and bigotry. Before he condemned the Manichaeans and their kindred sects, he resolved to make an accurate inquiry into the nature of their religious principles. As if he distrusted the impartiality of his ecclesiastical counsellors, this delicate commission was intrusted to a civil magistrate, whose learning and moderation he justly esteemed, and of whose venal character he was probably ignorant. [3] The emperor was soon convinced, that he had too hastily proscribed the orthodox faith and the exemplary morals of the Novatians, who had dissented from the church in some articles of discipline which were not perhaps essential to salvation. By a particular edict, he exempted them from the general penalties of the law; [4] allowed them to build a church at Constantinople, respected the miracles of their saints, invited their bishop Acesius to the council of Nice; and gently ridiculed the narrow tenets of his sect by a familiar jest; which, from the mouth of a sovereign, must have been received with applause and gratitude. [5]

[Footnote 1: Eusebius in Vit. Constantin. l. iii. c. 63, 64, 65, 66.]

[Footnote 2: After some examination of the various opinions of Tillemont, Beausobre, Lardner, &c., I am convinced that Manes did not propagate his sect, even in Persia, before the year 270. It is strange, that a philosophic and foreign heresy should have penetrated so rapidly into the African provinces; yet I cannot easily reject the edict of Diocletian against the Manichaeans, which may be found in Baronius. (Annal Eccl. A. D. 287.)]

[Footnote 3: Constantinus enim, cum limatius superstitionum quaeroret sectas, Manichaeorum et similium, &c. Ammian. xv. 15. Strategius, who from this commission obtained the surname of Musonianus, was a Christian of the Arian sect. He acted as one of the counts at the council of Sardica. Libanius praises his mildness and prudence. Vales. ad locum Ammian.]

[Footnote 4: Cod. Theod. l. xvi. tit. 5, leg. 2. As the general law is not inserted in the Theodosian Code, it probable that, in the year 438, the sects which it had condemned were already extinct.]

[Footnote 5: Sozomen, l. i. c. 22. Socrates, l. i. c. 10. These historians have been suspected, but I think without reason, of an attachment to the Novatian doctrine. The emperor said to the bishop, "Acesius, take a ladder, and get up to heaven by yourself." Most of the Christian sects have, by turns, borrowed the ladder of Acesius.]

The complaints and mutual accusations which assailed the throne of Constantine, as soon as the death of Maxentius had submitted Africa to his victorious arms, were ill adapted to edify an imperfect proselyte. He learned, with surprise, that the provinces of that great country, from the confines of Cyrene to the columns of Hercules, were distracted with religious discord. [6] The source of the division was derived from a double election in the church of Carthage; the second, in rank and opulence, of the ecclesiastical thrones of the West. Caecilian and Majorinus were the two rival prelates of Africa; and the death of the latter soon made room for Donatus, who, by his superior abilities and apparent virtues, was the firmest support of his party. The advantage which Caecilian might claim from the priority of his ordination, was destroyed by the illegal, or at least indecent, haste, with which it had been performed, without expecting the arrival of the bishops of Numidia. The authority of these bishops, who, to the number of seventy, condemned Caecilian, and consecrated Majorinus, is again weakened by the infamy of some of their personal characters; and by the female intrigues, sacrilegious bargains, and tumultuous proceedings, which are imputed to this Numidian council. [7] The bishops of the contending factions maintained, with equal ardor and obstinacy, that their adversaries were degraded, or at least dishonored, by the odious crime of delivering the Holy Scriptures to the officers of Diocletian. From their mutual reproaches, as well as from the story of this dark transaction, it may justly be inferred, that the late persecution had imbittered the zeal, without reforming the manners, of the African Christians. That divided church was incapable of affording an impartial judicature; the controversy was solemnly tried in five successive tribunals, which were appointed by the emperor; and the whole proceeding, from the first appeal to the final sentence, lasted above three years. A severe inquisition, which was taken by the Praetorian vicar, and the proconsul of Africa, the report of two episcopal visitors who had been sent to Carthage, the decrees of the councils of Rome and of Arles, and the supreme judgment of Constantine himself in his sacred consistory, were all favorable to the cause of Caecilian; and he was unanimously acknowledged by the civil and ecclesiastical powers, as the true and lawful primate of Africa. The honors and estates of the church were attributed to his suffragan bishops, and it was not without difficulty, that Constantine was satisfied with inflicting the punishment of exile on the principal leaders of the Donatist faction. As their cause was examined with attention, perhaps it was determined with justice. Perhaps their complaint was not without foundation, that the credulity of the emperor had been abused by the insidious arts of his favorite Osius. The influence of falsehood and corruption might procure the condemnation of the innocent, or aggravate the sentence of the guilty. Such an act, however, of injustice, if it concluded an importunate dispute, might be numbered among the transient evils of a despotic administration, which are neither felt nor remembered by posterity.

[Footnote 6: The best materials for this part of ecclesiastical history may be found in the edition of Optatus Milevitanus, published (Paris, 1700) by M. Dupin, who has enriched it with critical notes, geographical discussions, original records, and an accurate abridgment of the whole controversy. M. de Tillemont has bestowed on the Donatists the greatest part of a volume, (tom. vi. part i.;) and I am indebted to him for an ample collection of all the passages of his favorite St. Augustin, which relate to those heretics.]

[Footnote 7: Schisma igitur illo tempore confusae mulieris iracundia peperit; ambitus nutrivit; avaritia roboravit. Optatus, l. i. c. 19. The language of Purpurius is that of a furious madman. Dicitur te necasse lilios sororis tuae duos. Purpurius respondit: Putas me terreri a te.. occidi; et occido eos qui contra me faciunt. Acta Concil. Cirtenais, ad calc. Optat. p. 274. When Caecilian was invited to an assembly of bishops, Purpurius said to his brethren, or rather to his accomplices, "Let him come hither to receive our imposition of hands, and we will break his head by way of penance." Optat. l. i. c. 19.]

But this incident, so inconsiderable that it scarcely deserves a place in history, was productive of a memorable schism which afflicted the provinces of Africa above three hundred years, and was extinguished only with Christianity itself. The inflexible zeal of freedom and fanaticism animated the Donatists to refuse obedience to the usurpers, whose election they disputed, and whose spiritual powers they denied. Excluded from the civil and religious communion of mankind, they boldly excommunicated the rest of mankind, who had embraced the impious party of Caecilian, and of the Traditors, from which he derived his pretended ordination. They asserted with confidence, and almost with exultation, that the Apostolical succession was interrupted; that all the bishops of Europe and Asia were infected by the contagion of guilt and schism; and that the prerogatives of the Catholic church were confined to the chosen portion of the African believers, who alone had preserved inviolate the integrity of their faith and discipline. This rigid theory was supported by the most uncharitable conduct. Whenever they acquired a proselyte, even from the distant provinces of the East, they carefully repeated the sacred rites of baptism [8] and ordination; as they rejected the validity of those which he had already received from the hands of heretics or schismatics. Bishops, virgins, and even spotless infants, were subjected to the disgrace of a public penance, before they could be admitted to the communion of the Donatists. If they obtained possession of a church which had been used by their Catholic adversaries, they purified the unhallowed building with the same zealous care which a temple of idols might have required. They washed the pavement, scraped the walls, burnt the altar, which was commonly of wood, melted the consecrated plate, and cast the Holy Eucharist to the dogs, with every circumstance of ignominy which could provoke and perpetuate the animosity of religious factions. [9] Notwithstanding this irreconcilable aversion, the two parties, who were mixed and separated in all the cities of Africa, had the same language and manners, the same zeal and learning, the same faith and worship. Proscribed by the civil and ecclesiastical powers of the empire, the Donatists still maintained in some provinces, particularly in Numidia, their superior numbers; and four hundred bishops acknowledged the jurisdiction of their primate. But the invincible spirit of the sect sometimes preyed on its own vitals: and the bosom of their schismatical church was torn by intestine divisions. A fourth part of the Donatist bishops followed the independent standard of the Maximianists. The narrow and solitary path which their first leaders had marked out, continued to deviate from the great society of mankind. Even the imperceptible sect of the Rogatians could affirm, without a blush, that when Christ should descend to judge the earth, he would find his true religion preserved only in a few nameless villages of the Caesarean Mauritania. [10]

[Footnote 8: The councils of Arles, of Nice, and of Trent, confirmed the wise and moderate practice of the church of Rome. The Donatists, however, had the advantage of maintaining the sentiment of Cyprian, and of a considerable part of the primitive church. Vincentius Lirinesis (p. 532, ap. Tillemont, Mem. Eccles. tom. vi. p. 138) has explained why the Donatists are eternally burning with the Devil, while St. Cyprian reigns in heaven with Jesus Christ.]

[Footnote 9: See the sixth book of Optatus Milevitanus, p. 91-100.]

[Footnote 10: Tillemont, Mem. Ecclesiastiques, tom. vi. part i. p. 253. He laughs at their partial credulity. He revered Augustin, the great doctor of the system of predestination.]

The schism of the Donatists was confined to Africa: the more diffusive mischief of the Trinitarian controversy successively penetrated into every part of the Christian world. The former was an accidental quarrel, occasioned by the abuse of freedom; the latter was a high and mysterious argument, derived from the abuse of philosophy. From the age of Constantine to that of Clovis and Theodoric, the temporal interests both of the Romans and Barbarians were deeply involved in the theological disputes of Arianism. The historian may therefore be permitted respectfully to withdraw the veil of the sanctuary; and to deduce the progress of reason and faith, of error and passion from the school of Plato, to the decline and fall of the empire.

The genius of Plato, informed by his own meditation, or by the traditional knowledge of the priests of Egypt, [11] had ventured to explore the mysterious nature of the Deity. When he had elevated his mind to the sublime contemplation of the first self-existent, necessary cause of the universe, the Athenian sage was incapable of conceiving how the simple unity of his essence could admit the infinite variety of distinct and successive ideas which compose the model of the intellectual world; how a Being purely incorporeal could execute that perfect model, and mould with a plastic hand the rude and independent chaos. The vain hope of extricating himself from these difficulties, which must ever oppress the feeble powers of the human mind, might induce Plato to consider the divine nature under the threefold modification—of the first cause, the reason, or Logos, and the soul or spirit of the universe. His poetical imagination sometimes fixed and animated these metaphysical abstractions; the three archical on original principles were represented in the Platonic system as three Gods, united with each other by a mysterious and ineffable generation; and the Logos was particularly considered under the more accessible character of the Son of an Eternal Father, and the Creator and Governor of the world. Such appear to have been the secret doctrines which were cautiously whispered in the gardens of the academy; and which, according to the more recent disciples of Plato, [11a] could not be perfectly understood, till after an assiduous study of thirty years. [12]

[Footnote 11: Plato Aegyptum peragravit ut a sacerdotibus Barbaris numeros et coelestia acciperet. Cicero de Finibus, v. 25. The Egyptians might still preserve the traditional creed of the Patriarchs. Josephus has persuaded many of the Christian fathers, that Plato derived a part of his knowledge from the Jews; but this vain opinion cannot be reconciled with the obscure state and unsocial manners of the Jewish people, whose scriptures were not accessible to Greek curiosity till more than one hundred years after the death of Plato. See Marsham Canon. Chron. p. 144 Le Clerc, Epistol. Critic. vii. p. 177-194.]

[Footnote 11a: This exposition of the doctrine of Plato appears to me contrary to the true sense of that philosopher's writings. The brilliant imagination which he carried into metaphysical inquiries, his style, full of allegories and figures, have misled those interpreters who did not seek, from the whole tenor of his works and beyond the images which the writer employs, the system of this philosopher. In my opinion, there is no Trinity in Plato; he has established no mysterious generation between the three pretended principles which he is made to distinguish. Finally, he conceives only as attributes of the Deity, or of matter, those ideas, of which it is supposed that he made substances, real beings—According to Plato, God and matter existed from all eternity. Before the creation of the world, matter had in itself a principle of motion, but without end or laws: it is this principle which Plato calls the irrational soul of the world, because, according to his doctrine, every spontaneous and original principle of motion is called soul. God wished to impress form upon matter, that is to say, 1. To mould matter, and make it into a body; 2. To regulate its motion, and subject it to some end and to certain laws. The Deity, in this operation, could not act but according to the ideas existing in his intelligence: their union filled this, and formed the ideal type of the world. It is this ideal world, this divine intelligence, existing with God from all eternity, and called by Plato which he is supposed to personify, to substantialize; while an attentive examination is sufficient to convince us that he has never assigned it an existence external to the Deity, (hors de la Divinite,) and that he considered the as the aggregate of the ideas of God, the divine understanding in its relation to the world. The contrary opinion is irreconcilable with all his philosophy; thus he says that to the idea of the Deity is essentially united that of intelligence, or a logos. He would thus have admitted a double logos; one inherent in the Deity as an attribute, the other independently existing as a substance. He affirms that the intelligence, the principle of order cannot exist but as an attribute of a soul, the principle of motion and of life, of which the nature is unknown to us. How, then, according to this, could he consider the logos as a substance endowed with an independent existence? In other places, he explains it by these two words, knowledge, science, which signify the attributes of the Deity. When Plato separates God, the ideal archetype of the world and matter, it is to explain how, according to his system, God has proceeded, at the creation, to unite the principle of order which he had within himself, his proper intelligence, the principle of motion, to the principle of motion, the irrational soul which was in matter.

When he speaks of the place occupied by the ideal world, it is to designate the divine intelligence, which is its cause. Finally, in no part of his writings do we find a true personification of the pretended beings of which he is said to have formed a trinity: and if this personification existed, it would equally apply to many other notions, of which might be formed many different trinities. This error, into which many ancient as well as modern interpreters of Plato have fallen, was very natural. Besides the snares which were concealed in his figurative style; besides the necessity of comprehending as a whole the system of his ideas, and not to explain isolated passages, the nature of his doctrine itself would conduce to this error. When Plato appeared, the uncertainty of human knowledge, and the continual illusions of the senses, were acknowledged, and had given rise to a general scepticism. Socrates had aimed at raising morality above the influence of this scepticism: Plato endeavored to save metaphysics, by seeking in the human intellect a source of certainty which the senses could not furnish. He invented the system of innate ideas, of which the aggregate formed, according to him, the ideal world, and affirmed that these ideas were real attributes, not only attached to our conceptions of objects, but to the nature of the objects themselves; a nature of which from them we might obtain a knowledge. He gave, then, to these ideas a positive existence as attributes; his commentators could easily give them a real existence as substances; especially as the terms which he used to designate them, essential beauty, essential goodness, lent themselves to this substantialization, (hypostasis.)—G. —We have retained this view of the original philosophy of Plato, in which there is probably much truth. The genius of Plato was rather metaphysical than impersonative: his poetry was in his language, rather than, like that of the Orientals, in his conceptions—M.]

[Footnote 12: The modern guides who lead me to the knowledge of the Platonic system are Cudworth, Basnage, Le Clerc, and Brucker. As the learning of these writers was equal, and their intention different, an inquisitive observer may derive instruction from their disputes, and certainty from their agreement.]

The arms of the Macedonians diffused over Asia and Egypt the language and learning of Greece; and the theological system of Plato was taught, with less reserve, and perhaps with some improvements, in the celebrated school of Alexandria. [13] A numerous colony of Jews had been invited, by the favor of the Ptolemies, to settle in their new capital. [14] While the bulk of the nation practised the legal ceremonies, and pursued the lucrative occupations of commerce, a few Hebrews, of a more liberal spirit, devoted their lives to religious and philosophical contemplation. [15] They cultivated with diligence, and embraced with ardor, the theological system of the Athenian sage. But their national pride would have been mortified by a fair confession of their former poverty: and they boldly marked, as the sacred inheritance of their ancestors, the gold and jewels which they had so lately stolen from their Egyptian masters. One hundred years before the birth of Christ, a philosophical treatise, which manifestly betrays the style and sentiments of the school of Plato, was produced by the Alexandrian Jews, and unanimously received as a genuine and valuable relic of the inspired Wisdom of Solomon. [16] A similar union of the Mosaic faith and the Grecian philosophy, distinguishes the works of Philo, which were composed, for the most part, under the reign of Augustus. [17] The material soul of the universe [18] might offend the piety of the Hebrews: but they applied the character of the Logos to the Jehovah of Moses and the patriarchs; and the Son of God was introduced upon earth under a visible, and even human appearance, to perform those familiar offices which seem incompatible with the nature and attributes of the Universal Cause. [19]

[Footnote 13: Brucker, Hist. Philosoph. tom. i. p. 1349-1357. The Alexandrian school is celebrated by Strabo (l. xvii.) and Ammianus, (xxii. 6.) Note: The philosophy of Plato was not the only source of that professed in the school of Alexandria. That city, in which Greek, Jewish, and Egyptian men of letters were assembled, was the scene of a strange fusion of the system of these three people. The Greeks brought a

Platonism, already much changed; the Jews, who had acquired at Babylon a great number of Oriental notions, and whose theological opinions had undergone great changes by this intercourse, endeavored to reconcile Platonism with their new doctrine, and disfigured it entirely: lastly, the Egyptians, who were not willing to abandon notions for which the Greeks themselves entertained respect, endeavored on their side to reconcile their own with those of their neighbors. It is in Ecclesiasticus and the Wisdom of Solomon that we trace the influence of Oriental philosophy rather than that of Platonism. We find in these books, and in those of the later prophets, as in Ezekiel, notions unknown to the Jews before the Babylonian captivity, of which we do not discover the germ in Plato, but which are manifestly derived from the Orientals. Thus God represented under the image of light, and the principle of evil under that of darkness; the history of the good and bad angels; paradise and hell, &c., are doctrines of which the origin, or at least the positive determination, can only be referred to the Oriental philosophy. Plato supposed matter eternal; the Orientals and the Jews considered it as a creation of God, who alone was eternal. It is impossible to explain the philosophy of the Alexandrian school solely by the blending of the Jewish theology with the Greek philosophy. The Oriental philosophy, however little it may be known, is recognized at every instant. Thus, according to the Zend Avesta, it is by the Word (honover) more ancient than the world, that Ormuzd created the universe. This word is the logos of Philo, consequently very different from that of Plato. I have shown that Plato never personified the logos as the ideal archetype of the world: Philo ventured this personification. The Deity, according to him, has a double logos; the first is the ideal archetype of the world, the ideal world, the first-born of the Deity; the second is the word itself of God, personified under the image of a being acting to create the sensible world, and to make it like to the ideal world: it is the second-born of God. Following out his imaginations, Philo went so far as to personify anew the ideal world, under the image of a celestial man, the primitive type of man, and the sensible world under the image of another man less perfect than the celestial man. Certain notions of the Oriental philosophy may have given rise to this strange abuse of allegory, which it is sufficient to relate, to show what alterations Platonism had already undergone, and what was their source. Philo, moreover, of all the Jews of Alexandria, is the one whose Platonism is the most pure. It is from this mixture of Orientalism, Platonism, and Judaism, that Gnosticism arose, which had produced so many theological and philosophical extravagancies, and in which Oriental notions evidently predominate—G.]

[Footnote 14: Joseph. Antiquitat, l. xii. c. 1, 3. Basnage, Hist. des Juifs, l. vii. c. 7.]

[Footnote 15: For the origin of the Jewish philosophy, see Eusebius, Praeparat. Evangel. viii. 9, 10. According to Philo, the Therapeutae studied philosophy; and Brucker has proved (Hist. Philosoph. tom. ii. p. 787) that they gave the preference to that of Plato.]

[Footnote 16: See Calmet, Dissertations sur la Bible, tom. ii. p. 277. The book of the Wisdom of Solomon was received by many of the fathers as the work of that monarch: and although rejected by the Protestants for want of a Hebrew original, it has obtained, with the rest of the Vulgate, the sanction of the council of Trent.]

[Footnote 17: The Platonism of Philo, which was famous to a proverb, is proved beyond a doubt by Le Clerc, (Epist. Crit. viii. p. 211-228.) Basnage (Hist. des Juifs, l. iv. c. 5) has clearly ascertained, that the theological works of Philo were composed before the death, and most probably before the birth, of Christ. In such a time of darkness, the knowledge of Philo is more astonishing than his errors. Bull, Defens. Fid. Nicen. s. i. c. i. p. 12.]

[Footnote 18: Mens agitat molem, et magno se corpore miscet. Besides this material soul, Cudworth has discovered (p. 562) in Amelius, Porphyry, Plotinus, and, as he thinks, in Plato himself, a superior, spiritual upercosmian soul of the universe. But this double soul is exploded by Brucker, Basnage, and Le Clerc, as an idle fancy of the latter Platonists.]

[Footnote 19: Petav. Dogmata Theologica, tom. ii. l. viii. c. 2, p. 791. Bull, Defens. Fid. Nicen. s. i. c. l. p. 8, 13. This notion, till it was abused by the Arians, was freely adopted in the Christian theology. Tertullian (adv. Praxeam, c. 16) has a remarkable and dangerous passage. After contrasting, with indiscreet wit, the nature of God, and the actions of Jehovah, he concludes: Scilicet ut haec de filio Dei non credenda fuisse, si non scripta essent; fortasse non credenda de l'atre licet scripta. Note: Tertullian is here arguing against the Patripassians; those who asserted that the Father was born of the Virgin, died and was buried—M.]

PART II

The eloquence of Plato, the name of Solomon, the authority of the school of Alexandria, and the consent of the Jews and Greeks, were insufficient to establish the truth of a mysterious doctrine, which might please, but could not satisfy, a rational mind. A prophet, or apostle, inspired by the Deity, can alone exercise a lawful dominion over the faith of mankind: and the theology of Plato might have been forever confounded with the philosophical visions of the Academy, the Porch, and the Lycaeum, if the name and divine attributes of the Logos had not been confirmed by the celestial pen of the last and most sublime of the Evangelists. [20] The Christian Revelation, which was consummated under the reign of Nerva, disclosed to the world the amazing secret, that the Logos, who was with God from the beginning, and was God, who had made all things, and for whom all things had been made, was incarnate in the person of Jesus of Nazareth; who had been born of a virgin, and suffered death on the cross. Besides the genera design of fixing on a perpetual basis the divine honors of Christ, the most ancient and respectable of the ecclesiastical writers have ascribed to the evangelic theologian a particular intention to confute two opposite heresies, which disturbed the peace of the primitive church. [21] I. The faith of the Ebionites, [22] perhaps of the Nazarenes, [23] was gross and imperfect. They revered Jesus as the greatest of the prophets, endowed with supernatural virtue and power. They ascribed to his person and to his future reign all the predictions of the Hebrew oracles which relate to the spiritual and everlasting kingdom of the promised Messiah. [24] Some of them might confess that he was born of a virgin; but they obstinately rejected the preceding existence and divine perfections of the Logos, or Son of God, which are so clearly defined in the Gospel of St. John. About fifty years afterwards, the Ebionites, whose errors are mentioned by Justin Martyr with less severity than they seem to deserve, [25] formed a very inconsiderable portion of the Christian name. II. The Gnostics, who were distinguished by the epithet of Docetes, deviated into the contrary extreme; and betrayed the human, while they asserted the divine, nature of Christ. Educated in the school of Plato, accustomed to the sublime idea of the Logos, they readily conceived that the brightest Aeon, or Emanation of the Deity, might assume the outward shape and visible appearances of a mortal; [26] but they vainly pretended, that the imperfections of matter are incompatible with the purity of a celestial substance.

While the blood of Christ yet smoked on Mount Calvary, the Docetes invented the impious and extravagant hypothesis, that, instead of issuing from the womb of the Virgin, [27] he had descended on the banks of the Jordan in the form of perfect manhood; that he had imposed on the senses of his enemies, and of his disciples; and that the ministers of Pilate had wasted their impotent rage on an ury phantom, who seemed to expire on the cross, and, after three days, to rise from the dead. [28]

[Footnote 20: The Platonists admired the beginning of the Gospel of St. John as containing an exact transcript of their own principles. Augustin de Civitat. Dei, x. 29. Amelius apud Cyril. advers. Julian. l. viii. p. 283. But in the third and fourth centuries, the Platonists of Alexandria might improve their Trinity by the secret study of the Christian theology. Note: A short discussion on the sense in which St. John has used the word Logos, will prove that he has not borrowed it from the philosophy of Plato. The evangelist adopts this word without previous explanation, as a term with which his contemporaries were already familiar, and which they could at once comprehend. To know the sense which he gave to it, we must inquire that which it generally bore in his time. We find two: the one attached to the word logos by the Jews of Palestine, the other by the school of Alexandria, particularly by Philo. The Jews had feared at all times to pronounce the name of Jehovah; they had formed a habit of designating God by one of his attributes; they called him sometimes Wisdom, sometimes the Word. By the word of the Lord were the heavens made. (Psalm xxxiii. 6.) Accustomed to allegories, they often addressed themselves to this attribute of the Deity as a real being. Solomon makes Wisdom say "The Lord possessed me in the beginning of his way, before his works of old. I was set up from everlasting, from the beginning, or ever the earth was." (Prov. viii. 22, 23.) Their residence in Persia only increased this inclination to sustained allegories. In the Ecclesiasticus of the son of Sirach, and the Book of Wisdom, we find allegorical descriptions of Wisdom like the following: "I came out of the mouth of the Most High; I covered the earth as a cloud;... I alone compassed the circuit of heaven, and walked in the bottom of the deep... The Creator created me from the beginning, before the world, and I shall never fail." (Eccles. xxiv. 35- 39.) See also the Wisdom of Solomon, c. vii. v. 9. [The latter book is clearly Alexandrian—M.] We see from this that the Jews understood from the Hebrew and Chaldaic words which signify Wisdom, the Word, and which were translated into Greek, a simple attribute of the Deity, allegorically personified, but of which they did not make a real particular being separate from the Deity. The school of Alexandria, on the contrary, and Philo among the rest, mingling Greek with Jewish and Oriental notions, and abandoning himself to his inclination to mysticism, personified the logos, and represented it a distinct being, created by God, and intermediate between God and man. This is the second logos of Philo, that which acts from the beginning of the world, alone in its kind, creator of the sensible world, formed by God according to the ideal world which he had in himself, and which was the first logos, the first- born of the Deity. The logos taken in this sense, then, was a created being, but, anterior to the creation of the world, near to God, and charged with his revelations to mankind—Which of these two senses is that which St. John intended to assign to the word logos in the first chapter of his Gospel, and in all his writings? St. John was a Jew, born and educated in Palestine; he had no knowledge, at least very little, of the philosophy of the Greeks, and that of the Grecizing Jews: he would naturally, then, attach to the word logos the sense attached to it by the Jews of Palestine. If, in fact, we compare the attributes which he assigns to the logos with those which are assigned to it in Proverbs, in the Wisdom of Solomon, in Ecclesiasticus, we shall see that they are the same. The Word was in the world, and the world was made by him; in him was life, and the life was the light of men, (c. i. v. 10-14.) It is impossible not to trace in this chapter the ideas which the Jews had formed of the allegorized logos. The evangelist afterwards really personifies that which his predecessors have personified only poetically; for he affirms "that the Word became flesh," (V. 14.) It was to prove this that he wrote. Closely examined, the ideas which he gives of the logos cannot agree with those of Philo and the school of Alexandria; they correspond, on the contrary, with those of the Jews of Palestine. Perhaps St. John, employing a well-known term to explain a doctrine which was yet unknown, has slightly altered the sense; it is this alteration which we appear to discover on comparing different passages of his writings—It is worthy of remark, that the Jews of Palestine, who did not perceive this alteration, could find nothing extraordinary in what St. John said of the Logos; at least they comprehended it without difficulty, while the Greeks and Grecizing Jews, on their part, brought to it prejudices and preconceptions easily reconciled with those of the evangelist, who did not expressly contradict them. This circumstance must have much favored the progress of Christianity. Thus the fathers of the church in the two first centuries and later, formed almost all in the school of Alexandria, gave to the Logos of St. John a sense nearly similar to that which it received from Philo. Their doctrine approached very near to that which in the fourth century the council of Nice condemned in the person of Arius—G—M. Guizot has forgotten the long residence of St. John at Ephesus, the centre of the mingling opinions of the East and West, which were gradually growing up into Gnosticism. (See Matter. Hist. du Gnosticisme, vol. i. p. 154.) St. John's sense of the Logos seems as far removed from the simple allegory ascribed to the Palestinian Jews as from the Oriental impersonation of the Alexandrian. The simple truth may be that St. John took the familiar term, and, as it were infused into it the peculiar and Christian sense in which it is used in his writings. —M.]

[Footnote 21: See Beausobre, Hist. Critique du Manicheisme, tom. i. p. 377. The Gospel according to St. John is supposed to have been published about seventy years after the death of Christ.]

[Footnote 22: The sentiments of the Ebionites are fairly stated by Mosheim (p. 331) and Le Clerc, (Hist. Eccles. p. 535.) The Clementines, published among the apostolical fathers, are attributed by the critics to one of these sectaries.]

[Footnote 23: Stanch polemics, like a Bull, (Judicium Eccles. Cathol. c. 2,) insist on the orthodoxy of the Nazarenes; which appears less pure and certain in the eyes of Mosheim, (p. 330.)]

[Footnote 24: The humble condition and sufferings of Jesus have always been a stumbling-block to the Jews. "Deus... contrariis coloribus Messiam depinxerat: futurus erat Rex, Judex, Pastor," &c. See Limborch et Orobio Amica Collat. p. 8, 19, 53-76, 192-234. But this objection has obliged the believing Christians to lift up their eyes to a spiritual and everlasting kingdom.]

[Footnote 25: Justin Martyr, Dialog. cum Tryphonte, p. 143, 144. See Le Clerc, Hist. Eccles. p. 615. Bull and his editor Grabe (Judicium Eccles. Cathol. c. 7, and Appendix) attempt to distort either the sentiments or the words of Justin; but their violent correction of the text is rejected even by the Benedictine editors.]

[Footnote 26: The Arians reproached the orthodox party with borrowing their Trinity from the Valentinians and Marcionites. See Beausobre, Hist. de Manicheisme, l. iii. c. 5, 7.]

[Footnote 27: Non dignum est ex utero credere Deum, et Deum Christum.... non dignum est ut tanta majestas per sordes et squalores muli eris transire credatur. The Gnostics asserted the impurity of matter, and of marriage; and they were scandalized by the gross interpretations of the fathers, and even of Augustin himself. See Beausobre, tom. ii. p. 523, Note: The greater part of the Docetae rejected the true divinity of Jesus Christ, as well as his human nature. They belonged to the Gnostics, whom some philosophers, in whose party Gibbon has enlisted, make to derive their opinions from those of Plato. These philosophers did not consider that Platonism had undergone continual alterations, and that those who gave it some analogy with the notions of the Gnostics were later in their origin than most of the sects comprehended under this name Mosheim has proved (in his Instit. Histor. Eccles. Major. s. i. p. 136, sqq and p. 339, sqq.) that the Oriental philosophy, combined with the cabalistical philosophy of the Jews, had given birth to Gnosticism. The relations which exist between this doctrine and the records which remain to us of that of the Orientals, the Chaldean and Persian, have been the source of the errors of the Gnostic Christians, who wished to reconcile their ancient notions with their new belief. It is on this account that, denying the human nature of Christ, they also denied his intimate union with God, and took him for one of the substances (aeons) created by God. As they believed in the eternity of matter, and considered it to be the principle of evil, in opposition to the Deity, the first cause and principle of good, they were unwilling to admit that one of the pure substances, one of the aeons which came forth from God, had, by partaking in the material nature, allied himself to the principle of evil; and this was their motive for rejecting the real humanity of Jesus Christ. See Ch. G. F. Walch, Hist. of Heresies in Germ. t. i. p. 217, sqq. Brucker, Hist. Crit. Phil. ii. p 639—G.]

[Footnote 28: Apostolis adhuc in saeculo superstitibus apud Judaeam Christi sanguine recente, et phanlasma corpus Domini asserebatur. Cotelerius thinks (Patres Apostol. tom. ii. p. 24) that those who will not allow the Docetes to have arisen in the time of the Apostles, may with equal reason deny that the sun shines at noonday. These Docetes, who formed the most considerable party among the Gnostics, were so called, because they granted only a seeming body to Christ. Note: The name of Docetae was given to these sectaries only in the course of the second century: this name did not designate a sect, properly so called; it applied to all the sects who taught the non- reality of the material body of Christ; of this number were the Valentinians, the Basilidians, the Ophites, the Marcionites, (against whom Tertullian wrote his book, De Carne Christi,) and other Gnostics. In truth, Clement of Alexandria (l. iii. Strom. c. 13, p. 552) makes express mention of a sect of Docetae, and even names as one of its heads a certain Cassianus; but every thing leads us to believe that it was not a distinct sect. Philastrius (de Haeres, c. 31) reproaches Saturninus with being a Docete. Irenaeus (adv. Haer. c. 23) makes the same reproach against Basilides. Epiphanius and Philastrius, who have treated in detail on each particular heresy, do not specially name that of the Docetae. Serapion, bishop of Antioch, (Euseb. Hist. Eccles. l. vi. c. 12,) and Clement of Alexandria, (l. vii. Strom. p. 900,) appear to be the first who have used the generic name. It is not found in any earlier record, though the error which it points out existed even in the time of the Apostles. See Ch. G. F. Walch, Hist. of Her. v. i. p. 283. Tillemont, Mempour servir a la Hist Eccles. ii. p. 50. Buddaeus de Eccles. Apost. c. 5 & 7—G.]

The divine sanction, which the Apostle had bestowed on the fundamental principle of the theology of Plato, encouraged the learned proselytes of the second and third centuries to admire and study the writings of the Athenian sage, who had thus marvellously anticipated one of the most surprising discoveries of the Christian revelation. The respectable name of Plato was used by the orthodox, [29] and abused by the heretics, [30] as the common support of truth and error: the authority of his skilful commentators, and the science of dialectics, were employed to justify the remote consequences of his opinions and to supply the discreet silence of the inspired writers. The same subtle and profound questions concerning the nature, the generation, the distinction, and the equality of the three divine persons of the mysterious Triad, or Trinity, [31] were agitated in the philosophical and in the Christian schools of Alexandria. An eager spirit of curiosity urged them to explore the secrets of the abyss; and the pride of the professors, and of their disciples, was satisfied with the sciences of words. But the most sagacious of the Christian theologians, the great Athanasius himself, has candidly confessed, [32] that whenever he forced his understanding to meditate on the divinity of the Logos, his toilsome and unavailing efforts recoiled on themselves; that the more he thought, the less he comprehended, and the more he wrote, the less capable was he of expressing his thoughts. In every step of the inquiry, we are compelled to feel and acknowledge the immeasurable disproportion between the size of the object and the capacity of the human mind. We may strive to abstract the notions of time, of space, and of matter, which so closely adhere to all the perceptions of our experimental knowledge. But as soon as we presume to reason of infinite substance, of spiritual generation; as often as we deduce any positive conclusions from a negative idea, we are involved in darkness, perplexity, and inevitable contradiction. As these difficulties arise from the nature of the subject, they oppress, with the same insuperable weight, the philosophic and the theological disputant; but we may observe two essential and peculiar circumstances, which discriminated the doctrines of the Catholic church from the opinions of the Platonic school.

[Footnote 29: Some proofs of the respect which the Christians entertained for the person and doctrine of Plato may be found in De la Mothe le Vayer, tom. v. p. 135, &c., edit. 1757; and Basnage, Hist. des Juifs tom. iv. p. 29, 79, &c.]

[Footnote 30: Doleo bona fide, Platonem omnium heraeticorum condimentarium factum. Tertullian. de Anima, c. 23. Petavius (Dogm. Theolog. tom. iii. proleg. 2) shows that this was a general complaint. Beausobre (tom. i. l. iii. c. 9, 10) has deduced the Gnostic errors from Platonic principles; and as, in the school of Alexandria, those principles were blended with the Oriental philosophy, (Brucker, tom. i. p. 1356,) the sentiment of Beausobre may be reconciled with the opinion of Mosheim, (General History of the Church, vol. i. p. 37.)]

[Footnote 31: If Theophilus, bishop of Antioch, (see Dupin, Bibliotheque Ecclesiastique, tom. i. p. 66,) was the first who employed the word Triad, Trinity, that abstract term, which was already familiar to the schools of philosophy, must have been introduced into the theology of the Christians after the middle of the second century.]

[Footnote 32: Athanasius, tom. i. p. 808. His expressions have an uncommon energy; and as he was writing to monks, there could not be any occasion for him to affect a rational language.]

I. A chosen society of philosophers, men of a liberal education and curious disposition, might silently meditate, and temperately discuss in the gardens of Athens or the library of Alexandria, the abstruse questions of metaphysical science. The lofty speculations, which neither convinced the understanding, nor agitated the passions, of the Platonists themselves, were carelessly overlooked by the idle, the busy, and even the studious part of mankind. [33] But after the Logos had been revealed as the sacred object of the faith, the hope, and the religious worship of the Christians, the mysterious system was embraced by a numerous and increasing multitude in every province of the Roman world. Those persons who, from their age, or sex, or occupations, were the least qualified to judge, who were the least exercised in the habits of abstract reasoning, aspired to contemplate the economy of the Divine Nature: and it is the boast of Tertullian, [34] that a Christian mechanic could readily answer such questions as had perplexed the wisest of the Grecian sages. Where the subject lies so far beyond our reach, the difference between the highest and the lowest of human understandings may indeed be calculated as infinitely small; yet the degree of weakness may perhaps be measured by the degree of obstinacy and dogmatic confidence. These speculations, instead of being treated as the amusement of a vacant hour, became the most serious business of the present, and the most useful preparation for a future, life. A theology, which it was incumbent to believe, which it was impious to doubt, and which it might be dangerous, and even fatal, to mistake, became the familiar topic of private meditation and popular discourse. The cold indifference of philosophy was inflamed by the fervent spirit of devotion; and even the metaphors of common language suggested the fallacious prejudices of sense and experience. The Christians, who abhorred the gross and impure generation of the Greek mythology, [35] were tempted to argue from the familiar analogy of the filial and paternal relations. The character of Son seemed to imply a perpetual subordination to the voluntary author of his existence; [36] but as the act of generation, in the most spiritual and abstracted sense, must be supposed to transmit the properties of a common nature, [37] they durst not presume to circumscribe the powers or the duration of the Son of an eternal and omnipotent Father. Fourscore years after the death of Christ, the Christians of Bithynia, declared before the tribunal of Pliny, that they invoked him as a god: and his divine honors have been perpetuated in every age and country, by the various sects who assume the name of his disciples. [38] Their tender reverence for the memory of Christ, and their horror for the profane worship of any created being, would have engaged them to assert the equal and absolute divinity of the Logos, if their rapid ascent towards the throne of heaven had not been imperceptibly checked by the apprehension of violating the unity and sole supremacy of the great Father of Christ and of the Universe. The suspense and fluctuation produced in the minds of the Christians by these opposite tendencies, may be observed in the writings of the theologians who flourished after the end of the apostolic age, and before the origin of the Arian controversy. Their suffrage is claimed, with equal confidence, by the orthodox and by the heretical parties; and the most inquisitive critics have fairly allowed, that if they had the good fortune of possessing the Catholic verity, they have delivered their conceptions in loose, inaccurate, and sometimes contradictory language. [39]

[Footnote 33: In a treatise, which professed to explain the opinions of the ancient philosophers concerning the nature of the gods we might expect to discover the theological Trinity of Plato. But Cicero very honestly confessed, that although he had translated the Timaeus, he could never understand that mysterious dialogue. See Hieronym. praef. ad l. xii. in Isaiam, tom. v. p. 154.]

[Footnote 34: Tertullian. in Apolog. c. 46. See Bayle, Dictionnaire, au mot Simonide. His remarks on the presumption of Tertullian are profound and interesting.]

[Footnote 35: Lactantius, iv. 8. Yet the Probole, or Prolatio, which the most orthodox divines borrowed without scruple from the Valentinians, and illustrated by the comparisons of a fountain and stream, the sun and its rays, &c., either meant nothing, or favored a material idea of the divine generation. See Beausobre, tom. i. l. iii. c. 7, p. 548.]

[Footnote 36: Many of the primitive writers have frankly confessed, that the Son owed his being to the will of the Father—See Clarke's Scripture Trinity, p. 280-287. On the other hand, Athanasius and his followers seem unwilling to grant what they are afraid to deny. The schoolmen extricate themselves from this difficulty by the distinction of a preceding and a concomitant will. Petav. Dogm. Theolog. tom. ii. l. vi. c. 8, p. 587-603.]

[Footnote 37: See Petav. Dogm. Theolog. tom. ii. l. ii. c. 10, p. 159.]

[Footnote 38: Carmenque Christo quasi Deo dicere secum invicem. Plin. Epist. x. 97. The sense of Deus, Elohim, in the ancient languages, is critically examined by Le Clerc, (Ars Critica, p. 150-156,) and the propriety of worshipping a very excellent creature is ably defended by the Socinian Emlyn, (Tracts, p. 29-36, 51-145.)]

[Footnote 39: See Daille de Usu Patrum, and Le Clerc, Bibliotheque Universelle, tom. x. p. 409. To arraign the faith of the Ante-Nicene fathers, was the object, or at least has been the effect, of the stupendous work of Petavius on the Trinity, (Dogm. Theolog. tom. ii.;) nor has the deep impression been erased by the learned defence of Bishop Bull. Note: Dr. Burton's work on the doctrine of the Ante-Nicene fathers must be consulted by those who wish to obtain clear notions on this subject—M.]

II. The devotion of individuals was the first circumstance which distinguished the Christians from the Platonists: the second was the authority of the church. The disciples of philosophy asserted the rights of intellectual freedom, and their respect for the sentiments of their teachers was a liberal and voluntary tribute, which they offered to superior reason. But the Christians formed a numerous and disciplined society; and the jurisdiction of their laws and magistrates was strictly exercised over the minds of the faithful. The loose wanderings of the imagination were gradually confined by creeds and confessions; [40] the freedom of private judgment submitted to the public wisdom of synods; the authority of a theologian was determined by his ecclesiastical rank; and the episcopal successors of the apostles inflicted the censures of the church on those who deviated from the orthodox belief. But in an age of religious controversy, every act of oppression adds new force to the elastic vigor of the mind; and the zeal or obstinacy of a spiritual rebel was sometimes stimulated by secret motives of ambition or avarice. A metaphysical argument became the cause or pretence of political contests; the subtleties of the Platonic school were used as the badges of popular factions, and the distance which separated their respective tenets were enlarged or magnified by the acrimony of dispute. As long as the dark heresies of Praxeas and Sabellius labored to confound the Father with the Son, [41] the orthodox party might be excused if they adhered more strictly and more earnestly to the distinction, than to the equality, of the divine persons. But as soon as the heat of controversy had subsided, and the progress of the Sabellians was no longer an object of terror to the churches of Rome, of Africa, or of Egypt, the tide of theological opinion began to flow with a gentle but steady motion towards the contrary extreme; and the most orthodox doctors allowed themselves the use of the terms and definitions which had been censured in the mouth of the sectaries. [42] After the edict of toleration had restored peace and leisure to the Christians, the Trinitarian controversy was revived in the ancient seat of Platonism, the learned, the opulent, the tumultuous city of Alexandria; and the flame of religious discord was rapidly communicated from the schools to the clergy, the people, the province, and the East. The abstruse question of the eternity of the Logos was agitated in ecclesiastic conferences and popular sermons; and the heterodox opinions of Arius [43] were soon made public by his own zeal, and by that of his adversaries. His most implacable adversaries have acknowledged the learning and blameless life of that eminent presbyter, who, in a former election, had declared, and perhaps generously declined, his pretensions to the episcopal throne. [44] His competitor Alexander assumed the office of his judge. The important cause was argued before him; and if at first he seemed to hesitate, he at length pronounced his final sentence, as an absolute rule of faith. [45] The undaunted presbyter, who presumed to resist the authority of his angry bishop, was separated from the community of the church. But the pride of Arius was supported by the applause of a numerous party. He reckoned among his immediate followers two bishops of Egypt, seven presbyters, twelve deacons, and (what may appear almost incredible) seven hundred virgins. A large majority of the bishops of Asia appeared to support or favor his cause; and their measures were conducted by Eusebius of Caesarea, the most learned of the Christian prelates; and by Eusebius of Nicomedia, who had acquired the reputation of a statesman without forfeiting that of a saint. Synods in Palestine and Bithynia were opposed to the synods of Egypt. The attention of the prince and people was attracted by this theological dispute; and the decision, at the end of six years, [46] was referred to the supreme authority of the general council of Nice.

[Footnote 40: The most ancient creeds were drawn up with the greatest latitude. See Bull, (Judicium Eccles. Cathol.,) who tries to prevent Episcopius from deriving any advantage from this observation.]

[Footnote 41: The heresies of Praxeas, Sabellius, &c., are accurately explained by Mosheim (p. 425, 680-714.) Praxeas, who came to Rome about the end of the second century, deceived, for some time, the simplicity of the bishop, and was confuted by the pen of the angry Tertullian.]

[Footnote 42: Socrates acknowledges, that the heresy of Arius proceeded from his strong desire to embrace an opinion the most diametrically opposite to that of Sabellius.]

[Footnote 43: The figure and manners of Arius, the character and numbers of his first proselytes, are painted in very lively colors by Epiphanius, (tom. i. Haeres. lxix. 3, p. 729,) and we cannot but regret that he should soon forget the historian, to assume the task of controversy.]

[Footnote 44: See Philostorgius (l. i. c. 3,) and Godefroy's ample Commentary. Yet the credibility of Philostorgius is lessened, in the eyes of the orthodox, by his Arianism; and in those of rational critics, by his passion, his prejudice, and his ignorance.]

[Footnote 45: Sozomen (l. i. c. 15) represents Alexander as indifferent, and even ignorant, in the beginning of the controversy; while Socrates (l. i. c. 5) ascribes the origin of the dispute to the vain curiosity of his theological speculations. Dr. Jortin (Remarks on Ecclesiastical History, vol. ii. p. 178) has censured, with his usual freedom, the conduct of Alexander.]

[Footnote 46: The flames of Arianism might burn for some time in secret; but there is reason to believe that they burst out with violence as early as the year 319. Tillemont, Mem. Eccles. tom. vi. p. 774-780.]

When the mysteries of the Christian faith were dangerously exposed to public debate, it might be observed, that the human understanding was capable of forming three district, though imperfect systems, concerning the nature of the Divine Trinity; and it was pronounced, that none of these systems, in a pure and absolute sense, were exempt from heresy and error. [47] I. According to the first hypothesis, which was maintained by Arius and his disciples, the Logos was a dependent and spontaneous production, created from nothing by the will of the father. The Son, by whom all things were made, [48] had been begotten before all worlds, and the longest of the astronomical periods could be compared only as a fleeting moment to the extent of his duration; yet this duration was not infinite, [49] and there had been a time which preceded the ineffable generation of the Logos. On this only-begotten Son, the Almighty Father had transfused his ample spirit, and impressed the effulgence of his glory. Visible image of invisible perfection, he saw, at an immeasurable distance beneath his feet, the thrones of the brightest archangels; yet he shone only with a reflected light, and, like the sons of the Romans emperors, who were invested with the titles of Caesar or Augustus, [50] he governed the universe in obedience to the will of his Father and Monarch. II. In the second hypothesis, the Logos possessed all the inherent, incommunicable perfections, which religion and philosophy appropriate to the Supreme God. Three distinct and infinite minds or substances, three coequal and coeternal beings, composed the Divine Essence; [51] and it would have implied contradiction, that any of them should not have existed, or that they should ever cease to exist. [52] The advocates of a system which seemed to establish three independent Deities, attempted to preserve the unity of the First Cause, so conspicuous in the design and order of the world, by the perpetual concord of their administration, and the essential agreement of their will. A faint resemblance of this unity of action may be discovered in the societies of men, and even of animals. The causes which disturb their harmony, proceed only from the imperfection and inequality of their faculties; but the omnipotence which is guided by infinite wisdom and goodness, cannot fail of choosing the same means for the accomplishment of the same ends. III. Three beings, who, by the self-derived necessity of their existence, possess all the divine attributes in the most perfect degree; who are eternal in duration, infinite in space, and intimately present to each other, and to the whole universe; irresistibly force themselves on the astonished mind, as one and the same being, [53] who, in the economy of grace, as well as in that of nature, may manifest himself under different forms, and be considered under different aspects. By this hypothesis, a real substantial trinity is refined into a trinity of names, and abstract modifications, that subsist only in the mind which conceives them. The Logos is no longer a person, but an attribute; and it is only in a figurative sense that the epithet of Son can be applied to the eternal reason, which was with God from the beginning, and by which, not by whom, all things were made. The incarnation of the Logos is reduced to a mere inspiration of the Divine Wisdom, which filled the soul, and directed all the actions, of the man Jesus. Thus, after revolving around the theological circle, we are surprised to find that the Sabellian ends where the Ebionite had begun; and that the incomprehensible mystery which excites our adoration, eludes our inquiry. [54]

[Footnote 47: Quid credidit? Certe, aut tria nomina audiens tres Deos esse credidit, et idololatra effectus est; aut in tribus vocabulis trinominem credens Deum, in Sabellii haeresim incurrit; aut edoctus ab Arianis unum esse verum Deum Patrem, filium et spiritum sanctum credidit creaturas. Aut extra haec quid credere potuerit nescio. Hieronym adv. Luciferianos. Jerom reserves for the last the orthodox system, which is more complicated and difficult.]

[Footnote 48: As the doctrine of absolute creation from nothing was gradually introduced among the Christians, (Beausobre, tom. ii. p. 165- 215,) the dignity of the workman very naturally rose with that of the work.]

[Footnote 49: The metaphysics of Dr. Clarke (Scripture Trinity, p. 276-280) could digest an eternal generation from an infinite cause.]

[Footnote 50: This profane and absurd simile is employed by several of the primitive fathers, particularly by Athenagoras, in his Apology to the emperor Marcus and his son; and it is alleged, without censure, by Bull himself. See Defens. Fid. Nicen. sect. iii. c. 5, No. 4.]

[Footnote 51: See Cudworth's Intellectual System, p. 559, 579. This dangerous hypothesis was countenanced by the two Gregories, of Nyssa and Nazianzen, by Cyril of Alexandria, John of Damascus, &c. See Cudworth, p. 603. Le Clerc, Bibliotheque Universelle, tom xviii. p. 97-105.]

[Footnote 52: Augustin seems to envy the freedom of the Philosophers. Liberis verbis loquuntur philosophi.... Nos autem non dicimus duo vel tria principia, duos vel tres Deos. De Civitat. Dei, x. 23.]

[Footnote 53: Boetius, who was deeply versed in the philosophy of Plato and Aristotle, explains the unity of the Trinity by the indifference of the three persons. See the judicious remarks of Le Clerc, Bibliotheque Choisie, tom. xvi. p. 225, &c.]

[Footnote 54: If the Sabellians were startled at this conclusion, they were driven another precipice into the confession, that the Father was born of a virgin, that he had suffered on the cross; and thus deserved the epithet of Patripassians, with which they were branded by their adversaries. See the invectives of Tertullian against Praxeas, and the temperate reflections of Mosheim, (p. 423, 681;) and Beausobre, tom. i. l. iii. c. 6, p. 533.]

If the bishops of the council of Nice [55] had been permitted to follow the unbiased dictates of their conscience, Arius and his associates could scarcely have flattered themselves with the hopes of obtaining a majority of votes, in favor of an hypothesis so directly averse to the two most popular opinions of the Catholic world. The Arians soon perceived the danger of their situation, and prudently assumed those modest virtues, which, in the fury of civil and religious dissensions, are seldom practised, or even praised, except by the weaker party. They recommended the exercise of Christian charity and moderation; urged the incomprehensible nature of the controversy, disclaimed the use of any terms or definitions which could not be found in the Scriptures; and offered, by very liberal concessions, to satisfy their adversaries without renouncing the integrity of their own principles. The victorious faction received all their proposals with haughty suspicion; and anxiously sought for some irreconcilable mark of distinction, the rejection of which might involve the Arians in the guilt and consequences of heresy. A letter was publicly read, and ignominiously torn, in which their patron, Eusebius of Nicomedia, ingenuously confessed, that the admission of the Homoousion, or Consubstantial, a word already familiar to the Platonists, was incompatible with the principles of their theological system. The fortunate opportunity was eagerly embraced by the bishops, who governed the resolutions of the synod; and, according to the lively expression of Ambrose, [56] they used the sword, which heresy itself had drawn from the scabbard, to cut off the head of the hated monster. The consubstantiality of the Father and the Son was established by the council of Nice, and has been unanimously received as a fundamental article of the Christian faith, by the consent of the Greek, the Latin, the Oriental, and the Protestant churches. But if the same word had not served to stigmatize the heretics, and to unite the Catholics, it would have been inadequate to the purpose of the majority, by whom it was introduced into the orthodox creed. This majority was divided into two parties, distinguished by a contrary tendency to the sentiments of the Tritheists and of the Sabellians. But as those opposite extremes seemed to overthrow the foundations either of natural or revealed religion, they mutually agreed to qualify the rigor of their principles; and to disavow the just, but invidious, consequences, which might be urged by their antagonists. The interest of the common cause inclined them to join their numbers, and to conceal their differences; their animosity was softened by the healing counsels of toleration, and their disputes were suspended by the use of the mysterious Homoousion, which either party was free to interpret according to their peculiar tenets. The Sabellian sense, which, about fifty years before, had obliged the council of Antioch [57] to prohibit this celebrated term, had endeared it to those theologians who entertained a secret but partial affection for a nominal Trinity. But the more fashionable saints of the Arian times, the intrepid Athanasius, the learned Gregory Nazianzen, and the other pillars of the church, who supported with ability and success the Nicene doctrine, appeared to consider the expression of substance as if it had been synonymous with that of nature; and they ventured to illustrate their meaning, by affirming that three men, as they belong to the same common species, are consubstantial, or homoousian to each other. [58] This pure and distinct equality was tempered, on the one hand, by the internal connection, and spiritual penetration which indissolubly unites the divine persons; [59] and, on the other, by the preeminence of the Father, which was acknowledged as far as it is compatible with the independence of the Son. [60] Within these limits, the almost invisible and tremulous ball of orthodoxy was allowed securely to vibrate. On either side, beyond this consecrated ground, the heretics and the daemons lurked in ambush to surprise and devour the unhappy wanderer. But as the degrees of theological hatred depend on the spirit of the war, rather than on the importance of the controversy, the heretics who degraded, were treated with more severity than those who annihilated, the person of the Son. The life of Athanasius was consumed in irreconcilable opposition to the impious madness of the Arians; [61] but he defended above twenty years the Sabellianism of Marcellus of Ancyra; and when at last he was compelled to withdraw himself from his communion, he continued to mention, with an ambiguous smile, the venial errors of his respectable friend. [62]

[Footnote 55: The transactions of the council of Nice are related by the ancients, not only in a partial, but in a very imperfect manner. Such a picture as Fra Paolo would have drawn, can never be recovered; but such rude sketches as have been traced by the pencil of bigotry, and that of reason, may be seen in Tillemont, (Mem. Eccles. tom. v. p. 669-759,) and in Le Clerc, (Bibliotheque Universelle, tom. x p. 435-454.)]

[Footnote 56: We are indebted to Ambrose (De Fide, l. iii.) knowledge of this curious anecdote. Hoc verbum quod viderunt adversariis esse formidini; ut ipsis gladio, ipsum nefandae caput haereseos.]

[Footnote 57: See Bull, Defens. Fid. Nicen. sect. ii. c. i. p. 25-36. He thinks it his duty to reconcile two orthodox synods.]

[Footnote 58: According to Aristotle, the stars were homoousian to each other. "That Homoousios means of one substance in kind, hath been shown by Petavius, Curcellaeus, Cudworth, Le Clerc, &c., and to prove it would be actum agere." This is the just remark of Dr. Jortin, (vol. ii p. 212,) who examines the Arian controversy with learning, candor, and ingenuity.]

[Footnote 59: See Petavius, (Dogm. Theolog. tom. ii. l. iv. c. 16, p. 453, &c.,) Cudworth, (p. 559,) Bull, (sect. iv. p. 285-290, edit. Grab.) The circumincessio, is perhaps the deepest and darkest he whole theological abyss.]

[Footnote 60: The third section of Bull's Defence of the Nicene Faith, which some of his antagonists have called nonsense, and others heresy, is consecrated to the supremacy of the Father.]

[Footnote 61: The ordinary appellation with which Athanasius and his followers chose to compliment the Arians, was that of Ariomanites.]

[Footnote 62: Epiphanius, tom i. Haeres. lxxii. 4, p. 837. See the adventures of Marcellus, in Tillemont, (Mem. Eccles. tom. v. i. p. 880- 899.) His work, in one book, of the unity of God, was answered in the three books, which are still extant, of Eusebius—After a long and careful examination, Petavius (tom. ii. l. i. c. 14, p. 78) has reluctantly pronounced the condemnation of Marcellus.]

The authority of a general council, to which the Arians themselves had been compelled to submit, inscribed on the banners of the orthodox party the mysterious characters of the word Homoousion, which essentially contributed, notwithstanding some obscure disputes, some nocturnal combats, to maintain and perpetuate the uniformity of faith, or at least of language. The consubstantialists, who by their success have deserved and obtained the title of Catholics, gloried in the simplicity and steadiness of their own creed, and insulted the repeated variations of their adversaries, who were destitute of any certain rule of faith. The sincerity or the cunning of the Arian chiefs, the fear of the laws or of the people, their reverence for Christ, their hatred of Athanasius, all the causes, human and divine, that influence and disturb the counsels of a theological faction, introduced among the sectaries a spirit of discord and inconstancy, which, in the course of a few years, erected eighteen different models of religion, [63] and avenged the violated dignity of the church. The zealous Hilary, [64] who, from the peculiar hardships of his situation, was inclined to extenuate rather than to aggravate the errors of the Oriental clergy, declares, that in the wide extent of the ten provinces of Asia, to which he had been banished, there could be found very few prelates who had preserved the knowledge of the true God. [65] The oppression which he had felt, the disorders of which he was the spectator and the victim, appeased, during a short interval, the angry passions of his soul; and in the following passage, of which I shall transcribe a few lines, the bishop of Poitiers unwarily deviates into the style of a Christian philosopher. "It is a thing," says Hilary, "equally deplorable and dangerous, that there are as many creeds as opinions among men, as many doctrines as inclinations, and as many sources of blasphemy as there are faults among us; because we make creeds arbitrarily, and explain them as arbitrarily. The Homoousion is rejected, and received, and explained away by successive synods. The partial or total resemblance of the Father and of the Son is a subject of dispute for these unhappy times. Every year, nay, every moon, we make new creeds to describe invisible mysteries. We repent of what we have done, we defend those who repent, we anathematize those whom we defended. We condemn either the doctrine of others in ourselves, or our own in that of others; and reciprocally tearing one another to pieces, we have been the cause of each other's ruin." [66]

[Footnote 63: Athanasius, in his epistle concerning the Synods of Seleucia and Rimini, (tom. i. p. 886-905,) has given an ample list of Arian creeds, which has been enlarged and improved by the labors of the indefatigable Tillemont, (Mem. Eccles. tom. vi. p. 477.)]

[Footnote 64: Erasmus, with admirable sense and freedom, has delineated the just character of Hilary. To revise his text, to compose the annals of his life, and to justify his sentiments and conduct, is the province of the Benedictine editors.]

[Footnote 65: Absque episcopo Eleusio et paucis cum eo, ex majore parte Asianae decem provinciae, inter quas consisto, vere Deum nesciunt. Atque utinam penitus nescirent! cum procliviore enim venia ignorarent quam obtrectarent. Hilar. de Synodis, sive de Fide Orientalium, c. 63, p. 1186, edit. Benedict. In the celebrated parallel between atheism and superstition, the bishop of Poitiers would have been surprised in the philosophic society of Bayle and Plutarch.]

[Footnote 66: Hilarius ad Constantium, l. i. c. 4, 5, p. 1227, 1228. This remarkable passage deserved the attention of Mr. Locke, who has transcribed it (vol. iii. p. 470) into the model of his new common-place book.]

It will not be expected, it would not perhaps be endured, that I should swell this theological digression, by a minute examination of the eighteen creeds, the authors of which, for the most part, disclaimed the odious name of their parent Arius. It is amusing enough to delineate the form, and to trace the vegetation, of a singular plant; but the tedious detail of leaves without flowers, and of branches without fruit, would soon exhaust the patience, and disappoint the curiosity, of the laborious student. One question, which gradually arose from the Arian controversy, may, however, be noticed, as it served to produce and discriminate the three sects, who were united only by their common aversion to the Homoousion of the Nicene synod. 1. If they were asked whether the Son was like unto the Father, the question was resolutely answered in the negative, by the heretics who adhered to the principles of Arius, or indeed to those of philosophy; which seem to establish an infinite difference between the Creator and the most excellent of his creatures. This obvious consequence was maintained by Aetius, [67] on whom the zeal of his adversaries bestowed the surname of the Atheist. His restless and aspiring spirit urged him to try almost every profession of human life. He was successively a slave, or at least a husbandman, a travelling tinker, a goldsmith, a physician, a schoolmaster, a theologian, and at last the apostle of a new church, which was propagated by the abilities of his disciple Eunomius. [68] Armed with texts of Scripture, and with captious syllogisms from the logic of Aristotle, the subtle Aetius had acquired the fame of an invincible disputant, whom it was impossible either to silence or to convince. Such talents engaged the friendship of the Arian bishops, till they were forced to renounce, and even to persecute, a dangerous ally, who, by the accuracy of his reasoning, had prejudiced their cause in the popular opinion, and offended the piety of their most devoted followers. 2. The omnipotence of the Creator suggested a specious and respectful solution of the likeness of the Father and the Son; and faith might humbly receive what reason could not presume to deny, that the Supreme God might communicate his infinite perfections, and create a being similar only to himself. [69] These Arians were powerfully supported by the weight and abilities of their leaders, who had succeeded to the management of the Eusebian interest, and who occupied the principal thrones of the East. They detested, perhaps with some affectation, the impiety of Aetius; they professed to believe, either without reserve, or according to the Scriptures, that the Son was different from all other creatures, and similar only to the Father. But they denied, the he was either of the same, or of a similar substance; sometimes boldly justifying their dissent, and sometimes objecting to the use of the word substance, which seems to imply an adequate, or at least, a distinct, notion of the nature of the Deity. 3. The sect which deserted the doctrine of a similar substance, was the most numerous, at least in the provinces of Asia; and when the leaders of both parties were assembled in the council of Seleucia, [70] their opinion would have prevailed by a majority of one hundred and five to forty-three bishops. The Greek word, which was chosen to express this mysterious resemblance, bears so close an affinity to the orthodox symbol, that the profane of every age have derided the furious contests which the difference of a single diphthong excited between the Homoousians and the Homoiousians. As it frequently happens, that the sounds and characters which approach the nearest to each other accidentally represent the most opposite ideas, the observation would be itself ridiculous, if it were possible to mark any real and sensible distinction between the doctrine of the Semi-Arians, as they were improperly styled, and that of the Catholics themselves. The bishop of Poitiers, who in his Phrygian exile very wisely aimed at a coalition of parties, endeavors to prove that by a pious and faithful interpretation, [71] the Homoiousion may be reduced to a consubstantial sense. Yet he confesses that the word has a dark and suspicious aspect; and, as if darkness were congenial to theological disputes, the Semi-Arians, who advanced to the doors of the church, assailed them with the most unrelenting fury.

[Footnote 67: In Philostorgius (l. iii. c. 15) the character and adventures of Aetius appear singular enough, though they are carefully softened by the hand of a friend. The editor, Godefroy, (p. 153,) who was more attached to his principles than to his author, has collected the odious circumstances which his various adversaries have preserved or invented.]

[Footnote 68: According to the judgment of a man who respected both these sectaries, Aetius had been endowed with a stronger understanding and Eunomius had acquired more art and learning. (Philostorgius l. viii. c. 18.) The confession and apology of Eunomius (Fabricius, Bibliot. Graec. tom. viii. p. 258-305) is one of the few heretical pieces which have escaped.]

[Footnote 69: Yet, according to the opinion of Estius and Bull, (p. 297,) there is one power—that of creation—which God cannot communicate to a creature. Estius, who so accurately defined the limits of Omnipotence was a Dutchman by birth, and by trade a scholastic divine. Dupin Bibliot. Eccles. tom. xvii. p. 45.]

[Footnote 70: Sabinus ap. Socrat. (l. ii. c. 39) had copied the acts: Athanasius and Hilary have explained the divisions of this Arian synod; the other circumstances which are relative to it are carefully collected by Baro and Tillemont]

[Footnote 71: Fideli et pia intelligentia... De Synod. c. 77, p. 1193. In his his short apologetical notes (first published by the Benedictines from a MS. of Chartres) he observes, that he used this cautious expression, qui intelligerum et impiam, p. 1206. See p. 1146. Philostorgius, who saw those objects through a different medium, is inclined to forget the difference of the important diphthong. See in particular viii. 17, and Godefroy, p. 352.]

The provinces of Egypt and Asia, which cultivated the language and manners of the Greeks, had deeply imbibed the venom of the Arian controversy. The familiar study of the Platonic system, a vain and argumentative disposition, a copious and flexible idiom, supplied the clergy and people of the East with an inexhaustible flow of words and distinctions; and, in the midst of their fierce contentions, they easily forgot the doubt which is recommended by philosophy, and the submission which is enjoined by religion. The inhabitants of the West were of a less inquisitive spirit; their passions were not so forcibly moved by invisible objects, their minds were less frequently exercised by the habits of dispute; and such was the happy ignorance of the Gallican church, that Hilary himself, above thirty years after the first general council, was still a stranger to the Nicene creed. [72] The Latins had received the rays of divine knowledge through the dark and doubtful medium of a translation. The poverty and stubbornness of their native tongue was not always capable of affording just equivalents for the Greek terms, for the technical words of the Platonic philosophy, [73] which had been consecrated, by the gospel or by the church, to express the mysteries of the Christian faith; and a verbal defect might introduce into the Latin theology a long train of error or perplexity. [74] But as the western provincials had the good fortune of deriving their religion from an orthodox source, they preserved with steadiness the doctrine which they had accepted with docility; and when the Arian pestilence approached their frontiers, they were supplied with the seasonable preservative of the Homoousion, by the paternal care of the Roman pontiff. Their sentiments and their temper were displayed in the memorable synod of Rimini, which surpassed in numbers the council of Nice, since it was composed of above four hundred bishops of Italy, Africa, Spain, Gaul, Britain, and Illyricum. From the first debates it appeared, that only fourscore prelates adhered to the party, though they affected to anathematize the name and memory, of Arius. But this inferiority was compensated by the advantages of skill, of experience, and of discipline; and the minority was conducted by Valens and Ursacius, two bishops of Illyricum, who had spent their lives in the intrigues of courts and councils, and who had been trained under the Eusebian banner in the religious wars of the East. By their arguments and negotiations, they embarrassed, they confounded, they at last deceived, the honest simplicity of the Latin bishops; who suffered the palladium of the faith to be extorted from their hand by fraud and importunity, rather than by open violence. The council of Rimini was not allowed to separate, till the members had imprudently subscribed a captious creed, in which some expressions, susceptible of an heretical sense, were inserted in the room of the Homoousion. It was on this occasion, that, according to Jerom, the world was surprised to find itself Arian. [75] But the bishops of the Latin provinces had no sooner reached their respective dioceses, than they discovered their mistake, and repented of their weakness. The ignominious capitulation was rejected with disdain and abhorrence; and the Homoousian standard, which had been shaken but not overthrown, was more firmly replanted in all the churches of the West. [76]

[Footnote 72: Testor Deumcoeli atque terrae me cum neutrum audissem, semper tamen utrumque sensisse.... Regeneratus pridem et in episcopatu aliquantisper manens fidem Nicenam nunquam nisi exsulaturus audivi. Hilar. de Synodis, c. xci. p. 1205. The Benedictines are persuaded that he governed the diocese of Poitiers several years before his exile.]

[Footnote 73: Seneca (Epist. lviii.) complains that even the of the Platonists (the ens of the bolder schoolmen) could not be expressed by a Latin noun.]

[Footnote 74: The preference which the fourth council of the Lateran at length gave to a numerical rather than a generical unity (See Petav. tom. ii. l. v. c. 13, p. 424) was favored by the Latin language: seems to excite the idea of substance, trinitas of qualities.]

[Footnote 75: Ingemuit totus orbis, et Arianum se esse miratus est. Hieronym. adv. Lucifer. tom. i. p. 145.]

[Footnote 76: The story of the council of Rimini is very elegantly told by Sulpicius Severus, (Hist. Sacra, l. ii. p. 419-430, edit. Lugd. Bat. 1647,) and by Jerom, in his dialogue against the Luciferians. The design of the latter is to apologize for the conduct of the Latin bishops, who were deceived, and who repented.]

PART IV

Such was the rise and progress, and such were the natural revolutions of those theological disputes, which disturbed the peace of Christianity under the reigns of Constantine and of his sons. But as those princes presumed to extend their despotism over the faith, as well as over the lives and fortunes, of their subjects, the weight of their suffrage sometimes inclined the ecclesiastical balance: and the prerogatives of the King of Heaven were settled, or changed, or modified, in the cabinet of an earthly monarch. The unhappy spirit of discord which pervaded the provinces of the East, interrupted the triumph of Constantine; but the emperor continued for some time to view, with cool and careless indifference, the object of the dispute. As he was yet ignorant of the difficulty of appeasing the quarrels of theologians, he addressed to the contending parties, to Alexander and to Arius, a moderating epistle; [77] which may be ascribed, with far greater reason, to the untutored sense of a soldier and statesman, than to the dictates of any of his episcopal counsellors. He attributes the origin of the whole controversy to a trifling and subtle question, concerning an incomprehensible point of law, which was foolishly asked by the bishop, and imprudently resolved by the presbyter. He laments that the Christian people, who had the same God, the same religion, and the same worship, should be divided by such inconsiderable distinctions; and he seriously recommend to the clergy of Alexandria the example of the Greek philosophers; who could maintain their arguments without losing their temper, and assert their freedom without violating their friendship. The indifference and contempt of the sovereign would have been, perhaps, the most effectual method of silencing the dispute, if the popular current had been less rapid and impetuous, and if Constantine himself, in the midst of faction and fanaticism, could have preserved the calm possession of his own mind. But his ecclesiastical ministers soon contrived to seduce the impartiality of the magistrate, and to awaken the zeal of the proselyte. He was provoked by the insults which had been offered to his statues; he was alarmed by the real, as well as the imaginary magnitude of the spreading mischief; and he extinguished the hope of peace and toleration, from the moment that he assembled three hundred bishops within the walls of the same palace. The presence of the monarch swelled the importance of the debate; his attention multiplied the arguments; and he exposed his person with a patient intrepidity, which animated the valor of the combatants. Notwithstanding the applause which has been bestowed on the eloquence and sagacity of Constantine, [78] a Roman general, whose religion might be still a subject of doubt, and whose mind had not been enlightened either by study or by inspiration, was indifferently qualified to discuss, in the Greek language, a metaphysical question, or an article of faith. But the credit of his favorite Osius, who appears to have presided in the council of Nice, might dispose the emperor in favor of the orthodox party; and a well-timed insinuation, that the same Eusebius of Nicomedia, who now protected the heretic, had lately assisted the tyrant, [79] might exasperate him against their adversaries. The Nicene creed was ratified by Constantine; and his firm declaration, that those who resisted the divine judgment of the synod, must prepare themselves for an immediate exile, annihilated the murmurs of a feeble opposition; which, from seventeen, was almost instantly reduced to two, protesting bishops. Eusebius of Caesarea yielded a reluctant and ambiguous consent to the Homoousion; [80] and the wavering conduct of the Nicomedian Eusebius served only to delay, about three months, his disgrace and exile. [81] The impious Arius was banished into one of the remote provinces of Illyricum; his person and disciples were branded by law with the odious name of Porphyrians; his writings were condemned to the flames, and a capital punishment was denounced against those in whose possession they should be found. The emperor had now imbibed the spirit of controversy, and the angry, sarcastic style of his edicts was designed to inspire his subjects with the hatred which he had conceived against the enemies of Christ. [82]

[Footnote 77: Eusebius, in Vit. Constant. l. ii. c. 64-72. The principles of toleration and religious indifference, contained in this epistle, have given great offence to Baronius, Tillemont, &c., who suppose that the emperor had some evil counsellor, either Satan or Eusebius, at his elbow. See Cortin's Remarks, tom. ii. p. 183. Note: Heinichen (Excursus xi.) quotes with approbation the term "golden words," applied by Ziegler to this moderate and tolerant letter of Constantine. May an English clergyman venture to express his regret that "the fine gold soon became dim" in the Christian church?—M.]

[Footnote 78: Eusebius in Vit. Constantin. l. iii. c. 13.]

[Footnote 79: Theodoret has preserved (l. i. c. 20) an epistle from Constantine to the people of Nicomedia, in which the monarch declares himself the public accuser of one of his subjects; he styles Eusebius and complains of his hostile behavior during the civil war.]

[Footnote 80: See in Socrates, (l. i. c. 8,) or rather in Theodoret, (l. i. c. 12,) an original letter of Eusebius of Caesarea, in which he attempts to justify his subscribing the Homoousion. The character of Eusebius has always been a problem; but those who have read the second critical epistle of Le Clerc, (Ars Critica, tom. iii. p. 30-69,) must entertain a very unfavorable opinion of the orthodoxy and sincerity of the bishop of Caesarea.]

[Footnote 81: Athanasius, tom. i. p. 727. Philostorgius, l. i. c. 10, and Godefroy's Commentary, p. 41.]

[Footnote 82: Socrates, l. i. c. 9. In his circular letters, which were addressed to the several cities, Constantine employed against the heretics the arms of ridicule and comic raillery.]

But, as if the conduct of the emperor had been guided by passion instead of principle, three years from the council of Nice were scarcely elapsed before he discovered some symptoms of mercy, and even of indulgence, towards the proscribed sect, which was secretly protected by his favorite sister. The exiles were recalled, and Eusebius, who gradually resumed his influence over the mind of Constantine, was restored to the episcopal throne, from which he had been ignominiously degraded. Arius himself was treated by the whole court with the respect which would have been due to an innocent and oppressed man. His faith was approved by the synod of Jerusalem; and the emperor seemed impatient to repair his injustice, by issuing an absolute command, that he should be solemnly admitted to the communion in the cathedral of Constantinople. On the same day, which had been fixed for the triumph of Arius, he expired; and the strange and horrid circumstances of his death might excite a suspicion, that the orthodox saints had contributed more efficaciously than by their prayers, to deliver the church from the most formidable of her enemies [83] The three principal leaders of the Catholics, Athanasius of Alexandria, Eustathius of Antioch, and Paul of Constantinople were deposed on various f accusations, by the sentence of numerous councils; and were afterwards banished into distant provinces by the first of the Christian emperors, who, in the last moments of his life, received the rites of baptism from the Arian bishop of Nicomedia. The ecclesiastical government of Constantine cannot be justified from the reproach of levity and weakness. But the credulous monarch, unskilled in the stratagems of theological warfare, might be deceived by the modest and specious professions of the heretics, whose sentiments he never perfectly understood; and while he protected Arius, and persecuted Athanasius, he still considered the council of Nice as the bulwark of the Christian faith, and the peculiar glory of his own reign. [84]

[Footnote 83: We derive the original story from Athanasius, (tom. i. p. 670,) who expresses some reluctance to stigmatize the memory of the dead. He might exaggerate; but the perpetual commerce of Alexandria and Constantinople would have rendered it dangerous to invent. Those who press the literal narrative of the death of Arius (his bowels suddenly burst out in a privy) must make their option between poison and miracle.]

[Footnote 84: The change in the sentiments, or at least in the conduct, of Constantine, may be traced in Eusebius, (in Vit. Constant. l. iii. c. 23, l. iv. c. 41,) Socrates, (l. i. c. 23-39,) Sozomen, (l. ii. c. 16-34,) Theodoret, (l. i. c. 14-34,) and Philostorgius, (l. ii. c. 1-17.) But the first of these writers was too near the scene of action, and the others were too remote from it. It is singular enough, that the important task of continuing the history of the church should have been left for two laymen and a heretic.]

The sons of Constantine must have been admitted from their childhood into the rank of catechumens; but they imitated, in the delay of their baptism, the example of their father. Like him they presumed to pronounce their judgment on mysteries into which they had never been regularly initiated; [85] and the fate of the Trinitarian controversy depended, in a great measure, on the sentiments of Constantius; who inherited the provinces of the East, and acquired the possession of the whole empire. The Arian presbyter or bishop, who had secreted for his use the testament of the deceased emperor, improved the fortunate occasion which had introduced him to the familiarity of a prince, whose public counsels were always swayed by his domestic favorites. The eunuchs and slaves diffused the spiritual poison through the palace, and the dangerous infection was communicated by the female attendants to the guards, and by the empress to her unsuspicious husband. [86] The partiality which Constantius always expressed towards the Eusebian faction, was insensibly fortified by the dexterous management of their leaders; and his victory over the tyrant Magnentius increased his inclination, as well as ability, to employ the arms of power in the cause of Arianism. While the two armies were engaged in the plains of Mursa, and the fate of the two rivals depended on the chance of war, the son of Constantine passed the anxious moments in a church of the martyrs under the walls of the city. His spiritual comforter, Valens, the Arian bishop of the diocese, employed the most artful precautions to obtain such early intelligence as might secure either his favor or his escape. A secret chain of swift and trusty messengers informed him of the vicissitudes of the battle; and while the courtiers stood trembling round their affrighted master, Valens assured him that the Gallic legions gave way; and insinuated with some presence of mind, that the glorious event had been revealed to him by an angel. The grateful emperor ascribed his success to the merits and intercession of the bishop of Mursa, whose faith had deserved the public and miraculous approbation of Heaven. [87] The Arians, who considered as their own the victory of Constantius, preferred his glory to that of his father. [88] Cyril, bishop of Jerusalem, immediately composed the description of a celestial cross, encircled with a splendid rainbow; which during the festival of Pentecost, about the third hour of the day, had appeared over the Mount of Olives, to the edification of the devout pilgrims, and the people of the holy city. [89] The size of the meteor was gradually magnified; and the Arian historian has ventured to affirm, that it was conspicuous to the two armies in the plains of Pannonia; and that the tyrant, who is purposely represented as an idolater, fled before the auspicious sign of orthodox Christianity. [90]

[Footnote 85: Quia etiam tum catechumenus sacramentum fidei merito videretiu potuisse nescire. Sulp. Sever. Hist. Sacra, l. ii. p. 410.]

[Footnote 86: Socrates, l. ii. c. 2. Sozomen, l. iii. c. 18. Athanas. tom. i. p. 813, 834. He observes that the eunuchs are the natural enemies of the Son. Compare Dr. Jortin's Remarks on Ecclesiastical History, vol. iv. p. 3 with a certain genealogy in Candide, (ch. iv.,) which ends with one of the first companions of Christopher Columbus.]

[Footnote 87: Sulpicius Severus in Hist. Sacra, l. ii. p. 405, 406.]

[Footnote 88: Cyril (apud Baron. A. D. 353, No. 26) expressly observes that in the reign of Constantine, the cross had been found in the bowels of the earth; but that it had appeared, in the reign of Constantius, in the midst of the heavens. This opposition evidently proves, that Cyril was ignorant of the stupendous miracle to which the conversion of Constantine is attributed; and this ignorance is the more surprising, since it was no more than twelve years after his death that Cyril was consecrated bishop of Jerusalem, by the immediate successor of Eusebius of Caesarea. See Tillemont, Mem. Eccles. tom. viii. p. 715.]

[Footnote 89: It is not easy to determine how far the ingenuity of Cyril might be assisted by some natural appearances of a solar halo.]

[Footnote 90: Philostorgius, l. iii. c. 26. He is followed by the author of the Alexandrian Chronicle, by Cedrenus, and by Nicephorus. (See Gothofred. Dissert. p. 188.) They could not refuse a miracle, even from the hand of an enemy.]

The sentiments of a judicious stranger, who has impartially considered the progress of civil or ecclesiastical discord, are always entitled to our notice; and a short passage of Ammianus, who served in the armies, and studied the character of Constantius, is perhaps of more value than many pages of theological invectives. "The Christian religion, which, in itself," says that moderate historian, "is plain and simple, he confounded by the dotage of superstition. Instead of reconciling the parties by the weight of his authority, he cherished and promulgated, by verbal disputes, the differences which his vain curiosity had excited. The highways were covered with troops of bishops galloping from every side to the assemblies, which they call synods; and while they labored to reduce the whole sect to their own particular opinions, the public establishment of the posts was almost ruined by their hasty and repeated journeys." [91] Our more intimate knowledge of the ecclesiastical transactions of the reign of Constantius would furnish an ample commentary on this remarkable passage, which justifies the rational apprehensions of Athanasius, that the restless activity of the clergy, who wandered round the empire in search of the true faith, would excite the contempt and laughter of the unbelieving world. [92] As soon as the emperor was relieved from the terrors of the civil war, he devoted the leisure of his winter quarters at Arles, Milan, Sirmium, and Constantinople, to the amusement or toils of controversy: the sword of the magistrate, and even of the tyrant, was unsheathed, to enforce the reasons of the theologian; and as he opposed the orthodox faith of Nice, it is readily confessed that his incapacity and ignorance were equal to his presumption. [93] The eunuchs, the women, and the bishops, who governed the vain and feeble mind of the emperor, had inspired him with an insuperable dislike to the Homoousion; but his timid conscience was alarmed by the impiety of Aetius. The guilt of that atheist was aggravated by the suspicious favor of the unfortunate Gallus; and even the death of the Imperial ministers, who had been massacred at Antioch, were imputed to the suggestions of that dangerous sophist. The mind of Constantius, which could neither be moderated by reason, nor fixed by faith, was blindly impelled to either side of the dark and empty abyss, by his horror of the opposite extreme; he alternately embraced and condemned the sentiments, he successively banished and recalled the leaders, of the Arian and Semi-Arian factions. [94] During the season of public business or festivity, he employed whole days, and even nights, in selecting the words, and weighing the syllables, which composed his fluctuating creeds. The subject of his meditations still pursued and occupied his slumbers: the incoherent dreams of the emperor were received as celestial visions, and he accepted with complacency the lofty title of bishop of bishops, from those ecclesiastics who forgot the interest of their order for the gratification of their passions. The design of establishing a uniformity of doctrine, which had engaged him to convene so many synods in Gaul, Italy, Illyricum, and Asia, was repeatedly baffled by his own levity, by the divisions of the Arians, and by the resistance of the Catholics; and he resolved, as the last and decisive effort, imperiously to dictate the decrees of a general council. The destructive earthquake of Nicomedia, the difficulty of finding a convenient place, and perhaps some secret motives of policy, produced an alteration in the summons. The bishops of the East were directed to meet at Seleucia, in Isauria; while those of the West held their deliberations at Rimini, on the coast of the Hadriatic; and instead of two or three deputies from each province, the whole episcopal body was ordered to march. The Eastern council, after consuming four days in fierce and unavailing debate, separated without any definitive conclusion. The council of the West was protracted till the seventh month. Taurus, the Praetorian praefect was instructed not to dismiss the prelates till they should all be united in the same opinion; and his efforts were supported by the power of banishing fifteen of the most refractory, and a promise of the consulship if he achieved so difficult an adventure. His prayers and threats, the authority of the sovereign, the sophistry of Valens and Ursacius, the distress of cold and hunger, and the tedious melancholy of a hopeless exile, at length extorted the reluctant consent of the bishops of Rimini. The deputies of the East and of the West attended the emperor in the palace of Constantinople, and he enjoyed the satisfaction of imposing on the world a profession of faith which established the likeness, without expressing the consubstantiality, of the Son of God. [95] But the triumph of Arianism had been preceded by the removal of the orthodox clergy, whom it was impossible either to intimidate or to corrupt; and the reign of Constantius was disgraced by the unjust and ineffectual persecution of the great Athanasius.

[Footnote 91: So curious a passage well deserves to be transcribed. Christianam religionem absolutam et simplicem, anili superstitione confundens; in qua scrutanda perplexius, quam componenda gravius excitaret discidia plurima; quae progressa fusius aluit concertatione verborum, ut catervis antistium jumentis publicis ultro citroque discarrentibus, per synodos (quas appellant) dum ritum omnem ad suum sahere conantur (Valesius reads conatur) rei vehiculariae concideret servos. Ammianus, xxi. 16.]

[Footnote 92: Athanas. tom. i. p. 870.]

[Footnote 93: Socrates, l. ii. c. 35-47. Sozomen, l. iv. c. 12-30. Theodore li. c. 18-32. Philostorg. l. iv. c. 4— 12, l. v. c. 1-4, l. vi. c. 1-5]

[Footnote 94: Sozomen, l. iv. c. 23. Athanas. tom. i. p. 831. Tillemont (Mem Eccles. tom. vii. p. 947) has collected several instances of the haughty fanaticism of Constantius from the detached treatises of Lucifer of Cagliari. The very titles of these treaties inspire zeal and terror; "Moriendum pro Dei Filio." "De Regibus Apostaticis." "De non conveniendo cum Haeretico." "De non parcendo in Deum delinquentibus."]

[Footnote 95: Sulp. Sever. Hist. Sacra, l. ii. p. 418-430. The Greek historians were very ignorant of the affairs of the West.]

We have seldom an opportunity of observing, either in active or speculative life, what effect may be produced, or what obstacles may be surmounted, by the force of a single mind, when it is inflexibly applied to the pursuit of a single object. The immortal name of Athanasius [96] will never be separated from the Catholic doctrine of the Trinity, to whose defence he consecrated every moment and every faculty of his being. Educated in the family of Alexander, he had vigorously opposed the early progress of the Arian heresy: he exercised the important functions of secretary under the aged prelate; and the fathers of the Nicene council beheld with surprise and respect the rising virtues of the young deacon. In a time of public danger, the dull claims of age and of rank are sometimes superseded; and within five months after his return from Nice, the deacon Athanasius was seated on the archiepiscopal throne of Egypt. He filled that eminent station above forty-six years, and his long administration was spent in a perpetual combat against the powers of Arianism. Five times was Athanasius expelled from his throne; twenty years he passed as an exile or a fugitive: and almost every province of the Roman empire was successively witness to his merit, and his sufferings in the cause of the Homoousion, which he considered as the sole pleasure and business, as the duty, and as the glory of his life. Amidst the storms of persecution, the archbishop of Alexandria was patient of labor, jealous of fame, careless of safety; and although his mind was tainted by the contagion of fanaticism, Athanasius displayed a superiority of character and abilities, which would have qualified him, far better than the degenerate sons of Constantine, for the government of a great monarchy. His learning was much less profound and extensive than that of Eusebius of Caesarea, and his rude eloquence could not be compared with the polished oratory of Gregory of Basil; but whenever the primate of Egypt was called upon to justify his sentiments, or his conduct, his unpremeditated style, either of speaking or writing, was clear, forcible, and persuasive. He has always been revered, in the orthodox school, as one of the most accurate masters of the Christian theology; and he was supposed to possess two profane sciences, less adapted to the episcopal character, the knowledge of jurisprudence, [97] and that of divination. [98] Some fortunate conjectures of future events, which impartial reasoners might ascribe to the experience and judgment of Athanasius, were attributed by his friends to heavenly inspiration, and imputed by his enemies to infernal magic.

[Footnote 96: We may regret that Gregory Nazianzen composed a panegyric instead of a life of Athanasius; but we should enjoy and improve the advantage of drawing our most authentic materials from the rich fund of his own epistles and apologies, (tom. i. p. 670-951.) I shall not imitate the example of Socrates, (l. ii. c. l.) who published the first edition of the history, without giving himself the trouble to consult the writings of Athanasius. Yet even Socrates, the more curious Sozomen, and the learned Theodoret, connect the life of Athanasius with the series of ecclesiastical history. The diligence of Tillemont, (tom. viii,) and of the Benedictine editors, has collected every fact, and examined every difficulty]

[Footnote 97: Sulpicius Severus (Hist. Sacra, l. ii. p. 396) calls him a lawyer, a jurisconsult. This character cannot now be discovered either in the life or writings of Athanasius.]

[Footnote 98: Dicebatur enim fatidicarum sortium fidem, quaeve augurales portenderent alites scientissime callens aliquoties praedixisse futura. Ammianus, xv. 7. A prophecy, or rather a joke, is related by Sozomen, (l. iv c. 10,) which evidently proves (if the crows speak Latin) that Athanasius understood the language of the crows.]

But as Athanasius was continually engaged with the prejudices and passions of every order of men, from the monk to the emperor, the knowledge of human nature was his first and most important science. He preserved a distinct and unbroken view of a scene which was incessantly shifting; and never failed to improve those decisive moments which are irrecoverably past before they are perceived by a common eye. The archbishop of Alexandria was capable of distinguishing how far he might boldly command, and where he must dexterously insinuate; how long he might contend with power, and when he must withdraw from persecution; and while he directed the thunders of the church against heresy and rebellion, he could assume, in the bosom of his own party, the flexible and indulgent temper of a prudent leader. The election of Athanasius has not escaped the reproach of irregularity and precipitation; [99] but the propriety of his behavior conciliated the affections both of the clergy and of the people. The Alexandrians were impatient to rise in arms for the defence of an eloquent and liberal pastor. In his distress he always derived support, or at least consolation, from the faithful attachment of his parochial clergy; and the hundred bishops of Egypt adhered, with unshaken zeal, to the cause of Athanasius. In the modest equipage which pride and policy would affect, he frequently performed the episcopal visitation of his provinces, from the mouth of the Nile to the confines of Aethiopia; familiarly conversing with the meanest of the populace, and humbly saluting the saints and hermits of the desert. [100] Nor was it only in ecclesiastical assemblies, among men whose education and manners were similar to his own, that Athanasius displayed the ascendancy of his genius. He appeared with easy and respectful firmness in the courts of princes; and in the various turns of his prosperous and adverse fortune he never lost the confidence of his friends, or the esteem of his enemies.

[Footnote 99: The irregular ordination of Athanasius was slightly mentioned in the councils which were held against him. See Philostorg. l. ii. c. 11, and Godefroy, p. 71; but it can scarcely be supposed that the assembly of the bishops of Egypt would solemnly attest a public falsehood. Athanas. tom. i. p. 726.]

[Footnote 100: See the history of the Fathers of the Desert, published by Rosweide; and Tillemont, Mem. Eccles. tom. vii., in the lives of Antony, Pachomius, &c. Athanasius himself, who did not disdain to compose the life of his friend Antony, has carefully observed how often the holy monk deplored and prophesied the mischiefs of the Arian heresy Athanas. tom. ii. p. 492, 498, &c.]

In his youth, the primate of Egypt resisted the great Constantine, who had repeatedly signified his will, that Arius should be restored to the Catholic communion. [101] The emperor respected, and might forgive, this inflexible resolution; and the faction who considered Athanasius as their most formidable enemy, was constrained to dissemble their hatred, and silently to prepare an indirect and distant assault. They scattered rumors and suspicions, represented the archbishop as a proud and oppressive tyrant, and boldly accused him of violating the treaty which had been ratified in the Nicene council, with the schismatic followers of Meletius. [102] Athanasius had openly disapproved that ignominious peace, and the emperor was disposed to believe that he had abused his ecclesiastical and civil power, to prosecute those odious sectaries: that he had sacrilegiously broken a chalice in one of their churches of Mareotis; that he had whipped or imprisoned six of their bishops; and that Arsenius, a seventh bishop of the same party, had been murdered, or at least mutilated, by the cruel hand of the primate. [103] These charges, which affected his honor and his life, were referred by Constantine to his brother Dalmatius the censor, who resided at Antioch; the synods of Caesarea and Tyre were successively convened; and the bishops of the East were instructed to judge the cause of Athanasius, before they proceeded to consecrate the new church of the Resurrection at Jerusalem. The primate might be conscious of his innocence; but he was sensible that the same implacable spirit which had dictated the accusation, would direct the proceeding, and pronounce the sentence. He prudently declined the tribunal of his enemies; despised the summons of the synod of Caesarea; and, after a long and artful delay, submitted to the peremptory commands of the emperor, who threatened to punish his criminal disobedience if he refused to appear in the council of Tyre. [104] Before Athanasius, at the head of fifty Egyptian prelates, sailed from Alexandria, he had wisely secured the alliance of the Meletians; and Arsenius himself, his imaginary victim, and his secret friend, was privately concealed in his train. The synod of Tyre was conducted by Eusebius of Caesarea, with more passion, and with less art, than his learning and experience might promise; his numerous faction repeated the names of homicide and tyrant; and their clamors were encouraged by the seeming patience of Athanasius, who expected the decisive moment to produce Arsenius alive and unhurt in the midst of the assembly. The nature of the other charges did not admit of such clear and satisfactory replies; yet the archbishop was able to prove, that in the village, where he was accused of breaking a consecrated chalice, neither church nor altar nor chalice could really exist.

The Arians, who had secretly determined the guilt and condemnation of their enemy, attempted, however, to disguise their injustice by the imitation of judicial forms: the synod appointed an episcopal commission of six delegates to collect evidence on the spot; and this measure which was vigorously opposed by the Egyptian bishops, opened new scenes of violence and perjury. [105] After the return of the deputies from Alexandria, the majority of the council pronounced the final sentence of degradation and exile against the primate of Egypt. The decree, expressed in the fiercest language of malice and revenge, was communicated to the emperor and the Catholic church; and the bishops immediately resumed a mild and devout aspect, such as became their holy pilgrimage to the Sepulchre of Christ. [106]

[Footnote 101: At first Constantine threatened in speaking, but requested in writing. His letters gradually assumed a menacing tone; by while he required that the entrance of the church should be open to all, he avoided the odious name of Arius. Athanasius, like a skilful politician, has accurately marked these distinctions, (tom. i. p. 788.) which allowed him some scope for excuse and delay]

[Footnote 102: The Meletians in Egypt, like the Donatists in Africa, were produced by an episcopal quarrel which arose from the persecution. I have not leisure to pursue the obscure controversy, which seems to have been misrepresented by the partiality of Athanasius and the ignorance of Epiphanius. See Mosheim's General History of the Church, vol. i. p. 201.]

[Footnote 103: The treatment of the six bishops is specified by Sozomen, (l. ii. c. 25;) but Athanasius himself, so copious on the subject of Arsenius and the chalice, leaves this grave accusation without a reply. Note: This grave charge, if made, (and it rests entirely on the authority of Sozomen,) seems to have been silently dropped by the parties themselves: it is never alluded to in the subsequent investigations. From Sozomen himself, who gives the unfavorable report of the commission of inquiry sent to Egypt concerning the cup. it does not appear that they noticed this accusation of personal violence—M]

[Footnote 104: Athanas, tom. i. p. 788. Socrates, l. i.c. 28. Sozomen, l. ii. c 25. The emperor, in his Epistle of Convocation, (Euseb. in Vit. Constant. l. iv. c. 42,) seems to prejudge some members of the clergy and it was more than probable that the synod would apply those reproaches to Athanasius.]

[Footnote 105: See, in particular, the second Apology of Athanasius, (tom. i. p. 763-808,) and his Epistles to the Monks, (p. 808-866.) They are justified by original and authentic documents; but they would inspire more confidence if he appeared less innocent, and his enemies less absurd.]

[Footnote 106: Eusebius in Vit. Constantin. l. iv. c. 41-47.]

PART V

But the injustice of these ecclesiastical judges had not been countenanced by the submission, or even by the presence, of Athanasius. He resolved to make a bold and dangerous experiment, whether the throne was inaccessible to the voice of truth; and before the final sentence could be pronounced at Tyre, the intrepid primate threw himself into a bark which was ready to hoist sail for the Imperial city. The request of a formal audience might have been opposed or eluded; but Athanasius concealed his arrival, watched the moment of Constantine's return from an adjacent villa, and boldly encountered his angry sovereign as he passed on horseback through the principal street of Constantinople. So strange an apparition excited his surprise and indignation; and the guards were ordered to remove the importunate suitor; but his resentment was subdued by involuntary respect; and the haughty spirit of the emperor was awed by the courage and eloquence of a bishop, who implored his justice and awakened his conscience. [107] Constantine listened to the complaints of Athanasius with impartial and even gracious attention; the members of the synod of Tyre were summoned to justify their proceedings; and the arts of the Eusebian faction would have been confounded, if they had not aggravated the guilt of the primate, by the dexterous supposition of an unpardonable offence; a criminal design to intercept and detain the corn-fleet of Alexandria, which supplied the subsistence of the new capital. [108] The emperor was satisfied that the peace of Egypt would be secured by the absence of a popular leader; but he refused to fill the vacancy of the archiepiscopal throne; and the sentence, which, after long hesitation, he pronounced, was that of a jealous ostracism, rather than of an ignominious exile. In the remote province of Gaul, but in the hospitable court of Treves, Athanasius passed about twenty eight months. The death of the emperor changed the face of public affairs and, amidst the general indulgence of a young reign, the primate was restored to his country by an honorable edict of the younger Constantine, who expressed a deep sense of the innocence and merit of his venerable guest. [109]

[Footnote 107: Athanas. tom. i. p. 804. In a church dedicated to St. Athanasius this situation would afford a better subject for a picture, than most of the stories of miracles and martyrdoms.]

[Footnote 108: Athanas. tom. i. p. 729. Eunapius has related (in Vit. Sophist. p. 36, 37, edit. Commelin) a strange example of the cruelty and credulity of Constantine on a similar occasion. The eloquent Sopater, a Syrian philosopher, enjoyed his friendship, and provoked the resentment of Ablavius, his Praetorian praefect. The corn-fleet was detained for want of a south wind; the people of Constantinople were discontented; and Sopater was beheaded, on a charge that he had bound the winds by the power of magic. Suidas adds, that Constantine wished to prove, by this execution, that he had absolutely renounced the superstition of the Gentiles.]

[Footnote 109: In his return he saw Constantius twice, at Viminiacum, and at Caesarea in Cappadocia, (Athanas. tom. i. p. 676.) Tillemont supposes that Constantine introduced him to the meeting of the three royal brothers in Pannonia, (Memoires Eccles. tom. viii. p. 69.)]

The death of that prince exposed Athanasius to a second persecution; and the feeble Constantius, the sovereign of the East, soon became the secret accomplice of the Eusebians. Ninety bishops of that sect or faction assembled at Antioch, under the specious pretence of dedicating the cathedral. They composed an ambiguous creed, which is faintly tinged with the colors of Semi-Arianism, and twenty-five canons, which still regulate the discipline of the orthodox Greeks. [110] It was decided, with some appearance of equity, that a bishop, deprived by a synod, should not resume his episcopal functions till he had been absolved by the judgment of an equal synod; the law was immediately applied to the case of Athanasius; the council of Antioch pronounced, or rather confirmed, his degradation: a stranger, named Gregory, was seated on his throne; and Philagrius, [111] the praefect of Egypt, was instructed to support the new primate with the civil and military powers of the province. Oppressed by the conspiracy of the Asiatic prelates, Athanasius withdrew from Alexandria, and passed three years [112] as an exile and a suppliant on the holy threshold of the Vatican. [113] By the assiduous study of the Latin language, he soon qualified himself to negotiate with the western clergy; his decent flattery swayed and directed the haughty Julius; the Roman pontiff was persuaded to consider his appeal as the peculiar interest of the Apostolic see: and his innocence was unanimously declared in a council of fifty bishops of Italy. At the end of three years, the primate was summoned to the court of Milan by the emperor Constans, who, in the indulgence of unlawful pleasures, still professed a lively regard for the orthodox faith. The cause of truth and justice was promoted by the influence of gold, [114] and the ministers of Constans advised their sovereign to require the convocation of an ecclesiastical assembly, which might act as the representatives of the Catholic church. Ninety-four bishops of the West, seventy-six bishops of the East, encountered each other at Sardica, on the verge of the two empires, but in the dominions of the protector of Athanasius. Their debates soon degenerated into hostile altercations; the Asiatics, apprehensive for their personal safety, retired to Philippopolis in Thrace; and the rival synods reciprocally hurled their spiritual thunders against their enemies, whom they piously condemned as the enemies of the true God. Their decrees were published and ratified in their respective provinces: and Athanasius, who in the West was revered as a saint, was exposed as a criminal to the abhorrence of the East. [115] The council of Sardica reveals the first symptoms of discord and schism between the Greek and Latin churches which were separated by the accidental difference of faith, and the permanent distinction of language.

[Footnote 110: See Beveridge, Pandect. tom. i. p. 429-452, and tom. ii. Annotation. p. 182. Tillemont, Mem. Eccles. tom. vi. p. 310-324. St. Hilary of Poitiers has mentioned this synod of Antioch with too much favor and respect. He reckons ninety-seven bishops.]

[Footnote 111: This magistrate, so odious to Athanasius, is praised by Gregory Nazianzen, tom. i. Orat. xxi. p. 390, 391.

Saepe premente Deo fert Deus alter opem.

For the credit of human nature, I am always pleased to discover some good qualities in those men whom party has represented as tyrants and monsters.]

[Footnote 112: The chronological difficulties which perplex the residence of Athanasius at Rome, are strenuously agitated by Valesius (Observat ad Calcem, tom. ii. Hist. Eccles. l. i. c. 1-5) and Tillemont, (Men: Eccles. tom. viii. p. 674, &c.) I have followed the simple hypothesis of Valesius, who allows only one journey, after the intrusion Gregory.]

[Footnote 113: I cannot forbear transcribing a judicious observation of Wetstein, (Prolegomen. N.S. p. 19:) Si tamen Historiam Ecclesiasticam velimus consulere, patebit jam inde a seculo quarto, cum, ortis controversiis, ecclesiae Graeciae doctores in duas partes scinderentur, ingenio, eloquentia, numero, tantum non aequales, eam partem quae vincere cupiebat Romam confugisse, majestatemque pontificis comiter coluisse, eoque pacto oppressis per pontificem et episcopos Latinos adversariis praevaluisse, atque orthodoxiam in conciliis stabilivisse. Eam ob causam Athanasius, non sine comitatu, Roman petiit, pluresque annos ibi haesit.]

[Footnote 114: Philostorgius, l. iii. c. 12. If any corruption was used to promote the interest of religion, an advocate of Athanasius might justify or excuse this questionable conduct, by the example of Cato and

Sidney; the former of whom is said to have given, and the latter to have received, a bribe in the cause of liberty.]

[Footnote 115: The canon which allows appeals to the Roman pontiffs, has almost raised the council of Sardica to the dignity of a general council; and its acts have been ignorantly or artfully confounded with those of the Nicene synod. See Tillemont, tom. vii. p. 689, and Geddos's Tracts, vol. ii. p. 419-460.]

During his second exile in the West, Athanasius was frequently admitted to the Imperial presence; at Capua, Lodi, Milan, Verona, Padua, Aquileia, and Treves. The bishop of the diocese usually assisted at these interviews; the master of the offices stood before the veil or curtain of the sacred apartment; and the uniform moderation of the primate might be attested by these respectable witnesses, to whose evidence he solemnly appeals. [116] Prudence would undoubtedly suggest the mild and respectful tone that became a subject and a bishop. In these familiar conferences with the sovereign of the West, Athanasius might lament the error of Constantius, but he boldly arraigned the guilt of his eunuchs and his Arian prelates; deplored the distress and danger of the Catholic church; and excited Constans to emulate the zeal and glory of his father. The emperor declared his resolution of employing the troops and treasures of Europe in the orthodox cause; and signified, by a concise and peremptory epistle to his brother Constantius, that unless he consented to the immediate restoration of Athanasius, he himself, with a fleet and army, would seat the archbishop on the throne of Alexandria. [117] But this religious war, so horrible to nature, was prevented by the timely compliance of Constantius; and the emperor of the East condescended to solicit a reconciliation with a subject whom he had injured. Athanasius waited with decent pride, till he had received three successive epistles full of the strongest assurances of the protection, the favor, and the esteem of his sovereign; who invited him to resume his episcopal seat, and who added the humiliating precaution of engaging his principal ministers to attest the sincerity of his intentions. They were manifested in a still more public manner, by the strict orders which were despatched into Egypt to recall the adherents of Athanasius, to restore their privileges, to proclaim their innocence, and to erase from the public registers the illegal proceedings which had been obtained during the prevalence of the Eusebian faction. After every satisfaction and security had been given, which justice or even delicacy could require, the primate proceeded, by slow journeys, through the provinces of Thrace, Asia, and Syria; and his progress was marked by the abject homage of the Oriental bishops, who excited his contempt without deceiving his penetration. [118] At Antioch he saw the emperor Constantius; sustained, with modest firmness, the embraces and protestations of his master, and eluded the proposal of allowing the Arians a single church at Alexandria, by claiming, in the other cities of the empire, a similar toleration for his own party; a reply which might have appeared just and moderate in the mouth of an independent prince. The entrance of the archbishop into his capital was a triumphal procession; absence and persecution had endeared him to the Alexandrians; his authority, which he exercised with rigor, was more firmly established; and his fame was diffused from Aethiopia to Britain, over the whole extent of the Christian world. [119]

[Footnote 116: As Athanasius dispersed secret invectives against Constantius, (see the Epistle to the Monks,) at the same time that he assured him of his profound respect, we might distrust the professions of the archbishop. Tom. i. p. 677.]

[Footnote 117: Notwithstanding the discreet silence of Athanasius, and the manifest forgery of a letter inserted by Socrates, these menaces are proved by the unquestionable evidence of Lucifer of Cagliari, and even of Constantius himself. See Tillemont, tom. viii. p. 693]

[Footnote 118: I have always entertained some doubts concerning the retraction of Ursacius and Valens, (Athanas. tom. i. p. 776.) Their epistles to Julius, bishop of Rome, and to Athanasius himself, are of so different a cast from each other, that they cannot both be genuine. The one speaks the language of criminals who confess their guilt and infamy; the other of enemies, who solicit on equal terms an honorable reconciliation. Note: I cannot quite comprehend the ground of Gibbon's doubts. Athanasius distinctly asserts the fact of their retractation. (Athan. Op. i. p. 124, edit. Benedict.) The epistles are apparently translations from the Latin, if, in fact, more than the substance of the epistles. That to Athanasius is brief, almost abrupt. Their retractation is likewise mentioned in the address of the orthodox bishops of Rimini to Constantius. Athan. de Synodis, Op t. i. p 723-M.]

[Footnote 119: The circumstances of his second return may be collected from Athanasius himself, tom. i. p. 769, and 822, 843. Socrates, l. ii. c. 18, Sozomen, l. iii. c. 19. Theodoret, l. ii. c. 11, 12. Philostorgius, l. iii. c. 12.]

But the subject who has reduced his prince to the necessity of dissembling, can never expect a sincere and lasting forgiveness; and the tragic fate of Constans soon deprived Athanasius of a powerful and generous protector. The civil war between the assassin and the only surviving brother of Constans, which afflicted the empire above three years, secured an interval of repose to the Catholic church; and the two contending parties were desirous to conciliate the friendship of a bishop, who, by the weight of his personal authority, might determine the fluctuating resolutions of an important province. He gave audience to the ambassadors of the tyrant, with whom he was afterwards accused of holding a secret correspondence; [120] and the emperor Constantius repeatedly assured his dearest father, the most reverend Athanasius, that, notwithstanding the malicious rumors which were circulated by their common enemies, he had inherited the sentiments, as well as the throne, of his deceased brother. [121] Gratitude and humanity would have disposed the primate of Egypt to deplore the untimely fate of Constans, and to abhor the guilt of Magnentius; but as he clearly understood that the apprehensions of Constantius were his only safeguard, the fervor of his prayers for the success of the righteous cause might perhaps be somewhat abated. The ruin of Athanasius was no longer contrived by the obscure malice of a few bigoted or angry bishops, who abused the authority of a credulous monarch. The monarch himself avowed the resolution, which he had so long suppressed, of avenging his private injuries; [122] and the first winter after his victory, which he passed at Arles, was employed against an enemy more odious to him than the vanquished tyrant of Gaul.

[Footnote 120: Athanasius (tom. i. p. 677, 678) defends his innocence by pathetic complaints, solemn assertions, and specious arguments. He admits that letters had been forged in his name, but he requests that his own secretaries and those of the tyrant might be examined, whether those letters had been written by the former, or received by the latter.]

[Footnote 121: Athanas. tom. i. p. 825-844.]

[Footnote 122: Athanas. tom. i. p. 861. Theodoret, l. ii. c. 16. The emperor declared that he was more desirous to subdue Athanasius, than he had been to vanquish Magnentius or Sylvanus.]

If the emperor had capriciously decreed the death of the most eminent and virtuous citizen of the republic, the cruel order would have been executed without hesitation, by the ministers of open violence or of specious injustice. The caution, the delay, the difficulty with which he proceeded in the condemnation and punishment of a popular bishop, discovered to the world that the privileges of the church had already revived a sense of order and freedom in the Roman government. The sentence which was pronounced in the synod of Tyre, and subscribed by a large majority of the Eastern bishops, had never been expressly repealed; and as Athanasius had been once degraded from his episcopal dignity by the judgment of his brethren, every subsequent act might be considered as irregular, and even criminal. But the memory of the firm and effectual support which the primate of Egypt had derived from the attachment of the Western church, engaged Constantius to suspend the execution of the sentence till he had obtained the concurrence of the Latin bishops. Two years were consumed in ecclesiastical negotiations; and the important cause between the emperor and one of his subjects was solemnly debated, first in the synod of Arles, and afterwards in the great council of Milan, [123] which consisted of above three hundred bishops. Their integrity was gradually undermined by the arguments of the Arians, the dexterity of the eunuchs, and the pressing solicitations of a prince who gratified his revenge at the expense of his dignity, and exposed his own passions, whilst he influenced those of the clergy. Corruption, the most infallible symptom of constitutional liberty, was successfully practised; honors, gifts, and immunities were offered and accepted as the price of an episcopal vote; [124] and the condemnation of the Alexandrian primate was artfully represented as the only measure which could restore the peace and union of the Catholic church. The friends of Athanasius were not, however, wanting to their leader, or to their cause. With a manly spirit, which the sanctity of their character rendered less dangerous, they maintained, in public debate, and in private conference with the emperor, the eternal obligation of religion and justice. They declared, that neither the hope of his favor, nor the fear of his displeasure, should prevail on them to join in the condemnation of an absent, an innocent, a respectable brother. [125] They affirmed, with apparent reason, that the illegal and obsolete decrees of the council of Tyre had long since been tacitly abolished by the Imperial edicts, the honorable reestablishment of the archbishop of Alexandria, and the silence or recantation of his most clamorous adversaries. They alleged, that his innocence had been attested by the unanimous bishops of Egypt, and had been acknowledged in the councils of Rome and Sardica, [126] by the impartial judgment of the Latin church. They deplored the hard condition of Athanasius, who, after enjoying so many years his seat, his reputation, and the seeming confidence of his sovereign, was again called upon to confute the most groundless and extravagant accusations. Their language was specious; their conduct was honorable: but in this long and obstinate contest, which fixed the eyes of the whole empire on a single bishop, the ecclesiastical factions were prepared to sacrifice truth and justice to the more interesting object of defending or removing the intrepid champion of the Nicene faith. The Arians still thought it prudent to disguise, in ambiguous language, their real sentiments and designs; but the orthodox bishops, armed with the favor of the people, and the decrees of a general council, insisted on every occasion, and particularly at Milan, that their adversaries should purge themselves from the suspicion of heresy, before they presumed to arraign the conduct of the great Athanasius. [127]

[Footnote 123: *The affairs of the council of Milan are so imperfectly and erroneously related by the Greek writers, that we must rejoice in the supply of some letters of Eusebius, extracted by Baronius from the archives of the church of Vercellae, and of an old life of Dionysius of Milan, published by Bollandus. See Baronius, A.D. 355, and Tillemont, tom. vii. p. 1415.*]

[Footnote 124: *The honors, presents, feasts, which seduced so many bishops, are mentioned with indignation by those who were too pure or too proud to accept them. "We combat (says Hilary of Poitiers) against Constantius the Antichrist; who strokes the belly instead of scourging the back;" qui non dorsa caedit; sed ventrem palpat. Hilarius contra Constant c. 5, p. 1240.*]

[Footnote 125: *Something of this opposition is mentioned by Ammianus (x. 7,) who had a very dark and superficial knowledge of ecclesiastical history. Liberius... perseveranter renitebatur, nec visum hominem,* nec auditum damnare, nefas ultimum saepe exclamans; aperte scilicet recalcitrans Imperatoris arbitrio. Id enim ille Athanasio semper infestus, &c.]

[Footnote 126: More properly by the orthodox part of the council of Sardica. If the bishops of both parties had fairly voted, the division would have been 94 to 76. M. de Tillemont (see tom. viii. p. 1147-1158) is justly surprised that so small a majority should have proceeded as vigorously against their adversaries, the principal of whom they immediately deposed.]

[Footnote 127: Sulp. Severus in Hist. Sacra, l. ii. p. 412.]

But the voice of reason (if reason was indeed on the side of Athanasius) was silenced by the clamors of a factious or venal majority; and the councils of Arles and Milan were not dissolved, till the archbishop of Alexandria had been solemnly condemned and deposed by the judgment of the Western, as well as of the Eastern, church. The bishops who had opposed, were required to subscribe, the sentence, and to unite in religious communion with the suspected leaders of the adverse party. A formulary of consent was transmitted by the messengers of state to the absent bishops: and all those who refused to submit their private opinion to the public and inspired wisdom of the councils of Arles and Milan, were immediately banished by the emperor, who affected to execute the decrees of the Catholic church. Among those prelates who led the honorable band of confessors and exiles, Liberius of Rome, Osius of Cordova, Paulinus of Treves, Dionysius of Milan, Eusebius of Vercellae, Lucifer of Cagliari and Hilary of Poitiers, may deserve to be particularly distinguished. The eminent station of Liberius, who governed the capital of the empire; the personal merit and long experience of the venerable Osius, who was revered as the favorite of the great Constantine, and the father of the Nicene faith, placed those prelates at the head of the Latin church: and their example, either of submission or resistance, would probable be imitated by the episcopal crowd. But the repeated attempts of the emperor to seduce or to intimidate the bishops of Rome and Cordova, were for some time ineffectual. The Spaniard declared himself ready to suffer under Constantius, as he had suffered threescore years before under his grandfather Maximian. The Roman, in the presence of his sovereign, asserted the innocence of Athanasius and his own freedom. When he was banished to Beraea in Thrace, he sent back a large sum which had been offered for the accommodation of his journey; and insulted the court of Milan by the haughty remark, that the emperor and his eunuchs might want that gold to pay their soldiers and their bishops. [128] The resolution of Liberius and Osius was at length subdued by the hardships of exile and confinement. The Roman pontiff purchased his return by some criminal compliances; and afterwards expiated his guilt by a seasonable repentance. Persuasion and violence were employed to extort the reluctant signature of the decrepit bishop of Cordova, whose strength was broken, and whose faculties were perhaps impaired by the weight of a hundred years; and the insolent triumph of the Arians provoked some of the orthodox party to treat with inhuman severity the character, or rather the memory, of an unfortunate old man, to whose former services Christianity itself was so deeply indebted. [129]

[Footnote 128: The exile of Liberius is mentioned by Ammianus, xv. 7. See Theodoret, l. ii. c. 16. Athanas. tom. i. p. 834-837. Hilar. Fragment l.]

[Footnote 129: The life of Osius is collected by Tillemont, (tom. vii. p. 524-561,) who in the most extravagant terms first admires, and then reprobates, the bishop of Cordova. In the midst of their lamentations on his fall, the prudence of Athanasius may be distinguished from the blind and intemperate zeal of Hilary.]

The fall of Liberius and Osius reflected a brighter lustre on the firmness of those bishops who still adhered, with unshaken fidelity, to the cause of Athanasius and religious truth. The ingenious malice of their enemies had deprived them of the benefit of mutual comfort and advice, separated those illustrious exiles into distant provinces, and carefully selected the most inhospitable spots of a great empire. [130] Yet they soon experienced that the deserts of Libya, and the most barbarous tracts of Cappadocia, were less inhospitable than the residence of those cities in which an Arian bishop could satiate, without restraint, the exquisite rancor of theological hatred. [131] Their consolation was derived from the consciousness of rectitude and independence, from the applause, the visits, the letters, and the liberal alms of their adherents, [132] and from the satisfaction which they soon enjoyed of observing the intestine divisions of the adversaries of the Nicene faith. Such was the nice and capricious taste of the emperor Constantius; and so easily was he offended by the slightest deviation from his imaginary standard of Christian truth, that he persecuted, with equal zeal, those who defended the consubstantiality, those who asserted the similar substance, and those who denied the likeness of the Son of God. Three bishops, degraded and banished for those adverse opinions, might possibly meet in the same place of exile; and, according to the difference of their temper, might either pity or insult the blind enthusiasm of their antagonists, whose present sufferings would never be compensated by future happiness.

[Footnote 130: *The confessors of the West were successively banished to the deserts of Arabia or Thebais, the lonely places of Mount Taurus, the wildest parts of Phrygia, which were in the possession of the impious Montanists, &c. When the heretic Aetius was too favorably entertained at Mopsuestia in Cilicia, the place of his exile was changed, by the advice of Acacius, to Amblada, a district inhabited by savages and infested by war and pestilence. Philostorg. l. v. c. 2.*]

[Footnote 131: *See the cruel treatment and strange obstinacy of Eusebius, in his own letters, published by Baronius, A.D. 356, No. 92-102.*]

[Footnote 132: *Caeterum exules satis constat, totius orbis studiis celebratos pecuniasque eis in sumptum affatim congestas, legationibus quoque plebis Catholicae ex omnibus fere provinciis frequentatos. Sulp. Sever Hist. Sacra, p. 414. Athanas. tom. i. p. 836, 840.*]

The disgrace and exile of the orthodox bishops of the West were designed as so many preparatory steps to the ruin of Athanasius himself. [133] Six-and-twenty months had elapsed, during which the Imperial court secretly labored, by the most insidious arts, to remove him from Alexandria, and to withdraw the allowance which supplied his popular liberality. But when the primate of Egypt, deserted and proscribed by the Latin church, was left destitute of any foreign support, Constantius despatched two of his secretaries with a verbal commission to announce and execute the order of his banishment. As the justice of the sentence was publicly avowed by the whole party, the only motive which could restrain Constantius from giving his messengers the sanction of a written mandate, must be imputed to his doubt of the event; and to a sense of the danger to which he might expose the second city, and the most fertile province, of the empire, if the people should persist in the resolution of defending, by force of arms, the innocence of their spiritual father. Such extreme caution afforded Athanasius a specious pretence respectfully to dispute the truth of an order, which he could not reconcile, either with the equity, or with the former declarations, of his gracious master. The civil powers of Egypt found themselves inadequate to the task of persuading or compelling the primate to abdicate his episcopal throne; and they were obliged to conclude a treaty with the popular leaders of Alexandria, by which it was stipulated, that all proceedings and all hostilities should be suspended till the emperor's pleasure had been more distinctly ascertained. By this seeming moderation, the Catholics were deceived into a false and fatal security; while the legions of the Upper Egypt, and of Libya, advanced, by secret orders and hasty marches, to besiege, or rather to surprise, a capital habituated to sedition, and inflamed by religious zeal. [134] The position of Alexandria, between the sea and the Lake Mareotis, facilitated the approach and landing of the troops; who were introduced into the heart of the city, before any effectual measures could be taken either to shut the gates or to occupy the important posts of defence. At the hour of midnight, twenty-three days after the signature of the treaty, Syrianus, duke of Egypt, at the head of five thousand soldiers, armed and prepared for an assault, unexpectedly invested the church of St. Theonas, where the archbishop, with a part of his clergy and people, performed their nocturnal devotions. The doors of the sacred edifice yielded to the impetuosity of the attack, which was accompanied with every horrid circumstance of tumult and bloodshed; but, as the bodies of the slain, and the fragments of military weapons, remained the next day an unexceptionable evidence in the possession of the Catholics, the enterprise of Syrianus may be considered as a successful irruption rather than as an absolute conquest. The other churches of the city were profaned by similar outrages; and, during at least four months, Alexandria was exposed to the insults of a licentious army, stimulated by the ecclesiastics of a hostile faction. Many of the faithful were killed; who may deserve the name of martyrs, if their deaths were neither provoked nor revenged; bishops and presbyters were treated with cruel ignominy; consecrated virgins were stripped naked, scourged and violated; the houses of wealthy citizens were plundered; and, under the mask of religious zeal, lust, avarice, and private resentment were gratified with impunity, and even with applause. The Pagans of Alexandria, who still formed a numerous and discontented party, were easily persuaded to desert a bishop whom they feared and esteemed. The hopes of some peculiar favors, and the apprehension of being involved in the general penalties of rebellion, engaged them to promise their support to the destined successor of Athanasius, the famous George of Cappadocia. The usurper, after receiving the consecration of an Arian synod, was placed on the episcopal throne by the arms of Sebastian, who had been appointed Count of Egypt for the execution of that important design. In the use, as well as in the acquisition, of power, the tyrant, George disregarded the laws of religion, of justice, and of humanity; and the same scenes of violence and scandal which had been exhibited in the capital, were repeated in more than ninety episcopal cities of Egypt. Encouraged by success, Constantius ventured to approve the conduct of his minister. By a public and passionate epistle, the emperor congratulates the deliverance of Alexandria from a popular tyrant, who deluded his blind votaries by the magic of his eloquence; expatiates on the virtues and piety of the most reverend George, the elected bishop; and aspires, as the patron and benefactor of the city to surpass the fame of Alexander himself. But he solemnly declares his unalterable resolution to pursue with fire and sword the seditious adherents of the wicked Athanasius, who, by flying from justice, has confessed his guilt, and escaped the ignominious death which he had so often deserved. [135]

[Footnote 133: Ample materials for the history of this third persecution of Athanasius may be found in his own works. See particularly his very able Apology to Constantius, (tom. i. p. 673,) his first Apology for his flight (p. 701,) his prolix Epistle to the Solitaries, (p. 808,) and the original protest of the people of Alexandria against the violences committed by Syrianus, (p. 866.) Sozomen (l. iv. c. 9) has thrown into the narrative two or three luminous and important circumstances.]

[Footnote 134: Athanasius had lately sent for Antony, and some of his chosen monks. They descended from their mountains, announced to the Alexandrians the sanctity of Athanasius, and were honorably conducted by the archbishop as far as the gates of the city. Athanas tom. ii. p. 491, 492. See likewise Rufinus, iii. 164, in Vit. Patr. p. 524.]

[Footnote 135: Athanas. tom. i. p. 694. The emperor, or his Arian secretaries while they express their resentment, betray their fears and esteem of Athanasius.]

PART VI

Athanasius had indeed escaped from the most imminent dangers; and the adventures of that extraordinary man deserve and fix our attention. On the memorable night when the church of St. Theonas was invested by the troops of Syrianus, the archbishop, seated on his throne, expected, with calm and intrepid dignity, the approach of death. While the public devotion was interrupted by shouts of rage and cries of terror, he animated his trembling congregation to express their religious confidence, by chanting one of the psalms of David which celebrates the triumph of the God of Israel over the haughty and impious tyrant of Egypt. The doors were at length burst open: a cloud of arrows was discharged among the people; the soldiers, with drawn swords, rushed forwards into the sanctuary; and the dreadful gleam of their arms was reflected by the holy luminaries which burnt round the altar. [136] Athanasius still rejected the pious importunity of the monks and presbyters, who were attached to his person; and nobly refused to desert his episcopal station, till he had dismissed in safety the last of the congregation. The darkness and tumult of the night favored the retreat of the archbishop; and though he was oppressed by the waves of an agitated multitude, though he was thrown to the ground, and left without sense or motion, he still recovered his undaunted courage, and eluded the eager search of the soldiers, who were instructed by their Arian guides, that the head of Athanasius would be the most acceptable present to the emperor. From that moment the primate of Egypt disappeared from the eyes of his enemies, and remained above six years concealed in impenetrable obscurity. [137]

[Footnote 136: These minute circumstances are curious, as they are literally transcribed from the protest, which was publicly presented three days afterwards by the Catholics of Alexandria. See Athanas. tom. l. n. 867]

[Footnote 137: The Jansenists have often compared Athanasius and Arnauld, and have expatiated with pleasure on the faith and zeal, the merit and exile, of those celebrated doctors. This concealed parallel is very dexterously managed by the Abbe de la Bleterie, Vie de Jovien, tom. i. p. 130.]

The despotic power of his implacable enemy filled the whole extent of the Roman world; and the exasperated monarch had endeavored, by a very pressing epistle to the Christian princes of Ethiopia, [137a] to exclude Athanasius from the most remote and sequestered regions of the earth. Counts, praefects, tribunes, whole armies, were successively employed to pursue a bishop and a fugitive; the vigilance of the civil and military powers was excited by the Imperial edicts; liberal rewards were promised to the man who should produce Athanasius, either alive or dead; and the most severe penalties were denounced against those who should dare to protect the public enemy. [138] But the deserts of Thebais were now peopled by a race of wild, yet submissive fanatics, who preferred the commands of their abbot to the laws of their sovereign. The numerous disciples of Antony and Pachonnus received the fugitive primate as their father, admired the patience and humility with which he conformed to their strictest institutions, collected every word which dropped from his lips as the genuine effusions of inspired wisdom; and persuaded themselves that their prayers, their fasts, and their vigils, were less meritorious than the zeal which they expressed, and the dangers which they braved, in the defence of truth and innocence. [139] The monasteries of Egypt were seated in lonely and desolate places, on the summit of mountains, or in the islands of the Nile; and the sacred horn or trumpet of Tabenne was the well-known signal which assembled several thousand robust and determined monks, who, for the most part, had been the peasants of the adjacent country. When their dark retreats were invaded by a military force, which it was impossible to resist, they silently stretched out their necks to the executioner; and supported their national character, that tortures could never wrest from an Egyptian the confession of a secret which he was resolved not to disclose. [140] The archbishop of Alexandria, for whose safety they eagerly devoted their lives, was lost among a uniform and well-disciplined multitude; and on the nearer approach of danger, he was swiftly removed, by their officious hands, from one place of concealment to another, till he reached the formidable deserts, which the gloomy and credulous temper of superstition had peopled with daemons and savage monsters. The retirement of Athanasius, which ended only with the life of Constantius, was spent, for the most part, in the society of the monks, who faithfully served him as guards, as secretaries, and as messengers; but the importance of maintaining a more intimate connection with the Catholic party tempted him, whenever the diligence of the pursuit was abated, to emerge from the desert, to introduce himself into Alexandria, and to trust his person to the discretion of his friends and adherents. His various adventures might have furnished the subject of a very entertaining romance. He was once secreted in a dry cistern, which he had scarcely left before he was betrayed by the treachery of a female slave; [141] and he was once concealed in a still more extraordinary asylum, the house of a virgin, only twenty years of age, and who was celebrated in the whole city for her exquisite beauty. At the hour of midnight, as she related the story many years afterwards, she was surprised by the appearance of the archbishop in a loose undress, who, advancing with hasty steps, conjured her to afford him the protection which he had been directed by a celestial vision to seek under her hospitable roof. The pious maid accepted and preserved the sacred pledge which was intrusted to her prudence and courage. Without imparting the secret to any one, she instantly conducted Athanasius into her most secret chamber, and watched over his safety with the tenderness of a friend and the assiduity of a servant. As long as the danger continued, she regularly supplied him with books and provisions, washed his feet, managed his correspondence, and dexterously concealed from the eye of suspicion this familiar and solitary intercourse between a saint whose character required the most unblemished chastity, and a female whose charms might excite the most dangerous emotions. [142] During the six years of persecution and exile, Athanasius repeated his visits to his fair and faithful companion; and the formal declaration, that he saw the councils of Rimini and Seleucia, [143] forces us to believe that he was secretly present at the time and place of their convocation. The advantage of personally negotiating with his friends, and of observing and improving the divisions of his enemies, might justify, in a prudent statesman, so bold and dangerous an enterprise: and Alexandria was connected by trade and navigation with every seaport of the Mediterranean. From the depth of his inaccessible retreat the intrepid primate waged an incessant and offensive war against the protector of the Arians; and his seasonable writings, which were diligently circulated and eagerly perused, contributed to unite and animate the orthodox party. In his public apologies, which he addressed to the emperor himself, he sometimes affected the praise of moderation; whilst at the same time, in secret and vehement invectives, he exposed Constantius as a weak and wicked prince, the executioner of his family, the tyrant of the republic, and the Antichrist of the church. In the height of his prosperity, the victorious monarch, who had chastised the rashness of Gallus, and suppressed the revolt of Sylvanus, who had taken the diadem from the head of Vetranio, and vanquished in the field the legions of Magnentius, received from an invisible hand a wound, which he could neither heal nor revenge; and the son of Constantine was the first of the Christian princes who experienced the strength of those principles, which, in the cause of religion, could resist the most violent exertions [144] of the civil power.

[Footnote 137a: These princes were called Aeizanas and Saiazanas. Athanasius calls them the kings of Axum. In the superscription of his letter, Constantius gives them no title. Mr. Salt, during his first journey in Ethiopia, (in 1806,) discovered, in the ruins of Axum, a long and very interesting inscription relating to these princes. It was erected to commemorate the victory of Aeizanas over the Bougaitae, (St. Martin

considers them the Blemmyes, whose true name is Bedjah or Bodjah.) Aeizanas is styled king of the Axumites, the Homerites, of Raeidan, of the Ethiopians, of the Sabsuites, of Silea, of Tiamo, of the Bougaites. and of Kaei. It appears that at this time the king of the Ethiopians ruled over the Homerites, the inhabitants of Yemen. He was not yet a Christian, as he calls himself son of the invincible Mars. Another brother besides Saiazanas, named Adephas, is mentioned, though Aeizanas seems to have been sole king. See St. Martin, note on Le Beau, ii. 151. Salt's Travels. De Sacy, note in Annales des Voyages, xii. p. 53—M.]

[Footnote 138: Hinc jam toto orbe profugus Athanasius, nec ullus ci tutus ad latendum supererat locus. Tribuni, Praefecti, Comites, exercitus quoque ad pervestigandum cum moventur edictis Imperialibus; praemia dela toribus proponuntur, si quis eum vivum, si id minus, caput certe Atha casii detulisset. Rufin. l. i. c. 16.]

[Footnote 139: Gregor. Nazianzen. tom. i. Orat. xxi. p. 384, 385. See Tillemont Mem. Eccles. tom. vii. p. 176-410, 820-830.]

[Footnote 140: Et nulla tormentorum vis inveneri, adhuc potuit, quae obdurato illius tractus latroni invito elicere potuit, ut nomen proprium dicat Ammian. xxii. 16, and Valesius ad locum.]

[Footnote 141: Rufin. l. i. c. 18. Sozomen, l. iv. c. 10. This and the following story will be rendered impossible, if we suppose that Athanasius always inhabited the asylum which he accidentally or occasionally had used.]

[Footnote 142: Paladius, (Hist. Lausiac. c. 136, in Vit. Patrum, p. 776,) the original author of this anecdote, had conversed with the damsel, who in her old age still remembered with pleasure so pious and honorable a connection. I cannot indulge the delicacy of Baronius, Valesius, Tillemont, &c., who almost reject a story so unworthy, as they deem it, of the gravity of ecclesiastical history.]

[Footnote 143: Athanas. tom. i. p. 869. I agree with Tillemont, (tom. iii. p. 1197,) that his expressions imply a personal, though perhaps secret visit to the synods.]

[Footnote 144: The epistle of Athanasius to the monks is filled with reproaches, which the public must feel to be true, (vol. i. p. 834, 856;) and, in compliment to his readers, he has introduced the comparisons of Pharaoh, Ahab, Belshazzar, &c. The boldness of Hilary was attended with less danger, if he published his invective in Gaul after the revolt of Julian; but Lucifer sent his libels to Constantius, and almost challenged the reward of martyrdom. See Tillemont, tom. vii. p. 905.]

The persecution of Athanasius, and of so many respectable bishops, who suffered for the truth of their opinions, or at least for the integrity of their conscience, was a just subject of indignation and discontent to all Christians, except those who were blindly devoted to the Arian faction. The people regretted the loss of their faithful pastors, whose banishment was usually followed by the intrusion of a stranger [145] into the episcopal chair; and loudly complained, that the right of election was violated, and that they were condemned to obey a mercenary usurper, whose person was unknown, and whose principles were suspected. The Catholics might prove to the world, that they were not involved in the guilt and heresy of their ecclesiastical governor, by publicly testifying their dissent, or by totally separating themselves from his communion. The first of these methods was invented at Antioch, and practised with such success, that it was soon diffused over the Christian world. The doxology or sacred hymn, which celebrates the glory of the Trinity, is susceptible of very nice, but material, inflections; and the substance of an orthodox, or an heretical, creed, may be expressed by the difference of a disjunctive, or a copulative, particle. Alternate responses, and a more regular psalmody, [146] were introduced into the public service by Flavianus and Diodorus, two devout and active laymen, who were attached to the Nicene faith. Under their conduct a swarm of monks issued from the adjacent desert, bands of well-disciplined singers were stationed in the cathedral of Antioch, the Glory to the Father, And the Son, And the Holy Ghost, [147] was triumphantly chanted by a full chorus of voices; and the Catholics insulted, by the purity of their doctrine, the Arian prelate, who had usurped the throne of the venerable Eustathius. The same zeal which inspired their songs prompted the more scrupulous members of the orthodox party to form separate assemblies, which were governed by the presbyters, till the death of their exiled bishop allowed the election and consecration of a new episcopal pastor. [148] The revolutions of the court multiplied the number of pretenders; and the same city was often disputed, under the reign of Constantius, by two, or three, or even four, bishops, who exercised their spiritual jurisdiction over their respective followers, and alternately lost and regained the temporal possessions of the church. The abuse of Christianity introduced into the Roman government new causes of tyranny and sedition; the bands of civil society were torn asunder by the fury of religious factions; and the obscure citizen, who might calmly have surveyed the elevation and fall of successive emperors, imagined and experienced, that his own life and fortune were connected with the interests of a popular ecclesiastic. The example of the two capitals, Rome and Constantinople, may serve to represent the state of the empire, and the temper of mankind, under the reign of the sons of Constantine.

[Footnote 145: Athanasius (tom. i. p. 811) complains in general of this practice, which he afterwards exemplifies (p. 861) in the pretended election of Faelix. Three eunuchs represented the Roman people, and three prelates, who followed the court, assumed the functions of the bishops of the Suburbicarian provinces.]

[Footnote 146: Thomassin (Discipline de l'Eglise, tom. i. l. ii. c. 72, 73, p. 966-984) has collected many curious facts concerning the origin and progress of church singing, both in the East and West. Note: Arius appears to have been the first who availed himself of this means of impressing his doctrines on the popular ear: he composed songs for sailors, millers, and travellers, and set them to common airs; "beguiling the ignorant, by the sweetness of his music, into the impiety of his doctrines." Philostorgius, ii. 2. Arian singers used to parade the streets of Constantinople by night, till Chrysostom arrayed against them a band of orthodox choristers. Sozomen, viii. 8—M.]

[Footnote 147: Philostorgius, l. iii. c. 13. Godefroy has examined this subject with singular accuracy, (p. 147, &c.) There were three heterodox forms: "To the Father by the Son, and in the Holy Ghost." "To the Father, and the Son in the Holy Ghost;" and "To the Father in the Son and the Holy Ghost."]

[Footnote 148: After the exile of Eustathius, under the reign of Constantine, the rigid party of the orthodox formed a separation which afterwards degenerated into a schism, and lasted about fourscore years. See Tillemont, Mem. Eccles. tom. vii. p. 35-54, 1137-1158, tom. viii. p. 537-632, 1314-1332. In many churches, the Arians and Homoousians, who had renounced each other's communion, continued for some time to join in prayer. Philostorgius, l. iii. c. 14.]

I. The Roman pontiff, as long as he maintained his station and his principles, was guarded by the warm attachment of a great people; and could reject with scorn the prayers, the menaces, and the oblations of an heretical prince. When the eunuchs had secretly pronounced the exile of Liberius, the well-grounded apprehension of a tumult engaged them to use the utmost precautions in the execution of the sentence. The capital was invested on every side, and the praefect was commanded to seize the person of the bishop, either by stratagem or by open force. The order was obeyed, and Liberius, with the greatest difficulty, at the hour of midnight, was swiftly conveyed beyond the reach of the Roman people, before their consternation was turned into rage. As soon as they were informed of his banishment into Thrace, a general assembly was convened, and the clergy of Rome bound themselves, by a public and solemn oath, never to desert their bishop, never to acknowledge the usurper Faelix; who, by the influence of the eunuchs, had been irregularly chosen and consecrated within the walls of a profane palace. At the end of two years, their pious obstinacy subsisted entire and unshaken; and when Constantius visited Rome, he was assailed by the importunate solicitations of a people, who had preserved, as the last remnant of their ancient freedom, the right of treating their sovereign with familiar insolence. The wives of many of the senators and most honorable citizens, after pressing their husbands to intercede in favor of Liberius, were advised to undertake a commission, which in their hands would be less dangerous, and might prove more successful. The emperor received with politeness these female deputies, whose wealth and dignity were displayed in the magnificence of their dress and ornaments: he admired their inflexible resolution of following their beloved pastor to the most distant regions of the earth; and consented that the two bishops, Liberius and Faelix, should govern in peace their respective congregations. But the ideas of toleration were so repugnant to the practice, and even to the sentiments, of those times, that when the answer of Constantius was publicly read in the Circus of Rome, so reasonable a project of accommodation was rejected with contempt and ridicule. The eager vehemence which animated the spectators in the decisive moment of a horse-race, was now directed towards a different object; and the Circus resounded with the shout of thousands, who repeatedly exclaimed, "One God, One Christ, One Bishop!" The zeal of the Roman people in the cause of Liberius was not confined to words alone; and the dangerous and bloody sedition which they excited soon after the departure of Constantius determined that prince to accept the submission of the exiled prelate, and to restore him to the undivided dominion of the capital. After some ineffectual resistance, his rival was expelled from the city by the permission of the emperor and the power of the opposite faction; the adherents of Faelix were inhumanly murdered in the streets, in the public places, in the baths, and even in the churches; and the face of Rome, upon the return of a Christian bishop, renewed the horrid image of the massacres of Marius, and the proscriptions of Sylla. [149]

[Footnote 149: See, on this ecclesiastical revolution of Rome, Ammianus, xv. 7 Athanas. tom. i. p. 834, 861. Sozomen, l. iv. c. 15. Theodoret, l. ii c. 17. Sulp. Sever. Hist. Sacra, l. ii. p. 413. Hieronym. Chron. Marcellin. et Faustin. Libell. p. 3, 4. Tillemont, Mem. Eccles. tom. vi. p.]

II. Notwithstanding the rapid increase of Christians under the reign of the Flavian family, Rome, Alexandria, and the other great cities of the empire, still contained a strong and powerful faction of Infidels, who envied the prosperity, and who ridiculed, even in their theatres, the theological disputes of the church. Constantinople alone enjoyed the advantage of being born and educated in the bosom of the faith. The capital of the East had never been polluted by the worship of idols; and the whole body of the people had deeply imbibed the opinions, the virtues, and the passions, which distinguished the Christians of that age from the rest of mankind. After the death of Alexander, the episcopal throne was disputed by Paul and Macedonius. By their zeal and abilities they both deserved the eminent station to which they aspired; and if the moral character of Macedonius was less exceptionable, his competitor had the advantage of a prior election and a more orthodox doctrine. His firm attachment to the Nicene creed, which has given Paul a place in the calendar among saints and martyrs, exposed him to the resentment of the Arians. In the space of fourteen years he was five times driven from his throne; to which he was more frequently restored by the violence of the people, than by the permission of the prince; and the power of Macedonius could be secured only by the death of his rival. The unfortunate Paul was dragged in chains from the sandy deserts of Mesopotamia to the most desolate places of

Mount Taurus, [150] confined in a dark and narrow dungeon, left six days without food, and at length strangled, by the order of Philip, one of the principal ministers of the emperor Constantius. [151] The first blood which stained the new capital was spilt in this ecclesiastical contest; and many persons were slain on both sides, in the furious and obstinate seditions of the people. The commission of enforcing a sentence of banishment against Paul had been intrusted to Hermogenes, the master-general of the cavalry; but the execution of it was fatal to himself. The Catholics rose in the defence of their bishop; the palace of Hermogenes was consumed; the first military officer of the empire was dragged by the heels through the streets of Constantinople, and, after he expired, his lifeless corpse was exposed to their wanton insults. [152] The fate of Hermogenes instructed Philip, the Praetorian praefect, to act with more precaution on a similar occasion. In the most gentle and honorable terms, he required the attendance of Paul in the baths of Xeuxippus, which had a private communication with the palace and the sea. A vessel, which lay ready at the garden stairs, immediately hoisted sail; and, while the people were still ignorant of the meditated sacrilege, their bishop was already embarked on his voyage to Thessalonica. They soon beheld, with surprise and indignation, the gates of the palace thrown open, and the usurper Macedonius seated by the side of the praefect on a lofty chariot, which was surrounded by troops of guards with drawn swords. The military procession advanced towards the cathedral; the Arians and the Catholics eagerly rushed to occupy that important post; and three thousand one hundred and fifty persons lost their lives in the confusion of the tumult. Macedonius, who was supported by a regular force, obtained a decisive victory; but his reign was disturbed by clamor and sedition; and the causes which appeared the least connected with the subject of dispute, were sufficient to nourish and to kindle the flame of civil discord. As the chapel in which the body of the great Constantine had been deposited was in a ruinous condition, the bishop transported those venerable remains into the church of St. Acacius. This prudent and even pious measure was represented as a wicked profanation by the whole party which adhered to the Homoousian doctrine. The factions immediately flew to arms, the consecrated ground was used as their field of battle; and one of the ecclesiastical historians has observed, as a real fact, not as a figure of rhetoric, that the well before the church overflowed with a stream of blood, which filled the porticos and the adjacent courts. The writer who should impute these tumults solely to a religious principle, would betray a very imperfect knowledge of human nature; yet it must be confessed that the motive which misled the sincerity of zeal, and the pretence which disguised the licentiousness of passion, suppressed the remorse which, in another cause, would have succeeded to the rage of the Christians at Constantinople. [153]

[Footnote 150: Cucusus was the last stage of his life and sufferings. The situation of that lonely town, on the confines of Cappadocia, Cilicia, and the Lesser Armenia, has occasioned some geographical perplexity; but we are directed to the true spot by the course of the Roman road from Caesarea to Anazarbus. See Cellarii Geograph. tom. ii. p. 213. Wesseling ad Itinerar. p. 179, 703.]

[Footnote 151: Athanasius (tom. i. p. 703, 813, 814) affirms, in the most positive terms, that Paul was murdered; and appeals, not only to common fame, but even to the unsuspicious testimony of Philagrius, one of the Arian persecutors. Yet he acknowledges that the heretics attributed to disease the death of the bishop of Constantinople. Athanasius is servilely copied by Socrates, (l. ii. c. 26;) but Sozomen, who discovers a more liberal temper. presumes (l. iv. c. 2) to insinuate a prudent doubt.]

[Footnote 152: Ammianus (xiv. 10) refers to his own account of this tragic event. But we no longer possess that part of his history. Note: The murder of Hermogenes took place at the first expulsion of Paul from the see of Constantinople—M.]

[Footnote 153: See Socrates, l. ii. c. 6, 7, 12, 13, 15, 16, 26, 27, 38, and Sozomen, l. iii. 3, 4, 7, 9, l. iv. c. ii. 21. The acts of St. Paul of Constantinople, of which Photius has made an abstract, (Phot. Bibliot. p. 1419-1430,) are an indifferent copy of these historians; but a modern Greek, who could write the life of a saint without adding fables and miracles, is entitled to some commendation.]

PART VII

The cruel and arbitrary disposition of Constantius, which did not always require the provocations of guilt and resistance, was justly exasperated by the tumults of his capital, and the criminal behavior of a faction, which opposed the authority and religion of their sovereign. The ordinary punishments of death, exile, and confiscation, were inflicted with partial vigor; and the Greeks still revere the holy memory of two clerks, a reader, and a sub-deacon, who were accused of the murder of Hermogenes, and beheaded at the gates of Constantinople. By an edict of Constantius against the Catholics which has not been judged worthy of a place in the Theodosian code, those who refused to communicate with the Arian bishops, and particularly with Macedonius, were deprived of the immunities of ecclesiastics, and of the rights of Christians; they were compelled to relinquish the possession of the churches; and were strictly prohibited from holding their assemblies within the walls of the city. The execution of this unjust law, in the provinces of Thrace and Asia Minor, was committed to the zeal of Macedonius; the civil and military powers were directed to obey his commands; and the cruelties exercised by this Semi-Arian tyrant in the support of the Homoiousion, exceeded the commission, and disgraced the reign, of Constantius. The sacraments of the church were administered to the reluctant victims, who denied the vocation, and abhorred the principles, of Macedonius. The rites of baptism were conferred on women and children, who, for that purpose, had been torn from the arms of their friends and parents; the mouths of the communicants were held open by a wooden engine, while the consecrated bread was forced down their throat; the breasts of tender virgins were either burnt with red-hot egg-shells, or inhumanly compressed betweens harp and heavy boards. [154] The Novatians of Constantinople and the adjacent country, by their firm attachment to the Homoousian standard, deserved to be confounded with the Catholics themselves. Macedonius was informed, that a large district of Paphlagonia [155] was almost entirely inhabited by those sectaries. He resolved either to convert or to extirpate them; and as he distrusted, on this occasion, the efficacy of an ecclesiastical mission, he commanded a body of four thousand legionaries to march against the rebels, and to reduce the territory of Mantinium under his spiritual dominion. The Novatian peasants, animated by despair and religious fury, boldly encountered the invaders of their country; and though many of the Paphlagonians were slain, the Roman legions were vanquished by an irregular multitude, armed only with scythes and axes; and, except a few who escaped by an ignominious flight, four thousand soldiers were left dead on the field of battle. The successor of Constantius has expressed, in a concise but lively manner, some of the theological calamities which afflicted the empire, and more especially the East, in the reign of a prince who was the slave of his own passions, and of those of his eunuchs: "Many were imprisoned, and persecuted, and driven into exile. Whole troops of those who are styled heretics, were massacred, particularly at Cyzicus, and at Samosata. In Paphlagonia, Bithynia, Galatia, and in many other provinces, towns and villages were laid waste, and utterly destroyed." [156]

[Footnote 154: Socrates, l. ii. c. 27, 38. Sozomen, l. iv. c. 21. The principal assistants of Macedonius, in the work of persecution, were the two bishops of Nicomedia and Cyzicus, who were esteemed for their virtues, and especially for their charity. I cannot forbear reminding the reader, that the difference between the Homoousion and Homoiousion, is almost invisible to the nicest theological eye.]

[Footnote 155: We are ignorant of the precise situation of Mantinium. In speaking of these four bands of legionaries, Socrates, Sozomen, and the author of the acts of St. Paul, use the indefinite terms of, which Nicephorus very properly translates thousands. Vales. ad Socrat. l. ii. c. 38.]

[Footnote 156: Julian. Epist. lii. p. 436, edit. Spanheim.]

While the flames of the Arian controversy consumed the vitals of the empire, the African provinces were infested by their peculiar enemies, the savage fanatics, who, under the name of Circumcellions, formed the strength and scandal of the Donatist party. [157] The severe execution of the laws of Constantine had excited a spirit of discontent and resistance, the strenuous efforts of his son Constans, to restore the unity of the church, exasperated the sentiments of mutual hatred, which had first occasioned the separation; and the methods of force and corruption employed by the two Imperial commissioners, Paul and Macarius, furnished the schismatics with a specious contrast between the maxims of the apostles and the conduct of their pretended successors. [158] The peasants who inhabited the villages of Numidia and Mauritania, were a ferocious race, who had been imperfectly reduced under the authority of the Roman laws; who were imperfectly converted to the Christian faith; but who were actuated by a blind and furious enthusiasm in the cause of their Donatist teachers. They indignantly supported the exile of their bishops, the demolition of their churches, and the interruption of their secret assemblies. The violence of the officers of justice, who were usually sustained by a military guard, was sometimes repelled with equal violence; and the blood of some popular ecclesiastics, which had been shed in the quarrel, inflamed their rude followers with an eager desire of revenging the death of these holy martyrs. By their own cruelty and rashness, the ministers of persecution sometimes provoked their fate; and the guilt of an accidental tumult precipitated the criminals into despair and rebellion. Driven from their native villages, the Donatist peasants assembled in formidable gangs on the edge of the Getulian desert; and readily exchanged the habits of labor for a life of idleness and rapine, which was consecrated by the name of religion, and faintly condemned by the doctors of the sect. The leaders of the Circumcellions assumed the title of captains of the saints; their principal weapon, as they were indifferently provided with swords and spears, was a huge and weighty club, which they termed an Israelite; and the well-known sound of "Praise be to God," which they used as their cry of war, diffused consternation over the unarmed provinces of Africa. At first their depredations were colored by the plea of necessity; but they soon exceeded the measure of subsistence, indulged without control their intemperance and avarice, burnt the villages which they had pillaged, and reigned the licentious tyrants of the open country. The occupations of husbandry, and the administration of justice, were interrupted; and as the Circumcellions pretended to restore the primitive equality of mankind, and to reform the abuses of civil society, they opened a secure asylum for the slaves and debtors, who flocked in crowds to their holy standard. When they were not resisted, they usually contented themselves with plunder, but the slightest opposition provoked them to acts of violence and murder; and some Catholic priests, who had imprudently signalized their zeal, were tortured by the fanatics with the most refined and wanton barbarity. The spirit of the Circumcellions was not always exerted against their defenceless enemies; they engaged, and sometimes defeated, the troops of the province; and in the bloody action of Bagai, they attacked in the open field, but with unsuccessful valor, an advanced guard of the Imperial cavalry. The Donatists who were taken in arms, received, and they soon deserved, the same treatment which might have been shown to the wild beasts of the desert. The captives died, without a murmur, either by the sword, the axe, or the fire; and the measures of retaliation were multiplied in a rapid proportion, which aggravated the horrors of rebellion, and excluded the hope of mutual forgiveness. In the beginning of the present century, the example of the Circumcellions has been renewed in the persecution, the boldness, the crimes, and the enthusiasm of the Camisards; and if the fanatics of Languedoc surpassed those of

Numidia, by their military achievements, the Africans maintained their fierce independence with more resolution and perseverance. [159]

[Footnote 157: See Optatus Milevitanus, (particularly iii. 4,) with the Donatis history, by M. Dupin, and the original pieces at the end of his edition. The numerous circumstances which Augustin has mentioned, of the fury of the Circumcellions against others, and against themselves, have been laboriously collected by Tillemont, Mem. Eccles. tom. vi. p. 147-165; and he has often, though without design, exposed injuries which had provoked those fanatics.]

[Footnote 158: It is amusing enough to observe the language of opposite parties, when they speak of the same men and things. Gratus, bishop of Carthage, begins the acclamations of an orthodox synod, "Gratias Deo omnipotenti et Christu Jesu... qui imperavit religiosissimo Constanti Imperatori, ut votum gereret unitatis, et mitteret ministros sancti operis famulos Dei Paulum et Macarium." Monument. Vet. ad Calcem Optati, p. 313. "Ecce subito," (says the Donatist author of the Passion of Marculus), "de Constantis regif tyrannica domo.. pollutum Macarianae persecutionis murmur increpuit, et duabus bestiis ad Africam missis, eodem scilicet Macario et Paulo, execrandum prorsus ac dirum ecclesiae certamen indictum est; ut populus Christianus ad unionem cum traditoribus faciendam, nudatis militum gladiis et draconum praesentibus signis, et tubarum vocibus cogeretur." Monument. p. 304.]

[Footnote 159: The Histoire des Camisards, in 3 vols. 12mo. Villefranche, 1760 may be recommended as accurate and impartial. It requires some attention to discover the religion of the author.]

Such disorders are the natural effects of religious tyranny, but the rage of the Donatists was inflamed by a frenzy of a very extraordinary kind; and which, if it really prevailed among them in so extravagant a degree, cannot surely be paralleled in any country or in any age. Many of these fanatics were possessed with the horror of life, and the desire of martyrdom; and they deemed it of little moment by what means, or by what hands, they perished, if their conduct was sanctified by the intention of devoting themselves to the glory of the true faith, and the hope of eternal happiness. [160] Sometimes they rudely disturbed the festivals, and profaned the temples of Paganism, with the design of exciting the most zealous of the idolaters to revenge the insulted honor of their gods. They sometimes forced their way into the courts of justice, and compelled the affrighted judge to give orders for their immediate execution. They frequently stopped travellers on the public highways, and obliged them to inflict the stroke of martyrdom, by the promise of a reward, if they consented, and by the threat of instant death, if they refused to grant so very singular a favor. When they were disappointed of every other resource, they announced the day on which, in the presence of their friends and brethren, they should cast themselves headlong from some lofty rock; and many precipices were shown, which had acquired fame by the number of religious suicides. In the actions of these desperate enthusiasts, who were admired by one party as the martyrs of God, and abhorred by the other as the victims of Satan, an impartial philosopher may discover the influence and the last abuse of that inflexible spirit which was originally derived from the character and principles of the Jewish nation.

[Footnote 160: The Donatist suicides alleged in their justification the example of Razias, which is related in the 14th chapter of the second book of the Maccabees.]

The simple narrative of the intestine divisions, which distracted the peace, and dishonored the triumph, of the church, will confirm the remark of a Pagan historian, and justify the complaint of a venerable bishop. The experience of Ammianus had convinced him, that the enmity of the Christians towards each other, surpassed the fury of savage beasts against man; [161] and Gregory Nazianzen most pathetically laments, that the kingdom of heaven was converted, by discord, into the image of chaos, of a nocturnal tempest, and of hell itself. [162] The fierce and partial writers of the times, ascribing all virtue to themselves, and imputing all guilt to their adversaries, have painted the battle of the angels and daemons. Our calmer reason will reject such pure and perfect monsters of vice or sanctity, and will impute an equal, or at least an indiscriminate, measure of good and evil to the hostile sectaries, who assumed and bestowed the appellations of orthodox and heretics. They had been educated in the same religion and the same civil society. Their hopes and fears in the present, or in a future life, were balanced in the same proportion. On either side, the error might be innocent, the faith sincere, the practice meritorious or corrupt. Their passions were excited by similar objects; and they might alternately abuse the favor of the court, or of the people. The metaphysical opinions of the Athanasians and the Arians could not influence their moral character; and they were alike actuated by the intolerant spirit which has been extracted from the pure and simple maxims of the gospel.

[Footnote 161: Nullus infestas hominibus bestias, ut sunt sibi ferales plerique Christianorum, expertus. Ammian. xxii. 5.]

[Footnote 162: Gregor, Nazianzen, Orav. i. p. 33. See Tillemont, tom vi. p. 501, qua to edit.]

A modern writer, who, with a just confidence, has prefixed to his own history the honorable epithets of political and philosophical, [163] accuses the timid prudence of Montesquieu, for neglecting to enumerate, among the causes of the decline of the empire, a law of Constantine, by which the exercise of the Pagan worship was absolutely suppressed, and a considerable part of his subjects was left destitute of priests, of temples, and of any public religion. The zeal of the philosophic historian for the rights of mankind, has induced him to acquiesce in the ambiguous testimony of those ecclesiastics, who have too lightly ascribed to their favorite hero the merit of a general persecution. [164] Instead of alleging this imaginary law, which would have blazed in the front of the Imperial codes, we may safely appeal to the original epistle, which Constantine addressed to the followers of the ancient religion; at a time when he no longer disguised his conversion, nor dreaded the rivals of his throne. He invites and exhorts, in the most pressing terms, the subjects of the Roman empire to imitate the example of their master; but he declares, that those who still refuse to open their eyes to the celestial light, may freely enjoy their temples and their fancied gods. A report, that the ceremonies of paganism were suppressed, is formally contradicted by the emperor himself, who wisely assigns, as the principle of his moderation, the invincible force of habit, of prejudice, and of superstition. [165] Without violating the sanctity of his promise, without alarming the fears of the Pagans, the artful monarch advanced, by slow and cautious steps, to undermine the irregular and decayed fabric of polytheism. The partial acts of severity which he occasionally exercised, though they were secretly promoted by a Christian zeal, were colored by the fairest pretences of justice and the public good; and while Constantine designed to ruin the foundations, he seemed to reform the abuses, of the ancient religion. After the example of the wisest of his predecessors, he condemned, under the most rigorous penalties, the occult and impious arts of divination; which excited the vain hopes, and sometimes the criminal attempts, of those who were discontented with their present condition. An ignominious silence was imposed on the oracles, which had been publicly convicted of fraud and falsehood; the effeminate priests of the Nile were abolished; and Constantine discharged the duties of a Roman censor, when he gave orders for the demolition of several temples of Phoenicia; in which every mode of prostitution was devoutly practised in the face of day, and to the honor of Venus. [166] The Imperial city of Constantinople was, in some measure, raised at the expense, and was adorned with the spoils, of the opulent temples of Greece and Asia; the sacred property was confiscated; the statues of gods and heroes were transported, with rude familiarity, among a people who considered them as objects, not of adoration, but of curiosity; the gold and silver were restored to circulation; and the magistrates, the bishops, and the eunuchs, improved the fortunate occasion of gratifying, at once, their zeal, their avarice, and their resentment. But these depredations were confined to a small part of the Roman world; and the provinces had been long since accustomed to endure the same sacrilegious rapine, from the tyranny of princes and proconsuls, who could not be suspected of any design to subvert the established religion. [167]

[Footnote 163: Histoire Politique et Philosophique des Etablissemens des Europeens dans les deux Indes, tom. i. p. 9.]

[Footnote 164: According to Eusebius, (in Vit. Constantin. l. ii. c. 45,) the emperor prohibited, both in cities and in the country, the abominable acts or parts of idolatry. I Socrates (l. i. c. 17) and Sozomen (l. ii. c. 4, 5) have represented the conduct of Constantine with a just regard to truth and history; which has been neglected by Theodoret (l. v. c. 21) and Orosius, (vii. 28.) Tum deinde (says the latter) primus Constantinus justo ordine et pio vicem vertit edicto; siquidem statuit citra ullam hominum caedem, paganorum templa claudi.]

[Footnote 165: See Eusebius in Vit. Constantin. l. ii. c. 56, 60. In the sermon to the assembly of saints, which the emperor pronounced when he was mature in years and piety, he declares to the idolaters (c. xii.) that they are permitted to offer sacrifices, and to exercise every part of their religious worship.]

[Footnote 166: See Eusebius, in Vit. Constantin. l. iii. c. 54-58, and l. iv. c. 23, 25. These acts of authority may be compared with the suppression of the Bacchanals, and the demolition of the temple of Isis, by the magistrates of Pagan Rome.]

[Footnote 167: Eusebius (in Vit. Constan. l. iii. c. 54-58) and Libanius (Orat. pro Templis, p. 9, 10, edit. Gothofred) both mention the pious sacrilege of Constantine, which they viewed in very different lights. The latter expressly declares, that "he made use of the sacred money, but made no alteration in the legal worship; the temples indeed were impoverished, but the sacred rites were performed there." Lardner's Jewish and Heathen Testimonies, vol. iv. p. 140.]

The sons of Constantine trod in the footsteps of their father, with more zeal, and with less discretion. The pretences of rapine and oppression were insensibly multiplied; [168] every indulgence was shown to the illegal behavior of the Christians; every doubt was explained to the disadvantage of Paganism; and the demolition of the temples was celebrated as one of the auspicious events of the reign of Constans and Constantius. [169] The name of Constantius is prefixed to a concise law, which might have superseded the necessity of any future prohibitions. "It is our pleasure, that in all places, and in all cities, the temples be immediately shut, and carefully guarded, that none may have the power of offending. It is likewise our pleasure, that all our subjects should abstain from sacrifices. If any one should be guilty of such an act, let him feel the sword of vengeance, and after his execution, let his property be confiscated to the public use. We denounce the same penalties against the governors of the provinces, if they neglect to punish the criminals." [170] But there is the strongest reason to believe, that this formidable edict was either composed without being published, or was published without being executed. The evidence of facts, and the monuments which are still extant of brass and marble, continue to prove the public exercise of the Pagan worship during the whole reign of the sons of Constantine. In the East, as well as in the West, in cities, as well as in the country, a great number of temples were respected, or at least were spared; and the devout multitude still enjoyed the luxury of sacrifices, of festivals, and of processions, by the permission, or by the connivance, of the civil government. About four years after the supposed date of this bloody edict, Constantius visited the temples of Rome; and the decency of his behavior is recommended by a pagan orator as an example worthy of the imitation of succeeding princes. "That emperor," says Symmachus, "suffered the privileges of the vestal virgins to remain inviolate; he bestowed the sacerdotal dignities on the nobles of Rome, granted the customary allowance to defray the expenses of the public rites and sacrifices; and, though he had embraced a different religion, he never attempted to deprive the empire of the sacred worship of antiquity." [171] The senate still presumed to consecrate, by solemn decrees, the divine memory of their sovereigns; and Constantine himself was associated, after his death, to those gods whom he had renounced and insulted during his life. The title, the ensigns, the prerogatives, of sovereign pontiff, which had been instituted by Numa, and assumed by Augustus, were accepted, without hesitation, by seven Christian emperors; who were invested with a more absolute authority over the religion which they had deserted, than over that which they professed. [172]

[Footnote 168: Ammianus (xxii. 4) speaks of some court eunuchs who were spoliis templorum pasti. Libanius says (Orat. pro Templ. p. 23) that the emperor often gave away a temple, like a dog, or a horse, or a slave, or a gold cup; but the devout philosopher takes care to observe that these sacrilegious favorites very seldom prospered.]

[Footnote 169: See Gothofred. Cod. Theodos. tom. vi. p. 262. Liban. Orat. Parental c. x. in Fabric. Bibl. Graec. tom. vii. p. 235.]

[Footnote 170: Placuit omnibus locis atque urbibus universis claudi protinus empla, et accessu vetitis omnibus licentiam delinquendi perditis abnegari. Volumus etiam cunctos a sacrificiis abstinere. Quod siquis aliquid forte hujusmodi perpetraverit, gladio sternatur: facultates etiam perempti fisco decernimus vindicari: et similiter adfligi rectores provinciarum si facinora vindicare neglexerint. Cod. Theodos. l. xvi. tit. x. leg. 4. Chronology has discovered some contradiction in the date of this extravagant law; the only one, perhaps, by which the negligence of magistrates is punished by death and confiscation. M. de la Bastie (Mem. de l'Academie, tom. xv. p. 98) conjectures, with a show of reason, that this was no more than the minutes of a law, the heads of an intended bill, which were found in Scriniis Memoriae among the papers of Constantius, and afterwards inserted, as a worthy model, in the Theodosian Code.]

[Footnote 171: Symmach. Epistol. x. 54.]

[Footnote 172: The fourth Dissertation of M. de la Bastie, sur le Souverain Pontificat des Empereurs Romains, (in the Mem. de l'Acad. tom. xv. p. 75- 144,) is a very learned and judicious performance, which explains the state, and prove the toleration, of Paganism from Constantino to Gratian. The assertion of Zosimus, that Gratian was the first who refused the pontifical robe, is confirmed beyond a doubt; and the murmurs of bigotry on that subject are almost silenced.]

The divisions of Christianity suspended the ruin of Paganism; [173] and the holy war against the infidels was less vigorously prosecuted by princes and bishops, who were more immediately alarmed by the guilt and danger of domestic rebellion. The extirpation of idolatry [174] might have been justified by the established principles of intolerance: but the hostile sects, which alternately reigned in the Imperial court were mutually apprehensive of alienating, and perhaps exasperating, the minds of a powerful, though declining faction. Every motive of authority and fashion, of interest and reason, now militated on the side of Christianity; but two or three generations elapsed, before their victorious influence was universally felt. The religion which had so long and so lately been established in the Roman empire was still revered by a numerous people, less attached indeed to speculative opinion, than to ancient custom. The honors of the state and army were indifferently bestowed on all the subjects of Constantine and

Constantius; and a considerable portion of knowledge and wealth and valor was still engaged in the service of polytheism. The superstition of the senator and of the peasant, of the poet and the philosopher, was derived from very different causes, but they met with equal devotion in the temples of the gods. Their zeal was insensibly provoked by the insulting triumph of a proscribed sect; and their hopes were revived by the well-grounded confidence, that the presumptive heir of the empire, a young and valiant hero, who had delivered Gaul from the arms of the Barbarians, had secretly embraced the religion of his ancestors.

[Footnote 173: As I have freely anticipated the use of pagans and paganism, I shall now trace the singular revolutions of those celebrated words. 1. in the Doric dialect, so familiar to the Italians, signifies a fountain; and the rural neighborhood, which frequented the same fountain, derived the common appellation of pagus and pagans. (Festus sub voce, and Servius ad Virgil. Georgic. ii. 382.) 2. By an easy extension of the word, pagan and rural became almost synonymous, (Plin. Hist. Natur. xxviii. 5;) and the meaner rustics acquired that name, which has been corrupted into peasants in the modern languages of Europe. 3. The amazing increase of the military order introduced the necessity of a correlative term, (Hume's Essays, vol. i. p. 555;) and all the people who were not enlisted in the service of the prince were branded with the contemptuous epithets of pagans. (Tacit. Hist. iii. 24, 43, 77. Juvenal. Satir. 16. Tertullian de Pallio, c. 4.) 4. The Christians were the soldiers of Christ; their adversaries, who refused his sacrament, or military oath of baptism might deserve the metaphorical name of pagans; and this popular reproach was introduced as early as the reign of Valentinian (A. D. 365) into Imperial laws (Cod. Theodos. l. xvi. tit. ii. leg. 18) and theological writings. 5. Christianity gradually filled the cities of the empire: the old religion, in the time of Prudentius (advers. Symmachum, l. i. ad fin.) and Orosius, (in Praefat. Hist.,) retired and languished in obscure villages; and the word pagans, with its new signification, reverted to its primitive origin. 6. Since the worship of Jupiter and his family has expired, the vacant title of pagans has been successively applied to all the idolaters and polytheists of the old and new world. 7. The Latin Christians bestowed it, without scruple, on their mortal enemies, the Mahometans; and the purest Unitarians were branded with the unjust reproach of idolatry and paganism. See Gerard Vossius, Etymologicon Linguae Latinae, in his works, tom. i. p. 420; Godefroy's Commentary on the Theodosian Code, tom. vi. p. 250; and Ducange, Mediae et Infimae Latinitat. Glossar.]

[Footnote 174: In the pure language of Ionia and Athens were ancient and familiar words. The former expressed a likeness, an apparition (Homer. Odys. xi. 601,) a representation, an image, created either by fancy or art. The latter denoted any sort of service or slavery. The Jews of Egypt, who translated the Hebrew Scriptures, restrained the use of these words (Exod. xx. 4, 5) to the religious worship of an image. The peculiar idiom of the Hellenists, or Grecian Jews, has been adopted by the sacred and ecclesiastical writers and the reproach of idolatry has stigmatized that visible and abject mode of superstition, which some sects of Christianity should not hastily impute to the polytheists of Greece and Rome.]

CHAPTER XXII

JULIAN DECLARED EMPEROR

PART I

Julian IS DECLARED EMPEROR BY THE LEGIONS OF GAUL—HIS MARCH AND SUCCESS—THE DEATH OF CONSTANTIUS—CIVIL ADMINISTRATION OF JULIAN

While the Romans languished under the ignominious tyranny of eunuchs and bishops, the praises of Julian were repeated with transport in every part of the empire, except in the palace of Constantius. The barbarians of Germany had felt, and still dreaded, the arms of the young Caesar; his soldiers were the companions of his victory; the grateful provincials enjoyed the blessings of his reign; but the favorites, who had opposed his elevation, were offended by his virtues; and they justly considered the friend of the people as the enemy of the court. As long as the fame of Julian was doubtful, the buffoons of the palace, who were skilled in the language of satire, tried the efficacy of those arts which they had so often practised with success. They easily discovered, that his simplicity was not exempt from affectation: the ridiculous epithets of a hairy savage, of an ape invested with the purple, were applied to the dress and person of the philosophic warrior; and his modest despatches were stigmatized as the vain and elaborate fictions of a loquacious Greek, a speculative soldier, who had studied the art of war amidst the groves of the academy. [1] The voice of malicious folly was at length silenced by the shouts of victory; the conqueror of the Franks and Alemanni could no longer be painted as an object of contempt; and the monarch himself was meanly ambitious of stealing from his lieutenant the honorable reward of his labors. In the letters crowned with laurel, which, according to ancient custom, were addressed to the provinces, the name of Julian was omitted. "Constantius had made his dispositions in person; he had signalized his valor in the foremost ranks; his military conduct had secured the victory; and the captive king of the barbarians was presented to him on the field of battle," from which he was at that time distant about forty days' journey. [2] So extravagant a fable was incapable, however, of deceiving the public credulity, or even of satisfying the pride of the emperor himself. Secretly conscious that the applause and favor of the Romans accompanied the rising fortunes of Julian, his discontented mind was prepared to receive the subtle poison of those artful sycophants, who colored their mischievous designs with the fairest appearances of truth and candor. [3] Instead of depreciating the merits of Julian, they acknowledged, and even exaggerated, his popular fame, superior talents, and important services. But they darkly insinuated, that the virtues of the Caesar might instantly be converted into the most dangerous crimes, if the inconstant multitude should prefer their inclinations to their duty; or if the general of a victorious army should be tempted from his allegiance by the hopes of revenge and independent greatness. The personal fears of Constantius were interpreted by his council as a laudable anxiety for the public safety; whilst in private, and perhaps in his own breast, he disguised, under the less odious appellation of fear, the sentiments of hatred and envy, which he had secretly conceived for the inimitable virtues of Julian.

[Footnote 1: *Omnes qui plus poterant in palatio, adulandi professores jam docti, recte consulta, prospereque completa vertebant in deridiculum: talia sine modo strepentes insulse; in odium venit cum victoriis suis; capella, non homo; ut hirsutum Julianum carpentes, appellantesque loquacem talpam, et purpuratam simiam, et litterionem Graecum: et his congruentia plurima atque vernacula principi resonantes, audire haec taliaque gestienti, virtutes ejus obruere verbis impudentibus conabantur, et segnem incessentes et timidum et umbratilem, gestaque secus verbis comptioribus exornantem.* Ammianus, s. xvii. 11. Note: The philosophers retaliated on the courtiers. Marius (says Eunapius in a newly-discovered fragment) was wont to call his antagonist Sylla a beast half lion and half fox. Constantius had nothing of the lion, but was surrounded by a whole litter of foxes. Mai. Script. Byz. Nov. Col. ii. 238. Niebuhr. Byzant. Hist. 66—M.]

[Footnote 2: Ammian. xvi. 12. The orator Themistius (iv. p. 56, 57) believed whatever was contained in the Imperial letters, which were addressed to the senate of Constantinople Aurelius Victor, who published his Abridgment in the last year of Constantius, ascribes the German victories to the wisdom of the emperor, and the fortune of the Caesar. Yet the historian, soon afterwards, was indebted to the favor or esteem of Julian for the honor of a brass statue, and the important offices of consular of the second Pannonia, and praefect of the city, Ammian. xxi. 10.]

[Footnote 3: Callido nocendi artificio, accusatoriam diritatem laudum titulis peragebant. .. Hae voces fuerunt ad inflammanda odia probria omnibus potentiores. See Mamertin, in Actione Gratiarum in Vet Panegyr. xi. 5, 6.]

The apparent tranquillity of Gaul, and the imminent danger of the eastern provinces, offered a specious pretence for the design which was artfully concerted by the Imperial ministers. They resolved to disarm the Caesar; to recall those faithful troops who guarded his person and dignity; and to employ, in a distant war against the Persian monarch, the hardy veterans who had vanquished, on the banks of the Rhine, the fiercest nations of Germany. While Julian used the laborious hours of his winter quarters at Paris in the administration of power, which, in his hands, was the exercise of virtue, he was surprised by the hasty arrival of a tribune and a notary, with positive orders, from the emperor, which they were directed to execute, and he was commanded not to oppose. Constantius signified his pleasure, that four entire legions, the Celtae, and Petulants, the Heruli, and the Batavians, should be separated from the standard of Julian, under which they had acquired their fame and discipline; that in each of the remaining bands three hundred of the bravest youths should be selected; and that this numerous detachment, the strength of the Gallic army, should instantly begin their march, and exert their utmost diligence to arrive, before the opening of the campaign, on the frontiers of Persia. [4] The Caesar foresaw and lamented the consequences of this fatal mandate. Most of the auxiliaries, who engaged their voluntary service, had stipulated, that they should never be obliged to pass the Alps. The public faith of Rome, and the personal honor of Julian, had been pledged for the observance of this condition. Such an act of treachery and oppression would destroy the confidence, and excite the resentment, of the independent warriors of Germany, who considered truth as the noblest of their virtues, and freedom as the most valuable of their possessions. The legionaries, who enjoyed the title and privileges of Romans, were enlisted for the general defence of the republic; but those mercenary troops heard with cold indifference the antiquated names of the republic and of Rome. Attached, either from birth or long habit, to the climate and manners of Gaul, they loved and admired Julian; they despised, and perhaps hated, the emperor; they dreaded the laborious march, the Persian arrows, and the burning deserts of Asia. They claimed as their own the country which they had saved; and excused their want of spirit, by pleading the sacred and more immediate duty of protecting their families and friends.

The apprehensions of the Gauls were derived from the knowledge of the impending and inevitable danger. As soon as the provinces were exhausted of their military strength, the Germans would violate a treaty which had been imposed on their fears; and notwithstanding the abilities and valor of Julian, the general of a nominal army, to whom the public calamities would be imputed, must find himself, after a vain resistance, either a prisoner in the camp of the barbarians, or a criminal in the palace of Constantius. If Julian complied with the orders which he had received, he subscribed his own destruction, and that of a people who deserved his affection. But a positive refusal was an act of rebellion, and a declaration of war. The inexorable jealousy of the emperor, the peremptory, and perhaps insidious, nature of his commands, left not any room for a fair apology, or candid interpretation; and the dependent station of the Caesar scarcely allowed him to pause or to deliberate. Solitude increased the perplexity of Julian; he could no longer apply to the faithful counsels of Sallust, who had been removed from his office by the judicious malice of the eunuchs: he could not even enforce his representations by the concurrence of the ministers, who would have been afraid or ashamed to approve the ruin of Gaul. The moment had been chosen, when Lupicinus, [5] the general of the cavalry, was despatched into Britain, to repulse the inroads of the Scots and Picts; and Florentius was occupied at Vienna by the assessment of the tribute. The latter, a crafty and corrupt statesman, declining to assume a responsible part on this dangerous occasion, eluded the pressing and repeated invitations of Julian, who represented to him, that in every important measure, the presence of the praefect was indispensable in the council of the prince. In the mean while the Caesar was oppressed by the rude and importunate solicitations of the Imperial messengers, who presumed to suggest, that if he expected the return of his ministers, he would charge himself with the guilt of the delay, and reserve for them the merit of the execution. Unable to resist, unwilling to comply, Julian expressed, in the most serious terms, his wish, and even his intention, of resigning the purple, which he could not preserve with honor, but which he could not abdicate with safety.

[Footnote 4: The minute interval, which may be interposed, between the hyeme adulta and the primo vere of Ammianus, (xx. l. 4,) instead of allowing a sufficient space for a march of three thousand miles, would render the orders of Constantius as extravagant as they were unjust. The troops of Gaul could not have reached Syria till the end of autumn. The memory of Ammianus must have been inaccurate, and his language incorrect. Note: The late editor of Ammianus attempts to vindicate his author from the charge of inaccuracy. "It is clear, from the whole course of the narrative, that Constantius entertained this design of demanding his troops from Julian, immediately after the taking of Amida, in the autumn of the preceding year, and had transmitted his orders into Gaul, before it was known that Lupicinus had gone into Britain with the Herulians and Batavians." Wagner, note to Amm. xx. 4. But it seems also clear that the troops were in winter quarters (hiemabant) when the orders arrived. Ammianus can scarcely be acquitted of incorrectness in his language at least—M]

[Footnote 5: Ammianus, xx. l. The valor of Lupicinus, and his military skill, are acknowledged by the historian, who, in his affected language, accuses the general of exalting the horns of his pride, bellowing in a tragic tone, and exciting a doubt whether he was more cruel or avaricious. The danger from the Scots and Picts was so serious that Julian himself had some thoughts of passing over into the island.]

After a painful conflict, Julian was compelled to acknowledge, that obedience was the virtue of the most eminent subject, and that the sovereign alone was entitled to judge of the public welfare. He issued the necessary orders for carrying into execution the commands of Constantius; a part of the troops began their march for the Alps; and the detachments from the several garrisons moved towards their respective places of assembly. They advanced with difficulty through the trembling and affrighted crowds of provincials, who attempted to excite their pity by silent despair, or loud lamentations, while the wives of the soldiers, holding their infants in their arms, accused the desertion of their husbands, in the mixed language of grief, of tenderness, and of indignation. This scene of general distress afflicted the humanity of the Caesar; he granted a sufficient number of post-wagons to transport the wives and families of the soldiers, [6] endeavored to alleviate the hardships which he was constrained to inflict, and increased, by the most laudable arts, his own popularity, and the discontent of the exiled troops. The grief of an armed multitude is soon converted into rage; their licentious murmurs, which every hour were communicated from tent to tent with more boldness and effect, prepared their minds for the most daring acts of sedition; and by the connivance of their tribunes, a seasonable libel was secretly dispersed, which painted in lively colors the disgrace of the Caesar, the oppression of the Gallic army, and the feeble vices of the tyrant of Asia. The servants of Constantius were astonished and alarmed by the progress of this dangerous spirit. They pressed the Caesar to hasten the departure of the troops; but they imprudently rejected the honest and judicious advice of Julian; who proposed that they should not march through Paris, and suggested the danger and temptation of a last interview.

[Footnote 6: He granted them the permission of the cursus clavularis, or clabularis. These post-wagons are often mentioned in the Code, and were supposed to carry fifteen hundred pounds weight. See Vales. ad Ammian. xx. 4.]

As soon as the approach of the troops was announced, the Caesar went out to meet them, and ascended his tribunal, which had been erected in a plain before the gates of the city. After distinguishing the officers and soldiers, who by their rank or merit deserved a peculiar attention, Julian addressed himself in a studied oration to the surrounding multitude: he celebrated their exploits with grateful applause; encouraged them to accept, with alacrity, the honor of serving under the eye of a powerful and liberal monarch; and admonished them, that the commands of Augustus required an instant and cheerful obedience. The soldiers, who were apprehensive of offending their general by an indecent clamor, or of belying their sentiments by false and venal acclamations, maintained an obstinate silence; and after a short pause, were dismissed to their quarters. The principal officers were entertained by the Caesar, who professed, in the warmest language of friendship, his desire and his inability to reward, according to their deserts, the brave companions of his victories. They retired from the feast, full of grief and perplexity; and lamented the hardship of their fate, which tore them from their beloved general and their native country. The only expedient which could prevent their separation was boldly agitated and approved the popular resentment was insensibly moulded into a regular conspiracy; their just reasons of complaint were heightened by passion, and their passions were inflamed by wine; as, on the eve of their departure, the troops were indulged in licentious festivity. At the hour of midnight, the impetuous multitude, with swords, and bows, and torches in their hands, rushed into the suburbs; encompassed the palace; [7] and, careless of future dangers, pronounced the fatal and irrevocable words, Julian Augustus! The prince, whose anxious suspense was interrupted by their disorderly acclamations, secured the doors against their intrusion; and as long as it was in his power, secluded his person and dignity from the accidents of a nocturnal tumult. At the dawn of day, the soldiers, whose zeal was irritated by opposition, forcibly entered the palace, seized, with respectful violence, the object of their choice, guarded Julian with drawn swords through the streets of Paris, placed him on the tribunal, and with repeated shouts saluted him as their emperor. Prudence, as well as loyalty, inculcated the propriety of resisting their treasonable designs; and of preparing, for his oppressed virtue, the excuse of violence. Addressing himself by turns to the multitude and to individuals, he sometimes implored their mercy, and sometimes expressed his indignation; conjured them not to sully the fame of their immortal victories; and ventured to promise, that if they would immediately return to their allegiance, he would undertake to obtain from the emperor not only a free and gracious pardon, but even the revocation of the orders which had excited their resentment. But the soldiers, who were conscious of their guilt, chose rather to depend on the gratitude of Julian, than on the clemency of the emperor. Their zeal was insensibly turned into impatience, and their impatience into rage. The inflexible Caesar sustained, till the third hour of the day, their prayers, their reproaches, and their menaces; nor did he yield, till he had been repeatedly assured, that if he wished to live, he must consent to reign. He was exalted on a shield in the presence, and amidst the unanimous acclamations, of the troops; a rich military collar, which was offered by chance, supplied the want of a diadem; [8] the ceremony was concluded by the promise of a moderate donative; and the new emperor, overwhelmed with real or affected grief retired into the most secret recesses of his apartment. [10]

[Footnote 7: Most probably the palace of the baths, (Thermarum,) of which a solid and lofty hall still subsists in the Rue de la Harpe. The buildings covered a considerable space of the modern quarter of the university; and the gardens, under the Merovingian kings, communicated with the abbey of St. Germain

des Prez. By the injuries of time and the Normans, this ancient palace was reduced, in the twelfth century, to a maze of ruins, whose dark recesses were the scene of licentious love.

Explicat aula sinus montemque amplectitur alis;
Multiplici latebra scelerum tersura ruborem.
.... pereuntis saepe pudoris Celatura nefas,
Venerisque accommoda furtis.

(These lines are quoted from the Architrenius, l. iv. c. 8, a poetical work of John de Hauteville, or Hanville, a monk of St. Alban's, about the year 1190. See Warton's History of English Poetry, vol. i. dissert. ii.) Yet such thefts might be less pernicious to mankind than the theological disputes of the Sorbonne, which have been since agitated on the same ground. Bonamy, Mem. de l'Academie, tom. xv. p. 678-632]

[Footnote 8: Even in this tumultuous moment, Julian attended to the forms of superstitious ceremony, and obstinately refused the inauspicious use of a female necklace, or a horse collar, which the impatient soldiers would have employed in the room of a diadem.]

[Footnote 9: An equal proportion of gold and silver, five pieces of the former one pound of the latter; the whole amounting to about five pounds ten shillings of our money.]

[Footnote 10: For the whole narrative of this revolt, we may appeal to authentic and original materials; Julian himself, (ad S. P. Q. Atheniensem, p. 282, 283, 284,) Libanius, (Orat. Parental. c. 44-48, in Fabricius, Bibliot. Graec. tom. vii. p. 269-273,) Ammianus, (xx. 4,) and Zosimus, (l. iii. p. 151, 152, 153.) who, in the reign of Julian, appears to follow the more respectable authority of Eunapius. With such guides we might neglect the abbreviators and ecclesiastical historians.]

The grief of Julian could proceed only from his innocence; out his innocence must appear extremely doubtful [11] in the eyes of those who have learned to suspect the motives and the professions of princes. His lively and active mind was susceptible of the various impressions of hope and fear, of gratitude and revenge, of duty and of ambition, of the love of fame, and of the fear of reproach. But it is impossible for us to calculate the respective weight and operation of these sentiments; or to ascertain the principles of action which might escape the observation, while they guided, or rather impelled, the steps of Julian himself. The discontent of the troops was produced by the malice of his enemies; their tumult was the natural effect of interest and of passion; and if Julian had tried to conceal a deep design under the appearances of chance, he must have employed the most consummate artifice without necessity, and probably without success. He solemnly declares, in the presence of Jupiter, of the Sun, of Mars, of Minerva, and of all the other deities, that till the close of the evening which preceded his elevation, he was utterly ignorant of the designs of the soldiers; [12] and it may seem ungenerous to distrust the honor of a hero and the truth of a philosopher. Yet the superstitious confidence that Constantius was the enemy, and that he himself was the favorite, of the gods, might prompt him to desire, to solicit, and even to hasten the auspicious moment of his reign, which was predestined to restore the ancient religion of mankind. When Julian had received the intelligence of the conspiracy, he resigned himself to a short slumber; and afterwards related to his friends that he had seen the genius of the empire waiting with some impatience at his door, pressing for admittance, and reproaching his want of spirit and ambition. [13] Astonished and perplexed, he addressed his prayers to the great Jupiter, who immediately signified, by a clear and manifest omen, that he should submit to the will of heaven and of the army. The conduct which disclaims the ordinary maxims of reason, excites our suspicion and eludes our inquiry. Whenever the spirit of fanaticism, at once so credulous and so crafty, has insinuated itself into a noble mind, it insensibly corrodes the vital principles of virtue and veracity.

[Footnote 11: Eutropius, a respectable witness, uses a doubtful expression, "consensu militum." (x. 15.) Gregory Nazianzen, whose ignorance night excuse his fanaticism, directly charges the apostate with presumption, madness, and impious rebellion, Orat. iii. p. 67.]

[Footnote 12: Julian. ad S. P. Q. Athen. p. 284. The devout Abbe de la Bleterie (Vie de Julien, p. 159) is almost inclined to respect the devout protestations of a Pagan.]

[Footnote 13: Ammian. xx. 5, with the note of Lindenbrogius on the Genius of the empire. Julian himself, in a confidential letter to his friend and physician, Oribasius, (Epist. xvii. p. 384,) mentions another dream, to which, before the event, he gave credit; of a stately tree thrown to the ground, of a small plant striking a deep root into the earth. Even in his sleep, the mind of the Caesar must have been agitated by the hopes and fears of his fortune. Zosimus (l. iii. p. 155) relates a subsequent dream.]

To moderate the zeal of his party, to protect the persons of his enemies, [14] to defeat and to despise the secret enterprises which were formed against his life and dignity, were the cares which employed the first days of the reign of the new emperor. Although he was firmly resolved to maintain the station which he had assumed, he was still desirous of saving his country from the calamities of civil war, of declining a contest with the superior forces of Constantius, and of preserving his own character from the reproach of perfidy and ingratitude. Adorned with the ensigns of military and imperial pomp, Julian showed himself in the field of Mars to the soldiers, who glowed with ardent enthusiasm in the cause of their pupil, their leader, and their friend. He recapitulated their victories, lamented their sufferings, applauded their resolution, animated their hopes, and checked their impetuosity; nor did he dismiss the assembly, till he had obtained a solemn promise from the troops, that if the emperor of the East would subscribe an equitable treaty, they would renounce any views of conquest, and satisfy themselves with the tranquil possession of the Gallic provinces. On this foundation he composed, in his own name, and in that of the army, a specious and moderate epistle, [15] which was delivered to Pentadius, his master of the offices, and to his chamberlain Eutherius; two ambassadors whom he appointed to receive the answer, and observe the dispositions of Constantius. This epistle is inscribed with the modest appellation of Caesar; but Julian solicits in a peremptory, though respectful, manner, the confirmation of the title of Augustus. He acknowledges the irregularity of his own election, while he justifies, in some measure, the resentment and violence of the troops which had extorted his reluctant consent. He allows the supremacy of his brother Constantius; and engages to send him an annual present of Spanish horses, to recruit his army with a select number of barbarian youths, and to accept from his choice a Praetorian praefect of approved discretion and fidelity. But he reserves for himself the nomination of his other civil and military officers, with the troops, the revenue, and the sovereignty of the provinces beyond the Alps. He admonishes the emperor to consult the dictates of justice; to distrust the arts of those venal flatterers, who subsist only by the discord of princes; and to embrace the offer of a fair and honorable treaty, equally advantageous to the republic and to the house of Constantine. In this negotiation Julian claimed no more than he already possessed. The delegated authority which he had long exercised over the provinces of Gaul, Spain, and Britain, was still obeyed under a name more independent and august. The soldiers and the people rejoiced in a revolution which was not stained even with the blood of the guilty. Florentius was a fugitive; Lupicinus a prisoner. The persons who were disaffected to the new government were disarmed and secured; and the vacant offices were distributed, according to the recommendation of merit, by a prince who despised the intrigues of the palace, and the clamors of the soldiers. [16]

[Footnote 14: The difficult situation of the prince of a rebellious army is finely described by Tacitus, (Hist. 1, 80-85.) But Otho had much more guilt, and much less abilities, than Julian.]

[Footnote 15: To this ostensible epistle he added, says Ammianus, private letters, objurgatorias et mordaces, which the historian had not seen, and would not have published. Perhaps they never existed.]

[Footnote 16: See the first transactions of his reign, in Julian. ad S. P. Q. Athen. p. 285, 286. Ammianus, xx. 5, 8. Liban. Orat. Parent. c. 49, 50, p. 273-275.]

The negotiations of peace were accompanied and supported by the most vigorous preparations for war. The army, which Julian held in readiness for immediate action, was recruited and augmented by the disorders of the times. The cruel persecutions of the faction of Magnentius had filled Gaul with numerous bands of outlaws and robbers. They cheerfully accepted the offer of a general pardon from a prince whom they could trust, submitted to the restraints of military discipline, and retained only their implacable hatred to the person and government of Constantius. [17] As soon as the season of the year permitted Julian to take the field, he appeared at the head of his legions; threw a bridge over the Rhine in the neighborhood of Cleves; and prepared to chastise the perfidy of the Attuarii, a tribe of Franks, who presumed that they might ravage, with impunity, the frontiers of a divided empire. The difficulty, as well as glory, of this enterprise, consisted in a laborious march; and Julian had conquered, as soon as he could penetrate into a country, which former princes had considered as inaccessible. After he had given peace to the Barbarians, the emperor carefully visited the fortifications along the Qhine from Cleves to Basil; surveyed, with peculiar attention, the territories which he had recovered from the hands of the Alemanni, passed through Besancon, [18] which had severely suffered from their fury, and fixed his headquarters at Vienna for the ensuing winter. The barrier of Gaul was improved and strengthened with additional fortifications; and Julian entertained some hopes that the Germans, whom he had so often vanquished, might, in his absence, be restrained by the terror of his name. Vadomair [19] was the only prince of the Alemanni whom he esteemed or feared and while the subtle Barbarian affected to observe the faith of treaties, the progress of his arms threatened the state with an unseasonable and dangerous war. The policy of Julian condescended to surprise the prince of the Alemanni by his own arts: and Vadomair, who, in the character of a friend, had incautiously accepted an invitation from the Roman governors, was seized in the midst of the entertainment, and sent away prisoner into the heart of Spain. Before the Barbarians were recovered from their amazement, the emperor appeared in arms on the banks of the Rhine, and, once more crossing the river, renewed the deep impressions of terror and respect which had been already made by four preceding expeditions. [20]

[Footnote 17: Liban. Orat. Parent. c. 50, p. 275, 276. A strange disorder, since it continued above seven years. In the factions of the Greek republics, the exiles amounted to 20,000 persons; and Isocrates assures Philip, that it would be easier to raise an army from the vagabonds than from the cities. See Hume's Essays, tom. i. p. 426, 427.]

[Footnote 18: Julian (Epist. xxxviii. p. 414) gives a short description of Vesontio, or Besancon; a rocky peninsula almost encircled by the River Doux; once a magnificent city, filled with temples, &c., now reduced to a small town, emerging, however, from its ruins.]

[Footnote 19: Vadomair entered into the Roman service, and was promoted from a barbarian kingdom to the military rank of duke of Phoenicia. He still retained the same artful character, (Ammian. xxi. 4;) but under the reign of Valens, he signalized his valor in the Armenian war, (xxix. 1.)]

[Footnote 20: Ammian. xx. 10, xxi. 3, 4. Zosimus, l. iii. p. 155.]

PART II

The ambassadors of Julian had been instructed to execute, with the utmost diligence, their important commission. But, in their passage through Italy and Illyricum, they were detained by the tedious and affected delays of the provincial governors; they were conducted by slow journeys from Constantinople to Caesarea in Cappadocia; and when at length they were admitted to the presence of Constantius, they found that he had already conceived, from the despatches of his own officers, the most unfavorable opinion of the conduct of Julian, and of the Gallic army. The letters were heard with impatience; the trembling messengers were dismissed with indignation and contempt; and the looks, gestures, the furious language of the monarch, expressed the disorder of his soul. The domestic connection, which might have reconciled the brother and the husband of Helena, was recently dissolved by the death of that princess, whose pregnancy had been several times fruitless, and was at last fatal to herself. [21] The empress Eusebia had preserved, to the last moment of her life, the warm, and even jealous, affection which she had conceived for Julian; and her mild influence might have moderated the resentment of a prince, who, since her death, was abandoned to his own passions, and to the arts of his eunuchs. But the terror of a foreign invasion obliged him to suspend the punishment of a private enemy: he continued his march towards the confines of Persia, and thought it sufficient to signify the conditions which might entitle Julian and his guilty followers to the clemency of their offended sovereign. He required, that the presumptuous Caesar should expressly renounce the appellation and rank of Augustus, which he had accepted from the rebels; that he should descend to his former station of a limited and dependent minister; that he should vest the powers of the state and army in the hands of those officers who were appointed by the Imperial court; and that he should trust his safety to the assurances of pardon, which were announced by Epictetus, a Gallic bishop, and one of the Arian favorites of Constantius. Several months were ineffectually consumed in a treaty which was negotiated at the distance of three thousand miles between Paris and Antioch; and, as soon as Julian perceived that his modest and respectful behavior served only to irritate the pride of an implacable adversary, he boldly resolved to commit his life and fortune to the chance of a civil war. He gave a public and military audience to the quaestor Leonas: the haughty epistle of Constantius was read to the attentive multitude; and Julian protested, with the most flattering deference, that he was ready to resign the title of Augustus, if he could obtain the consent of those whom he acknowledged as the authors of his elevation. The faint proposal was impetuously silenced; and the acclamations of "Julian Augustus, continue to reign, by the authority of the army, of the people, of the republic which you have saved," thundered at once from every part of the field, and terrified the pale ambassador of Constantius. A part of the letter was afterwards read, in which the emperor arraigned the ingratitude of Julian, whom he had invested with the honors of the purple; whom he had educated with so much care and tenderness; whom he had preserved in his infancy, when he was left a helpless orphan.

"An orphan!" interrupted Julian, who justified his cause by indulging his passions: "does the assassin of my family reproach me that I was left an orphan? He urges me to revenge those injuries which I have long studied to forget." The assembly was dismissed; and Leonas, who, with some difficulty, had been protected from the popular fury, was sent back to his master with an epistle, in which Julian expressed, in a strain of the most vehement eloquence, the sentiments of contempt, of hatred, and of resentment, which had been suppressed and imbittered by the dissimulation of twenty years. After this message, which might be considered as a signal of irreconcilable war, Julian, who, some weeks before, had celebrated the Christian festival of the Epiphany, [22] made a public declaration that he committed the care of his safety to the Immortal Gods; and thus publicly renounced the religion as well as the friendship of Constantius. [23]

[Footnote 21: Her remains were sent to Rome, and interred near those of her sister Constantina, in the suburb of the Via Nomentana. Ammian. xxi. 1. Libanius has composed a very weak apology, to justify his hero from a very absurd charge of poisoning his wife, and rewarding her physician with his mother's jewels. (See the seventh of seventeen new orations, published at Venice, 1754, from a MS. in St. Mark's Library, p. 117-127.) Elpidius, the Praetorian praefect of the East, to whose evidence the accuser of Julian appeals, is arraigned by Libanius, as effeminate and ungrateful; yet the religion of Elpidius is praised by Jerom, (tom. i. p. 243,) and his Ammianus (xxi. 6.)]

[Footnote 22: Feriarum die quem celebrantes mense Januario, Christiani Epiphania dictitant, progressus in eorum ecclesiam, solemniter numine orato discessit. Ammian. xxi. 2. Zonaras observes, that it was on Christmas day, and his assertion is not inconsistent; since the churches of Egypt, Asia, and perhaps Gaul, celebrated on the same day (the sixth of January) the nativity and the baptism of their Savior. The Romans, as ignorant as their brethren of the real date of his birth, fixed the solemn festival to the 25th of December, the Brumalia, or winter solstice, when the Pagans annually celebrated the birth of the sun. See Bingham's Antiquities of the Christian Church, l. xx. c. 4, and Beausobre, Hist. Critique du Manicheismo tom. ii. p. 690-700.]

[Footnote 23: The public and secret negotiations between Constantius and Julian must be extracted, with some caution, from Julian himself. (Orat. ad S. P. Q. Athen. p. 286.) Libanius, (Orat. Parent. c. 51, p. 276,) Ammianus, (xx. 9,) Zosimus, (l. iii. p. 154,) and even Zonaras, (tom. ii. l. xiii. p. 20, 21, 22,) who, on this occasion, appears to have possessed and used some valuable materials.]

The situation of Julian required a vigorous and immediate resolution. He had discovered, from intercepted letters, that his adversary, sacrificing the interest of the state to that of the monarch, had again excited the Barbarians to invade the provinces of the West. The position of two magazines, one of them collected on the banks of the Lake of Constance, the other formed at the foot of the Cottian Alps, seemed to indicate the march of two armies; and the size of those magazines, each of which consisted of six hundred thousand quarters of wheat, or rather flour, [24] was a threatening evidence of the strength and numbers of the enemy who prepared to surround him. But the Imperial legions were still in their distant quarters of Asia; the Danube was feebly guarded; and if Julian could occupy, by a sudden incursion, the important provinces of Illyricum, he might expect that a people of soldiers would resort to his standard, and that the rich mines of gold and silver would contribute to the expenses of the civil war. He proposed this bold enterprise to the assembly of the soldiers; inspired them with a just confidence in their general, and in themselves; and exhorted them to maintain their reputation of being terrible to the enemy, moderate to their fellow-citizens, and obedient to their officers. His spirited discourse was received with the loudest acclamations, and the same troops which had taken up arms against Constantius, when he summoned them to leave Gaul, now declared with alacrity, that they would follow Julian to the farthest extremities of Europe or Asia. The oath of fidelity was administered; and the soldiers, clashing their shields, and pointing their drawn swords to their throats, devoted themselves, with horrid imprecations, to the service of a leader whom they celebrated as the deliverer of Gaul and the conqueror of the Germans. [25] This solemn engagement, which seemed to be dictated by affection rather than by duty, was singly opposed by Nebridius, who had been admitted to the office of Praetorian praefect. That faithful minister, alone and unassisted, asserted the rights of Constantius, in the midst of an armed and angry multitude, to whose fury he had almost fallen an honorable, but useless sacrifice. After losing one of his hands by the stroke of a sword, he embraced the knees of the prince whom he had offended. Julian covered the praefect with his Imperial mantle, and, protecting him from the zeal of his followers, dismissed him to his own house, with less respect than was perhaps due to the virtue of an enemy. [26] The high office of Nebridius was bestowed on Sallust; and the provinces of Gaul, which were now delivered from the intolerable oppression of taxes, enjoyed the mild and equitable administration of the friend of Julian, who was permitted to practise those virtues which he had instilled into the mind of his pupil. [27]

[Footnote 24: Three hundred myriads, or three millions of medimni, a corn measure familiar to the Athenians, and which contained six Roman modii. Julian explains, like a soldier and a statesman, the danger of his situation, and the necessity and advantages of an offensive war, (ad S. P. Q. Athen. p. 286, 287.)]

[Footnote 25: See his oration, and the behavior of the troops, in Ammian. xxi. 5.]

[Footnote 26: He sternly refused his hand to the suppliant praefect, whom he sent into Tuscany. (Ammian. xxi. 5.) Libanius, with savage fury, insults Nebridius, applauds the soldiers, and almost censures the humanity of Julian. (Orat. Parent. c. 53, p. 278.)]

[Footnote 27: Ammian. xxi. 8. In this promotion, Julian obeyed the law which he publicly imposed on himself. Neque civilis quisquam judex nec militaris rector, alio quodam praeter merita suffragante, ad potiorem veniat gradum. (Ammian. xx. 5.) Absence did not weaken his regard for Sallust, with whose name (A. D. 363) he honored the consulship.]

The hopes of Julian depended much less on the number of his troops, than on the celerity of his motions. In the execution of a daring enterprise, he availed himself of every precaution, as far as prudence could suggest; and where prudence could no longer accompany his steps, he trusted the event to valor and to fortune. In the neighborhood of Basil he assembled and divided his army. [28] One body, which consisted of ten thousand men, was directed under the command of Nevitta, general of the cavalry, to advance through the midland parts of Rhaetia and Noricum. A similar division of troops, under the orders of Jovius and Jovinus, prepared to follow the oblique course of the highways, through the Alps, and the northern confines of Italy. The instructions to the generals were conceived with energy and precision: to hasten their march in close and compact columns, which, according to the disposition of the ground, might readily be changed into any order of battle; to secure themselves against the surprises of the night by strong posts and vigilant guards; to prevent resistance by their unexpected arrival; to elude examination by their sudden departure; to spread the opinion of their strength, and the terror of his name; and to join their sovereign under the walls of Sirmium. For himself Julian had reserved a more difficult and extraordinary part. He selected three thousand brave and active volunteers, resolved, like their leader, to cast behind them every hope of a retreat; at the head of this faithful band, he fearlessly plunged into the recesses of the Marcian, or Black Forest, which conceals the sources of the Danube; [29] and, for many days, the fate of Julian was unknown to the world. The secrecy of his march, his diligence, and vigor, surmounted every obstacle; he forced his way over mountains and morasses, occupied the bridges or swam the rivers, pursued his direct course, [30] without reflecting whether he traversed the territory of the Romans or of the Barbarians, and at length emerged, between Ratisbon and Vienna, at the place where he designed to embark his troops on the Danube. By a well-concerted stratagem, he seized a fleet of light brigantines, [31] as it lay at anchor; secured a apply of coarse provisions sufficient to satisfy the indelicate, and voracious, appetite of a

Gallic army; and boldly committed himself to the stream of the Danube. The labors of the mariners, who plied their oars with incessant diligence, and the steady continuance of a favorable wind, carried his fleet above seven hundred miles in eleven days; [32] and he had already disembarked his troops at Bononia, [32a] only nineteen miles from Sirmium, before his enemies could receive any certain intelligence that he had left the banks of the Rhine. In the course of this long and rapid navigation, the mind of Julian was fixed on the object of his enterprise; and though he accepted the deputations of some cities, which hastened to claim the merit of an early submission, he passed before the hostile stations, which were placed along the river, without indulging the temptation of signalizing a useless and ill-timed valor. The banks of the Danube were crowded on either side with spectators, who gazed on the military pomp, anticipated the importance of the event, and diffused through the adjacent country the fame of a young hero, who advanced with more than mortal speed at the head of the innumerable forces of the West. Lucilian, who, with the rank of general of the cavalry, commanded the military powers of Illyricum, was alarmed and perplexed by the doubtful reports, which he could neither reject nor believe. He had taken some slow and irresolute measures for the purpose of collecting his troops, when he was surprised by Dagalaiphus, an active officer, whom Julian, as soon as he landed at Bononia, had pushed forwards with some light infantry. The captive general, uncertain of his life or death, was hastily thrown upon a horse, and conducted to the presence of Julian; who kindly raised him from the ground, and dispelled the terror and amazement which seemed to stupefy his faculties. But Lucilian had no sooner recovered his spirits, than he betrayed his want of discretion, by presuming to admonish his conqueror that he had rashly ventured, with a handful of men, to expose his person in the midst of his enemies. "Reserve for your master Constantius these timid remonstrances," replied Julian, with a smile of contempt: "when I gave you my purple to kiss, I received you not as a counsellor, but as a suppliant." Conscious that success alone could justify his attempt, and that boldness only could command success, he instantly advanced, at the head of three thousand soldiers, to attack the strongest and most populous city of the Illyrian provinces. As he entered the long suburb of Sirmium, he was received by the joyful acclamations of the army and people; who, crowned with flowers, and holding lighted tapers in their hands, conducted their acknowledged sovereign to his Imperial residence. Two days were devoted to the public joy, which was celebrated by the games of the circus; but, early on the morning of the third day, Julian marched to occupy the narrow pass of Succi, in the defiles of Mount Haemus; which, almost in the midway between Sirmium and Constantinople, separates the provinces of Thrace and Dacia, by an abrupt descent towards the former, and a gentle declivity on the side of the latter. [33] The defence of this important post was intrusted to the brave Nevitta; who, as well as the generals of the Italian division, successfully executed the plan of the march and junction which their master had so ably conceived. [34]

[Footnote 28: *Ammianus (xxi. 8) ascribes the same practice, and the same motive, to Alexander the Great and other skilful generals.*]

[Footnote 29: *This wood was a part of the great Hercynian forest, which, is the time of Caesar, stretched away from the country of the Rauraci (Basil) into the boundless regions of the north. See Cluver, Germania Antiqua. l. iii. c. 47.*]

[Footnote 30: *Compare Libanius, Orat. Parent. c. 53, p. 278, 279, with Gregory Nazianzen, Orat. iii. p. 68. Even the saint admires the speed and secrecy of this march. A modern divine might apply to the progress of Julian the lines which were originally designed for another apostate:—*

*—So eagerly the fiend,
O'er bog, or steep, through strait, rough, dense, or rare,*

With head, hands, wings, or feet, pursues his way,
And swims, or sinks, or wades, or creeps, or flies.]

[Footnote 31: In that interval the Notitia places two or three fleets, the Lauriacensis, (at Lauriacum, or Lorch,) the Arlapensis, the Maginensis; and mentions five legions, or cohorts, of Libernarii, who should be a sort of marines. Sect. lviii. edit. Labb.]

[Footnote 32: Zosimus alone (l. iii. p. 156) has specified this interesting circumstance. Mamertinus, (in Panegyr. Vet. xi. 6, 7, 8,) who accompanied Julian, as count of the sacred largesses, describes this voyage in a florid and picturesque manner, challenges Triptolemus and the Argonauts of Greece, &c.]

[Footnote 32a: Banostar. Mannert—M.]

[Footnote 33: The description of Ammianus, which might be supported by collateral evidence, ascertains the precise situation of the Angustine Succorum, or passes of Succi. M. d'Anville, from the trifling resemblance of names, has placed them between Sardica and Naissus. For my own justification I am obliged to mention the only error which I have discovered in the maps or writings of that admirable geographer.]

[Footnote 34: Whatever circumstances we may borrow elsewhere, Ammianus (xx. 8, 9, 10) still supplies the series of the narrative.]

The homage which Julian obtained, from the fears or the inclination of the people, extended far beyond the immediate effect of his arms. [35] The praefectures of Italy and Illyricum were administered by Taurus and Florentius, who united that important office with the vain honors of the consulship; and as those magistrates had retired with precipitation to the court of Asia, Julian, who could not always restrain the levity of his temper, stigmatized their flight by adding, in all the Acts of the Year, the epithet of fugitive to the names of the two consuls. The provinces which had been deserted by their first magistrates acknowledged the authority of an emperor, who, conciliating the qualities of a soldier with those of a philosopher, was equally admired in the camps of the Danube and in the cities of Greece. From his palace, or, more properly, from his head-quarters of Sirmium and Naissus, he distributed to the principal cities of the empire, a labored apology for his own conduct; published the secret despatches of Constantius; and solicited the judgment of mankind between two competitors, the one of whom had expelled, and the other had invited, the Barbarians. [36] Julian, whose mind was deeply wounded by the reproach of ingratitude, aspired to maintain, by argument as well as by arms, the superior merits of his cause; and to excel, not only in the arts of war, but in those of composition. His epistle to the senate and people of Athens [37] seems to have been dictated by an elegant enthusiasm; which prompted him to submit his actions and his motives to the degenerate Athenians of his own times, with the same humble deference as if he had been pleading, in the days of Aristides, before the tribunal of the Areopagus. His application to the senate of Rome, which was still permitted to bestow the titles of Imperial power, was agreeable to the forms of the expiring republic. An assembly was summoned by Tertullus, praefect of the city; the epistle of Julian was read; and, as he appeared to be master of Italy his claims were admitted without a dissenting voice. His oblique censure of the innovations of Constantine, and his passionate invective against the vices of Constantius, were heard with less satisfaction; and the senate, as if Julian had been present, unanimously exclaimed, "Respect, we beseech you, the author of your own fortune." [38] An artful expression, which, according to the chance of war, might be differently explained; as a manly reproof of the ingratitude of the usurper, or as a flattering confession, that a single act of such benefit to the state ought to atone for all the failings of Constantius.

[Footnote 35: Ammian. xxi. 9, 10. Libanius, Orat. Parent. c. 54, p. 279, 280. Zosimus, l. iii. p. 156, 157.]

[Footnote 36: Julian (ad S. P. Q. Athen. p. 286) positively asserts, that he intercepted the letters of Constantius to the Barbarians; and Libanius as positively affirms, that he read them on his march to the troops and the cities. Yet Ammianus (xxi. 4) expresses himself with cool and candid hesitation, si famoe solius admittenda est fides. He specifies, however, an intercepted letter from Vadomair to Constantius, which supposes an intimate correspondence between them. "disciplinam non habet."]

[Footnote 37: Zosimus mentions his epistles to the Athenians, the Corinthians, and the Lacedaemonians. The substance was probably the same, though the address was properly varied. The epistle to the Athenians is still extant, (p. 268-287,) and has afforded much valuable information. It deserves the praises of the Abbe de la Bleterie, (Pref. a l'Histoire de Jovien, p. 24, 25,) and is one of the best manifestoes to be found in any language.]

[Footnote 38: Auctori tuo reverentiam rogamus. Ammian. xxi. 10. It is amusing enough to observe the secret conflicts of the senate between flattery and fear. See Tacit. Hist. i. 85.]

The intelligence of the march and rapid progress of Julian was speedily transmitted to his rival, who, by the retreat of Sapor, had obtained some respite from the Persian war. Disguising the anguish of his soul under the semblance of contempt, Constantius professed his intention of returning into Europe, and of giving chase to Julian; for he never spoke of his military expedition in any other light than that of a hunting party. [39] In the camp of Hierapolis, in Syria, he communicated this design to his army; slightly mentioned the guilt and rashness of the Caesar; and ventured to assure them, that if the mutineers of Gaul presumed to meet them in the field, they would be unable to sustain the fire of their eyes, and the irresistible weight of their shout of onset. The speech of the emperor was received with military applause, and Theodotus, the president of the council of Hierapolis, requested, with tears of adulation, that his city might be adorned with the head of the vanquished rebel. [40] A chosen detachment was despatched away in post-wagons, to secure, if it were yet possible, the pass of Succi; the recruits, the horses, the arms, and the magazines, which had been prepared against Sapor, were appropriated to the service of the civil war; and the domestic victories of Constantius inspired his partisans with the most sanguine assurances of success. The notary Gaudentius had occupied in his name the provinces of Africa; the subsistence of Rome was intercepted; and the distress of Julian was increased by an unexpected event, which might have been productive of fatal consequences. Julian had received the submission of two legions and a cohort of archers, who were stationed at Sirmium; but he suspected, with reason, the fidelity of those troops which had been distinguished by the emperor; and it was thought expedient, under the pretence of the exposed state of the Gallic frontier, to dismiss them from the most important scene of action. They advanced, with reluctance, as far as the confines of Italy; but as they dreaded the length of the way, and the savage fierceness of the Germans, they resolved, by the instigation of one of their tribunes, to halt at Aquileia, and to erect the banners of Constantius on the walls of that impregnable city. The vigilance of Julian perceived at once the extent of the mischief, and the necessity of applying an immediate remedy. By his order, Jovinus led back a part of the army into Italy; and the siege of Aquileia was formed with diligence, and prosecuted with vigor. But the legionaries, who seemed to have rejected the yoke of discipline, conducted the defence of the place with skill and perseverance; vited the rest of Italy to imitate the example of their courage and loyalty; and threatened the retreat of Julian, if he should be forced to yield to the superior numbers of the armies of the East. [41]

[Footnote 39: *Tanquam venaticiam praedam caperet: hoc enim ad Jeniendum suorum metum subinde praedicabat. Ammian. xxii. 7.*]

[Footnote 40: See the speech and preparations in Ammianus, xxi. 13. The vile Theodotus afterwards implored and obtained his pardon from the merciful conqueror, who signified his wish of diminishing his enemies and increasing the numbers of his friends, (xxii. 14.)]

[Footnote 41: Ammian. xxi. 7, 11, 12. He seems to describe, with superfluous labor, the operations of the siege of Aquileia, which, on this occasion, maintained its impregnable fame. Gregory Nazianzen (Orat. iii. p. 68) ascribes this accidental revolt to the wisdom of Constantius, whose assured victory he announces with some appearance of truth. *Constantio quem credebat procul dubio fore victorem; nemo enim omnium tunc ab hac constanti sententia discrepebat. Ammian. xxi. 7.*]

But the humanity of Julian was preserved from the cruel alternative which he pathetically laments, of destroying or of being himself destroyed: and the seasonable death of Constantius delivered the Roman empire from the calamities of civil war. The approach of winter could not detain the monarch at Antioch; and his favorites durst not oppose his impatient desire of revenge. A slight fever, which was perhaps occasioned by the agitation of his spirits, was increased by the fatigues of the journey; and Constantius was obliged to halt at the little town of Mopsucrene, twelve miles beyond Tarsus, where he expired, after a short illness, in the forty-fifth year of his age, and the twenty-fourth of his reign. [42] His genuine character, which was composed of pride and weakness, of superstition and cruelty, has been fully displayed in the preceding narrative of civil and ecclesiastical events. The long abuse of power rendered him a considerable object in the eyes of his contemporaries; but as personal merit can alone deserve the notice of posterity, the last of the sons of Constantine may be dismissed from the world, with the remark, that he inherited the defects, without the abilities, of his father. Before Constantius expired, he is said to have named Julian for his successor; nor does it seem improbable, that his anxious concern for the fate of a young and tender wife, whom he left with child, may have prevailed, in his last moments, over the harsher passions of hatred and revenge. Eusebius, and his guilty associates, made a faint attempt to prolong the reign of the eunuchs, by the election of another emperor; but their intrigues were rejected with disdain, by an army which now abhorred the thought of civil discord; and two officers of rank were instantly despatched, to assure Julian, that every sword in the empire would be drawn for his service. The military designs of that prince, who had formed three different attacks against Thrace, were prevented by this fortunate event. Without shedding the blood of his fellow-citizens, he escaped the dangers of a doubtful conflict, and acquired the advantages of a complete victory. Impatient to visit the place of his birth, and the new capital of the empire, he advanced from Naissus through the mountains of Haemus, and the cities of Thrace. When he reached Heraclea, at the distance of sixty miles, all Constantinople was poured forth to receive him; and he made his triumphal entry amidst the dutiful acclamations of the soldiers, the people, and the senate. At innumerable multitude pressed around him with eager respect and were perhaps disappointed when they beheld the small stature and simple garb of a hero, whose unexperienced youth had vanquished the Barbarians of Germany, and who had now traversed, in a successful career, the whole continent of Europe, from the shores of the Atlantic to those of the Bosphorus. [43] A few days afterwards, when the remains of the deceased emperor were landed in the harbor, the subjects of Julian applauded the real or affected humanity of their sovereign. On foot, without his diadem, and clothed in a mourning habit, he accompanied the funeral as far as the church of the Holy Apostles, where the body was deposited: and if these marks of respect may be interpreted as a selfish tribute to the birth and dignity of his Imperial kinsman, the tears of Julian professed to the world that he had forgot the injuries, and remembered only the obligations, which he had received from Constantius. [44] As soon as the legions of Aquileia were assured of the death of the emperor, they opened the gates of the city, and, by the sacrifice of their guilty leaders, obtained an easy pardon from the prudence or lenity of Julian; who, in the thirty-second year of his age, acquired the undisputed possession of the Roman empire. [45]

[Footnote 42: His death and character are faithfully delineated by Ammianus, (xxi. 14, 15, 16;) and we are authorized to despise and detest the foolish calumny of Gregory, (Orat. iii. p. 68,) who accuses Julian of contriving the death of his benefactor. The private repentance of the emperor, that he had spared and promoted Julian, (p. 69, and Orat. xxi. p. 389,) is not improbable in itself, nor incompatible with the public verbal testament which prudential considerations might dictate in the last moments of his life. Note: Wagner thinks this sudden change of sentiment altogether a fiction of the attendant courtiers and chiefs of the army. who up to this time had been hostile to Julian. Note in loco Ammian—M.]

[Footnote 43: In describing the triumph of Julian, Ammianus (xxii. l, 2) assumes the lofty tone of an orator or poet; while Libanius (Orat. Parent. c. 56, p. 281) sinks to the grave simplicity of an historian.]

[Footnote 44: The funeral of Constantius is described by Ammianus, (xxi. 16.) Gregory Nazianzen, (Orat. iv. p. 119,) Mamertinus, in (Panegyr. Vet. xi. 27,) Libanius, (Orat. Parent. c. lvi. p. 283,) and Philostorgius, (l. vi. c. 6, with Godefroy's Dissertations, p. 265.) These writers, and their followers, Pagans, Catholics, Arians, beheld with very different eyes both the dead and the living emperor.]

[Footnote 45: The day and year of the birth of Julian are not perfectly ascertained. The day is probably the sixth of November, and the year must be either 331 or 332. Tillemont, Hist. des Empereurs, tom. iv. p. 693. Ducange, Fam. Byzantin. p. 50. I have preferred the earlier date.]

PART III

Philosophy had instructed Julian to compare the advantages of action and retirement; but the elevation of his birth, and the accidents of his life, never allowed him the freedom of choice. He might perhaps sincerely have preferred the groves of the academy, and the society of Athens; but he was constrained, at first by the will, and afterwards by the injustice, of Constantius, to expose his person and fame to the dangers of Imperial greatness; and to make himself accountable to the world, and to posterity, for the happiness of millions. [46] Julian recollected with terror the observation of his master Plato, [47] that the government of our flocks and herds is always committed to beings of a superior species; and that the conduct of nations requires and deserves the celestial powers of the gods or of the genii. From this principle he justly concluded, that the man who presumes to reign, should aspire to the perfection of the divine nature; that he should purify his soul from her mortal and terrestrial part; that he should extinguish his appetites, enlighten his understanding, regulate his passions, and subdue the wild beast, which, according to the lively metaphor of Aristotle, [48] seldom fails to ascend the throne of a despot. The throne of Julian, which the death of Constantius fixed on an independent basis, was the seat of reason, of virtue, and perhaps of vanity. He despised the honors, renounced the pleasures, and discharged with incessant diligence the duties, of his exalted station; and there were few among his subjects who would have consented to relieve him from the weight of the diadem, had they been obliged to submit their time and their actions to the rigorous laws which that philosophic emperor imposed on himself. One of his most intimate friends, [49] who had often shared the frugal simplicity of his table, has remarked, that his light and sparing diet (which was usually of the vegetable kind) left his mind and body always free and active, for the various and important business of an author, a pontiff, a magistrate, a general, and a prince. In one and the same day, he gave audience to several ambassadors, and wrote, or dictated, a great number of letters to his generals, his civil magistrates, his private friends, and the different cities of his dominions. He listened to the memorials which had been received, considered the subject of the petitions, and signified his intentions more rapidly than they could be taken in short-hand by the diligence of his secretaries. He possessed such flexibility of thought, and such firmness of attention, that he could employ his hand to write, his ear to listen, and his voice to dictate; and pursue at once three several trains of ideas without hesitation, and without error. While his ministers reposed, the prince flew with agility from one labor to another, and, after a hasty dinner, retired into his library, till the public business, which he had appointed for the evening, summoned him to interrupt the prosecution of his studies. The supper of the emperor was still less substantial than the former meal; his sleep was never clouded by the fumes of indigestion; and except in the short interval of a marriage, which was the effect of policy rather than love, the chaste Julian never shared his bed with a female companion. [50] He was soon awakened by the entrance of fresh secretaries, who had slept the preceding day; and his servants were obliged to wait alternately while their indefatigable master allowed himself scarcely any other refreshment than the change of occupation. The predecessors of Julian, his uncle, his brother, and his cousin, indulged their puerile taste for the games of the Circus, under the specious pretence of complying with the inclinations of the people; and they frequently remained the greatest part of the day as idle spectators, and as a part of the splendid spectacle, till the ordinary round of twenty-four races [51] was completely finished. On solemn festivals, Julian, who felt and professed an unfashionable dislike to these frivolous amusements, condescended to appear in the Circus; and after bestowing a careless glance at five or six of the races, he hastily withdrew with the impatience of a philosopher, who considered every moment as lost that was not devoted to the advantage of the public or the improvement of his own mind. [52] By this avarice of time, he seemed to protract the short duration of his reign; and if the dates were less securely ascertained, we should refuse to believe, that only sixteen months elapsed between the death of Constantius and the departure of his successor for the Persian war. The actions of Julian can only be preserved by the care of the historian; but the portion of his voluminous writings, which is still extant, remains as a monument of the application, as well as of the genius, of the emperor. The Misopogon, the Caesars, several of his orations, and his elaborate work against the Christian religion, were composed in the long nights of the two winters, the former of which he passed at Constantinople, and the latter at Antioch.

[Footnote 46: Julian himself (p. 253-267) has expressed these philosophical ideas with much eloquence and some affectation, in a very elaborate epistle to Themistius. The Abbe de la Bleterie, (tom. ii. p. 146-193,) who has given an elegant translation, is inclined to believe that it was the celebrated Themistius, whose orations are still extant.]

[Footnote 47: Julian. ad Themist. p. 258. Petavius (not. p. 95) observes that this passage is taken from the fourth book De Legibus; but either Julian quoted from memory, or his MSS. were different from ours Xenophon opens the Cyropaedia with a similar reflection.]

[Footnote 48: Aristot. ap. Julian. p. 261. The MS. of Vossius, unsatisfied with the single beast, affords the stronger reading of which the experience of despotism may warrant.]

[Footnote 49: Libanius (Orat. Parentalis, c. lxxxiv. lxxxv. p. 310, 311, 312) has given this interesting detail of the private life of Julian. He himself (in Misopogon, p. 350) mentions his vegetable diet, and upbraids the gross and sensual appetite of the people of Antioch.]

[Footnote 50: Lectulus... Vestalium toris purior, is the praise which Mamertinus (Panegyr. Vet. xi. 13) addresses to Julian himself. Libanius affirms, in sober peremptory language, that Julian never knew a woman before his marriage, or after the death of his wife, (Orat. Parent. c. lxxxviii. p. 313.) The chastity of Julian is confirmed by the impartial testimony of Ammianus, (xxv. 4,) and the partial silence of the Christians. Yet Julian ironically urges the reproach of the people of Antioch, that he almost always (in Misopogon, p. 345) lay alone. This suspicious expression is explained by the Abbe de la Bleterie (Hist. de Jovien, tom. ii. p. 103-109) with candor and ingenuity.]

[Footnote 51: See Salmasius ad Sueton in Claud. c. xxi. A twenty-fifth race, or missus, was added, to complete the number of one hundred chariots, four of which, the four colors, started each heat.

Centum quadrijugos agitabo ad flumina currus.

It appears, that they ran five or seven times round the Mota (Sueton in Domitian. c. 4;) and (from the measure of the Circus Maximus at Rome, the Hippodrome at Constantinople, &c.) it might be about a four mile course.]

[Footnote 52: Julian. in Misopogon, p. 340. Julius Caesar had offended the Roman people by reading his despatches during the actual race. Augustus indulged their taste, or his own, by his constant attention to the important business of the Circus, for which he professed the warmest inclination. Sueton. in August. c. xlv.]

The reformation of the Imperial court was one of the first and most necessary acts of the government of Julian. [53] Soon after his entrance into the palace of Constantinople, he had occasion for the service of a barber. An officer, magnificently dressed, immediately presented himself. "It is a barber," exclaimed the prince, with affected surprise, "that I want, and not a receiver-general of the finances." [54] He questioned the man concerning the profits of his employment and was informed, that besides a large salary, and some valuable perquisites, he enjoyed a daily allowance for twenty servants, and as many horses. A thousand barbers, a thousand cup-bearers, a thousand cooks, were distributed in the several offices of luxury; and the number of eunuchs could be compared only with the insects of a summer's day. The monarch who resigned to his subjects the superiority of merit and virtue, was distinguished by the oppressive magnificence of his dress, his table, his buildings, and his train. The stately palaces erected by Constantine and his sons, were decorated with many colored marbles, and ornaments of massy gold. The most exquisite dainties were procured, to gratify their pride, rather than their taste; birds of the most distant climates, fish from the most remote seas, fruits out of their natural season, winter roses, and summer snows. [56] The domestic crowd of the palace surpassed the expense of the legions; yet the smallest part of this costly multitude was subservient to the use, or even to the splendor, of the throne. The monarch was disgraced, and the people was injured, by the creation and sale of an infinite number of obscure, and even titular employments; and the most worthless of mankind might purchase the privilege of being maintained, without the necessity of labor, from the public revenue. The waste of an enormous household, the increase of fees and perquisites, which were soon claimed as a lawful debt, and the bribes which they extorted from those who feared their enmity, or solicited their favor, suddenly enriched these haughty menials. They abused their fortune, without considering their past, or their future, condition; and their rapine and venality could be equalled only by the extravagance of their dissipations. Their silken robes were embroidered with gold, their tables were served with delicacy and profusion; the houses which they built for their own use, would have covered the farm of an ancient consul; and the most honorable citizens were obliged to dismount from their horses, and respectfully to salute a eunuch whom they met on the public highway. The luxury of the palace excited the contempt and indignation of Julian, who usually slept on the ground, who yielded with reluctance to the indispensable calls of nature; and who placed his vanity, not in emulating, but in despising, the pomp of royalty.

[Footnote 53: *The reformation of the palace is described by Ammianus, (xxii. 4,) Libanius, Orat. (Parent. c. lxii. p. 288, &c.,) Mamertinus, in Panegyr. (Vet. xi. 11,) Socrates, (l. iii. c. l.,) and Zonaras, (tom. ii. l. xiii. p. 24.)*]

[Footnote 54: *Ego non rationalem jussi sed tonsorem acciri. Zonaras uses the less natural image of a senator. Yet an officer of the finances, who was satisfied with wealth, might desire and obtain the honors of the senate.*]

[Footnote 56: *The expressions of Mamertinus are lively and forcible. Quis etiam prandiorum et caenarum laboratas magnitudines Romanus populus sensit; cum quaesitissimae dapes non gustu sed difficultatibus aestimarentur; miracula avium, longinqui maris pisces, aheni temporis poma, aestivae nives, hybernae rosae*]

By the total extirpation of a mischief which was magnified even beyond its real extent, he was impatient to relieve the distress, and to appease the murmurs of the people; who support with less uneasiness the weight of taxes, if they are convinced that the fruits of their industry are appropriated to the service of the state. But in the execution of this salutary work, Julian is accused of proceeding with too much haste and inconsiderate severity. By a single edict, he reduced the palace of Constantinople to an immense desert, and dismissed with ignominy the whole train of slaves and dependants, [57] without providing any just, or at least benevolent, exceptions, for the age, the services, or the poverty, of the faithful domestics of the Imperial family. Such indeed was the temper of Julian, who seldom recollected the fundamental maxim of Aristotle, that true virtue is placed at an equal distance between the opposite vices.

The splendid and effeminate dress of the Asiatics, the curls and paint, the collars and bracelets, which had appeared so ridiculous in the person of Constantine, were consistently rejected by his philosophic successor. But with the fopperies, Julian affected to renounce the decencies of dress; and seemed to value himself for his neglect of the laws of cleanliness. In a satirical performance, which was designed for the public eye, the emperor descants with pleasure, and even with pride, on the length of his nails, and the inky blackness of his hands; protests, that although the greatest part of his body was covered with hair, the use of the razor was confined to his head alone; and celebrates, with visible complacency, the shaggy and populous [58] beard, which he fondly cherished, after the example of the philosophers of Greece. Had Julian consulted the simple dictates of reason, the first magistrate of the Romans would have scorned the affectation of Diogenes, as well as that of Darius.

[Footnote 57: *Yet Julian himself was accused of bestowing whole towns on the eunuchs, (Orat. vii. against Polyclet. p. 117-127.) Libanius contents himself with a cold but positive denial of the fact, which seems indeed to belong more properly to Constantius. This charge, however, may allude to some unknown circumstance.*]

[Footnote 58: *In the Misopogon (p. 338, 339) he draws a very singular picture of himself, and the following words are strangely characteristic. The friends of the Abbe de la Bleterie adjured him, in the name of the French nation, not to translate this passage, so offensive to their delicacy, (Hist. de Jovien,* tom. ii. p. 94.) Like him, I have contented myself with a transient allusion; but the little animal which Julian names, is a beast familiar to man, and signifies love.]

But the work of public reformation would have remained imperfect, if Julian had only corrected the abuses, without punishing the crimes, of his predecessor's reign. "We are now delivered," says he, in a familiar letter to one of his intimate friends, "we are now surprisingly delivered from the voracious jaws of the Hydra. [59] I do not mean to apply the epithet to my brother Constantius. He is no more; may the earth lie light on his head! But his artful and cruel favorites studied to deceive and exasperate a prince, whose natural mildness cannot be praised without some efforts of adulation. It is not, however, my intention, that even those men should be oppressed: they are accused, and they shall enjoy the benefit of a fair and impartial trial." To conduct this inquiry, Julian named six judges of the highest rank in the state and army; and as he wished to escape the reproach of condemning his personal enemies, he fixed this extraordinary tribunal at Chalcedon, on the Asiatic side of the Bosphorus; and transferred to the commissioners an absolute power to pronounce and execute their final sentence, without delay, and without appeal. The office of president was exercised by the venerable praefect of the East, a second Sallust, [60] whose virtues conciliated the esteem of Greek sophists, and of Christian bishops. He was assisted by the eloquent Mamertinus, [61] one of the consuls elect, whose merit is loudly celebrated by the doubtful evidence of his own applause. But the civil wisdom of two magistrates was overbalanced by the ferocious violence of four generals, Nevitta, Agilo, Jovinus, and Arbetio. Arbetio, whom the public would have seen with less surprise at the bar than on the bench, was supposed to possess the secret of the commission; the armed and angry leaders of the Jovian and Herculian bands encompassed the tribunal; and the judges were alternately swayed by the laws of justice, and by the clamors of faction. [62]

[Footnote 59: Julian, epist. xxiii. p. 389. He uses the words in writing to his friend Hermogenes, who, like himself, was conversant with the Greek poets.]

[Footnote 60: The two Sallusts, the praefect of Gaul, and the praefect of the East, must be carefully distinguished, (Hist. des Empereurs, tom. iv. p. 696.) I have used the surname of Secundus, as a convenient epithet. The second Sallust extorted the esteem of the Christians themselves; and Gregory Nazianzen, who condemned his religion, has celebrated his virtues, (Orat. iii. p. 90.) See a curious note of the Abbe de la Bleterie, Vie de Julien, p. 363. Note: Gibbonus secundum habet pro numero, quod tamen est viri agnomen Wagner, nota in loc. Amm. It is not a mistake; it is rather an error in taste. Wagner inclines to transfer the chief guilt to Arbetio—M.]

[Footnote 61: Mamertinus praises the emperor (xi. l.) for bestowing the offices of Treasurer and Praefect on a man of wisdom, firmness, integrity, &c., like himself. Yet Ammianus ranks him (xxi. l.) among the ministers of Julian, quorum merita norat et fidem.]

[Footnote 62: The proceedings of this chamber of justice are related by Ammianus, (xxii. 3,) and praised by Libanius, (Orat. Parent. c. 74, p. 299, 300.)]

The chamberlain Eusebius, who had so long abused the favor of Constantius, expiated, by an ignominious death, the insolence, the corruption, and cruelty of his servile reign. The executions of Paul and Apodemius (the former of whom was burnt alive) were accepted as an inadequate atonement by the widows and orphans of so many hundred Romans, whom those legal tyrants had betrayed and murdered. But justice herself (if we may use the pathetic expression of Ammianus) [63] appeared to weep over the fate of Ursulus, the treasurer of the empire; and his blood accused the ingratitude of

Julian, whose distress had been seasonably relieved by the intrepid liberality of that honest minister. The rage of the soldiers, whom he had provoked by his indiscretion, was the cause and the excuse of his death; and the emperor, deeply wounded by his own reproaches and those of the public, offered some consolation to the family of Ursulus, by the restitution of his confiscated fortunes. Before the end of the year in which they had been adorned with the ensigns of the prefecture and consulship, [64] Taurus and Florentius were reduced to implore the clemency of the inexorable tribunal of Chalcedon. The former was banished to Vercellae in Italy, and a sentence of death was pronounced against the latter. A wise prince should have rewarded the crime of Taurus: the faithful minister, when he was no longer able to oppose the progress of a rebel, had taken refuge in the court of his benefactor and his lawful sovereign. But the guilt of Florentius justified the severity of the judges; and his escape served to display the magnanimity of Julian, who nobly checked the interested diligence of an informer, and refused to learn what place concealed the wretched fugitive from his just resentment. [65] Some months after the tribunal of Chalcedon had been dissolved, the praetorian vicegerent of Africa, the notary Gaudentius, and Artemius [66] duke of Egypt, were executed at Antioch. Artemius had reigned the cruel and corrupt tyrant of a great province; Gaudentius had long practised the arts of calumny against the innocent, the virtuous, and even the person of Julian himself. Yet the circumstances of their trial and condemnation were so unskillfully managed, that these wicked men obtained, in the public opinion, the glory of suffering for the obstinate loyalty with which they had supported the cause of Constantius. The rest of his servants were protected by a general act of oblivion; and they were left to enjoy with impunity the bribes which they had accepted, either to defend the oppressed, or to oppress the friendless. This measure, which, on the soundest principles of policy, may deserve our approbation, was executed in a manner which seemed to degrade the majesty of the throne. Julian was tormented by the importunities of a multitude, particularly of Egyptians, who loudly redemanded the gifts which they had imprudently or illegally bestowed; he foresaw the endless prosecution of vexatious suits; and he engaged a promise, which ought always to have been sacred, that if they would repair to Chalcedon, he would meet them in person, to hear and determine their complaints. But as soon as they were landed, he issued an absolute order, which prohibited the watermen from transporting any Egyptian to Constantinople; and thus detained his disappointed clients on the Asiatic shore till, their patience and money being utterly exhausted, they were obliged to return with indignant murmurs to their native country. [67]

[Footnote 63: Ursuli vero necem ipsa mihi videtur flesse justitia. Libanius, who imputes his death to the soldiers, attempts to criminate the court of the largesses.]

[Footnote 64: Such respect was still entertained for the venerable names of the commonwealth, that the public was surprised and scandalized to hear Taurus summoned as a criminal under the consulship of Taurus. The summons of his colleague Florentius was probably delayed till the commencement of the ensuing year.]

[Footnote 65: Ammian. xx. 7.]

[Footnote 66: For the guilt and punishment of Artemius, see Julian (Epist. x. p. 379) and Ammianus, (xxii. 6, and Vales, ad hoc.) The merit of Artemius, who demolished temples, and was put to death by an apostate, has tempted the Greek and Latin churches to honor him as a martyr. But as ecclesiastical history attests that he was not only a tyrant, but an Arian, it is not altogether easy to justify this indiscreet promotion. Tillemont, Mem. Eccles. tom. vii. p. 1319.]

[Footnote 67: See Ammian. xxii. 6, and Vales, ad locum; and the Codex Theodosianus, l. ii. tit. xxxix. leg. i.; and Godefroy's Commentary, tom. i. p. 218, ad locum.]

PART IV

The numerous army of spies, of agents, and informers enlisted by Constantius to secure the repose of one man, and to interrupt that of millions, was immediately disbanded by his generous successor. Julian was slow in his suspicions, and gentle in his punishments; and his contempt of treason was the result of judgment, of vanity, and of courage. Conscious of superior merit, he was persuaded that few among his subjects would dare to meet him in the field, to attempt his life, or even to seat themselves on his vacant throne. The philosopher could excuse the hasty sallies of discontent; and the hero could despise the ambitious projects which surpassed the fortune or the abilities of the rash conspirators. A citizen of Ancyra had prepared for his own use a purple garment; and this indiscreet action, which, under the reign of Constantius, would have been considered as a capital offence, [68] was reported to Julian by the officious importunity of a private enemy. The monarch, after making some inquiry into the rank and character of his rival, despatched the informer with a present of a pair of purple slippers, to complete the magnificence of his Imperial habit. A more dangerous conspiracy was formed by ten of the domestic guards, who had resolved to assassinate Julian in the field of exercise near Antioch. Their intemperance revealed their guilt; and they were conducted in chains to the presence of their injured sovereign, who, after a lively representation of the wickedness and folly of their enterprise, instead of a death of torture, which they deserved and expected, pronounced a sentence of exile against the two principal offenders. The only instance in which Julian seemed to depart from his accustomed clemency, was the execution of a rash youth, who, with a feeble hand, had aspired to seize the reins of empire. But that youth was the son of Marcellus, the general of cavalry, who, in the first campaign of the Gallic war, had deserted the standard of the Caesar and the republic. Without appearing to indulge his personal resentment, Julian might easily confound the crime of the son and of the father; but he was reconciled by the distress of Marcellus, and the liberality of the emperor endeavored to heal the wound which had been inflicted by the hand of justice. [69]

[Footnote 68: The president Montesquieu (Considerations sur la Grandeur, &c., des Romains, c. xiv. in his works, tom. iii. p. 448, 449,) excuses this minute and absurd tyranny, by supposing that actions the most indifferent in our eyes might excite, in a Roman mind, the idea of guilt and danger. This strange apology is supported by a strange misapprehension of the English laws, "chez une nation.... ou il est defendu da boire a la sante d'une certaine personne."]

[Footnote 69: The clemency of Julian, and the conspiracy which was formed against his life at Antioch, are described by Ammianus (xxii. 9, 10, and Vales, ad loc.) and Libanius, (Orat. Parent. c. 99, p. 323.)]

Julian was not insensible of the advantages of freedom. [70] From his studies he had imbibed the spirit of ancient sages and heroes; his life and fortunes had depended on the caprice of a tyrant; and when he ascended the throne, his pride was sometimes mortified by the reflection, that the slaves who would not dare to censure his defects were not worthy to applaud his virtues. [71] He sincerely abhorred the system of Oriental despotism, which Diocletian, Constantine, and the patient habits of fourscore years, had established in the empire. A motive of superstition prevented the execution of the design, which Julian had frequently meditated, of relieving his head from the weight of a costly diadem; [72] but he absolutely refused the title of Dominus, or Lord, [73] a word which was grown so familiar to the ears of the Romans, that they no longer remembered its servile and humiliating origin. The office, or rather the name, of consul, was cherished by a prince who contemplated with reverence the ruins of the republic;

and the same behavior which had been assumed by the prudence of Augustus was adopted by Julian from choice and inclination. On the calends of January, at break of day, the new consuls, Mamertinus and Nevitta, hastened to the palace to salute the emperor. As soon as he was informed of their approach, he leaped from his throne, eagerly advanced to meet them, and compelled the blushing magistrates to receive the demonstrations of his affected humility. From the palace they proceeded to the senate. The emperor, on foot, marched before their litters; and the gazing multitude admired the image of ancient times, or secretly blamed a conduct, which, in their eyes, degraded the majesty of the purple. [74] But the behavior of Julian was uniformly supported. During the games of the Circus, he had, imprudently or designedly, performed the manumission of a slave in the presence of the consul. The moment he was reminded that he had trespassed on the jurisdiction of another magistrate, he condemned himself to pay a fine of ten pounds of gold; and embraced this public occasion of declaring to the world, that he was subject, like the rest of his fellow-citizens, to the laws, [75] and even to the forms, of the republic. The spirit of his administration, and his regard for the place of his nativity, induced Julian to confer on the senate of Constantinople the same honors, privileges, and authority, which were still enjoyed by the senate of ancient Rome. [76] A legal fiction was introduced, and gradually established, that one half of the national council had migrated into the East; and the despotic successors of Julian, accepting the title of Senators, acknowledged themselves the members of a respectable body, which was permitted to represent the majesty of the Roman name. From Constantinople, the attention of the monarch was extended to the municipal senates of the provinces. He abolished, by repeated edicts, the unjust and pernicious exemptions which had withdrawn so many idle citizens from the services of their country; and by imposing an equal distribution of public duties, he restored the strength, the splendor, or, according to the glowing expression of Libanius, [77] the soul of the expiring cities of his empire. The venerable age of Greece excited the most tender compassion in the mind of Julian, which kindled into rapture when he recollected the gods, the heroes, and the men superior to heroes and to gods, who have bequeathed to the latest posterity the monuments of their genius, or the example of their virtues. He relieved the distress, and restored the beauty, of the cities of Epirus and Peloponnesus. [78] Athens acknowledged him for her benefactor; Argos, for her deliverer. The pride of Corinth, again rising from her ruins with the honors of a Roman colony, exacted a tribute from the adjacent republics, for the purpose of defraying the games of the Isthmus, which were celebrated in the amphitheatre with the hunting of bears and panthers. From this tribute the cities of Elis, of Delphi, and of Argos, which had inherited from their remote ancestors the sacred office of perpetuating the Olympic, the Pythian, and the Nemean games, claimed a just exemption. The immunity of Elis and Delphi was respected by the Corinthians; but the poverty of Argos tempted the insolence of oppression; and the feeble complaints of its deputies were silenced by the decree of a provincial magistrate, who seems to have consulted only the interest of the capital in which he resided. Seven years after this sentence, Julian [79] allowed the cause to be referred to a superior tribunal; and his eloquence was interposed, most probably with success, in the defence of a city, which had been the royal seat of Agamemnon, [80] and had given to Macedonia a race of kings and conquerors. [81]

[Footnote 70: According to some, says Aristotle, (as he is quoted by Julian ad Themist. p. 261,) the form of absolute government is contrary to nature. Both the prince and the philosopher choose, how ever to involve this eternal truth in artful and labored obscurity.]

[Footnote 71: That sentiment is expressed almost in the words of Julian himself. Ammian. xxii. 10.]

[Footnote 72: Libanius, (Orat. Parent. c. 95, p. 320,) who mentions the wish and design of Julian, insinuates, in mysterious language that the emperor was restrained by some particular revelation.]

[Footnote 73: Julian in Misopogon, p. 343. As he never abolished, by any public law, the proud appellations of Despot, or Dominus, they are still extant on his medals, (Ducange, Fam. Byzantin. p. 38, 39;) and the private displeasure which he affected to express, only gave a different tone to the servility of the court. The Abbe de la Bleterie (Hist. de Jovien, tom. ii. p. 99-102) has curiously traced the origin and progress of the word Dominus under the Imperial government.]

[Footnote 74: Ammian. xxii. 7. The consul Mamertinus (in Panegyr. Vet. xi. 28, 29, 30) celebrates the auspicious day, like an elegant slave, astonished and intoxicated by the condescension of his master.]

[Footnote 75: Personal satire was condemned by the laws of the twelve tables: Si male condiderit in quem quis carmina, jus est Judiciumque—Horat. Sat. ii. 1. 82. —Julian (in Misopogon, p. 337) owns himself subject to the law; and the Abbe de la Bleterie (Hist. de Jovien, tom. ii. p. 92) has eagerly embraced a declaration so agreeable to his own system, and, indeed, to the true spirit of the Imperial constitution.]

[Footnote 76: Zosimus, l. iii. p. 158.]

[Footnote 77: See Libanius, (Orat. Parent. c. 71, p. 296,) Ammianus, (xxii. 9,) and the Theodosian Code (l. xii. tit. i. leg. 50-55.) with Godefroy's Commentary, (tom. iv. p. 390-402.) Yet the whole subject of the Curia, notwithstanding very ample materials, still remains the most obscure in the legal history of the empire.]

[Footnote 78: Quae paulo ante arida et siti anhelantia visebantur, ea nunc perlui, mundari, madere; Fora, Deambulacra, Gymnasia, laetis et gaudentibus populis frequentari; dies festos, et celebrari veteres, et novos in honorem principis consecrari, (Mamertin. xi. 9.) He particularly restored the city of Nicopolis and the Actiac games, which had been instituted by Augustus.]

[Footnote 79: Julian. Epist. xxxv. p. 407-411. This epistle, which illustrates the declining age of Greece, is omitted by the Abbe de la Bleterie, and strangely disfigured by the Latin translator, who, by rendering tributum, and populus, directly contradicts the sense of the original.]

[Footnote 80: He reigned in Mycenae at the distance of fifty stadia, or six miles from Argos: but these cities, which alternately flourished, are confounded by the Greek poets. Strabo, l. viii. p. 579, edit. Amstel. 1707.]

[Footnote 81: Marsham, Canon. Chron. p. 421. This pedigree from Temenus and Hercules may be suspicious; yet it was allowed, after a strict inquiry, by the judges of the Olympic games, (Herodot. l. v. c. 22,) at a time when the Macedonian kings were obscure and unpopular in Greece. When the Achaean league declared against Philip, it was thought decent that the deputies of Argos should retire, (T. Liv. xxxii. 22.)]

The laborious administration of military and civil affairs, which were multiplied in proportion to the extent of the empire, exercised the abilities of Julian; but he frequently assumed the two characters of Orator [82] and of Judge, [83] which are almost unknown to the modern sovereigns of Europe. The arts of persuasion, so diligently cultivated by the first Caesars, were neglected by the military ignorance and Asiatic pride of their successors; and if they condescended to harangue the soldiers, whom they feared, they treated with silent disdain the senators, whom they despised. The assemblies of the senate, which Constantius had avoided, were considered by Julian as the place where he could exhibit, with the most propriety, the maxims of a republican, and the talents of a rhetorician. He alternately practised, as in a school of declamation, the several modes of praise, of censure, of exhortation; and his friend Libanius has remarked, that the study of Homer taught him to imitate the simple, concise style of Menelaus, the copiousness of Nestor, whose words descended like the flakes of a winter's snow, or the pathetic and forcible eloquence of Ulysses. The functions of a judge, which are sometimes incompatible with those of a prince, were exercised by Julian, not only as a duty, but as an amusement; and although he might have trusted the integrity and discernment of his Praetorian praefects, he often placed himself by their side on the seat of judgment. The acute penetration of his mind was agreeably occupied in detecting and defeating the chicanery of the advocates, who labored to disguise the truths of facts, and to pervert the sense of the laws. He sometimes forgot the gravity of his station, asked indiscreet or unseasonable questions, and betrayed, by the loudness of his voice, and the agitation of his body, the earnest vehemence with which he maintained his opinion against the judges, the advocates, and their clients. But his knowledge of his own temper prompted him to encourage, and even to solicit, the reproof of his friends and ministers; and whenever they ventured to oppose the irregular sallies of his passions, the spectators could observe the shame, as well as the gratitude, of their monarch. The decrees of Julian were almost always founded on the principles of justice; and he had the firmness to resist the two most dangerous temptations, which assault the tribunal of a sovereign, under the specious forms of compassion and equity. He decided the merits of the cause without weighing the circumstances of the parties; and the poor, whom he wished to relieve, were condemned to satisfy the just demands of a wealthy and noble adversary. He carefully distinguished the judge from the legislator; [84] and though he meditated a necessary reformation of the Roman jurisprudence, he pronounced sentence according to the strict and literal interpretation of those laws, which the magistrates were bound to execute, and the subjects to obey.

[Footnote 82: His eloquence is celebrated by Libanius, (Orat. Parent. c. 75, 76, p. 300, 301,) who distinctly mentions the orators of Homer. Socrates (l. iii. c. 1) has rashly asserted that Julian was the only prince, since Julius Caesar, who harangued the senate. All the predecessors of Nero, (Tacit. Annal. xiii. 3,) and many of his successors, possessed the faculty of speaking in public; and it might be proved by various examples, that they frequently exercised it in the senate.]

[Footnote 83: Ammianus (xxi. 10) has impartially stated the merits and defects of his judicial proceedings. Libanius (Orat. Parent. c. 90, 91, p. 315, &c.) has seen only the fair side, and his picture, if it flatters the person, expresses at least the duties, of the judge. Gregory Nazianzen, (Orat. iv. p. 120,) who suppresses the virtues, and exaggerates even the venial faults of the Apostate, triumphantly asks, whether such a judge was fit to be seated between Minos and Rhadamanthus, in the Elysian Fields.]

[Footnote 84: Of the laws which Julian enacted in a reign of sixteen months, fifty-four have been admitted into the codes of Theodosius and Justinian. (Gothofred. Chron. Legum, p. 64-67.) The Abbe de la Bleterie (tom. ii. p. 329-336) has chosen one of these laws to give an idea of Julian's Latin style, which is forcible and elaborate, but less pure than his Greek.]

The generality of princes, if they were stripped of their purple, and cast naked into the world, would immediately sink to the lowest rank of society, without a hope of emerging from their obscurity. But the personal merit of Julian was, in some measure, independent of his fortune. Whatever had been his choice of life, by the force of intrepid courage, lively wit, and intense application, he would have obtained, or at least he would have deserved, the highest honors of his profession; and Julian might have raised himself to the rank of minister, or general, of the state in which he was born a private citizen. If the jealous caprice of power had disappointed his expectations, if he had prudently declined the paths of greatness, the employment of the same talents in studious solitude would have placed beyond the reach of kings his present happiness and his immortal fame. When we inspect, with minute, or perhaps malevolent attention, the portrait of Julian, something seems wanting to the grace and perfection of the whole figure. His genius was less powerful and sublime than that of Caesar; nor did he possess the consummate prudence of Augustus. The virtues of Trajan appear more steady and natural, and the philosophy of Marcus is more simple and consistent. Yet Julian sustained adversity with firmness, and prosperity with moderation. After an interval of one hundred and twenty years from the death of Alexander Severus, the Romans beheld an emperor who made no distinction between his duties and his pleasures; who labored to relieve the distress, and to revive the spirit, of his subjects; and who endeavored always to connect authority with merit, and happiness with virtue. Even faction, and religious faction, was constrained to acknowledge the superiority of his genius, in peace as well as in war, and to confess, with a sigh, that the apostate Julian was a lover of his country, and that he deserved the empire of the world. [85]

[Footnote 85:
... Ductor fortissimus armis;
Conditor et legum celeberrimus; ore manuque
Consultor patriae; sed non consultor habendae
Religionis; amans tercentum millia Divum.
Pertidus ille Deo, sed non et perfidus orbi.
Prudent. Apotheosis, 450, &c.

The consciousness of a generous sentiment seems to have raised the Christian post above his usual mediocrity.]

CHAPTER XXIII

REIGN OF JULIAN

PART I

THE RELIGION OF JULIAN—UNIVERSAL TOLERATION—HE ATTEMPTS TO RESTORE AND REFORM THE PAGAN WORSHIP—TO REBUILD THE TEMPLE OF JERSUSALEM—HIS ARTFUL PERSECUTION OF THE CHRISTIANS—MUTUAL ZEAL AND INJUSTICE

The character of Apostate has injured the reputation of Julian; and the enthusiasm which clouded his virtues has exaggerated the real and apparent magnitude of his faults. Our partial ignorance may represent him as a philosophic monarch, who studied to protect, with an equal hand, the religious factions of the empire; and to allay the theological fever which had inflamed the minds of the people, from the edicts of Diocletian to the exile of Athanasius. A more accurate view of the character and conduct of Julian will remove this favorable prepossession for a prince who did not escape the general contagion of the times. We enjoy the singular advantage of comparing the pictures which have been delineated by his fondest admirers and his implacable enemies. The actions of Julian are faithfully related by a judicious and candid historian, the impartial spectator of his life and death. The unanimous evidence of his contemporaries is confirmed by the public and private declarations of the emperor himself; and his various writings express the uniform tenor of his religious sentiments, which policy would have prompted him to dissemble rather than to affect. A devout and sincere attachment for the gods of Athens and Rome constituted the ruling passion of Julian; [1] the powers of an enlightened understanding were betrayed and corrupted by the influence of superstitious prejudice; and the phantoms which existed only in the mind of the emperor had a real and pernicious effect on the government of the empire. The vehement zeal of the Christians, who despised the worship, and overturned the altars of those fabulous deities, engaged their votary in a state of irreconcilable hostility with a very numerous party of his subjects; and he was sometimes tempted by the desire of victory, or the shame of a repulse, to violate the laws of prudence, and even of justice. The triumph of the party, which he deserted and opposed, has fixed a stain of infamy on the name of Julian; and the unsuccessful apostate has been overwhelmed with a torrent of pious invectives, of which the signal was given by the sonorous trumpet [2] of Gregory Nazianzen. [3] The interesting nature of the events which were crowded into the short reign of this active emperor, deserve a just and circumstantial narrative. His motives, his counsels, and his actions, as far as they are connected with the history of religion, will be the subject of the present chapter.

[Footnote 1: *I shall transcribe some of his own expressions from a short religious discourse which the Imperial pontiff composed to censure the bold impiety of a Cynic. Orat. vii. p. 212. The variety and copiousness of the Greek tongue seem inadequate to the fervor of his devotion.*]

[Footnote 2: *The orator, with some eloquence, much enthusiasm, and more vanity, addresses his discourse to heaven and earth, to men and angels, to the living and the dead; and above all, to the great Constantius, an odd Pagan expression. He concludes with a bold assurance, that he has erected a monument not less durable, and much more portable, than the columns of Hercules. See Greg. Nazianzen, Orat. iii. p. 50, iv. p. 134.*]

[Footnote 3: *See this long invective, which has been injudiciously divided into two orations in Gregory's works, tom. i. p. 49-134, Paris, 1630. It was published by Gregory and his friend Basil, (iv. p. 133,) about six months after the death of Julian, when his remains had been carried to Tarsus, (iv. p. 120;) but while Jovian was still on the throne, (iii. p. 54, iv. p. 117) I have derived much assistance from a French version and remarks, printed at Lyons, 1735.*]

The cause of his strange and fatal apostasy may be derived from the early period of his life, when he was left an orphan in the hands of the murderers of his family. The names of Christ and of Constantius, the ideas of slavery and of religion, were soon associated in a youthful imagination, which was susceptible of the most lively impressions. The care of his infancy was intrusted to Eusebius, bishop of Nicomedia, [4] who was related to him on the side of his mother; and till Julian reached the twentieth year of his age, he received from his Christian preceptors the education, not of a hero, but of a saint. The emperor, less jealous of a heavenly than of an earthly crown, contented himself with the imperfect character of a catechumen, while he bestowed the advantages of baptism [5] on the nephews of Constantine. [6] They were even admitted to the inferior offices of the ecclesiastical order; and Julian publicly read the Holy Scriptures in the church of Nicomedia. The study of religion, which they assiduously cultivated, appeared to produce the fairest fruits of faith and devotion. [7] They prayed, they fasted, they distributed alms to the poor, gifts to the clergy, and oblations to the tombs of the martyrs; and the splendid monument of St. Mamas, at Caesarea, was erected, or at least was undertaken, by the joint labor of Gallus and Julian. [8] They respectfully conversed with the bishops, who were eminent for superior sanctity, and solicited the benediction of the monks and hermits, who had introduced into Cappadocia the voluntary hardships of the ascetic life. [9] As the two princes advanced towards the years of manhood, they discovered, in their religious sentiments, the difference of their characters. The dull and obstinate understanding of

Gallus embraced, with implicit zeal, the doctrines of Christianity; which never influenced his conduct, or moderated his passions. The mild disposition of the younger brother was less repugnant to the precepts of the gospel; and his active curiosity might have been gratified by a theological system, which explains the mysterious essence of the Deity, and opens the boundless prospect of invisible and future worlds. But the independent spirit of Julian refused to yield the passive and unresisting obedience which was required, in the name of religion, by the haughty ministers of the church. Their speculative opinions were imposed as positive laws, and guarded by the terrors of eternal punishments; but while they prescribed the rigid formulary of the thoughts, the words, and the actions of the young prince; whilst they silenced his objections, and severely checked the freedom of his inquiries, they secretly provoked his impatient genius to disclaim the authority of his ecclesiastical guides. He was educated in the Lesser Asia, amidst the scandals of the Arian controversy. [10] The fierce contests of the Eastern bishops, the incessant alterations of their creeds, and the profane motives which appeared to actuate their conduct, insensibly strengthened the prejudice of Julian, that they neither understood nor believed the religion for which they so fiercely contended. Instead of listening to the proofs of Christianity with that favorable attention which adds weight to the most respectable evidence, he heard with suspicion, and disputed with obstinacy and acuteness, the doctrines for which he already entertained an invincible aversion. Whenever the young princes were directed to compose declamations on the subject of the prevailing controversies, Julian always declared himself the advocate of Paganism; under the specious excuse that, in the defence of the weaker cause, his learning and ingenuity might be more advantageously exercised and displayed.

[Footnote 4: Nicomediae ab Eusebio educatus Episcopo, quem genere longius contingebat, (Ammian. xxii. 9.) Julian never expresses any gratitude towards that Arian prelate; but he celebrates his preceptor, the eunuch Mardonius, and describes his mode of education, which inspired his pupil with a passionate admiration for the genius, and perhaps the religion of Homer. Misopogon, p. 351, 352.]

[Footnote 5: Greg. Naz. iii. p. 70. He labored to effect that holy mark in the blood, perhaps of a Taurobolium. Baron. Annal. Eccles. A. D. 361, No. 3, 4.]

[Footnote 6: Julian himself (Epist. li. p. 454) assures the Alexandrians that he had been a Christian (he must mean a sincere one) till the twentieth year of his age.]

[Footnote 7: See his Christian, and even ecclesiastical education, in Gregory, (iii. p. 58,) Socrates, (l. iii. c. 1,) and Sozomen, (l. v. c. 2.) He escaped very narrowly from being a bishop, and perhaps a saint.]

[Footnote 8: The share of the work which had been allotted to Gallus, was prosecuted with vigor and success; but the earth obstinately rejected and subverted the structures which were imposed by the sacrilegious hand of Julian. Greg. iii. p. 59, 60, 61. Such a partial earthquake, attested by many living spectators, would form one of the clearest miracles in ecclesiastical story.]

[Footnote 9: The philosopher (Fragment, p. 288,) ridicules the iron chains, &c, of these solitary fanatics, (see Tillemont, Mem. Eccles. tom. ix. p. 661, 632,) who had forgot that man is by nature a gentle and social animal. The Pagan supposes, that because they had renounced the gods, they were possessed and tormented by evil daemons.]

[Footnote 10: See Julian apud Cyril, l. vi. p. 206, l. viii. p. 253, 262. "You persecute," says he, "those heretics who do not mourn the dead man precisely in the way which you approve." He shows himself a

tolerable theologian; but he maintains that the Christian Trinity is not derived from the doctrine of Paul, of Jesus, or of Moses.]

As soon as Gallus was invested with the honors of the purple, Julian was permitted to breathe the air of freedom, of literature, and of Paganism. [11] The crowd of sophists, who were attracted by the taste and liberality of their royal pupil, had formed a strict alliance between the learning and the religion of Greece; and the poems of Homer, instead of being admired as the original productions of human genius, were seriously ascribed to the heavenly inspiration of Apollo and the muses. The deities of Olympus, as they are painted by the immortal bard, imprint themselves on the minds which are the least addicted to superstitious credulity. Our familiar knowledge of their names and characters, their forms and attributes, seems to bestow on those airy beings a real and substantial existence; and the pleasing enchantment produces an imperfect and momentary assent of the imagination to those fables, which are the most repugnant to our reason and experience. In the age of Julian, every circumstance contributed to prolong and fortify the illusion; the magnificent temples of Greece and Asia; the works of those artists who had expressed, in painting or in sculpture, the divine conceptions of the poet; the pomp of festivals and sacrifices; the successful arts of divination; the popular traditions of oracles and prodigies; and the ancient practice of two thousand years. The weakness of polytheism was, in some measure, excused by the moderation of its claims; and the devotion of the Pagans was not incompatible with the most licentious scepticism. [12] Instead of an indivisible and regular system, which occupies the whole extent of the believing mind, the mythology of the Greeks was composed of a thousand loose and flexible parts, and the servant of the gods was at liberty to define the degree and measure of his religious faith. The creed which Julian adopted for his own use was of the largest dimensions; and, by strange contradiction, he disdained the salutary yoke of the gospel, whilst he made a voluntary offering of his reason on the altars of Jupiter and Apollo. One of the orations of Julian is consecrated to the honor of Cybele, the mother of the gods, who required from her effeminate priests the bloody sacrifice, so rashly performed by the madness of the Phrygian boy. The pious emperor condescends to relate, without a blush, and without a smile, the voyage of the goddess from the shores of Pergamus to the mouth of the Tyber, and the stupendous miracle, which convinced the senate and people of Rome that the lump of clay, which their ambassadors had transported over the seas, was endowed with life, and sentiment, and divine power. [13] For the truth of this prodigy he appeals to the public monuments of the city; and censures, with some acrimony, the sickly and affected taste of those men, who impertinently derided the sacred traditions of their ancestors. [14]

[Footnote 11: Libanius, Orat. Parentalis, c. 9, 10, p. 232, &c. Greg. Nazianzen. Orat. iii. p 61. Eunap. Vit. Sophist. in Maximo, p. 68, 69, 70, edit Commelin.]

[Footnote 12: A modern philosopher has ingeniously compared the different operation of theism and polytheism, with regard to the doubt or conviction which they produce in the human mind. See Hume's Essays vol. ii. p. 444- 457, in 8vo. edit. 1777.]

[Footnote 13: The Idaean mother landed in Italy about the end of the second Punic war. The miracle of Claudia, either virgin or matron, who cleared her fame by disgracing the graver modesty of the Roman Indies, is attested by a cloud of witnesses. Their evidence is collected by Drakenborch, (ad Silium Italicum, xvii. 33;) but we may observe that Livy (xxix. 14) slides over the transaction with discreet ambiguity.]

[Footnote 14: I cannot refrain from transcribing the emphatical words of Julian: Orat. v. p. 161. Julian likewise declares his firm belief in the ancilia, the holy shields, which dropped from heaven on the

Quirinal hill; and pities the strange blindness of the Christians, who preferred the cross to these celestial trophies. Apud Cyril. l. vi. p. 194.]

But the devout philosopher, who sincerely embraced, and warmly encouraged, the superstition of the people, reserved for himself the privilege of a liberal interpretation; and silently withdrew from the foot of the altars into the sanctuary of the temple. The extravagance of the Grecian mythology proclaimed, with a clear and audible voice, that the pious inquirer, instead of being scandalized or satisfied with the literal sense, should diligently explore the occult wisdom, which had been disguised, by the prudence of antiquity, under the mask of folly and of fable. [15] The philosophers of the Platonic school, [16] Plotinus, Porphyry, and the divine Iamblichus, were admired as the most skilful masters of this allegorical science, which labored to soften and harmonize the deformed features of Paganism. Julian himself, who was directed in the mysterious pursuit by Aedesius, the venerable successor of Iamblichus, aspired to the possession of a treasure, which he esteemed, if we may credit his solemn asseverations, far above the empire of the world. [17] It was indeed a treasure, which derived its value only from opinion; and every artist who flattered himself that he had extracted the precious ore from the surrounding dross, claimed an equal right of stamping the name and figure the most agreeable to his peculiar fancy. The fable of Atys and Cybele had been already explained by Porphyry; but his labors served only to animate the pious industry of Julian, who invented and published his own allegory of that ancient and mystic tale. This freedom of interpretation, which might gratify the pride of the Platonists, exposed the vanity of their art. Without a tedious detail, the modern reader could not form a just idea of the strange allusions, the forced etymologies, the solemn trifling, and the impenetrable obscurity of these sages, who professed to reveal the system of the universe. As the traditions of Pagan mythology were variously related, the sacred interpreters were at liberty to select the most convenient circumstances; and as they translated an arbitrary cipher, they could extract from any fable any sense which was adapted to their favorite system of religion and philosophy. The lascivious form of a naked Venus was tortured into the discovery of some moral precept, or some physical truth; and the castration of Atys explained the revolution of the sun between the tropics, or the separation of the human soul from vice and error. [18]

[Footnote 15: See the principles of allegory, in Julian, (Orat. vii. p. 216, 222.) His reasoning is less absurd than that of some modern theologians, who assert that an extravagant or contradictory doctrine must be divine; since no man alive could have thought of inventing it.]

[Footnote 16: Eunapius has made these sophists the subject of a partial and fanatical history; and the learned Brucker (Hist. Philosoph. tom. ii. p. 217-303) has employed much labor to illustrate their obscure lives and incomprehensible doctrines.]

[Footnote 17: Julian, Orat. vii p 222. He swears with the most fervent and enthusiastic devotion; and trembles, lest he should betray too much of these holy mysteries, which the profane might deride with an impious Sardonic laugh.]

[Footnote 18: See the fifth oration of Julian. But all the allegories which ever issued from the Platonic school are not worth the short poem of Catullus on the same extraordinary subject. The transition of Atys, from the wildest enthusiasm to sober, pathetic complaint, for his irretrievable loss, must inspire a man with pity, a eunuch with despair.]

The theological system of Julian appears to have contained the sublime and important principles of natural religion. But as the faith, which is not founded on revelation, must remain destitute of any firm assurance, the disciple of Plato imprudently relapsed into the habits of vulgar superstition; and the popular and philosophic notion of the Deity seems to have been confounded in the practice, the writings, and even in the mind of Julian. [19] The pious emperor acknowledged and adored the Eternal Cause of the universe, to whom he ascribed all the perfections of an infinite nature, invisible to the eyes and inaccessible to the understanding, of feeble mortals. The Supreme God had created, or rather, in the Platonic language, had generated, the gradual succession of dependent spirits, of gods, of daemons, of heroes, and of men; and every being which derived its existence immediately from the First Cause, received the inherent gift of immortality. That so precious an advantage might be lavished upon unworthy objects, the Creator had intrusted to the skill and power of the inferior gods the office of forming the human body, and of arranging the beautiful harmony of the animal, the vegetable, and the mineral kingdoms. To the conduct of these divine ministers he delegated the temporal government of this lower world; but their imperfect administration is not exempt from discord or error. The earth and its inhabitants are divided among them, and the characters of Mars or Minerva, of Mercury or Venus, may be distinctly traced in the laws and manners of their peculiar votaries. As long as our immortal souls are confined in a mortal prison, it is our interest, as well as our duty, to solicit the favor, and to deprecate the wrath, of the powers of heaven; whose pride is gratified by the devotion of mankind; and whose grosser parts may be supposed to derive some nourishment from the fumes of sacrifice. [20] The inferior gods might sometimes condescend to animate the statues, and to inhabit the temples, which were dedicated to their honor. They might occasionally visit the earth, but the heavens were the proper throne and symbol of their glory. The invariable order of the sun, moon, and stars, was hastily admitted by Julian, as a proof of their eternal duration; and their eternity was a sufficient evidence that they were the workmanship, not of an inferior deity, but of the Omnipotent King. In the system of Platonists, the visible was a type of the invisible world. The celestial bodies, as they were informed by a divine spirit, might be considered as the objects the most worthy of religious worship. The Sun, whose genial influence pervades and sustains the universe, justly claimed the adoration of mankind, as the bright representative of the Logos, the lively, the rational, the beneficent image of the intellectual Father. [21]

[Footnote 19: The true religion of Julian may be deduced from the Caesars, p. 308, with Spanheim's notes and illustrations, from the fragments in Cyril, l. ii. p. 57, 58, and especially from the theological oration in Solem Regem, p. 130-158, addressed in the confidence of friendship, to the praefect Sallust.]

[Footnote 20: Julian adopts this gross conception by ascribing to his favorite Marcus Antoninus, (Caesares, p. 333.) The Stoics and Platonists hesitated between the analogy of bodies and the purity of spirits; yet the gravest philosophers inclined to the whimsical fancy of Aristophanes and Lucian, that an unbelieving age might starve the immortal gods. See Observations de Spanheim, p. 284, 444, &c.]

[Footnote 21: Julian. Epist. li. In another place, (apud Cyril. l. ii. p. 69,) he calls the Sun God, and the throne of God. Julian believed the Platonician Trinity; and only blames the Christians for preferring a mortal to an immortal Logos.]

In every age, the absence of genuine inspiration is supplied by the strong illusions of enthusiasm, and the mimic arts of imposture. If, in the time of Julian, these arts had been practised only by the pagan priests, for the support of an expiring cause, some indulgence might perhaps be allowed to the interest and habits of the sacerdotal character. But it may appear a subject of surprise and scandal, that the philosophers themselves should have contributed to abuse the superstitious credulity of mankind, [22] and that the Grecian mysteries should have been supported by the magic or theurgy of the modern Platonists. They arrogantly pretended to control the order of nature, to explore the secrets of futurity, to command the service of the inferior daemons, to enjoy the view and conversation of the superior gods, and by disengaging the soul from her material bands, to reunite that immortal particle with the Infinite and Divine Spirit.

[Footnote 22: The sophists of Eunapias perform as many miracles as the saints of the desert; and the only circumstance in their favor is, that they are of a less gloomy complexion. Instead of devils with horns and tails, Iamblichus evoked the genii of love, Eros and Anteros, from two adjacent fountains. Two beautiful boys issued from the water, fondly embraced him as their father, and retired at his command, p. 26, 27.]

The devout and fearless curiosity of Julian tempted the philosophers with the hopes of an easy conquest; which, from the situation of their young proselyte, might be productive of the most important consequences. [23] Julian imbibed the first rudiments of the Platonic doctrines from the mouth of Aedesius, who had fixed at Pergamus his wandering and persecuted school. But as the declining strength of that venerable sage was unequal to the ardor, the diligence, the rapid conception of his pupil, two of his most learned disciples, Chrysanthes and Eusebius, supplied, at his own desire, the place of their aged master. These philosophers seem to have prepared and distributed their respective parts; and they artfully contrived, by dark hints and affected disputes, to excite the impatient hopes of the aspirant, till they delivered him into the hands of their associate, Maximus, the boldest and most skilful master of the Theurgic science. By his hands, Julian was secretly initiated at Ephesus, in the twentieth year of his age. His residence at Athens confirmed this unnatural alliance of philosophy and superstition.

He obtained the privilege of a solemn initiation into the mysteries of Eleusis, which, amidst the general decay of the Grecian worship, still retained some vestiges of their primaeval sanctity; and such was the zeal of Julian, that he afterwards invited the Eleusinian pontiff to the court of Gaul, for the sole purpose of consummating, by mystic rites and sacrifices, the great work of his sanctification. As these ceremonies were performed in the depth of caverns, and in the silence of the night, and as the inviolable secret of the mysteries was preserved by the discretion of the initiated, I shall not presume to describe the horrid sounds, and fiery apparitions, which were presented to the senses, or the imagination, of the credulous aspirant, [24] till the visions of comfort and knowledge broke upon him in a blaze of celestial light. [25] In the caverns of Ephesus and Eleusis, the mind of Julian was penetrated with sincere, deep, and unalterable enthusiasm; though he might sometimes exhibit the vicissitudes of pious fraud and hypocrisy, which may be observed, or at least suspected, in the characters of the most conscientious fanatics. From that moment he consecrated his life to the service of the gods; and while the occupations of war, of government, and of study, seemed to claim the whole measure of his time, a stated portion of the hours of the night was invariably reserved for the exercise of private devotion. The temperance which adorned the severe manners of the soldier and the philosopher was connected with some strict and frivolous rules of religious abstinence; and it was in honor of Pan or Mercury, of Hecate or Isis, that Julian, on particular days, denied himself the use of some particular food, which might have been offensive to his tutelar deities. By these voluntary fasts, he prepared his senses and his understanding for the frequent and familiar visits with which he was honored by the celestial powers. Notwithstanding the modest silence of Julian himself, we may learn from his faithful friend, the orator Libanius, that he lived in a perpetual intercourse with the gods and goddesses; that they descended upon earth to enjoy the conversation of their favorite hero; that they gently interrupted his slumbers by touching his hand or his hair; that they warned him of every impending danger, and conducted him, by their infallible wisdom, in every action of his life; and that he had acquired such an intimate knowledge of his heavenly guests, as readily to distinguish the voice of Jupiter from that of Minerva, and the form of Apollo from the figure of Hercules. [26] These sleeping or waking visions, the ordinary effects of abstinence and fanaticism, would almost degrade the emperor to the level of an Egyptian monk. But the useless lives of Antony or Pachomius were consumed in these vain occupations. Julian could break from the dream of superstition to arm himself for battle; and after vanquishing in the field the enemies of Rome, he calmly retired into his tent, to dictate the wise and salutary laws of an empire, or to indulge his genius in the elegant pursuits of literature and philosophy.

[Footnote 23: *The dexterous management of these sophists, who played their credulous pupil into each other's hands, is fairly told by Eunapius (p. 69- 79) with unsuspecting simplicity. The Abbe de la Bleterie understands, and neatly describes, the whole comedy, (Vie de Julian, p. 61-67.)*]

[Footnote 24: *When Julian, in a momentary panic, made the sign of the cross the daemons instantly disappeared, (Greg. Naz. Orat. iii. p. 71.) Gregory supposes that they were frightened, but the priests declared that they were indignant. The reader, according to the measure of his faith, will determine this profound question.*]

[Footnote 25: *A dark and distant view of the terrors and joys of initiation is shown by Dion Chrysostom, Themistius, Proclus, and Stobaeus. The learned author of the Divine Legation has exhibited their words, (vol. i. p. 239, 247, 248, 280, edit. 1765,) which he dexterously or forcibly applies to his own hypothesis.*]

[Footnote 26: *Julian's modesty confined him to obscure and occasional hints: but Libanius expiates with pleasure on the facts and visions of the religious hero. (Legat. ad Julian. p. 157, and Orat. Parental. c. lxxxiii. p. 309, 310.)*]

The important secret of the apostasy of Julian was intrusted to the fidelity of the initiated, with whom he was united by the sacred ties of friendship and religion. [27] The pleasing rumor was cautiously circulated among the adherents of the ancient worship; and his future greatness became the object of the hopes, the prayers, and the predictions of the Pagans, in every province of the empire. From the zeal and virtues of their royal proselyte, they fondly expected the cure of every evil, and the restoration of every blessing; and instead of disapproving of the ardor of their pious wishes, Julian ingenuously confessed, that he was ambitious to attain a situation in which he might be useful to his country and to his religion. But this religion was viewed with a hostile eye by the successor of Constantine, whose capricious passions altercately saved and threatened the life of Julian. The arts of magic and divination were strictly prohibited under a despotic government, which condescended to fear them; and if the Pagans were reluctantly indulged in the exercise of their superstition, the rank of Julian would have excepted him from the general toleration. The apostate soon became the presumptive heir of the monarchy, and his death could alone have appeased the just apprehensions of the Christians. [28] But the young prince, who aspired to the glory of a hero rather than of a martyr, consulted his safety by dissembling his religion; and the easy temper of polytheism permitted him to join in the public worship of a sect which he inwardly despised. Libanius has considered the hypocrisy of his friend as a subject, not of censure, but of praise. "As the statues of the gods," says that orator, "which have been defiled with filth, are again placed in a magnificent temple, so the beauty of truth was seated in the mind of Julian, after it had been purified from the errors and follies of his education. His sentiments were changed; but as it would have been dangerous to have avowed his sentiments, his conduct still continued the same. Very different from the ass in Aesop, who disguised himself with a lion's hide, our lion was obliged to conceal himself under the skin of an ass; and, while he embraced the dictates of reason, to obey the laws of prudence and necessity." [29] The dissimulation of Julian lasted about ten years, from his secret initiation at Ephesus to the beginning of the civil war; when he declared himself at once the implacable enemy of Christ and of Constantius. This state of constraint might contribute to strengthen his devotion; and as soon as he had satisfied the obligation of assisting, on solemn festivals, at the assemblies of the Christians, Julian returned, with the impatience of a lover, to burn his free and voluntary incense on the domestic chapels of Jupiter and Mercury. But as every act of dissimulation must be painful to an ingenuous spirit, the profession of Christianity increased the aversion of Julian for a religion which oppressed the freedom of his mind, and compelled him to hold a conduct repugnant to the noblest attributes of human nature, sincerity and courage.

[Footnote 27: Libanius, Orat. Parent. c. x. p. 233, 234. Gallus had some reason to suspect the secret apostasy of his brother; and in a letter, which may be received as genuine, he exhorts Julian to adhere to the religion of their ancestors; an argument which, as it should seem, was not yet perfectly ripe. See Julian, Op. p. 454, and Hist. de Jovien tom ii. p. 141.]

[Footnote 28: Gregory, (iii. p. 50,) with inhuman zeal, censures Constantius for paring the infant apostate. His French translator (p. 265) cautiously observes, that such expressions must not be prises a la lettre.]

[Footnote 29: Libanius, Orat. Parental. c ix. p. 233.]

PART II

The inclination of Julian might prefer the gods of Homer, and of the Scipios, to the new faith, which his uncle had established in the Roman empire; and in which he himself had been sanctified by the sacrament of baptism. But, as a philosopher, it was incumbent on him to justify his dissent from Christianity, which was supported by the number of its converts, by the chain of prophecy, the splendor of or miracles, and the weight of evidence. The elaborate work, [30] which he composed amidst the preparations of the Persian war, contained the substance of those arguments which he had long revolved in his mind. Some fragments have been transcribed and preserved, by his adversary, the vehement Cyril of Alexandria; [31] and they exhibit a very singular mixture of wit and learning, of sophistry and fanaticism. The elegance of the style and the rank of the author, recommended his writings to the public attention; [32] and in the impious list of the enemies of Christianity, the celebrated name of Porphyry was effaced by the superior merit or reputation of Julian. The minds of the faithful were either seduced, or scandalized, or alarmed; and the pagans, who sometimes presumed to engage in the unequal dispute, derived, from the popular work of their Imperial missionary, an inexhaustible supply of fallacious objections. But in the assiduous prosecution of these theological studies, the emperor of the Romans imbibed the illiberal prejudices and passions of a polemic divine. He contracted an irrevocable obligation to maintain and propagate his religious opinions; and whilst he secretly applauded the strength and dexterity with which he wielded the weapons of controversy, he was tempted to distrust the sincerity, or to despise the understandings, of his antagonists, who could obstinately resist the force of reason and eloquence.

[Footnote 30: Fabricius (Biblioth. Graec. l. v. c. viii, p. 88-90) and Lardner (Heathen Testimonies, vol. iv. p. 44-47) have accurately compiled all that can now be discovered of Julian's work against the Christians.]

[Footnote 31: About seventy years after the death of Julian, he executed a task which had been feebly attempted by Philip of Side, a prolix and contemptible writer. Even the work of Cyril has not entirely satisfied the most favorable judges; and the Abbe de la Bleterie (Preface a l'Hist. de Jovien, p. 30, 32) wishes that some theologien philosophe (a strange centaur) would undertake the refutation of Julian.]

[Footnote 32: Libanius, (Orat. Parental. c. lxxxvii. p. 313,) who has been suspected of assisting his friend, prefers this divine vindication (Orat. ix in necem Julian. p. 255, edit. Morel.) to the writings of Porphyry. His judgment may be arraigned, (Socrates, l. iii. c. 23,) but Libanius cannot be accused of flattery to a dead prince.]

The Christians, who beheld with horror and indignation the apostasy of Julian, had much more to fear from his power than from his arguments. The pagans, who were conscious of his fervent zeal, expected, perhaps with impatience, that the flames of persecution should be immediately kindled against the enemies of the gods; and that the ingenious malice of Julian would invent some cruel refinements of death and torture which had been unknown to the rude and inexperienced fury of his predecessors. But the hopes, as well as the fears, of the religious factions were apparently disappointed, by the prudent humanity of a prince, [33] who was careful of his own fame, of the public peace, and of the rights of mankind. Instructed by history and reflection, Julian was persuaded, that if the diseases of the body may sometimes be cured by salutary violence, neither steel nor fire can eradicate the erroneous opinions of the mind. The reluctant victim may be dragged to the foot of the altar; but the heart still abhors and disclaims the sacrilegious act of the hand. Religious obstinacy is hardened and exasperated by oppression; and, as soon as the persecution subsides, those who have yielded are restored as penitents, and those who have resisted are honored as saints and martyrs. If Julian adopted the unsuccessful cruelty of Diocletian and his colleagues, he was sensible that he should stain his memory with the name of a tyrant, and add new glories to the Catholic church, which had derived strength and increase from the severity of the pagan magistrates. Actuated by these motives, and apprehensive of disturbing the repose of an unsettled reign, Julian surprised the world by an edict, which was not unworthy of a statesman, or a philosopher. He extended to all the inhabitants of the Roman world the benefits of a free and equal toleration; and the only hardship which he inflicted on the Christians, was to deprive them of the power of tormenting their fellow-subjects, whom they stigmatized with the odious titles of idolaters and heretics. The pagans received a gracious permission, or rather an express order, to open All their temples; [34] and they were at once delivered from the oppressive laws, and arbitrary vexations, which they had sustained under the reign of Constantine, and of his sons. At the same time the bishops and clergy, who had been banished by the Arian monarch, were recalled from exile, and restored to their respective churches; the Donatists, the Novatians, the Macedonians, the Eunomians, and those who, with a more prosperous fortune, adhered to the doctrine of the Council of Nice. Julian, who understood and derided their theological disputes, invited to the palace the leaders of the hostile sects, that he might enjoy the agreeable spectacle of their furious encounters. The clamor of controversy sometimes provoked the emperor to exclaim, "Hear me! the Franks have heard me, and the Alemanni;" but he soon discovered that he was now engaged with more obstinate and implacable enemies; and though he exerted the powers of oratory to persuade them to live in concord, or at least in peace, he was perfectly satisfied, before he dismissed them from his presence, that he had nothing to dread from the union of the Christians. The impartial Ammianus has ascribed this affected clemency to the desire of fomenting the intestine divisions of the church, and the insidious design of undermining the foundations of Christianity, was inseparably connected with the zeal which Julian professed, to restore the ancient religion of the empire. [35]

[Footnote 33: Libanius (Orat. Parent. c. lviii. p. 283, 284) has eloquently explained the tolerating principles and conduct of his Imperial friend. In a very remarkable epistle to the people of Bostra, Julian himself (Epist. lii.) professes his moderation, and betrays his zeal, which is acknowledged by Ammianus, and exposed by Gregory (Orat. iii. p.72)]

[Footnote 34: In Greece the temples of Minerva were opened by his express command, before the death of Constantius, (Liban. Orat. Parent. c. 55, p. 280;) and Julian declares himself a Pagan in his public manifesto to the Athenians. This unquestionable evidence may correct the hasty assertion of Ammianus, who seems to suppose Constantinople to be the place where he discovered his attachment to the gods]

[Footnote 35: Ammianus, xxii. 5. Sozomen, l. v. c. 5. Bestia moritur, tranquillitas redit.... omnes episcopi qui de propriis sedibus fuerant exterminati per indulgentiam novi principis ad acclesias redeunt. Jerom. adversus Luciferianos, tom. ii. p. 143. Optatus accuses the Donatists for owing their safety to an apostate, (l. ii. c. 16, p. 36, 37, edit. Dupin.)]

As soon as he ascended the throne, he assumed, according to the custom of his predecessors, the character of supreme pontiff; not only as the most honorable title of Imperial greatness, but as a sacred and important office; the duties of which he was resolved to execute with pious diligence. As the business of the state prevented the emperor from joining every day in the public devotion of his subjects, he dedicated a domestic chapel to his tutelar deity the Sun; his gardens were filled with statues and altars of the gods; and each apartment of the palace displaced the appearance of a magnificent temple. Every morning he saluted the parent of light with a sacrifice; the blood of another victim was shed at the moment when the Sun sunk below the horizon; and the Moon, the Stars, and the Genii of the night received their respective and seasonable honors from the indefatigable devotion of Julian. On solemn festivals, he regularly visited the temple of the god or goddess to whom the day was peculiarly consecrated, and endeavored to excite the religion of the magistrates and people by the example of his own zeal. Instead of maintaining the lofty state of a monarch, distinguished by the splendor of his purple, and encompassed by the golden shields of his guards, Julian solicited, with respectful eagerness, the meanest offices which contributed to the worship of the gods. Amidst the sacred but licentious crowd of priests, of inferior ministers, and of female dancers, who were dedicated to the service of the temple, it was the business of the emperor to bring the wood, to blow the fire, to handle the knife, to slaughter the victim, and, thrusting his bloody hands into the bowels of the expiring animal, to draw forth the heart or liver, and to read, with the consummate skill of an haruspex, imaginary signs of future events. The wisest of the Pagans censured this extravagant superstition, which affected to despise the restraints of prudence and decency. Under the reign of a prince, who practised the rigid maxims of economy, the expense of religious worship consumed a very large portion of the revenue a constant supply of the scarcest and most beautiful birds was transported from distant climates, to bleed on the altars of the gods; a hundred oxen were frequently sacrificed by Julian on one and the same day; and it soon became a popular jest, that if he should return with conquest from the Persian war, the breed of horned cattle must infallibly be extinguished. Yet this expense may appear inconsiderable, when it is compared with the splendid presents which were offered either by the hand, or by order, of the emperor, to all the celebrated places of devotion in the Roman world; and with the sums allotted to repair and decorate the ancient temples, which had suffered the silent decay of time, or the recent injuries of Christian rapine. Encouraged by the example, the exhortations, the liberality, of their pious sovereign, the cities and families resumed the practice of their neglected ceremonies. "Every part of the world," exclaims Libanius, with devout transport, "displayed the triumph of religion; and the grateful prospect of flaming altars, bleeding victims, the smoke of incense, and a solemn train of priests and prophets, without fear and without danger. The sound of prayer and of music was heard on the tops of the highest mountains; and the same ox afforded a sacrifice for the gods, and a supper for their joyous votaries." [36]

[Footnote 36: The restoration of the Pagan worship is described by Julian, (Misopogon, p. 346,) Libanius, (Orat. Parent. c. 60, p. 286, 287, and Orat. Consular. ad Julian. p. 245, 246, edit. Morel.,) Ammianus, (xxii.

12,) and Gregory Nazianzen, (Orat. iv. p. 121.) These writers agree in the essential, and even minute, facts; but the different lights in which they view the extreme devotion of Julian, are expressive of the gradations of self-applause, passionate admiration, mild reproof, and partial invective.]

But the genius and power of Julian were unequal to the enterprise of restoring a religion which was destitute of theological principles, of moral precepts, and of ecclesiastical discipline; which rapidly hastened to decay and dissolution, and was not susceptible of any solid or consistent reformation. The jurisdiction of the supreme pontiff, more especially after that office had been united with the Imperial dignity, comprehended the whole extent of the Roman empire. Julian named for his vicars, in the several provinces, the priests and philosophers whom he esteemed the best qualified to cooperate in the execution of his great design; and his pastoral letters, [37] if we may use that name, still represent a very curious sketch of his wishes and intentions. He directs, that in every city the sacerdotal order should be composed, without any distinction of birth and fortune, of those persons who were the most conspicuous for the love of the gods, and of men. "If they are guilty," continues he, "of any scandalous offence, they should be censured or degraded by the superior pontiff; but as long as they retain their rank, they are entitled to the respect of the magistrates and people. Their humility may be shown in the plainness of their domestic garb; their dignity, in the pomp of holy vestments. When they are summoned in their turn to officiate before the altar, they ought not, during the appointed number of days, to depart from the precincts of the temple; nor should a single day be suffered to elapse, without the prayers and the sacrifice, which they are obliged to offer for the prosperity of the state, and of individuals. The exercise of their sacred functions requires an immaculate purity, both of mind and body; and even when they are dismissed from the temple to the occupations of common life, it is incumbent on them to excel in decency and virtue the rest of their fellow-citizens. The priest of the gods should never be seen in theatres or taverns. His conversation should be chaste, his diet temperate, his friends of honorable reputation; and if he sometimes visits the Forum or the Palace, he should appear only as the advocate of those who have vainly solicited either justice or mercy. His studies should be suited to the sanctity of his profession. Licentious tales, or comedies, or satires, must be banished from his library, which ought solely to consist of historical or philosophical writings; of history, which is founded in truth, and of philosophy, which is connected with religion. The impious opinions of the Epicureans and sceptics deserve his abhorrence and contempt; [38] but he should diligently study the systems of Pythagoras, of Plato, and of the Stoics, which unanimously teach that there are gods; that the world is governed by their providence; that their goodness is the source of every temporal blessing; and that they have prepared for the human soul a future state of reward or punishment." The Imperial pontiff inculcates, in the most persuasive language, the duties of benevolence and hospitality; exhorts his inferior clergy to recommend the universal practice of those virtues; promises to assist their indigence from the public treasury; and declares his resolution of establishing hospitals in every city, where the poor should be received without any invidious distinction of country or of religion. Julian beheld with envy the wise and humane regulations of the church; and he very frankly confesses his intention to deprive the Christians of the applause, as well as advantage, which they had acquired by the exclusive practice of charity and beneficence. [39] The same spirit of imitation might dispose the emperor to adopt several ecclesiastical institutions, the use and importance of which were approved by the success of his enemies. But if these imaginary plans of reformation had been realized, the forced and imperfect copy would have been less beneficial to Paganism, than honorable to Christianity. [40] The Gentiles, who peaceably followed the customs of their ancestors, were rather surprised than pleased with the introduction of foreign manners; and in the short period of his reign, Julian had frequent occasions to complain of the want of fervor of his own party. [41]

[Footnote 37: See Julian. Epistol. xlix. lxii. lxiii., and a long and curious fragment, without beginning or end, (p. 288-305.) The supreme pontiff derides the Mosaic history and the Christian discipline, prefers the Greek poets to the Hebrew prophets, and palliates, with the skill of a Jesuit the relative worship of images.]

[Footnote 38: The exultation of Julian (p. 301) that these impious sects and even their writings, are extinguished, may be consistent enough with the sacerdotal character; but it is unworthy of a philosopher to wish that any opinions and arguments the most repugnant to his own should be concealed from the knowledge of mankind.]

[Footnote 39: Yet he insinuates, that the Christians, under the pretence of charity, inveigled children from their religion and parents, conveyed them on shipboard, and devoted those victims to a life of poverty or pervitude in a remote country, (p. 305.) Had the charge been proved it was his duty, not to complain, but to punish.]

[Footnote 40: Gregory Nazianzen is facetious, ingenious, and argumentative, (Orat. iii. p. 101, 102, &c.) He ridicules the folly of such vain imitation; and amuses himself with inquiring, what lessons, moral or theological, could be extracted from the Grecian fables.]

[Footnote 41: He accuses one of his pontiffs of a secret confederacy with the Christian bishops and presbyters, (Epist. lxii.) &c. Epist. lxiii.]

The enthusiasm of Julian prompted him to embrace the friends of Jupiter as his personal friends and brethren; and though he partially overlooked the merit of Christian constancy, he admired and rewarded the noble perseverance of those Gentiles who had preferred the favor of the gods to that of the emperor. [42] If they cultivated the literature, as well as the religion, of the Greeks, they acquired an additional claim to the friendship of Julian, who ranked the Muses in the number of his tutelar deities. In the religion which he had adopted, piety and learning were almost synonymous; [43] and a crowd of poets, of rhetoricians, and of philosophers, hastened to the Imperial court, to occupy the vacant places of the bishops, who had seduced the credulity of Constantius. His successor esteemed the ties of common initiation as far more sacred than those of consanguinity; he chose his favorites among the sages, who were deeply skilled in the occult sciences of magic and divination; and every impostor, who pretended to reveal the secrets of futurity, was assured of enjoying the present hour in honor and affluence. [44] Among the philosophers, Maximus obtained the most eminent rank in the friendship of his royal disciple, who communicated, with unreserved confidence, his actions, his sentiments, and his religious designs, during the anxious suspense of the civil war. [45] As soon as Julian had taken possession of the palace of Constantinople, he despatched an honorable and pressing invitation to Maximus, who then resided at Sardes in Lydia, with Chrysanthius, the associate of his art and studies. The prudent and superstitious Chrysanthius refused to undertake a journey which showed itself, according to the rules of divination, with the most threatening and malignant aspect: but his companion, whose fanaticism was of a bolder cast, persisted in his interrogations, till he had extorted from the gods a seeming consent to his own wishes, and those of the emperor. The journey of Maximus through the cities of Asia displayed the triumph of philosophic vanity; and the magistrates vied with each other in the honorable reception which they prepared for the friend of their sovereign. Julian was pronouncing an oration before the senate, when he was informed of the arrival of Maximus. The emperor immediately interrupted his discourse, advanced to meet him, and after a tender embrace, conducted him by the hand into the midst of the assembly; where he publicly acknowledged the benefits which he had derived from the instructions of the philosopher. Maximus, [46] who soon acquired the confidence, and influenced the councils of Julian, was insensibly corrupted by the temptations of a court. His dress became more splendid, his demeanor more lofty, and he was exposed, under a succeeding reign, to a disgraceful inquiry into the means by which the disciple of Plato had accumulated, in the short duration of his favor, a very scandalous proportion of wealth. Of the other philosophers and sophists, who were invited to the Imperial residence by the choice of Julian, or by the success of Maximus, few were able to preserve their innocence or their reputation. The liberal gifts of money, lands, and houses, were insufficient to satiate their rapacious avarice; and the indignation of the people was justly excited by the remembrance of their abject poverty and disinterested professions. The penetration of Julian could not always be deceived: but he was unwilling to despise the characters of those men whose talents deserved his esteem: he desired to escape the double reproach of imprudence and inconstancy; and he was apprehensive of degrading, in the eyes of the profane, the honor of letters and of religion. [48]

[Footnote 42: He praises the fidelity of Callixene, priestess of Ceres, who had been twice as constant as Penelope, and rewards her with the priesthood of the Phrygian goddess at Pessinus, (Julian. Epist. xxi.) He applauds the firmness of Sopater of Hierapolis, who had been repeatedly pressed by Constantius and Gallus to apostatize, (Epist. xxvii p. 401.)]

[Footnote 43: Orat. Parent. c. 77, p. 202. The same sentiment is frequently inculcated by Julian, Libanius, and the rest of their party.]

[Footnote 44: The curiosity and credulity of the emperor, who tried every mode of divination, are fairly exposed by Ammianus, xxii. 12.]

[Footnote 45: Julian. Epist. xxxviii. Three other epistles, (xv. xvi. xxxix.,) in the same style of friendship and confidence, are addressed to the philosopher Maximus.]

[Footnote 46: Eunapius (in Maximo, p. 77, 78, 79, and in Chrysanthio, p. 147, 148) has minutely related these anecdotes, which he conceives to be the most important events of the age. Yet he fairly confesses the frailty of Maximus. His reception at Constantinople is described by Libanius (Orat. Parent. c. 86, p. 301) and Ammianus, (xxii. 7.) Note: Eunapius wrote a continuation of the History of Dexippus. Some valuable fragments of this work have been recovered by M. Mai, and reprinted in Niebuhr's edition of the Byzantine Historians—M.]

[Footnote 47: Chrysanthius, who had refused to quit Lydia, was created high priest of the province. His cautious and temperate use of power secured him after the revolution; and he lived in peace, while Maximus, Priscus, &c., were persecuted by the Christian ministers. See the adventures of those fanatic sophists, collected by Brucker, tom ii. p. 281-293.]

[Footnote 48: Sec Libanius (Orat. Parent. c. 101, 102, p. 324, 325, 326) and Eunapius, (Vit. Sophist. in Proaeresio, p. 126.) Some students, whose expectations perhaps were groundless, or extravagant, retired in disgust, (Greg. Naz. Orat. iv. p. 120.) It is strange that we should not be able to contradict the title of one of Tillemont's chapters, (Hist. des Empereurs, tom. iv. p. 960,) "La Cour de Julien est pleine de philosphes et de gens perdus."]

The favor of Julian was almost equally divided between the Pagans, who had firmly adhered to the worship of their ancestors, and the Christians, who prudently embraced the religion of their sovereign. The acquisition of new proselytes [49] gratified the ruling passions of his soul, superstition and vanity; and he was heard to declare, with the enthusiasm of a missionary, that if he could render each individual richer than Midas, and every city greater than Babylon, he should not esteem himself the benefactor of mankind, unless, at the same time, he could reclaim his subjects from their impious revolt against the immortal gods. [50] A prince who had studied human nature, and who possessed the treasures of the Roman empire, could adapt his arguments, his promises, and his rewards, to every order of Christians; [51] and the merit of a seasonable conversion was allowed to supply the defects of a candidate, or even to expiate the guilt of a criminal. As the army is the most forcible engine of absolute power, Julian applied himself, with peculiar diligence, to corrupt the religion of his troops, without whose hearty concurrence every measure must be dangerous and unsuccessful; and the natural temper of soldiers made this conquest as easy as it was important. The legions of Gaul devoted themselves to the faith, as well as to the fortunes, of their victorious leader; and even before the death of Constantius, he had the satisfaction of announcing to his friends, that they assisted with fervent devotion, and voracious appetite, at the sacrifices, which were repeatedly offered in his camp, of whole hecatombs of fat oxen. [52] The armies of the East, which had been trained under the standard of the cross, and of Constantius, required a more artful and expensive mode of persuasion. On the days of solemn and public festivals, the emperor received the homage, and rewarded the merit, of the troops. His throne of state was encircled with the military ensigns of Rome and the republic; the holy name of Christ was erased from the Labarum; and the symbols of war, of majesty, and of pagan superstition, were so dexterously blended, that the faithful subject incurred the guilt of idolatry, when he respectfully saluted the person or image of his sovereign. The soldiers passed successively in review; and each of them, before he received from the hand of Julian a liberal donative, proportioned to his rank and services, was required to cast a few grains of incense into the flame which burnt upon the altar. Some Christian confessors might resist, and others might repent; but the far greater number, allured by the prospect of gold, and awed by the presence of the emperor, contracted the criminal engagement; and their future perseverance in the worship of the gods was enforced by every consideration of duty and of interest.

By the frequent repetition of these arts, and at the expense of sums which would have purchased the service of half the nations of Scythia, Julian gradually acquired for his troops the imaginary protection of the gods, and for himself the firm and effectual support of the Roman legions. [53] It is indeed more than probable, that the restoration and encouragement of Paganism revealed a multitude of pretended Christians, who, from motives of temporal advantage, had acquiesced in the religion of the former reign; and who afterwards returned, with the same flexibility of conscience, to the faith which was professed by the successors of Julian.

[Footnote 49: *Under the reign of Lewis XIV. his subjects of every rank aspired to the glorious title of Convertisseur, expressive of their zea and success in making proselytes. The word and the idea are growing obsolete in France may they never be introduced into England.*]

[Footnote 50: *See the strong expressions of Libanius, which were probably those of Julian himself, (Orat. Parent. c. 59, p. 285.)*]

[Footnote 51: *When Gregory Nazianzen (Orat. x. p. 167) is desirous to magnify the Christian firmness of his brother Caesarius, physician to the Imperial court, he owns that Caesarius disputed with a formidable adversary. In his invectives he scarcely allows any share of wit or courage to the apostate.*]

[Footnote 52: *Julian, Epist. xxxviii. Ammianus, xxii. 12. Adeo ut in dies paene singulos milites carnis distentiore sagina victitantes incultius, potusque aviditate correpti, humeris impositi transeuntium per plateas, ex publicis aedibus..... ad sua diversoria portarentur. The devout prince and the indignant* historian describe the same scene; and in Illyricum or Antioch, similar causes must have produced similar effects.]

[Footnote 53: Gregory (Orat. iii. p. 74, 75, 83-86) and Libanius, (Orat. Parent. c. lxxxi. lxxxii. p. 307, 308,). The sophist owns and justifies the expense of these military conversions.]

While the devout monarch incessantly labored to restore and propagate the religion of his ancestors, he embraced the extraordinary design of rebuilding the temple of Jerusalem. In a public epistle [54] to the nation or community of the Jews, dispersed through the provinces, he pities their misfortunes, condemns their oppressors, praises their constancy, declares himself their gracious protector, and expresses a pious hope, that after his return from the Persian war, he may be permitted to pay his grateful vows to the Almighty in his holy city of Jerusalem. The blind superstition, and abject slavery, of those unfortunate exiles, must excite the contempt of a philosophic emperor; but they deserved the friendship of Julian, by their implacable hatred of the Christian name. The barren synagogue abhorred and envied the fecundity of the rebellious church; the power of the Jews was not equal to their malice; but their gravest rabbis approved the private murder of an apostate; [55] and their seditious clamors had often awakened the indolence of the Pagan magistrates. Under the reign of Constantine, the Jews became the subjects of their revolted children nor was it long before they experienced the bitterness of domestic tyranny. The civil immunities which had been granted, or confirmed, by Severus, were gradually repealed by the Christian princes; and a rash tumult, excited by the Jews of Palestine, [56] seemed to justify the lucrative modes of oppression which were invented by the bishops and eunuchs of the court of Constantius. The Jewish patriarch, who was still permitted to exercise a precarious jurisdiction, held his residence at Tiberias; [57] and the neighboring cities of Palestine were filled with the remains of a people who fondly adhered to the promised land. But the edict of Hadrian was renewed and enforced; and they viewed from afar the walls of the holy city, which were profaned in their eyes by the triumph of the cross and the devotion of the Christians. [58]

[Footnote 54: Julian's epistle (xxv.) is addressed to the community of the Jews. Aldus (Venet. 1499) has branded it with an; but this stigma is justly removed by the subsequent editors, Petavius and Spanheim. This epistle is mentioned by Sozomen, (l. v. c. 22,) and the purport of it is confirmed by Gregory, (Orat. iv. p. 111.) and by Julian himself (Fragment. p. 295.)]

[Footnote 55: The Misnah denounced death against those who abandoned the foundation. The judgment of zeal is explained by Marsham (Canon. Chron. p. 161, 162, edit. fol. London, 1672) and Basnage, (Hist. des Juifs, tom. viii. p. 120.) Constantine made a law to protect Christian converts from Judaism. Cod. Theod. l. xvi. tit. viii. leg. 1. Godefroy, tom. vi. p. 215.]

[Footnote 56: Et interea (during the civil war of Magnentius) Judaeorum seditio, qui Patricium, nefarie in regni speciem sustulerunt, oppressa. Aurelius Victor, in Constantio, c. xlii. See Tillemont, Hist. des Empereurs, tom. iv. p. 379, in 4to.]

[Footnote 57: The city and synagogue of Tiberias are curiously described by Reland. Palestin. tom. ii. p. 1036-1042.]

[Footnote 58: Basnage has fully illustrated the state of the Jews under Constantine and his successors, (tom. viii. c. iv. p. 111-153.)]

PART III

In the midst of a rocky and barren country, the walls of Jerusalem [59] enclosed the two mountains of Sion and Acra, within an oval figure of about three English miles. [60] Towards the south, the upper town, and the fortress of David, were erected on the lofty ascent of Mount Sion: on the north side, the buildings of the lower town covered the spacious summit of Mount Acra; and a part of the hill, distinguished by the name of Moriah, and levelled by human industry, was crowned with the stately temple of the Jewish nation. After the final destruction of the temple by the arms of Titus and Hadrian, a ploughshare was drawn over the consecrated ground, as a sign of perpetual interdiction. Sion was deserted; and the vacant space of the lower city was filled with the public and private edifices of the Aelian colony, which spread themselves over the adjacent hill of Calvary. The holy places were polluted with mountains of idolatry; and, either from design or accident, a chapel was dedicated to Venus, on the spot which had been sanctified by the death and resurrection of Christ. [61] [61a] Almost three hundred years after those stupendous events, the profane chapel of Venus was demolished by the order of Constantine; and the removal of the earth and stones revealed the holy sepulchre to the eyes of mankind. A magnificent church was erected on that mystic ground, by the first Christian emperor; and the effects of his pious munificence were extended to every spot which had been consecrated by the footstep of patriarchs, of prophets, and of the Son of God. [62]

[Footnote 59: Reland (Palestin. l. i. p. 309, 390, l. iii. p. 838) describes, with learning and perspicuity, Jerusalem, and the face of the adjacent country.]

[Footnote 60: I have consulted a rare and curious treatise of M. D'Anville, (sur l'Ancienne Jerusalem, Paris, 1747, p. 75.) The circumference of the ancient city (Euseb. Preparat. Evangel. l. ix. c. 36) was 27 stadia, or 2550 toises. A plan, taken on the spot, assigns no more than 1980 for the modern town. The circuit is defined by natural landmarks, which cannot be mistaken or removed.]

[Footnote 61: See two curious passages in Jerom, (tom. i. p. 102, tom. vi. p. 315,) and the ample details of Tillemont, (Hist, des Empereurs, tom. i. p. 569. tom. ii. p. 289, 294, 4to edition.)]

[Footnote 61a: On the site of the Holy Sepulchre, compare the chapter in Professor Robinson's Travels in Palestine, which has renewed the old controversy with great vigor. To me, this temple of Venus, said to have been erected by Hadrian to insult the Christians, is not the least suspicious part of the whole legend.-M. 1845.]

[Footnote 62: Eusebius in Vit. Constantin. l. iii. c. 25-47, 51-53. The emperor likewise built churches at Bethlem, the Mount of Olives, and the oa of Mambre. The holy sepulchre is described by Sandys, (Travels, p. 125-133,) and curiously delineated by Le Bruyn, (Voyage au Levant, p. 28-296.)]

The passionate desire of contemplating the original monuments of their redemption attracted to Jerusalem a successive crowd of pilgrims, from the shores of the Atlantic Ocean, and the most distant countries of the East; [63] and their piety was authorized by the example of the empress Helena, who appears to have united the credulity of age with the warm feelings of a recent conversion. Sages and heroes, who have visited the memorable scenes of ancient wisdom or glory, have confessed the inspiration of the genius of the place; [64] and the Christian who knelt before the holy sepulchre, ascribed his lively faith, and his fervent devotion, to the more immediate influence of the Divine Spirit. The zeal, perhaps the avarice, of the clergy of Jerusalem, cherished and multiplied these beneficial visits.

They fixed, by unquestionable tradition, the scene of each memorable event. They exhibited the instruments which had been used in the passion of Christ; the nails and the lance that had pierced his hands, his feet, and his side; the crown of thorns that was planted on his head; the pillar at which he was scourged; and, above all, they showed the cross on which he suffered, and which was dug out of the earth in the reign of those princes, who inserted the symbol of Christianity in the banners of the Roman legions. [65] Such miracles as seemed necessary to account for its extraordinary preservation, and seasonable discovery, were gradually propagated without opposition. The custody of the true cross, which on Easter Sunday was solemnly exposed to the people, was intrusted to the bishop of Jerusalem; and he alone might gratify the curious devotion of the pilgrims, by the gift of small pieces, which they encased in gold or gems, and carried away in triumph to their respective countries. But as this gainful branch of commerce must soon have been annihilated, it was found convenient to suppose, that the marvelous wood possessed a secret power of vegetation; and that its substance, though continually diminished, still remained entire and unimpaired. [66] It might perhaps have been expected, that the influence of the place and the belief of a perpetual miracle, should have produced some salutary effects on the morals, as well as on the faith, of the people. Yet the most respectable of the ecclesiastical writers have been obliged to confess, not only that the streets of Jerusalem were filled with the incessant tumult of business and pleasure, [67] but that every species of vice—adultery, theft, idolatry, poisoning, murder—was familiar to the inhabitants of the holy city. [68] The wealth and preeminence of the church of Jerusalem excited the ambition of Arian, as well as orthodox, candidates; and the virtues of Cyril, who, since his death, has been honored with the title of Saint, were displayed in the exercise, rather than in the acquisition, of his episcopal dignity. [69]

[Footnote 63: The Itinerary from Bourdeaux to Jerusalem was composed in the year 333, for the use of pilgrims; among whom Jerom (tom. i. p. 126) mentions the Britons and the Indians. The causes of this superstitious fashion are discussed in the learned and judicious preface of Wesseling. (Itinarar. p. 537-545.) —Much curious information on this subject is collected in the first chapter of Wilken, Geschichte der Kreuzzuge—M.]

[Footnote 64: Cicero (de Finibus, v. 1) has beautifully expressed the common sense of mankind.]

[Footnote 65: Baronius (Annal. Eccles. A. D. 326, No. 42-50) and Tillemont (Mem. Eccles. tom. xii. p. 8-16) are the historians and champions of the miraculous invention of the cross, under the reign of Constantine. Their oldest witnesses are Paulinus, Sulpicius Severus, Rufinus, Ambrose, and perhaps Cyril of Jerusalem. The silence of Eusebius, and the Bourdeaux pilgrim, which satisfies those who think perplexes those who believe. See Jortin's sensible remarks, vol. ii. p 238-248.]

[Footnote 66: This multiplication is asserted by Paulinus, (Epist. xxxvi. See Dupin. Bibliot. Eccles. tom. iii. p. 149,) who seems to have improved a rhetorical flourish of Cyril into a real fact. The same supernatural privilege must have been communicated to the Virgin's milk, (Erasmi Opera, tom. i. p. 778, Lugd. Batav. 1703, in Colloq. de Peregrinat. Religionis ergo,) saints' heads, &c. and other relics, which are repeated in so many different churches. Note: Lord Mahon, in a memoir read before the Society of Antiquaries, (Feb. 1831,) has traced in a brief but interesting manner, the singular adventures of the "true" cross. It is curious to inquire, what authority we have, except of late tradition, for the Hill of Calvary. There is none in the sacred writings; the uniform use of the common word, instead of any word expressing assent or acclivity, is against the notion—M.]

[Footnote 67: Jerom, (tom. i. p. 103,) who resided in the neighboring village of Bethlem, describes the vices of Jerusalem from his personal experience.]

[Footnote 68: Gregor. Nyssen, apud Wesseling, p. 539. The whole epistle, which condemns either the use or the abuse of religious pilgrimage, is painful to the Catholic divines, while it is dear and familiar to our Protestant polemics.]

[Footnote 69: He renounced his orthodox ordination, officiated as a deacon, and was re-ordained by the hands of the Arians. But Cyril afterwards changed with the times, and prudently conformed to the Nicene faith. Tillemont, (Mem. Eccles. tom. viii.,) who treats his memory with tenderness and respect, has thrown his virtues into the text, and his faults into the notes, in decent obscurity, at the end of the volume.]

The vain and ambitious mind of Julian might aspire to restore the ancient glory of the temple of Jerusalem. [70] As the Christians were firmly persuaded that a sentence of everlasting destruction had been pronounced against the whole fabric of the Mosaic law, the Imperial sophist would have converted the success of his undertaking into a specious argument against the faith of prophecy, and the truth of revelation. [71] He was displeased with the spiritual worship of the synagogue; but he approved the institutions of Moses, who had not disdained to adopt many of the rites and ceremonies of Egypt. [72] The local and national deity of the Jews was sincerely adored by a polytheist, who desired only to multiply the number of the gods; [73] and such was the appetite of Julian for bloody sacrifice, that his emulation might be excited by the piety of Solomon, who had offered, at the feast of the dedication, twenty-two thousand oxen, and one hundred and twenty thousand sheep. [74] These considerations might influence his designs; but the prospect of an immediate and important advantage would not suffer the impatient monarch to expect the remote and uncertain event of the Persian war. He resolved to erect, without delay, on the commanding eminence of Moriah, a stately temple, which might eclipse the splendor of the church of the resurrection on the adjacent hill of Calvary; to establish an order of priests, whose interested zeal would detect the arts, and resist the ambition, of their Christian rivals; and to invite a numerous colony of Jews, whose stern fanaticism would be always prepared to second, and even to anticipate, the hostile measures of the Pagan government. Among the friends of the emperor (if the names of emperor, and of friend, are not incompatible) the first place was assigned, by Julian himself, to the virtuous and learned Alypius. [75] The humanity of Alypius was tempered by severe justice and manly fortitude; and while he exercised his abilities in the civil administration of Britain, he imitated, in his poetical compositions, the harmony and softness of the odes of Sappho. This minister, to whom Julian communicated, without reserve, his most careless levities, and his most serious counsels, received an extraordinary commission to restore, in its pristine beauty, the temple of Jerusalem; and the diligence of Alypius required and obtained the strenuous support of the governor of Palestine. At the call of their great deliverer, the Jews, from all the provinces of the empire, assembled on the holy mountain of their fathers; and their insolent triumph alarmed and exasperated the Christian inhabitants of Jerusalem. The desire of rebuilding the temple has in every age been the ruling passion of the children of Israel. In this propitious moment the men forgot their avarice, and the women their delicacy; spades and pickaxes of silver were provided by the vanity of the rich, and the rubbish was transported in mantles of silk and purple. Every purse was opened in liberal contributions, every hand claimed a share in the pious labor, and the commands of a great monarch were executed by the enthusiasm of a whole people. [76]

[Footnote 70: Imperii sui memoriam magnitudine operum gestiens propagare Ammian. xxiii. 1. The temple of Jerusalem had been famous even among the Gentiles. They had many temples in each city, (at Sichem five, at Gaza eight, at Rome four hundred and twenty-four;) but the wealth and religion of the Jewish nation was centred in one spot.]

[Footnote 71: The secret intentions of Julian are revealed by the late bishop of Gloucester, the learned and dogmatic Warburton; who, with the authority of a theologian, prescribes the motives and conduct of the Supreme Being. The discourse entitled Julian (2d edition, London, 1751) is strongly marked with all the peculiarities which are imputed to the Warburtonian school.]

[Footnote 72: I shelter myself behind Maimonides, Marsham, Spencer, Le Clerc, Warburton, &c., who have fairly derided the fears, the folly, and the falsehood of some superstitious divines. See Divine Legation, vol. iv. p. 25, &c.]

[Footnote 73: Julian (Fragment. p. 295) respectfully styles him, and mentions him elsewhere (Epist. lxiii.) with still higher reverence. He doubly condemns the Christians for believing, and for renouncing, the religion of the Jews. Their Deity was a true, but not the only, God Apul Cyril. l. ix. p. 305, 306.]

[Footnote 74: 1 Kings, viii. 63. 2 Chronicles, vii. 5. Joseph. Antiquitat. Judaic. l. viii. c. 4, p. 431, edit. Havercamp. As the blood and smoke of so many hecatombs might be inconvenient, Lightfoot, the Christian Rabbi, removes them by a miracle. Le Clerc (ad loca) is bold enough to suspect to fidelity of the numbers. Note: According to the historian Kotobeddym, quoted by Burckhardt, (Travels in Arabia, p. 276,) the Khalif Mokteder sacrificed, during his pilgrimage to Mecca, in the year of the Hejira 350, forty thousand camels and cows, and fifty thousand sheep. Barthema describes thirty thousand oxen slain, and their carcasses given to the poor. Quarterly Review, xiii.p.39—M.]

[Footnote 75: Julian, epist. xxix. xxx. La Bleterie has neglected to translate the second of these epistles.]

[Footnote 76: See the zeal and impatience of the Jews in Gregory Nazianzen (Orat. iv. p. 111) and Theodoret. (l. iii. c. 20.)]

Yet, on this occasion, the joint efforts of power and enthusiasm were unsuccessful; and the ground of the Jewish temple, which is now covered by a Mahometan mosque, [77] still continued to exhibit the same edifying spectacle of ruin and desolation. Perhaps the absence and death of the emperor, and the new maxims of a Christian reign, might explain the interruption of an arduous work, which was attempted only in the last six months of the life of Julian. [78] But the Christians entertained a natural and pious expectation, that, in this memorable contest, the honor of religion would be vindicated by some signal miracle. An earthquake, a whirlwind, and a fiery eruption, which overturned and scattered the new foundations of the temple, are attested, with some variations, by contemporary and respectable evidence. [79] This public event is described by Ambrose, [80] bishop of Milan, in an epistle to the emperor Theodosius, which must provoke the severe animadversion of the Jews; by the eloquent Chrysostom, [81] who might appeal to the memory of the elder part of his congregation at Antioch; and by Gregory Nazianzen, [82] who published his account of the miracle before the expiration of the same year. The last of these writers has boldly declared, that this preternatural event was not disputed by the infidels; and his assertion, strange as it may seem is confirmed by the unexceptionable testimony of Ammianus Marcellinus. [83] The philosophic soldier, who loved the virtues, without adopting the prejudices, of his master, has recorded, in his judicious and candid history of his own times, the extraordinary obstacles which interrupted the restoration of the temple of Jerusalem. "Whilst Alypius, assisted by the governor of the province, urged, with vigor and diligence, the execution of the work, horrible balls of fire breaking out near the foundations, with frequent and reiterated attacks, rendered the place, from time to time, inaccessible to the scorched and blasted workmen; and the victorious element continuing in this manner obstinately and resolutely bent, as it were, to drive them to a distance, the undertaking was abandoned." [83a] Such authority should satisfy a believing, and must astonish an incredulous, mind. Yet a philosopher may still require the original evidence of impartial and intelligent spectators. At this important crisis, any singular accident of nature would assume the appearance, and produce the effects of a real prodigy. This glorious deliverance would be speedily improved and magnified by the pious art of the clergy of Jerusalem, and the active credulity of the Christian world and, at the distance of twenty years, a Roman historian, care less of theological disputes, might adorn his work with the specious and splendid miracle. [84]

[Footnote 77: Built by Omar, the second Khalif, who died A. D. 644. This great mosque covers the whole consecrated ground of the Jewish temple, and constitutes almost a square of 760 toises, or one Roman mile in circumference. See D'Anville, Jerusalem, p. 45.]

[Footnote 78: Ammianus records the consults of the year 363, before he proceeds to mention the thoughts of Julian. Templum. ... instaurare sumptibus cogitabat immodicis. Warburton has a secret wish to anticipate the design; but he must have understood, from former examples, that the execution of such a work would have demanded many years.]

[Footnote 79: The subsequent witnesses, Socrates, Sozomen, Theodoret, Philostorgius, &c., add contradictions rather than authority. Compare the objections of Basnage (Hist. des Juifs, tom. viii. p. 156-168) with Warburton's answers, (Julian, p. 174-258.) The bishop has ingeniously explained the miraculous crosses which appeared on the garments of the spectators by a similar instance, and the natural effects of lightning.]

[Footnote 80: Ambros. tom. ii. epist. xl. p. 946, edit. Benedictin. He composed this fanatic epistle (A. D. 388) to justify a bishop who had been condemned by the civil magistrate for burning a synagogue.]

[Footnote 81: Chrysostom, tom. i. p. 580, advers. Judaeos et Gentes, tom. ii. p. 574, de Sto Babyla, edit. Montfaucon. I have followed the common and natural supposition; but the learned Benedictine, who dates the composition of these sermons in the year 383, is confident they were never pronounced from the pulpit.]

[Footnote 82: Greg. Nazianzen, Orat. iv. p. 110-113.]

[Footnote 83: Ammian. xxiii. 1. Cum itaque rei fortiter instaret Alypius, juvaretque provinciae rector, metuendi globi flammarum prope fundamenta crebris assultibus erumpentes fecere locum exustis aliquoties operantibus inaccessum; hocque modo elemento destinatius repellente, cessavit inceptum. Warburton labors (p. 60-90) to extort a confession of the miracle from the mouths of Julian and Libanius, and to employ the evidence of a rabbi who lived in the fifteenth century. Such witnesses can only be received by a very favorable judge.]

[Footnote 83a: Michaelis has given an ingenious and sufficiently probable explanation of this remarkable incident, which the positive testimony of Ammianus, a contemporary and a pagan, will not permit us to call in question. It was suggested by a passage in Tacitus. That historian, speaking of Jerusalem, says, [I omit the first part of the quotation adduced by M. Guizot, which only by a most extraordinary mistranslation of muri introrsus sinuati by "enfoncemens" could be made to bear on the question—M.] The Temple itself was a kind of citadel, which had its own walls, superior in their workmanship and construction to those of the city. The porticos themselves, which surrounded the temple, were an excellent fortification. There was a fountain of constantly running water; subterranean excavations under the mountain; reservoirs and cisterns to collect the rain-water. Tac. Hist. v. ii. 12. These excavations and reservoirs must have been very considerable. The latter furnished water during the whole siege of Jerusalem to 1,100,000 inhabitants, for whom the fountain of Siloe could not have sufficed, and who had no fresh rain-water, the siege having taken place from the month of April to the month of August, a period of the year during which it rarely rains in Jerusalem. As to the excavations, they served after, and even before, the return of the Jews from Babylon, to contain not only magazines of oil, wine, and corn, but also the treasures which were laid up in the Temple. Josephus has related several incidents which show their extent. When Jerusalem was on the point of being taken by Titus, the rebel chiefs, placing their last hopes in these vast subterranean cavities, formed a design of concealing themselves there, and remaining during the conflagration of the city, and until the Romans had retired to a distance. The greater part had not time to execute their design; but one of them, Simon, the Son of Gioras, having provided himself with food, and tools to excavate the earth descended into this retreat with some companions: he remained there till Titus had set out for Rome: under the pressure of famine he issued forth on a sudden in the very place where the Temple had stood, and appeared in the midst of the Roman guard. He was seized and carried to Rome for the triumph. His appearance made it be suspected that other Jews might have chosen the same asylum; search was made, and a great number discovered. Joseph. de Bell. Jud. l. vii. c. 2. It is probable that the greater part of these excavations were the remains of the time of Solomon, when it was the custom to work to a great extent under ground: no other date can be assigned to them. The Jews, on their return from the captivity, were too poor to undertake such works; and, although Herod, on rebuilding the Temple, made some excavations, (Joseph. Ant. Jud. xv. 11, vii.,) the haste with which that building was completed will not allow us to suppose that they belonged to that period. Some were used for sewers and drains, others served to conceal the immense treasures of which Crassus, a hundred and twenty years before, plundered the Jews, and which doubtless had been since replaced. The Temple was destroyed A. C. 70; the attempt of Julian to rebuild it, and the fact related by Ammianus, coincide with the year 363. There had then elapsed between these two epochs an interval of near 300 years, during which the excavations, choked up with ruins, must have become full of inflammable air. The workmen employed by Julian as they were digging, arrived at the excavations of the Temple; they would take torches to explore them; sudden flames repelled those who approached; explosions were heard, and these phenomena were renewed every time that they penetrated into new subterranean passages. This explanation is confirmed by the relation of an event nearly similar, by Josephus. King Herod having heard that immense treasures had been concealed in the sepulchre of David, he descended into it with a few confidential persons; he found in the first subterranean chamber only jewels and precious stuffs: but having wished to penetrate into a second chamber, which had been long closed, he was repelled, when he opened it, by flames which killed those who accompanied him. (Ant. Jud. xvi. 7, i.) As here there is no room for miracle, this fact may be considered as a new proof of the veracity of that related by Ammianus and the contemporary writers—G. —To the illustrations of the extent of the subterranean chambers adduced by Michaelis, may be added, that when John of Gischala, during the siege, surprised the Temple, the party of Eleazar took refuge within them. Bell. Jud. vi. 3, i. The sudden sinking of the hill of Sion when Jerusalem was occupied by Barchocab, may have been connected with similar excavations. Hist. of Jews, vol. iii. 122 and 186—M. —It is a fact now popularly known, that when mines which have been long closed are opened, one of two things takes place; either the torches are extinguished and the men fall first into a swoor and soon die; or, if the air is inflammable, a little flame is seen to flicker round the lamp, which spreads and multiplies till the conflagration becomes general, is followed by an explosion, and kill all who are in the way—G.]

[Footnote 84: Dr. Lardner, perhaps alone of the Christian critics, presumes to doubt the truth of this famous miracle. (Jewish and Heathen Testimonies, vol. iv. p. 47-71.)]

The silence of Jerom would lead to a suspicion that the same story which was celebrated at a distance, might be despised on the spot. Note: Gibbon has forgotten Basnage, to whom Warburton replied—M.

PART IV

The restoration of the Jewish temple was secretly connected with the ruin of the Christian church. Julian still continued to maintain the freedom of religious worship, without distinguishing whether this universal toleration proceeded from his justice or his clemency. He affected to pity the unhappy Christians, who were mistaken in the most important object of their lives; but his pity was degraded by contempt, his contempt was embittered by hatred; and the sentiments of Julian were expressed in a style of sarcastic wit, which inflicts a deep and deadly wound, whenever it issues from the mouth of a sovereign. As he was sensible that the Christians gloried in the name of their Redeemer, he countenanced, and perhaps enjoined, the use of the less honorable appellation of Galilaeans. [85] He declared, that by the folly of the Galilaeans, whom he describes as a sect of fanatics, contemptible to men, and odious to the gods, the empire had been reduced to the brink of destruction; and he insinuates in a public edict, that a frantic patient might sometimes be cured by salutary violence. [86] An ungenerous distinction was admitted into the mind and counsels of Julian, that, according to the difference of their religious sentiments, one part of his subjects deserved his favor and friendship, while the other was entitled only to the common benefits that his justice could not refuse to an obedient people. According to a principle, pregnant with mischief and oppression, the emperor transferred to the pontiffs of his own religion the management of the liberal allowances for the public revenue, which had been granted to the church by the piety of Constantine and his sons. The proud system of clerical honors and immunities, which had been constructed with so much art and labor, was levelled to the ground; the hopes of testamentary donations were intercepted by the rigor of the laws; and the priests of the Christian sect were confounded with the last and most ignominious class of the people. Such of these regulations as appeared necessary to check the ambition and avarice of the ecclesiastics, were soon afterwards imitated by the wisdom of an orthodox prince. The peculiar distinctions which policy has bestowed, or superstition has lavished, on the sacerdotal order, must be confined to those priests who profess the religion of the state. But the will of the legislator was not exempt from prejudice and passion; and it was the object of the insidious policy of Julian, to deprive the Christians of all the temporal honors and advantages which rendered them respectable in the eyes of the world. [88]

[Footnote 85: Greg. Naz. Orat. iii. p. 81. And this law was confirmed by the invariable practice of Julian himself. Warburton has justly observed (p. 35,) that the Platonists believed in the mysterious virtue of words and Julian's dislike for the name of Christ might proceed from superstition, as well as from contempt.]

[Footnote 86: Fragment. Julian. p. 288. He derides the (Epist. vii.,) and so far loses sight of the principles of toleration, as to wish (Epist. xlii.).]

[Footnote 88: These laws, which affected the clergy, may be found in the slight hints of Julian himself, (Epist. lii.) in the vague declamations of Gregory, (Orat. iii. p. 86, 87,) and in the positive assertions of Sozomen, (l. v. c. 5.)]

A just and severe censure has been inflicted on the law which prohibited the Christians from teaching the arts of grammar and rhetoric. [89] The motives alleged by the emperor to justify this partial and oppressive measure, might command, during his lifetime, the silence of slaves and the applause of Gatterers. Julian abuses the ambiguous meaning of a word which might be indifferently applied to the language and the religion of the Greeks: he contemptuously observes, that the men who exalt the merit of implicit faith are unfit to claim or to enjoy the advantages of science; and he vainly contends, that if they refuse to adore the gods of Homer and Demosthenes, they ought to content themselves with expounding Luke and Matthew in the church of the Galilaeans. [90] In all the cities of the Roman world, the education of the youth was intrusted to masters of grammar and rhetoric; who were elected by the magistrates, maintained at the public expense, and distinguished by many lucrative and honorable privileges. The edict of Julian appears to have included the physicians, and professors of all the liberal arts; and the emperor, who reserved to himself the approbation of the candidates, was authorized by the laws to corrupt, or to punish, the religious constancy of the most learned of the Christians. [91] As soon as the resignation of the more obstinate [92] teachers had established the unrivalled dominion of the Pagan sophists, Julian invited the rising generation to resort with freedom to the public schools, in a just confidence, that their tender minds would receive the impressions of literature and idolatry. If the greatest part of the Christian youth should be deterred by their own scruples, or by those of their parents, from accepting this dangerous mode of instruction, they must, at the same time, relinquish the benefits of a liberal education. Julian had reason to expect that, in the space of a few years, the church would relapse into its primaeval simplicity, and that the theologians, who possessed an adequate share of the learning and eloquence of the age, would be succeeded by a generation of blind and ignorant fanatics, incapable of defending the truth of their own principles, or of exposing the various follies of Polytheism. [93]

[Footnote 89: Inclemens.... perenni obruendum silentio. Ammian. xxii. 10, ixv. 5.]

[Footnote 90: The edict itself, which is still extant among the epistles of Julian, (xlii.,) may be compared with the loose invectives of Gregory (Orat. iii. p. 96.) Tillemont (Mem. Eccles. tom. vii. p. 1291-1294) has collected the seeming differences of ancients and moderns. They may be easily reconciled. The Christians were directly forbid to teach, they were indirectly forbid to learn; since they would not frequent the schools of the Pagans.]

[Footnote 91: Codex Theodos. l. xiii. tit. iii. de medicis et professoribus, leg. 5, (published the 17th of June, received, at Spoleto in Italy, the 29th of July, A. D. 363,) with Godefroy's Illustrations, tom. v. p. 31.]

[Footnote 92: Orosius celebrates their disinterested resolution, Sicut a majori bus nostris compertum habemus, omnes ubique propemodum... officium quam fidem deserere maluerunt, vii. 30. Proaeresius, a Christian sophist, refused to accept the partial favor of the emperor Hieronym. in Chron. p. 185, edit. Scaliger. Eunapius in Proaeresio p. 126.]

[Footnote 93: They had recourse to the expedient of composing books for their own schools. Within a few months Apollinaris produced his Christian imitations of Homer, (a sacred history in twenty-four books,) Pindar, Euripides, and Menander; and Sozomen is satisfied, that they equalled, or excelled, the originals. Note: Socrates, however, implies that, on the death of Julian, they were contemptuously thrown aside by the Christians. Socr. Hist. iii.16—M.]

It was undoubtedly the wish and design of Julian to deprive the Christians of the advantages of wealth, of knowledge, and of power; but the injustice of excluding them from all offices of trust and profit seems to have been the result of his general policy, rather than the immediate consequence of any positive law. [94] Superior merit might deserve and obtain, some extraordinary exceptions; but the greater part of the Christian officers were gradually removed from their employments in the state, the army, and the provinces. The hopes of future candidates were extinguished by the declared partiality of a prince, who maliciously reminded them, that it was unlawful for a Christian to use the sword, either of justice, or of war; and who studiously guarded the camp and the tribunals with the ensigns of idolatry. The powers of government were intrusted to the pagans, who professed an ardent zeal for the religion of their ancestors; and as the choice of the emperor was often directed by the rules of divination, the favorites whom he preferred as the most agreeable to the gods, did not always obtain the approbation of mankind. [95] Under the administration of their enemies, the Christians had much to suffer, and more to apprehend. The temper of Julian was averse to cruelty; and the care of his reputation, which was exposed to the eyes of the universe, restrained the philosophic monarch from violating the laws of justice and toleration, which he himself had so recently established. But the provincial ministers of his authority were placed in a less conspicuous station. In the exercise of arbitrary power, they consulted the wishes, rather than the commands, of their sovereign; and ventured to exercise a secret and vexatious tyranny against the sectaries, on whom they were not permitted to confer the honors of martyrdom. The emperor, who dissembled as long as possible his knowledge of the injustice that was exercised in his name, expressed his real sense of the conduct of his officers, by gentle reproofs and substantial rewards. [96]

[Footnote 94: It was the instruction of Julian to his magistrates, (Epist. vii.,). Sozomen (l. v. c. 18) and Socrates (l. iii. c. 13) must be reduced to the standard of Gregory, (Orat. iii. p. 95,) not less prone to exaggeration, but more restrained by the actual knowledge of his contemporary readers.]

[Footnote 95: Libanius, Orat. Parent. 88, p. 814.]

[Footnote 96: Greg. Naz. Orat. iii. p. 74, 91, 92. Socrates, l. iii. c. 14. The doret, l. iii. c. 6. Some drawback may, however, be allowed for the violence of their zeal, not less partial than the zeal of Julian]

The most effectual instrument of oppression, with which they were armed, was the law that obliged the Christians to make full and ample satisfaction for the temples which they had destroyed under the preceding reign. The zeal of the triumphant church had not always expected the sanction of the public authority; and the bishops, who were secure of impunity, had often marched at the head of their congregation, to attack and demolish the fortresses of the prince of darkness. The consecrated lands, which had increased the patrimony of the sovereign or of the clergy, were clearly defined, and easily restored. But on these lands, and on the ruins of Pagan superstition, the Christians had frequently erected their own religious edifices: and as it was necessary to remove the church before the temple could be rebuilt, the justice and piety of the emperor were applauded by one party, while the other deplored and execrated his sacrilegious violence. [97] After the ground was cleared, the restitution of those stately structures which had been levelled with the dust, and of the precious ornaments which had been converted to Christian uses, swelled into a very large account of damages and debt. The authors of the injury had neither the ability nor the inclination to discharge this accumulated demand: and the impartial wisdom of a legislator would have been displayed in balancing the adverse claims and complaints, by an equitable and temperate arbitration.

But the whole empire, and particularly the East, was thrown into confusion by the rash edicts of Julian; and the Pagan magistrates, inflamed by zeal and revenge, abused the rigorous privilege of the Roman law, which substitutes, in the place of his inadequate property, the person of the insolvent debtor. Under the preceding reign, Mark, bishop of Arethusa, [98] had labored in the conversion of his people with arms more effectual than those of persuasion. [99] The magistrates required the full value of a temple which had been destroyed by his intolerant zeal: but as they were satisfied of his poverty, they desired only to bend his inflexible spirit to the promise of the slightest compensation. They apprehended the aged prelate, they inhumanly scourged him, they tore his beard; and his naked body, annointed with honey, was suspended, in a net, between heaven and earth, and exposed to the stings of insects and the rays of a Syrian sun. [100] From this lofty station, Mark still persisted to glory in his crime, and to insult the impotent rage of his persecutors. He was at length rescued from their hands, and dismissed to enjoy the honor of his divine triumph. The Arians celebrated the virtue of their pious confessor; the Catholics ambitiously claimed his alliance; [101] and the Pagans, who might be susceptible of shame or remorse, were deterred from the repetition of such unavailing cruelty. [102] Julian spared his life: but if the bishop of Arethusa had saved the infancy of Julian, [103] posterity will condemn the ingratitude, instead of praising the clemency, of the emperor.

[Footnote 97: If we compare the gentle language of Libanius (Orat. Parent c. 60. p. 286) with the passionate exclamations of Gregory, (Orat. iii. p. 86, 87,) we may find it difficult to persuade ourselves that the two orators are really describing the same events.]

[Footnote 98: Restan, or Arethusa, at the equal distance of sixteen miles between Emesa (Hems) and Epiphania, (Hamath,) was founded, or at least named, by Seleucus Nicator. Its peculiar aera dates from the year of Rome 685, according to the medals of the city. In the decline of the Seleucides, Emesa and Arethusa were usurped by the Arab Sampsiceramus, whose posterity, the vassals of Rome, were not extinguished in the reign of Vespasian—See D'Anville's Maps and Geographie Ancienne, tom. ii. p. 134. Wesseling, Itineraria, p. 188, and Noris. Epoch Syro-Macedon, p. 80, 481, 482.]

[Footnote 99: Sozomen, l. v. c. 10. It is surprising, that Gregory and Theodoret should suppress a circumstance, which, in their eyes, must have enhanced the religious merit of the confessor.]

[Footnote 100: The sufferings and constancy of Mark, which Gregory has so tragically painted, (Orat. iii. p. 88-91,) are confirmed by the unexceptionable and reluctant evidence of Libanius. Epist. 730, p. 350, 351. Edit. Wolf. Amstel. 1738.]

[Footnote 101: Certatim eum sibi (Christiani) vindicant. It is thus that La Croze and Wolfius (ad loc.) have explained a Greek word, whose true signification had been mistaken by former interpreters, and even by Le Clerc, (Bibliotheque Ancienne et Moderne, tom. iii. p. 371.) Yet Tillemont is strangely puzzled to understand (Mem. Eccles. tom. vii. p. 1390) how Gregory and Theodoret could mistake a Semi-Arian bishop for a saint.]

[Footnote 102: See the probable advice of Sallust, (Greg. Nazianzen, Orat. iii. p. 90, 91.) Libanius intercedes for a similar offender, lest they should find many Marks; yet he allows, that if Orion had secreted the consecrated wealth, he deserved to suffer the punishment of Marsyas; to be flayed alive, (Epist. 730, p. 349-351.)]

[Footnote 103: Gregory (Orat. iii. p. 90) is satisfied that, by saving the apostate, Mark had deserved still more than he had suffered.]

At the distance of five miles from Antioch, the Macedonian kings of Syria had consecrated to Apollo one of the most elegant places of devotion in the Pagan world. [104] A magnificent temple rose in honor of the god of light; and his colossal figure [105] almost filled the capacious sanctuary, which was enriched with gold and gems, and adorned by the skill of the Grecian artists. The deity was represented in a bending attitude, with a golden cup in his hand, pouring out a libation on the earth; as if he supplicated the venerable mother to give to his arms the cold and beauteous Daphne: for the spot was ennobled by fiction; and the fancy of the Syrian poets had transported the amorous tale from the banks of the Peneus to those of the Orontes. The ancient rites of Greece were imitated by the royal colony of Antioch. A stream of prophecy, which rivalled the truth and reputation of the Delphic oracle, flowed from the Castalian fountain of Daphne. [106] In the adjacent fields a stadium was built by a special privilege, [107] which had been purchased from Elis; the Olympic games were celebrated at the expense of the city; and a revenue of thirty thousand pounds sterling was annually applied to the public pleasures. [108] The perpetual resort of pilgrims and spectators insensibly formed, in the neighborhood of the temple, the stately and populous village of Daphne, which emulated the splendor, without acquiring the title, of a provincial city. The temple and the village were deeply bosomed in a thick grove of laurels and cypresses, which reached as far as a circumference of ten miles, and formed in the most sultry summers a cool and impenetrable shade. A thousand streams of the purest water, issuing from every hill, preserved the verdure of the earth, and the temperature of the air; the senses were gratified with harmonious sounds and aromatic odors; and the peaceful grove was consecrated to health and joy, to luxury and love. The vigorous youth pursued, like Apollo, the object of his desires; and the blushing maid was warned, by the fate of Daphne, to shun the folly of unseasonable coyness. The soldier and the philosopher wisely avoided the temptation of this sensual paradise: [109] where pleasure, assuming the character of religion, imperceptibly dissolved the firmness of manly virtue. But the groves of Daphne continued for many ages to enjoy the veneration of natives and strangers; the privileges of the holy ground were enlarged by the munificence of succeeding emperors; and every generation added new ornaments to the splendor of the temple. [110]

[Footnote 104: The grove and temple of Daphne are described by Strabo, (l. xvi. p. 1089, 1090, edit. Amstel. 1707,) Libanius, (Naenia, p. 185-188. Antiochic. Orat. xi. p. 380, 381,) and Sozomen, (l. v. c. 19.) Wesseling (Itinerar. p. 581) and Casaubon (ad Hist. August. p. 64) illustrate this curious subject.]

[Footnote 105: Simulacrum in eo Olympiaci Jovis imitamenti aequiparans magnitudinem. Ammian. xxii. 13. The Olympic Jupiter was sixty feet high, and his bulk was consequently equal to that of a thousand men. See a curious Memoire of the Abbe Gedoyn, (Academie des Inscriptions, tom. ix. p. 198.)]

[Footnote 106: Hadrian read the history of his future fortunes on a leaf dipped in the Castalian stream; a trick which, according to the physician Vandale, (de Oraculis, p. 281, 282,) might be easily performed by chemical preparations. The emperor stopped the source of such dangerous knowledge; which was again opened by the devout curiosity of Julian.]

[Footnote 107: It was purchased, A. D. 44, in the year 92 of the aera of Antioch, (Noris. Epoch. Syro-Maced. p. 139-174,) for the term of ninety Olympiads. But the Olympic games of Antioch were not regularly celebrated till the reign of Commodus. See the curious details in the Chronicle of John Malala, (tom. i. p. 290, 320, 372-381,) a writer whose merit and authority are confined within the limits of his native city.]

[Footnote 108: Fifteen talents of gold, bequeathed by Sosibius, who died in the reign of Augustus. The theatrical merits of the Syrian cities in the reign of Constantine, are computed in the Expositio totius Murd, p. 8, (Hudson, Geograph. Minor tom. iii.)]

[Footnote 109: Avidio Cassio Syriacas legiones dedi luxuria diffluentes et Daphnicis moribus. These are the words of the emperor Marcus Antoninus in an original letter preserved by his biographer in Hist. August. p. 41. Cassius dismissed or punished every soldier who was seen at Daphne.]

[Footnote 110: Aliquantum agrorum Daphnensibus dedit, (Pompey,) quo lucus ibi spatiosior fieret; delectatus amoenitate loci et aquarum abundantiz, Eutropius, vi. 14. Sextus Rufus, de Provinciis, c. 16.]

When Julian, on the day of the annual festival, hastened to adore the Apollo of Daphne, his devotion was raised to the highest pitch of eagerness and impatience. His lively imagination anticipated the grateful pomp of victims, of libations and of incense; a long procession of youths and virgins, clothed in white robes, the symbol of their innocence; and the tumultuous concourse of an innumerable people. But the zeal of Antioch was diverted, since the reign of Christianity, into a different channel. Instead of hecatombs of fat oxen sacrificed by the tribes of a wealthy city to their tutelar deity the emperor complains that he found only a single goose, provided at the expense of a priest, the pale and solitary in habitant of this decayed temple. [111] The altar was deserted, the oracle had been reduced to silence, and the holy ground was profaned by the introduction of Christian and funereal rites. After Babylas [112] (a bishop of Antioch, who died in prison in the persecution of Decius) had rested near a century in his grave, his body, by the order of Caesar Gallus, was transported into the midst of the grove of Daphne. A magnificent church was erected over his remains; a portion of the sacred lands was usurped for the maintenance of the clergy, and for the burial of the Christians at Antioch, who were ambitious of lying at the feet of their bishop; and the priests of Apollo retired, with their affrighted and indignant votaries. As soon as another revolution seemed to restore the fortune of Paganism, the church of St. Babylas was demolished, and new buildings were added to the mouldering edifice which had been raised by the piety of Syrian kings. But the first and most serious care of Julian was to deliver his oppressed deity from the odious presence of the dead and living Christians, who had so effectually suppressed the voice of fraud or enthusiasm. [113] The scene of infection was purified, according to the forms of ancient rituals; the bodies were decently removed; and the ministers of the church were permitted to convey the remains of St. Babylas to their former habitation within the walls of Antioch. The modest behavior which might have assuaged the jealousy of a hostile government was neglected, on this occasion, by the zeal of the Christians. The lofty car, that transported the relics of Babylas, was followed, and accompanied, and received, by an innumerable multitude; who chanted, with thundering acclamations, the Psalms of David the most expressive of their contempt for idols and idolaters. The return of the saint was a triumph; and the triumph was an insult on the religion of the emperor, who exerted his pride to dissemble his resentment. During the night which terminated this indiscreet procession, the temple of Daphne was in flames; the statue of Apollo was consumed; and the walls of the edifice were left a naked and awful monument of ruin. The Christians of Antioch asserted, with religious confidence, that the powerful intercession of St. Babylas had pointed the lightnings of heaven against the devoted roof: but as Julian was reduced to the alternative of believing either a crime or a miracle, he chose, without hesitation, without evidence, but with some color of probability, to impute the fire of Daphne to the revenge of the Galilaeans. [114] Their offence, had it been sufficiently proved, might have justified the retaliation, which was immediately executed by the order of Julian, of shutting the doors, and confiscating the wealth, of the cathedral of Antioch. To discover the criminals who were guilty of the tumult, of the fire, or of secreting the riches of the church, several of the ecclesiastics were tortured; [115] and a Presbyter, of the name of Theodoret, was beheaded by the sentence of the Count of the East. But this hasty act was blamed by the emperor; who lamented, with real or affected concern, that the imprudent zeal of his ministers would tarnish his reign with the disgrace of persecution. [116]

[Footnote 111: Julian (Misopogon, p. 367, 362) discovers his own character with naivete, that unconscious simplicity which always constitutes genuine humor.]

[Footnote 112: Babylas is named by Eusebius in the succession of the bishops of Antioch, (Hist. Eccles. l. vi. c. 29, 39.) His triumph over two emperors (the first fabulous, the second historical) is diffusely celebrated by Chrysostom, (tom. ii. p. 536-579, edit. Montfaucon.) Tillemont (Mem. Eccles. tom. iii. part ii. p. 287-302, 459-465) becomes almost a sceptic.]

[Footnote 113: Ecclesiastical critics, particularly those who love relics, exult in the confession of Julian (Misopogon, p. 361) and Libanius, (Laenia, p. 185,) that Apollo was disturbed by the vicinity of one dead man. Yet Ammianus (xxii. 12) clears and purifies the whole ground, according to the rites which the Athenians formerly practised in the Isle of Delos.]

[Footnote 114: Julian (in Misopogon, p. 361) rather insinuates, than affirms, their guilt. Ammianus (xxii. 13) treats the imputation as levissimus rumor, and relates the story with extraordinary candor.]

[Footnote 115: Quo tam atroci casu repente consumpto, ad id usque e imperatoris ira provexit, ut quaestiones agitare juberet solito acriores, (yet Julian blames the lenity of the magistrates of Antioch,) et majorem ecclesiam Antiochiae claudi. This interdiction was performed with some circumstances of indignity and profanation; and the seasonable death of the principal actor, Julian's uncle, is related with much superstitious complacency by the Abbe de la Bleterie. Vie de Julien, p. 362-369.]

[Footnote 116: Besides the ecclesiastical historians, who are more or less to be suspected, we may allege the passion of St. Theodore, in the Acta Sincera of Ruinart, p. 591. The complaint of Julian gives it an original and authentic air.]

PART V

The zeal of the ministers of Julian was instantly checked by the frown of their sovereign; but when the father of his country declares himself the leader of a faction, the license of popular fury cannot easily be restrained, nor consistently punished. Julian, in a public composition, applauds the devotion and loyalty of the holy cities of Syria, whose pious inhabitants had destroyed, at the first signal, the sepulchres of the Galilaeans; and faintly complains, that they had revenged the injuries of the gods with less moderation than he should have recommended. [117] This imperfect and reluctant confession may appear to confirm the ecclesiastical narratives; that in the cities of Gaza, Ascalon, Caesarea, Heliopolis, &c., the Pagans abused, without prudence or remorse, the moment of their prosperity. That the unhappy objects of their cruelty were released from torture only by death; and as their mangled bodies were dragged through the streets, they were pierced (such was the universal rage) by the spits of cooks, and the distaffs of enraged women; and that the entrails of Christian priests and virgins, after they had been tasted by those bloody fanatics, were mixed with barley, and contemptuously thrown to the unclean animals of the city. [118] Such scenes of religious madness exhibit the most contemptible and odious picture of human nature; but the massacre of Alexandria attracts still more attention, from the certainty of the fact, the rank of the victims, and the splendor of the capital of Egypt.

[Footnote 117: Julian. Misopogon, p. 361.]

[Footnote 118: See Gregory Nazianzen, (Orat. iii. p. 87.) Sozomen (l. v. c. 9) may be considered as an original, though not impartial, witness. He was a native of Gaza, and had conversed with the confessor Zeno, who, as bishop of Maiuma, lived to the age of a hundred, (l. vii. c. 28.) Philostorgius (l. vii. c. 4, with Godefroy's Dissertations, p. 284) adds some tragic circumstances, of Christians who were literally sacrificed at the altars of the gods, &c.]

George, [119] from his parents or his education, surnamed the Cappadocian, was born at Epiphania in Cilicia, in a fuller's shop. From this obscure and servile origin he raised himself by the talents of a parasite; and the patrons, whom he assiduously flattered, procured for their worthless dependent a lucrative commission, or contract, to supply the army with bacon. His employment was mean; he rendered it infamous. He accumulated wealth by the basest arts of fraud and corruption; but his malversations were so notorious, that George was compelled to escape from the pursuits of justice. After this disgrace, in which he appears to have saved his fortune at the expense of his honor, he embraced, with real or affected zeal, the profession of Arianism. From the love, or the ostentation, of learning, he collected a valuable library of history rhetoric, philosophy, and theology, [120] and the choice of the prevailing faction promoted George of Cappadocia to the throne of Athanasius. The entrance of the new archbishop was that of a Barbarian conqueror; and each moment of his reign was polluted by cruelty and avarice. The Catholics of Alexandria and Egypt were abandoned to a tyrant, qualified, by nature and education, to exercise the office of persecution; but he oppressed with an impartial hand the various inhabitants of his extensive diocese. The primate of Egypt assumed the pomp and insolence of his lofty station; but he still betrayed the vices of his base and servile extraction. The merchants of Alexandria were impoverished by the unjust, and almost universal, monopoly, which he acquired, of nitre, salt, paper, funerals, &c.: and the spiritual father of a great people condescended to practise the vile and pernicious arts of an informer. The Alexandrians could never forget, nor forgive, the tax, which he suggested, on all the houses of the city; under an obsolete claim, that the royal founder had conveyed to his successors, the Ptolemies and the Caesars, the perpetual property of the soil. The Pagans, who had been flattered with the hopes of freedom and toleration, excited his devout avarice; and the rich temples of Alexandria were either pillaged or insulted by the haughty prince, who exclaimed, in a loud and threatening tone, "How long will these sepulchres be permitted to stand?" Under the reign of Constantius, he was expelled by the fury, or rather by the justice, of the people; and it was not without a violent struggle, that the civil and military powers of the state could restore his authority, and gratify his revenge. The messenger who proclaimed at Alexandria the accession of Julian, announced the downfall of the archbishop. George, with two of his obsequious ministers, Count Diodorus, and Dracontius, master of the mint were ignominiously dragged in chains to the public prison. At the end of twenty-four days, the prison was forced open by the rage of a superstitious multitude, impatient of the tedious forms of judicial proceedings. The enemies of gods and men expired under their cruel insults; the lifeless bodies of the archbishop and his associates were carried in triumph through the streets on the back of a camel; [120] and the inactivity of the Athanasian party [121] was esteemed a shining example of evangelical patience. The remains of these guilty wretches were thrown into the sea; and the popular leaders of the tumult declared their resolution to disappoint the devotion of the Christians, and to intercept the future honors of these martyrs, who had been punished, like their predecessors, by the enemies of their religion. [122] The fears of the Pagans were just, and their precautions ineffectual. The meritorious death of the archbishop obliterated the memory of his life. The rival of Athanasius was dear and sacred to the Arians, and the seeming conversion of those sectaries introduced his worship into the bosom of the Catholic church. [123] The odious stranger, disguising every circumstance of time and place, assumed the mask of a martyr, a saint, and a Christian hero; [124] and the infamous George of Cappadocia has been transformed [125] into the renowned St. George of England, the patron of arms, of chivalry, and of the garter. [126]

[Footnote 119: The life and death of George of Cappadocia are described by Ammianus, (xxii. 11,) Gregory of Nazianzen, (Orat. xxi. p. 382, 385, 389, 390,) and Epiphanius, (Haeres. lxxvi.) The invectives of the two saints might not deserve much credit, unless they were confirmed by the testimony of the cool and impartial infidel.]

[Footnote 120: After the massacre of George, the emperor Julian repeatedly sent orders to preserve the library for his own use, and to torture the slaves who might be suspected of secreting any books. He praises the merit of the collection, from whence he had borrowed and transcribed several manuscripts while he pursued his studies in Cappadocia. He could wish, indeed, that the works of the Galiaeans might perish but he requires an exact account even of those theological volumes lest other treatises more valuable should be confounded in their less Julian. Epist. ix. xxxvi.]

[Footnote 120a: Julian himself says, that they tore him to pieces like dogs, Epist. x—M.]

[Footnote 121: Philostorgius, with cautious malice, insinuates their guilt, l. vii. c. ii. Godefroy p. 267.]

[Footnote 122: Cineres projecit in mare, id metuens ut clamabat, ne, collectis supremis, aedes illis exstruerentur ut reliquis, qui deviare a religione compulsi, pertulere, cruciabiles poenas, adusque gloriosam mortem intemerata fide progressi, et nunc Martyres appellantur. Ammian. xxii. 11. Epiphanius proves to the Arians, that George was not a martyr.]

[Footnote 123: Some Donatists (Optatus Milev. p. 60, 303, edit. Dupin; and Tillemont, Mem. Eccles. tom. vi. p. 713, in 4to.) and Priscillianists (Tillemont, Mem. Eccles. tom. viii. p. 517, in 4to.) have in like manner usurped the honors of the Catholic saints and martyrs.]

[Footnote 124: The saints of Cappadocia, Basil, and the Gregories, were ignorant of their holy companion. Pope Gelasius, (A. D. 494,) the first Catholic who acknowledges St. George, places him among the martyrs "qui Deo magis quam hominibus noti sunt." He rejects his Acts as the composition of heretics. Some, perhaps, not the oldest, of the spurious Acts, are still extant; and, through a cloud of fiction, we may yet distinguish the combat which St. George of Cappadocia sustained, in the presence of Queen Alexandria, against the magician Afhanasius.]

[Footnote 125: This transformation is not given as absolutely certain, but as extremely probable. See the Longueruana, tom. i. p. 194. —Note: The late Dr. Milner (the Roman Catholic bishop) wrote a tract to vindicate the existence and the orthodoxy of the tutelar saint of England. He succeeds, I think, in tracing the worship of St. George up to a period which makes it improbable that so notorious an Arian could be palmed upon the Catholic church as a saint and a martyr. The Acts rejected by Gelasius may have been of Arian origin, and designed to ingraft the story of their hero on the obscure adventures of some earlier saint. See an Historical and Critical Inquiry into the Existence and Character of Saint George, in a letter to the Earl of Leicester, by the Rev. J. Milner. F. S. A. London 1792—M.]

[Footnote 126: A curious history of the worship of St. George, from the sixth century, (when he was already revered in Palestine, in Armenia at Rome, and at Treves in Gaul,) might be extracted from Dr. Heylin (History of St. George, 2d edition, London, 1633, in 4to. p. 429) and the Bollandists, (Act. Ss. Mens. April. tom. iii. p. 100-163.) His fame and popularity in Europe, and especially in England, proceeded from the Crusades.]

About the same time that Julian was informed of the tumult of Alexandria, he received intelligence from Edessa, that the proud and wealthy faction of the Arians had insulted the weakness of the Valentinians, and committed such disorders as ought not to be suffered with impunity in a well-regulated state. Without expecting the slow forms of justice, the exasperated prince directed his mandate to the magistrates of Edessa, [127] by which he confiscated the whole property of the church: the money was distributed among the soldiers; the lands were added to the domain; and this act of oppression was aggravated by the most ungenerous irony. "I show myself," says Julian, "the true friend of the Galilaeans. Their admirable law has promised the kingdom of heaven to the poor; and they will advance with more diligence in the paths of virtue and salvation, when they are relieved by my assistance from the load of temporal possessions. Take care," pursued the monarch, in a more serious tone, "take care how you provoke my patience and humanity. If these disorders continue, I will revenge on the magistrates the crimes of the people; and you will have reason to dread, not only confiscation and exile, but fire and the sword." The tumults of Alexandria were doubtless of a more bloody and dangerous nature: but a Christian bishop had fallen by the hands of the Pagans; and the public epistle of Julian affords a very lively proof of the partial spirit of his administration. His reproaches to the citizens of Alexandria are mingled with expressions of esteem and tenderness; and he laments, that, on this occasion, they should have departed from the gentle and generous manners which attested their Grecian extraction. He gravely censures the offence which they had committed against the laws of justice and humanity; but he recapitulates, with visible complacency, the intolerable provocations which they had so long endured from the impious tyranny of George of Cappadocia. Julian admits the principle, that a wise and vigorous government should chastise the insolence of the people; yet, in consideration of their founder Alexander, and of Serapis their tutelar deity, he grants a free and gracious pardon to the guilty city, for which he again feels the affection of a brother. [128]

[Footnote 127: Julian. Epist. xliii.]

[Footnote 128: Julian. Epist. x. He allowed his friends to assuage his anger Ammian. xxii. 11.]

After the tumult of Alexandria had subsided, Athanasius, amidst the public acclamations, seated himself on the throne from whence his unworthy competitor had been precipitated: and as the zeal of the archbishop was tempered with discretion, the exercise of his authority tended not to inflame, but to reconcile, the minds of the people. His pastoral labors were not confined to the narrow limits of Egypt. The state of the Christian world was present to his active and capacious mind; and the age, the merit, the reputation of Athanasius, enabled him to assume, in a moment of danger, the office of Ecclesiastical Dictator. [129] Three years were not yet elapsed since the majority of the bishops of the West had ignorantly, or reluctantly, subscribed the Confession of Rimini. They repented, they believed, but they dreaded the unseasonable rigor of their orthodox brethren; and if their pride was stronger than their faith, they might throw themselves into the arms of the Arians, to escape the indignity of a public penance, which must degrade them to the condition of obscure laymen. At the same time the domestic differences concerning the union and distinction of the divine persons, were agitated with some heat among the Catholic doctors; and the progress of this metaphysical controversy seemed to threaten a public and lasting division of the Greek and Latin churches. By the wisdom of a select synod, to which the name and presence of Athanasius gave the authority of a general council, the bishops, who had unwarily deviated into error, were admitted to the communion of the church, on the easy condition of subscribing the Nicene Creed; without any formal acknowledgment of their past fault, or any minute definition of their scholastic opinions. The advice of the primate of Egypt had already prepared the clergy of Gaul and Spain, of Italy and Greece, for the reception of this salutary measure; and, notwithstanding the opposition of some ardent spirits, [130] the fear of the common enemy promoted the peace and harmony of the Christians. [131]

[Footnote 129: See Athanas. ad Rufin. tom. ii. p. 40, 41, and Greg. Nazianzen Orat. iii. p. 395, 396; who justly states the temperate zeal of the primate, as much more meritorious than his prayers, his fasts, his persecutions, &c.]

[Footnote 130: I have not leisure to follow the blind obstinacy of Lucifer of Cagliari. See his adventures in Tillemont, (Mem. Eccles. tom. vii. p. 900-926;) and observe how the color of the narrative insensibly changes, as the confessor becomes a schismatic.]

[Footnote 131: Assensus est huic sententiae Occidens, et, per tam necessarium conilium, Satanae faucibus mundus ereptus. The lively and artful dialogue of Jerom against the Luciferians (tom. ii. p. 135-155) exhibits an original picture of the ecclesiastical policy of the times.]

The skill and diligence of the primate of Egypt had improved the season of tranquillity, before it was interrupted by the hostile edicts of the emperor. [132] Julian, who despised the Christians, honored Athanasius with his sincere and peculiar hatred. For his sake alone, he introduced an arbitrary distinction, repugnant at least to the spirit of his former declarations. He maintained, that the Galilaeans, whom he had recalled from exile, were not restored, by that general indulgence, to the possession of their respective churches; and he expressed his astonishment, that a criminal, who had been repeatedly condemned by the judgment of the emperors, should dare to insult the majesty of the laws, and insolently usurp the archiepiscopal throne of Alexandria, without expecting the orders of his sovereign. As a punishment for the imaginary offence, he again banished Athanasius from the city; and he was pleased to suppose, that this act of justice would be highly agreeable to his pious subjects. The pressing solicitations of the people soon convinced him, that the majority of the Alexandrians were Christians; and that the greatest part of the Christians were firmly attached to the cause of their oppressed primate. But the knowledge of their sentiments, instead of persuading him to recall his decree, provoked him to extend to all Egypt the term of the exile of Athanasius. The zeal of the multitude rendered Julian still more inexorable: he was alarmed by the danger of leaving at the head of a tumultuous city, a daring and popular leader; and the language of his resentment discovers the opinion which he entertained of the courage and abilities of Athanasius. The execution of the sentence was still delayed, by the caution or negligence of Ecdicius, praefect of Egypt, who was at length awakened from his lethargy by a severe reprimand. "Though you neglect," says Julian, "to write to me on any other subject, at least it is your duty to inform me of your conduct towards Athanasius, the enemy of the gods. My intentions have been long since communicated to you. I swear by the great Serapis, that unless, on the calends of December, Athanasius has departed from Alexandria, nay, from Egypt, the officers of your government shall pay a fine of one hundred pounds of gold. You know my temper: I am slow to condemn, but I am still slower to forgive." This epistle was enforced by a short postscript, written with the emperor's own hand. "The contempt that is shown for all the gods fills me with grief and indignation. There is nothing that I should see, nothing that I should hear, with more pleasure, than the expulsion of Athanasius from all Egypt. The abominable wretch! Under my reign, the baptism of several Grecian ladies of the highest rank has been the effect of his persecutions." [133] The death of Athanasius was not expressly commanded; but the praefect of Egypt understood that it was safer for him to exceed, than to neglect, the orders of an irritated master. The archbishop prudently retired to the monasteries of the Desert; eluded, with his usual dexterity, the snares of the enemy; and lived to triumph over the ashes of a prince, who, in words of formidable import, had declared his wish that the whole venom of the Galilaean school were contained in the single person of Athanasius. [134] [134a]

[Footnote 132: Tillemont, who supposes that George was massacred in August crowds the actions of Athanasius into a narrow space, (Mem. Eccles. tom. viii. p. 360.) An original fragment, published by the Marquis Maffei, from the old Chapter library of Verona, (Osservazioni Letterarie, tom. iii. p. 60-92,) affords many important dates, which are authenticated by the computation of Egyptian months.]

[Footnote 133: I have preserved the ambiguous sense of the last word, the ambiguity of a tyrant who wished to find, or to create, guilt.]

[Footnote 134: The three epistles of Julian, which explain his intentions and conduct with regard to Athanasius, should be disposed in the following chronological order, xxvi. x. vi. See likewise, Greg. Nazianzen xxi. p. 393. Sozomen, l. v. c. 15. Socrates, l. iii. c. 14. Theodoret, l iii. c. 9, and Tillemont, Mem. Eccles. tom. viii. p. 361-368, who has used some materials prepared by the Bollandists.]

[Footnote 134a: The sentence in the text is from Epist. li. addressed to the people of Alexandria—M.]

I have endeavored faithfully to represent the artful system by which Julian proposed to obtain the effects, without incurring the guilt, or reproach, of persecution. But if the deadly spirit of fanaticism perverted the heart and understanding of a virtuous prince, it must, at the same time, be confessed that the real sufferings of the Christians were inflamed and magnified by human passions and religious enthusiasm. The meekness and resignation which had distinguished the primitive disciples of the gospel, was the object of the applause, rather than of the imitation of their successors. The Christians, who had now possessed above forty years the civil and ecclesiastical government of the empire, had contracted the insolent vices of prosperity, [135] and the habit of believing that the saints alone were entitled to reign over the earth. As soon as the enmity of Julian deprived the clergy of the privileges which had been conferred by the favor of Constantine, they complained of the most cruel oppression; and the free toleration of idolaters and heretics was a subject of grief and scandal to the orthodox party. [136] The acts of violence, which were no longer countenanced by the magistrates, were still committed by the zeal of the people. At Pessinus, the altar of Cybele was overturned almost in the presence of the emperor; and in the city of Caesarea in Cappadocia, the temple of Fortune, the sole place of worship which had been left to the Pagans, was destroyed by the rage of a popular tumult. On these occasions, a prince, who felt for the honor of the gods, was not disposed to interrupt the course of justice; and his mind was still more deeply exasperated, when he found that the fanatics, who had deserved and suffered the punishment of incendiaries, were rewarded with the honors of martyrdom. [137] The Christian subjects of Julian were assured of the hostile designs of their sovereign; and, to their jealous apprehension, every circumstance of his government might afford some grounds of discontent and suspicion. In the ordinary administration of the laws, the Christians, who formed so large a part of the people, must frequently be condemned: but their indulgent brethren, without examining the merits of the cause, presumed their innocence, allowed their claims, and imputed the severity of their judge to the partial malice of religious persecution. [138] These present hardships, intolerable as they might appear, were represented as a slight prelude of the impending calamities. The Christians considered Julian as a cruel and crafty tyrant; who suspended the execution of his revenge till he should return victorious from the Persian war. They expected, that as soon as he had triumphed over the foreign enemies of Rome, he would lay aside the irksome mask of dissimulation; that the amphitheatre would stream with the blood of hermits and bishops; and that the Christians who still persevered in the profession of the faith, would be deprived of the common benefits of nature and society. [139] Every calumny [140] that could wound the reputation of the Apostate, was credulously embraced by the fears and hatred of his adversaries; and their indiscreet clamors provoked the temper of a sovereign, whom it was their duty to respect, and their interest to flatter.

They still protested, that prayers and tears were their only weapons against the impious tyrant, whose head they devoted to the justice of offended Heaven. But they insinuated, with sullen resolution, that their submission was no longer the effect of weakness; and that, in the imperfect state of human virtue, the patience, which is founded on principle, may be exhausted by persecution. It is impossible to determine how far the zeal of Julian would have prevailed over his good sense and humanity; but if we seriously reflect on the strength and spirit of the church, we shall be convinced, that before the emperor could have extinguished the religion of Christ, he must have involved his country in the horrors of a civil war. [141]

[Footnote 135: See the fair confession of Gregory, (Orat. iii. p. 61, 62.)]

[Footnote 136: Hear the furious and absurd complaint of Optatus, (de Schismat Denatist. l. ii. c. 16, 17.)]

[Footnote 137: Greg. Nazianzen, Orat. iii. p. 91, iv. p. 133. He praises the rioters of Caesarea. See Sozomen, l. v. 4, 11. Tillemont (Mem. Eccles. tom. vii. p. 649, 650) owns, that their behavior was not dans l'ordre commun: but he is perfectly satisfied, as the great St. Basil always celebrated the festival of these blessed martyrs.]

[Footnote 138: Julian determined a lawsuit against the new Christian city at Maiuma, the port of Gaza; and his sentence, though it might be imputed to bigotry, was never reversed by his successors. Sozomen, l. v. c. 3. Reland, Palestin. tom. ii. p. 791.]

[Footnote 139: Gregory (Orat. iii. p. 93, 94, 95. Orat. iv. p. 114) pretends to speak from the information of Julian's confidants, whom Orosius (vii. 30) could not have seen.]

[Footnote 140: Gregory (Orat. iii. p. 91) charges the Apostate with secret sacrifices of boys and girls; and positively affirms, that the dead bodies were thrown into the Orontes. See Theodoret, l. iii. c. 26, 27; and the equivocal candor of the Abbe de la Bleterie, Vie de Julien, p. 351, 352. Yet contemporary malice could not impute to Julian the troops of martyrs, more especially in the West, which Baronius so greedily swallows, and Tillemont so faintly rejects, (Mem. Eccles. tom. vii. p. 1295-1315.)]

[Footnote 141: The resignation of Gregory is truly edifying, (Orat. iv. p. 123, 124.) Yet, when an officer of Julian attempted to seize the church of Nazianzus, he would have lost his life, if he had not yielded to the zeal of the bishop and people, (Orat. xix. p. 308.) See the reflections of Chrysostom, as they are alleged by Tillemont, (Mem. Eccles. tom. vii. p. 575.)]

CHAPTER XXIV

THE RETREAT AND DEATH OF JULIAN

PART I

RESIDENCE OF JULIAN AT ANTIOCH—HIS SUCCESSFUL EXPEDITION AGAINST THE PERSIANS—PASSAGE OF THE TIGRIS—THE RETREAT AND DEATH OF JULIAN—ELECTION OF JOVIAN—HE SAVES THE ROMAN ARMY BY A DISGRACEFUL TREATY

The philosophical fable which Julian composed under the name of the Caesars, [1] is one of the most agreeable and instructive productions of ancient wit. [2] During the freedom and equality of the days of the Saturnalia, Romulus prepared a feast for the deities of Olympus, who had adopted him as a worthy associate, and for the Roman princes, who had reigned over his martial people, and the vanquished nations of the earth. The immortals were placed in just order on their thrones of state, and the table of the Caesars was spread below the Moon in the upper region of the air. The tyrants, who would have disgraced the society of gods and men, were thrown headlong, by the inexorable Nemesis, into the Tartarean abyss. The rest of the Caesars successively advanced to their seats; and as they passed, the vices, the defects, the blemishes of their respective characters, were maliciously noticed by old Silenus, a laughing moralist, who disguised the wisdom of a philosopher under the mask of a Bacchanal. [3] As soon as the feast was ended, the voice of Mercury proclaimed the will of Jupiter, that a celestial crown should be the reward of superior merit. Julius Caesar, Augustus, Trajan, and Marcus Antoninus, were selected as the most illustrious candidates; the effeminate Constantine [4] was not excluded from this honorable competition, and the great Alexander was invited to dispute the prize of glory with the Roman heroes. Each of the candidates was allowed to display the merit of his own exploits; but, in the judgment of the gods, the modest silence of Marcus pleaded more powerfully than the elaborate orations of his haughty rivals. When the judges of this awful contest proceeded to examine the heart, and to scrutinize the springs of action, the superiority of the Imperial Stoic appeared still more decisive and conspicuous. [5] Alexander and Caesar, Augustus, Trajan, and Constantine, acknowledged, with a blush, that fame, or power, or pleasure had been the important object of their labors: but the gods themselves beheld, with reverence and love, a virtuous mortal, who had practised on the throne the lessons of philosophy; and who, in a state of human imperfection, had aspired to imitate the moral attributes of the Deity. The value of this agreeable composition (the Caesars of Julian) is enhanced by the rank of the author. A prince, who delineates, with freedom, the vices and virtues of his predecessors, subscribes, in every line, the censure or approbation of his own conduct.

[Footnote 1: See this fable or satire, p. 306-336 of the Leipsig edition of Julian's works. The French version of the learned Ezekiel Spanheim (Paris, 1683) is coarse, languid, and correct; and his notes, proofs, illustrations, &c., are piled on each other till they form a mass of 557 close-printed quarto pages. The Abbe' de la Bleterie (Vie de Jovien, tom. i. p. 241-393) has more happily expressed the spirit, as well as the sense, of the original, which he illustrates with some concise and curious notes.]

[Footnote 2: Spanheim (in his preface) has most learnedly discussed the etymology, origin, resemblance, and disagreement of the Greek satyrs, a dramatic piece, which was acted after the tragedy; and the Latin satires, (from Satura,) a miscellaneous composition, either in prose or verse. But the Caesars of Julian are of such an original cast, that the critic is perplexed to which class he should ascribe them. Note: See also Casaubon de Satira, with Rambach's observations—M.]

[Footnote 3: This mixed character of Silenus is finely painted in the sixth eclogue of Virgil.]

[Footnote 4: Every impartial reader must perceive and condemn the partiality of Julian against his uncle Constantine, and the Christian religion. On this occasion, the interpreters are compelled, by a most sacred interest, to renounce their allegiance, and to desert the cause of their author.]

[Footnote 5: Julian was secretly inclined to prefer a Greek to a Roman. But when he seriously compared a hero with a philosopher, he was sensible that mankind had much greater obligations to Socrates than to Alexander, (Orat. ad Themistium, p. 264.)]

In the cool moments of reflection, Julian preferred the useful and benevolent virtues of Antoninus; but his ambitious spirit was inflamed by the glory of Alexander; and he solicited, with equal ardor, the esteem of the wise, and the applause of the multitude. In the season of life when the powers of the mind and body enjoy the most active vigor, the emperor who was instructed by the experience, and animated by the success, of the German war, resolved to signalize his reign by some more splendid and memorable achievement. The ambassadors of the East, from the continent of India, and the Isle of Ceylon, [6] had respectfully saluted the Roman purple. [7] The nations of the West esteemed and dreaded the personal virtues of Julian, both in peace and war. He despised the trophies of a Gothic victory, and was satisfied that the rapacious Barbarians of the Danube would be restrained from any future violation of the faith of treaties by the terror of his name, and the additional fortifications with which he strengthened the Thracian and Illyrian frontiers. The successor of Cyrus and Artaxerxes was the only rival whom he deemed worthy of his arms; and he resolved, by the final conquest of Persia, to chastise the naughty nation which had so long resisted and insulted the majesty of Rome. [9] As soon as the Persian monarch was informed that the throne of Constantius was filed by a prince of a very different character, he condescended to make some artful, or perhaps sincere, overtures towards a negotiation of peace. But the pride of Sapor was astonished by the firmness of Julian; who sternly declared, that he would never consent to hold a peaceful conference among the flames and ruins of the cities of Mesopotamia; and who added, with a smile of contempt, that it was needless to treat by ambassadors, as he himself had determined to visit speedily the court of Persia. The impatience of the emperor urged the diligence of the military preparations. The generals were named; and Julian, marching from Constantinople through the provinces of Asia Minor, arrived at Antioch about eight months after the death of his predecessor. His ardent desire to march into the heart of Persia, was checked by the indispensable duty of regulating the state of the empire; by his zeal to revive the worship of the gods; and by the advice of his wisest friends; who represented the necessity of allowing the salutary interval of winter quarters, to restore the exhausted strength of the legions of Gaul, and the discipline and spirit of the Eastern troops. Julian was persuaded to fix, till the ensuing spring, his residence at Antioch, among a people maliciously disposed to deride the haste, and to censure the delays, of their sovereign. [10]

[Footnote 6: Inde nationibus Indicis certatim cum aonis optimates mittentibus.... ab usque Divis et Serendivis. Ammian. xx. 7. This island, to which the names of Taprobana, Serendib, and Ceylon, have been successively applied, manifests how imperfectly the seas and lands to the east of Cape Comorin were known to the Romans. 1. Under the reign of Claudius, a freedman, who farmed the customs of the Red Sea, was accidentally driven by the winds upon this strange and undiscovered coast: he conversed six months with the natives; and the king of Ceylon, who heard, for the first time, of the power and justice of Rome, was persuaded to send an embassy to the emperor. (Plin. Hist. Nat. vi. 24.) 2. The geographers (and even Ptolemy) have magnified, above fifteen times, the real size of this new world, which they extended as far as the equator, and the neighborhood of China. Note: The name of Diva gens or Divorum regio, according to the probable conjecture of M. Letronne, (Trois Mem. Acad. p. 127,) was applied by the ancients to the whole eastern coast of the Indian Peninsula, from Ceylon to the Canges. The name may be traced in Devipatnam, Devidan, Devicotta, Divinelly, the point of Divy—M. Letronne, p.121, considers the freedman with his embassy from Ceylon to have been an impostor—M.]

[Footnote 7: These embassies had been sent to Constantius. Ammianus, who unwarily deviates into gross flattery, must have forgotten the length of the way, and the short duration of the reign of Julian.]

[Footnote 8: Gothos saepe fallaces et perfidos; hostes quaerere se meliores aiebat: illis enim sufficere mercators Galatas per quos ubique sine conditionis discrimine venumdantur. (Ammian. xxii. 7.) Within less than fifteen years, these Gothic slaves threatened and subdued their masters.]

[Footnote 9: Alexander reminds his rival Caesar, who depreciated the fame and merit of an Asiatic victory, that Crassus and Antony had felt the Persian arrows; and that the Romans, in a war of three hundred years, had not yet subdued the single province of Mesopotamia or Assyria, (Caesares, p. 324.)]

[Footnote 10: The design of the Persian war is declared by Ammianus, (xxii. 7, 12,) Libanius, (Orat. Parent. c. 79, 80, p. 305, 306,) Zosimus, (l. iii. p. 158,) and Socrates, (l. iii. c. 19.)]

If Julian had flattered himself, that his personal connection with the capital of the East would be productive of mutual satisfaction to the prince and people, he made a very false estimate of his own character, and of the manners of Antioch. [11] The warmth of the climate disposed the natives to the most intemperate enjoyment of tranquillity and opulence; and the lively licentiousness of the Greeks was blended with the hereditary softness of the Syrians. Fashion was the only law, pleasure the only pursuit, and the splendor of dress and furniture was the only distinction of the citizens of Antioch. The arts of luxury were honored; the serious and manly virtues were the subject of ridicule; and the contempt for female modesty and reverent age announced the universal corruption of the capital of the East. The love of spectacles was the taste, or rather passion, of the Syrians; the most skilful artists were procured from the adjacent cities; [12] a considerable share of the revenue was devoted to the public amusements; and the magnificence of the games of the theatre and circus was considered as the happiness and as the glory of Antioch. The rustic manners of a prince who disdained such glory, and was insensible of such happiness, soon disgusted the delicacy of his subjects; and the effeminate Orientals could neither imitate, nor admire, the severe simplicity which Julian always maintained, and sometimes affected. The days of festivity, consecrated, by ancient custom, to the honor of the gods, were the only occasions in which Julian relaxed his philosophic severity; and those festivals were the only days in which the Syrians of Antioch could reject the allurements of pleasure. The majority of the people supported the glory of the Christian name, which had been first invented by their ancestors: [13] they contended themselves with disobeying the moral precepts, but they were scrupulously attached to the speculative doctrines of their religion. The church of Antioch was distracted by heresy and schism; but the Arians and the Athanasians, the followers of Meletius and those of Paulinus, [14] were actuated by the same pious hatred of their common adversary.

[Footnote 11: The Satire of Julian, and the Homilies of St. Chrysostom, exhibit the same picture of Antioch. The miniature which the Abbe de la Bleterie has copied from thence, (Vie de Julian, p. 332,) is elegant and correct.]

[Footnote 12: Laodicea furnished charioteers; Tyre and Berytus, comedians; Caesarea, pantomimes; Heliopolis, singers; Gaza, gladiators, Ascalon, wrestlers; and Castabala, rope-dancers. See the Expositio totius Mundi, p. 6, in the third tome of Hudson's Minor Geographers.]

[Footnote 13: The people of Antioch ingenuously professed their attachment to the Chi, (Christ,) and the Kappa, (Constantius.) Julian in Misopogon, p. 357.]

[Footnote 14: The schism of Antioch, which lasted eighty-five years, (A. D. 330-415,) was inflamed, while Julian resided in that city, by the indiscreet ordination of Paulinus. See Tillemont, Mem. Eccles. tom. iii. p. 803 of the quarto edition, (Paris, 1701, &c,) which henceforward I shall quote.]

The strongest prejudice was entertained against the character of an apostate, the enemy and successor of a prince who had engaged the affections of a very numerous sect; and the removal of St. Babylas excited an implacable opposition to the person of Julian. His subjects complained, with superstitious indignation, that famine had pursued the emperor's steps from Constantinople to Antioch; and the discontent of a hungry people was exasperated by the injudicious attempt to relieve their distress. The inclemency of the season had affected the harvests of Syria; and the price of bread, [15] in the markets of Antioch, had naturally risen in proportion to the scarcity of corn. But the fair and reasonable proportion was soon violated by the rapacious arts of monopoly. In this unequal contest, in which the produce of the land is claimed by one party as his exclusive property, is used by another as a lucrative object of trade, and is required by a third for the daily and necessary support of life, all the profits of the intermediate agents are accumulated on the head of the defenceless customers. The hardships of their situation were exaggerated and increased by their own impatience and anxiety; and the apprehension of a scarcity gradually produced the appearances of a famine. When the luxurious citizens of Antioch complained of the high price of poultry and fish, Julian publicly declared, that a frugal city ought to be satisfied with a regular supply of wine, oil, and bread; but he acknowledged, that it was the duty of a sovereign to provide for the subsistence of his people. With this salutary view, the emperor ventured on a very dangerous and doubtful step, of fixing, by legal authority, the value of corn. He enacted, that, in a time of scarcity, it should be sold at a price which had seldom been known in the most plentiful years; and that his own example might strengthen his laws, he sent into the market four hundred and twenty-two thousand modii, or measures, which were drawn by his order from the granaries of Hierapolis, of Chalcis, and even of Egypt. The consequences might have been foreseen, and were soon felt. The Imperial wheat was purchased by the rich merchants; the proprietors of land, or of corn, withheld from the city the accustomed supply; and the small quantities that appeared in the market were secretly sold at an advanced and illegal price. Julian still continued to applaud his own policy, treated the complaints of the people as a vain and ungrateful murmur, and convinced Antioch that he had inherited the obstinacy, though not the cruelty, of his brother Gallus. [16] The remonstrances of the municipal senate served only to exasperate his inflexible mind. He was persuaded, perhaps with truth, that the senators of Antioch who possessed lands, or were concerned in trade, had themselves contributed to the calamities of their country; and he imputed the disrespectful boldness which they assumed, to the sense, not of public duty, but of private interest. The whole body, consisting of two hundred of the most noble and wealthy citizens, were sent, under a guard, from the palace to the prison; and though they were permitted, before the close of evening, to return to their respective houses, [17] the emperor himself could not obtain the forgiveness which he had so easily granted. The same grievances were still the subject of the same complaints, which were industriously circulated by the wit and levity of the Syrian Greeks. During the licentious days of the Saturnalia, the streets of the city resounded with insolent songs, which derided the laws, the religion, the personal conduct, and even the beard, of the emperor; the spirit of Antioch was manifested by the connivance of the magistrates, and the applause of the multitude. [18] The disciple of Socrates was too deeply affected by these popular insults; but the monarch, endowed with a quick sensibility, and possessed of absolute power, refused his passions the gratification of revenge. A tyrant might have proscribed, without distinction, the lives and fortunes of the citizens of Antioch; and the unwarlike Syrians must have patiently submitted to the lust, the rapaciousness and the cruelty, of the faithful legions of Gaul. A milder sentence might have deprived the capital of the East of its honors and privileges; and the courtiers, perhaps the subjects, of Julian, would have applauded an act of justice, which asserted the dignity of the supreme magistrate of the republic.

[19] But instead of abusing, or exerting, the authority of the state, to revenge his personal injuries, Julian contented himself with an inoffensive mode of retaliation, which it would be in the power of few princes to employ. He had been insulted by satires and libels; in his turn, he composed, under the title of the Enemy of the Beard, an ironical confession of his own faults, and a severe satire on the licentious and effeminate manners of Antioch. This Imperial reply was publicly exposed before the gates of the palace; and the Misopogon [20] still remains a singular monument of the resentment, the wit, the humanity, and the indiscretion of Julian. Though he affected to laugh, he could not forgive. [21] His contempt was expressed, and his revenge might be gratified, by the nomination of a governor [22] worthy only of such subjects; and the emperor, forever renouncing the ungrateful city, proclaimed his resolution to pass the ensuing winter at Tarsus in Cilicia. [23]

[Footnote 15: Julian states three different proportions, of five, ten, or fifteen medii of wheat for one piece of gold, according to the degrees of plenty and scarcity, (in Misopogon, p. 369.) From this fact, and from some collateral examples, I conclude, that under the successors of Constantine, the moderate price of wheat was about thirty-two shillings the English quarter, which is equal to the average price of the sixty-four first years of the present century. See Arbuthnot's Tables of Coins, Weights, and Measures, p. 88, 89. Plin. Hist. Natur. xviii. 12. Mem. de l'Academie des Inscriptions, tom. xxviii. p. 718-721. Smith's Inquiry into the Nature and Causes of the Wealth of Nations, vol. i. p 246. This last I am proud to quote as the work of a sage and a friend.]

[Footnote 16: Nunquam a proposito declinabat, Galli similis fratris, licet incruentus. Ammian. xxii. 14. The ignorance of the most enlightened princes may claim some excuse; but we cannot be satisfied with Julian's own defence, (in Misopogon, p. 363, 369,) or the elaborate apology of Libanius, (Orat. Parental c. xcvii. p. 321.)]

[Footnote 17: Their short and easy confinement is gently touched by Libanius, (Orat. Parental. c. xcviii. p. 322, 323.)]

[Footnote 18: Libanius, (ad Antiochenos de Imperatoris ira, c. 17, 18, 19, in Fabricius, Bibliot. Graec. tom. vii. p. 221-223,) like a skilful advocate, severely censures the folly of the people, who suffered for the crime of a few obscure and drunken wretches.]

[Footnote 19. Libanius (ad Antiochen. c. vii. p. 213) reminds Antioch of the recent chastisement of Caesarea; and even Julian (in Misopogon, p. 355) insinuates how severely Tarentum had expiated the insult to the Roman ambassadors.]

[Footnote 20: On the subject of the Misopogon, see Ammianus, (xxii. 14,) Libanius, (Orat. Parentalis, c. xcix. p. 323,) Gregory Nazianzen, (Orat. iv. p. 133) and the Chronicle of Antioch, by John Malala, (tom. ii. p. 15, 16.) I have essential obligations to the translation and notes of the Abbe de la Bleterie, (Vie de Jovien, tom. ii. p. 1-138.)]

[Footnote 21: Ammianus very justly remarks, Coactus dissimulare pro tempore ira sufflabatur interna. The elaborate irony of Julian at length bursts forth into serious and direct invective.]

[Footnote 22: Ipse autem Antiochiam egressurus, Heliopoliten quendam Alexandrum Syriacae jurisdictioni praefecit, turbulentum et saevum; dicebatque non illum meruisse, sed Antiochensibus avaris et contumeliosis hujusmodi judicem convenire. Ammian. xxiii. 2. Libanius, (Epist. 722, p. 346, 347,) who confesses to Julian himself, that he had shared the general discontent, pretends that Alexander was a useful, though harsh, reformer of the manners and religion of Antioch.]

[Footnote 23: Julian, in Misopogon, p. 364. Ammian. xxiii. 2, and Valesius, ad loc. Libanius, in a professed oration, invites him to return to his loyal and penitent city of Antioch.]

Yet Antioch possessed one citizen, whose genius and virtues might atone, in the opinion of Julian, for the vice and folly of his country. The sophist Libanius was born in the capital of the East; he publicly professed the arts of rhetoric and declamation at Nice, Nicomedia, Constantinople, Athens, and, during the remainder of his life, at Antioch. His school was assiduously frequented by the Grecian youth; his disciples, who sometimes exceeded the number of eighty, celebrated their incomparable master; and the jealousy of his rivals, who persecuted him from one city to another, confirmed the favorable opinion which Libanius ostentatiously displayed of his superior merit. The preceptors of Julian had extorted a rash but solemn assurance, that he would never attend the lectures of their adversary: the curiosity of the royal youth was checked and inflamed: he secretly procured the writings of this dangerous sophist, and gradually surpassed, in the perfect imitation of his style, the most laborious of his domestic pupils. [24] When Julian ascended the throne, he declared his impatience to embrace and reward the Syrian sophist, who had preserved, in a degenerate age, the Grecian purity of taste, of manners, and of religion. The emperor's prepossession was increased and justified by the discreet pride of his favorite. Instead of pressing, with the foremost of the crowd, into the palace of Constantinople, Libanius calmly expected his arrival at Antioch; withdrew from court on the first symptoms of coldness and indifference; required a formal invitation for each visit; and taught his sovereign an important lesson, that he might command the obedience of a subject, but that he must deserve the attachment of a friend. The sophists of every age, despising, or affecting to despise, the accidental distinctions of birth and fortune, [25] reserve their esteem for the superior qualities of the mind, with which they themselves are so plentifully endowed. Julian might disdain the acclamations of a venal court, who adored the Imperial purple; but he was deeply flattered by the praise, the admonition, the freedom, and the envy of an independent philosopher, who refused his favors, loved his person, celebrated his fame, and protected his memory. The voluminous writings of Libanius still exist; for the most part, they are the vain and idle compositions of an orator, who cultivated the science of words; the productions of a recluse student, whose mind, regardless of his contemporaries, was incessantly fixed on the Trojan war and the Athenian commonwealth. Yet the sophist of Antioch sometimes descended from this imaginary elevation; he entertained a various and elaborate correspondence; [26] he praised the virtues of his own times; he boldly arraigned the abuse of public and private life; and he eloquently pleaded the cause of Antioch against the just resentment of Julian and Theodosius. It is the common calamity of old age, [27] to lose whatever might have rendered it desirable; but Libanius experienced the peculiar misfortune of surviving the religion and the sciences, to which he had consecrated his genius. The friend of Julian was an indignant spectator of the triumph of Christianity; and his bigotry, which darkened the prospect of the visible world, did not inspire Libanius with any lively hopes of celestial glory and happiness. [28]

[Footnote 24: Libanius, Orat. Parent. c. vii. p. 230, 231.]

[Footnote 25: Eunapius reports, that Libanius refused the honorary rank of Praetorian praefect, as less illustrious than the title of Sophist, (in Vit. Sophist. p. 135.) The critics have observed a similar sentiment in one of the epistles (xviii. edit. Wolf) of Libanius himself.]

[Footnote 26: Near two thousand of his letters—a mode of composition in which Libanius was thought to excel—are still extant, and already published. The critics may praise their subtle and elegant brevity; yet

Dr. Bentley (Dissertation upon Phalaris, p. 48) might justly, though quaintly observe, that "you feel, by the emptiness and deadness of them, that you converse with some dreaming pedant, with his elbow on his desk."]

[Footnote 27: His birth is assigned to the year 314. He mentions the seventy-sixth year of his age, (A. D. 390,) and seems to allude to some events of a still later date.]

[Footnote 28: Libanius has composed the vain, prolix, but curious narrative of his own life, (tom. ii. p. 1-84, edit. Morell,) of which Eunapius (p. 130-135) has left a concise and unfavorable account. Among the moderns, Tillemont, (Hist. des Empereurs, tom. iv. p. 571-576,) Fabricius, (Bibliot. Graec. tom. vii. p. 376-414,) and Lardner, (Heathen Testimonies, tom. iv. p. 127-163,) have illustrated the character and writings of this famous sophist.]

PART II

The martial impatience of Julian urged him to take the field in the beginning of the spring; and he dismissed, with contempt and reproach, the senate of Antioch, who accompanied the emperor beyond the limits of their own territory, to which he was resolved never to return. After a laborious march of two days, [29] he halted on the third at Beraea, or Aleppo, where he had the mortification of finding a senate almost entirely Christian; who received with cold and formal demonstrations of respect the eloquent sermon of the apostle of paganism. The son of one of the most illustrious citizens of Beraea, who had embraced, either from interest or conscience, the religion of the emperor, was disinherited by his angry parent. The father and the son were invited to the Imperial table. Julian, placing himself between them, attempted, without success, to inculcate the lesson and example of toleration; supported, with affected calmness, the indiscreet zeal of the aged Christian, who seemed to forget the sentiments of nature, and the duty of a subject; and at length, turning towards the afflicted youth, "Since you have lost a father," said he, "for my sake, it is incumbent on me to supply his place." [30] The emperor was received in a manner much more agreeable to his wishes at Batnae, [30a] a small town pleasantly seated in a grove of cypresses, about twenty miles from the city of Hierapolis. The solemn rites of sacrifice were decently prepared by the inhabitants of Batnae, who seemed attached to the worship of their tutelar deities, Apollo and Jupiter; but the serious piety of Julian was offended by the tumult of their applause; and he too clearly discerned, that the smoke which arose from their altars was the incense of flattery, rather than of devotion. The ancient and magnificent temple which had sanctified, for so many ages, the city of Hierapolis, [31] no longer subsisted; and the consecrated wealth, which afforded a liberal maintenance to more than three hundred priests, might hasten its downfall. Yet Julian enjoyed the satisfaction of embracing a philosopher and a friend, whose religious firmness had withstood the pressing and repeated solicitations of Constantius and Gallus, as often as those princes lodged at his house, in their passage through Hierapolis. In the hurry of military preparation, and the careless confidence of a familiar correspondence, the zeal of Julian appears to have been lively and uniform. He had now undertaken an important and difficult war; and the anxiety of the event rendered him still more attentive to observe and register the most trifling presages, from which, according to the rules of divination, any knowledge of futurity could be derived. [32] He informed Libanius of his progress as far as Hierapolis, by an elegant epistle, [33] which displays the facility of his genius, and his tender friendship for the sophist of Antioch.

[Footnote 29: From Antioch to Litarbe, on the territory of Chalcis, the road, over hills and through morasses, was extremely bad; and the loose stones were cemented only with sand, (Julian. epist. xxvii.) It is singular enough that the Romans should have neglected the great communication between Antioch and the Euphrates. See Wesseling Itinerar. p. 190 Bergier, Hist des Grands Chemins, tom. ii. p. 100]

[Footnote 30: Julian alludes to this incident, (epist. xxvii.,) which is more distinctly related by Theodoret, (l. iii. c. 22.) The intolerant spirit of the father is applauded by Tillemont, (Hist. des Empereurs, tom. iv. p. 534.) and even by La Bleterie, (Vie de Julien, p. 413.)]

[Footnote 30a: This name, of Syriac origin, is found in the Arabic, and means a place in a valley where waters meet. Julian says, the name of the city is Barbaric, the situation Greek. The geographer Abulfeda (tab. Syriac. p. 129, edit. Koehler) speaks of it in a manner to justify the praises of Julian—St. Martin. Notes to Le Beau, iii. 56—M.]

[Footnote 31: See the curious treatise de Dea Syria, inserted among the works of Lucian, (tom. iii. p. 451-490, edit. Reitz.) The singular appellation of Ninus vetus (Ammian. xiv. 8) might induce a suspicion, that Heirapolis had been the royal seat of the Assyrians.]

[Footnote 32: Julian (epist. xxviii.) kept a regular account of all the fortunate omens; but he suppresses the inauspicious signs, which Ammianus (xxiii. 2) has carefully recorded.]

[Footnote 33: Julian. epist. xxvii. p. 399-402.]

Hierapolis, [33a] situate almost on the banks of the Euphrates, [34] had been appointed for the general rendezvous of the Roman troops, who immediately passed the great river on a bridge of boats, which was previously constructed. [35] If the inclinations of Julian had been similar to those of his predecessor, he might have wasted the active and important season of the year in the circus of Samosata or in the churches of Edessa. But as the warlike emperor, instead of Constantius, had chosen Alexander for his model, he advanced without delay to Carrhae, [36] a very ancient city of Mesopotamia, at the distance of fourscore miles from Hierapolis. The temple of the Moon attracted the devotion of Julian; but the halt of a few days was principally employed in completing the immense preparations of the Persian war. The secret of the expedition had hitherto remained in his own breast; but as Carrhae is the point of separation of the two great roads, he could no longer conceal whether it was his design to attack the dominions of Sapor on the side of the Tigris, or on that of the Euphrates. The emperor detached an army of thirty thousand men, under the command of his kinsman Procopius, and of Sebastian, who had been duke of Egypt. They were ordered to direct their march towards Nisibis, and to secure the frontier from the desultory incursions of the enemy, before they attempted the passage of the Tigris. Their subsequent operations were left to the discretion of the generals; but Julian expected, that after wasting with fire and sword the fertile districts of Media and Adiabene, they might arrive under the walls of Ctesiphon at the same time that he himself, advancing with equal steps along the banks of the Euphrates, should besiege the capital of the Persian monarchy. The success of this well-concerted plan depended, in a great measure, on the powerful and ready assistance of the king of Armenia, who, without exposing the safety of his own dominions, might detach an army of four thousand horse, and twenty thousand foot, to the assistance of the Romans. [37] But the feeble Arsaces Tiranus, [38] king of Armenia, had degenerated still more shamefully than his father Chosroes, from the manly virtues of the great Tiridates; and as the pusillanimous monarch was averse to any enterprise of danger and glory, he could disguise his timid indolence by the more decent excuses of religion and gratitude. He expressed a pious attachment to the memory of Constantius, from whose hands he had received in marriage

Olympias, the daughter of the praefect Ablavius; and the alliance of a female, who had been educated as the destined wife of the emperor Constans, exalted the dignity of a Barbarian king. [39] Tiranus professed the Christian religion; he reigned over a nation of Christians; and he was restrained, by every principle of conscience and interest, from contributing to the victory, which would consummate the ruin of the church. The alienated mind of Tiranus was exasperated by the indiscretion of Julian, who treated the king of Armenia as his slave, and as the enemy of the gods. The haughty and threatening style of the Imperial mandates [40] awakened the secret indignation of a prince, who, in the humiliating state of dependence, was still conscious of his royal descent from the Arsacides, the lords of the East, and the rivals of the Roman power. [40a]

[Footnote 33a: Or Bambyce, now Bambouch; Manbedj Arab., or Maboug, Syr. It was twenty-four Roman miles from the Euphrates—M.]

[Footnote 34: I take the earliest opportunity of acknowledging my obligations to M. d'Anville, for his recent geography of the Euphrates and Tigris, (Paris, 1780, in 4to.,) which particularly illustrates the expedition of Julian.]

[Footnote 35: There are three passages within a few miles of each other; 1. Zeugma, celebrated by the ancients; 2. Bir, frequented by the moderns; and, 3. The bridge of Menbigz, or Hierapolis, at the distance of four parasangs from the city. — Djisr Manbedj is the same with the ancient Zeugma. St. Martin, iii. 58—M.]

[Footnote 36: Haran, or Carrhae, was the ancient residence of the Sabaeans, and of Abraham. See the Index Geographicus of Schultens, (ad calcem Vit. Saladin.,) a work from which I have obtained much Oriental knowledge concerning the ancient and modern geography of Syria and the adjacent countries. —On an inedited medal in the collection of the late M. Tochon. of the Academy of Inscriptions, it is read Xappan. St. Martin. iii 60—M.]

[Footnote 37: See Xenophon. Cyropaed. l. iii. p. 189, edit. Hutchinson. Artavasdes might have supplied Marc Antony with 16,000 horse, armed and disciplined after the Parthian manner, (Plutarch, in M. Antonio. tom. v. p. 117.)]

[Footnote 38: Moses of Chorene (Hist. Armeniac. l. iii. c. 11, p. 242) fixes his accession (A. D. 354) to the 17th year of Constantius. —Arsaces Tiranus, or Diran, had ceased to reign twenty-five years before, in 337. The intermediate changes in Armenia, and the character of this Arsaces, the son of Diran, are traced by M. St. Martin, at considerable length, in his supplement to Le Beau, ii. 208-242. As long as his Grecian queen Olympias maintained her influence, Arsaces was faithful to the Roman and Christian alliance. On the accession of Julian, the same influence made his fidelity to waver; but Olympias having been poisoned in the sacramental bread by the agency of Pharandcem, the former wife of Arsaces, another change took place in Armenian politics unfavorable to the Christian interest. The patriarch Narses retired from the impious court to a safe seclusion. Yet Pharandsem was equally hostile to the Persian influence, and Arsaces began to support with vigor the cause of Julian. He made an inroad into the Persian dominions with a body of Rans and Alans as auxiliaries; wasted Aderbidgan and Sapor, who had been defeated near Tauriz, was engaged in making head against his troops in Persarmenia, at the time of the death of Julian. Such is M. St. Martin's view, (ii. 276, et sqq.,) which rests on the Armenian historians, Faustos of Byzantium, and Mezrob the biographer of the Partriarch Narses. In the history of Armenia by Father Chamitch, and translated by Avdall, Tiran is still king of Armenia, at the time of Julian's death. F. Chamitch follows Moses of Chorene, The authority of Gibbon—M.]

[Footnote 39: Ammian. xx. 11. Athanasius (tom. i. p. 856) says, in general terms, that Constantius gave to his brother's widow, an expression more suitable to a Roman than a Christian.]

[Footnote 40: Ammianus (xxiii. 2) uses a word much too soft for the occasion, monuerat. Muratori (Fabricius, Bibliothec. Graec. tom. vii. p. 86) has published an epistle from Julian to the satrap Arsaces; fierce, vulgar, and (though it might deceive Sozomen, l. vi. c. 5) most probably spurious. La Bleterie (Hist. de Jovien, tom. ii. p. 339) translates and rejects it. Note: St. Martin considers it genuine: the Armenian writers mention such a letter, iii. 37—M.]

[Footnote 40a: Arsaces did not abandon the Roman alliance, but gave it only feeble support. St. Martin, iii. 41—M.]

The military dispositions of Julian were skilfully contrived to deceive the spies and to divert the attention of Sapor. The legions appeared to direct their march towards Nisibis and the Tigris. On a sudden they wheeled to the right; traversed the level and naked plain of Carrhae; and reached, on the third day, the banks of the Euphrates, where the strong town of Nicephorium, or Callinicum, had been founded by the Macedonian kings. From thence the emperor pursued his march, above ninety miles, along the winding stream of the Euphrates, till, at length, about one month after his departure from Antioch, he discovered the towers of Circesium, [40b] the extreme limit of the Roman dominions. The army of Julian, the most numerous that any of the Caesars had ever led against Persia, consisted of sixty-five thousand effective and well-disciplined soldiers. The veteran bands of cavalry and infantry, of Romans and Barbarians, had been selected from the different provinces; and a just preeminence of loyalty and valor was claimed by the hardy Gauls, who guarded the throne and person of their beloved prince. A formidable body of Scythian auxiliaries had been transported from another climate, and almost from another world, to invade a distant country, of whose name and situation they were ignorant. The love of rapine and war allured to the Imperial standard several tribes of Saracens, or roving Arabs, whose service Julian had commanded, while he sternly refuse the payment of the accustomed subsidies. The broad channel of the Euphrates [41] was crowded by a fleet of eleven hundred ships, destined to attend the motions, and to satisfy the wants, of the Roman army. The military strength of the fleet was composed of fifty armed galleys; and these were accompanied by an equal number of flat-bottomed boats, which might occasionally be connected into the form of temporary bridges. The rest of the ships, partly constructed of timber, and partly covered with raw hides, were laden with an almost inexhaustible supply of arms and engines, of utensils and provisions. The vigilant humanity of Julian had embarked a very large magazine of vinegar and biscuit for the use of the soldiers, but he prohibited the indulgence of wine; and rigorously stopped a long string of superfluous camels that attempted to follow the rear of the army. The River Chaboras falls into the Euphrates at Circesium; [42] and as soon as the trumpet gave the signal of march, the Romans passed the little stream which separated two mighty and hostile empires. The custom of ancient discipline required a military oration; and Julian embraced every opportunity of displaying his eloquence. He animated the impatient and attentive legions by the example of the inflexible courage and glorious triumphs of their ancestors. He excited their resentment by a lively picture of the insolence of the Persians; and he exhorted them to imitate his firm resolution, either to extirpate that perfidious nation, or to devote his life in the cause of the republic. The eloquence of Julian was enforced by a donative of one hundred and thirty pieces of silver to every soldier; and the bridge of the Chaboras was instantly cut away, to convince the troops that they must place their hopes of safety in the success of their arms. Yet the prudence of the emperor induced him to secure a remote frontier, perpetually exposed to the inroads of the hostile Arabs. A detachment of four thousand men was left at Circesium, which completed, to the number of ten thousand, the regular garrison of that important fortress. [43]

[Footnote 40b: Kirkesia the Carchemish of the Scriptures—M.]

[Footnote 41: Latissimum flumen Euphraten artabat. Ammian. xxiii. 3 Somewhat higher, at the fords of Thapsacus, the river is four stadia or 800 yards, almost half an English mile, broad. (Xenophon, Anabasis, l. i. p. 41, edit. Hutchinson, with Foster's Observations, p. 29, &c., in the 2d volume of Spelman's translation.) If the breadth of the Euphrates at Bir and Zeugma is no more than 130 yards, (Voyages de Niebuhr, tom. ii. p. 335,) the enormous difference must chiefly arise from the depth of the channel.]

[Footnote 42: Munimentum tutissimum et fabre politum, Abora (the Orientals aspirate Chaboras or Chabour) et Euphrates ambiunt flumina, velut spatium insulare fingentes. Ammian. xxiii. 5.]

[Footnote 43: The enterprise and armament of Julian are described by himself, (Epist. xxvii.,) Ammianus Marcellinus, (xxiii. 3, 4, 5,) Libanius, (Orat. Parent. c. 108, 109, p. 332, 333,) Zosimus, (l. iii. p. 160, 161, 162) Sozomen, (l. vi. c. l,) and John Malala, (tom. ii. p. 17.)]

From the moment that the Romans entered the enemy's country, [44] the country of an active and artful enemy, the order of march was disposed in three columns. [45] The strength of the infantry, and consequently of the whole army was placed in the centre, under the peculiar command of their master-general Victor. On the right, the brave Nevitta led a column of several legions along the banks of the Euphrates, and almost always in sight of the fleet. The left flank of the army was protected by the column of cavalry. Hormisdas and Arinthaeus were appointed generals of the horse; and the singular adventures of Hormisdas [46] are not undeserving of our notice. He was a Persian prince, of the royal race of the Sassanides, who, in the troubles of the minority of Sapor, had escaped from prison to the hospitable court of the great Constantine. Hormisdas at first excited the compassion, and at length acquired the esteem, of his new masters; his valor and fidelity raised him to the military honors of the Roman service; and though a Christian, he might indulge the secret satisfaction of convincing his ungrateful country, than at oppressed subject may prove the most dangerous enemy. Such was the disposition of the three principal columns. The front and flanks of the army were covered by Lucilianus with a flying detachment of fifteen hundred light-armed soldiers, whose active vigilance observed the most distant signs, and conveyed the earliest notice, of any hostile approach. Dagalaiphus, and Secundinus duke of Osrhoene, conducted the troops of the rear-guard; the baggage securely proceeded in the intervals of the columns; and the ranks, from a motive either of use or ostentation, were formed in such open order, that the whole line of march extended almost ten miles. The ordinary post of Julian was at the head of the centre column; but as he preferred the duties of a general to the state of a monarch, he rapidly moved, with a small escort of light cavalry, to the front, the rear, the flanks, wherever his presence could animate or protect the march of the Roman army. The country which they traversed from the Chaboras, to the cultivated lands of Assyria, may be considered as a part of the desert of Arabia, a dry and barren waste, which could never be improved by the most powerful arts of human industry. Julian marched over the same ground which had been trod above seven hundred years before by the footsteps of the younger Cyrus, and which is described by one of the companions of his expedition, the sage and heroic Xenophon. [47] "The country was a plain throughout, as even as the sea, and full of wormwood; and if any other kind of shrubs or reeds grew there, they had all an aromatic smell, but no trees could be seen. Bustards and ostriches, antelopes and wild asses, [48] appeared to be the only inhabitants of the desert; and the fatigues of the march were alleviated by the amusements of the chase." The loose sand of the desert was frequently raised by the wind into clouds of dust; and a great number of the soldiers of Julian, with their tents, were suddenly thrown to the ground by the violence of an unexpected hurricane.

[Footnote 44: Before he enters Persia, Ammianus copiously describes (xxiii. p. 396-419, edit. Gronov. in 4to.) the eighteen great provinces, (as far as the Seric, or Chinese frontiers,) which were subject to the Sassanides.]

[Footnote 45: Ammianus (xxiv. 1) and Zosimus (l. iii. p. 162, 163) rately expressed the order of march.]

[Footnote 46: The adventures of Hormisdas are related with some mixture of fable, (Zosimus, l. ii. p. 100-102; Tillemont, Hist. des Empereurs tom. iv. p. 198.) It is almost impossible that he should be the brother (frater germanus) of an eldest and posthumous child: nor do I recollect that Ammianus ever gives him that title. Note: St. Martin conceives that he was an elder brother by another mother who had several children, ii. 24—M.]

[Footnote 47: See the first book of the Anabasis, p. 45, 46. This pleasing work is original and authentic. Yet Xenophon's memory, perhaps many years after the expedition, has sometimes betrayed him; and the distances which he marks are often larger than either a soldier or a geographer will allow.]

[Footnote 48: Mr. Spelman, the English translator of the Anabasis, (vol. i. p. 51,) confounds the antelope with the roebuck, and the wild ass with the zebra.]

The sandy plains of Mesopotamia were abandoned to the antelopes and wild asses of the desert; but a variety of populous towns and villages were pleasantly situated on the banks of the Euphrates, and in the islands which are occasionally formed by that river. The city of Annah, or Anatho, [49] the actual residence of an Arabian emir, is composed of two long streets, which enclose, within a natural fortification, a small island in the midst, and two fruitful spots on either side, of the Euphrates. The warlike inhabitants of Anatho showed a disposition to stop the march of a Roman emperor; till they were diverted from such fatal presumption by the mild exhortations of Prince Hormisdas, and the approaching terrors of the fleet and army. They implored, and experienced, the clemency of Julian, who transplanted the people to an advantageous settlement, near Chalcis in Syria, and admitted Pusaeus, the governor, to an honorable rank in his service and friendship. But the impregnable fortress of Thilutha could scorn the menace of a siege; and the emperor was obliged to content himself with an insulting promise, that, when he had subdued the interior provinces of Persia, Thilutha would no longer refuse to grace the triumph of the emperor. The inhabitants of the open towns, unable to resist, and unwilling to yield, fled with precipitation; and their houses, filled with spoil and provisions, were occupied by the soldiers of Julian, who massacred, without remorse and without punishment, some defenceless women. During the march, the Surenas, [49a] or Persian general, and Malek Rodosaces, the renowned emir of the tribe of Gassan, [50] incessantly hovered round the army; every straggler was intercepted; every detachment was attacked; and the valiant Hormisdas escaped with some difficulty from their hands. But the Barbarians were finally repulsed; the country became every day less favorable to the operations of cavalry; and when the Romans arrived at Macepracta, they perceived the ruins of the wall, which had been constructed by the ancient kings of Assyria, to secure their dominions from the incursions of the Medes. These preliminaries of the expedition of Julian appear to have employed about fifteen days; and we may compute near three hundred miles from the fortress of Circesium to the wall of Macepracta. [1]

[Footnote 49: See Voyages de Tavernier, part i. l. iii. p. 316, and more especially Viaggi di Pietro della Valle, tom. i. lett. xvii. p. 671, &c. He was ignorant of the old name and condition of Annah. Our blind travellers seldom possess any previous knowledge of the countries which they visit. Shaw and Tournefort deserve an honorable exception.]

[Footnote 49a: This is not a title, but the name of a great Persian family. St. Martin, iii. 79—M.]

[Footnote 50: Famosi nominis latro, says Ammianus; a high encomium for an Arab. The tribe of Gassan had settled on the edge of Syria, and reigned some time in Damascus, under a dynasty of thirty-one kings, or emirs, from the time of Pompey to that of the Khalif Omar. D'Herbelot, Bibliotheque Orientale, p. 360. Pococke, Specimen Hist. Arabicae, p. 75-78. The name of Rodosaces does not appear in the list. Note: Rodosaces-malek is king. St. Martin considers that Gibbon has fallen into an error in bringing the tribe of Gassan to the Euphrates. In Ammianus it is Assan. M. St. Martin would read Massanitarum, the same with the Mauzanitae of Malala—M.]

[Footnote 51: See Ammianus, (xxiv. 1, 2,) Libanius, (Orat. Parental. c. 110, 111, p. 334,) Zosimus, (l. iii. p. 164-168.) Note: This Syriac or Chaldaic has relation to its position; it easily bears the signification of the division of the waters. M. St. M. considers it the Missice of Pliny, v. 26. St. Martin, iii. 83—M.]

The fertile province of Assyria, [52] which stretched beyond the Tigris, as far as the mountains of Media, [53] extended about four hundred miles from the ancient wall of Macepracta, to the territory of Basra, where the united streams of the Euphrates and Tigris discharge themselves into the Persian Gulf. [54] The whole country might have claimed the peculiar name of Mesopotamia; as the two rivers, which are never more distant than fifty, approach, between Bagdad and Babylon, within twenty-five miles, of each other. A multitude of artificial canals, dug without much labor in a soft and yielding soil connected the rivers, and intersected the plain of Assyria. The uses of these artificial canals were various and important. They served to discharge the superfluous waters from one river into the other, at the season of their respective inundations. Subdividing themselves into smaller and smaller branches, they refreshed the dry lands, and supplied the deficiency of rain. They facilitated the intercourse of peace and commerce; and, as the dams could be speedily broke down, they armed the despair of the Assyrians with the means of opposing a sudden deluge to the progress of an invading army. To the soil and climate of Assyria, nature had denied some of her choicest gifts, the vine, the olive, and the fig-tree; [54a] but the food which supports the life of man, and particularly wheat and barley, were produced with inexhaustible fertility; and the husbandman, who committed his seed to the earth, was frequently rewarded with an increase of two, or even of three, hundred. The face of the country was interspersed with groves of innumerable palm-trees; [55] and the diligent natives celebrated, either in verse or prose, the three hundred and sixty uses to which the trunk, the branches, the leaves, the juice, and the fruit, were skilfully applied. Several manufactures, especially those of leather and linen, employed the industry of a numerous people, and afforded valuable materials for foreign trade; which appears, however, to have been conducted by the hands of strangers. Babylon had been converted into a royal park; but near the ruins of the ancient capital, new cities had successively arisen, and the populousness of the country was displayed in the multitude of towns and villages, which were built of bricks dried in the sun, and strongly cemented with bitumen; the natural and peculiar production of the Babylonian soil. While the successors of Cyrus reigned over Asia, the province of Syria alone maintained, during a third part of the year, the luxurious plenty of the table and household of the Great King. Four considerable villages were assigned for the subsistence of his Indian dogs; eight hundred stallions, and sixteen thousand mares, were constantly kept, at the expense of the country, for the royal stables; and as the daily tribute, which was paid to the satrap, amounted to one English bushe of silver, we may compute the annual revenue of Assyria at more than twelve hundred thousand pounds sterling. [56]

[Footnote 52: The description of Assyria, is furnished by Herodotus, (l. i. c. 192, &c.,) who sometimes writes for children, and sometimes for philosophers; by Strabo, (l. xvi. p. 1070-1082,) and by Ammianus, (l.xxiii. c. 6.) The most useful of the modern travellers are Tavernier, (part i. l. ii. p. 226-258,) Otter, (tom. ii. p. 35-69, and 189-224,) and Niebuhr, (tom. ii. p. 172-288.) Yet I much regret that the Irak Arabi of Abulfeda has not been translated.]

[Footnote 53: Ammianus remarks, that the primitive Assyria, which comprehended Ninus, (Nineveh,) and Arbela, had assumed the more recent and peculiar appellation of Adiabene; and he seems to fix Teredon, Vologesia, and Apollonia, as the extreme cities of the actual province of Assyria.]

[Footnote 54: The two rivers unite at Apamea, or Corna, (one hundred miles from the Persian Gulf,) into the broad stream of the Pasitigris, or Shutul-Arab. The Euphrates formerly reached the sea by a separate channel, which was obstructed and diverted by the citizens of Orchoe, about twenty miles to the south-east of modern Basra. (D'Anville, in the Memoires de l'Acad. des Inscriptions, tom.xxx. p. 171-191.)]

[Footnote 54a: We are informed by Mr. Gibbon, that nature has denied to the soil an climate of Assyria some of her choicest gifts, the vine, the olive, and the fig-tree. This might have been the case ir the age of Ammianus Marcellinus, but it is not so at the present day; and it is a curious fact that the grape, the olive, and the fig, are the most common fruits in the province, and may be seen in every garden. Macdonald Kinneir, Geogr. Mem. on Persia 239—M.]

[Footnote 55: The learned Kaempfer, as a botanist, an antiquary, and a traveller, has exhausted (Amoenitat. Exoticae, Fasicul. iv. p. 660-764) the whole subject of palm-trees.]

[Footnote 56: Assyria yielded to the Persian satrap an Artaba of silver each day. The well-known proportion of weights and measures (see Bishop Hooper's elaborate Inquiry,) the specific gravity of water and silver, and the value of that metal, will afford, after a short process, the annual revenue which I have stated. Yet the Great King received no more than 1000 Euboic, or Tyrian, talents (252,000l.) from Assyria. The comparison of two passages in Herodotus, (l. i. c. 192, l. iii. c. 89-96) reveals an important difference between the gross, and the net, revenue of Persia; the sums paid by the province, and the gold or silver deposited in the royal treasure. The monarch might annually save three millions six hundred thousand pounds, of the seventeen or eighteen millions raised upon the people.]

PART III

The fields of Assyria were devoted by Julian to the calamities of war; and the philosopher retaliated on a guiltless people the acts of rapine and cruelty which had been committed by their haughty master in the Roman provinces. The trembling Assyrians summoned the rivers to their assistance; and completed, with their own hands, the ruin of their country. The roads were rendered impracticable; a flood of waters was poured into the camp; and, during several days, the troops of Julian were obliged to contend with the most discouraging hardships. But every obstacle was surmounted by the perseverance of the legionaries, who were inured to toil as well as to danger, and who felt themselves animated by the spirit of their leader. The damage was gradually repaired; the waters were restored to their proper channels;

whole groves of palm-trees were cut down, and placed along the broken parts of the road; and the army passed over the broad and deeper canals, on bridges of floating rafts, which were supported by the help of bladders. Two cities of Assyria presumed to resist the arms of a Roman emperor: and they both paid the severe penalty of their rashness. At the distance of fifty miles from the royal residence of Ctesiphon, Perisabor, [57a] or Anbar, held the second rank in the province; a city, large, populous, and well fortified, surrounded with a double wall, almost encompassed by a branch of the Euphrates, and defended by the valor of a numerous garrison. The exhortations of Hormisdas were repulsed with contempt; and the ears of the Persian prince were wounded by a just reproach, that, unmindful of his royal birth, he conducted an army of strangers against his king and country. The Assyrians maintained their loyalty by a skilful, as well as vigorous, defence; till the lucky stroke of a battering-ram, having opened a large breach, by shattering one of the angles of the wall, they hastily retired into the fortifications of the interior citadel. The soldiers of Julian rushed impetuously into the town, and after the full gratification of every military appetite, Perisabor was reduced to ashes; and the engines which assaulted the citadel were planted on the ruins of the smoking houses. The contest was continued by an incessant and mutual discharge of missile weapons; and the superiority which the Romans might derive from the mechanical powers of their balistae and catapultae was counterbalanced by the advantage of the ground on the side of the besieged. But as soon as an Helepolis had been constructed, which could engage on equal terms with the loftiest ramparts, the tremendous aspect of a moving turret, that would leave no hope of resistance or mercy, terrified the defenders of the citadel into an humble submission; and the place was surrendered only two days after Julian first appeared under the walls of Perisabor. Two thousand five hundred persons, of both sexes, the feeble remnant of a flourishing people, were permitted to retire; the plentiful magazines of corn, of arms, and of splendid furniture, were partly distributed among the troops, and partly reserved for the public service; the useless stores were destroyed by fire or thrown into the stream of the Euphrates; and the fate of Amida was revenged by the total ruin of Perisabor.

[Footnote 57a: *Libanius says that it was a great city of Assyria, called after the name of the reigning king. The orator of Antioch is not mistaken. The Persians and Syrians called it Fyrouz Schapour or Fyrouz Schahbour; in Persian, the victory of Schahpour. It owed that name to Sapor the First. It was before called Anbar St. Martin, iii. 85—M.*]

The city or rather fortress, of Maogamalcha, which was defended by sixteen large towers, a deep ditch, and two strong and solid walls of brick and bitumen, appears to have been constructed at the distance of eleven miles, as the safeguard of the capital of Persia. The emperor, apprehensive of leaving such an important fortress in his rear, immediately formed the siege of Maogamalcha; and the Roman army was distributed, for that purpose, into three divisions. Victor, at the head of the cavalry, and of a detachment of heavy-armed foot, was ordered to clear the country, as far as the banks of the Tigris, and the suburbs of Ctesiphon. The conduct of the attack was assumed by Julian himself, who seemed to place his whole dependence in the military engines which he erected against the walls; while he secretly contrived a more efficacious method of introducing his troops into the heart of the city Under the direction of Nevitta and Dagalaiphus, the trenches were opened at a considerable distance, and gradually prolonged as far as the edge of the ditch. The ditch was speedily filled with earth; and, by the incessant labor of the troops, a mine was carried under the foundations of the walls, and sustained, at sufficient intervals, by props of timber. Three chosen cohorts, advancing in a single file, silently explored the dark and dangerous passage; till their intrepid leader whispered back the intelligence, that he was ready to issue from his confinement into the streets of the hostile city. Julian checked their ardor, that he might insure their success; and immediately diverted the attention of the garrison, by the tumult and clamor of a general assault. The Persians, who, from their walls, contemptuously beheld the progress of an impotent attack, celebrated with songs of triumph the glory of Sapor; and ventured to assure the emperor, that he might ascend the starry mansion of Ormusd, before he could hope to take the impregnable city of Maogamalcha. The city was already taken. History has recorded the name of a private soldier the first who ascended from the mine into a deserted tower. The passage was widened by his companions, who pressed forwards with impatient valor. Fifteen hundred enemies were already in the midst of the city. The astonished garrison abandoned the walls, and their only hope of safety; the gates were instantly burst open; and the revenge of the soldier, unless it were suspended by lust or avarice, was satiated by an undistinguishing massacre. The governor, who had yielded on a promise of mercy, was burnt alive, a few days afterwards, on a charge of having uttered some disrespectful words against the honor of Prince Hormisdas. The fortifications were razed to the ground; and not a vestige was left, that the city of Maogamalcha had ever existed. The neighborhood of the capital of Persia was adorned with three stately palaces, laboriously enriched with every production that could gratify the luxury and pride of an Eastern monarch. The pleasant situation of the gardens along the banks of the Tigris, was improved, according to the Persian taste, by the symmetry of flowers, fountains, and shady walks: and spacious parks were enclosed for the reception of the bears, lions, and wild boars, which were maintained at a considerable expense for the pleasure of the royal chase. The park walls were broken down, the savage game was abandoned to the darts of the soldiers, and the palaces of Sapor were reduced to ashes, by the command of the Roman emperor. Julian, on this occasion, showed himself ignorant, or careless, of the laws of civility, which the prudence and refinement of polished ages have established between hostile princes. Yet these wanton ravages need not excite in our breasts any vehement emotions of pity or resentment. A simple, naked statue, finished by the hand of a Grecian artist, is of more genuine value than all these rude and costly monuments of Barbaric labor; and, if we are more deeply affected by the ruin of a palace than by the conflagration of a cottage, our humanity must have formed a very erroneous estimate of the miseries of human life. [57]

[Footnote 57a: And as guilty of a double treachery, having first engaged to surrender the city, and afterwards valiantly defended it. Gibbon, perhaps, should have noticed this charge, though he may have rejected it as improbable Compare Zosimus. iii. 23—M.]

[Footnote 57: The operations of the Assyrian war are circumstantially related by Ammianus, (xxiv. 2, 3, 4, 5,) Libanius, (Orat. Parent. c. 112-123, p. 335-347,) Zosimus, (l. iii. p. 168-180,) and Gregory Nazianzen, (Orat iv. p. 113, 144.) The military criticisms of the saint are devoutly copied by Tillemont, his faithful slave.]

Julian was an object of hatred and terror to the Persian and the painters of that nation represented the invader of their country under the emblem of a furious lion, who vomited from his mouth a consuming fire. [58] To his friends and soldiers the philosophic hero appeared in a more amiable light; and his virtues were never more conspicuously displayed, than in the last and most active period of his life. He practised, without effort, and almost without merit, the habitual qualities of temperance and sobriety. According to the dictates of that artificial wisdom, which assumes an absolute dominion over the mind and body, he sternly refused himself the indulgence of the most natural appetites. [59] In the warm climate of Assyria, which solicited a luxurious people to the gratification of every sensual desire, [60] a youthful conqueror preserved his chastity pure and inviolate; nor was Julian ever tempted, even by a motive of curiosity, to visit his female captives of exquisite beauty, [61] who, instead of resisting his power, would have disputed with each other the honor of his embraces. With the same firmness that he resisted the allurements of love, he sustained the hardships of war. When the Romans marched through the flat and flooded country, their sovereign, on foot, at the head of his legions, shared their fatigues and animated their diligence. In every useful labor, the hand of Julian was prompt and strenuous; and the Imperial purple was wet and dirty as the coarse garment of the meanest soldier. The two sieges allowed him some remarkable opportunities of signalizing his personal valor, which, in the improved state of the military art, can seldom be exerted by a prudent general. The emperor stood before the citadel before the citadel of Perisabor, insensible of his extreme danger, and encouraged his troops to burst open the gates of iron, till he was almost overwhelmed under a cloud of missile weapons and huge stones, that were directed against his person. As he examined the exterior fortifications of Maogamalcha, two Persians, devoting themselves for their country, suddenly rushed upon him with drawn cimeters: the emperor dexterously received their blows on his uplifted shield; and, with a steady and well-aimed thrust, laid one of his adversaries dead at his feet. The esteem of a prince who possesses the virtues which he approves, is the noblest recompense of a deserving subject; and the authority which Julian derived from his personal merit, enabled him to revive and enforce the rigor of ancient discipline. He punished with death or ignominy the misbehavior of three troops of horse, who, in a skirmish with the Surenas, had lost their honor and one of their standards: and he distinguished with obsidional [62] crowns the valor of the foremost soldiers, who had ascended into the city of Maogamalcha.

After the siege of Perisabor, the firmness of the emperor was exercised by the insolent avarice of the army, who loudly complained, that their services were rewarded by a trifling donative of one hundred pieces of silver. His just indignation was expressed in the grave and manly language of a Roman. "Riches are the object of your desires; those riches are in the hands of the Persians; and the spoils of this fruitful country are proposed as the prize of your valor and discipline. Believe me," added Julian, "the Roman republic, which formerly possessed such immense treasures, is now reduced to want and wretchedness once our princes have been persuaded, by weak and interested ministers, to purchase with gold the tranquillity of the Barbarians. The revenue is exhausted; the cities are ruined; the provinces are dispeopled. For myself, the only inheritance that I have received from my royal ancestors is a soul incapable of fear; and as long as I am convinced that every real advantage is seated in the mind, I shall not blush to acknowledge an honorable poverty, which, in the days of ancient virtue, was considered as the glory of Fabricius. That glory, and that virtue, may be your own, if you will listen to the voice of Heaven and of your leader. But if you will rashly persist, if you are determined to renew the shameful and mischievous examples of old seditions, proceed. As it becomes an emperor who has filled the first rank among men, I am prepared to die, standing; and to despise a precarious life, which, every hour, may depend on an accidental fever. If I have been found unworthy of the command, there are now among you, (I speak it with pride and pleasure,) there are many chiefs whose merit and experience are equal to the conduct of the most important war. Such has been the temper of my reign, that I can retire, without regret, and without apprehension, to the obscurity of a private station" [63] The modest resolution of Julian was answered by the unanimous applause and cheerful obedience of the Romans, who declared their confidence of victory, while they fought under the banners of their heroic prince. Their courage was kindled by his frequent and familiar asseverations, (for such wishes were the oaths of Julian,) "So may I reduce the Persians under the yoke!" "Thus may I restore the strength and splendor of the republic!" The love of fame was the ardent passion of his soul: but it was not before he trampled on the ruins of Maogamalcha, that he allowed himself to say, "We have now provided some materials for the sophist of Antioch." [64]

[Footnote 58: Libanius de ulciscenda Juliani nece, c. 13, p. 162.]

[Footnote 59: The famous examples of Cyrus, Alexander, and Scipio, were acts of justice. Julian's chastity was voluntary, and, in his opinion, meritorious.]

[Footnote 60: Sallust (ap. Vet. Scholiast. Juvenal. Satir. i. 104) observes, that nihil corruptius moribus. The matrons and virgins of Babylon freely mingled with the men in licentious banquets; and as they felt the intoxication of wine and love, they gradually, and almost completely, threw aside the encumbrance of dress; ad ultimum ima corporum velamenta projiciunt. Q. Curtius, v. 1.]

[Footnote 61: Ex virginibus autem quae speciosae sunt captae, et in Perside, ubi faeminarum pulchritudo excellit, nec contrectare aliquam votuit nec videre. Ammian. xxiv. 4. The native race of Persians is small and ugly; but it has been improved by the perpetual mixture of Circassian blood, (Herodot. l. iii. c. 97. Buffon, Hist. Naturelle, tom. iii. p. 420.)]

[Footnote 62: Obsidionalibus coronis donati. Ammian. xxiv. 4. Either Julian or his historian were unskillful antiquaries. He should have given mural crowns. The obsidional were the reward of a general who had delivered a besieged city, (Aulus Gellius, Noct. Attic. v. 6.)]

[Footnote 63: I give this speech as original and genuine. Ammianus might hear, could transcribe, and was incapable of inventing, it. I have used some slight freedoms, and conclude with the most forcibic sentence.]

[Footnote 64: Ammian. xxiv. 3. Libanius, Orat. Parent. c. 122, p. 346.]

The successful valor of Julian had triumphed over all the obstacles that opposed his march to the gates of Ctesiphon. But the reduction, or even the siege, of the capital of Persia, was still at a distance: nor can the military conduct of the emperor be clearly apprehended, without a knowledge of the country which was the theatre of his bold and skilful operations. [65] Twenty miles to the south of Bagdad, and on the eastern bank of the Tigris, the curiosity of travellers has observed some ruins of the palaces of Ctesiphon, which, in the time of Julian, was a great and populous city. The name and glory of the adjacent Seleucia were forever extinguished; and the only remaining quarter of that Greek colony had resumed, with the Assyrian language and manners, the primitive appellation of Coche. Coche was situate on the western side of the Tigris; but it was naturally considered as a suburb of Ctesiphon, with which we may suppose it to have been connected by a permanent bridge of boats.

The united parts contribute to form the common epithet of Al Modain, the cities, which the Orientals have bestowed on the winter residence of the Sassinadees; and the whole circumference of the Persian capital was strongly fortified by the waters of the river, by lofty walls, and by impracticable morasses. Near the ruins of Seleucia, the camp of Julian was fixed, and secured, by a ditch and rampart, against the sallies of the numerous and enterprising garrison of Coche. In this fruitful and pleasant country, the Romans were plentifully supplied with water and forage: and several forts, which might have embarrassed the motions of the army, submitted, after some resistance, to the efforts of their valor. The fleet passed from the Euphrates into an artificial derivation of that river, which pours a copious and navigable stream into the Tigris, at a small distance below the great city. If they had followed this royal canal, which bore the name of Nahar-Malcha, [66] the intermediate situation of Coche would have separated the fleet and army of Julian; and the rash attempt of steering against the current of the Tigris, and forcing their way through the midst of a hostile capital, must have been attended with the total destruction of the Roman navy. The prudence of the emperor foresaw the danger, and provided the remedy. As he had minutely studied the operations of Trajan in the same country, he soon recollected that his warlike predecessor had dug a new and navigable canal, which, leaving Coche on the right hand, conveyed the waters of the Nahar-Malcha into the river Tigris, at some distance above the cities. From the information of the peasants, Julian ascertained the vestiges of this ancient work, which were almost obliterated by design or accident. By the indefatigable labor of the soldiers, a broad and deep channel was speedily prepared for the reception of the Euphrates. A strong dike was constructed to interrupt the ordinary current of the Nahar-Malcha: a flood of waters rushed impetuously into their new bed; and the Roman fleet, steering their triumphant course into the Tigris, derided the vain and ineffectual barriers which the Persians of Ctesiphon had erected to oppose their passage.

[Footnote 65: M. d'Anville, (Mem. de l'Academie des Inscriptions, tom. xxxviii p. 246-259) has ascertained the true position and distance of Babylon, Seleucia, Ctesiphon, Bagdad, &c. The Roman traveller, Pietro della Valle, (tom. i. lett. xvii. p. 650-780,) seems to be the most intelligent spectator of that famous province. He is a gentleman and a scholar, but intolerably vain and prolix.]

[Footnote 66: The Royal Canal (Nahar-Malcha) might be successively restored, altered, divided, &c., (Cellarius, Geograph. Antiq. tom. ii. p. 453;) and these changes may serve to explain the seeming contradictions of antiquity. In the time of Julian, it must have fallen into the Euphrates below Ctesiphon.]

As it became necessary to transport the Roman army over the Tigris, another labor presented itself, of less toil, but of more danger, than the preceding expedition. The stream was broad and rapid; the ascent steep and difficult; and the intrenchments which had been formed on the ridge of the opposite bank, were lined with a numerous army of heavy cuirrasiers, dexterous archers, and huge elephants; who (according to the extravagant hyperbole of Libanius) could trample with the same ease a field of corn, or a legion of Romans. [67] In the presence of such an enemy, the construction of a bridge was impracticable; and the intrepid prince, who instantly seized the only possible expedient, concealed his design, till the moment of execution, from the knowledge of the Barbarians, of his own troops, and even of his generals themselves. Under the specious pretence of examining the state of the magazines, fourscore vessels [67a] were gradually unladen; and a select detachment, apparently destined for some secret expedition, was ordered to stand to their arms on the first signal. Julian disguised the silent anxiety of his own mind with smiles of confidence and joy; and amused the hostile nations with the spectacle of military games, which he insultingly celebrated under the walls of Coche. The day was consecrated to pleasure; but, as soon as the hour of supper was passed, the emperor summoned the generals to his tent, and acquainted them that he had fixed that night for the passage of the Tigris. They stood in silent and respectful astonishment; but, when the venerable Sallust assumed the privilege of his age and experience, the rest of the chiefs supported with freedom the weight of his prudent remonstrances. [68] Julian contented himself with observing, that conquest and safety depended on the attempt; that instead of diminishing, the number of their enemies would be increased, by successive reenforcements; and that a longer delay would neither contract the breadth of the stream, nor level the height of the bank. The signal was instantly given, and obeyed; the most impatient of the legionaries leaped into five vessels that lay nearest to the bank; and as they plied their oars with intrepid diligence, they were lost, after a few moments, in the darkness of the night. A flame arose on the opposite side; and Julian, who too clearly understood that his foremost vessels, in attempting to land, had been fired by the enemy, dexterously converted their extreme danger into a presage of victory. "Our fellow-soldiers," he eagerly exclaimed, "are already masters of the bank; see—they make the appointed signal; let us hasten to emulate and assist their courage." The united and rapid motion of a great fleet broke the violence of the current, and they reached the eastern shore of the Tigris with sufficient speed to extinguish the flames, and rescue their adventurous companions. The difficulties of a steep and lofty ascent were increased by the weight of armor, and the darkness of the night. A shower of stones, darts, and fire, was incessantly discharged on the heads of the assailants; who, after an arduous struggle, climbed the bank and stood victorious upon the rampart. As soon as they possessed a more equal field, Julian, who, with his light infantry, had led the attack, [69] darted through the ranks a skilful and experienced eye: his bravest soldiers, according to the precepts of Homer, [70] were distributed in the front and rear: and all the trumpets of the Imperial army sounded to battle. The Romans, after sending up a military shout, advanced in measured steps to the animating notes of martial music; launched their formidable javelins; and rushed forwards with drawn swords, to deprive the Barbarians, by a closer onset, of the advantage of their missile weapons. The whole engagement lasted above twelve hours; till the gradual retreat of the Persians was changed into a disorderly flight, of which the shameful example was given by the principal leader, and the Surenas himself. They were pursued to the gates of Ctesiphon; and the conquerors might have entered the dismayed city, [71] if their general, Victor, who was dangerously wounded with an arrow, had not conjured them to desist from a rash attempt, which must be fatal, if it were not successful. On their side, the Romans acknowledged the loss of only seventy-five men; while they affirmed, that the Barbarians had left on the field of battle two thousand five hundred, or even six thousand, of their bravest soldiers. The spoil was such as might be expected from the riches and luxury of an Oriental camp; large quantities of silver and gold, splendid arms and trappings, and beds and tables of massy silver. [71a] The victorious emperor distributed, as the rewards of valor, some honorable gifts, civic, and mural, and naval crowns; which he, and perhaps he alone, esteemed more precious than the wealth of Asia. A solemn sacrifice was offered to the god of war, but the appearances of the victims threatened the most inauspicious events; and Julian soon discovered, by less ambiguous signs, that he had now reached the term of his prosperity. [72]

[Footnote 67: Rien n'est beau que le vrai; a maxim which should be inscribed on the desk of every rhetorician.]

[Footnote 67a: This is a mistake; each vessel (according to Zosimus two, according to Ammianus five) had eighty men. Amm. xxiv. 6, with Wagner's note. Gibbon must have read octogenas for octogenis. The five vessels selected for this service were remarkably large and strong provision transports. The strength of the fleet remained with Julian to carry over the army—M.]

[Footnote 68: Libanius alludes to the most powerful of the generals. I have ventured to name Sallust. Ammianus says, of all the leaders, quod acri metu territ acrimetu territi duces concordi precatu precaut fieri prohibere tentarent. Note: It is evident that Gibbon has mistaken the sense of Libanius; his words can only apply to a commander of a detachment, not to so eminent a person as the Praefect of the East. St. Martin, iii. 313—M.]

[Footnote 69: Hinc Imperator.... (says Ammianus) ipse cum levis armaturae auxiliis per prima postremaque discurrens, &c. Yet Zosimus, his friend, does not allow him to pass the river till two days after the battle.]

[Footnote 70: Secundum Homericam dispositionem. A similar disposition is ascribed to the wise Nestor, in the fourth book of the Iliad; and Homer was never absent from the mind of Julian.]

[Footnote 71: Persas terrore subito miscuerunt, versisque agminibus totius gentis, apertas Ctesiphontis portas victor miles intrasset, ni major praedarum occasio fuisset, quam cura victoriae, (Sextus Rufus de Provinciis c. 28.) Their avarice might dispose them to hear the advice of Victor.]

[Footnote 71a: The suburbs of Ctesiphon, according to a new fragment of Eunapius, were so full of provisions, that the soldiers were in danger of suffering from excess. Mai, p. 260. Eunapius in Niebuhr. Nov. Byz. Coll. 68. Julian exhibited warlike dances and games in his camp to recreate the soldiers Ibid—M.]

[Footnote 72: *The labor of the canal, the passage of the Tigris, and the victory, are described by Ammianus, (xxiv. 5, 6,) Libanius, (Orat. Parent. c. 124-128, p. 347-353,) Greg. Nazianzen, (Orat. iv. p. 115,) Zosimus, (l. iii. p. 181-183,) and Sextus Rufus, (de Provinciis, c. 28.)*]

On the second day after the battle, the domestic guards, the Jovians and Herculians, and the remaining troops, which composed near two thirds of the whole army, were securely wafted over the Tigris. [73] While the Persians beheld from the walls of Ctesiphon the desolation of the adjacent country, Julian cast many an anxious look towards the North, in full expectation, that as he himself had victoriously penetrated to the capital of Sapor, the march and junction of his lieutenants, Sebastian and Procopius, would be executed with the same courage and diligence. His expectations were disappointed by the treachery of the Armenian king, who permitted, and most probably directed, the desertion of his auxiliary troops from the camp of the Romans; [74] and by the dissensions of the two generals, who were incapable of forming or executing any plan for the public service. When the emperor had relinquished the hope of this important reenforcement, he condescended to hold a council of war, and approved, after a full debate, the sentiment of those generals, who dissuaded the siege of Ctesiphon, as a fruitless and pernicious undertaking. It is not easy for us to conceive, by what arts of fortification a city thrice besieged and taken by the predecessors of Julian could be rendered impregnable against an army of sixty thousand Romans, commanded by a brave and experienced general, and abundantly supplied with ships, provisions, battering engines, and military stores. But we may rest assured, from the love of glory, and contempt of danger, which formed the character of Julian, that he was not discouraged by any trivial or imaginary obstacles. [75] At the very time when he declined the siege of Ctesiphon, he rejected, with obstinacy and disdain, the most flattering offers of a negotiation of peace. Sapor, who had been so long accustomed to the tardy ostentation of Constantius, was surprised by the intrepid diligence of his successor. As far as the confines of India and Scythia, the satraps of the distant provinces were ordered to assemble their troops, and to march, without delay, to the assistance of their monarch. But their preparations were dilatory, their motions slow; and before Sapor could lead an army into the field, he received the melancholy intelligence of the devastation of Assyria, the ruin of his palaces, and the slaughter of his bravest troops, who defended the passage of the Tigris. The pride of royalty was humbled in the dust; he took his repasts on the ground; and the disorder of his hair expressed the grief and anxiety of his mind. Perhaps he would not have refused to purchase, with one half of his kingdom, the safety of the remainder; and he would have gladly subscribed himself, in a treaty of peace, the faithful and dependent ally of the Roman conqueror. Under the pretence of private business, a minister of rank and confidence was secretly despatched to embrace the knees of Hormisdas, and to request, in the language of a suppliant, that he might be introduced into the presence of the emperor. The Sassanian prince, whether he listened to the voice of pride or humanity, whether he consulted the sentiments of his birth, or the duties of his situation, was equally inclined to promote a salutary measure, which would terminate the calamities of Persia, and secure the triumph of Rome. He was astonished by the inflexible firmness of a hero, who remembered, most unfortunately for himself and for his country, that Alexander had uniformly rejected the propositions of Darius. But as Julian was sensible, that the hope of a safe and honorable peace might cool the ardor of his troops, he earnestly requested that Hormisdas would privately dismiss the minister of Sapor, and conceal this dangerous temptation from the knowledge of the camp. [76]

[Footnote 73: *The fleet and army were formed in three divisions, of which the first only had passed during the night.*]

[Footnote 74: Moses of Chorene (Hist. Armen. l. iii. c. 15, p. 246) supplies us with a national tradition, and a spurious letter. I have borrowed only the leading circumstance, which is consistent with truth, probability, and Libanius, (Orat. Parent. c. 131, p. 355.)]

[Footnote 75: Civitas inexpugnabilis, facinus audax et importunum. Ammianus, xxiv. 7. His fellow-soldier, Eutropius, turns aside from the difficulty, Assyriamque populatus, castra apud Ctesiphontem stativa aliquandiu habuit: remeansbue victor, &c. x. 16. Zosimus is artful or ignorant, and Socrates inaccurate.]

[Footnote 76: Libanius, Orat. Parent. c. 130, p. 354, c. 139, p. 361. Socrates, l. iii. c. 21. The ecclesiastical historian imputes the refusal of peace to the advice of Maximus. Such advice was unworthy of a philosopher; but the philosopher was likewise a magician, who flattered the hopes and passions of his master.]

PART IV

The honor, as well as interest, of Julian, forbade him to consume his time under the impregnable walls of Ctesiphon and as often as he defied the Barbarians, who defended the city, to meet him on the open plain, they prudently replied, that if he desired to exercise his valor, he might seek the army of the Great King. He felt the insult, and he accepted the advice. Instead of confining his servile march to the banks of the Euphrates and Tigris, he resolved to imitate the adventurous spirit of Alexander, and boldly to advance into the inland provinces, till he forced his rival to contend with him, perhaps in the plains of Arbela, for the empire of Asia. The magnanimity of Julian was applauded and betrayed, by the arts of a noble Persian, who, in the cause of his country, had generously submitted to act a part full of danger, of falsehood, and of shame. [77] With a train of faithful followers, he deserted to the Imperial camp; exposed, in a specious tale, the injuries which he had sustained; exaggerated the cruelty of Sapor, the discontent of the people, and the weakness of the monarchy; and confidently offered himself as the hostage and guide of the Roman march. The most rational grounds of suspicion were urged, without effect, by the wisdom and experience of Hormisdas; and the credulous Julian, receiving the traitor into his bosom, was persuaded to issue a hasty order, which, in the opinion of mankind, appeared to arraign his prudence, and to endanger his safety. He destroyed, in a single hour, the whole navy, which had been transported above five hundred miles, at so great an expense of toil, of treasure, and of blood. Twelve, or, at the most, twenty-two small vessels were saved, to accompany, on carriages, the march of the army, and to form occasional bridges for the passage of the rivers. A supply of twenty days' provisions was reserved for the use of the soldiers; and the rest of the magazines, with a fleet of eleven hundred vessels, which rode at anchor in the Tigris, were abandoned to the flames, by the absolute command of the emperor. The Christian bishops, Gregory and Augustin, insult the madness of the Apostate, who executed, with his own hands, the sentence of divine justice. Their authority, of less weight, perhaps, in a military question, is confirmed by the cool judgment of an experienced soldier, who was himself spectator of the conflagration, and who could not disapprove the reluctant murmurs of the troops. [78] Yet there are not wanting some specious, and perhaps solid, reasons, which might justify the resolution of Julian. The navigation of the Euphrates never ascended above Babylon, nor that of the Tigris above Opis. [79] The distance of the last-mentioned city from the Roman camp was not very considerable: and Julian must soon have renounced the vain and impracticable attempt of forcing upwards a great fleet against the stream of a rapid river, [80] which in several places was embarrassed by natural or artificial cataracts. [81] The power of sails and oars was insufficient; it became necessary to tow the ships against the current of the river; the strength of twenty thousand soldiers was exhausted in this tedious and servile labor, and if the Romans continued to march along the banks of the Tigris, they could only expect to return home without achieving any enterprise worthy of the genius or fortune of their leader. If, on the contrary, it was advisable to advance into the inland country, the destruction of the fleet and magazines was the only measure which could save that valuable prize from the hands of the numerous and active troops which might suddenly be poured from the gates of Ctesiphon. Had the arms of Julian been victorious, we should now admire the conduct, as well as the courage, of a hero, who, by depriving his soldiers of the hopes of a retreat, left them only the alternative of death or conquest. [82]

[Footnote 77: The arts of this new Zopyrus (Greg. Nazianzen, Orat. iv. p. 115, 116) may derive some credit from the testimony of two abbreviators, (Sextus Rufus and Victor,) and the casual hints of Libanius (Orat. Parent. c. 134, p. 357) and Ammianus, (xxiv. 7.) The course of genuine history is interrupted by a most unseasonable chasm in the text of Ammianus.]

[Footnote 78: See Ammianus, (xxiv. 7,) Libanius, (Orat. Parentalis, c. 132, 133, p. 356, 357,) Zosimus, (l. iii. p. 183,) Zonaras, (tom. ii. l. xiii. p. 26) Gregory, (Orat. iv. p. 116,) and Augustin, (de Civitate Dei, l. iv. c. 29, l. v. c. 21.) Of these Libanius alone attempts a faint apology for his hero; who, according to Ammianus, pronounced his own condemnation by a tardy and ineffectual attempt to extinguish the flames.]

[Footnote 79: Consult Herodotus, (l. i. c. 194,) Strabo, (l. xvi. p. 1074,) and Tavernier, (part i. l. ii. p. 152.)]

[Footnote 80: A celeritate Tigris incipit vocari, ita appellant Medi sagittam. Plin. Hist. Natur. vi. 31.]

[Footnote 81: One of these dikes, which produces an artificial cascade or cataract, is described by Tavernier (part i. l. ii. p. 226) and Thevenot, (part ii. l. i. p. 193.) The Persians, or Assyrians, labored to interrupt the navigation of the river, (Strabo, l. xv. p. 1075. D'Anville, l'Euphrate et le Tigre, p. 98, 99.)]

[Footnote 82: Recollect the successful and applauded rashness of Agathocles and Cortez, who burnt their ships on the coast of Africa and Mexico.]

The cumbersome train of artillery and wagons, which retards the operations of a modern army, were in a great measure unknown in the camps of the Romans. [83] Yet, in every age, the subsistence of sixty thousand men must have been one of the most important cares of a prudent general; and that subsistence could only be drawn from his own or from the enemy's country. Had it been possible for Julian to maintain a bridge of communication on the Tigris, and to preserve the conquered places of Assyria, a desolated province could not afford any large or regular supplies, in a season of the year when the lands were covered by the inundation of the Euphrates, [84] and the unwholesome air was darkened with swarms of innumerable insects. [85] The appearance of the hostile country was far more inviting. The extensive region that lies between the River Tigris and the mountains of Media, was filled with villages and towns; and the fertile soil, for the most part, was in a very improved state of cultivation. Julian might expect, that a conqueror, who possessed the two forcible instruments of persuasion, steel and gold, would easily procure a plentiful subsistence from the fears or avarice of the natives. But, on the approach of the Romans, the rich and smiling prospect was instantly blasted. Wherever they moved, the inhabitants deserted the open villages, and took shelter in the fortified towns; the cattle was driven away; the grass and ripe corn were consumed with fire; and, as soon as the flames had subsided which interrupted the march of Julian, he beheld the melancholy face of a smoking and naked desert. This desperate but effectual method of defence can only be executed by the enthusiasm of a people who prefer their independence to their property; or by the rigor of an arbitrary government, which consults the public safety without submitting to their inclinations the liberty of choice. On the present occasion the zeal and obedience of the Persians seconded the commands of Sapor; and the emperor was soon reduced to the scanty stock of provisions, which continually wasted in his hands. Before they were entirely consumed, he might still have reached the wealthy and unwarlike cities of Ecbatana or Susa, by the effort of a rapid and well-directed march; [86] but he was deprived of this last resource by his ignorance of the roads, and by the perfidy of his guides. The Romans wandered several days in the country to the eastward of Bagdad; the Persian deserter, who had artfully led them into the spare, escaped from their resentment; and his followers, as soon as they were put to the torture, confessed the secret of the conspiracy. The visionary conquests of Hyrcania and India, which had so long amused, now tormented, the mind of Julian. Conscious that his own imprudence was the cause of the public distress, he anxiously balanced the hopes of safety or success, without obtaining a satisfactory answer, either from gods or men. At length, as the only practicable measure, he embraced the resolution of directing his steps towards the banks of the Tigris, with the design of saving the army by a hasty march to the confines of Corduene; a fertile and friendly province, which acknowledged the sovereignty of Rome. The desponding troops obeyed the signal of the retreat, only seventy days after they had passed the Chaboras, with the sanguine expectation of subverting the throne of Persia. [87]

[Footnote 83: See the judicious reflections of the author of the Essai sur la Tactique, tom. ii. p. 287-353, and the learned remarks of M. Guichardt Nouveaux Memoires Militaires, tom. i. p. 351-382, on the baggage and subsistence of the Roman armies.]

[Footnote 84: The Tigris rises to the south, the Euphrates to the north, of the Armenian mountains. The former overflows in March, the latter in July. These circumstances are well explained in the Geographical Dissertation of Foster, inserted in Spelman's Expedition of Cyras, vol. ii. p. 26.]

[Footnote 85: Ammianus (xxiv. 8) describes, as he had felt, the inconveniency of the flood, the heat, and the insects. The lands of Assyria, oppressed by the Turks, and ravaged by the Curds or Arabs, yield an increase of ten, fifteen, and twenty fold, for the seed which is cast into the ground by the wretched and unskillful husbandmen. Voyage de Niebuhr, tom. ii. p. 279, 285.]

[Footnote 86: Isidore of Charax (Mansion. Parthic. p. 5, 6, in Hudson, Geograph. Minor. tom. ii.) reckons 129 schaeni from Seleucia, and Thevenot, (part i. l. i. ii. p. 209-245,) 128 hours of march from Bagdad to Ecbatana, or Hamadan. These measures cannot exceed an ordinary parasang, or three Roman miles.]

[Footnote 87: The march of Julian from Ctesiphon is circumstantially, but not clearly, described by Ammianus, (xxiv. 7, 8,) Libanius, (Orat. Parent. c. 134, p. 357,) and Zosimus, (l. iii. p. 183.) The two last seem ignorant that their conqueror was retreating; and Libanius absurdly confines him to the banks of the Tigris.]

As long as the Romans seemed to advance into the country, their march was observed and insulted from a distance, by several bodies of Persian cavalry; who, showing themselves sometimes in loose, and sometimes in close order, faintly skirmished with the advanced guards. These detachments were, however, supported by a much greater force; and the heads of the columns were no sooner pointed towards the Tigris than a cloud of dust arose on the plain. The Romans, who now aspired only to the permission of a safe and speedy retreat, endeavored to persuade themselves, that this formidable appearance was occasioned by a troop of wild asses, or perhaps by the approach of some friendly Arabs. They halted, pitched their tents, fortified their camp, passed the whole night in continual alarms; and discovered at the dawn of day, that they were surrounded by an army of Persians. This army, which might be considered only as the van of the Barbarians, was soon followed by the main body of cuirassiers, archers, and elephants, commanded by Meranes, a general of rank and reputation. He was accompanied by two of the king's sons, and many of the principal satraps; and fame and expectation exaggerated the strength of the remaining powers, which slowly advanced under the conduct of Sapor himself. As the Romans continued their march, their long array, which was forced to bend or divide, according to the varieties of the ground, afforded frequent and favorable opportunities to their vigilant enemies. The Persians repeatedly charged with fury; they were repeatedly repulsed with firmness; and the action at Maronga, which almost deserved the name of a battle, was marked by a considerable loss of satraps and elephants, perhaps of equal value in the eyes of their monarch. These splendid advantages were not obtained without an adequate slaughter on the side of the Romans: several officers of distinction were either killed or wounded; and the emperor himself, who, on all occasions of danger, inspired and guided the valor of his troops, was obliged to expose his person, and exert his abilities. The weight of offensive and defensive arms, which still constituted the strength and safety of the Romans, disabled them from making any long or effectual pursuit; and as the horsemen of the East were trained to dart their javelins, and shoot their arrows, at full speed, and in every possible direction, [88] the cavalry of Persia was never more formidable than in the moment of a rapid and disorderly flight. But the most certain and irreparable loss of the Romans was that of time. The hardy veterans, accustomed to the cold climate of Gaul and Germany, fainted under the sultry heat of an Assyrian summer; their vigor was exhausted by the incessant repetition of march and combat; and the progress of the army was suspended by the precautions of a slow and dangerous retreat, in the presence of an active enemy. Every day, every hour, as the supply diminished, the value and price of subsistence increased in the Roman camp. [89] Julian, who always contented himself with such food as a hungry soldier would have disdained, distributed, for the use of the troops, the provisions of the Imperial household, and whatever could be spared, from the sumpter-horses, of the tribunes and generals. But this feeble relief served only to aggravate the sense of the public distress; and the Romans began to entertain the most gloomy apprehensions that, before they could reach the frontiers of the empire, they should all perish, either by famine, or by the sword of the Barbarians. [90]

[Footnote 88: Chardin, the most judicious of modern travellers, describes (tom. ii. p. 57, 58, &c., edit. in 4to.) the education and dexterity of the Persian horsemen. Brissonius (de Regno Persico, p. 650 651, &c.,) has collected the testimonies of antiquity.]

[Footnote 89: In Mark Antony's retreat, an attic choenix sold for fifty drachmae, or, in other words, a pound of flour for twelve or fourteen shillings barley bread was sold for its weight in silver. It is impossible to peruse the interesting narrative of Plutarch, (tom. v. p. 102-116,) without perceiving that Mark Antony and Julian were pursued by the same enemies, and involved in the same distress.]

[Footnote 90: Ammian. xxiv. 8, xxv. 1. Zosimus, l. iii. p. 184, 185, 186. Libanius, Orat. Parent. c. 134, 135, p. 357, 358, 359. The sophist of Antioch appears ignorant that the troops were hungry.]

While Julian struggled with the almost insuperable difficulties of his situation, the silent hours of the night were still devoted to study and contemplation. Whenever he closed his eyes in short and interrupted slumbers, his mind was agitated with painful anxiety; nor can it be thought surprising, that the Genius of the empire should once more appear before him, covering with a funeral veil his head, and his horn of abundance, and slowly retiring from the Imperial tent. The monarch started from his couch, and stepping forth to refresh his wearied spirits with the coolness of the midnight air, he beheld a fiery meteor, which shot athwart the sky, and suddenly vanished. Julian was convinced that he had seen the menacing countenance of the god of war; [91] the council which he summoned, of Tuscan Haruspices, [92] unanimously pronounced that he should abstain from action; but on this occasion, necessity and reason were more prevalent than superstition; and the trumpets sounded at the break of day. The army marched through a hilly country; and the hills had been secretly occupied by the Persians. Julian led the van with the skill and attention of a consummate general; he was alarmed by the intelligence that his rear was suddenly attacked. The heat of the weather had tempted him to lay aside his cuirass; but he snatched a shield from one of his attendants, and hastened, with a sufficient reenforcement, to the relief of the rear-guard. A similar danger recalled the intrepid prince to the defence of the front; and, as he galloped through the columns, the centre of the left was attacked, and almost overpowered by the furious charge of the Persian cavalry and elephants. This huge body was soon defeated, by the well-timed evolution of the light infantry, who aimed their weapons, with dexterity and effect, against the backs of the horsemen, and the legs of the elephants. The Barbarians fled; and Julian, who was foremost in every danger, animated the pursuit with his voice and gestures. His trembling guards, scattered and oppressed by the disorderly throng of friends and enemies, reminded their fearless sovereign that he was without armor; and conjured him to decline the fall of the impending ruin. As they exclaimed, [93] a cloud of darts and arrows was discharged from the flying squadrons; and a javelin, after razing the skin of his arm, transpierced the ribs, and fixed in the inferior part of the liver. Julian attempted to draw the deadly weapon from his side; but his fingers were cut by the sharpness of the steel, and he fell senseless from his horse. His guards flew to his relief; and the wounded emperor was gently raised from the ground, and conveyed out of the tumult of the battle into an adjacent tent. The report of the melancholy event passed from rank to rank; but the grief of the Romans inspired them with invincible valor, and the desire of revenge. The bloody and obstinate conflict was maintained by the two armies, till they were separated by the total darkness of the night. The Persians derived some honor from the advantage which they obtained against the left wing, where Anatolius, master of the offices, was slain, and the praefect Sallust very narrowly escaped. But the event of the day was adverse to the Barbarians. They abandoned the field; their two generals, Meranes and Nohordates, [94] fifty nobles or satraps, and a multitude of their bravest soldiers; and the success of the Romans, if Julian had survived, might have been improved into a decisive and useful victory.

[Footnote 91: Ammian. xxv. 2. Julian had sworn in a passion, nunquam se Marti sacra facturum, (xxiv. 6.) Such whimsical quarrels were not uncommon between the gods and their insolent votaries; and even the prudent Augustus, after his fleet had been twice shipwrecked, excluded Neptune from the honors of public processions. See Hume's Philosophical Reflections. Essays, vol. ii. p. 418.]

[Footnote 92: They still retained the monopoly of the vain but lucrative science, which had been invented in Hetruria; and professed to derive their knowledge of signs and omens from the ancient books of Tarquitius, a Tuscan sage.]

[Footnote 93: Clambant hinc inde candidati (see the note of Valesius) quos terror, ut fugientium molem tanquam ruinam male compositi culminis declinaret. Ammian. xxv 3.]

[Footnote 94: Sapor himself declared to the Romans, that it was his practice to comfort the families of his deceased satraps, by sending them, as a present, the heads of the guards and officers who had not fallen by their master's side. Libanius, de nece Julian. ulcis. c. xiii. p. 163.]

The first words that Julian uttered, after his recovery from the fainting fit into which he had been thrown by loss of blood, were expressive of his martial spirit. He called for his horse and arms, and was impatient to rush into the battle. His remaining strength was exhausted by the painful effort; and the surgeons, who examined his wound, discovered the symptoms of approaching death. He employed the awful moments with the firm temper of a hero and a sage; the philosophers who had accompanied him in this fatal expedition, compared the tent of Julian with the prison of Socrates; and the spectators, whom duty, or friendship, or curiosity, had assembled round his couch, listened with respectful grief to the funeral oration of their dying emperor. [95] "Friends and fellow-soldiers, the seasonable period of my departure is now arrived, and I discharge, with the cheerfulness of a ready debtor, the demands of nature. I have learned from philosophy, how much the soul is more excellent than the body; and that the separation of the nobler substance should be the subject of joy, rather than of affliction. I have learned from religion, that an early death has often been the reward of piety; [96] and I accept, as a favor of the gods, the mortal stroke that secures me from the danger of disgracing a character, which has hitherto been supported by virtue and fortitude. I die without remorse, as I have lived without guilt. I am pleased to reflect on the innocence of my private life; and I can affirm with confidence, that the supreme authority, that emanation of the Divine Power, has been preserved in my hands pure and immaculate. Detesting the corrupt and destructive maxims of despotism, I have considered the happiness of the people as the end of government. Submitting my actions to the laws of prudence, of justice, and of moderation, I have trusted the event to the care of Providence. Peace was the object of my counsels, as long as peace was consistent with the public welfare; but when the imperious voice of my country summoned me to arms, I exposed my person to the dangers of war, with the clear foreknowledge (which I had acquired from the art of divination) that I was destined to fall by the sword. I now offer my tribute of gratitude to the Eternal Being, who has not suffered me to perish by the cruelty of a tyrant, by the secret dagger of conspiracy, or by the slow tortures of lingering disease. He has given me, in the midst of an honorable career, a splendid and glorious departure from this world; and I hold it equally absurd, equally base, to solicit, or to decline, the stroke of fate. This much I have attempted to say; but my strength fails me, and I feel the approach of death. I shall cautiously refrain from any word that may tend to influence your suffrages in the election of an emperor. My choice might be imprudent or injudicious; and if it should not be ratified by the consent of the army, it might be fatal to the person whom I should recommend. I shall only, as a good citizen, express my hopes, that the Romans may be blessed with the government of a virtuous sovereign." After this discourse, which Julian pronounced in a firm and gentle tone of voice, he distributed, by a military testament, [97] the remains of his private fortune; and making some inquiry why Anatolius was not present, he understood, from the answer of Sallust, that Anatolius was killed; and bewailed, with amiable inconsistency, the loss of his friend. At the same time he reproved the immoderate grief of the spectators; and conjured them not to disgrace, by unmanly tears, the fate of a prince, who in a few moments would be united with heaven, and with the stars. [98] The spectators were silent; and Julian entered into a metaphysical argument with the philosophers Priscus and Maximus, on the nature of the soul. The efforts which he made, of mind as well as body, most probably hastened his death. His wound began to bleed with fresh violence; his respiration was embarrassed by the swelling of the veins; he called for a draught of cold water, and, as soon as he had drank it, expired without pain, about the hour of midnight. Such was the end of that extraordinary man, in the thirty-second year of his age, after a reign of one year and about eight months, from the death of Constantius. In his last moments he displayed, perhaps with some ostentation, the love of virtue and of fame, which had been the ruling passions of his life. [99]

[Footnote 95: The character and situation of Julian might countenance the suspicion that he had previously composed the elaborate oration, which Ammianus heard, and has transcribed. The version of the Abbe de la Bleterie is faithful and elegant. I have followed him in expressing the Platonic idea of emanations, which is darkly insinuated in the original.]

[Footnote 96: Herodotus (l. i. c. 31,) has displayed that doctrine in an agreeable tale. Yet the Jupiter, (in the 16th book of the Iliad,) who laments with tears of blood the death of Sarpedon his son, had a very imperfect notion of happiness or glory beyond the grave.]

[Footnote 97: The soldiers who made their verbal or nuncupatory testaments, upon actual service, (in procinctu,) were exempted from the formalities of the Roman law. See Heineccius, (Antiquit. Jur. Roman. tom. i. p. 504,) and Montesquieu, (Esprit des Loix, l. xxvii.)]

[Footnote 98: This union of the human soul with the divine aethereal substance of the universe, is the ancient doctrine of Pythagoras and Plato: but it seems to exclude any personal or conscious immortality. See Warburton's learned and rational observations. Divine Legation, vol ii. p. 199-216.]

[Footnote 99: The whole relation of the death of Julian is given by Ammianus, (xxv. 3,) an intelligent spectator. Libanius, who turns with horror from the scene, has supplied some circumstances, (Orat. Parental. c 136-140, p. 359-362.) The calumnies of Gregory, and the legends of more recent saints, may now be silently despised. Note: A very remarkable fragment of Eunapius describes, not without spirit, the struggle between the terror of the army on account of their perilous situation, and their grief for the death of Julian. "Even the vulgar felt that they would soon provide a general, but such a general as Julian they would never find, even though a god in the form of man—Julian, who, with a mind equal to the divinity, triumphed over the evil propensities of human nature,—who held commerce with immaterial beings while yet in the material body—who condescended to rule because a ruler was necessary to the welfare of mankind." Mai, Nov. Coll. ii. 261. Eunapius in Niebuhr, 69.]

The triumph of Christianity, and the calamities of the empire, may, in some measure, be ascribed to Julian himself, who had neglected to secure the future execution of his designs, by the timely and judicious nomination of an associate and successor. But the royal race of Constantius Chlorus was reduced to his own person; and if he entertained any serious thoughts of investing with the purple the most worthy among the Romans, he was diverted from his resolution by the difficulty of the choice, the jealousy of power, the fear of ingratitude, and the natural presumption of health, of youth, and of prosperity. His unexpected death left the empire without a master, and without an heir, in a state of perplexity and danger, which, in the space of fourscore years, had never been experienced, since the election of Diocletian. In a government which had almost forgotten the distinction of pure and noble blood, the superiority of birth was of little moment; the claims of official rank were accidental and precarious; and the candidates, who might aspire to ascend the vacant throne could be supported only by the consciousness of personal merit, or by the hopes of popular favor. But the situation of a famished army, encompassed on all sides by a host of Barbarians, shortened the moments of grief and deliberation. In this scene of terror and distress, the body of the deceased prince, according to his own directions, was decently embalmed; and, at the dawn of day, the generals convened a military senate, at which the commanders of the legions, and the officers both of cavalry and infantry, were invited to assist. Three or four hours of the night had not passed away without some secret cabals; and when the election of an emperor was proposed, the spirit of faction began to agitate the assembly. Victor and Arinthaeus collected the remains of the court of Constantius; the friends of Julian attached themselves to the Gallic chiefs, Dagalaiphus and Nevitta; and the most fatal consequences might be apprehended from the discord of two factions, so opposite in their character and interest, in their maxims of government, and perhaps in their religious principles. The superior virtues of Sallust could alone reconcile their divisions, and unite their suffrages; and the venerable praefect would immediately have been declared the successor of Julian, if he himself, with sincere and modest firmness, had not alleged his age and infirmities, so unequal to the weight of the diadem. The generals, who were surprised and perplexed by his refusal, showed some disposition to adopt the salutary advice of an inferior officer, [100] that they should act as they would have acted in the absence of the emperor; that they should exert their abilities to extricate the army from the present distress; and, if they were fortunate enough to reach the confines of Mesopotamia, they should proceed with united and deliberate counsels in the election of a lawful sovereign. While they debated, a few voices saluted Jovian, who was no more than first [101] of the domestics, with the names of Emperor and Augustus. The tumultuary acclamation [101a] was instantly repeated by the guards who surrounded the tent, and passed, in a few minutes, to the extremities of the line. The new prince, astonished with his own fortune was hastily invested with the Imperial ornaments, and received an oath of fidelity from the generals, whose favor and protection he so lately solicited. The strongest recommendation of Jovian was the merit of his father, Count Varronian, who enjoyed, in honorable retirement, the fruit of his long services. In the obscure freedom of a private station, the son indulged his taste for wine and women; yet he supported, with credit, the character of a Christian [102] and a soldier. Without being conspicuous for any of the ambitious qualifications which excite the admiration and envy of mankind, the comely person of Jovian, his cheerful temper, and familiar wit, had gained the affection of his fellow-soldiers; and the generals of both parties acquiesced in a popular election, which had not been conducted by the arts of their enemies. The pride of this unexpected elevation was moderated by the just apprehension, that the same day might terminate the life and reign of the new emperor. The pressing voice of necessity was obeyed without delay; and the first orders issued by Jovian, a few hours after his predecessor had expired, were to prosecute a march, which could alone extricate the Romans from their actual distress. [103]

[Footnote 100: Honoratior aliquis miles; perhaps Ammianus himself. The modest and judicious historian describes the scene of the election, at which he was undoubtedly present, (xxv. 5.)]

[Footnote 101: The primus or primicerius enjoyed the dignity of a senator, and though only a tribune, he ranked with the military dukes. Cod. Theodosian. l. vi. tit. xxiv. These privileges are perhaps more recent than the time of Jovian.]

[Footnote 101a: The soldiers supposed that the acclamations proclaimed the name of Julian, restored, as they fondly thought, to health, not that of Jovian. loc—M.]

[Footnote 102: The ecclesiastical historians, Socrates, (l. iii. c. 22,) Sozomen, (l. vi. c. 3,) and Theodoret, (l. iv. c. 1,) ascribe to Jovian the merit of a confessor under the preceding reign; and piously suppose that he refused the purple, till the whole army unanimously exclaimed that they were Christians. Ammianus, calmly pursuing his narrative, overthrows the legend by a single sentence. Hostiis pro Joviano extisque inspectis, pronuntiatum est, &c., xxv. 6.]

[Footnote 103: Ammianus (xxv. 10) has drawn from the life an impartial portrait of Jovian; to which the younger Victor has added some remarkable strokes. The Abbe de la Bleterie (Histoire de Jovien, tom. i. p. 1-238) has composed an elaborate history of his short reign; a work remarkably distinguished by elegance of style, critical disquisition, and religious prejudice.]

PART V

The esteem of an enemy is most sincerely expressed by his fears; and the degree of fear may be accurately measured by the joy with which he celebrates his deliverance. The welcome news of the death of Julian, which a deserter revealed to the camp of Sapor, inspired the desponding monarch with a sudden confidence of victory. He immediately detached the royal cavalry, perhaps the ten thousand Immortals, [104] to second and support the pursuit; and discharged the whole weight of his united forces on the rear-guard of the Romans. The rear-guard was thrown into disorder; the renowned legions, which derived their titles from Diocletian, and his warlike colleague, were broke and trampled down by the elephants; and three tribunes lost their lives in attempting to stop the flight of their soldiers. The battle was at length restored by the persevering valor of the Romans; the Persians were repulsed with a great slaughter of men and elephants; and the army, after marching and fighting a long summer's day, arrived, in the evening, at Samara, on the banks of the Tigris, about one hundred miles above Ctesiphon. [105] On the ensuing day, the Barbarians, instead of harassing the march, attacked the camp, of Jovian; which had been seated in a deep and sequestered valley. From the hills, the archers of Persia insulted and annoyed the wearied legionaries; and a body of cavalry, which had penetrated with desperate courage through the Praetorian gate, was cut in pieces, after a doubtful conflict, near the Imperial tent. In the succeeding night, the camp of Carche was protected by the lofty dikes of the river; and the Roman army, though incessantly exposed to the vexatious pursuit of the Saracens, pitched their tents near the city of Dura, [106] four days after the death of Julian. The Tigris was still on their left; their hopes and provisions were almost consumed; and the impatient soldiers, who had fondly persuaded themselves that the frontiers of the empire were not far distant, requested their new sovereign, that they might be permitted to hazard the passage of the river. With the assistance of his wisest officers, Jovian endeavored to check their rashness; by representing, that if they possessed sufficient skill and vigor to stem the torrent of a deep and rapid stream, they would only deliver themselves naked and defenceless to the Barbarians, who had occupied the opposite banks, Yielding at length to their clamorous importunities, he consented, with reluctance, that five hundred Gauls and Germans, accustomed from their infancy to the waters of the Rhine and Danube, should attempt the bold adventure, which might serve either as an encouragement, or as a warning, for the rest of the army. In the silence of the night, they swam the Tigris, surprised an unguarded post of the enemy, and displayed at the dawn of day the signal of their resolution and fortune. The success of this trial disposed the emperor to listen to the promises of his architects, who propose to construct a floating bridge of the inflated skins of sheep, oxen, and goats, covered with a floor of earth and fascines. [107] Two important days were spent in the ineffectual labor; and the Romans, who already endured the miseries of famine, cast a look of despair on the Tigris, and upon the Barbarians; whose numbers and obstinacy increased with the distress of the Imperial army. [108]

[Footnote 104: Regius equitatus. It appears, from Irocopius, that the Immortals, so famous under Cyrus and his successors, were revived, if we may use that improper word, by the Sassanides. Brisson de Regno Persico, p. 268, &c.]

[Footnote 105: The obscure villages of the inland country are irrecoverably lost; nor can we name the field of battle where Julian fell: but M. D'Anville has demonstrated the precise situation of Sumere, Carche, and Dura, along the banks of the Tigris, (Geographie Ancienne, tom. ii. p. 248 L'Euphrate et le Tigre, p. 95, 97.) In the ninth century, Sumere, or Samara, became, with a slight change of name, the royal residence of the khalifs of the house of Abbas. Note: Sormanray, called by the Arabs Samira, where D'Anville placed Samara, is too much to the south; and is a modern town built by Caliph Morasen. Serraman-rai means, in Arabic, it rejoices every one who sees it. St. Martin, iii. 133—M.]

[Footnote 106: Dura was a fortified place in the wars of Antiochus against the rebels of Media and Persia, (Polybius, l. v. c. 48, 52, p. 548, 552 edit. Casaubon, in 8vo.)]

[Footnote 107: A similar expedient was proposed to the leaders of the ten thousand, and wisely rejected. Xenophon, Anabasis, l. iii. p. 255, 256, 257. It appears, from our modern travellers, that rafts floating on bladders perform the trade and navigation of the Tigris.]

[Footnote 108: The first military acts of the reign of Jovian are related by Ammianus, (xxv. 6,) Libanius, (Orat. Parent. c. 146, p. 364,) and Zosimus, (l. iii. p. 189, 190, 191.) Though we may distrust the fairness of Libanius, the ocular testimony of Eutropius (uno a Persis atque altero proelio victus, x. 17) must incline us to suspect that Ammianus had been too jealous of the honor of the Roman arms.]

In this hopeless condition, the fainting spirits of the Romans were revived by the sound of peace. The transient presumption of Sapor had vanished: he observed, with serious concern, that, in the repetition of doubtful combats, he had lost his most faithful and intrepid nobles, his bravest troops, and the greatest part of his train of elephants: and the experienced monarch feared to provoke the resistance of despair, the vicissitudes of fortune, and the unexhausted powers of the Roman empire; which might soon advance to elieve, or to revenge, the successor of Julian. The Surenas himself, accompanied by another satrap, appeared in the camp of Jovian; [109] and declared, that the clemency of his sovereign was not averse to signify the conditions on which he would consent to spare and to dismiss the Caesar with the relics of his captive army. [109a] The hopes of safety subdued the firmness of the Romans; the emperor was compelled, by the advice of his council, and the cries of his soldiers, to embrace the offer of peace; [109b] and the praefect Sallust was immediately sent, with the general Arinthaeus, to understand the pleasure of the Great King. The crafty Persian delayed, under various pretenses, the conclusion of the agreement; started difficulties, required explanations, suggested expedients, receded from his concessions, increased his demands, and wasted four days in the arts of negotiation, till he had consumed the stock of provisions which yet remained in the camp of the Romans. Had Jovian been capable of executing a bold and prudent measure, he would have continued his march, with unremitting diligence; the progress of the treaty would have suspended the attacks of the Barbarians; and, before the expiration of the fourth day, he might have safely reached the fruitful province of Corduene, at the distance only of one hundred miles. [110] The irresolute emperor, instead of breaking through the toils of the enemy, expected his fate with patient resignation; and accepted the humiliating conditions of peace, which it was no longer in his power to refuse. The five provinces beyond the Tigris, which had been ceded by the grandfather of Sapor, were restored to the Persian monarchy. He acquired, by a single article, the impregnable city of Nisibis; which had sustained, in three successive sieges, the effort of his arms. Singara, and the castle of the Moors, one of the strongest places of Mesopotamia, were likewise dismembered from the empire. It was considered as an indulgence, that the inhabitants of those fortresses were permitted to retire with their effects; but the conqueror rigorously insisted, that the Romans should forever abandon the king and kingdom of Armenia. [110a] A peace, or rather a long truce, of thirty years, was stipulated between the hostile nations; the faith of the treaty was ratified by solemn oaths and religious ceremonies; and hostages of distinguished rank were reciprocally delivered to secure the performance of the conditions. [111]

[Footnote 109: Sextus Rufus (de Provinciis, c. 29) embraces a poor subterfuge of national vanity. Tanta reverentia nominis Romani fuit, ut a Persis primus de pace sermo haberetur. —He is called Junius by John Malala; the same, M. St. Martin conjectures, with a satrap of Gordyene named Jovianus, or Jovinianus; mentioned in Ammianus Marcellinus, xviii. 6—M.]

[Footnote 109a: The Persian historians couch the message of Shah-pour in these Oriental terms: "I have reassembled my numerous army. I am resolved to revenge my subjects, who have been plundered, made captives, and slain. It is for this that I have bared my arm, and girded my loins. If you consent to pay the price of the blood which has been shed, to deliver up the booty which has been plundered, and to restore the city of Nisibis, which is in Irak, and belongs to our empire, though now in your possession, I will sheathe the sword of war; but should you refuse these terms, the hoofs of my horse, which are hard as steel, shall efface the name of the Romans from the earth; and my glorious cimeter, that destroys like fire, shall exterminate the people of your empire." These authorities do not mention the death of Julian. Malcolm's Persia, i. 87—M.]

[Footnote 109b: The Paschal chronicle, not, as M. St. Martin says, supported by John Malala, places the mission of this ambassador before the death of Julian. The king of Persia was then in Persarmenia, ignorant of the death of Julian; he only arrived at the army subsequent to that event. St. Martin adopts this view, and finds or extorts support for it, from Libanius and Ammianus, iii. 158—M.]

[Footnote 110: It is presumptuous to controvert the opinion of Ammianus, a soldier and a spectator. Yet it is difficult to understand how the mountains of Corduene could extend over the plains of Assyria, as low as the conflux of the Tigris and the great Zab; or how an army of sixty thousand men could march one hundred miles in four days. Note: Yet this appears to be the case (in modern maps:) the march is the difficulty—M.]

[Footnote 110a: Sapor availed himself, a few years after, of the dissolution of the alliance between the Romans and the Armenians. See St. M. iii. 163—M.]

[Footnote 111: The treaty of Dura is recorded with grief or indignation by Ammianus, (xxv. 7,) Libanius, (Orat. Parent. c. 142, p. 364,) Zosimus, (l. iii. p. 190, 191,) Gregory Nazianzen, (Orat. iv. p. 117, 118, who imputes the distress to Julian, the deliverance to Jovian,) and Eutropius, (x. 17.) The last-mentioned writer, who was present in military station, styles this peace necessarium quidem sed ignoblem.]

The sophist of Antioch, who saw with indignation the sceptre of his hero in the feeble hand of a Christian successor, professes to admire the moderation of Sapor, in contenting himself with so small a portion of the Roman empire. If he had stretched as far as the Euphrates the claims of his ambition, he might have been secure, says Libanius, of not meeting with a refusal. If he had fixed, as the boundary of Persia, the Orontes, the Cydnus, the Sangarius, or even the Thracian Bosphorus, flatterers would not have been wanting in the court of Jovian to convince the timid monarch, that his remaining provinces would still afford the most ample gratifications of power and luxury. [112] Without adopting in its full force this malicious insinuation, we must acknowledge, that the conclusion of so ignominious a treaty was facilitated by the private ambition of Jovian. The obscure domestic, exalted to the throne by fortune, rather than by merit, was impatient to escape from the hands of the Persians, that he might prevent the designs of Procopius, who commanded the army of Mesopotamia, and establish his doubtful reign over the legions and provinces which were still ignorant of the hasty and tumultuous choice of the camp beyond the Tigris. [113] In the neighborhood of the same river, at no very considerable distance from the fatal station of Dura, [114] the ten thousand Greeks, without generals, or guides, or provisions, were abandoned, above twelve hundred miles from their native country, to the resentment of a victorious monarch. The difference of their conduct and success depended much more on their character than on their situation. Instead of tamely resigning themselves to the secret deliberations and private views of a single person, the united councils of the Greeks were inspired by the generous enthusiasm of a popular assembly; where the mind of each citizen is filled with the love of glory, the pride of freedom, and the contempt of death. Conscious of their superiority over the Barbarians in arms and discipline, they disdained to yield, they refused to capitulate: every obstacle was surmounted by their patience, courage, and military skill; and the memorable retreat of the ten thousand exposed and insulted the weakness of the Persian monarchy. [115]

[Footnote 112: Libanius, Orat. Parent. c. 143, p. 364, 365.]

[Footnote 113: Conditionibus..... dispendiosis Romanae reipublicae impositis.... quibus cupidior regni quam gloriae Jovianus, imperio rudis, adquievit. Sextus Rufus de Provinciis, c. 29. La Bleterie has expressed, in a long, direct oration, these specious considerations of public and private interest, (Hist. de Jovien, tom. i. p. 39, &c.)]

[Footnote 114: The generals were murdered on the bauks of the Zabatus, (Ana basis, l. ii. p. 156, l. iii. p. 226,) or great Zab, a river of Assyria, 400 feet broad, which falls into the Tigris fourteen hours below Mosul. The error of the Greeks bestowed on the greater and lesser Zab the names of the Wolf, (Lycus,) and the Goat, (Capros.) They created these animals to attend the Tiger of the East.]

[Footnote 115: The Cyropoedia is vague and languid; the Anabasis circumstance and animated. Such is the eternal difference between fiction and truth.]

As the price of his disgraceful concessions, the emperor might perhaps have stipulated, that the camp of the hungry Romans should be plentifully supplied; [116] and that they should be permitted to pass the Tigris on the bridge which was constructed by the hands of the Persians. But, if Jovian presumed to solicit those equitable terms, they were sternly refused by the haughty tyrant of the East, whose clemency had pardoned the invaders of his country. The Saracens sometimes intercepted the stragglers of the march; but the generals and troops of Sapor respected the cessation of arms; and Jovian was suffered to explore the most convenient place for the passage of the river. The small vessels, which had been saved from the conflagration of the fleet, performed the most essential service. They first conveyed the emperor and his favorites; and afterwards transported, in many successive voyages, a great part of the army. But, as every man was anxious for his personal safety, and apprehensive of being left on the hostile shore, the soldiers, who were too impatient to wait the slow returns of the boats, boldly ventured themselves on light hurdles, or inflated skins; and, drawing after them their horses, attempted, with various success, to swim across the river. Many of these daring adventurers were swallowed by the waves; many others, who were carried along by the violence of the stream, fell an easy prey to the avarice or cruelty of the wild Arabs: and the loss which the army sustained in the passage of the Tigris, was not inferior to the carnage of a day of battle. As soon as the Romans were landed on the western bank, they were delivered from the hostile pursuit of the Barbarians; but, in a laborious march of two hundred miles over the plains of Mesopotamia, they endured the last extremities of thirst and hunger. They were obliged to traverse the sandy desert, which, in the extent of seventy miles, did not afford a single blade of sweet grass, nor a single spring of fresh water; and the rest of the inhospitable waste was untrod by the footsteps either of friends or enemies. Whenever a small measure of flour could be discovered in the camp, twenty pounds weight were greedily purchased with ten pieces of gold: [117] the beasts of burden were slaughtered and devoured; and the desert was strewed with the arms and baggage of the Roman soldiers, whose tattered garments and meagre countenances displayed their past sufferings and actual misery. A small convoy of provisions advanced to meet the army as far as the castle of Ur; and the supply was the more grateful, since it declared the fidelity of Sebastian and Procopius. At Thilsaphata, [118] the emperor most graciously received the generals of Mesopotamia; and the remains of a once flourishing army at length reposed themselves under the walls of Nisibis. The messengers of Jovian had already proclaimed, in the language of flattery, his election, his treaty, and his return; and the new prince had taken the most effectual measures to secure the allegiance of the armies and provinces of Europe, by placing the military command in the hands of those officers, who, from motives of interest, or inclination, would firmly support the cause of their benefactor. [119]

[Footnote 116: According to Rufinus, an immediate supply of provisions was stipulated by the treaty, and Theodoret affirms, that the obligation was faithfully discharged by the Persians. Such a fact is probable but undoubtedly false. See Tillemont, Hist. des Empereurs, tom. iv. p. 702.]

[Footnote 117: We may recollect some lines of Lucan, (Pharsal. iv. 95,) who describes a similar distress of Caesar's army in Spain:—Saeva fames aderat—Miles eget: toto censu non prodigus emit Exiguam Cererem. Proh lucri pallida tabes! Non deest prolato jejunus venditor auro. See Guichardt (Nouveaux Memoires Militaires, tom. i. p. 370-382.) His analysis of the two campaigns in Spain and Africa is the noblest monument that has ever been raised to the fame of Caesar.]

[Footnote 118: M. d'Anville (see his Maps, and l'Euphrate et le Tigre, p. 92, 93) traces their march, and assigns the true position of Hatra, Ur, and Thilsaphata, which Ammianus has mentioned. —He does not complain of the Samiel, the deadly hot wind, which Thevenot (Voyages, part ii. l. i. p. 192) so much dreaded. —Hatra, now Kadhr. Ur, Kasr or Skervidgi. Thilsaphata is unknown—M.]

[Footnote 119: The retreat of Jovian is described by Ammianus, (xxv. 9,) Libanius, (Orat. Parent. c. 143, p. 365,) and Zosimus, (l. iii. p. 194.)]

The friends of Julian had confidently announced the success of his expedition. They entertained a fond persuasion that the temples of the gods would be enriched with the spoils of the East; that Persia would be reduced to the humble state of a tributary province, governed by the laws and magistrates of Rome; that the Barbarians would adopt the dress, and manners, and language of their conquerors; and that the youth of Ecbatana and Susa would study the art of rhetoric under Grecian masters. [120] The progress of the arms of Julian interrupted his communication with the empire; and, from the moment that he passed the Tigris, his affectionate subjects were ignorant of the fate and fortunes of their prince. Their contemplation of fancied triumphs was disturbed by the melancholy rumor of his death; and they persisted to doubt, after they could no longer deny, the truth of that fatal event. [121] The messengers of Jovian promulgated the specious tale of a prudent and necessary peace; the voice of fame, louder and more sincere, revealed the disgrace of the emperor, and the conditions of the ignominious treaty. The minds of the people were filled with astonishment and grief, with indignation and terror, when they were informed, that the unworthy successor of Julian relinquished the five provinces which had been acquired by the victory of Galerius; and that he shamefully surrendered to the Barbarians the important city of Nisibis, the firmest bulwark of the provinces of the East. [122] The deep and dangerous question, how far the public faith should be observed, when it becomes incompatible with the public safety, was freely agitated in popular conversation; and some hopes were entertained that the emperor would redeem his pusillanimous behavior by a splendid act of patriotic perfidy. The inflexible spirit of the Roman senate had always disclaimed the unequal conditions which were extorted from the distress of their captive armies; and, if it were necessary to satisfy the national honor, by delivering the guilty general into the hands of the Barbarians, the greatest part of the subjects of Jovian would have cheerfully acquiesced in the precedent of ancient times. [123]

[Footnote 120: Libanius, (Orat. Parent. c. 145, p. 366.) Such were the natural hopes and wishes of a rhetorician.]

[Footnote 121: The people of Carrhae, a city devoted to Paganism, buried the inauspicious messenger under a pile of stones, (Zosimus, l. iii. p. 196.) Libanius, when he received the fatal intelligence, cast his eye on his sword; but he recollected that Plato had condemned suicide, and that he must live to compose the Panegyric of Julian, (Libanius de Vita sua, tom. ii. p. 45, 46.)]

[Footnote 122: Ammianus and Eutropius may be admitted as fair and credible witnesses of the public language and opinions. The people of Antioch reviled an ignominious peace, which exposed them to the Persians, on a naked and defenceless frontier, (Excerpt. Valesiana, p. 845, ex Johanne Antiocheno.)]

[Footnote 123: The Abbe de la Bleterie, (Hist. de Jovien, tom. i. p. 212-227.) though a severe casuist, has pronounced that Jovian was not bound to execute his promise; since he could not dismember the empire, nor alienate, without their consent, the allegiance of his people. I have never found much delight or instruction in such political metaphysics.]

But the emperor, whatever might be the limits of his constitutional authority, was the absolute master of the laws and arms of the state; and the same motives which had forced him to subscribe, now pressed him to execute, the treaty of peace. He was impatient to secure an empire at the expense of a few provinces; and the respectable names of religion and honor concealed the personal fears and ambition of Jovian. Notwithstanding the dutiful solicitations of the inhabitants, decency, as well as prudence, forbade the emperor to lodge in the palace of Nisibis; but the next morning after his arrival. Bineses, the ambassador of Persia, entered the place, displayed from the citadel the standard of the Great King, and proclaimed, in his name, the cruel alternative of exile or servitude. The principal citizens of Nisibis, who, till that fatal moment, had confided in the protection of their sovereign, threw themselves at his feet. They conjured him not to abandon, or, at least, not to deliver, a faithful colony to the rage of a Barbarian tyrant, exasperated by the three successive defeats which he had experienced under the walls of Nisibis. They still possessed arms and courage to repel the invaders of their country: they requested only the permission of using them in their own defence; and, as soon as they had asserted their independence, they should implore the favor of being again admitted into the ranks of his subjects. Their arguments, their eloquence, their tears, were ineffectual. Jovian alleged, with some confusion, the sanctity of oaths; and, as the reluctance with which he accepted the present of a crown of gold, convinced the citizens of their hopeless condition, the advocate Sylvanus was provoked to exclaim, "O emperor! may you thus be crowned by all the cities of your dominions!" Jovian, who in a few weeks had assumed the habits of a prince, [124] was displeased with freedom, and offended with truth: and as he reasonably supposed, that the discontent of the people might incline them to submit to the Persian government, he published an edict, under pain of death, that they should leave the city within the term of three days. Ammianus has delineated in lively colors the scene of universal despair, which he seems to have viewed with an eye of compassion. [125] The martial youth deserted, with indignant grief, the walls which they had so gloriously defended: the disconsolate mourner dropped a last tear over the tomb of a son or husband, which must soon be profaned by the rude hand of a Barbarian master; and the aged citizen kissed the threshold, and clung to the doors, of the house where he had passed the cheerful and careless hours of infancy. The highways were crowded with a trembling multitude: the distinctions of rank, and sex, and age, were lost in the general calamity. Every one strove to bear away some fragment from the wreck of his fortunes; and as they could not command the immediate service of an adequate number of horses or wagons, they were obliged to leave behind them the greatest part of their valuable effects. The savage insensibility of Jovian appears to have aggravated the hardships of these unhappy fugitives. They were seated, however, in a new-built quarter of Amida; and that rising city, with the reenforcement of a very considerable colony, soon recovered its former splendor, and became the capital of Mesopotamia. [126] Similar orders were despatched by the emperor for the evacuation of Singara and the castle of the Moors; and for the restitution of the five provinces beyond the Tigris. Sapor enjoyed the glory and the fruits of his victory; and this ignominious peace has justly been considered as a memorable aera in the decline and fall of the Roman empire. The predecessors of Jovian had sometimes relinquished the dominion of distant and unprofitable provinces; but, since the foundation of the city, the genius of Rome, the god Terminus, who guarded the boundaries of the republic, had never retired before the sword of a victorious enemy. [127]

[Footnote 124: At Nisibis he performed a royal act. A brave officer, his namesake, who had been thought worthy of the purple, was dragged from supper, thrown into a well, and stoned to death without any form of trial or evidence of guilt. Anomian. xxv. 8.]

[Footnote 125: See xxv. 9, and Zosimus, l. iii. p. 194, 195.]

[Footnote 126: Chron. Paschal. p. 300. The ecclesiastical Notitie may be consulted.]

[Footnote 127: Zosimus, l. iii. p. 192, 193. Sextus Rufus de Provinciis, c. 29. Augustin de Civitat. Dei, l. iv. c. 29. This general position must be applied and interpreted with some caution.]

After Jovian had performed those engagements which the voice of his people might have tempted him to violate, he hastened away from the scene of his disgrace, and proceeded with his whole court to enjoy the luxury of Antioch. [128] Without consulting the dictates of religious zeal, he was prompted, by humanity and gratitude, to bestow the last honors on the remains of his deceased sovereign: [129] and Procopius, who sincerely bewailed the loss of his kinsman, was removed from the command of the army, under the decent pretence of conducting the funeral. The corpse of Julian was transported from Nisibis to Tarsus, in a slow march of fifteen days; and, as it passed through the cities of the East, was saluted by the hostile factions, with mournful lamentations and clamorous insults. The Pagans already placed their beloved hero in the rank of those gods whose worship he had restored; while the invectives of the Christians pursued the soul of the Apostate to hell, and his body to the grave. [130] One party lamented the approaching ruin of their altars; the other celebrated the marvellous deliverance of their church. The Christians applauded, in lofty and ambiguous strains, the stroke of divine vengeance, which had been so long suspended over the guilty head of Julian. They acknowledge, that the death of the tyrant, at the instant he expired beyond the Tigris, was revealed to the saints of Egypt, Syria, and Cappadocia; [131] and instead of suffering him to fall by the Persian darts, their indiscretion ascribed the heroic deed to the obscure hand of some mortal or immortal champion of the faith. [132] Such imprudent declarations were eagerly adopted by the malice, or credulity, of their adversaries; [133] who darkly insinuated, or confidently asserted, that the governors of the church had instigated and directed the fanaticism of a domestic assassin. [134] Above sixteen years after the death of Julian, the charge was solemnly and vehemently urged, in a public oration, addressed by Libanius to the emperor Theodosius. His suspicions are unsupported by fact or argument; and we can only esteem the generous zeal of the sophist of Antioch for the cold and neglected ashes of his friend. [135]

[Footnote 128: Ammianus, xxv. 9. Zosimus, l. iii. p. 196. He might be edax, vino Venerique indulgens. But I agree with La Bleterie (tom. i. p. 148-154) in rejecting the foolish report of a Bacchanalian riot (ap. Suidam) celebrated at Antioch, by the emperor, his wife, and a troop of concubines.]

[Footnote 129: The Abbe de la Bleterie (tom. i. p. 156-209) handsomely exposes the brutal bigotry of Baronius, who would have thrown Julian to the dogs, ne cespititia quidem sepultura dignus.]

[Footnote 130: Compare the sophist and the saint, (Libanius, Monod. tom. ii. p. 251, and Orat. Parent. c. 145, p. 367, c. 156, p. 377, with Gregory Nazianzen, Orat. iv. p. 125-132.) The Christian orator faintly mutters some exhortations to modesty and forgiveness; but he is well satisfied, that the real sufferings of Julian will far exceed the fabulous torments of Ixion or Tantalus.]

[Footnote 131: Tillemont (Hist. des Empereurs, tom. iv. p. 549) has collected these visions. Some saint or angel was observed to be absent in the night, on a secret expedition, &c.]

[Footnote 132: Sozomen (l. vi. 2) applauds the Greek doctrine of tyrannicide; but the whole passage, which a Jesuit might have translated, is prudently suppressed by the president Cousin.]

[Footnote 133: Immediately after the death of Julian, an uncertain rumor was scattered, telo cecidisse Romano. It was carried, by some deserters to the Persian camp; and the Romans were reproached as the assassins of the emperor by Sapor and his subjects, (Ammian. xxv. 6. Libanius de ulciscenda Juliani nece, c. xiii. p. 162, 163.) It was urged, as a decisive proof, that no Persian had appeared to claim the promised reward, (Liban. Orat. Parent. c. 141, p. 363.) But the flying horseman, who darted the fatal javelin, might be ignorant of its effect; or he might be slain in the same action. Ammianus neither feels nor inspires a suspicion.]

[Footnote 134: This dark and ambiguous expression may point to Athanasius, the first, without a rival, of the Christian clergy, (Libanius de ulcis. Jul. nece, c. 5, p. 149. La Bleterie, Hist. de Jovien, tom. i. p. 179.)]

[Footnote 135: The orator (Fabricius, Bibliot. Graec. tom. vii. p. 145-179) scatters suspicions, demands an inquiry, and insinuates, that proofs might still be obtained. He ascribes the success of the Huns to the criminal neglect of revenging Julian's death.]

It was an ancient custom in the funerals, as well as in the triumphs, of the Romans, that the voice of praise should be corrected by that of satire and ridicule; and that, in the midst of the splendid pageants, which displayed the glory of the living or of the dead, their imperfections should not be concealed from the eyes of the world. [136] This custom was practised in the funeral of Julian. The comedians, who resented his contempt and aversion for the theatre, exhibited, with the applause of a Christian audience, the lively and exaggerated representation of the faults and follies of the deceased emperor. His various character and singular manners afforded an ample scope for pleasantry and ridicule. [137] In the exercise of his uncommon talents, he often descended below the majesty of his rank. Alexander was transformed into Diogenes; the philosopher was degraded into a priest. The purity of his virtue was sullied by excessive vanity; his superstition disturbed the peace, and endangered the safety, of a mighty empire; and his irregular sallies were the less entitled to indulgence, as they appeared to be the laborious efforts of art, or even of affectation. The remains of Julian were interred at Tarsus in Cilicia; but his stately tomb, which arose in that city, on the banks of the cold and limpid Cydnus, [138] was displeasing to the faithful friends, who loved and revered the memory of that extraordinary man. The philosopher expressed a very reasonable wish, that the disciple of Plato might have reposed amidst the groves of the academy; [139] while the soldier exclaimed, in bolder accents, that the ashes of Julian should have been mingled with those of Caesar, in the field of Mars, and among the ancient monuments of Roman virtue. [140] The history of princes does not very frequently renew the examples of a similar competition.

[Footnote 136: At the funeral of Vespasian, the comedian who personated that frugal emperor, anxiously inquired how much it cost. Fourscore thousand pounds, (centies.) Give me the tenth part of the sum, and throw my body into the Tiber. Sueton, in Vespasian, c. 19, with the notes of Casaubon and Gronovius.]

[Footnote 137: Gregory (Orat. iv. p. 119, 120) compares this supposed ignominy and ridicule to the funeral honors of Constantius, whose body was chanted over Mount Taurus by a choir of angels.]

[Footnote 138: Quintus Curtius, l. iii. c. 4. The luxuriancy of his descriptions has been often censured. Yet it was almost the duty of the historian to describe a river, whose waters had nearly proved fatal to Alexander.]

[Footnote 139: Libanius, Orat. Parent. c. 156, p. 377. Yet he acknowledges with gratitude the liberality of the two royal brothers in decorating the tomb of Julian, (de ulcis. Jul. nece, c. 7, p. 152.)]

[Footnote 140: Cujus suprema et cineres, si qui tunc juste consuleret, non Cydnus videre deberet, quamvis gratissimus amnis et liquidus: sed ad perpetuandam gloriam recte factorum praeterlambere Tiberis, intersecans urbem aeternam, divorumque veterum monumenta praestringens Ammian. xxv. 10.]

CHAPTER XXV

REIGNS OF JOVIAN AND VALENTINIAN, DIVISION OF THE EMPIRE

PART I

THE GOVERNMENT AND DEATH OF JOVIAN—ELECTION OF VALENTINIAN, WHO ASSOCIATES HIS BROTHER VALENS, AND MAKES THE FINAL DIVISION OF THE EASTERN AND EMPIRES—REVOLT OF PROCOPIUS—CIVIL AND ECCLESIASTICAL ADMINISTRATION—GERMANY—BRITIAN—AFRICA—The EAST—THE DANUBE—DEATH OF VALENTINIAN—HIS TWO SONS, GRATIAN AND VALENTINIAN II., SUCCEED TO THE WESTERN EMPIRE

The death of Julian had left the public affairs of the empire in a very doubtful and dangerous situation. The Roman army was saved by an inglorious, perhaps a necessary treaty; [1] and the first moments of peace were consecrated by the pious Jovian to restore the domestic tranquility of the church and state. The indiscretion of his predecessor, instead of reconciling, had artfully fomented the religious war: and the balance which he affected to preserve between the hostile factions, served only to perpetuate the contest, by the vicissitudes of hope and fear, by the rival claims of ancient possession and actual favor. The Christians had forgotten the spirit of the gospel; and the Pagans had imbibed the spirit of the church. In private families, the sentiments of nature were extinguished by the blind fury of zeal and revenge: the majesty of the laws was violated or abused; the cities of the East were stained with blood; and the most implacable enemies of the Romans were in the bosom of their country. Jovian was educated in the profession of Christianity; and as he marched from Nisibis to Antioch, the banner of the Cross, the Labarum of Constantine, which was again displayed at the head of the legions, announced to the people the faith of their new emperor. As soon as he ascended the throne, he transmitted a circular epistle to all the governors of provinces; in which he confessed the divine truth, and secured the legal establishment, of the Christian religion. The insidious edicts of Julian were abolished; the ecclesiastical immunities were restored and enlarged; and Jovian condescended to lament, that the distress of the times obliged him to diminish the measure of charitable distributions. [2] The Christians were unanimous in the loud and sincere applause which they bestowed on the pious successor of Julian. But they were still ignorant what creed, or what synod, he would choose for the standard of orthodoxy; and the peace of the church immediately revived those eager disputes which had been suspended during the season of persecution. The episcopal leaders of the contending sects, convinced, from experience, how much their fate would depend on the earliest impressions that were made on the mind of an untutored soldier, hastened to the court of Edessa, or Antioch. The highways of the East were crowded with Homoousian, and Arian, and Semi-Arian, and Eunomian bishops, who struggled to outstrip each other in the holy race: the apartments of the palace resounded with their clamors; and the ears of the prince were assaulted, and perhaps astonished, by the singular mixture of metaphysical argument and passionate invective. [3] The moderation of Jovian, who recommended concord and charity, and referred the disputants to the sentence of a future council, was interpreted as a symptom of indifference: but his attachment to the Nicene creed was at length discovered and declared, by the reverence which he expressed for the celestial [4] virtues of the great Athanasius. The intrepid veteran of the faith, at the age of seventy, had issued from his retreat on the first intelligence of the tyrant's death. The acclamations of the people seated him once more on the archiepiscopal throne; and he wisely accepted, or anticipated, the invitation of Jovian. The venerable figure of Athanasius, his calm courage, and insinuating eloquence, sustained the reputation which he had already acquired in the courts of four successive princes. [5] As soon as he had gained the confidence, and secured the faith, of the Christian emperor, he returned in triumph to his diocese, and continued, with mature counsels and undiminished vigor, to direct, ten years longer, [6] the ecclesiastical government of Alexandria, Egypt, and the Catholic church. Before his departure from Antioch, he assured Jovian that his orthodox devotion would be rewarded with a long and peaceful reign. Athanasius, had reason to hope, that he should be allowed either the merit of a successful prediction, or the excuse of a grateful though ineffectual prayer. [7]

[Footnote 1: The medals of Jovian adorn him with victories, laurel crowns, and prostrate captives. Ducange, Famil. Byzantin. p. 52. Flattery is a foolish suicide; she destroys herself with her own hands.]

[Footnote 2: Jovian restored to the church a forcible and comprehensive expression, (Philostorgius, l. viii. c. 5, with Godefroy's Dissertations, p. 329. Sozomen, l. vi. c. 3.) The new law which condemned the rape or marriage of nuns (Cod. Theod. l. ix. tit. xxv. leg. 2) is exaggerated by Sozomen; who supposes, that an amorous glance, the adultery of the heart, was punished with death by the evangelic legislator.]

[Footnote 3: Compare Socrates, l. iii. c. 25, and Philostorgius, l. viii. c. 6, with Godefroy's Dissertations, p. 330.]

[Footnote 4: The word celestial faintly expresses the impious and extravagant flattery of the emperor to the archbishop. (See the original epistle in Athanasius, tom. ii. p. 33.) Gregory Nazianzen (Orat. xxi. p. 392) celebrates the friendship of Jovian and Athanasius. The primate's journey was advised by the Egyptian monks, (Tillemont, Mem. Eccles. tom. viii. p. 221.)]

[Footnote 5: Athanasius, at the court of Antioch, is agreeably represented by La Bleterie, (Hist. de Jovien, tom. i. p. 121-148;) he translates the singular and original conferences of the emperor, the primate of Egypt, and the Arian deputies. The Abbe is not satisfied with the coarse pleasantry of Jovian; but his partiality for Athanasius assumes, in his eyes, the character of justice.]

[Footnote 6: The true area of his death is perplexed with some difficulties, (Tillemont, Mem. Eccles. tom. viii. p. 719-723.) But the date (A. D. 373, May 2) which seems the most consistent with history and reason, is ratified by his authentic life, (Maffei Osservazioni Letterarie, tom. iii. p. 81.)]

[Footnote 7: See the observations of Valesius and Jortin (Remarks on Ecclesiastical History, vol. iv. p. 38) on the original letter of Athanasius; which is preserved by Theodoret, (l. iv. c. 3.) In some Mss. this indiscreet promise is omitted; perhaps by the Catholics, jealous of the prophetic fame of their leader.]

The slightest force, when it is applied to assist and guide the natural descent of its object, operates with irresistible weight; and Jovian had the good fortune to embrace the religious opinions which were supported by the spirit of the times, and the zeal and numbers of the most powerful sect. [8] Under his reign, Christianity obtained an easy and lasting victory; and as soon as the smile of royal patronage was withdrawn, the genius of Paganism, which had been fondly raised and cherished by the arts of Julian, sunk irrecoverably in the. In many cities, the temples were shut or deserted: the philosophers who had abused their transient favor, thought it prudent to shave their beards, and disguise their profession; and the Christians rejoiced, that they were now in a condition to forgive, or to revenge, the injuries which they had suffered under the preceding reign. [9] The consternation of the Pagan world was dispelled by a wise and gracious edict of toleration; in which Jovian explicitly declared, that although he should severely punish the sacrilegious rites of magic, his subjects might exercise, with freedom and safety, the ceremonies of the ancient worship. The memory of this law has been preserved by the orator Themistius, who was deputed by the senate of Constantinople to express their royal devotion for the new emperor. Themistius expatiates on the clemency of the Divine Nature, the facility of human error, the rights of conscience, and the independence of the mind; and, with some eloquence, inculcates the principles of philosophical toleration; whose aid Superstition herself, in the hour of her distress, is not ashamed to implore. He justly observes, that in the recent changes, both religions had been alternately disgraced by the seeming acquisition of worthless proselytes, of those votaries of the reigning purple, who could pass, without a reason, and without a blush, from the church to the temple, and from the altars of Jupiter to the sacred table of the Christians. [10]

[Footnote 8: Athanasius (apud Theodoret, l. iv. c. 3) magnifies the number of the orthodox, who composed the whole world. This assertion was verified in the space of thirty and forty years.]

[Footnote 9: Socrates, l. iii. c. 24. Gregory Nazianzen (Orat. iv. p. 131) and Libanius (Orat. Parentalis, c. 148, p. 369) expresses the living sentiments of their respective factions.]

[Footnote 10: Themistius, Orat. v. p. 63-71, edit. Harduin, Paris, 1684. The Abbe de la Bleterie judiciously remarks, (Hist. de Jovien, tom. i. p. 199,) that Sozomen has forgot the general toleration; and Themistius the establishment of the Catholic religion. Each of them turned away from the object which he disliked, and wished to suppress the part of the edict the least honorable, in his opinion, to the emperor.]

In the space of seven months, the Roman troops, who were now returned to Antioch, had performed a march of fifteen hundred miles; in which they had endured all the hardships of war, of famine, and of climate. Notwithstanding their services, their fatigues, and the approach of winter, the timid and impatient Jovian allowed only, to the men and horses, a respite of six weeks. The emperor could not sustain the indiscreet and malicious raillery of the people of Antioch. [11] He was impatient to possess the palace of Constantinople; and to prevent the ambition of some competitor, who might occupy the vacant allegiance of Europe. But he soon received the grateful intelligence, that his authority was acknowledged from the Thracian Bosphorus to the Atlantic Ocean. By the first letters which he despatched from the camp of Mesopotamia, he had delegated the military command of Gaul and Illyricum to Malarich, a brave and faithful officer of the nation of the Franks; and to his father-in-law, Count Lucillian, who had formerly distinguished his courage and conduct in the defence of Nisibis. Malarich had declined an office to which he thought himself unequal; and Lucillian was massacred at Rheims, in an accidental mutiny of the Batavian cohorts. [12] But the moderation of Jovinus, master-general of the cavalry, who forgave the intention of his disgrace, soon appeased the tumult, and confirmed the uncertain minds of the soldiers. The oath of fidelity was administered and taken, with loyal acclamations; and the deputies of the Western armies [13] saluted their new sovereign as he descended from Mount Taurus to the city of Tyana in Cappadocia. From Tyana he continued his hasty march to Ancyra, capital of the province of Galatia; where Jovian assumed, with his infant son, the name and ensigns of the consulship. [14] Dadastana, [15] an obscure town, almost at an equal distance between Ancyra and Nice, was marked for the fatal term of his journey and life. After indulging himself with a plentiful, perhaps an intemperate, supper, he retired to rest; and the next morning the emperor Jovian was found dead in his bed. The cause of this sudden death was variously understood. By some it was ascribed to the consequences of an indigestion, occasioned either by the quantity of the wine, or the quality of the mushrooms, which he had swallowed in the evening. According to others, he was suffocated in his sleep by the vapor of charcoal, which extracted from the walls of the apartment the unwholesome moisture of the fresh plaster. [16] But the want of a regular inquiry into the death of a prince, whose reign and person were soon forgotten, appears to have been the only circumstance which countenanced the malicious whispers of poison and domestic guilt. [17] The body of Jovian was sent to Constantinople, to be interred with his predecessors, and the sad procession was met on the road by his wife Charito, the daughter of Count Lucillian; who still wept the recent death of her father, and was hastening to dry her tears in the embraces of an Imperial husband. Her disappointment and grief were imbittered by the anxiety of maternal tenderness. Six weeks before the death of Jovian, his infant son had been placed in the curule chair, adorned with the title of Nobilissimus, and the vain ensigns of the consulship. Unconscious of his fortune, the royal youth, who, from his grandfather, assumed the name of Varronian, was reminded only by the jealousy of the government, that he was the son of an emperor. Sixteen years afterwards he was still alive, but he had already been deprived of an eye; and his afflicted mother expected every hour, that the innocent victim would be torn from her arms, to appease, with his blood, the suspicions of the reigning prince. [18]

[Footnote 11: Johan. Antiochen. in Excerpt. Valesian. p. 845. The libels of Antioch may be admitted on very slight evidence.]

[Footnote 12: Compare Ammianus, (xxv. 10,) who omits the name of the Batarians, with Zosimus, (l. iii. p. 197,) who removes the scene of action from Rheims to Sirmium.]

[Footnote 13: Quos capita scholarum ordo castrensis appellat. Ammian. xxv. 10, and Vales. ad locum.]

[Footnote 14: Cugus vagitus, pertinaciter reluctantis, ne in curuli sella veheretur ex more, id quod mox accidit protendebat. Augustus and his successors respectfully solicited a dispensation of age for the sons or nephews whom they raised to the consulship. But the curule chair of the first Brutus had never been dishonored by an infant.]

[Footnote 15: The Itinerary of Antoninus fixes Dadastana 125 Roman miles from Nice; 117 from Ancyra, (Wesseling, Itinerar. p. 142.) The pilgrim of Bourdeaux, by omitting some stages, reduces the whole space from 242 to 181 miles. Wesseling, p. 574. Note: Dadastana is supposed to be Castabat—M.]

[Footnote 16: See Ammianus, (xxv. 10,) Eutropius, (x. 18.) who might likewise be present, Jerom, (tom. i. p. 26, ad Heliodorum.) Orosius, (vii. 31,) Sozomen, (l. vi. c. 6,) Zosimus, (l. iii. p. 197, 198,) and Zonaras, (tom. ii. l. xiii. p. 28, 29.) We cannot expect a perfect agreement, and we shall not discuss minute differences.]

[Footnote 17: Ammianus, unmindful of his usual candor and good sense, compares the death of the harmless Jovian to that of the second Africanus, who had excited the fears and resentment of the popular faction.]

[Footnote 18: Chrysostom, tom. i. p. 336, 344, edit. Montfaucon. The Christian orator attempts to comfort a widow by the examples of illustrious misfortunes; and observes, that of nine emperors (including the Caesar Gallus) who had reigned in his time, only two (Constantine and Constantius) died a natural death. Such vague consolations have never wiped away a single tear.]

After the death of Jovian, the throne of the Roman world remained ten days, [19] without a master. The ministers and generals still continued to meet in council; to exercise their respective functions; to maintain the public order; and peaceably to conduct the army to the city of Nice in Bithynia, which was chosen for the place of the election. [20] In a solemn assembly of the civil and military powers of the empire, the diadem was again unanimously offered to the praefect Sallust. He enjoyed the glory of a second refusal: and when the virtues of the father were alleged in favor of his son, the praefect, with the firmness of a disinterested patriot, declared to the electors, that the feeble age of the one, and the unexperienced youth of the other, were equally incapable of the laborious duties of government. Several candidates were proposed; and, after weighing the objections of character or situation, they were successively rejected; but, as soon as the name of Valentinian was pronounced, the merit of that officer united the suffrages of the whole assembly, and obtained the sincere approbation of Sallust himself. Valentinian [21] was the son of Count Gratian, a native of Cibalis, in Pannonia, who from an obscure condition had raised himself, by matchless strength and dexterity, to the military commands of Africa and Britain; from which he retired with an ample fortune and suspicious integrity. The rank and services of Gratian contributed, however, to smooth the first steps of the promotion of his son; and afforded him an early opportunity of displaying those solid and useful qualifications, which raised his character above the ordinary level of his fellow-soldiers. The person of Valentinian was tall, graceful, and majestic. His manly countenance, deeply marked with the impression of sense and spirit, inspired his friends with awe, and his enemies with fear; and to second the efforts of his undaunted courage, the son of Gratian had inherited the advantages of a strong and healthy constitution. By the habits of chastity and temperance, which restrain the appetites and invigorate the faculties, Valentinian preserved his own and the public esteem. The avocations of a military life had diverted his youth from the elegant pursuits of literature; [21a] he was ignorant of the Greek language, and the arts of rhetoric; but as the mind of the orator was never disconcerted by timid perplexity, he was able, as often as the occasion prompted him, to deliver his decided sentiments with bold and ready elocution. The laws of martial discipline were the only laws that he had studied; and he was soon distinguished by the laborious diligence, and inflexible severity, with which he discharged and enforced the duties of the camp. In the time of Julian he provoked the danger of disgrace, by the contempt which he publicly expressed for the reigning religion; [22] and it should seem, from his subsequent conduct, that the indiscreet and unseasonable freedom of Valentinian was the effect of military spirit, rather than of Christian zeal. He was pardoned, however, and still employed by a prince who esteemed his merit; [23] and in the various events of the Persian war, he improved the reputation which he had already acquired on the banks of the Rhine. The celerity and success with which he executed an important commission, recommended him to the favor of Jovian; and to the honorable command of the second school, or company, of Targetiers, of the domestic guards. In the march from Antioch, he had reached his quarters at Ancyra, when he was unexpectedly summoned, without guilt and without intrigue, to assume, in the forty-third year of his age, the absolute government of the Roman empire.

[Footnote 19: Ten days appear scarcely sufficient for the march and election. But it may be observed, 1. That the generals might command the expeditious use of the public posts for themselves, their attendants, and messengers. 2. That the troops, for the ease of the cities, marched in many divisions; and that the head of the column might arrive at Nice, when the rear halted at Ancyra.]

[Footnote 20: Ammianus, xxvi. 1. Zosimus, l. iii. p. 198. Philostorgius, l. viii. c. 8, and Godefroy, Dissertat. p. 334. Philostorgius, who appears to have obtained some curious and authentic intelligence, ascribes the choice of Valentinian to the praefect Sallust, the master-general Arintheus, Dagalaiphus count of the domestics, and the patrician Datianus, whose pressing recommendations from Ancyra had a weighty influence in the election.]

[Footnote 21: Ammianus (xxx. 7, 9) and the younger Victor have furnished the portrait of Valentinian, which naturally precedes and illustrates the history of his reign. Note: Symmachus, in a fragment of an oration published by M. Mai, describes Valentinian as born among the snows of Illyria, and habituated to military labor amid the heat and dust of Libya: genitus in frigoribus, educatus is solibus Sym. Orat. Frag. edit. Niebuhr, p. 5—M.]

[Footnote 21a: According to Ammianus, he wrote elegantly, and was skilled in painting and modelling. Scribens decore, venusteque pingens et fingens. xxx. 7—M.]

[Footnote 22: At Antioch, where he was obliged to attend the emperor to the table, he struck a priest, who had presumed to purify him with lustral water, (Sozomen, l. vi. c. 6. Theodoret, l. iii. c. 15.) Such public defiance might become Valentinian; but it could leave no room for the unworthy delation of the philosopher Maximus, which supposes some more private offence, (Zosimus, l. iv. p. 200, 201.)]

[Footnote 23: Socrates, l. iv. A previous exile to Melitene, or Thebais (the first might be possible,) is interposed by Sozomen (l. vi. c. 6) and Philostorgius, (l. vii. c. 7, with Godefroy's Dissertations, p. 293.)]

The invitation of the ministers and generals at Nice was of little moment, unless it were confirmed by the voice of the army.

The aged Sallust, who had long observed the irregular fluctuations of popular assemblies, proposed, under pain of death, that none of those persons, whose rank in the service might excite a party in their favor, should appear in public on the day of the inauguration. Yet such was the prevalence of ancient superstition, that a whole day was voluntarily added to this dangerous interval, because it happened to be the intercalation of the Bissextile. [24] At length, when the hour was supposed to be propitious, Valentinian showed himself from a lofty tribunal; the judicious choice was applauded; and the new prince was solemnly invested with the diadem and the purple, amidst the acclamation of the troops, who were disposed in martial order round the tribunal. But when he stretched forth his hand to address the armed multitude, a busy whisper was accidentally started in the ranks, and insensibly swelled into a loud and imperious clamor, that he should name, without delay, a colleague in the empire. The intrepid calmness of Valentinian obtained silence, and commanded respect; and he thus addressed the assembly: "A few minutes since it was in your power, fellow-soldiers, to have left me in the obscurity of a private station. Judging, from the testimony of my past life, that I deserved to reign, you have placed me on the throne. It is now my duty to consult the safety and interest of the republic. The weight of the universe is undoubtedly too great for the hands of a feeble mortal. I am conscious of the limits of my abilities, and the uncertainty of my life; and far from declining, I am anxious to solicit, the assistance of a worthy colleague. But, where discord may be fatal, the choice of a faithful friend requires mature and serious deliberation. That deliberation shall be my care. Let your conduct be dutiful and consistent. Retire to your quarters; refresh your minds and bodies; and expect the accustomed donative on the accession of a new emperor." [25] The astonished troops, with a mixture of pride, of satisfaction, and of terror, confessed the voice of their master.

Their angry clamors subsided into silent reverence; and Valentinian, encompassed with the eagles of the legions, and the various banners of the cavalry and infantry, was conducted, in warlike pomp, to the palace of Nice. As he was sensible, however, of the importance of preventing some rash declaration of the soldiers, he consulted the assembly of the chiefs; and their real sentiments were concisely expressed by the generous freedom of Dagalaiphus. "Most excellent prince," said that officer, "if you consider only your family, you have a brother; if you love the republic, look round for the most deserving of the Romans." [26] The emperor, who suppressed his displeasure, without altering his intention, slowly proceeded from Nice to Nicomedia and Constantinople. In one of the suburbs of that capital, [27] thirty days after his own elevation, he bestowed the title of Augustus on his brother Valens; [27a] and as the boldest patriots were convinced, that their opposition, without being serviceable to their country, would be fatal to themselves, the declaration of his absolute will was received with silent submission. Valens was now in the thirty-sixth year of his age; but his abilities had never been exercised in any employment, military or civil; and his character had not inspired the world with any sanguine expectations. He possessed, however, one quality, which recommended him to Valentinian, and preserved the domestic peace of the empire; devout and grateful attachment to his benefactor, whose superiority of genius, as well as of authority, Valens humbly and cheerfully acknowledged in every action of his life. [28]

[Footnote 24: *Ammianus, in a long, because unseasonable, digression, (xxvi. I, and Valesius, ad locum,) rashly supposes that he understands an astronomical question, of which his readers are ignorant. It is treated with more judgment and propriety by Censorinus (de Die Natali, c. 20) and Macrobius, (Saturnal. i. c. 12-16.) The appellation of Bissextile, which marks the inauspicious year, (Augustin. ad Januarium, Epist. 119,) is derived from the repetition of the sixth day of the calends of March.*]

[Footnote 25: *Valentinian's first speech is in Ammianus, (xxvi. 2;) concise and sententious in Philostorgius, (l. viii. c. 8.)*]

[Footnote 26: *Si tuos amas, Imperator optime, habes fratrem; si Rempublicam quaere quem vestias. Ammian. xxvi. 4. In the division of the empire, Valentinian retained that sincere counsellor for himself, (c.6.)*]

[Footnote 27: *In suburbano, Ammian. xxvi. 4. The famous Hebdomon, or field of Mars, was distant from Constantinople either seven stadia, or seven miles. See Valesius, and his brother, ad loc., and Ducange, Const. l. ii. p. 140, 141, 172, 173.*]

[Footnote 27a: *Symmachus praises the liberality of Valentinian in raising his brother at once to the rank of Augustus, not training him through the slow and probationary degree of Caesar. Exigui animi vices munerum partiuntur, liberalitas desideriis nihil reliquit. Symm. Orat. p. 7. edit. Niebuhr, 1816, reprinted from Mai—M.*]

[Footnote 28: Participem quidem legitimum potestatis; sed in modum apparitoris morigerum, ut progrediens aperiet textus. Ammian. xxvi. 4.]

PART II

Before Valentinian divided the provinces, he reformed the administration of the empire. All ranks of subjects, who had been injured or oppressed under the reign of Julian, were invited to support their public accusations. The silence of mankind attested the spotless integrity of the praefect Sallust; [29] and his own pressing solicitations, that he might be permitted to retire from the business of the state, were rejected by Valentinian with the most honorable expressions of friendship and esteem. But among the favorites of the late emperor, there were many who had abused his credulity or superstition; and who could no longer hope to be protected either by favor or justice. [30] The greater part of the ministers of the palace, and the governors of the provinces, were removed from their respective stations; yet the eminent merit of some officers was distinguished from the obnoxious crowd; and, notwithstanding the opposite clamors of zeal and resentment, the whole proceedings of this delicate inquiry appear to have been conducted with a reasonable share of wisdom and moderation. [31] The festivity of a new reign received a short and suspicious interruption from the sudden illness of the two princes; but as soon as their health was restored, they left Constantinople in the beginning of the spring. In the castle, or palace, of Mediana, only three miles from Naissus, they executed the solemn and final division of the Roman empire. [32] Valentinian bestowed on his brother the rich praefecture of the East, from the Lower Danube to the confines of Persia; whilst he reserved for his immediate government the warlike [3a] praefectures of Illyricum, Italy, and Gaul, from the extremity of Greece to the Caledonian rampart, and from the rampart of Caledonia to the foot of Mount Atlas. The provincial administration remained on its former basis; but a double supply of generals and magistrates was required for two councils, and two courts: the division was made with a just regard to their peculiar merit and situation, and seven master-generals were soon created, either of the cavalry or infantry. When this important business had been amicably transacted, Valentinian and Valens embraced for the last time. The emperor of the West established his temporary residence at Milan; and the emperor of the East returned to Constantinople, to assume the dominion of fifty provinces, of whose language he was totally ignorant. [33]

[Footnote 29: Notwithstanding the evidence of Zonaras, Suidas, and the Paschal Chronicle, M. de Tillemont (Hist. des Empereurs, tom. v. p. 671) wishes to disbelieve those stories, si avantageuses a un payen.]

[Footnote 30: Eunapius celebrates and exaggerates the sufferings of Maximus. (p. 82, 83;) yet he allows that the sophist or magician, the guilty favorite of Julian, and the personal enemy of Valentinian, was dismissed on the payment of a small fine.]

[Footnote 31: The loose assertions of a general disgrace (Zosimus, l. iv. p. 201), are detected and refuted by Tillemont, (tom. v. p. 21.)]

[Footnote 32: Ammianus, xxvi. 5.]

[Footnote 32a:
Ipae supra impacati Rhen semibarbaras ripas raptim vexilla constituens

Princeps creatus ad difficilem militiam revertisti. Symm. Orat. 81—M.]

[Footnote 33: Ammianus says, in general terms, subagrestis ingenii, nec bellicis nec liberalibus studiis eruditus. Ammian. xxxi. 14. The orator Themistius, with the genuine impertinence of a Greek, wishes for the first time to speak the Latin language, the dialect of his sovereign. Orat. vi. p. 71.]

The tranquility of the East was soon disturbed by rebellion; and the throne of Valens was threatened by the daring attempts of a rival whose affinity to the emperor Julian [34] was his sole merit, and had been his only crime. Procopius had been hastily promoted from the obscure station of a tribune, and a notary, to the joint command of the army of Mesopotamia; the public opinion already named him as the successor of a prince who was destitute of natural heirs; and a vain rumor was propagated by his friends, or his enemies, that Julian, before the altar of the Moon at Carrhae, had privately invested Procopius with the Imperial purple. [35] He endeavored, by his dutiful and submissive behavior, to disarm the jealousy of Jovian; resigned, without a contest, his military command; and retired, with his wife and family, to cultivate the ample patrimony which he possessed in the province of Cappadocia. These useful and innocent occupations were interrupted by the appearance of an officer with a band of soldiers, who, in the name of his new sovereigns, Valentinian and Valens, was despatched to conduct the unfortunate Procopius either to a perpetual prison or an ignominious death. His presence of mind procured him a longer respite, and a more splendid fate. Without presuming to dispute the royal mandate, he requested the indulgence of a few moments to embrace his weeping family; and while the vigilance of his guards was relaxed by a plentiful entertainment, he dexterously escaped to the sea-coast of the Euxine, from whence he passed over to the country of Bosphorus. In that sequestered region he remained many months, exposed to the hardships of exile, of solitude, and of want; his melancholy temper brooding over his misfortunes, and his mind agitated by the just apprehension, that, if any accident should discover his name, the faithless Barbarians would violate, without much scruple, the laws of hospitality. In a moment of impatience and despair, Procopius embarked in a merchant vessel, which made sail for Constantinople; and boldly aspired to the rank of a sovereign, because he was not allowed to enjoy the security of a subject. At first he lurked in the villages of Bithynia, continually changing his habitation and his disguise. [36] By degrees he ventured into the capital, trusted his life and fortune to the fidelity of two friends, a senator and a eunuch, and conceived some hopes of success, from the intelligence which he obtained of the actual state of public affairs. The body of the people was infected with a spirit of discontent: they regretted the justice and the abilities of Sallust, who had been imprudently dismissed from the praefecture of the East. They despised the character of Valens, which was rude without vigor, and feeble without mildness. They dreaded the influence of his father-in-law, the patrician Petronius, a cruel and rapacious minister, who rigorously exacted all the arrears of tribute that might remain unpaid since the reign of the emperor Aurelian. The circumstances were propitious to the designs of a usurper. The hostile measures of the Persians required the presence of Valens in Syria: from the Danube to the Euphrates the troops were in motion; and the capital was occasionally filled with the soldiers who passed or repassed the Thracian Bosphorus. Two cohorts of Gaul were persuaded to listen to the secret proposals of the conspirators; which were recommended by the promise of a liberal donative; and, as they still revered the memory of Julian, they easily consented to support the hereditary claim of his proscribed kinsman. At the dawn of day they were drawn up near the baths of Anastasia; and Procopius, clothed in a purple garment, more suitable to a player than to a monarch, appeared, as if he rose from the dead, in the midst of Constantinople. The soldiers, who were prepared for his reception, saluted their trembling prince with shouts of joy and vows of fidelity. Their numbers were soon increased by a band of sturdy peasants, collected from the adjacent country; and Procopius, shielded by the arms of his adherents, was successively conducted to the tribunal, the senate, and the palace. During the first moments of his tumultuous reign, he was astonished and terrified by the gloomy silence of the people; who were either ignorant of the cause, or apprehensive of the event. But his military strength was superior to any actual resistance: the malecontents flocked to the standard of rebellion; the poor were excited by the hopes, and the rich were intimidated by the fear, of a general pillage; and the obstinate credulity of the multitude was once more deceived by the promised advantages of a revolution. The magistrates were seized; the prisons and arsenals broke open; the gates, and the entrance of the harbor, were diligently occupied; and, in a few hours, Procopius became the absolute, though precarious, master of the Imperial city. [36a] The usurper improved this unexpected success with some degree of courage and dexterity. He artfully propagated the rumors and opinions the most favorable to his interest; while he deluded the populace by giving audience to the frequent, but imaginary, ambassadors of distant nations. The large bodies of troops stationed in the cities of Thrace and the fortresses of the Lower Danube, were gradually involved in the guilt of rebellion: and the Gothic princes consented to supply the sovereign of Constantinople with the formidable strength of several thousand auxiliaries. His generals passed the Bosphorus, and subdued, without an effort, the unarmed, but wealthy provinces of Bithynia and Asia. After an honorable defence, the city and island of Cyzicus yielded to his power; the renowned legions of the Jovians and Herculeans embraced the cause of the usurper, whom they were ordered to crush; and, as the veterans were continually augmented with new levies, he soon appeared at the head of an army, whose valor, as well as numbers, were not unequal to the greatness of the contest. The son of Hormisdas, [37] a youth of spirit and ability, condescended to draw his sword against the lawful emperor of the East; and the Persian prince was immediately invested with the ancient and extraordinary powers of a Roman Proconsul. The alliance of Faustina, the widow of the emperor Constantius, who intrusted herself and her daughter to the hands of the usurper, added dignity and reputation to his cause. The princess Constantia, who was then about five years of age, accompanied, in a litter, the march of the army. She was shown to the multitude in the arms of her adopted father; and, as often as she passed through the ranks, the tenderness of the soldiers was inflamed into martial fury: [38] they recollected the glories of the house of Constantine, and they declared, with loyal acclamation, that they would shed the last drop of their blood in the defence of the royal infant. [39]

[Footnote 34: The uncertain degree of alliance, or consanguinity, is expressed by the words, cognatus, consobrinus, (see Valesius ad Ammian. xxiii. 3.) The mother of Procopius might be a sister of Basilina and Count Julian, the mother and uncle of the Apostate. Ducange, Fam. Byzantin. p. 49.]

[Footnote 35: Ammian. xxiii. 3, xxvi. 6. He mentions the report with much hesitation: susurravit obscurior fama; nemo enim dicti auctor exstitit verus. It serves, however, to remark, that Procopius was a Pagan. Yet his religion does not appear to have promoted, or obstructed, his pretensions.]

[Footnote 36: One of his retreats was a country-house of Eunomius, the heretic. The master was absent, innocent, ignorant; yet he narrowly escaped a sentence of death, and was banished into the remote parts of Mauritania, (Philostorg. l. ix. c. 5, 8, and Godefroy's Dissert. p. 369-378.)]

[Footnote 36a: It may be suspected, from a fragment of Eunapius, that the heathen and philosophic party espoused the cause of Procopius. Heraclius, the Cynic, a man who had been honored by a philosophic controversy with Julian, striking the ground with his staff, incited him to courage with the line of Homer Eunapius. Mai, p. 207 or in Niebuhr's edition, p. 73—M.]

[Footnote 37: Hormisdae maturo juveni Hormisdae regalis illius filio, potestatem Proconsulis detulit; et civilia, more veterum, et bella, recturo. Ammian. xxvi. 8. The Persian prince escaped with honor and safety, and was afterwards (A. D. 380) restored to the same extraordinary office of proconsul of Bithynia,

(Tillemont, Hist. des Empereurs, tom. v. p. 204) I am ignorant whether the race of Sassan was propagated. I find (A. D. 514) a pope Hormisdas; but he was a native of Frusino, in Italy, (Pagi Brev. Pontific. tom. i. p. 247)]

[Footnote 38: The infant rebel was afterwards the wife of the emperor Gratian but she died young, and childless. See Ducange, Fam. Byzantin. p. 48, 59.]

[Footnote 39: Sequimini culminis summi prosapiam, was the language of Procopius, who affected to despise the obscure birth, and fortuitous election of the upstart Pannonian. Ammian. xxvi. 7.]

In the mean while Valentinian was alarmed and perplexed by the doubtful intelligence of the revolt of the East. [39a] The difficulties of a German was forced him to confine his immediate care to the safety of his own dominions; and, as every channel of communication was stopped or corrupted, he listened, with doubtful anxiety, to the rumors which were industriously spread, that the defeat and death of Valens had left Procopius sole master of the Eastern provinces. Valens was not dead: but on the news of the rebellion, which he received at Caesarea, he basely despaired of his life and fortune; proposed to negotiate with the usurper, and discovered his secret inclination to abdicate the Imperial purple. The timid monarch was saved from disgrace and ruin by the firmness of his ministers, and their abilities soon decided in his favor the event of the civil war. In a season of tranquillity, Sallust had resigned without a murmur; but as soon as the public safety was attacked, he ambitiously solicited the preeminence of toil and danger; and the restoration of that virtuous minister to the praefecture of the East, was the first step which indicated the repentance of Valens, and satisfied the minds of the people. The reign of Procopius was apparently supported by powerful armies and obedient provinces. But many of the principal officers, military as well as civil, had been urged, either by motives of duty or interest, to withdraw themselves from the guilty scene; or to watch the moment of betraying, and deserting, the cause of the usurper. Lupicinus advanced by hasty marches, to bring the legions of Syria to the aid of Valens. Arintheus, who, in strength, beauty, and valor, excelled all the heroes of the age, attacked with a small troop a superior body of the rebels. When he beheld the faces of the soldiers who had served under his banner, he commanded them, with a loud voice, to seize and deliver up their pretended leader; and such was the ascendant of his genius, that this extraordinary order was instantly obeyed. [40] Arbetio, a respectable veteran of the great Constantine, who had been distinguished by the honors of the consulship, was persuaded to leave his retirement, and once more to conduct an army into the field. In the heat of action, calmly taking off his helmet, he showed his gray hairs and venerable countenance: saluted the soldiers of Procopius by the endearing names of children and companions, and exhorted them no longer to support the desperate cause of a contemptible tyrant; but to follow their old commander, who had so often led them to honor and victory. In the two engagements of Thyatira [41] and Nacolia, the unfortunate Procopius was deserted by his troops, who were seduced by the instructions and example of their perfidious officers. After wandering some time among the woods and mountains of Phyrgia, he was betrayed by his desponding followers, conducted to the Imperial camp, and immediately beheaded. He suffered the ordinary fate of an unsuccessful usurper; but the acts of cruelty which were exercised by the conqueror, under the forms of legal justice, excited the pity and indignation of mankind. [42]

[Footnote 39a: Symmachus describes his embarrassment. "The Germans are the common enemies of the state, Procopius the private foe of the Emperor; his first care must be victory, his second revenge." Symm. Orat. p. 11—M.]

[Footnote 40: Et dedignatus hominem superare certamine despicabilem, auctoritatis et celsi fiducia corporis ipsis hostibus jussit, suum vincire rectorem: atque ita turmarum, antesignanus umbratilis comprensus suorum manibus. The strength and beauty of Arintheus, the new Hercules, are celebrated by St. Basil, who supposed that God had created him as an inimitable model of the human species. The painters and sculptors could not express his figure: the historians appeared fabulous when they related his exploits, (Ammian. xxvi. and Vales. ad loc.)]

[Footnote 41: The same field of battle is placed by Ammianus in Lycia, and by Zosimus at Thyatira, which are at the distance of 150 miles from each other. But Thyatira alluitur Lyco, (Plin. Hist. Natur. v. 31, Cellarius, Geograph. Antiq. tom. ii. p. 79;) and the transcribers might easily convert an obscure river into a well-known province. Note: Ammianus and Zosimus place the last battle at Nacolia in Phrygia; Ammianus altogether omits the former battle near Thyatira. Procopius was on his march (iter tendebat) towards Lycia. See Wagner's note, in c—M.]

[Footnote 42: The adventures, usurpation, and fall of Procopius, are related, in a regular series, by Ammianus, (xxvi. 6, 7, 8, 9, 10,) and Zosimus, (l. iv. p. 203-210.) They often illustrate, and seldom contradict, each other. Themistius (Orat. vii. p. 91, 92) adds some base panegyric; and Euna pius (p. 83, 84) some malicious satire. —Symmachus joins with Themistius in praising the clemency of Valens dic victoriae moderatus est, quasi contra se nemo pugnavit. Symm. Orat. p. 12—M.]

Such indeed are the common and natural fruits of despotism and rebellion. But the inquisition into the crime of magic, [42a] which, under the reign of the two brothers, was so rigorously prosecuted both at Rome and Antioch, was interpreted as the fatal symptom, either of the displeasure of Heaven, or of the depravity of mankind. [43] Let us not hesitate to indulge a liberal pride, that, in the present age, the enlightened part of Europe has abolished [44] a cruel and odious prejudice, which reigned in every climate of the globe, and adhered to every system of religious opinions. [45] The nations, and the sects, of the Roman world, admitted with equal credulity, and similar abhorrence, the reality of that infernal art, [46] which was able to control the eternal order of the planets, and the voluntary operations of the human mind. They dreaded the mysterious power of spells and incantations, of potent herbs, and execrable rites; which could extinguish or recall life, inflame the passions of the soul, blast the works of creation, and extort from the reluctant daemons the secrets of futurity. They believed, with the wildest inconsistency, that this preternatural dominion of the air, of earth, and of hell, was exercised, from the vilest motives of malice or gain, by some wrinkled hags and itinerant sorcerers, who passed their obscure lives in penury and contempt. [47] The arts of magic were equally condemned by the public opinion, and by the laws of Rome; but as they tended to gratify the most imperious passions of the heart of man, they were continually proscribed, and continually practised. [48] An imaginary cause as capable of producing the most serious and mischievous effects. The dark predictions of the death of an emperor, or the success of a conspiracy, were calculated only to stimulate the hopes of ambition, and to dissolve the ties of fidelity; and the intentional guilt of magic was aggravated by the actual crimes of treason and sacrilege. [49] Such vain terrors disturbed the peace of society, and the happiness of individuals; and the harmless flame which insensibly melted a waxen image, might derive a powerful and pernicious energy from the affrighted fancy of the person whom it was maliciously designed to represent. [50] From the infusion of those herbs, which were supposed to possess a supernatural influence, it was an easy step to the use of more substantial poison; and the folly of mankind sometimes became the instrument, and the mask, of the most atrocious crimes. As soon as the zeal of informers was encouraged by the ministers of Valens and Valentinian, they could not refuse to listen to another charge, too frequently mingled in the scenes of domestic guilt; a charge of a softer and less malignant nature, for which the pious, though excessive, rigor of Constantine had recently decreed the punishment of death. [51] This deadly and incoherent mixture of treason and magic, of poison and adultery, afforded infinite gradations of guilt and innocence, of excuse and aggravation, which in these proceedings appear to have been confounded by the angry or corrupt passions of the judges. They easily discovered that the degree of their industry and discernment was estimated, by the Imperial court, according to the number of executions that were furnished from the respective tribunals. It was not without extreme reluctance that they pronounced a sentence of acquittal; but they eagerly admitted such evidence as was stained with perjury, or procured by torture, to prove the most improbable charges against the most respectable characters. The progress of the inquiry continually opened new subjects of criminal prosecution; the audacious informer, whose falsehood was detected, retired with impunity; but the wretched victim, who discovered his real or pretended accomplices, were seldom permitted to receive the price of his infamy. From the extremity of Italy and Asia, the young, and the aged, were dragged in chains to the tribunals of Rome and Antioch. Senators, matrons, and philosophers, expired in ignominious and cruel tortures. The soldiers, who were appointed to guard the prisons, declared, with a murmur of pity and indignation, that their numbers were insufficient to oppose the flight, or resistance, of the multitude of captives. The wealthiest families were ruined by fines and confiscations; the most innocent citizens trembled for their safety; and we may form some notion of the magnitude of the evil, from the extravagant assertion of an ancient writer, that, in the obnoxious provinces, the prisoners, the exiles, and the fugitives, formed the greatest part of the inhabitants. [52]

[Footnote 42a: This infamous inquisition into sorcery and witchcraft has been of greater influence on human affairs than is commonly supposed. The persecutions against philosophers and their libraries was carried on with so much fury, that from this time (A. D. 374) the names of the Gentile philosophers became almost extinct; and the Christian philosophy and religion, particularly in the East, established their ascendency. I am surprised that Gibbon has not made this observation. Heyne, Note on Zosimus, l. iv. 14, p. 637. Besides vast heaps of manuscripts publicly destroyed throughout the East, men of letters burned their whole libraries, lest some fatal volume should expose them to the malice of the informers and the extreme penalty of the law. Amm. Marc. xxix. 11—M.]

[Footnote 43: Libanius de ulciscend. Julian. nece, c. ix. p. 158, 159. The sophist deplores the public frenzy, but he does not (after their deaths) impeach the justice of the emperors.]

[Footnote 44: The French and English lawyers, of the present age, allow the theory, and deny the practice, of witchcraft, (Denisart, Recueil de Decisions de Jurisprudence, au mot Sorciers, tom. iv. p. 553. Blackstone's Commentaries, vol. iv. p. 60.) As private reason always prevents, or outstrips, public wisdom, the president Montesquieu (Esprit des Loix, l. xii. c. 5, 6) rejects the existence of magic.]

[Footnote 45: See Oeuvres de Bayle, tom. iii. p. 567-589. The sceptic of Rotterdam exhibits, according to his custom, a strange medley of loose knowledge and lively wit.]

[Footnote 46: The Pagans distinguished between good and bad magic, the Theurgic and the Goetic, (Hist. de l'Academie, &c., tom. vii. p. 25.) But they could not have defended this obscure distinction against the acute logic of Bayle. In the Jewish and Christian system, all daemons are infernal spirits; and all commerce with them is idolatry, apostasy &c., which deserves death and damnation.]

[Footnote 47: The Canidia of Horace (Carm. l. v. Od. 5, with Dacier's and Sanadon's illustrations) is a vulgar witch. The Erictho of Lucan (Pharsal. vi. 430-830) is tedious, disgusting, but sometimes sublime. She chides the delay of the Furies, and threatens, with tremendous obscurity, to pronounce their real

names; to reveal the true infernal countenance of Hecate; to invoke the secret powers that lie below hell, &c.]

[Footnote 48: Genus hominum potentibus infidum, sperantibus fallax, quod in civitate nostra et vetabitur semper et retinebitur. Tacit. Hist. i. 22. See Augustin. de Civitate Dei, l. viii. c. 19, and the Theodosian Code l. ix. tit. xvi., with Godefroy's Commentary.]

[Footnote 49: The persecution of Antioch was occasioned by a criminal consultation. The twenty-four letters of the alphabet were arranged round a magic tripod: and a dancing ring, which had been placed in the centre, pointed to the four first letters in the name of the future emperor, O. E. O Triangle. Theodorus (perhaps with many others, who owned the fatal syllables) was executed. Theodosius succeeded. Lardner (Heathen Testimonies, vol. iv. p. 353-372) has copiously and fairly examined this dark transaction of the reign of Valens.]

[Footnote 50: Limus ut hic durescit, et haec ut cera liquescit
Uno eodemque igni—Virgil. Bucolic. viii. 80.

Devovet absentes, simulacraque cerea figit.
—Ovid. in Epist. Hypsil. ad Jason 91.

Such vain incantations could affect the mind, and increase the disease of Germanicus. Tacit. Annal. ii. 69.]

[Footnote 51: See Heineccius, Antiquitat. Juris Roman. tom. ii. p. 353, &c. Cod. Theodosian. l. ix. tit. 7, with Godefroy's Commentary.]

[Footnote 52: The cruel persecution of Rome and Antioch is described, and most probably exaggerated, by Ammianus (xxvii. 1. xxix. 1, 2) and Zosimus, (l. iv. p. 216-218.) The philosopher Maximus, with some justice, was involved in the charge of magic, (Eunapius in Vit. Sophist. p. 88, 89;) and young Chrysostom, who had accidentally found one of the proscribed books, gave himself up for lost, (Tillemont, Hist. des Empereurs, tom. v. p. 340.)]

When Tacitus describes the deaths of the innocent and illustrious Romans, who were sacrificed to the cruelty of the first Caesars, the art of the historian, or the merit of the sufferers, excites in our breast the most lively sensations of terror, of admiration, and of pity. The coarse and undistinguishing pencil of Ammianus has delineated his bloody figures with tedious and disgusting accuracy. But as our attention is no longer engaged by the contrast of freedom and servitude, of recent greatness and of actual misery, we should turn with horror from the frequent executions, which disgraced, both at Rome and Antioch, the reign of the two brothers. [53] Valens was of a timid, [54] and Valentinian of a choleric, disposition. [55] An anxious regard to his personal safety was the ruling principle of the administration of Valens. In the condition of a subject, he had kissed, with trembling awe, the hand of the oppressor; and when he ascended the throne, he reasonably expected, that the same fears, which had subdued his own mind, would secure the patient submission of his people. The favorites of Valens obtained, by the privilege of rapine and confiscation, the wealth which his economy would have refused. [56] They urged, with persuasive eloquence, that, in all cases of treason, suspicion is equivalent to proof; that the power supposes the intention, of mischief; that the intention is not less criminal than the act; and that a subject no longer deserves to live, if his life may threaten the safety, or disturb the repose, of his sovereign. The judgment of Valentinian was sometimes deceived, and his confidence abused; but he would have silenced the informers with a contemptuous smile, had they presumed to alarm his fortitude by the sound of danger. They praised his inflexible love of justice; and, in the pursuit of justice, the emperor was easily tempted to consider clemency as a weakness, and passion as a virtue. As long as he wrestled with his equals, in the bold competition of an active and ambitious life, Valentinian was seldom injured, and never insulted, with impunity: if his prudence was arraigned, his spirit was applauded; and the proudest and most powerful generals were apprehensive of provoking the resentment of a fearless soldier. After he became master of the world, he unfortunately forgot, that where no resistance can be made, no courage can be exerted; and instead of consulting the dictates of reason and magnanimity, he indulged the furious emotions of his temper, at a time when they were disgraceful to himself, and fatal to the defenceless objects of his displeasure. In the government of his household, or of his empire, slight, or even imaginary, offences—a hasty word, a casual omission, an involuntary delay—were chastised by a sentence of immediate death. The expressions which issued the most readily from the mouth of the emperor of the West were, "Strike off his head;" "Burn him alive;" "Let him be beaten with clubs till he expires;" [57] and his most favored ministers soon understood, that, by a rash attempt to dispute, or suspend, the execution of his sanguinary commands, they might involve themselves in the guilt and punishment of disobedience. The repeated gratification of this savage justice hardened the mind of Valentinian against pity and remorse; and the sallies of passion were confirmed by the habits of cruelty. [58] He could behold with calm satisfaction the convulsive agonies of torture and death; he reserved his friendship for those faithful servants whose temper was the most congenial to his own. The merit of Maximin, who had slaughtered the noblest families of Rome, was rewarded with the royal approbation, and the praefecture of Gaul.

Two fierce and enormous bears, distinguished by the appellations of Innocence, and Mica Aurea, could alone deserve to share the favor of Maximin. The cages of those trusty guards were always placed near the bed-chamber of Valentinian, who frequently amused his eyes with the grateful spectacle of seeing them tear and devour the bleeding limbs of the malefactors who were abandoned to their rage. Their diet and exercises were carefully inspected by the Roman emperor; and when Innocence had earned her discharge, by a long course of meritorious service, the faithful animal was again restored to the freedom of her native woods. [59]

[Footnote 53: Consult the six last books of Ammianus, and more particularly the portraits of the two royal brothers, (xxx. 8, 9, xxxi. 14.) Tillemont has collected (tom. v. p. 12-18, p. 127-133) from all antiquity their virtues and vices.]

[Footnote 54: The younger Victor asserts, that he was valde timidus: yet he behaved, as almost every man would do, with decent resolution at the head of an army. The same historian attempts to prove that his anger was harmless. Ammianus observes, with more candor and judgment, incidentia crimina ad contemptam vel laesam principis amplitudinem trahens, in sanguinem saeviebat.]

[Footnote 55: Cum esset ad acerbitatem naturae calore propensior. .. poenas perignes augebat et gladios. Ammian. xxx. 8. See xxvii. 7]

[Footnote 56: I have transferred the reproach of avarice from Valens to his servant. Avarice more properly belongs to ministers than to kings; in whom that passion is commonly extinguished by absolute possession.]

[Footnote 57: He sometimes expressed a sentence of death with a tone of pleasantry: "Abi, Comes, et muta ei caput, qui sibi mutari provinciam cupit." A boy, who had slipped too hastily a Spartan bound; an armorer, who had made a polished cuirass that wanted some grains of the legitimate weight, &c., were the victims of his fury.]

[Footnote 58: The innocents of Milan were an agent and three apparitors, whom Valentinian condemned for signifying a legal summons. Ammianus (xxvii. 7) strangely supposes, that all who had been unjustly executed were worshipped as martyrs by the Christians. His impartial silence does not allow us to believe, that the great chamberlain Rhodanus was burnt alive for an act of oppression, (Chron. Paschal. p. 392.) Note: Ammianus does not say that they were worshipped as martyrs. Onorum memoriam apud Mediolanum colentes nunc usque Christiani loculos ubi sepulti sunt, ad innocentes appellant. Wagner's note in loco. Yet if the next paragraph refers to that transaction, which is not quite clear. Gibbon is right—M.]

[Footnote 59: Ut bene meritam in sylvas jussit abire Innoxiam. Ammian. xxix. and Valesius ad locum.]

PART III

But in the calmer moments of reflection, when the mind of Valens was not agitated by fear, or that of Valentinian by rage, the tyrant resumed the sentiments, or at least the conduct, of the father of his country. The dispassionate judgment of the Western emperor could clearly perceive, and accurately pursue, his own and the public interest; and the sovereign of the East, who imitated with equal docility the various examples which he received from his elder brother, was sometimes guided by the wisdom and virtue of the praefect Sallust. Both princes invariably retained, in the purple, the chaste and temperate simplicity which had adorned their private life; and, under their reign, the pleasures of the court never cost the people a blush or a sigh. They gradually reformed many of the abuses of the times of Constantius; judiciously adopted and improved the designs of Julian and his successor; and displayed a style and spirit of legislation which might inspire posterity with the most favorable opinion of their character and government. It is not from the master of Innocence, that we should expect the tender regard for the welfare of his subjects, which prompted Valentinian to condemn the exposition of new-born infants; [60] and to establish fourteen skilful physicians, with stipends and privileges, in the fourteen quarters of Rome. The good sense of an illiterate soldier founded a useful and liberal institution for the education of youth, and the support of declining science. [61] It was his intention, that the arts of rhetoric and grammar should be taught in the Greek and Latin languages, in the metropolis of every province; and as the size and dignity of the school was usually proportioned to the importance of the city, the academies of Rome and Constantinople claimed a just and singular preeminence. The fragments of the literary edicts of Valentinian imperfectly represent the school of Constantinople, which was gradually improved by subsequent regulations. That school consisted of thirty-one professors in different branches of learning. One philosopher, and two lawyers; five sophists, and ten grammarians for the Greek, and three orators, and ten grammarians for the Latin tongue; besides seven scribes, or, as they were then styled, antiquarians, whose laborious pens supplied the public library with fair and correct copies of the classic writers. The rule of conduct, which was prescribed to the students, is the more curious, as it affords the first outlines of the form and discipline of a modern university. It was required, that they should bring proper certificates from the magistrates of their native province. Their names, professions, and places of abode, were regularly entered in a public register.

The studious youth were severely prohibited from wasting their time in feasts, or in the theatre; and the term of their education was limited to the age of twenty. The praefect of the city was empowered to chastise the idle and refractory by stripes or expulsion; and he was directed to make an annual report to the master of the offices, that the knowledge and abilities of the scholars might be usefully applied to the public service. The institutions of Valentinian contributed to secure the benefits of peace and plenty; and the cities were guarded by the establishment of the Defensors; [62] freely elected as the tribunes and advocates of the people, to support their rights, and to expose their grievances, before the tribunals of the civil magistrates, or even at the foot of the Imperial throne. The finances were diligently administered by two princes, who had been so long accustomed to the rigid economy of a private fortune; but in the receipt and application of the revenue, a discerning eye might observe some difference between the government of the East and of the West. Valens was persuaded, that royal liberality can be supplied only by public oppression, and his ambition never aspired to secure, by their actual distress, the future strength and prosperity of his people. Instead of increasing the weight of taxes, which, in the space of forty years, had been gradually doubled, he reduced, in the first years of his reign, one fourth of the tribute of the East. [63] Valentinian appears to have been less attentive and less anxious to relieve the burdens of his people. He might reform the abuses of the fiscal administration; but he exacted, without scruple, a very large share of the private property; as he was convinced, that the revenues, which supported the luxury of individuals, would be much more advantageously employed for the defence and improvement of the state. The subjects of the East, who enjoyed the present benefit, applauded the indulgence of their prince. The solid but less splendid, merit of Valentinian was felt and acknowledged by the subsequent generation. [64]

[Footnote 60: See the Code of Justinian, l. viii. tit. lii. leg. 2. Unusquisque sabolem suam nutriat. Quod si exponendam putaverit animadversioni quae constituta est subjacebit. For the present I shall not interfere in the dispute between Noodt and Binkershoek; how far, or how long this unnatural practice had been condemned or abolished by law philosophy, and the more civilized state of society.]

[Footnote 61: These salutary institutions are explained in the Theodosian Code, l. xiii. tit. iii. De Professoribus et Medicis, and l. xiv. tit. ix. De Studiis liberalibus Urbis Romoe. Besides our usual guide, (Godefroy,) we may consult Giannone, (Istoria di Napoli, tom. i. p. 105-111,) who has treated the interesting subject with the zeal and curiosity of a man of latters who studies his domestic history.]

[Footnote 62: Cod. Theodos. l. i. tit. xi. with Godefroy's Paratitlon, which diligently gleans from the rest of the code.]

[Footnote 63: Three lines of Ammianus (xxxi. 14) countenance a whole oration of Themistius, (viii. p. 101-120,) full of adulation, pedantry, and common-place morality. The eloquent M. Thomas (tom. i. p. 366-396) has amused himself with celebrating the virtues and genius of Themistius, who was not unworthy of the age in which he lived.]

[Footnote 64: Zosimus, l. iv. p. 202. Ammian. xxx. 9. His reformation of costly abuses might entitle him to the praise of, in provinciales admodum parcus, tributorum ubique molliens sarcinas. By some his frugality was styled avarice, (Jerom. Chron. p. 186)]

But the most honorable circumstance of the character of Valentinian, is the firm and temperate impartiality which he uniformly preserved in an age of religious contention. His strong sense, unenlightened, but uncorrupted, by study, declined, with respectful indifference, the subtle questions of theological debate. The government of the Earth claimed his vigilance, and satisfied his ambition; and while he remembered that he was the disciple of the church, he never forgot that he was the sovereign of the clergy. Under the reign of an apostate, he had signalized his zeal for the honor of Christianity: he allowed to his subjects the privilege which he had assumed for himself; and they might accept, with gratitude and confidence, the general toleration which was granted by a prince addicted to passion, but incapable of fear or of disguise. [65] The Pagans, the Jews, and all the various sects which acknowledged the divine authority of Christ, were protected by the laws from arbitrary power or popular insult; nor was any mode of worship prohibited by Valentinian, except those secret and criminal practices, which abused the name of religion for the dark purposes of vice and disorder. The art of magic, as it was more cruelly punished, was more strictly proscribed: but the emperor admitted a formal distinction to protect the ancient methods of divination, which were approved by the senate, and exercised by the Tuscan haruspices. He had condemned, with the consent of the most rational Pagans, the license of nocturnal sacrifices; but he immediately admitted the petition of Praetextatus, proconsul of Achaia, who represented, that the life of the Greeks would become dreary and comfortless, if they were deprived of the invaluable blessing of the Eleusinian mysteries. Philosophy alone can boast, (and perhaps it is no more than the boast of philosophy,) that her gentle hand is able to eradicate from the human mind the latent and deadly principle of fanaticism. But this truce of twelve years, which was enforced by the wise and vigorous government of Valentinian, by suspending the repetition of mutual injuries, contributed to soften the manners, and abate the prejudices, of the religious factions.

[Footnote 65: Testes sunt leges a me in exordio Imperii mei datae; quibus unicuique quod animo imbibisset colendi libera facultas tributa est. Cod. Theodos. l. ix. tit. xvi. leg. 9. To this declaration of Valentinian, we may add the various testimonies of Ammianus, (xxx. 9,) Zosimus, (l. iv. p. 204,) and Sozomen, (l. vi. c. 7, 21.) Baronius would naturally blame such rational toleration, (Annal. Eccles A. D. 370, No. 129-132, A. D. 376, No. 3, 4.) —Comme il s'etait prescrit pour regle de ne point se meler de disputes de religion, son histoire est presque entierement degagee des affaires ecclesiastiques. Le Beau. iii. 214—M.]

The friend of toleration was unfortunately placed at a distance from the scene of the fiercest controversies. As soon as the Christians of the West had extricated themselves from the snares of the creed of Rimini, they happily relapsed into the slumber of orthodoxy; and the small remains of the Arian party, that still subsisted at Sirmium or Milan, might be considered rather as objects of contempt than of resentment. But in the provinces of the East, from the Euxine to the extremity of Thebais, the strength and numbers of the hostile factions were more equally balanced; and this equality, instead of recommending the counsels of peace, served only to perpetuate the horrors of religious war. The monks and bishops supported their arguments by invectives; and their invectives were sometimes followed by blows. Athanasius still reigned at Alexandria; the thrones of Constantinople and Antioch were occupied by Arian prelates, and every episcopal vacancy was the occasion of a popular tumult. The Homoousians were fortified by the reconciliation of fifty-nine Macedonian, or Semi-Arian, bishops; but their secret reluctance to embrace the divinity of the Holy Ghost, clouded the splendor of the triumph; and the declaration of Valens, who, in the first years of his reign, had imitated the impartial conduct of his brother, was an important victory on the side of Arianism. The two brothers had passed their private life in the condition of catechumens; but the piety of Valens prompted him to solicit the sacrament of baptism, before he exposed his person to the dangers of a Gothic war. He naturally addressed himself to Eudoxus, [66] [66a] bishop of the Imperial city; and if the ignorant monarch was instructed by that Arian pastor in the principles of heterodox theology, his misfortune, rather than his guilt, was the inevitable consequence of his erroneous choice. Whatever had been the determination of the emperor, he must have offended a numerous party of his Christian subjects; as the leaders both of the Homoousians and of the Arians believed, that, if they were not suffered to reign, they were most cruelly injured and oppressed. After he had taken this decisive step, it was extremely difficult for him to preserve either the virtue, or the reputation of impartiality. He never aspired, like Constantius, to the fame of a profound theologian; but as he had received with simplicity and respect the tenets of Euxodus, Valens resigned his conscience to the direction of his ecclesiastical guides, and promoted, by the influence of his authority, the reunion of the Athanasian heretics to the body of the Catholic church. At first, he pitied their blindness; by degrees he was provoked at their obstinacy; and he insensibly hated those sectaries to whom he was an object of hatred. [67] The feeble mind of Valens was always swayed by the persons with whom he familiarly conversed; and the exile or imprisonment of a private citizen are the favors the most readily granted in a despotic court. Such punishments were frequently inflicted on the leaders of the Homoousian party; and the misfortune of fourscore ecclesiastics of Constantinople, who, perhaps accidentally, were burned on shipboard, was imputed to the cruel and premeditated malice of the emperor, and his Arian ministers. In every contest, the Catholics (if we may anticipate that name) were obliged to pay the penalty of their own faults, and of those of their adversaries. In every election, the claims of the Arian candidate obtained the preference; and if they were opposed by the majority of the people, he was usually supported by the authority of the civil magistrate, or even by the terrors of a military force. The enemies of Athanasius attempted to disturb the last years of his venerable age; and his temporary retreat to his father's sepulchre has been celebrated as a fifth exile. But the zeal of a great people, who instantly flew to arms, intimidated the praefect: and the archbishop was permitted to end his life in peace and in glory, after a reign of forty-seven years. The death of Athanasius was the signal of the persecution of Egypt; and the Pagan minister of Valens, who forcibly seated the worthless Lucius on the archiepiscopal throne, purchased the favor of the reigning party, by the blood and sufferings of their Christian brethren. The free toleration of the heathen and Jewish worship was bitterly lamented, as a circumstance which aggravated the misery of the Catholics, and the guilt of the impious tyrant of the East. [68]

[Footnote 66: *Eudoxus was of a mild and timid disposition. When he baptized Valens, (A. D. 367,) he must have been extremely old; since he had studied theology fifty-five years before, under Lucian, a learned and pious martyr. Philostorg. l. ii. c. 14-16, l. iv. c. 4, with Godefroy, p 82, 206, and Tillemont, Mem. Eccles. tom. v. p. 471-480, &c.]*

[Footnote 66a: *Through the influence of his wife say the ecclesiastical writers—M.]*

[Footnote 67: *Gregory Nazianzen (Orat. xxv. p. 432) insults the persecuting spirit of the Arians, as an infallible symptom of error and heresy.]*

[Footnote 68: *This sketch of the ecclesiastical government of Valens is drawn from Socrates, (l. iv.,) Sozomen, (l. vi.,) Theodoret, (l. iv.,) and the immense compilations of Tillemont, (particularly tom. vi. viii. and ix.)]*

The triumph of the orthodox party has left a deep stain of persecution on the memory of Valens; and the character of a prince who derived his virtues, as well as his vices, from a feeble understanding and a pusillanimous temper, scarcely deserves the labor of an apology. Yet candor may discover some reasons to suspect that the ecclesiastical ministers of Valens often exceeded the orders, or even the intentions, of their master; and that the real measure of facts has been very liberally magnified by the vehement declamation and easy credulity of his antagonists. [69] 1. The silence of Valentinian may suggest a probable argument that the partial severities, which were exercised in the name and provinces of his colleague, amounted only to some obscure and inconsiderable deviations from the established system of religious toleration: and the judicious historian, who has praised the equal temper of the elder brother, has not thought himself obliged to contrast the tranquillity of the West with the cruel persecution of the East. [70] 2. Whatever credit may be allowed to vague and distant reports, the character, or at least the behavior, of Valens, may be most distinctly seen in his personal transactions with the eloquent Basil, archbishop of Caesarea, who had succeeded Athanasius in the management of the Trinitarian cause. [71] The circumstantial narrative has been composed by the friends and admirers of Basil; and as soon as we have stripped away a thick coat of rhetoric and miracle, we shall be astonished by the unexpected mildness of the Arian tyrant, who admired the firmness of his character, or was apprehensive, if he employed violence, of a general revolt in the province of Cappadocia. The archbishop, who asserted, with inflexible pride, [72] the truth of his opinions, and the dignity of his rank, was left in the free possession of his conscience and his throne. The emperor devoutly assisted at the solemn service of the cathedral; and, instead of a sentence of banishment, subscribed the donation of a valuable estate for the use of a hospital, which Basil had lately founded in the neighborhood of Caesarea. [73] 3. I am not able to discover, that any law (such as Theodosius afterwards enacted against the Arians) was published by Valens against the Athanasian sectaries; and the edict which excited the most violent clamors, may not appear so extremely reprehensible. The emperor had observed, that several of his subjects, gratifying their lazy disposition under the pretence of religion, had associated themselves with the monks of Egypt; and he directed the count of the East to drag them from their solitude; and to compel these deserters of society to accept the fair alternative of renouncing their temporal possessions, or of discharging the public duties of men and citizens. [74] The ministers of Valens seem to have extended the sense of this penal statute, since they claimed a right of enlisting the young and ablebodied monks in the Imperial armies. A detachment of cavalry and infantry, consisting of three thousand men, marched from Alexandria into the adjacent desert of Nitria, [75] which was peopled by five thousand monks. The soldiers were conducted by Arian priests; and it is reported, that a considerable slaughter was made in the monasteries which disobeyed the commands of their sovereign. [76]

[Footnote 69: Dr. Jortin (Remarks on Ecclesiastical History, vol. iv. p. 78) has already conceived and intimated the same suspicion.]

[Footnote 70: This reflection is so obvious and forcible, that Orosius (l. vii. c. 32, 33,) delays the persecution till after the death of Valentinian. Socrates, on the other hand, supposes, (l. iii. c. 32,) that it was appeased by a philosophical oration, which Themistius pronounced in the year 374, (Orat. xii. p. 154, in Latin only.) Such contradictions diminish the evidence, and reduce the term, of the persecution of Valens.]

[Footnote 71: Tillemont, whom I follow and abridge, has extracted (Mem. Eccles. tom. viii. p. 153-167) the most authentic circumstances from the Panegyrics of the two Gregories; the brother, and the friend, of Basil. The letters of Basil himself (Dupin, Bibliotheque, Ecclesiastique, tom. ii. p. 155-180) do not present the image of a very lively persecution.]

[Footnote 72: Basilius Caesariensis episcopus Cappadociae clarus habetur... qui multa continentiae et ingenii bona uno superbiae malo perdidit. This irreverent passage is perfectly in the style and character of St. Jerom. It does not appear in Scaliger's edition of his Chronicle; but Isaac Vossius found it in some old Mss. which had not been reformed by the monks.]

[Footnote 73: This noble and charitable foundation (almost a new city) surpassed in merit, if not in greatness, the pyramids, or the walls of Babylon. It was principally intended for the reception of lepers, (Greg. Nazianzen, Orat. xx. p. 439.)]

[Footnote 74: Cod. Theodos. l. xii. tit. i. leg. 63. Godefroy (tom. iv. p. 409-413) performs the duty of a commentator and advocate. Tillemont (Mem. Eccles. tom. viii. p. 808) supposes a second law to excuse his orthodox friends, who had misrepresented the edict of Valens, and suppressed the liberty of choice.]

[Footnote 75: See D'Anville, Description de l'Egypte, p. 74. Hereafter I shall consider the monastic institutions.]

[Footnote 76: Socrates, l. iv. c. 24, 25. Orosius, l. vii. c. 33. Jerom. in Chron. p. 189, and tom. ii. p. 212. The monks of Egypt performed many miracles, which prove the truth of their faith. Right, says Jortin, (Remarks, vol iv. p. 79,) but what proves the truth of those miracles.]

The strict regulations which have been framed by the wisdom of modern legislators to restrain the wealth and avarice of the clergy, may be originally deduced from the example of the emperor Valentinian. His edict, [77] addressed to Damasus, bishop of Rome, was publicly read in the churches of the city. He admonished the ecclesiastics and monks not to frequent the houses of widows and virgins; and menaced their disobedience with the animadversion of the civil judge. The director was no longer permitted to receive any gift, or legacy, or inheritance, from the liberality of his spiritual-daughter: every testament contrary to this edict was declared null and void; and the illegal donation was confiscated for the use of the treasury. By a subsequent regulation, it should seem, that the same provisions were extended to nuns and bishops; and that all persons of the ecclesiastical order were rendered incapable of receiving any testamentary gifts, and strictly confined to the natural and legal rights of inheritance. As the guardian of domestic happiness and virtue, Valentinian applied this severe remedy to the growing evil. In the capital of the empire, the females of noble and opulent houses possessed a very ample share of independent property: and many of those devout females had embraced the doctrines of Christianity, not only with the cold assent of the understanding, but with the warmth of affection, and perhaps with the eagerness of fashion. They sacrificed the pleasures of dress and luxury; and renounced, for the praise of chastity, the soft endearments of conjugal society. Some ecclesiastic, of real or apparent sanctity, was chosen to direct their timorous conscience, and to amuse the vacant tenderness of their heart: and the unbounded confidence, which they hastily bestowed, was often abused by knaves and enthusiasts; who hastened from the extremities of the East, to enjoy, on a splendid theatre, the privileges of the monastic profession. By their contempt of the world, they insensibly acquired its most desirable advantages; the lively attachment, perhaps of a young and beautiful woman, the delicate plenty of an opulent household, and the respectful homage of the slaves, the freedmen, and the clients of a senatorial family. The immense fortunes of the Roman ladies were gradually consumed in lavish alms and expensive pilgrimages; and the artful monk, who had assigned himself the first, or possibly the sole place, in the testament of his spiritual daughter, still presumed to declare, with the smooth face of hypocrisy, that he was only the instrument of charity, and the steward of the poor. The lucrative, but disgraceful, trade, [78] which was exercised by the clergy to defraud the expectations of the natural heirs, had provoked the indignation of a superstitious age: and two of the most respectable of the Latin fathers very honestly confess, that the ignominious edict of Valentinian was just and necessary; and that the Christian priests had deserved to lose a privilege, which was still enjoyed by comedians, charioteers, and the ministers of idols. But the wisdom and authority of the legislator are seldom victorious in a contest with the vigilant dexterity of private interest; and Jerom, or Ambrose, might patiently acquiesce in the justice of an ineffectual or salutary law. If the ecclesiastics were checked in the pursuit of personal emolument, they would exert a more laudable industry to increase the wealth of the church; and dignify their covetousness with the specious names of piety and patriotism. [79]

[Footnote 77: Cod. Theodos. l. xvi. tit. ii. leg. 20. Godefroy, (tom. vi. p. 49,) after the example of Baronius, impartially collects all that the fathers have said on the subject of this important law; whose spirit was long afterwards revived by the emperor Frederic II., Edward I. of England, and other Christian princes who reigned after the twelfth century.]

[Footnote 78: The expressions which I have used are temperate and feeble, if compared with the vehement invectives of Jerom, (tom. i. p. 13, 45, 144, &c.) In his turn he was reproached with the guilt which he imputed to his brother monks; and the Sceleratus, the Versipellis, was publicly accused as the lover of the widow Paula, (tom. ii. p. 363.) He undoubtedly possessed the affection, both of the mother and the daughter; but he declares that he never abused his influence to any selfish or sensual purpose.]

[Footnote 79: Pudet dicere, sacerdotes idolorum, mimi et aurigae, et scorta, haereditates capiunt: solis clericis ac monachis hac lege prohibetur. Et non prohibetur a persecutoribus, sed a principibus Christianis. Nec de lege queror; sed doleo cur meruerimus hanc legem. Jerom (tom. i. p. 13) discreetly insinuates the secret policy of his patron Damasus.]

Damasus, bishop of Rome, who was constrained to stigmatize the avarice of his clergy by the publication of the law of Valentinian, had the good sense, or the good fortune, to engage in his service the zeal and abilities of the learned Jerom; and the grateful saint has celebrated the merit and purity of a very ambiguous character. [80] But the splendid vices of the church of Rome, under the reign of Valentinian and Damasus, have been curiously observed by the historian Ammianus, who delivers his impartial sense in these expressive words: "The praefecture of Juventius was accompanied with peace and plenty, but the tranquillity of his government was soon disturbed by a bloody sedition of the distracted people. The ardor of Damasus and Ursinus, to seize the episcopal seat, surpassed the ordinary measure of human ambition. They contended with the rage of party; the quarrel was maintained by the wounds and death of their followers; and the praefect, unable to resist or appease the tumult, was constrained, by superior violence, to retire into the suburbs. Damasus prevailed: the well-disputed victory remained on the side of his faction; one hundred and thirty-seven dead bodies [81] were found in the Basilica of Sicininus, [82] where the Christians hold their religious assemblies; and it was long before the angry minds of the people resumed their accustomed tranquillity. When I consider the splendor of the capital, I am not astonished that so valuable a prize should inflame the desires of ambitious men, and produce the fiercest and most obstinate contests. The successful candidate is secure, that he will be enriched by the offerings of matrons; [83] that, as soon as his dress is composed with becoming care and elegance, he may proceed, in his chariot, through the streets of Rome; [84] and that the sumptuousness of the Imperial table will not equal the profuse and delicate entertainments provided by the taste, and at the expense, of the Roman pontiffs. How much more rationally (continues the honest Pagan) would those pontiffs consult their true happiness, if, instead of alleging the greatness of the city as an excuse for their manners, they would imitate the exemplary life of some provincial bishops, whose temperance and sobriety, whose mean apparel and downcast looks, recommend their pure and modest virtue to the Deity and his true worshippers!" [85] The schism of Damasus and Ursinus was extinguished by the exile of the latter; and the wisdom of the praefect Praetextatus [86] restored the tranquillity of the city. Praetextatus was a philosophic Pagan, a man of learning, of taste, and politeness; who disguised a reproach in the form of a jest, when he assured Damasus, that if he could obtain the bishopric of Rome, he himself would immediately embrace the Christian religion. [87] This lively picture of the wealth and luxury of the popes in the fourth century becomes the more curious, as it represents the intermediate degree between the humble poverty of the apostolic fishermen, and the royal state of a temporal prince, whose dominions extend from the confines of Naples to the banks of the Po.

[Footnote 80: Three words of Jerom, sanctoe memorioe Damasus (tom. ii. p. 109,) wash away all his stains, and blind the devout eyes of Tillemont. (Mem Eccles. tom. viii. p. 386-424.)]

[Footnote 81: Jerom himself is forced to allow, crudelissimae interfectiones diversi sexus perpetratae, (in Chron. p. 186.) But an original libel, or petition of two presbyters of the adverse party, has unaccountably escaped. They affirm that the doors of the Basilica were burnt, and that the roof was untiled; that Damasus marched at the head of his own clergy, grave-diggers, charioteers, and hired gladiators; that none of his party were killed, but that one hundred and sixty dead bodies were found. This petition is published by the P. Sirmond, in the first volume of his work.]

[Footnote 82: The Basilica of Sicininus, or Liberius, is probably the church of Sancta Maria Maggiore, on the Esquiline hill. Baronius, A. D. 367 No. 3; and Donatus, Roma Antiqua et Nova, l. iv. c. 3, p. 462.]

[Footnote 83: The enemies of Damasus styled him Auriscalpius Matronarum the ladies' ear-scratcher.]

[Footnote 84: Gregory Nazianzen (Orat. xxxii. p. 526) describes the pride and luxury of the prelates who reigned in the Imperial cities; their gilt car, fiery steeds, numerous train, &c. The crowd gave way as to a wild beast.]

[Footnote 85: Ammian. xxvii. 3. Perpetuo Numini, verisque ejus cultoribus. The incomparable pliancy of a polytheist!]

[Footnote 86: Ammianus, who makes a fair report of his praefecture (xxvii. 9) styles him praeclarae indolis, gravitatisque senator, (xxii. 7, and Vales. ad loc.) A curious inscription (Grutor MCII. No. 2) records, in two columns, his religious and civil honors. In one line he was Pontiff of the Sun, and of Vesta, Augur, Quindecemvir, Hierophant, &c., &c. In the other, 1. Quaestor candidatus, more probably titular. 2. Praetor. 3. Corrector of Tuscany and Umbria. 4. Consular of Lusitania. 5. Proconsul of Achaia. 6. Praefect of Rome. 7. Praetorian praefect of Italy. 8. Of Illyricum. 9. Consul elect; but he died before the beginning of the year 385. See Tillemont, Hist. des Empereurs, tom v. p. 241, 736.]

[Footnote 87: Facite me Romanae urbis episcopum; et ero protinus Christianus (Jerom, tom. ii. p. 165.) It is more than probable that Damasus would not have purchased his conversion at such a price.]

PART IV

When the suffrage of the generals and of the army committed the sceptre of the Roman empire to the hands of Valentinian, his reputation in arms, his military skill and experience, and his rigid attachment to the forms, as well as spirit, of ancient discipline, were the principal motives of their judicious choice.

The eagerness of the troops, who pressed him to nominate his colleague, was justified by the dangerous situation of public affairs; and Valentinian himself was conscious, that the abilities of the most active mind were unequal to the defence of the distant frontiers of an invaded monarchy. As soon as the death of Julian had relieved the Barbarians from the terror of his name, the most sanguine hopes of rapine and conquest excited the nations of the East, of the North, and of the South. Their inroads were often vexatious, and sometimes formidable; but, during the twelve years of the reign of Valentinian, his firmness and vigilance protected his own dominions; and his powerful genius seemed to inspire and direct the feeble counsels of his brother. Perhaps the method of annals would more forcibly express the urgent and divided cares of the two emperors; but the attention of the reader, likewise, would be distracted by a tedious and desultory narrative. A separate view of the five great theatres of war; I. Germany; II. Britain; III. Africa; IV. The East; and, V. The Danube; will impress a more distinct image of the military state of the empire under the reigns of Valentinian and Valens.

I. The ambassadors of the Alemanni had been offended by the harsh and haughty behavior of Ursacius, master of the offices; [88] who by an act of unseasonable parsimony, had diminished the value, as well as the quantity, of the presents to which they were entitled, either from custom or treaty, on the accession of a new emperor. They expressed, and they communicated to their countrymen, their strong sense of the national affront. The irascible minds of the chiefs were exasperated by the suspicion of contempt; and the martial youth crowded to their standard. Before Valentinian could pass the Alps, the villages of Gaul were in flames; before his general Degalaiphus could encounter the Alemanni, they had secured the captives and the spoil in the forests of Germany. In the beginning of the ensuing year, the military force of the whole nation, in deep and solid columns, broke through the barrier of the Rhine, during the severity of a northern winter. Two Roman counts were defeated and mortally wounded; and the standard of the Heruli and Batavians fell into the hands of the Heruli and Batavians fell into the hands of the conquerors, who displayed, with insulting shouts and menaces, the trophy of their victory. The standard was recovered; but the Batavians had not redeemed the shame of their disgrace and flight in the eyes of their severe judge. It was the opinion of Valentinian, that his soldiers must learn to fear their commander, before they could cease to fear the enemy. The troops were solemnly assembled; and the trembling Batavians were enclosed within the circle of the Imperial army. Valentinian then ascended his tribunal; and, as if he disdained to punish cowardice with death, he inflicted a stain of indelible ignominy on the officers, whose misconduct and pusillanimity were found to be the first occasion of the defeat. The Batavians were degraded from their rank, stripped of their arms, and condemned to be sold for slaves to the highest bidder. At this tremendous sentence, the troops fell prostrate on the ground, deprecated the indignation of their sovereign, and protested, that, if he would indulge them in another trial, they would approve themselves not unworthy of the name of Romans, and of his soldiers. Valentinian, with affected reluctance, yielded to their entreaties; the Batavians resumed their arms, and with their arms, the invincible resolution of wiping away their disgrace in the blood of the Alemanni. [89] The principal command was declined by Dagalaiphus; and that experienced general, who had represented, perhaps with too much prudence, the extreme difficulties of the undertaking, had the mortification, before the end of the campaign, of seeing his rival Jovinus convert those difficulties into a decisive advantage over the scattered forces of the Barbarians. At the head of a well-disciplined army of cavalry, infantry, and light troops, Jovinus advanced, with cautious and rapid steps, to Scarponna, [90] [90a] in the territory of Metz, where he surprised a large division of the Alemanni, before they had time to run to their arms; and flushed his soldiers with the confidence of an easy and bloodless victory. Another division, or rather army, of the enemy, after the cruel and wanton devastation of the adjacent country, reposed themselves on the shady banks of the Moselle. Jovinus, who had viewed the ground with the eye of a general, made a silent approach through a deep and woody vale, till he could distinctly perceive the indolent security of the Germans. Some were bathing their huge limbs in the river; others were combing their long and flaxen hair; others again were swallowing large draughts of rich and delicious wine. On a sudden they heard the sound of the Roman trumpet; they saw the enemy in their camp. Astonishment produced disorder; disorder was followed by flight and dismay; and the confused multitude of the bravest warriors was pierced by the swords and javelins of the legionaries and auxiliaries. The fugitives escaped to the third, and most considerable, camp, in the Catalonian plains, near Chalons in Champagne: the straggling detachments were hastily recalled to their standard; and the Barbarian chiefs, alarmed and admonished by the fate of their companions, prepared to encounter, in a decisive battle, the victorious forces of the lieutenant of Valentinian. The bloody and obstinate conflict lasted a whole summer's day, with equal valor, and with alternate success. The Romans at length prevailed, with the loss of about twelve hundred men. Six thousand of the Alemanni were slain, four thousand were wounded; and the brave Jovinus, after chasing the flying remnant of their host as far as the banks of the Rhine, returned to Paris, to receive the applause of his sovereign, and the ensigns of the consulship for the ensuing year. [91] The triumph of the Romans was indeed sullied by their treatment of the captive king, whom they hung on a gibbet, without the knowledge of their indignant general. This disgraceful act of cruelty, which might be imputed to the fury of the troops, was followed by the deliberate murder of Withicab, the son of Vadomair; a German prince, of a weak and sickly constitution, but of a daring and formidable spirit. The domestic assassin was instigated and protected by the Romans; [92] and the violation of the laws of humanity and justice betrayed their secret apprehension of the weakness of the declining empire. The use of the dagger is seldom adopted in public councils, as long as they retain any confidence in the power of the sword.

[Footnote 88: Ammian, xxvi. 5. Valesius adds a long and good note on the master of the offices.]

[Footnote 89: Ammian. xxvii. 1. Zosimus, l. iv. p. 208. The disgrace of the Batavians is suppressed by the contemporary soldier, from a regard for military honor, which could not affect a Greek rhetorician of the succeeding age.]

[Footnote 90: See D'Anville, Notice de l'Ancienne Gaule, p. 587. The name of the Moselle, which is not specified by Ammianus, is clearly understood by Mascou, (Hist. of the Ancient Germans, vii. 2)]

[Footnote 90a: Charpeigne on the Moselle. Mannert—M.]

[Footnote 91: The battles are described by Ammianus, (xxvii. 2,) and by Zosimus, (l. iv. p. 209,) who supposes Valentinian to have been present.]

[Footnote 92: Studio solicitante nostrorum, occubuit. Ammian xxvii. 10.]

While the Alemanni appeared to be humbled by their recent calamities, the pride of Valentinian was mortified by the unexpected surprisal of Moguntiacum, or Mentz, the principal city of the Upper Germany. In the unsuspicious moment of a Christian festival, [92a] Rando, a bold and artful chieftain, who had long meditated his attempt, suddenly passed the Rhine; entered the defenceless town, and retired with a multitude of captives of either sex. Valentinian resolved to execute severe vengeance on the whole body of the nation. Count Sebastian, with the bands of Italy and Illyricum, was ordered to invade their country, most probably on the side of Rhaetia. The emperor in person, accompanied by his son Gratian, passed the Rhine at the head of a formidable army, which was supported on both flanks by Jovinus and Severus, the two masters-general of the cavalry and infantry of the West. The Alemanni, unable to prevent the devastation of their villages, fixed their camp on a lofty, and almost inaccessible, mountain, in the modern duchy of Wirtemberg, and resolutely expected the approach of the Romans. The life of Valentinian was exposed to imminent danger by the intrepid curiosity with which he persisted to explore some secret and unguarded path. A troop of Barbarians suddenly rose from their ambuscade: and the emperor, who vigorously spurred his horse down a steep and slippery descent, was obliged to leave behind him his armor-bearer, and his helmet, magnificently enriched with gold and precious stones. At the signal of the general assault, the Roman troops encompassed and ascended the mountain of Solicinium on three different sides. [92b] Every step which they gained, increased their ardor, and abated the resistance of the enemy: and after their united forces had occupied the summit of the hill, they impetuously urged the Barbarians down the northern descent, where Count Sebastian was posted to intercept their retreat. After this signal victory, Valentinian returned to his winter quarters at Treves; where he indulged the public joy by the exhibition of splendid and triumphal games. [93] But the wise monarch, instead of aspiring to the conquest of Germany, confined his attention to the important and laborious defence of the Gallic frontier, against an enemy whose strength was renewed by a stream of daring volunteers, which incessantly flowed from the most distant tribes of the North. [94] The banks of the Rhine [94a] from its source to the straits of the ocean, were closely planted with strong castles and convenient towers; new works, and new arms, were invented by the ingenuity of a prince who was skilled in the mechanical arts; and his numerous levies of Roman and Barbarian youth were severely trained in all the exercises of war. The progress of the work, which was sometimes opposed by modest representations, and sometimes by hostile attempts, secured the tranquillity of Gaul during the nine subsequent years of the administration of Valentinian. [95]

[Footnote 92a: Probably Easter. Wagner—M.]

[Footnote 92b: Mannert is unable to fix the position of Solicinium. Haefelin (in Comm Acad Elect. Palat. v. 14) conjectures Schwetzingen, near Heidelberg. See Wagner's note. St. Martin, Sultz in Wirtemberg, near the sources of the Neckar St. Martin, iii. 339—M.]

[Footnote 93: The expedition of Valentinian is related by Ammianus, (xxvii. 10;) and celebrated by Ausonius, (Mosell. 421, &c.,) who foolishly supposes, that the Romans were ignorant of the sources of the Danube.]

[Footnote 94: Immanis enim natio, jam inde ab incunabulis primis varietate casuum imminuta; ita saepius adolescit, ut fuisse longis saeculis aestimetur intacta. Ammianus, xxviii. 5. The Count de Buat (Hist. des Peuples de l'Europe, tom. vi. p. 370) ascribes the fecundity of the Alemanni to their easy adoption of strangers. —Note: "This explanation," says Mr. Malthus, "only removes the difficulty a little farther off. It makes the earth rest upon the tortoise, but does not tell us on what the tortoise rests. We may still ask what northern reservoir supplied this incessant stream of daring adventurers. Montesquieu's solution of the problem will, I think, hardly be admitted, (Grandeur et Decadence des Romains, c. 16, p. 187.) The whole difficulty, however, is at once removed, if we apply to the German nations, at that time, a fact which is so generally known to have occurred in America, and suppose that, when not checked by wars and famine, they increased at a rate that would double their numbers in twenty-five or thirty years. The propriety, and even the necessity, of applying this rate of increase to the inhabitants of ancient Germany, will strikingly appear from that most valuable picture of their manners which has been left us by Tacitus, (Tac. de Mor. Germ. 16 to 20.) With these manners, and a habit of enterprise and emigration, which would naturally remove all fears about providing for a family, it is difficult to conceive a society with a stronger principle of increase in it, and we see at once that prolific source of armies and colonies against which the force of the Roman empire so long struggled with difficulty, and under which it ultimately sunk. It is not probable that, for two periods together, or even for one, the population within the confines of Germany ever doubled itself in twenty-five years. Their perpetual wars, the rude state of agriculture, and particularly the very strange custom adopted by most of the tribes of marking their barriers by extensive deserts, would prevent any very great actual increase of numbers. At no one period could the country be called well peopled, though it was often redundant in population. Instead of clearing their forests, draining their swamps, and rendering their soil fit to support an extended population, they found it more congenial to their martial habits and impatient dispositions to go in quest of food, of plunder, or of glory, into other countries." Malthus on Population, i. p. 128—G.]

[Footnote 94a: The course of the Neckar was likewise strongly guarded. The hyperbolical eulogy of Symmachus asserts that the Neckar first became known to the Romans by the conquests and fortifications of Valentinian. Nunc primum victoriis tuis externus fluvius publicatur. Gaudeat servitute, captivus innotuit. Symm. Orat. p. 22—M.]

[Footnote 95: Ammian. xxviii. 2. Zosimus, l. iv. p. 214. The younger Victor mentions the mechanical genius of Valentinian, nova arma meditari fingere terra seu limo simulacra.]

That prudent emperor, who diligently practised the wise maxims of Diocletian, was studious to foment and excite the intestine divisions of the tribes of Germany. About the middle of the fourth century, the countries, perhaps of Lusace and Thuringia, on either side of the Elbe, were occupied by the vague dominion of the Burgundians; a warlike and numerous people, [95a] of the Vandal race, [96] whose obscure name insensibly swelled into a powerful kingdom, and has finally settled on a flourishing province. The most remarkable circumstance in the ancient manners of the Burgundians appears to have been the difference of their civil and ecclesiastical constitution. The appellation of Hendinos was given to the king or general, and the title of Sinistus to the high priest, of the nation. The person of the priest was sacred, and his dignity perpetual; but the temporal government was held by a very precarious tenure. If the events of war accuses the courage or conduct of the king, he was immediately deposed; and the injustice of his subjects made him responsible for the fertility of the earth, and the regularity of the seasons, which seemed to fall more properly within the sacerdotal department. [97] The disputed possession of some salt-pits [98] engaged the Alemanni and the Burgundians in frequent contests: the latter were easily tempted, by the secret solicitations and liberal offers of the emperor; and their fabulous descent from the Roman soldiers, who had formerly been left to garrison the fortresses of Drusus, was admitted with mutual credulity, as it was conducive to mutual interest. [99] An army of fourscore thousand Burgundians soon appeared on the banks of the Rhine; and impatiently required the support and subsidies which Valentinian had promised: but they were amused with excuses and delays, till at length, after a fruitless expectation, they were compelled to retire. The arms and fortifications of the Gallic frontier checked the fury of their just resentment; and their massacre of the captives served to imbitter the hereditary feud of the Burgundians and the Alemanni. The inconstancy of a wise prince may, perhaps, be explained by some alteration of circumstances; and perhaps it was the original design of Valentinian to intimidate, rather than to destroy; as the balance of power would have been equally overturned by the extirpation of either of the German nations. Among the princes of the Alemanni, Macrianus, who, with a Roman name, had assumed the arts of a soldier and a statesman, deserved his hatred and esteem. The emperor himself, with a light and unencumbered band, condescended to pass the Rhine, marched fifty miles into the country, and would infallibly have seized the object of his pursuit, if his judicious measures had not been defeated by the impatience of the troops. Macrianus was afterwards admitted to the honor of a personal conference with the emperor; and the favors which he received, fixed him, till the hour of his death, a steady and sincere friend of the republic. [100]

[Footnote 95a: According to the general opinion, the Burgundians formed a Gothic o Vandalic tribe, who, from the banks of the Lower Vistula, made incursions, on one side towards Transylvania, on the other towards the centre of Germany. All that remains of the Burgundian language is Gothic. Nothing in their customs indicates a different origin. Malte Brun, Geog. tom. i. p. 396. (edit. 1831.)—M.]

[Footnote 96: Bellicosos et pubis immensae viribus affluentes; et ideo metuendos finitimis universis. Ammian. xxviii. 5.]

[Footnote 97: I am always apt to suspect historians and travellers of improving extraordinary facts into general laws. Ammianus ascribes a similar custom to Egypt; and the Chinese have imputed it to the Ta-tsin, or Roman empire, (De Guignes, Hist. des Huns, tom. ii. part. 79.)]

[Footnote 98: Salinarum finiumque causa Alemannis saepe jurgabant. Ammian xxviii. 5. Possibly they disputed the possession of the Sala, a river which produced salt, and which had been the object of ancient contention. Tacit. Annal. xiii. 57, and Lipsius ad loc.]

[Footnote 99: Jam inde temporibus priscis sobolem se esse Romanam Burgundii sciunt: and the vague tradition gradually assumed a more regular form, (Oros. l. vii. c. 32.) It is annihilated by the decisive authority of Pliny, who composed the History of Drusus, and served in Germany, (Plin. Secund. Epist. iii. 5,) within sixty years after the death of that hero. Germanorum genera quinque; Vindili, quorum pars Burgundiones, &c., (Hist. Natur. iv. 28.)]

[Footnote 100: The wars and negotiations relative to the Burgundians and Alemanni, are distinctly related by Ammianus Marcellinus, (xxviii. 5, xxix 4, xxx. 3.) Orosius, (l. vii. c. 32,) and the Chronicles of Jerom and Cassiodorus, fix some dates, and add some circumstances.]

The land was covered by the fortifications of Valentinian; but the sea-coast of Gaul and Britain was exposed to the depredations of the Saxons. That celebrated name, in which we have a dear and domestic interest, escaped the notice of Tacitus; and in the maps of Ptolemy, it faintly marks the narrow neck of the Cimbric peninsula, and three small islands towards the mouth of the Elbe. [101] This contracted territory, the present duchy of Sleswig, or perhaps of Holstein, was incapable of pouring forth the inexhaustible swarms of Saxons who reigned over the ocean, who filled the British island with their language, their laws, and their colonies; and who so long defended the liberty of the North against the arms of Charlemagne. [102] The solution of this difficulty is easily derived from the similar manners, and loose constitution, of the tribes of Germany; which were blended with each other by the slightest accidents of war or friendship. The situation of the native Saxons disposed them to embrace the hazardous professions of fishermen and pirates; and the success of their first adventures would naturally excite the emulation of their bravest countrymen, who were impatient of the gloomy solitude of their woods and mountains. Every tide might float down the Elbe whole fleets of canoes, filled with hardy and intrepid associates, who aspired to behold the unbounded prospect of the ocean, and to taste the wealth and luxury of unknown worlds. It should seem probable, however, that the most numerous auxiliaries of the Saxons were furnished by the nations who dwelt along the shores of the Baltic. They possessed arms and ships, the art of navigation, and the habits of naval war; but the difficulty of issuing through the northern columns of Hercules [103] (which, during several months of the year, are obstructed with ice) confined their skill and courage within the limits of a spacious lake. The rumor of the successful armaments which sailed from the mouth of the Elbe, would soon provoke them to cross the narrow isthmus of Sleswig, and to launch their vessels on the great sea. The various troops of pirates and adventurers, who fought under the same standard, were insensibly united in a permanent society, at first of rapine, and afterwards of government. A military confederation was gradually moulded into a national body, by the gentle operation of marriage and consanguinity; and the adjacent tribes, who solicited the alliance, accepted the name and laws, of the Saxons. If the fact were not established by the most unquestionable evidence, we should appear to abuse the credulity of our readers, by the description of the vessels in which the Saxon pirates ventured to sport in the waves of the German Ocean, the British Channel, and the Bay of Biscay. The keel of their large flat-bottomed boats were framed of light timber, but the sides and upper works consisted only of wicker, with a covering of strong hides. [104] In the course of their slow and distant navigations, they must always have been exposed to the danger, and very frequently to the misfortune, of shipwreck; and the naval annals of the Saxons were undoubtedly filled with the accounts of the losses which they sustained on the coasts of Britain and Gaul. But the daring spirit of the pirates braved the perils both of the sea and of the shore: their skill was confirmed by the habits of enterprise; the meanest of their mariners was alike capable of handling an oar, of rearing a sail, or of conducting a vessel, and the Saxons rejoiced in the appearance of a tempest, which concealed their design, and dispersed the fleets of the enemy. [105] After they had acquired an accurate knowledge of the maritime provinces of the West, they extended the scene of their depredations, and the most sequestered places had no reason to presume on their security. The Saxon boats drew so little water that they could easily proceed fourscore or a hundred miles up the great rivers; their weight was so inconsiderable, that they were transported on wagons from one river to another; and the pirates who had entered the mouth of the Seine, or of the Rhine, might descend, with the rapid stream of the Rhone, into the Mediterranean. Under the reign of Valentinian, the maritime provinces of Gaul were afflicted by the Saxons: a military count was stationed for the defence of the sea-coast, or Armorican limit; and that officer, who found his strength, or his abilities, unequal to the task, implored the assistance of Severus, master-general of the infantry. The Saxons, surrounded and outnumbered, were forced to relinquish their spoil, and to yield a select band of their tall and robust youth to serve in the Imperial armies. They stipulated only a safe and honorable retreat; and the condition was readily granted by the Roman general, who meditated an act of perfidy, [106] imprudent as it was inhuman, while a Saxon remained alive, and in arms, to revenge the fate of their countrymen. The premature eagerness of the infantry, who were secretly posted in a deep valley, betrayed the ambuscade; and they would perhaps have fallen the victims of their own treachery, if a large body of cuirassiers, alarmed by the noise of the combat, had not hastily advanced to extricate their companions, and to overwhelm the undaunted valor of the Saxons. Some of the prisoners were saved from the edge of the sword, to shed their blood in the amphitheatre; and the orator Symmachus complains, that twenty-nine of those desperate savages, by strangling themselves with their own hands, had disappointed the amusement of the public. Yet the polite and philosophic citizens of Rome were impressed with the deepest horror, when they were informed, that the Saxons consecrated to the gods the tithe of their human spoil; and that they ascertained by lot the objects of the barbarous sacrifice. [107]

[Footnote 101: At the northern extremity of the peninsula, (the Cimbric promontory of Pliny, iv. 27,) Ptolemy fixes the remnant of the Cimbri. He fills the interval between the Saxons and the Cimbri with six obscure tribes, who were united, as early as the sixth century, under the national appellation of Danes. See Cluver. German. Antiq. l. iii. c. 21, 22, 23.]

[Footnote 102: M. D'Anville (Establissement des Etats de l'Europe, &c., p. 19-26) has marked the extensive limits of the Saxony of Charlemagne.]

[Footnote 103: The fleet of Drusus had failed in their attempt to pass, or even to approach, the Sound, (styled, from an obvious resemblance, the columns of Hercules,) and the naval enterprise was never resumed, (Tacit. de Moribus German. c. 34.) The knowledge which the Romans acquired of the naval powers of the Baltic, (c. 44, 45) was obtained by their land journeys in search of amber.]

[Footnote 104:
Quin et Aremoricus piratam Saxona tractus
Sperabat; cui pelle salum sulcare Britannum
Ludus; et assuto glaucum mare findere lembo
Sidon. in Panegyr. Avit. 369.

The genius of Caesar imitated, for a particular service, these rude, but light vessels, which were likewise used by the natives of Britain. (Comment. de Bell. Civil. i. 51, and Guichardt, Nouveaux Memoires Militaires, tom. ii. p. 41, 42.) The British vessels would now astonish the genius of Caesar.]

[Footnote 105: The best original account of the Saxon pirates may be found in Sidonius Apollinaris, (l. viii. epist. 6, p. 223, edit. Sirmond,) and the best commentary in the Abbe du Bos, (Hist. Critique de la Monarchie Francoise, &c. tom. i. l. i. c. 16, p. 148-155. See likewise p. 77, 78.)]

[Footnote 106: Ammian. (xxviii. 5) justifies this breach of faith to pirates and robbers; and Orosius (l. vii. c. 32) more clearly expresses their real guilt; virtute atque agilitate terribeles.]

[Footnote 107: Symmachus (l. ii. epist. 46) still presumes to mention the sacred name of Socrates and philosophy. Sidonius, bishop of Clermont, might condemn, (l. viii. epist. 6,) with less inconsistency, the human sacrifices of the Saxons.]

II. The fabulous colonies of Egyptians and Trojans, of Scandinavians and Spaniards, which flattered the pride, and amused the credulity, of our rude ancestors, have insensibly vanished in the light of science and philosophy. [108] The present age is satisfied with the simple and rational opinion, that the islands of Great Britain and Ireland were gradually peopled from the adjacent continent of Gaul. From the coast of Kent, to the extremity of Caithness and Ulster, the memory of a Celtic origin was distinctly preserved, in the perpetual resemblance of language, of religion, and of manners; and the peculiar characters of the British tribes might be naturally ascribed to the influence of accidental and local circumstances. [109] The Roman Province was reduced to the state of civilized and peaceful servitude; the rights of savage freedom were contracted to the narrow limits of Caledonia. The inhabitants of that northern region were divided, as early as the reign of Constantine, between the two great tribes of the Scots and of the Picts, [110] who have since experienced a very different fortune. The power, and almost the memory, of the Picts have been extinguished by their successful rivals; and the Scots, after maintaining for ages the dignity of an independent kingdom, have multiplied, by an equal and voluntary union, the honors of the English name. The hand of nature had contributed to mark the ancient distinctions of the Scots and Picts. The former were the men of the hills, and the latter those of the plain. The eastern coast of Caledonia may be considered as a level and fertile country, which, even in a rude state of tillage, was capable of producing a considerable quantity of corn; and the epithet of cruitnich, or wheat-eaters, expressed the contempt or envy of the carnivorous highlander. The cultivation of the earth might introduce a more accurate separation of property, and the habits of a sedentary life; but the love of arms and rapine was still the ruling passion of the Picts; and their warriors, who stripped themselves for a day of battle, were distinguished, in the eyes of the Romans, by the strange fashion of painting their naked bodies with gaudy colors and fantastic figures. The western part of Caledonia irregularly rises into wild and barren hills, which scarcely repay the toil of the husbandman, and are most profitably used for the pasture of cattle. The highlanders were condemned to the occupations of shepherds and hunters; and, as they seldom were fixed to any permanent habitation, they acquired the expressive name of Scots, which, in the Celtic tongue, is said to be equivalent to that of wanderers, or vagrants. The inhabitants of a barren land were urged to seek a fresh supply of food in the waters. The deep lakes and bays which intersect their country, are plentifully supplied with fish; and they gradually ventured to cast their nets in the waves of the ocean. The vicinity of the Hebrides, so profusely scattered along the western coast of Scotland, tempted their curiosity, and improved their skill; and they acquired, by slow degrees, the art, or rather the habit, of managing their boats in a tempestuous sea, and of steering their nocturnal course by the light of the well-known stars. The two bold headlands of Caledonia almost touch the shores of a spacious island, which obtained, from its luxuriant vegetation, the epithet of Green; and has preserved, with a slight alteration, the name of Erin, or Ierne, or Ireland. It is probable, that in some remote period of antiquity, the fertile plains of Ulster received a colony of hungry Scots; and that the strangers of the North, who had dared to encounter the arms of the legions, spread their conquests over the savage and unwarlike natives of a solitary island. It is certain, that, in the declining age of the Roman empire, Caledonia, Ireland, and the Isle of Man, were inhabited by the Scots, and that the kindred tribes, who were often associated in military enterprise, were deeply affected by the various accidents of their mutual fortunes. They long cherished the lively tradition of their common name and origin; and the missionaries of the Isle of Saints, who diffused the light of Christianity over North Britain, established the vain opinion, that their Irish countrymen were the natural, as well as spiritual, fathers of the Scottish race. The loose and obscure tradition has been preserved by the venerable Bede, who scattered some rays of light over the darkness of the eighth century. On this slight foundation, a huge superstructure of fable was gradually reared, by the bards and the monks; two orders of men, who equally abused the privilege of fiction. The Scottish nation, with mistaken pride, adopted their Irish genealogy; and the annals of a long line of imaginary kings have been adorned by the fancy of Boethius, and the classic elegance of Buchanan. [111]

[Footnote 108: In the beginning of the last century, the learned Camden was obliged to undermine, with respectful scepticism, the romance of Brutus, the Trojan; who is now buried in silent oblivion with Scota the daughter of Pharaoh, and her numerous progeny. Yet I am informed, that some champions of the Milesian colony may still be found among the original natives of Ireland. A people dissatisfied with their present condition, grasp at any visions of their past or future glory.]

[Footnote 109: Tacitus, or rather his father-in-law, Agricola, might remark the German or Spanish complexion of some British tribes. But it was their sober, deliberate opinion: "In universum tamen aestimanti Gallos cicinum solum occupasse credibile est. Eorum sacra deprehendas.... ermo haud multum diversus," (in Vit. Agricol. c. xi.) Caesar had observed their common religion, (Comment. de Bello Gallico, vi. 13;) and in his time the emigration from the Belgic Gaul was a recent, or at least an historical event, (v. 10.) Camden, the British Strabo, has modestly ascertained our genuine antiquities, (Britannia, vol. i. Introduction, p. ii—xxxi.)]

[Footnote 110: In the dark and doubtful paths of Caledonian antiquity, I have chosen for my guides two learned and ingenious Highlanders, whom their birth and education had peculiarly qualified for that office. See Critical Dissertations on the Origin and Antiquities, &c., of the Caledonians, by Dr. John Macpherson, London 1768, in 4to.; and Introduction to the History of Great Britain and Ireland, by James Macpherson, Esq., London 1773, in 4to., third edit. Dr. Macpherson was a minister in the Isle of Sky: and it is a circumstance honorable for the present age, that a work, replete with erudition and criticism, should have been composed in the most remote of the Hebrides.]

[Footnote 111: The Irish descent of the Scots has been revived in the last moments of its decay, and strenuously supported, by the Rev. Mr. Whitaker, (Hist. of Manchester, vol. i. p. 430, 431; and Genuine History of the Britons asserted, &c., p. 154-293) Yet he acknowledges, 1. That the Scots of Ammianus Marcellinus (A.D. 340) were already settled in Caledonia; and that the Roman authors do not afford any hints of their emigration from another country. 2. That all the accounts of such emigrations, which have been asserted or received, by Irish bards, Scotch historians, or English antiquaries, (Buchanan, Camden, Usher, Stillingfleet, &c.,) are totally fabulous. 3. That three of the Irish tribes, which are mentioned by Ptolemy, (A.D. 150,) were of Caledonian extraction. 4. That a younger branch of Caledonian princes, of the house of Fingal, acquired and possessed the monarchy of Ireland. After these concessions, the

remaining difference between Mr. Whitaker and his adversaries is minute and obscure. The genuine history, which he produces, of a Fergus, the cousin of Ossian, who was transplanted (A.D. 320) from Ireland to Caledonia, is built on a conjectural supplement to the Erse poetry, and the feeble evidence of Richard of Cirencester, a monk of the fourteenth century. The lively spirit of the learned and ingenious antiquarian has tempted him to forget the nature of a question, which he so vehemently debates, and so absolutely decides. Note: This controversy has not slumbered since the days of Gibbon. We have strenuous advocates of the Phoenician origin of the Irish, and each of the old theories, with several new ones, maintains its partisans. It would require several pages fairly to bring down the dispute to our own days, and perhaps we should be no nearer to any satisfactory theory than Gibbon was.]

PART V

Six years after the death of Constantine, the destructive inroads of the Scots and Picts required the presence of his youngest son, who reigned in the Western empire. Constans visited his British dominions: but we may form some estimate of the importance of his achievements, by the language of panegyric, which celebrates only his triumph over the elements or, in other words, the good fortune of a safe and easy passage from the port of Boulogne to the harbor of Sandwich. [112] The calamities which the afflicted provincials continued to experience, from foreign war and domestic tyranny, were aggravated by the feeble and corrupt administration of the eunuchs of Constantius; and the transient relief which they might obtain from the virtues of Julian, was soon lost by the absence and death of their benefactor. The sums of gold and silver, which had been painfully collected, or liberally transmitted, for the payment of the troops, were intercepted by the avarice of the commanders; discharges, or, at least, exemptions, from the military service, were publicly sold; the distress of the soldiers, who were injuriously deprived of their legal and scanty subsistence, provoked them to frequent desertion; the nerves of discipline were relaxed, and the highways were infested with robbers. [113] The oppression of the good, and the impunity of the wicked, equally contributed to diffuse through the island a spirit of discontent and revolt; and every ambitious subject, every desperate exile, might entertain a reasonable hope of subverting the weak and distracted government of Britain. The hostile tribes of the North, who detested the pride and power of the King of the World, suspended their domestic feuds; and the Barbarians of the land and sea, the Scots, the Picts, and the Saxons, spread themselves with rapid and irresistible fury, from the wall of Antoninus to the shores of Kent. Every production of art and nature, every object of convenience and luxury, which they were incapable of creating by labor or procuring by trade, was accumulated in the rich and fruitful province of Britain. [114] A philosopher may deplore the eternal discords of the human race, but he will confess, that the desire of spoil is a more rational provocation than the vanity of conquest. From the age of Constantine to the Plantagenets, this rapacious spirit continued to instigate the poor and hardy Caledonians; but the same people, whose generous humanity seems to inspire the songs of Ossian, was disgraced by a savage ignorance of the virtues of peace, and of the laws of war. Their southern neighbors have felt, and perhaps exaggerated, the cruel depredations of the Scots and Picts; [115] and a valiant tribe of Caledonia, the Attacotti, [116] the enemies, and afterwards the soldiers, of Valentinian, are accused, by an eye-witness, of delighting in the taste of human flesh. When they hunted the woods for prey, it is said, that they attacked the shepherd rather than his flock; and that they curiously selected the most delicate and brawny parts, both of males and females, which they prepared for their horrid repasts. [117] If, in the neighborhood of the commercial and literary town of Glasgow, a race of cannibals has really existed, we may contemplate, in the period of the Scottish history, the opposite extremes of savage and civilized life.

Such reflections tend to enlarge the circle of our ideas; and to encourage the pleasing hope, that New Zealand may produce, in some future age, the Hume of the Southern Hemisphere.

[Footnote 112: Hyeme tumentes ac saevientes undas calcastis Oceani sub remis vestris;... insperatam imperatoris faciem Britannus expavit. Julius Fermicus Maternus de Errore Profan. Relig. p. 464. edit. Gronov. ad calcem Minuc. Fael. See Tillemont, (Hist. des Empereurs, tom. iv. p. 336.)]

[Footnote 113: Libanius, Orat. Parent. c. xxxix. p. 264. This curious passage has escaped the diligence of our British antiquaries.]

[Footnote 114: The Caledonians praised and coveted the gold, the steeds, the lights, &c., of the stranger. See Dr. Blair's Dissertation on Ossian, vol ii. p. 343; and Mr. Macpherson's Introduction, p. 242-286.]

[Footnote 115: Lord Lyttelton has circumstantially related, (History of Henry II. vol. i. p. 182,) and Sir David Dalrymple has slightly mentioned, (Annals of Scotland, vol. i. p. 69,) a barbarous inroad of the Scots, at a time (A.D. 1137) when law, religion, and society must have softened their primitive manners.]

[Footnote 116: Attacotti bellicosa hominum natio. Ammian. xxvii. 8. Camden (Introduct. p. clii.) has restored their true name in the text of Jerom. The bands of Attacotti, which Jerom had seen in Gaul, were afterwards stationed in Italy and Illyricum, (Notitia, S. viii. xxxix. xl.)]

[Footnote 117: Cum ipse adolescentulus in Gallia viderim Attacottos (or Scotos) gentem Britannicam humanis vesci carnibus; et cum per silvas porcorum greges, et armentorum percudumque reperiant, pastorum nates et feminarum papillas solere abscindere; et has solas ciborum delicias arbitrari. Such is the evidence of Jerom, (tom. ii. p. 75,) whose veracity I find no reason to question. Note: See Dr. Parr's works, iii. 93, where he questions the propriety of Gibbon's translation of this passage. The learned doctor approves of the version proposed by a Mr. Gaches, who would make out that it was the delicate parts of the swine and the cattle, which were eaten by these ancestors of the Scotch nation. I confess that even to acquit them of this charge. I cannot agree to the new version, which, in my opinion, is directly contrary both to the meaning of the words, and the general sense of the passage. But I would suggest, did Jerom, as a boy, accompany these savages in any of their hunting expeditions? If he did not, how could he be an eye-witness of this practice? The Attacotti in Gaul must have been in the service of Rome. Were they permitted to indulge these cannibal propensities at the expense, not of the flocks, but of the shepherds of the provinces? These sanguinary trophies of plunder would scarce'y have been publicly exhibited in a Roman city or a Roman camp. I must leave the hereditary pride of our northern neighbors at issue with the veracity of St. Jerom.]

Every messenger who escaped across the British Channel, conveyed the most melancholy and alarming tidings to the ears of Valentinian; and the emperor was soon informed that the two military commanders of the province had been surprised and cut off by the Barbarians. Severus, count of the domestics, was hastily despatched, and as suddenly recalled, by the court of Treves. The representations of Jovinus served only to indicate the greatness of the evil; and, after a long and serious consultation, the defence, or rather the recovery, of Britain was intrusted to the abilities of the brave Theodosius. The exploits of that general, the father of a line of emperors, have been celebrated, with peculiar complacency, by the writers of the age: but his real merit deserved their applause; and his nomination was received, by the army and province, as a sure presage of approaching victory. He seized the favorable moment of navigation, and securely landed the numerous and veteran bands of the Heruli and Batavians, the Jovians and the Victors. In his march from Sandwich to London, Theodosius defeated several parties of the Barbarians, released a multitude of captives, and, after distributing to his soldiers a small portion of the spoil, established the fame of disinterested justice, by the restitution of the remainder to the rightful proprietors. The citizens of London, who had almost despaired of their safety, threw open their gates; and as soon as Theodosius had obtained from the court of Treves the important aid of a military lieutenant, and a civil governor, he executed, with wisdom and vigor, the laborious task of the deliverance of Britain. The vagrant soldiers were recalled to their standard; an edict of amnesty dispelled the public apprehensions; and his cheerful example alleviated the rigor of martial discipline. The scattered and desultory warfare of the Barbarians, who infested the land and sea, deprived him of the glory of a signal victory; but the prudent spirit, and consummate art, of the Roman general, were displayed in the operations of two campaigns, which successively rescued every part of the province from the hands of a cruel and rapacious enemy. The splendor of the cities, and the security of the fortifications, were diligently restored, by the paternal care of Theodosius; who with a strong hand confined the trembling Caledonians to the northern angle of the island; and perpetuated, by the name and settlement of the new province of Valentia, the glories of the reign of Valentinian. [118] The voice of poetry and panegyric may add, perhaps with some degree of truth, that the unknown regions of Thule were stained with the blood of the Picts; that the oars of Theodosius dashed the waves of the Hyperborean ocean; and that the distant Orkneys were the scene of his naval victory over the Saxon pirates. [119] He left the province with a fair, as well as splendid, reputation; and was immediately promoted to the rank of master-general of the cavalry, by a prince who could applaud, without envy, the merit of his servants. In the important station of the Upper Danube, the conqueror of Britain checked and defeated the armies of the Alemanni, before he was chosen to suppress the revolt of Africa.

[Footnote 118: Ammianus has concisely represented (xx. l. xxvi. 4, xxvii. 8 xxviii. 3) the whole series of the British war.]

[Footnote 119: Horrescit.... ratibus.... impervia Thule. Ille.... nec falso nomine Pictos Edomuit. Scotumque vago mucrone secutus, Fregit Hyperboreas remis audacibus undas. Claudian, in iii. Cons. Honorii, ver. 53, &c—Madurunt Saxone fuso Orcades: incaluit Pictorum sanguine Thule, Scotorum cumulos flevit glacialis Ierne. In iv. Cons. Hon. ver. 31, &c. —See likewise Pacatus, (in Panegyr. Vet. xii. 5.) But it is not easy to appreciate the intrinsic value of flattery and metaphor. Compare the British victories of Bolanus (Statius, Silv. v. 2) with his real character, (Tacit. in Vit. Agricol. c. 16.)]

III. The prince who refuses to be the judge, instructs the people to consider him as the accomplice, of his ministers. The military command of Africa had been long exercised by Count Romanus, and his abilities were not inadequate to his station; but, as sordid interest was the sole motive of his conduct, he acted, on most occasions, as if he had been the enemy of the province, and the friend of the Barbarians of the desert. The three flourishing cities of Oea, Leptis, and Sobrata, which, under the name of Tripoli, had long constituted a federal union, [120] were obliged, for the first time, to shut their gates against a hostile invasion; several of their most honorable citizens were surprised and massacred; the villages, and even the suburbs, were pillaged; and the vines and fruit trees of that rich territory were extirpated by the malicious savages of Getulia. The unhappy provincials implored the protection of Romanus; but they soon found that their military governor was not less cruel and rapacious than the Barbarians. As they were incapable of furnishing the four thousand camels, and the exorbitant present, which he required, before he would march to the assistance of Tripoli; his demand was equivalent to a refusal, and he might justly be accused as the author of the public calamity. In the annual assembly of the three cities, they nominated two deputies, to lay at the feet of Valentinian the customary offering of a gold victory; and to accompany this tribute of duty, rather than of gratitude, with their humble complaint, that they were ruined by the enemy, and betrayed by their governor. If the severity of Valentinian had been rightly directed, it would have fallen on the guilty head of Romanus. But the count, long exercised in the arts of corruption, had despatched a swift and trusty messenger to secure the venal friendship of Remigius, master of the offices. The wisdom of the Imperial council was deceived by artifice; and their honest indignation was cooled by delay. At length, when the repetition of complaint had been justified by the repetition of public misfortunes, the notary Palladius was sent from the court of Treves, to examine the state of Africa, and the conduct of Romanus. The rigid impartiality of Palladius was easily disarmed: he was tempted to reserve for himself a part of the public treasure, which he brought with him for the payment of the troops; and from the moment that he was conscious of his own guilt, he could no longer refuse to attest the innocence and merit of the count. The charge of the Tripolitans was declared to be false and frivolous; and Palladius himself was sent back from Treves to Africa, with a special commission to discover and prosecute the authors of this impious conspiracy against the representatives of the sovereign. His inquiries were managed with so much dexterity and success, that he compelled the citizens of Leptis, who had sustained a recent siege of eight days, to contradict the truth of their own decrees, and to censure the behavior of their own deputies. A bloody sentence was pronounced, without hesitation, by the rash and headstrong cruelty of Valentinian. The president of Tripoli, who had presumed to pity the distress of the province, was publicly executed at Utica; four distinguished citizens were put to death, as the accomplices of the imaginary fraud; and the tongues of two others were cut out, by the express order of the emperor. Romanus, elated by impunity, and irritated by resistance, was still continued in the military command; till the Africans were provoked, by his avarice, to join the rebellious standard of Firmus, the Moor. [121]

[Footnote 120: Ammianus frequently mentions their concilium annuum, legitimum, &c. Leptis and Sabrata are long since ruined; but the city of Oea, the native country of Apuleius, still flourishes under the provincial denomination of Tripoli. See Cellarius (Geograph. Antiqua, tom. ii. part ii. p. 81,) D'Anville, (Geographie Ancienne, tom. iii. p. 71, 72,) and Marmol, (Arrique, tom. ii. p. 562.)]

[Footnote 121: Ammian. xviii. 6. Tillemont (Hist. des Empereurs, tom. v. p 25, 676) has discussed the chronological difficulties of the history of Count Romanus.]

His father Nabal was one of the richest and most powerful of the Moorish princes, who acknowledged the supremacy of Rome. But as he left, either by his wives or concubines, a very numerous posterity, the wealthy inheritance was eagerly disputed; and Zamma, one of his sons, was slain in a domestic quarrel by his brother Firmus. The implacable zeal, with which Romanus prosecuted the legal revenge of this murder, could be ascribed only to a motive of avarice, or personal hatred; but, on this occasion, his claims were just; his influence was weighty; and Firmus clearly understood, that he must either present his neck to the executioner, or appeal from the sentence of the Imperial consistory, to his sword, and to the people. [122] He was received as the deliverer of his country; and, as soon as it appeared that Romanus was formidable only to a submissive province, the tyrant of Africa became the object of universal contempt. The ruin of Caesarea, which was plundered and burnt by the licentious Barbarians, convinced the refractory cities of the danger of resistance; the power of Firmus was established, at least in the provinces of Mauritania and Numidia; and it seemed to be his only doubt whether he should assume the diadem of a Moorish king, or the purple of a Roman emperor. But the imprudent and unhappy Africans soon discovered, that, in this rash insurrection, they had not sufficiently consulted their own strength, or the abilities of their leader. Before he could procure any certain intelligence, that the emperor of the West had fixed the choice of a general, or that a fleet of transports was collected at the mouth of the Rhone, he was suddenly informed that the great Theodosius, with a small band of veterans, had landed near Igilgilis, or Gigeri, on the African coast; and the timid usurper sunk under the ascendant of virtue and military genius. Though Firmus possessed arms and treasures, his despair of victory immediately reduced him to the use of those arts, which, in the same country, and in a similar situation, had formerly been practised by the crafty Jugurtha. He attempted to deceive, by an apparent submission, the vigilance of the Roman general; to seduce the fidelity of his troops; and to protract the duration of the war, by successively engaging the independent tribes of Africa to espouse his quarrel, or to protect his flight. Theodosius imitated the example, and obtained the success, of his predecessor Metellus. When Firmus, in the character of a suppliant, accused his own rashness, and humbly solicited the clemency of the emperor, the lieutenant of Valentinian received and dismissed him with a friendly embrace: but he diligently required the useful and substantial pledges of a sincere repentance; nor could he be persuaded, by the assurances of peace, to suspend, for an instant, the operations of an active war. A dark conspiracy was detected by the penetration of Theodosius; and he satisfied, without much reluctance, the public indignation, which he had secretly excited. Several of the guilty accomplices of Firmus were abandoned, according to ancient custom, to the tumult of a military execution; many more, by the amputation of both their hands, continued to exhibit an instructive spectacle of horror; the hatred of the rebels was accompanied with fear; and the fear of the Roman soldiers was mingled with respectful admiration. Amidst the boundless plains of Getulia, and the innumerable valleys of Mount Atlas, it was impossible to prevent the escape of Firmus; and if the usurper could have tired the patience of his antagonist, he would have secured his person in the depth of some remote solitude, and expected the hopes of a future revolution. He was subdued by the perseverance of Theodosius; who had formed an inflexible determination, that the war should end only by the death of the tyrant; and that every nation of Africa, which presumed to support his cause, should be involved in his ruin. At the head of a small body of troops, which seldom exceeded three thousand five hundred men, the Roman general advanced, with a steady prudence, devoid of rashness or of fear, into the heart of a country, where he was sometimes attacked by armies of twenty thousand Moors. The boldness of his charge dismayed the irregular Barbarians; they were disconcerted by his seasonable and orderly retreats; they were continually baffled by the unknown resources of the military art; and they felt and confessed the just superiority which was assumed by the leader of a civilized nation. When Theodosius entered the extensive dominions of Igmazen, king of the Isaflenses, the haughty savage required, in words of defiance, his name, and the object of his expedition. "I am," replied the stern and disdainful count, "I am the general of Valentinian, the lord of the world; who has sent me hither to pursue and punish a desperate robber. Deliver him instantly into my hands; and be assured, that if thou dost not obey the commands of my invincible sovereign, thou, and the people over whom thou reignest, shall be utterly extirpated." [122a] As soon as Igmazen was satisfied, that his enemy had strength and resolution to execute the fatal menace, he consented to purchase a necessary peace by the sacrifice of a guilty fugitive. The guards that were placed to secure the person of Firmus deprived him of the hopes of escape; and the Moorish tyrant, after wine had extinguished the sense of danger, disappointed the insulting triumph of the Romans, by strangling himself in the night. His dead body, the only present which Igmazen could offer to the conqueror, was carelessly thrown upon a camel; and Theodosius, leading back his victorious troops to Sitifi, was saluted by the warmest acclamations of joy and loyalty. [123]

[Footnote 122: The Chronology of Ammianus is loose and obscure; and Orosius (i. vii. c. 33, p. 551, edit. Havercamp) seems to place the revolt of Firmus after the deaths of Valentinian and Valens. Tillemont (Hist. des. Emp. tom. v. p. 691) endeavors to pick his way. The patient and sure-foot mule of the Alps may be trusted in the most slippery paths.]

[Footnote 122a: The war was longer protracted than this sentence would lead us to suppose: it was not till defeated more than once that Igmazen yielded Amm. xxix. 5—M]

[Footnote 123: Ammian xxix. 5. The text of this long chapter (fifteen quarto pages) is broken and corrupted; and the narrative is perplexed by the want of chronological and geographical landmarks.]

Africa had been lost by the vices of Romanus; it was restored by the virtues of Theodosius; and our curiosity may be usefully directed to the inquiry of the respective treatment which the two generals received from the Imperial court. The authority of Count Romanus had been suspended by the master-general of the cavalry; and he was committed to safe and honorable custody till the end of the war. His crimes were proved by the most authentic evidence; and the public expected, with some impatience, the decree of severe justice. But the partial and powerful favor of Mellobaudes encouraged him to challenge his legal judges, to obtain repeated delays for the purpose of procuring a crowd of friendly witnesses, and, finally, to cover his guilty conduct, by the additional guilt of fraud and forgery. About the same time, the restorer of Britain and Africa, on a vague suspicion that his name and services were superior to the rank of a subject, was ignominiously beheaded at Carthage. Valentinian no longer reigned; and the death of Theodosius, as well as the impunity of Romanus, may justly be imputed to the arts of the ministers, who abused the confidence, and deceived the inexperienced youth, of his sons. [124]

[Footnote 124: Ammian xxviii. 4. Orosius, l. vii. c. 33, p. 551, 552. Jerom. in Chron. p. 187.]

If the geographical accuracy of Ammianus had been fortunately bestowed on the British exploits of Theodosius, we should have traced, with eager curiosity, the distinct and domestic footsteps of his march. But the tedious enumeration of the unknown and uninteresting tribes of Africa may be reduced to the general remark, that they were all of the swarthy race of the Moors; that they inhabited the back settlements of the Mauritanian and Numidian province, the country, as they have since been termed by the Arabs, of dates and of locusts; [125] and that, as the Roman power declined in Africa, the boundary of civilized manners and cultivated land was insensibly contracted. Beyond the utmost limits of the Moors, the vast and inhospitable desert of the South extends above a thousand miles to the banks of the Niger. The ancients, who had a very faint and imperfect knowledge of the great peninsula of Africa, were sometimes tempted to believe, that the torrid zone must ever remain destitute of inhabitants; [126] and they sometimes amused their fancy by filling the vacant space with headless men, or rather monsters; [127] with horned and cloven-footed satyrs; [128] with fabulous centaurs; [129] and with human pygmies, who waged a bold and doubtful warfare against the cranes. [130] Carthage would have trembled at the strange intelligence that the countries on either side of the equator were filled with innumerable nations, who differed only in their color from the ordinary appearance of the human species: and the subjects of the Roman empire might have anxiously expected, that the swarms of Barbarians, which issued from the North, would soon be encountered from the South by new swarms of Barbarians, equally fierce and equally formidable. These gloomy terrors would indeed have been dispelled by a more intimate acquaintance with the character of their African enemies. The inaction of the negroes does not seem to be the effect either of their virtue or of their pusillanimity. They indulge, like the rest of mankind, their passions and appetites; and the adjacent tribes are engaged in frequent acts of hostility. [131] But their rude ignorance has never invented any effectual weapons of defence, or of destruction; they appear incapable of forming any extensive plans of government, or conquest; and the obvious inferiority of their mental faculties has been discovered and abused by the nations of the temperate zone. Sixty thousand blacks are annually embarked from the coast of Guinea, never to return to their native country; but they are embarked in chains; [132] and this constant emigration, which, in the space of two centuries, might have furnished armies to overrun the globe, accuses the guilt of Europe, and the weakness of Africa.

[Footnote 125: Leo Africanus (in the Viaggi di Ramusio, tom. i. fol. 78-83) has traced a curious picture of the people and the country; which are more minutely described in the Afrique de Marmol, tom. iii. p. 1-54.]

[Footnote 126: This uninhabitable zone was gradually reduced by the improvements of ancient geography, from forty-five to twenty-four, or even sixteen degrees of latitude. See a learned and judicious note of Dr. Robertson, Hist. of America, vol. i. p. 426.]

[Footnote 127: Intra, si credere libet, vix jam homines et magis semiferi... Blemmyes, Satyri, &c. Pomponius Mela, i. 4, p. 26, edit. Voss. in 8vo. Pliny philosophically explains (vi. 35) the irregularities of nature, which he had credulously admitted, (v. 8.)]

[Footnote 128: If the satyr was the Orang-outang, the great human ape, (Buffon, Hist. Nat. tom. xiv. p. 43, &c.,) one of that species might actually be shown alive at Alexandria, in the reign of Constantine. Yet some difficulty will still remain about the conversation which St. Anthony held with one of these pious savages, in the desert of Thebais. (Jerom. in Vit. Paul. Eremit. tom. i. p. 238.)]

[Footnote 129: St. Anthony likewise met one of these monsters; whose existence was seriously asserted by the emperor Claudius. The public laughed; but his praefect of Egypt had the address to send an artful preparation, the embalmed corpse of a Hippocentaur, which was preserved almost a century afterwards in the Imperial palace. See Pliny, (Hist. Natur. vii. 3,) and the judicious observations of Freret. (Memoires de l'Acad. tom. vii. p. 321, &c.)]

[Footnote 130: The fable of the pygmies is as old as Homer, (Iliad. iii. 6) The pygmies of India and Aethiopia were (trispithami) twenty-seven inches high. Every spring their cavalry (mounted on rams and goats) marched, in battle array, to destroy the cranes' eggs, aliter (says Pliny) futuris gregibus non resisti. Their houses were built of mud, feathers, and egg-shells. See Pliny, (vi. 35, vii. 2,) and Strabo, (l. ii. p. 121.)]

[Footnote 131: The third and fourth volumes of the valuable Histoire des Voyages describe the present state of the Negroes. The nations of the sea-coast have been polished by European commerce; and those of the inland country have been improved by Moorish colonies. Note: The martial tribes in chain armor, discovered by Denham, are Mahometan; the great question of the inferiority of the African tribes in their mental faculties will probably be experimentally resolved before the close of the century; but the Slave Trade still continues, and will, it is to be feared, till the spirit of gain is subdued by the spirit of Christian humanity—M.]

[Footnote 132: Histoire Philosophique et Politique, &c., tom. iv. p. 192.]

PART VI

IV. The ignominious treaty, which saved the army of Jovian, had been faithfully executed on the side of the Romans; and as they had solemnly renounced the sovereignty and alliance of Armenia and Iberia, those tributary kingdoms were exposed, without protection, to the arms of the Persian monarch. [133] Sapor entered the Armenian territories at the head of a formidable host of cuirassiers, of archers, and of mercenary foot; but it was the invariable practice of Sapor to mix war and negotiation, and to consider falsehood and perjury as the most powerful instruments of regal policy. He affected to praise the prudent and moderate conduct of the king of Armenia; and the unsuspicious Tiranus was persuaded, by the repeated assurances of insidious friendship, to deliver his person into the hands of a faithless and cruel enemy. In the midst of a splendid entertainment, he was bound in chains of silver, as an honor due to the blood of the Arsacides; and, after a short confinement in the Tower of Oblivion at Ecbatana, he was released from the miseries of life, either by his own dagger, or by that of an assassin. [133a] The kingdom of Armenia was reduced to the state of a Persian province; the administration was shared between a distinguished satrap and a favorite eunuch; and Sapor marched, without delay, to subdue the martial spirit of the Iberians. Sauromaces, who reigned in that country by the permission of the emperors, was expelled by a superior force; and, as an insult on the majesty of Rome, the king of kings placed a diadem on the head of his abject vassal Aspacuras. The city of Artogerassa [134] was the only place of Armenia [134a] which presumed to resist the efforts of his arms. The treasure deposited in that strong fortress tempted the avarice of Sapor; but the danger of Olympias, the wife or widow of the Armenian king, excited the public compassion, and animated the desperate valor of her subjects and soldiers. [134b] The Persians were surprised and repulsed under the walls of Artogerassa, by a bold and well-concerted sally of the besieged. But the forces of Sapor were continually renewed and increased; the hopeless courage of the garrison was exhausted; the strength of the walls yielded to the assault; and the proud conqueror, after wasting the rebellious city with fire and sword, led away captive an unfortunate queen; who, in a more auspicious hour, had been the destined bride of the son of Constantine. [135] Yet if Sapor already triumphed in the easy conquest of two dependent kingdoms, he soon felt, that a country is unsubdued as long as the minds of the people are actuated by a hostile and contumacious spirit. The satraps, whom he was obliged to trust, embraced the first opportunity of regaining the affection of their countrymen, and of signalizing their immortal hatred to the Persian name. Since the conversion of the Armenians and Iberians, these nations considered the Christians as the favorites, and the Magians as the adversaries, of the Supreme Being: the influence of the clergy, over a superstitious people was uniformly exerted in the cause of Rome; and as long as the successors of Constantine disputed with those of Artaxerxes the sovereignty of the intermediate provinces, the religious connection always threw a decisive advantage into the scale of the empire. A numerous and active party acknowledged Para, the son of Tiranus, as the lawful sovereign of Armenia, and his title to the throne was deeply rooted in the hereditary succession of five hundred years. By the unanimous consent of the Iberians, the country was equally divided between the rival princes; and Aspacuras, who owed his diadem to the choice of Sapor, was obliged to declare, that his regard for his children, who were detained as hostages by the tyrant, was the only consideration which prevented him from openly renouncing the alliance of Persia. The emperor Valens, who respected the obligations of the treaty, and who was apprehensive of involving the East in a dangerous war, ventured, with slow and cautious measures, to support the Roman party in the kingdoms of Iberia and Armenia. [135a] Twelve legions established the authority of Sauromaces on the banks of the Cyrus. The Euphrates was protected by the valor of Arintheus. A powerful army, under the command of Count Trajan, and of Vadomair, king of the Alemanni, fixed their camp on the confines of Armenia. But they were strictly enjoined not to commit the first hostilities, which might be understood as a breach of the treaty: and such was the implicit obedience of the Roman general, that they retreated, with exemplary patience, under a shower of Persian arrows till they had clearly acquired a just title to an honorable and legitimate victory. Yet these appearances of war insensibly subsided in a vain and tedious negotiation. The contending parties supported their claims by mutual reproaches of perfidy and ambition; and it should seem, that the original treaty was expressed in very obscure terms, since they were reduced to the necessity of making their inconclusive appeal to the partial testimony of the generals of the two nations, who had assisted at the negotiations. [136] The invasion of the Goths and Huns which soon afterwards shook the foundations of the Roman empire, exposed the provinces of Asia to the arms of Sapor. But the declining age, and perhaps the infirmities, of the monarch suggested new maxims of tranquillity and moderation. His death, which happened in the full maturity of a reign of seventy years, changed in a moment the court and councils of Persia; and their attention was most probably engaged by domestic troubles, and the distant efforts of a Carmanian war. [137] The remembrance of ancient injuries was lost in the enjoyment of peace. The kingdoms of Armenia and Iberia were permitted, by the mutual,though tacit consent of both empires, to resume their doubtful neutrality. In the first years of the reign of Theodosius, a Persian embassy arrived at Constantinople, to excuse the unjustifiable measures of the former reign; and to offer, as the tribute of friendship, or even of respect, a splendid present of gems, of silk, and of Indian elephants. [138]

[Footnote 133: The evidence of Ammianus is original and decisive, (xxvii. 12.) Moses of Chorene, (l. iii. c. 17, p. 249, and c. 34, p. 269,) and Procopius, (de Bell. Persico, l. i. c. 5, p. 17, edit. Louvre,) have been consulted: but those historians who confound distinct facts, repeat the same events, and introduce strange stories, must be used with diffidence and caution. Note: The statement of Ammianus is more brief and succinct, but harmonizes with the more complicated history developed by M. St. Martin from the Armenian writers, and from Procopius, who wrote, as he states from Armenian authorities—M.]

[Footnote 133a: According to M. St. Martin, Sapor, though supported by the two apostate Armenian princes, Meroujan the Ardzronnian and Vahan the Mamigonian, was gallantly resisted by Arsaces, and his brave though impious wife Pharandsem. His troops were defeated by Vasag, the high constable of the kingdom. (See M. St. Martin.) But after four years' courageous defence of his kingdom, Arsaces was abandoned by his nobles, and obliged to accept the perfidious hospitality of Sapor. He was blinded and imprisoned in the "Castle of Oblivion;" his brave general Vasag was flayed alive; his skin stuffed and placed near the king in his lonely prison. It was not till many years after (A.D. 371) that he stabbed himself, according to the romantic story, (St. M. iii. 387, 389,) in a paroxysm of excitement at his restoration to royal honors. St. Martin, Additions to Le Beau, iii. 283, 296—M.]

[Footnote 134: Perhaps Artagera, or Ardis; under whose walls Caius, the grandson of Augustus, was wounded. This fortress was situate above Amida, near one of the sources of the Tigris. See D'Anville, Geographie Ancienue, tom. ii. p. 106. Note: St. Martin agrees with Gibbon, that it was the same fortress with Ardis Note, p. 373—M.]

[Footnote 134a: Artaxata, Vagharschabad, or Edchmiadzin, Erovantaschad, and many other cities, in all of which there was a considerable Jewish population were taken and destroyed—M.]

[Footnote 134b: Pharandsem, not Olympias, refusing the orders of her captive husband to surrender herself to Sapor, threw herself into Artogerassa St. Martin, iii. 293, 302. She defended herself for fourteen months, till famine and disease had left few survivors out of 11,000 soldiers and 6000 women who had taken refuge in the fortress. She then threw open the gates with her own hand. M. St. Martin adds, what even the horrors of Oriental warfare will scarcely permit us to credit, that she was exposed by Sapor on a public scaffold to the brutal lusts of his soldiery, and afterwards empaled, iii. 373, &c—M.]

[Footnote 135: Tillemont (Hist. des Empereurs, tom. v. p. 701) proves, from chronology, that Olympias must have been the mother of Para. Note : An error according to St. M. 273—M.]

[Footnote 135a: According to Themistius, quoted by St. Martin, he once advanced to the Tigris, iii. 436—M.]

[Footnote 136: Ammianus (xxvii. 12, xix. 1. xxx. 1, 2) has described the events, without the dates, of the Persian war. Moses of Chorene (Hist. Armen. l. iii. c. 28, p. 261, c. 31, p. 266, c. 35, p. 271) affords some additional facts; but it is extremely difficult to separate truth from fable.]

[Footnote 137: Artaxerxes was the successor and brother (the cousin-german) of the great Sapor; and the guardian of his son, Sapor III. (Agathias, l. iv. p. 136, edit. Louvre.) See the Universal History, vol. xi. p. 86, 161. The authors of that unequal work have compiled the Sassanian dynasty with erudition and diligence; but it is a preposterous arrangement to divide the Roman and Oriental accounts into two distinct histories. Note: On the war of Sapor with the Bactrians, which diverted from Armenia, see St. M. iii. 387—M.]

[Footnote 138: Pacatus in Panegyr. Vet. xii. 22, and Orosius, l. vii. c. 34. Ictumque tum foedus est, quo universus Oriens usque ad num (A. D. 416) tranquillissime fruitur.]

In the general picture of the affairs of the East under the reign of Valens, the adventures of Para form one of the most striking and singular objects. The noble youth, by the persuasion of his mother Olympias, had escaped through the Persian host that besieged Artogerassa, and implored the protection of the emperor of the East. By his timid councils, Para was alternately supported, and recalled, and restored, and betrayed. The hopes of the Armenians were sometimes raised by the presence of their natural sovereign, [138a] and the ministers of Valens were satisfied, that they preserved the integrity of the public faith, if their vassal was not suffered to assume the diadem and title of King. But they soon repented of their own rashness. They were confounded by the reproaches and threats of the Persian monarch. They found reason to distrust the cruel and inconstant temper of Para himself; who sacrificed, to the slightest suspicions, the lives of his most faithful servants, and held a secret and disgraceful correspondence with the assassin of his father and the enemy of his country. Under the specious pretence of consulting with the emperor on the subject of their common interest, Para was persuaded to descend from the mountains of Armenia, where his party was in arms, and to trust his independence and safety to the discretion of a perfidious court. The king of Armenia, for such he appeared in his own eyes and in those of his nation, was received with due honors by the governors of the provinces through which he passed; but when he arrived at Tarsus in Cilicia, his progress was stopped under various pretences; his motions were watched with respectful vigilance, and he gradually discovered, that he was a prisoner in the hands of the Romans. Para suppressed his indignation, dissembled his fears, and after secretly preparing his escape, mounted on horseback with three hundred of his faithful followers. The officer stationed at the door of his apartment immediately communicated his flight to the consular of Cilicia, who overtook him in the suburbs, and endeavored without success, to dissuade him from prosecuting his rash and dangerous design. A legion was ordered to pursue the royal fugitive; but the pursuit of infantry could not be very alarming to a body of light cavalry; and upon the first cloud of arrows that was discharged into the air, they retreated with precipitation to the gates of Tarsus. After an incessant march of two days and two nights, Para and his Armenians reached the banks of the Euphrates; but the passage of the river which they were obliged to swim, [138b] was attended with some delay and some loss. The country was alarmed; and the two roads, which were only separated by an interval of three miles had been occupied by a thousand archers on horseback, under the command of a count and a tribune. Para must have yielded to superior force, if the accidental arrival of a friendly traveller had not revealed the danger and the means of escape. A dark and almost impervious path securely conveyed the Armenian troop through the thicket; and Para had left behind him the count and the tribune, while they patiently expected his approach along the public highways. They returned to the Imperial court to excuse their want of diligence or success; and seriously alleged, that the king of

Armenia, who was a skilful magician, had transformed himself and his followers, and passed before their eyes under a borrowed shape. [138c] After his return to his native kingdom, Para still continued to profess himself the friend and ally of the Romans: but the Romans had injured him too deeply ever to forgive, and the secret sentence of his death was signed in the council of Valens. The execution of the bloody deed was committed to the subtle prudence of Count Trajan; and he had the merit of insinuating himself into the confidence of the credulous prince, that he might find an opportunity of stabbing him to the heart Para was invited to a Roman banquet, which had been prepared with all the pomp and sensuality of the East; the hall resounded with cheerful music, and the company was already heated with wine; when the count retired for an instant, drew his sword, and gave the signal of the murder. A robust and desperate Barbarian instantly rushed on the king of Armenia; and though he bravely defended his life with the first weapon that chance offered to his hand, the table of the Imperial general was stained with the royal blood of a guest, and an ally. Such were the weak and wicked maxims of the Roman administration, that, to attain a doubtful object of political interest the laws of nations, and the sacred rights of hospitality were inhumanly violated in the face of the world. [139]

[Footnote 138a: On the reconquest of Armenia by Para, or rather by Mouschegh, the Mamigonian see St. M. iii. 375, 383—M.]

[Footnote 138b: On planks floated by bladders—M.]

[Footnote 138c: It is curious enough that the Armenian historian, Faustus of Byzandum, represents Para as a magician. His impious mother Pharandac had devoted him to the demons on his birth. St. M. iv. 23—M.]

[Footnote 139: See in Ammianus (xxx. 1) the adventures of Para. Moses of Chorene calls him Tiridates; and tells a long, and not improbable story of his son Gnelus, who afterwards made himself popular in Armenia, and provoked the jealousy of the reigning king, (l. iii. c 21, &c., p. 253, &c.) Note: This note is a tissue of mistakes. Tiridates and Para are two totally different persons. Tiridates was the father of Gnel first husband of Pharandsem, the mother of Para. St. Martin, iv. 27—M.]

V. During a peaceful interval of thirty years, the Romans secured their frontiers, and the Goths extended their dominions. The victories of the great Hermanric, [140] king of the Ostrogoths, and the most noble of the race of the Amali, have been compared, by the enthusiasm of his countrymen, to the exploits of Alexander; with this singular, and almost incredible, difference, that the martial spirit of the Gothic hero, instead of being supported by the vigor of youth, was displayed with glory and success in the extreme period of human life, between the age of fourscore and one hundred and ten years. The independent tribes were persuaded, or compelled, to acknowledge the king of the Ostrogoths as the sovereign of the Gothic nation: the chiefs of the Visigoths, or Thervingi, renounced the royal title, and assumed the more humble appellation of Judges; and, among those judges, Athanaric, Fritigern, and Alavivus, were the most illustrious, by their personal merit, as well as by their vicinity to the Roman provinces. These domestic conquests, which increased the military power of Hermanric, enlarged his ambitious designs. He invaded the adjacent countries of the North; and twelve considerable nations, whose names and limits cannot be accurately defined, successively yielded to the superiority of the Gothic arms [141] The Heruli, who inhabited the marshy lands near the lake Maeotis, were renowned for their strength and agility; and the assistance of their light infantry was eagerly solicited, and highly esteemed, in all the wars of the Barbarians. But the active spirit of the Heruli was subdued by the slow and steady perseverance of the Goths; and, after a bloody action, in which the king was slain, the remains of that warlike tribe became a useful accession to the camp of Hermanric.

He then marched against the Venedi; unskilled in the use of arms, and formidable only by their numbers, which filled the wide extent of the plains of modern Poland. The victorious Goths, who were not inferior in numbers, prevailed in the contest, by the decisive advantages of exercise and discipline. After the submission of the Venedi, the conqueror advanced, without resistance, as far as the confines of the Aestii; [142] an ancient people, whose name is still preserved in the province of Esthonia. Those distant inhabitants of the Baltic coast were supported by the labors of agriculture, enriched by the trade of amber, and consecrated by the peculiar worship of the Mother of the Gods. But the scarcity of iron obliged the Aestian warriors to content themselves with wooden clubs; and the reduction of that wealthy country is ascribed to the prudence, rather than to the arms, of Hermanric. His dominions, which extended from the Danube to the Baltic, included the native seats, and the recent acquisitions, of the Goths; and he reigned over the greatest part of Germany and Scythia with the authority of a conqueror, and sometimes with the cruelty of a tyrant. But he reigned over a part of the globe incapable of perpetuating and adorning the glory of its heroes. The name of Hermanric is almost buried in oblivion; his exploits are imperfectly known; and the Romans themselves appeared unconscious of the progress of an aspiring power which threatened the liberty of the North, and the peace of the empire. [143]

[Footnote 140: The concise account of the reign and conquests of Hermanric seems to be one of the valuable fragments which Jornandes (c 28) borrowed from the Gothic histories of Ablavius, or Cassiodorus.]

[Footnote 141: M. d. Buat. (Hist. des Peuples de l'Europe, tom. vi. p. 311-329) investigates, with more industry than success, the nations subdued by the arms of Hermanric. He denies the existence of the Vasinobroncoe, on account of the immoderate length of their name. Yet the French envoy to Ratisbon, or Dresden, must have traversed the country of the Mediomatrici.]

[Footnote 142: The edition of Grotius (Jornandes, p. 642) exhibits the name of Aestri. But reason and the Ambrosian MS. have restored the Aestii, whose manners and situation are expressed by the pencil of Tacitus, (Germania, c. 45.)]

[Footnote 143: Ammianus (xxxi. 3) observes, in general terms, Ermenrichi.... nobilissimi Regis, et per multa variaque fortiter facta, vicinigentibus formidati, &c.]

The Goths had contracted an hereditary attachment for the Imperial house of Constantine, of whose power and liberality they had received so many signal proofs. They respected the public peace; and if a hostile band sometimes presumed to pass the Roman limit, their irregular conduct was candidly ascribed to the ungovernable spirit of the Barbarian youth. Their contempt for two new and obscure princes, who had been raised to the throne by a popular election, inspired the Goths with bolder hopes; and, while they agitated some design of marching their confederate force under the national standard, [144] they were easily tempted to embrace the party of Procopius; and to foment, by their dangerous aid, the civil discord of the Romans. The public treaty might stipulate no more than ten thousand auxiliaries; but the design was so zealously adopted by the chiefs of the Visigoths, that the army which passed the Danube amounted to the number of thirty thousand men. [145] They marched with the proud confidence, that their invincible valor would decide the fate of the Roman empire; and the provinces of Thrace groaned under the weight of the Barbarians, who displayed the insolence of masters and the licentiousness of enemies. But the intemperance which gratified their appetites, retarded their progress; and before the Goths could receive any certain intelligence of the defeat and death of

Procopius, they perceived, by the hostile state of the country, that the civil and military powers were resumed by his successful rival. A chain of posts and fortifications, skilfully disposed by Valens, or the generals of Valens, resisted their march, prevented their retreat, and intercepted their subsistence. The fierceness of the Barbarians was tamed and suspended by hunger; they indignantly threw down their arms at the feet of the conqueror, who offered them food and chains: the numerous captives were distributed in all the cities of the East; and the provincials, who were soon familiarized with their savage appearance, ventured, by degrees, to measure their own strength with these formidable adversaries, whose name had so long been the object of their terror. The king of Scythia (and Hermanric alone could deserve so lofty a title) was grieved and exasperated by this national calamity. His ambassadors loudly complained, at the court of Valens, of the infraction of the ancient and solemn alliance, which had so long subsisted between the Romans and the Goths. They alleged, that they had fulfilled the duty of allies, by assisting the kinsman and successor of the emperor Julian; they required the immediate restitution of the noble captives; and they urged a very singular claim, that the Gothic generals marching in arms, and in hostile array, were entitled to the sacred character and privileges of ambassadors. The decent, but peremptory, refusal of these extravagant demands, was signified to the Barbarians by Victor, master-general of the cavalry; who expressed, with force and dignity, the just complaints of the emperor of the East. [146] The negotiation was interrupted; and the manly exhortations of Valentinian encouraged his timid brother to vindicate the insulted majesty of the empire. [147]

[Footnote 144: Valens. ... docetur relationibus Ducum, gentem Gothorum, ea tempestate intactam ideoque saevissimam, conspirantem in unum, ad pervadenda parari collimitia Thraciarum. Ammian. xxi. 6.]

[Footnote 145: M. de Buat (Hist. des Peuples de l'Europe, tom. vi. p. 332) has curiously ascertained the real number of these auxiliaries. The 3000 of Ammianus, and the 10,000 of Zosimus, were only the first divisions of the Gothic army. Note: M. St. Martin (iii. 246) denies that there is any authority for these numbers—M.]

[Footnote 146: The march, and subsequent negotiation, are described in the Fragments of Eunapius, (Excerpt. Legat. p. 18, edit. Louvre.) The provincials who afterwards became familiar with the Barbarians, found that their strength was more apparent than real. They were tall of stature; but their legs were clumsy, and their shoulders were narrow.]

[Footnote 147: Valens enim, ut consulto placuerat fratri, cujus regebatur arbitrio, arma concussit in Gothos ratione justa permotus. Ammianus (xxvii. 4) then proceeds to describe, not the country of the Goths, but the peaceful and obedient province of Thrace, which was not affected by the war.]

The splendor and magnitude of this Gothic war are celebrated by a contemporary historian: [148] but the events scarcely deserve the attention of posterity, except as the preliminary steps of the approaching decline and fall of the empire. Instead of leading the nations of Germany and Scythia to the banks of the Danube, or even to the gates of Constantinople, the aged monarch of the Goths resigned to the brave Athanaric the danger and glory of a defensive war, against an enemy, who wielded with a feeble hand the powers of a mighty state. A bridge of boats was established upon the Danube; the presence of Valens animated his troops; and his ignorance of the art of war was compensated by personal bravery, and a wise deference to the advice of Victor and Arintheus, his masters-general of the cavalry and infantry. The operations of the campaign were conducted by their skill and experience; but they found it impossible to drive the Visigoths from their strong posts in the mountains; and the devastation of the plains obliged the Romans themselves to repass the Danube on the approach of winter. The incessant rains, which swelled the waters of the river, produced a tacit suspension of arms, and confined the emperor Valens, during the whole course of the ensuing summer, to his camp of Marcianopolis. The third year of the war was more favorable to the Romans, and more pernicious to the Goths. The interruption of trade deprived the Barbarians of the objects of luxury, which they already confounded with the necessaries of life; and the desolation of a very extensive tract of country threatened them with the horrors of famine. Athanaric was provoked, or compelled, to risk a battle, which he lost, in the plains; and the pursuit was rendered more bloody by the cruel precaution of the victorious generals, who had promised a large reward for the head of every Goth that was brought into the Imperial camp. The submission of the Barbarians appeased the resentment of Valens and his council: the emperor listened with satisfaction to the flattering and eloquent remonstrance of the senate of Constantinople, which assumed, for the first time, a share in the public deliberations; and the same generals, Victor and Arintheus, who had successfully directed the conduct of the war, were empowered to regulate the conditions of peace. The freedom of trade, which the Goths had hitherto enjoyed, was restricted to two cities on the Danube; the rashness of their leaders was severely punished by the suppression of their pensions and subsidies; and the exception, which was stipulated in favor of Athanaric alone, was more advantageous than honorable to the Judge of the Visigoths. Athanaric, who, on this occasion, appears to have consulted his private interest, without expecting the orders of his sovereign, supported his own dignity, and that of his tribe, in the personal interview which was proposed by the ministers of Valens. He persisted in his declaration, that it was impossible for him, without incurring the guilt of perjury, ever to set his foot on the territory of the empire; and it is more than probable, that his regard for the sanctity of an oath was confirmed by the recent and fatal examples of Roman treachery. The Danube, which separated the dominions of the two independent nations, was chosen for the scene of the conference. The emperor of the East, and the Judge of the Visigoths, accompanied by an equal number of armed followers, advanced in their respective barges to the middle of the stream. After the ratification of the treaty, and the delivery of hostages, Valens returned in triumph to Constantinople; and the Goths remained in a state of tranquillity about six years; till they were violently impelled against the Roman empire by an innumerable host of Scythians, who appeared to issue from the frozen regions of the North. [149]

[Footnote 148: Eunapius, in Excerpt. Legat. p. 18, 19. The Greek sophist must have considered as one and the same war, the whole series of Gothic history till the victories and peace of Theodosius.]

[Footnote 149: The Gothic war is described by Ammianus, (xxvii. 6,) Zosimus, (l. iv. p. 211-214,) and Themistius, (Orat. x. p. 129-141.) The orator Themistius was sent from the senate of Constantinople to congratulate the victorious emperor; and his servile eloquence compares Valens on the Danube to Achilles in the Scamander. Jornandes forgets a war peculiar to the Visi-Goths, and inglorious to the Gothic name, (Mascon's Hist. of the Germans, vii. 3.)]

The emperor of the West, who had resigned to his brother the command of the Lower Danube, reserved for his immediate care the defence of the Rhaetian and Illyrian provinces, which spread so many hundred miles along the greatest of the European rivers. The active policy of Valentinian was continually employed in adding new fortifications to the security of the frontier: but the abuse of this policy provoked the just resentment of the Barbarians. The Quadi complained, that the ground for an intended fortress had been marked out on their territories; and their complaints were urged with so much reason and moderation, that Equitius, master-general of Illyricum, consented to suspend the prosecution of the work, till he should be more clearly informed of the will of his sovereign. This fair occasion of injuring a rival, and of advancing the fortune of his son, was eagerly embraced by the inhuman Maximin, the praefect, or rather tyrant, of Gaul. The passions of Valentinian were impatient of control; and he credulously listened to the assurances of his favorite, that if the government of Valeria, and the direction of the work, were intrusted to the zeal of his son Marcellinus, the emperor should no longer be importuned with the audacious remonstrances of the Barbarians. The subjects of Rome, and the natives of Germany, were insulted by the arrogance of a young and worthless minister, who considered his rapid elevation as the proof and reward of his superior merit. He affected, however, to receive the modest application of Gabinius, king of the Quadi, with some attention and regard: but this artful civility concealed a dark and bloody design, and the credulous prince was persuaded to accept the pressing invitation of Marcellinus. I am at a loss how to vary the narrative of similar crimes; or how to relate, that, in the course of the same year, but in remote parts of the empire, the inhospitable table of two Imperial generals was stained with the royal blood of two guests and allies, inhumanly murdered by their order, and in their presence. The fate of Gabinius, and of Para, was the same: but the cruel death of their sovereign was resented in a very different manner by the servile temper of the Armenians, and the free and daring spirit of the Germans. The Quadi were much declined from that formidable power, which, in the time of Marcus Antoninus, had spread terror to the gates of Rome. But they still possessed arms and courage; their courage was animated by despair, and they obtained the usual reenforcement of the cavalry of their Sarmatian allies. So improvident was the assassin Marcellinus, that he chose the moment when the bravest veterans had been drawn away, to suppress the revolt of Firmus; and the whole province was exposed, with a very feeble defence, to the rage of the exasperated Barbarians. They invaded Pannonia in the season of harvest; unmercifully destroyed every object of plunder which they could not easily transport; and either disregarded, or demolished, the empty fortifications. The princess Constantia, the daughter of the emperor Constantius, and the granddaughter of the great Constantine, very narrowly escaped. That royal maid, who had innocently supported the revolt of Procopius, was now the destined wife of the heir of the Western empire. She traversed the peaceful province with a splendid and unarmed train. Her person was saved from danger, and the republic from disgrace, by the active zeal of Messala, governor of the provinces. As soon as he was informed that the village, where she stopped to dine, was almost encompassed by the Barbarians, he hastily placed her in his own chariot, and drove full speed till he reached the gates of Sirmium, which were at the distance of six-and-twenty miles. Even Sirmium might not have been secure, if the Quadi and Sarmatians had diligently advanced during the general consternation of the magistrates and people. Their delay allowed Probus, the Praetorian praefect, sufficient time to recover his own spirits, and to revive the courage of the citizens. He skilfully directed their strenuous efforts to repair and strengthen the decayed fortifications; and procured the seasonable and effectual assistance of a company of archers, to protect the capital of the Illyrian provinces. Disappointed in their attempts against the walls of Sirmium, the indignant Barbarians turned their arms against the master general of the frontier, to whom they unjustly attributed the murder of their king. Equitius could bring into the field no more than two legions; but they contained the veteran strength of the Maesian and Pannonian bands. The obstinacy with which they disputed the vain honors of rank and precedency, was the cause of their destruction; and while they acted with separate forces and divided councils, they were surprised and slaughtered by the active vigor of the Sarmatian horse. The success of this invasion provoked the emulation of the bordering tribes; and the province of Maesia would infallibly have been lost, if young Theodosius, the duke, or military commander, of the frontier, had not signalized, in the defeat of the public enemy, an intrepid genius, worthy of his illustrious father, and of his future greatness. [150]

[Footnote 150: Ammianus (xxix. 6) and Zosimus (l. iv. p. 219, 220) carefully mark the origin and progress of the Quadic and Sarmatian war.]

PART VII

The mind of Valentinian, who then resided at Treves, was deeply affected by the calamities of Illyricum; but the lateness of the season suspended the execution of his designs till the ensuing spring. He marched in person, with a considerable part of the forces of Gaul, from the banks of the Moselle: and to the suppliant ambassadors of the Sarmatians, who met him on the way, he returned a doubtful answer, that, as soon as he reached the scene of action, he should examine, and pronounce. When he arrived at Sirmium, he gave audience to the deputies of the Illyrian provinces; who loudly congratulated their own felicity under the auspicious government of Probus, his Praetorian praefect. [151] Valentinian, who was flattered by these demonstrations of their loyalty and gratitude, imprudently asked the deputy of Epirus, a Cynic philosopher of intrepid sincerity, [152] whether he was freely sent by the wishes of the province. "With tears and groans am I sent," replied Iphicles, "by a reluctant people." The emperor paused: but the impunity of his ministers established the pernicious maxim, that they might oppress his subjects, without injuring his service. A strict inquiry into their conduct would have relieved the public discontent. The severe condemnation of the murder of Gabinius, was the only measure which could restore the confidence of the Germans, and vindicate the honor of the Roman name. But the haughty monarch was incapable of the magnanimity which dares to acknowledge a fault. He forgot the provocation, remembered only the injury, and advanced into the country of the Quadi with an insatiate thirst of blood and revenge. The extreme devastation, and promiscuous massacre, of a savage war, were justified, in the eyes of the emperor, and perhaps in those of the world, by the cruel equity of retaliation: [153] and such was the discipline of the Romans, and the consternation of the enemy, that Valentinian repassed the Danube without the loss of a single man. As he had resolved to complete the destruction of the Quadi by a second campaign, he fixed his winter quarters at Bregetio, on the Danube, near the Hungarian city of Presburg. While the operations of war were suspended by the severity of the weather, the Quadi made an humble attempt to deprecate the wrath of their conqueror; and, at the earnest persuasion of Equitius, their ambassadors were introduced into the Imperial council. They approached the throne with bended bodies and dejected countenances; and without daring to complain of the murder of their king, they affirmed, with solemn oaths, that the late invasion was the crime of some irregular robbers, which the public council of the nation condemned and abhorred. The answer of the emperor left them but little to hope from his clemency or compassion. He reviled, in the most intemperate language, their baseness, their ingratitude, their insolence. His eyes, his voice, his color, his gestures, expressed the violence of his ungoverned fury; and while his whole frame was agitated with convulsive passion, a large blood vessel suddenly burst in his body; and Valentinian fell speechless into the arms of his attendants. Their pious care immediately concealed his situation from the crowd; but, in a few minutes, the emperor of the West expired in an agony of pain, retaining his senses till the last; and struggling, without success, to declare his intentions to the generals and ministers, who surrounded the royal couch. Valentinian was about fifty-four years of age; and he wanted only one hundred days to accomplish the twelve years of his reign. [154]

[Footnote 151: Ammianus, (xxx. 5,) who acknowledges the merit, has censured, with becoming asperity, the oppressive administration of Petronius Probus. When Jerom translated and continued the Chronicle of Eusebius, (A. D. 380; see Tillemont, Mem. Eccles. tom. xii. p. 53, 626,) he expressed the truth, or at least the public opinion of his country, in the following words: "Probus P. P. Illyrici inquissimus tributorum exactionibus, ante provincias quas regebat, quam a Barbaris vastarentur, erasit." (Chron. edit. Scaliger, p. 187. Animadvers p. 259.) The Saint afterwards formed an intimate and tender friendship with the widow of Probus; and the name of Count Equitius with less propriety, but without much injustice, has been substituted in the text.]

[Footnote 152: Julian (Orat. vi. p. 198) represents his friend Iphicles, as a man of virtue and merit, who had made himself ridiculous and unhappy by adopting the extravagant dress and manners of the Cynics.]

[Footnote 153: Ammian. xxx. v. Jerom, who exaggerates the misfortune of Valentinian, refuses him even this last consolation of revenge. Genitali vastato solo et inultam patriam derelinquens, (tom. i. p. 26.)]

[Footnote 154: See, on the death of Valentinian, Ammianus, (xxx. 6,) Zosimus, (l. iv. p. 221,) Victor, (in Epitom.,) Socrates, (l. iv. c. 31,) and Jerom, (in Chron. p. 187, and tom. i. p. 26, ad Heliodor.) There is much variety of circumstances among them; and Ammianus is so eloquent, that he writes nonsense.]

The polygamy of Valentinian is seriously attested by an ecclesiastical historian. [155] "The empress Severa (I relate the fable) admitted into her familiar society the lovely Justina, the daughter of an Italian governor: her admiration of those naked charms, which she had often seen in the bath, was expressed with such lavish and imprudent praise, that the emperor was tempted to introduce a second wife into his bed; and his public edict extended to all the subjects of the empire the same domestic privilege which he had assumed for himself." But we may be assured, from the evidence of reason as well as history, that the two marriages of Valentinian, with Severa, and with Justina, were successively contracted; and that he used the ancient permission of divorce, which was still allowed by the laws, though it was condemned by the church Severa was the mother of Gratian, who seemed to unite every claim which could entitle him to the undoubted succession of the Western empire. He was the eldest son of a monarch whose glorious reign had confirmed the free and honorable choice of his fellow-soldiers. Before he had attained the ninth year of his age, the royal youth received from the hands of his indulgent father the purple robe and diadem, with the title of Augustus; the election was solemnly ratified by the consent and applause of the armies of Gaul; [156] and the name of Gratian was added to the names of Valentinian and Valens, in all the legal transactions of the Roman government. By his marriage with the granddaughter of Constantine, the son of Valentinian acquired all the hereditary rights of the Flavian family; which, in a series of three Imperial generations, were sanctified by time, religion, and the reverence of the people. At the death of his father, the royal youth was in the seventeenth year of his age; and his virtues already justified the favorable opinion of the army and the people. But Gratian resided, without apprehension, in the palace of Treves; whilst, at the distance of many hundred miles, Valentinian suddenly expired in the camp of Bregetio. The passions, which had been so long suppressed by the presence of a master, immediately revived in the Imperial council; and the ambitious design of reigning in the name of an infant, was artfully executed by Mellobaudes and Equitius, who commanded the attachment of the Illyrian and Italian bands. They contrived the most honorable pretences to remove the popular leaders, and the troops of Gaul, who might have asserted the claims of the lawful successor; they suggested the necessity of extinguishing the hopes of foreign and domestic enemies, by a bold and decisive measure. The empress Justina, who had been left in a palace about one hundred miles from Bregetio, was respectively invited to appear in the camp, with the son of the deceased emperor. On the sixth day after the death of Valentinian, the infant prince of the same name, who was only four years old, was shown, in the arms of his mother, to the legions; and solemnly invested, by military acclamation, with the titles and ensigns of supreme power. The impending dangers of a civil war were seasonably prevented by the wise and moderate conduct of the emperor Gratian. He cheerfully accepted the choice of the army; declared that he should always consider the son of Justina as a brother, not as a rival; and advised the empress, with her son Valentinian to fix their residence at Milan, in the fair and peaceful province of Italy; while he assumed the more arduous command of the countries beyond the Alps. Gratian dissembled his resentment till he could safely punish, or disgrace, the authors of the conspiracy; and though he uniformly behaved with tenderness and regard to his infant colleague, he gradually confounded, in the administration of the

Western empire, the office of a guardian with the authority of a sovereign. The government of the Roman world was exercised in the united names of Valens and his two nephews; but the feeble emperor of the East, who succeeded to the rank of his elder brother, never obtained any weight or influence in the councils of the West. [157]

[Footnote 155: Socrates (l. iv. c. 31) is the only original witness of this foolish story, so repugnant to the laws and manners of the Romans, that it scarcely deserved the formal and elaborate dissertation of M. Bonamy, (Mem. de l'Academie, tom. xxx. p. 394-405.) Yet I would preserve the natural circumstance of the bath; instead of following Zosimus who represents Justina as an old woman, the widow of Magnentius.]

[Footnote 156: Ammianus (xxvii. 6) describes the form of this military election, and august investiture. Valentinian does not appear to have consulted, or even informed, the senate of Rome.]

[Footnote 157: Ammianus, xxx. 10. Zosimus, l. iv. p. 222, 223. Tillemont has proved (Hist. des Empereurs, tom. v. p. 707-709) that Gratian reignea in Italy, Africa, and Illyricum. I have endeavored to express his authority over his brother's dominions, as he used it, in an ambiguous style.]

CHAPTER XXVI

PROGRESS OF THE HUNS

PART I

MANNERS OF THE PASTORAL NATIONS—PROGRESS OF THE HUNS, FROM CHINA TO EUROPE—FLIGHT OF THE GOTHS—THEY PASS THE DANUBE—GOTHIC WAR—DEFEAT AND DEATH OF VALENS—GRATIAN INVESTS THEODOSIUS WITH THE EASTERN EMPIRE—HIS CHARACTER AND SUCCESS—PEACE AND SETTLEMENT OF THE GOTHS

In the second year of the reign of Valentinian and Valens, on the morning of the twenty-first day of July, the greatest part of the Roman world was shaken by a violent and destructive earthquake. The impression was communicated to the waters; the shores of the Mediterranean were left dry, by the sudden retreat of the sea; great quantities of fish were caught with the hand; large vessels were stranded on the mud; and a curious spectator [1] amused his eye, or rather his fancy, by contemplating the various appearance of valleys and mountains, which had never, since the formation of the globe, been exposed to the sun. But the tide soon returned, with the weight of an immense and irresistible deluge, which was severely felt on the coasts of Sicily, of Dalmatia, of Greece, and of Egypt: large boats were transported, and lodged on the roofs of houses, or at the distance of two miles from the shore; the people, with their habitations, were swept away by the waters; and the city of Alexandria annually commemorated the fatal day, on which fifty thousand persons had lost their lives in the inundation. This calamity, the report of which was magnified from one province to another, astonished and terrified the subjects of Rome; and their affrighted imagination enlarged the real extent of a momentary evil. They recollected the preceding earthquakes, which had subverted the cities of Palestine and Bithynia: they considered these alarming strokes as the prelude only of still more dreadful calamities, and their fearful vanity was disposed to confound the symptoms of a declining empire and a sinking world. [2] It was the fashion of the times to attribute every remarkable event to the particular will of the Deity; the alterations of nature were connected, by an invisible chain, with the moral and metaphysical opinions of the human mind; and the most sagacious divines could distinguish, according to the color of their respective prejudices, that the establishment of heresy tended to produce an earthquake; or that a deluge was the inevitable consequence of the progress of sin and error. Without presuming to discuss the truth or propriety of these lofty speculations, the historian may content himself with an observation, which seems to be justified by experience, that man has much more to fear from the passions of his fellow-creatures, than from the convulsions of the elements. [3] The mischievous effects of an earthquake, or deluge, a hurricane, or the eruption of a volcano, bear a very inconsiderable portion to the ordinary calamities of war, as they are now moderated by the prudence or humanity of the princes of Europe, who amuse their own leisure, and exercise the courage of their subjects, in the practice of the military art. But the laws and manners of modern nations protect the safety and freedom of the vanquished soldier; and the peaceful citizen has seldom reason to complain, that his life, or even his fortune, is exposed to the rage of war. In the disastrous period of the fall of the Roman empire, which may justly be dated from the reign of Valens, the happiness and security of each individual were personally attacked; and the arts and labors of ages were rudely defaced by the Barbarians of Scythia and Germany. The invasion of the Huns precipitated on the provinces of the West the Gothic nation, which advanced, in less than forty years, from the Danube to the Atlantic, and opened a way, by the success of their arms, to the inroads of so many hostile tribes, more savage than themselves. The original principle of motion was concealed in the remote countries of the North; and the curious observation of the pastoral life of the Scythians, [4] or Tartars, [5] will illustrate the latent cause of these destructive emigrations.

[Footnote 1: Such is the bad taste of Ammianus, (xxvi. 10,) that it is not easy to distinguish his facts from his metaphors. Yet he positively affirms, that he saw the rotten carcass of a ship, ad Modon, in Peloponnesus.]

[Footnote 2: The earthquakes and inundations are variously described by Libanius, (Orat. de ulciscenda Juliani nece, c. x., in Fabricius, Bibl. Graec. tom. vii. p. 158, with a learned note of Olearius,) Zosimus, (l. iv. p. 221,) Sozomen, (l. vi. c. 2,) Cedrenus, (p. 310, 314,) and Jerom, (in Chron. p. 186, and tom. i. p. 250, in Vit. Hilarion.) Epidaurus must have been overwhelmed, had not the prudent citizens placed St. Hilarion, an Egyptian monk, on the beach. He made the sign of the Cross; the mountain-wave stopped, bowed, and returned.]

[Footnote 3: Dicaearchus, the Peripatetic, composed a formal treatise, to prove this obvious truth; which is not the most honorable to the human species. (Cicero, de Officiis, ii. 5.)]

[Footnote 4: The original Scythians of Herodotus (l. iv. c. 47—57, 99—101) were confined, by the Danube and the Palus Maeotis, within a square of 4000 stadia, (400 Roman miles.) See D'Anville (Mem. de l'Academie, tom. xxxv. p. 573—591.) Diodorus Siculus (tom. i. l. ii. p. 155, edit. Wesseling) has marked the gradual progress of the name and nation.]

[Footnote 5: The Tatars, or Tartars, were a primitive tribe, the rivals, and at length the subjects, of the Moguls. In the victorious armies of Zingis Khan, and his successors, the Tartars formed the vanguard; and the name, which first reached the ears of foreigners, was applied to the whole nation, (Freret, in the Hist. de l'Academie, tom. xviii. p. 60.) In speaking of all, or any of the northern shepherds of Europe, or Asia, I indifferently use the appellations of Scythians or Tartars. Note: The Moguls, (Mongols,) according to M. Klaproth, are a tribe of the Tartar nation. Tableaux Hist. de l'Asie, p. 154—M.]

The different characters that mark the civilized nations of the globe, may be ascribed to the use, and the abuse, of reason; which so variously shapes, and so artificially composes, the manners and opinions of a European, or a Chinese. But the operation of instinct is more sure and simple than that of reason: it is much easier to ascertain the appetites of a quadruped than the speculations of a philosopher; and the savage tribes of mankind, as they approach nearer to the condition of animals, preserve a stronger resemblance to themselves and to each other. The uniform stability of their manners is the natural consequence of the imperfection of their faculties. Reduced to a similar situation, their wants, their desires, their enjoyments, still continue the same: and the influence of food or climate, which, in a more improved state of society, is suspended, or subdued, by so many moral causes, most powerfully contributes to form, and to maintain, the national character of Barbarians. In every age, the immense plains of Scythia, or Tartary, have been inhabited by vagrant tribes of hunters and shepherds, whose indolence refuses to cultivate the earth, and whose restless spirit disdains the confinement of a sedentary life. In every age, the Scythians, and Tartars, have been renowned for their invincible courage and rapid conquests. The thrones of Asia have been repeatedly overturned by the shepherds of the North; and their arms have spread terror and devastation over the most fertile and warlike countries of Europe. [6] On this occasion, as well as on many others, the sober historian is forcibly awakened from a pleasing vision; and is compelled, with some reluctance, to confess, that the pastoral manners, which have been adorned with the fairest attributes of peace and innocence, are much better adapted to the fierce and cruel habits of a military life. To illustrate this observation, I shall now proceed to consider a nation of shepherds and of warriors, in the three important articles of, I. Their diet; II. Their habitations; and, III. Their exercises. The narratives of antiquity are justified by the experience of modern times; [7] and the banks of the Borysthenes, of the Volga, or of the Selinga, will indifferently present the same uniform spectacle of similar and native manners. [8]

[Footnote 6: *Imperium Asiae ter quaesivere: ipsi perpetuo ab alieno imperio, aut intacti aut invicti, mansere.* Since the time of Justin, (ii. 2,) they have multiplied this account. Voltaire, in a few words, (tom. x. p. 64, Hist. Generale, c. 156,) has abridged the Tartar conquests. *Oft o'er the trembling nations from afar, Has Scythia breathed the living cloud of war.* Note : Gray—M.]

[Footnote 7: The fourth book of Herodotus affords a curious though imperfect, portrait of the Scythians. Among the moderns, who describe the uniform scene, the Khan of Khowaresm, Abulghazi Bahadur, expresses his native feelings; and his genealogical history of the Tartars has been copiously illustrated by the French and English editors. Carpin, Ascelin, and Rubruquis (in the Hist. des Voyages, tom. vii.) represent the Moguls of the fourteenth century. To these guides I have added Gerbillon, and the other Jesuits, (Description de la China par du Halde, tom. iv.,) who accurately surveyed the Chinese Tartary; and that honest and intelligent traveller, Bell, of Antermony, (two volumes in 4to. Glasgow, 1763.) Note: Of the various works published since the time of Gibbon, which throw fight on the nomadic population of Central Asia, may be particularly remarked the Travels and Dissertations of Pallas; and above all, the very curious work of Bergman, Nomadische Streifereyen. Riga, 1805—M.]

[Footnote 8: The Uzbecks are the most altered from their primitive manners; 1. By the profession of the Mahometan religion; and 2. By the possession of the cities and harvests of the great Bucharia.]

I. The corn, or even the rice, which constitutes the ordinary and wholesome food of a civilized people, can be obtained only by the patient toil of the husbandman. Some of the happy savages, who dwell between the tropics, are plentifully nourished by the liberality of nature; but in the climates of the North, a nation of shepherds is reduced to their flocks and herds. The skilful practitioners of the medical art will determine (if they are able to determine) how far the temper of the human mind may be affected by the use of animal, or of vegetable, food; and whether the common association of carniverous and cruel deserves to be considered in any other light than that of an innocent, perhaps a salutary, prejudice of humanity. [9] Yet, if it be true, that the sentiment of compassion is imperceptibly weakened by the sight and practice of domestic cruelty, we may observe, that the horrid objects which are disguised by the arts of European refinement, are exhibited in their naked and most disgusting simplicity in the tent of a Tartarian shepherd. The ox, or the sheep, are slaughtered by the same hand from which they were accustomed to receive their daily food; and the bleeding limbs are served, with very little preparation, on the table of their unfeeling murderer. In the military profession, and especially in the conduct of a numerous army, the exclusive use of animal food appears to be productive of the most solid advantages. Corn is a bulky and perishable commodity; and the large magazines, which are indispensably necessary for the subsistence of our troops, must be slowly transported by the labor of men or horses. But the flocks and herds, which accompany the march of the Tartars, afford a sure and increasing supply of flesh and milk: in the far greater part of the uncultivated waste, the vegetation of the grass is quick and luxuriant; and there are few places so extremely barren, that the hardy cattle of the North cannot find some tolerable pasture.

The supply is multiplied and prolonged by the undistinguishing appetite, and patient abstinence, of the Tartars. They indifferently feed on the flesh of those animals that have been killed for the table, or have died of disease. Horseflesh, which in every age and country has been proscribed by the civilized nations of Europe and Asia, they devour with peculiar greediness; and this singular taste facilitates the success of their military operations. The active cavalry of Scythia is always followed, in their most distant and rapid incursions, by an adequate number of spare horses, who may be occasionally used, either to redouble the speed, or to satisfy the hunger, of the Barbarians. Many are the resources of courage and poverty. When the forage round a camp of Tartars is almost consumed, they slaughter the greatest part of their cattle, and preserve the flesh, either smoked, or dried in the sun. On the sudden emergency of a hasty march, they provide themselves with a sufficient quantity of little balls of cheese, or rather of hard curd, which they occasionally dissolve in water; and this unsubstantial diet will support, for many days, the life, and even the spirits, of the patient warrior. But this extraordinary abstinence, which the Stoic would approve, and the hermit might envy, is commonly succeeded by the most voracious indulgence of appetite. The wines of a happier climate are the most grateful present, or the most valuable commodity, that can be offered to the Tartars; and the only example of their industry seems to consist in the art of extracting from mare's milk a fermented liquor, which possesses a very strong power of intoxication. Like the animals of prey, the savages, both of the old and new world, experience the alternate vicissitudes of famine and plenty; and their stomach is inured to sustain, without much inconvenience, the opposite extremes of hunger and of intemperance.

[Footnote 9: Il est certain que les grands mangeurs de viande sont en general cruels et feroces plus que les autres hommes. Cette observation est de tous les lieux, et de tous les temps: la barbarie Angloise est connue, &c. Emile de Rousseau, tom. i. p. 274. Whatever we may think of the general observation, we shall not easily allow the truth of his example. The good-natured complaints of Plutarch, and the pathetic lamentations of Ovid, seduce our reason, by exciting our sensibility.]

II. In the ages of rustic and martial simplicity, a people of soldiers and husbandmen are dispersed over the face of an extensive and cultivated country; and some time must elapse before the warlike youth of Greece or Italy could be assembled under the same standard, either to defend their own confines, or to invade the territories of the adjacent tribes. The progress of manufactures and commerce insensibly collects a large multitude within the walls of a city: but these citizens are no longer soldiers; and the arts which adorn and improve the state of civil society, corrupt the habits of the military life. The pastoral manners of the Scythians seem to unite the different advantages of simplicity and refinement. The individuals of the same tribe are constantly assembled, but they are assembled in a camp; and the native spirit of these dauntless shepherds is animated by mutual support and emulation. The houses of the Tartars are no more than small tents, of an oval form, which afford a cold and dirty habitation, for the promiscuous youth of both sexes. The palaces of the rich consist of wooden huts, of such a size that they may be conveniently fixed on large wagons, and drawn by a team perhaps of twenty or thirty oxen. The flocks and herds, after grazing all day in the adjacent pastures, retire, on the approach of night, within the protection of the camp. The necessity of preventing the most mischievous confusion, in such a perpetual concourse of men and animals, must gradually introduce, in the distribution, the order, and the guard, of the encampment, the rudiments of the military art. As soon as the forage of a certain district is consumed, the tribe, or rather army, of shepherds, makes a regular march to some fresh pastures; and thus acquires, in the ordinary occupations of the pastoral life, the practical knowledge of one of the most important and difficult operations of war. The choice of stations is regulated by the difference of the seasons: in the summer, the Tartars advance towards the North, and pitch their tents on the banks of a river, or, at least, in the neighborhood of a running stream. But in the winter, they return to the South, and shelter their camp, behind some convenient eminence, against the winds, which are chilled in their passage over the bleak and icy regions of Siberia. These manners are admirably adapted to diffuse, among the wandering tribes, the spirit of emigration and conquest. The connection between the people and their territory is of so frail a texture, that it may be broken by the slightest accident. The camp, and not the soil, is the native country of the genuine Tartar. Within the precincts of that camp, his family, his companions, his property, are always included; and, in the most distant marches, he is still surrounded by the objects which are dear, or valuable, or familiar in his eyes. The thirst of rapine, the fear, or the resentment of injury, the impatience of servitude, have, in every age, been sufficient causes to urge the tribes of Scythia boldly to advance into some unknown countries, where they might hope to find a more plentiful subsistence or a less formidable enemy. The revolutions of the North have frequently determined the fate of the South; and in the conflict of hostile nations, the victor and the vanquished have alternately drove, and been driven, from the confines of China to those of Germany. [10] These great emigrations, which have been sometimes executed with almost incredible diligence, were rendered more easy by the peculiar nature of the climate. It is well known that the cold of Tartary is much more severe than in the midst of the temperate zone might reasonably be expected; this uncommon rigor is attributed to the height of the plains, which rise, especially towards the East, more than half a mile above the level of the sea; and to the quantity of saltpetre with which the soil is deeply impregnated. [11] In the winter season, the broad and rapid rivers, that discharge their waters into the Euxine, the Caspian, or the Icy Sea, are strongly frozen; the fields are covered with a bed of snow; and the fugitive, or victorious, tribes may securely traverse, with their families, their wagons, and their cattle, the smooth and hard surface of an immense plain.

[Footnote 10: These Tartar emigrations have been discovered by M. de Guignes (Histoire des Huns, tom. i. ii.) a skilful and laborious interpreter of the Chinese language; who has thus laid open new and important scenes in the history of mankind.]

[Footnote 11: A plain in the Chinese Tartary, only eighty leagues from the great wall, was found by the missionaries to be three thousand geometrical paces above the level of the sea. Montesquieu, who has used, and abused, the relations of travellers, deduces the revolutions of Asia from this important circumstance, that heat and cold, weakness and strength, touch each other without any temperate zone, (Esprit des Loix, l. xvii. c. 3.)]

III. The pastoral life, compared with the labors of agriculture and manufactures, is undoubtedly a life of idleness; and as the most honorable shepherds of the Tartar race devolve on their captives the domestic management of the cattle, their own leisure is seldom disturbed by any servile and assiduous cares. But this leisure, instead of being devoted to the soft enjoyments of love and harmony, is use fully spent in the violent and sanguinary exercise of the chase. The plains of Tartary are filled with a strong and serviceable breed of horses, which are easily trained for the purposes of war and hunting. The Scythians of every age have been celebrated as bold and skilful riders; and constant practice had seated them so firmly on horseback, that they were supposed by strangers to perform the ordinary duties of civil life, to eat, to drink, and even to sleep, without dismounting from their steeds. They excel in the dexterous management of the lance; the long Tartar bow is drawn with a nervous arm; and the weighty arrow is directed to its object with unerring aim and irresistible force. These arrows are often pointed against the harmless animals of the desert, which increase and multiply in the absence of their most formidable enemy; the hare, the goat, the roebuck, the fallow-deer, the stag, the elk, and the antelope. The vigor and patience, both of the men and horses, are continually exercised by the fatigues of the chase; and the plentiful supply of game contributes to the subsistence, and even luxury, of a Tartar camp. But the exploits of the hunters of Scythia are not confined to the destruction of timid or innoxious beasts; they boldly encounter the angry wild boar, when he turns against his pursuers, excite the sluggish courage of the bear, and provoke the fury of the tiger, as he slumbers in the thicket. Where there is danger, there may be glory; and the mode of hunting, which opens the fairest field to the exertions of valor, may justly be considered as the image, and as the school, of war. The general hunting matches, the pride and delight of the Tartar princes, compose an instructive exercise for their numerous cavalry. A circle is drawn, of many miles in circumference, to encompass the game of an extensive district; and the troops that form the circle regularly advance towards a common centre; where the captive animals, surrounded on every side, are abandoned to the darts of the hunters. In this march, which frequently continues many days, the cavalry are obliged to climb the hills, to swim the rivers, and to wind through the valleys, without interrupting the prescribed order of their gradual progress. They acquire the habit of directing their eye, and their steps, to a remote object; of preserving their intervals of suspending or accelerating their pace, according to the motions of the troops on their right and left; and of watching and repeating the signals of their leaders. Their leaders study, in this practical school, the most important lesson of the military art; the prompt and accurate judgment of ground, of distance, and of time. To employ against a human enemy the same patience and valor, the same skill and discipline, is the only alteration which is required in real war; and the amusements of the chase serve as a prelude to the conquest of an empire. [12]

[Footnote 12: Petit de la Croix (Vie de Gengiscan, l. iii. c. 6) represents the full glory and extent of the Mogul chase. The Jesuits Gerbillon and Verbiest followed the emperor Khamhi when he hunted in Tartary, Duhalde, (Description de la Chine, tom. iv. p. 81, 290, &c., folio edit.) His grandson, Kienlong, who unites the Tartar discipline with the laws and learning of China, describes (Eloge de Moukden, p. 273—285) as a poet the pleasures which he had often enjoyed as a sportsman.]

The political society of the ancient Germans has the appearance of a voluntary alliance of independent warriors. The tribes of Scythia, distinguished by the modern appellation of Hords, assume the form of a numerous and increasing family; which, in the course of successive generations, has been propagated from the same original stock. The meanest, and most ignorant, of the Tartars, preserve, with conscious pride, the inestimable treasure of their genealogy; and whatever distinctions of rank may have been introduced, by the unequal distribution of pastoral wealth, they mutually respect themselves, and each other, as the descendants of the first founder of the tribe. The custom, which still prevails, of adopting the bravest and most faithful of the captives, may countenance the very probable suspicion, that this extensive consanguinity is, in a great measure, legal and fictitious. But the useful prejudice, which has obtained the sanction of time and opinion, produces the effects of truth; the haughty Barbarians yield a cheerful and voluntary obedience to the head of their blood; and their chief, or mursa, as the representative of their great father, exercises the authority of a judge in peace, and of a leader in war. In the original state of the pastoral world, each of the mursas (if we may continue to use a modern appellation) acted as the independent chief of a large and separate family; and the limits of their peculiar territories were gradually fixed by superior force, or mutual consent. But the constant operation of various and permanent causes contributed to unite the vagrant Hordes into national communities, under the command of a supreme head. The weak were desirous of support, and the strong were ambitious of dominion; the power, which is the result of union, oppressed and collected the divided force of the adjacent tribes; and, as the vanquished were freely admitted to share the advantages of victory, the most valiant chiefs hastened to range themselves and their followers under the formidable standard of a confederate nation. The most successful of the Tartar princes assumed the military command, to which he was entitled by the superiority, either of merit or of power. He was raised to the throne by the acclamations of his equals; and the title of Khan expresses, in the language of the North of Asia, the full extent of the regal dignity. The right of hereditary succession was long confined to the blood of the founder of the monarchy; and at this moment all the Khans, who reign from Crimea to the wall of China, are the lineal descendants of the renowned Zingis. [13] But, as it is the indispensable duty of a Tartar sovereign to lead his warlike subjects into the field, the claims of an infant are often disregarded; and some royal kinsman, distinguished by his age and valor, is intrusted with the sword and sceptre of his predecessor. Two distinct and regular taxes are levied on the tribes, to support the dignity of the national monarch, and of their peculiar chief; and each of those contributions amounts to the tithe, both of their property, and of their spoil. A Tartar sovereign enjoys the tenth part of the wealth of his people; and as his own domestic riches of flocks and herds increase in a much larger proportion, he is able plentifully to maintain the rustic splendor of his court, to reward the most deserving, or the most favored of his followers, and to obtain, from the gentle influence of corruption, the obedience which might be sometimes refused to the stern mandates of authority. The manners of his subjects, accustomed, like himself, to blood and rapine, might excuse, in their eyes, such partial acts of tyranny, as would excite the horror of a civilized people; but the power of a despot has never been acknowledged in the deserts of Scythia. The immediate jurisdiction of the khan is confined within the limits of his own tribe; and the exercise of his royal prerogative has been moderated by the ancient institution of a national council. The Coroulai, [14] or Diet, of the Tartars, was regularly held in the spring and autumn, in the midst of a plain; where the princes of the reigning family, and the mursas of the respective tribes, may conveniently assemble on horseback, with their martial and numerous trains; and the ambitious monarch, who reviewed the strength, must consult the inclination of an armed people. The rudiments of a feudal government may be discovered in the constitution of the Scythian or Tartar nations; but the perpetual conflict of those hostile nations has sometimes terminated in the establishment of a powerful and despotic empire. The victor, enriched by the tribute, and fortified by the arms of dependent kings, has spread his conquests over Europe or Asia: the successful shepherds of the North have submitted to the confinement of arts, of laws, and of cities; and the introduction of luxury, after destroying the freedom of the people, has undermined the foundations of the throne. [15]

[Footnote 13: See the second volume of the Genealogical History of the Tartars; and the list of the Khans, at the end of the life of Geng's, or Zingis. Under the reign of Timur, or Tamerlane, one of his subjects, a descendant of Zingis, still bore the regal appellation of Khan and the conqueror of Asia contented himself with the title of Emir or Sultan. Abulghazi, part v. c. 4. D'Herbelot, Bibliotheque Orien tale, p. 878.]

[Footnote 14: See the Diets of the ancient Huns, (De Guignes, tom. ii. p. 26,) and a curious description of those of Zingis, (Vie de Gengiscan, l. i. c. 6, l. iv. c. 11.) Such assemblies are frequently mentioned in the Persian history of Timur; though they served only to countenance the resolutions of their master.]

[Footnote 15: Montesquieu labors to explain a difference, which has not existed, between the liberty of the Arabs, and the perpetual slavery of the Tartars. (Esprit des Loix, l. xvii. c. 5, l. xviii. c. 19, &c.)]

The memory of past events cannot long be preserved in the frequent and remote emigrations of illiterate Barbarians. The modern Tartars are ignorant of the conquests of their ancestors; [16] and our knowledge of the history of the Scythians is derived from their intercourse with the learned and civilized nations of the South, the Greeks, the Persians, and the Chinese. The Greeks, who navigated the Euxine, and planted their colonies along the sea-coast, made the gradual and imperfect discovery of Scythia; from the Danube, and the confines of Thrace, as far as the frozen Maeotis, the seat of eternal winter, and Mount Caucasus, which, in the language of poetry, was described as the utmost boundary of the earth. They celebrated, with simple credulity, the virtues of the pastoral life: [17] they entertained a more rational apprehension of the strength and numbers of the warlike Barbarians, [18] who contemptuously baffled the immense armament of Darius, the son of Hystaspes. [19] The Persian monarchs had extended their western conquests to the banks of the Danube, and the limits of European Scythia. The eastern provinces of their empire were exposed to the Scythians of Asia; the wild inhabitants of the plains beyond the Oxus and the Jaxartes, two mighty rivers, which direct their course towards the Caspian Sea. The long and memorable quarrel of Iran and Touran is still the theme of history or romance: the famous, perhaps the fabulous, valor of the Persian heroes, Rustan and Asfendiar, was signalized, in the defence of their country, against the Afrasiabs of the North; [20] and the invincible spirit of the same Barbarians resisted, on the same ground, the victorious arms of Cyrus and Alexander. [21] In the eyes of the Greeks and Persians, the real geography of Scythia was bounded, on the East, by the mountains of Imaus, or Caf; and their distant prospect of the extreme and inaccessible parts of Asia was clouded by ignorance, or perplexed by fiction. But those inaccessible regions are the ancient residence of a powerful and civilized nation, [22] which ascends, by a probable tradition, above forty centuries; [23] and which is able to verify a series of near two thousand years, by the perpetual testimony of accurate and contemporary historians. [24] The annals of China [25] illustrate the state and revolutions of the pastoral tribes, which may still be distinguished by the vague appellation of Scythians, or Tartars; the vassals, the enemies, and sometimes the conquerors, of a great empire; whose policy has uniformly opposed the blind and impetuous valor of the Barbarians of the North. From the mouth of the Danube to the Sea of Japan, the whole longitude of Scythia is about one hundred and ten degrees, which, in that parallel, are equal to more than five thousand miles. The latitude of these extensive deserts cannot be so easily, or so accurately, measured; but, from the fortieth degree, which touches the wall of China, we may securely advance above a thousand miles to the northward, till our progress is stopped by the excessive cold of Siberia. In that dreary climate, instead of the animated picture of a Tartar camp, the smoke that issues from the earth, or rather from the snow, betrays the subterraneous dwellings of the Tongouses, and the Samoides: the want of horses and oxen is imperfectly supplied by the use of reindeer, and of large dogs; and the conquerors of the earth insensibly degenerate into a race of deformed and diminutive savages, who tremble at the sound of arms. [26]

[Footnote 16: Abulghasi Khan, in the two first parts of his Genealogical History, relates the miserable tales and traditions of the Uzbek Tartars concerning the times which preceded the reign of Zingis. Note: The differences between the various pastoral tribes and nations comprehended by the ancients under the vague name of Scythians, and by Gibbon under inst of Tartars, have received some, and still, perhaps, may receive more, light from the comparisons of their dialects and languages by modern scholars—M]

[Footnote 17: In the thirteenth book of the Iliad, Jupiter turns away his eyes from the bloody fields of Troy, to the plains of Thrace and Scythia. He would not, by changing the prospect, behold a more peaceful or innocent scene.]

[Footnote 18: Thucydides, l. ii. c. 97.]

[Footnote 19: See the fourth book of Herodotus. When Darius advanced into the Moldavian desert, between the Danube and the Niester, the king of the Scythians sent him a mouse, a frog, a bird, and five arrows; a tremendous allegory!]

[Footnote 20: These wars and heroes may be found under their respective titles, in the Bibliotheque Orientale of D'Herbelot. They have been celebrated in an epic poem of sixty thousand rhymed couplets, by Ferdusi, the Homer of Persia. See the history of Nadir Shah, p. 145, 165. The public must lament that Mr. Jones has suspended the pursuit of Oriental learning. Note: Ferdusi is yet imperfectly known to European readers. An abstract of the whole poem has been published by Goerres in German, under the title "das Heldenbuch des Iran." In English, an abstract with poetical translations, by Mr. Atkinson, has appeared, under the auspices of the Oriental Fund. But to translate a poet a man must be a poet. The best account of the poem is in an article by Von Hammer in the Vienna Jahrbucher, 1820: or perhaps in a masterly article in Cochrane's Foreign Quarterly Review, No. 1, 1835. A splendid and critical edition of the whole work has been published by a very learned English Orientalist, Captain Macan, at the expense of the king of Oude. As to the number of 60,000 couplets, Captain Macan (Preface, p. 39) states that he never saw a MS. containing more than 56,685, including doubtful and spurious passages and episodes—M. Note: The later studies of Sir W. Jones were more in unison with the wishes of the public, thus expressed by Gibbon—M.]

[Footnote 21: The Caspian Sea, with its rivers and adjacent tribes, are laboriously illustrated in the Examen Critique des Historiens d'Alexandre, which compares the true geography, and the errors produced by the vanity or ignorance of the Greeks.]

[Footnote 22: The original seat of the nation appears to have been in the Northwest of China, in the provinces of Chensi and Chansi. Under the two first dynasties, the principal town was still a movable camp; the villages were thinly scattered; more land was employed in pasture than in tillage; the exercise of hunting was ordained to clear the country from wild beasts; Petcheli (where Pekin stands) was a desert, and the Southern provinces were peopled with Indian savages. The dynasty of the Han (before Christ 206) gave the empire its actual form and extent.]

[Footnote 23: The aera of the Chinese monarchy has been variously fixed from 2952 to 2132 years before Christ; and the year 2637 has been chosen for the lawful epoch, by the authority of the present emperor. The difference arises from the uncertain duration of the two first dynasties; and the vacant space that lies beyond them, as far as the real, or fabulous, times of Fohi, or Hoangti. Sematsien dates his authentic chronology from the year 841; the thirty-six eclipses of Confucius (thirty-one of which have been verified) were observed between the years 722 and 480 before Christ. The historical period of China does not ascend above the Greek Olympiads.]

[Footnote 24: After several ages of anarchy and despotism, the dynasty of the Han (before Christ 206) was the aera of the revival of learning. The fragments of ancient literature were restored; the characters were improved and fixed; and the future preservation of books was secured by the useful inventions of ink, paper, and the art of printing. Ninety-seven years before Christ, Sematsien published the first history of China. His labors were illustrated, and continued, by a series of one hundred and eighty historians. The substance of their works is still extant; and the most considerable of them are now deposited in the king of France's library.]

[Footnote 25: China has been illustrated by the labors of the French; of the missionaries at Pekin, and Messrs. Freret and De Guignes at Paris. The substance of the three preceding notes is extracted from the Chou-king, with the preface and notes of M. de Guignes, Paris, 1770. The Tong-Kien-Kang-Mou, translated by P. de Mailla, under the name of Hist. Generale de la Chine, tom. i. p. xlix—cc.; the Memoires sur la Chine, Paris, 1776, &c., tom. i. p. 1—323; tom. ii. p. 5—364; the Histoire des Huns, tom. i. p. 4—131, tom. v. p. 345—362; and the Memoires de l'Academie des Inscriptions, tom. x. p. 377—402; tom. xv. p. 495—564; tom. xviii. p. 178—295; xxxvi. p. 164—238.]

[Footnote 26: See the Histoire Generale des Voyages, tom. xviii., and the Genealogical History, vol. ii. p. 620—664.]

PART II

The Huns, who under the reign of Valens threatened the empire of Rome, had been formidable, in a much earlier period, to the empire of China. [27] Their ancient, perhaps their original, seat was an extensive, though dry and barren, tract of country, immediately on the north side of the great wall. Their place is at present occupied by the forty-nine Hords or Banners of the Mongous, a pastoral nation, which consists of about two hundred thousand families. [28] But the valor of the Huns had extended the narrow limits of their dominions; and their rustic chiefs, who assumed the appellation of Tanjou, gradually became the conquerors, and the sovereigns of a formidable empire. Towards the East, their victorious arms were stopped only by the ocean; and the tribes, which are thinly scattered between the Amoor and the extreme peninsula of Corea, adhered, with reluctance, to the standard of the Huns. On the West, near the head of the Irtish, in the valleys of Imaus, they found a more ample space, and more numerous enemies. One of the lieutenants of the Tanjou subdued, in a single expedition, twenty-six nations; the Igours, [29] distinguished above the Tartar race by the use of letters, were in the number of his vassals; and, by the strange connection of human events, the flight of one of those vagrant tribes recalled the victorious Parthians from the invasion of Syria. [30] On the side of the North, the ocean was assigned as the limit of the power of the Huns. Without enemies to resist their progress, or witnesses to contradict their vanity, they might securely achieve a real, or imaginary, conquest of the frozen regions of Siberia. The Northren Sea was fixed as the remote boundary of their empire. But the name of that sea, on whose shores the patriot Sovou embraced the life of a shepherd and an exile, [31] may be transferred, with much more probability, to the Baikal, a capacious basin, above three hundred miles in length, which disdains the modest appellation of a lake [32] and which actually communicates with the seas of the North, by the long course of the Angara, the Tongusha, and the Jenissea. The submission of so many distant nations might flatter the pride of the Tanjou; but the valor of the Huns could be rewarded only by the enjoyment of the wealth and luxury of the empire of the South. In the third century [32a] before the Christian aera, a wall of fifteen hundred miles in length was constructed, to defend the frontiers of China against the inroads of the Huns; [33] but this stupendous work, which holds a conspicuous place in the map of the world, has never contributed to the safety of an unwarlike people. The cavalry of the Tanjou frequently consisted of two or three hundred thousand men, formidable by the matchless dexterity with which they managed their bows and their horses: by their hardy patience in supporting the inclemency of the weather; and by the incredible speed of their march, which was seldom checked by torrents, or precipices, by the deepest rivers, or by the most lofty mountains. They spread themselves at once over the face of the country; and their rapid impetuosity surprised, astonished, and disconcerted the grave and elaborate tactics of a Chinese army. The emperor Kaoti, [34] a soldier of fortune, whose personal merit had raised him to the throne, marched against the Huns with those veteran troops which had been trained in the civil wars of China. But he was soon surrounded by the Barbarians; and, after a siege of seven days, the monarch, hopeless of relief, was reduced to purchase his deliverance by an ignominious capitulation. The successors of Kaoti, whose lives were dedicated to the arts of peace, or the luxury of the palace, submitted to a more permanent disgrace. They too hastily confessed the insufficiency of arms and fortifications. They were too easily convinced, that while the blazing signals announced on every side the approach of the Huns, the Chinese troops, who slept with the helmet on their head, and the cuirass on their back, were destroyed by the incessant labor of ineffectual marches. [35] A regular payment of money, and silk, was stipulated as the condition of a temporary and precarious peace; and the wretched expedient of disguising a real tribute, under the names of a gift or subsidy, was practised by the emperors of China as well as by those of Rome. But there still remained a more disgraceful article of tribute, which violated the sacred feelings of humanity and nature. The hardships of the savage life, which destroy in their infancy the children who are born with a less healthy and robust constitution, introduced a remarkable disproportion between the numbers of the two sexes. The Tartars are an ugly and even deformed race; and while they consider their own women as the instruments of domestic labor, their desires, or rather their appetites, are directed to the enjoyment of more elegant beauty. A select band of the fairest maidens of China was annually devoted to the rude embraces of the Huns; [36] and the alliance of the haughty Tanjous was secured by their marriage with the genuine, or adopted, daughters of the Imperial family, which vainly attempted to escape the sacrilegious pollution. The situation of these unhappy victims is described in the verses of a Chinese princess, who laments that she had been condemned by her parents to a distant exile, under a Barbarian husband; who complains that sour milk was her only drink, raw flesh her only food, a tent her only palace; and who expresses, in a strain of pathetic simplicity, the natural wish, that she were transformed into a bird, to fly back to her dear country; the object of her tender and perpetual regret. [37]

[Footnote 27: M. de Guignes (tom. ii. p. 1—124) has given the original history of the ancient Hiong-nou, or Huns. The Chinese geography of their country (tom. i. part. p. lv—lxiii.) seems to comprise a part of their conquests. Note: The theory of De Guignes on the early history of the Huns is, in general, rejected by modern writers. De Guignes advanced no valid proof of the identity of the Hioung-nou of the Chinese writers with the Huns, except the similarity of name. Schlozer, (Allgemeine Nordische Geschichte, p. 252,) Klaproth, (Tableaux Historiques de l'Asie, p. 246,) St. Martin, iv. 61, and A. Remusat, (Recherches sur les Langues Tartares, D. P. xlvi, and p. 328; though in the latter passage he considers the theory of De Guignes not absolutely disproved,) concur in considering the Huns as belonging to the Finnish stock, distinct from the Moguls the Mandscheus, and the Turks. The Hiong-nou, according to Klaproth, were Turks. The names of the Hunnish chiefs could not be pronounced by a Turk; and, according to the same author, the Hioung-nou, which is explained in Chinese as detestable slaves, as early as the year 91 J. C., were dispersed by the Chinese, and assumed the name of Yue-po or Yue-pan. M. St. Martin does not consider it impossible that the appellation of Hioung-nou may have belonged to the Huns. But all agree in considering the Madjar or Magyar of modern Hungary the descendants of the Huns. Their language (compare Gibbon, c. lv. n. 22) is nearly related to the Lapponian and Vogoul. The noble forms of the

modern Hungarians, so strongly contrasted with the hideous pictures which the fears and the hatred of the Romans give of the Huns, M. Klaproth accounts for by the intermingling with other races, Turkish and Slavonian. The present state of the question is thus stated in the last edition of Malte Brun, and a new and ingenious hypothesis suggested to resolve all the difficulties of the question. Were the Huns Finns? This obscure question has not been debated till very recently, and is yet very far from being decided. We are of opinion that it will be so hereafter in the same manner as that with regard to the Scythians. We shall trace in the portrait of Attila a dominant tribe or Mongols, or Kalmucks, with all the hereditary ugliness of that race; but in the mass of the Hunnish army and nation will be recognized the Chuni and the Ounni of the Greek Geography. the Kuns of the Hungarians, the European Huns, and a race in close relationship with the Flemish stock. Malte Brun, vi. p. 94. This theory is more fully and ably developed, p. 743. Whoever has seen the emperor of Austria's Hungarian guard, will not readily admit their descent from the Huns described by Sidonius Appolinaris—M]

[Footnote 28: See in Duhalde (tom. iv. p. 18—65) a circumstantial description, with a correct map, of the country of the Mongous.]

[Footnote 29: The Igours, or Vigours, were divided into three branches; hunters, shepherds, and husbandmen; and the last class was despised by the two former. See Abulghazi, part ii. c. 7. Note: On the Ouigour or Igour characters, see the work of M. A. Remusat, Sur les Langues Tartares. He conceives the Ouigour alphabet of sixteen letters to have been formed from the Syriac, and introduced by the Nestorian Christians—Ch. ii. M.]

[Footnote 30: Memoires de l'Academie des Inscriptions, tom. xxv. p. 17—33. The comprehensive view of M. de Guignes has compared these distant events.]

[Footnote 31: The fame of Sovou, or So-ou, his merit, and his singular adventurers, are still celebrated in China. See the Eloge de Moukden, p. 20, and notes, p. 241—247; and Memoires sur la Chine, tom. iii. p. 317—360.]

[Footnote 32: See Isbrand Ives in Harris's Collection, vol. ii. p. 931; Bell's Travels, vol. i. p. 247—254; and Gmelin, in the Hist. Generale des Voyages, tom. xviii. 283—329. They all remark the vulgar opinion that the holy sea grows angry and tempestuous if any one presumes to call it a lake. This grammatical nicety often excites a dispute between the absurd superstition of the mariners and the absurd obstinacy of travellers.]

[Footnote 32a: 224 years before Christ. It was built by Chi-hoang-ti of the Dynasty Thsin. It is from twenty to twenty-five feet high. Ce monument, aussi gigantesque qu'impuissant, arreterait bien les incursions de quelques Nomades; mais il n'a jamais empeche les invasions des Turcs, des Mongols, et des Mandchous. Abe Remusat Rech. Asiat. 2d ser. vol. i. p. 58—M.]

[Footnote 33: The construction of the wall of China is mentioned by Duhalde (tom. ii. p. 45) and De Guignes, (tom. ii. p. 59.)]

[Footnote 34: See the life of Lieoupang, or Kaoti, in the Hist, de la Chine, published at Paris, 1777, &c., tom. i. p. 442—522. This voluminous work is the translation (by the P. de Mailla) of the Tong- Kien-Kang-Mou, the celebrated abridgment of the great History of Semakouang (A.D. 1084) and his continuators.]

[Footnote 35: See a free and ample memorial, presented by a Mandarin to the emperor Venti, (before Christ 180—157,) in Duhalde, (tom. ii. p. 412—426,) from a collection of State papers marked with the red pencil by Kamhi himself, (p. 354—612.) Another memorial from the minister of war (Kang-Mou, tom. ii. p 555) supplies some curious circumstances of the manners of the Huns.]

[Footnote 36: A supply of women is mentioned as a customary article of treaty and tribute, (Hist. de la Conquete de la Chine, par les Tartares Mantcheoux, tom. i. p. 186, 187, with the note of the editor.)]

[Footnote 37: De Guignes, Hist. des Huns, tom. ii. p. 62.]

The conquest of China has been twice achieved by the pastoral tribes of the North: the forces of the Huns were not inferior to those of the Moguls, or of the Mantcheoux; and their ambition might entertain the most sanguine hopes of success. But their pride was humbled, and their progress was checked, by the arms and policy of Vouti, [38] the fifth emperor of the powerful dynasty of the Han. In his long reign of fifty- four years, the Barbarians of the southern provinces submitted to the laws and manners of China; and the ancient limits of the monarchy were enlarged, from the great river of Kiang, to the port of Canton. Instead of confining himself to the timid operations of a defensive war, his lieutenants penetrated many hundred miles into the country of the Huns. In those boundless deserts, where it is impossible to form magazines, and difficult to transport a sufficient supply of provisions, the armies of Vouti were repeatedly exposed to intolerable hardships: and, of one hundred and forty thousand soldiers, who marched against the Barbarians, thirty thousand only returned in safety to the feet of their master. These losses, however, were compensated by splendid and decisive success. The Chinese generals improved the superiority which they derived from the temper of their arms, their chariots of war, and the service of their Tartar auxiliaries. The camp of the Tanjou was surprised in the midst of sleep and intemperance; and, though the monarch of the Huns bravely cut his way through the ranks of the enemy, he left above fifteen thousand of his subjects on the field of battle. Yet this signal victory, which was preceded and followed by many bloody engagements, contributed much less to the destruction of the power of the Huns than the effectual policy which was employed to detach the tributary nations from their obedience. Intimidated by the arms, or allured by the promises, of Vouti and his successors, the most considerable tribes, both of the East and of the West, disclaimed the authority of the Tanjou. While some acknowledged themselves the allies or vassals of the empire, they all became the implacable enemies of the Huns; and the numbers of that haughty people, as soon as they were reduced to their native strength, might, perhaps, have been contained within the walls of one of the great and populous cities of China. [39] The desertion of his subjects, and the perplexity of a civil war, at length compelled the Tanjou himself to renounce the dignity of an independent sovereign, and the freedom of a warlike and high-spirited nation. He was received at Sigan, the capital of the monarchy, by the troops, the mandarins, and the emperor himself, with all the honors that could adorn and disguise the triumph of Chinese vanity. [40] A magnificent palace was prepared for his reception; his place was assigned above all the princes of the royal family; and the patience of the Barbarian king was exhausted by the ceremonies of a banquet, which consisted of eight courses of meat, and of nine solemn pieces of music. But he performed, on his knees, the duty of a respectful homage to the emperor of China; pronounced, in his own name, and in the name of his successors, a perpetual oath of fidelity; and gratefully accepted a seal, which was bestowed as the emblem of his regal dependence. After this humiliating submission, the Tanjous sometimes departed from their allegiance and seized the favorable moments of war and rapine; but the monarchy of the Huns gradually declined, till it was broken, by civil dissension, into two hostile and separate kingdoms. One of the princes of the nation was urged, by fear and ambition, to retire towards the South with eight hords, which composed between forty and fifty thousand families. He obtained, with the title of Tanjou, a convenient territory on the verge of the

Chinese provinces; and his constant attachment to the service of the empire was secured by weakness, and the desire of revenge. From the time of this fatal schism, the Huns of the North continued to languish about fifty years; till they were oppressed on every side by their foreign and domestic enemies. The proud inscription [41] of a column, erected on a lofty mountain, announced to posterity, that a Chinese army had marched seven hundred miles into the heart of their country. The Sienpi, [42] a tribe of Oriental Tartars, retaliated the injuries which they had formerly sustained; and the power of the Tanjous, after a reign of thirteen hundred years, was utterly destroyed before the end of the first century of the Christian aera. [43]

[Footnote 38: See the reign of the emperor Vouti, in the Kang-Mou, tom. iii. p. 1—98. His various and inconsistent character seems to be impartially drawn.]

[Footnote 39: This expression is used in the memorial to the emperor Venti, (Duhalde, tom. ii. p. 411.) Without adopting the exaggerations of Marco Polo and Isaac Vossius, we may rationally allow for Pekin two millions of inhabitants. The cities of the South, which contain the manufactures of China, are still more populous.]

[Footnote 40: See the Kang-Mou, tom. iii. p. 150, and the subsequent events under the proper years. This memorable festival is celebrated in the Eloge de Moukden, and explained in a note by the P. Gaubil, p. 89, 90.]

[Footnote 41: This inscription was composed on the spot by Parkou, President of the Tribunal of History (Kang-Mou, tom. iii. p. 392.) Similar monuments have been discovered in many parts of Tartary, (Histoire des Huns, tom. ii. p. 122.)]

[Footnote 42: M. de Guignes (tom. i. p. 189) has inserted a short account of the Sienpi.]

[Footnote 43: The aera of the Huns is placed, by the Chinese, 1210 years before Christ. But the series of their kings does not commence till the year 230, (Hist. des Huns, tom. ii. p. 21, 123.)]

The fate of the vanquished Huns was diversified by the various influence of character and situation. [44] Above one hundred thousand persons, the poorest, indeed, and the most pusillanimous of the people, were contented to remain in their native country, to renounce their peculiar name and origin, and to mingle with the victorious nation of the Sienpi. Fifty-eight hordes, about two hundred thousand men, ambitious of a more honorable servitude, retired towards the South; implored the protection of the emperors of China; and were permitted to inhabit, and to guard, the extreme frontiers of the province of Chansi and the territory of Ortous. But the most warlike and powerful tribes of the Huns maintained, in their adverse fortune, the undaunted spirit of their ancestors. The Western world was open to their valor; and they resolved, under the conduct of their hereditary chieftains, to conquer and subdue some remote country, which was still inaccessible to the arms of the Sienpi, and to the laws of China. [45] The course of their emigration soon carried them beyond the mountains of Imaus, and the limits of the Chinese geography; but we are able to distinguish the two great divisions of these formidable exiles, which directed their march towards the Oxus, and towards the Volga. The first of these colonies established their dominion in the fruitful and extensive plains of Sogdiana, on the eastern side of the Caspian; where they preserved the name of Huns, with the epithet of Euthalites, or Nepthalites. [45a] Their manners were softened, and even their features were insensibly improved, by the mildness of the climate, and their long residence in a flourishing province, [46] which might still retain a faint impression of the arts of Greece. [47] The white Huns, a name which they derived from the change of their complexions, soon abandoned the pastoral life of Scythia. Gorgo, which, under the appellation of Carizme, has since enjoyed a temporary splendor, was the residence of the king, who exercised a legal authority over an obedient people. Their luxury was maintained by the labor of the Sogdians; and the only vestige of their ancient barbarism, was the custom which obliged all the companions, perhaps to the number of twenty, who had shared the liberality of a wealthy lord, to be buried alive in the same grave. [48] The vicinity of the Huns to the provinces of Persia, involved them in frequent and bloody contests with the power of that monarchy. But they respected, in peace, the faith of treaties; in war, she dictates of humanity; and their memorable victory over Peroses, or Firuz, displayed the moderation, as well as the valor, of the Barbarians. The second division of their countrymen, the Huns, who gradually advanced towards the North-west, were exercised by the hardships of a colder climate, and a more laborious march. Necessity compelled them to exchange the silks of China for the furs of Siberia; the imperfect rudiments of civilized life were obliterated; and the native fierceness of the Huns was exasperated by their intercourse with the savage tribes, who were compared, with some propriety, to the wild beasts of the desert. Their independent spirit soon rejected the hereditary succession of the Tanjous; and while each horde was governed by its peculiar mursa, their tumultuary council directed the public measures of the whole nation. As late as the thirteenth century, their transient residence on the eastern banks of the Volga was attested by the name of Great Hungary. [49] In the winter, they descended with their flocks and herds towards the mouth of that mighty river; and their summer excursions reached as high as the latitude of Saratoff, or perhaps the conflux of the Kama. Such at least were the recent limits of the black Calmucks, [50] who remained about a century under the protection of Russia; and who have since returned to their native seats on the frontiers of the Chinese empire. The march, and the return, of those wandering Tartars, whose united camp consists of fifty thousand tents or families, illustrate the distant emigrations of the ancient Huns. [51]

[Footnote 44: The various accidents, the downfall, and the flight of the Huns, are related in the Kang-Mou, tom. iii. p. 88, 91, 95, 139, &c. The small numbers of each horde may be due to their losses and divisions.]

[Footnote 45: M. de Guignes has skilfully traced the footsteps of the Huns through the vast deserts of Tartary, (tom. ii. p. 123, 277, &c., 325, &c.)]

[Footnote 45a: The Armenian authors often mention this people under the name of Hepthal. St. Martin considers that the name of Nepthalites is an error of a copyist. St. Martin, iv. 254—M.]

[Footnote 46: Mohammed, sultan of Carizme, reigned in Sogdiana when it was invaded (A.D. 1218) by Zingis and his moguls. The Oriental historians (see D'Herbelot, Petit de la Croix, &c.,) celebrate the populous cities which he ruined, and the fruitful country which he desolated. In the next century, the same provinces of Chorasmia and Nawaralnahr were described by Abulfeda, (Hudson, Geograph. Minor. tom. iii.) Their actual misery may be seen in the Genealogical History of the Tartars, p. 423—469.]

[Footnote 47: Justin (xli. 6) has left a short abridgment of the Greek kings of Bactriana. To their industry I should ascribe the new and extraordinary trade, which transported the merchandises of India into Europe, by the Oxus, the Caspian, the Cyrus, the Phasis, and the Euxine. The other ways, both of the land and sea, were possessed by the Seleucides and the Ptolemies. (See l'Esprit des Loix, l. xxi.)]

[Footnote 48: Procopius de Bell. Persico, l. i. c. 3, p. 9.]

[Footnote 49: In the thirteenth century, the monk Rubruquis (who traversed the immense plain of Kipzak, in his journey to the court of the Great Khan) observed the remarkable name of Hungary, with the traces of a common language and origin, (Hist. des Voyages, tom. vii. p. 269.)]

[Footnote 50: Bell, (vol. i. p. 29—34,) and the editors of the Genealogical History, (p. 539,) have described the Calmucks of the Volga in the beginning of the present century.]

[Footnote 51: This great transmigration of 300,000 Calmucks, or Torgouts, happened in the year 1771. The original narrative of Kien-long, the reigning emperor of China, which was intended for the inscription of a column, has been translated by the missionaries of Pekin, (Memoires sur la Chine, tom. i. p. 401—418.) The emperor affects the smooth and specious language of the Son of Heaven, and the Father of his People.]

It is impossible to fill the dark interval of time, which elapsed, after the Huns of the Volga were lost in the eyes of the Chinese, and before they showed themselves to those of the Romans. There is some reason, however, to apprehend, that the same force which had driven them from their native seats, still continued to impel their march towards the frontiers of Europe. The power of the Sienpi, their implacable enemies, which extended above three thousand miles from East to West, [52] must have gradually oppressed them by the weight and terror of a formidable neighborhood; and the flight of the tribes of Scythia would inevitably tend to increase the strength or to contract the territories, of the Huns. The harsh and obscure appellations of those tribes would offend the ear, without informing the understanding, of the reader; but I cannot suppress the very natural suspicion, that the Huns of the North derived a considerable reenforcement from the ruin of the dynasty of the South, which, in the course of the third century, submitted to the dominion of China; that the bravest warriors marched away in search of their free and adventurous countrymen; and that, as they had been divided by prosperity, they were easily reunited by the common hardships of their adverse fortune. [53] The Huns, with their flocks and herds, their wives and children, their dependents and allies, were transported to the west of the Volga, and they boldly advanced to invade the country of the Alani, a pastoral people, who occupied, or wasted, an extensive tract of the deserts of Scythia. The plains between the Volga and the Tanais were covered with the tents of the Alani, but their name and manners were diffused over the wide extent of their conquests; and the painted tribes of the Agathyrsi and Geloni were confounded among their vassals. Towards the North, they penetrated into the frozen regions of Siberia, among the savages who were accustomed, in their rage or hunger, to the taste of human flesh; and their Southern inroads were pushed as far as the confines of Persia and India. The mixture of Samartic and German blood had contributed to improve the features of the Alani, [53a] to whiten their swarthy complexions, and to tinge their hair with a yellowish cast, which is seldom found in the Tartar race. They were less deformed in their persons, less brutish in their manners, than the Huns; but they did not yield to those formidable Barbarians in their martial and independent spirit; in the love of freedom, which rejected even the use of domestic slaves; and in the love of arms, which considered war and rapine as the pleasure and the glory of mankind. A naked cimeter, fixed in the ground, was the only object of their religious worship; the scalps of their enemies formed the costly trappings of their horses; and they viewed, with pity and contempt, the pusillanimous warriors, who patiently expected the infirmities of age, and the tortures of lingering disease. [54] On the banks of the Tanais, the military power of the Huns and the Alani encountered each other with equal valor, but with unequal success. The Huns prevailed in the bloody contest; the king of the Alani was slain; and the remains of the vanquished nation were dispersed by the ordinary alternative of flight or submission. [55] A colony of exiles found a secure refuge in the mountains of Caucasus, between the Euxine and the Caspian, where they still preserve their name and their independence. Another colony advanced, with more intrepid courage, towards the shores of the Baltic; associated themselves with the Northern tribes of Germany; and shared the spoil of the Roman provinces of Gaul and Spain. But the greatest part of the nation of the Alani embraced the offers of an honorable and advantageous union; and the Huns, who esteemed the valor of their less fortunate enemies, proceeded, with an increase of numbers and confidence, to invade the limits of the Gothic empire.

[Footnote 52: The Khan-Mou (tom. iii. p. 447) ascribes to their conquests a space of 14,000 lis. According to the present standard, 200 lis (or more accurately 193) are equal to one degree of latitude; and one English mile consequently exceeds three miles of China. But there are strong reasons to believe that the ancient li scarcely equalled one half of the modern. See the elaborate researches of M. D'Anville, a geographer who is not a stranger in any age or climate of the globe. (Memoires de l'Acad. tom. ii. p. 125-502. Itineraires, p. 154-167.)]

[Footnote 53: See Histoire des Huns, tom. ii. p. 125—144. The subsequent history (p. 145—277) of three or four Hunnic dynasties evidently proves that their martial spirit was not impaired by a long residence in China.]

[Footnote 53a: Compare M. Klaproth's curious speculations on the Alani. He supposes them to have been the people, known by the Chinese, at the time of their first expeditions to the West, under the name of Yath-sai or A-lanna, the Alanan of Persian tradition, as preserved in Ferdusi; the same, according to Ammianus, with the Massagetae, and with the Albani. The remains of the nation still exist in the Ossetae of Mount Caucasus. Klaproth, Tableaux Historiques de l'Asie, p. 174—M. Compare Shafarik Slawische alterthumer, i. p. 350—M. 1845.]

[Footnote 54: Utque hominibus quietis et placidis otium est voluptabile, ita illos pericula juvent et bella. Judicatur ibi beatus qui in proelio profuderit animam: senescentes etiam et fortuitis mortibus mundo digressos, ut degeneres et ignavos, conviciis atrocibus insectantur. [Ammian. xxxi. 11.] We must think highly of the conquerors of such men.]

[Footnote 55: On the subject of the Alani, see Ammianus, (xxxi. 2,) Jornandes, (de Rebus Geticis, c. 24,) M. de Guignes, (Hist. des Huns, tom. ii. p. 279,) and the Genealogical History of the Tartars, (tom. ii. p. 617.)]

The great Hermanric, whose dominions extended from the Baltic to the Euxine, enjoyed, in the full maturity of age and reputation, the fruit of his victories, when he was alarmed by the formidable approach of a host of unknown enemies, [56] on whom his barbarous subjects might, without injustice, bestow the epithet of Barbarians. The numbers, the strength, the rapid motions, and the implacable cruelty of the Huns, were felt, and dreaded, and magnified, by the astonished Goths; who beheld their fields and villages consumed with flames, and deluged with indiscriminate slaughter. To these real terrors they added the surprise and abhorrence which were excited by the shrill voice, the uncouth gestures, and the strange deformity of the Huns. [56a] These savages of Scythia were compared (and the picture had some resemblance) to the animals who walk very awkwardly on two legs and to the misshapen figures, the Termini, which were often placed on the bridges of antiquity. They were distinguished from the rest of the human species by their broad shoulders, flat noses, and small black eyes, deeply buried in the head; and as they were almost destitute of beards, they never enjoyed either the manly grace of youth, or the venerable aspect of age. [57] A fabulous origin was assigned, worthy of their form and manners; that the witches of Scythia, who, for their foul and deadly practices, had been driven from society, had copulated in the desert with infernal spirits; and that the Huns were the offspring of this execrable conjunction. [58] The tale, so full of horror and absurdity, was greedily embraced by the credulous hatred of the Goths; but, while it gratified their hatred, it increased their fear, since the posterity of daemons and witches might be supposed to inherit some share of the praeternatural powers, as well as of the malignant temper, of their parents. Against these enemies, Hermanric prepared to exert the united forces of the Gothic state; but he soon discovered that his vassal tribes, provoked by oppression, were much more inclined to second, than to repel, the invasion of the Huns. One of the chiefs of the Roxolani [59] had formerly deserted the standard of Hermanric, and the cruel tyrant had condemned the innocent wife of the traitor to be torn asunder by wild horses. The brothers of that unfortunate woman seized the favorable moment of revenge.

The aged king of the Goths languished some time after the dangerous wound which he received from their daggers; but the conduct of the war was retarded by his infirmities; and the public councils of the nation were distracted by a spirit of jealousy and discord. His death, which has been imputed to his own despair, left the reins of government in the hands of Withimer, who, with the doubtful aid of some Scythian mercenaries, maintained the unequal contest against the arms of the Huns and the Alani, till he was defeated and slain in a decisive battle. The Ostrogoths submitted to their fate; and the royal race of the Amali will hereafter be found among the subjects of the haughty Attila. But the person of Witheric, the infant king, was saved by the diligence of Alatheus and Saphrax; two warriors of approved valor and fiedlity, who, by cautious marches, conducted the independent remains of the nation of the Ostrogoths towards the Danastus, or Niester; a considerable river, which now separates the Turkish dominions from the empire of Russia. On the banks of the Niester, the prudent Athanaric, more attentive to his own than to the general safety, had fixed the camp of the Visigoths; with the firm resolution of opposing the victorious Barbarians, whom he thought it less advisable to provoke. The ordinary speed of the Huns was checked by the weight of baggage, and the encumbrance of captives; but their military skill deceived, and almost destroyed, the army of Athanaric. While the Judge of the Visigoths defended the banks of the Niester, he was encompassed and attacked by a numerous detachment of cavalry, who, by the light of the moon, had passed the river in a fordable place; and it was not without the utmost efforts of courage and conduct, that he was able to effect his retreat towards the hilly country. The undaunted general had already formed a new and judicious plan of defensive war; and the strong lines, which he was preparing to construct between the mountains, the Pruth, and the Danube, would have secured the extensive and fertile territory that bears the modern name of Walachia, from the destructive inroads of the Huns. [60] But the hopes and measures of the Judge of the Visigoths was soon disappointed, by the trembling impatience of his dismayed countrymen; who were persuaded by their fears, that the interposition of the Danube was the only barrier that could save them from the rapid pursuit, and invincible valor, of the Barbarians of Scythia. Under the command of Fritigern and Alavivus, [61] the body of the nation hastily advanced to the banks of the great river, and implored the protection of the Roman emperor of the East. Athanaric himself, still anxious to avoid the guilt of perjury, retired, with a band of faithful followers, into the mountainous country of Caucaland; which appears to have been guarded, and almost concealed, by the impenetrable forests of Transylvania. [62] [62a]

[Footnote 56: As we are possessed of the authentic history of the Huns, it would be impertinent to repeat, or to refute, the fables which misrepresent their origin and progress, their passage of the mud or water of the Maeotis, in pursuit of an ox or stag, les Indes qu'ils avoient decouvertes, &c., (Zosimus, l. iv. p. 224. Sozomen, l. vi. c. 37. Procopius, Hist. Miscell. c. 5. Jornandes, c. 24. Grandeur et Decadence, &c., des Romains, c. 17.)]

[Footnote 56a: Art added to their native ugliness; in fact, it is difficult to ascribe the proper share in the features of this hideous picture to nature, to the barbarous skill with which they were self-disfigured, or

to the terror and hatred of the Romans. Their noses were flattened by their nurses, their cheeks were gashed by an iron instrument, that the scars might look more fearful, and prevent the growth of the beard. Jornandes and Sidonius Apollinaris:—

Obtundit teneras circumdata fascia nares,
Ut galeis cedant.

Yet he adds that their forms were robust and manly, their height of a middle size, but, from the habit of riding, disproportioned.

Stant pectora vasta,
Insignes humer, succincta sub ilibus alvus.
Forma quidem pediti media est, procera sed extat
Si cernas equites, sic longi saepe putantur
Si sedeant.]

[Footnote 57: Prodigiosae formae, et pandi; ut bipedes existimes bestias; vel quales in commarginandis pontibus, effigiati stipites dolantur incompte. Ammian. xxxi. i. Jornandes (c. 24) draws a strong caricature of a Calmuck face. Species pavenda nigredine... quaedam deformis offa, non fecies; habensque magis puncta quam lumina. See Buffon. Hist. Naturelle, tom. iii. 380.]

[Footnote 58: This execrable origin, which Jornandes (c. 24) describes with the rancor of a Goth, might be originally derived from a more pleasing fable of the Greeks. (Herodot. l. iv. c. 9, &c.)]

[Footnote 59: The Roxolani may be the fathers of the the Russians, (D'Anville, Empire de Russie, p. 1—10,) whose residence (A.D. 862) about Novogrod Veliki cannot be very remote from that which the Geographer of Ravenna (i. 12, iv. 4, 46, v. 28, 30) assigns to the Roxolani, (A.D. 886.) Note: See, on the origin of the Russ, Schlozer, Nordische Geschichte, p. 78—M.]

[Footnote 60: The text of Ammianus seems to be imperfect or corrupt; but the nature of the ground explains, and almost defines, the Gothic rampart. Memoires de l'Academie, &c., tom. xxviii. p. 444—462.]

[Footnote 61: M. de Buat (Hist. des Peuples de l'Europe, tom. vi. p. 407) has conceived a strange idea, that Alavivus was the same person as Ulphilas, the Gothic bishop; and that Ulphilas, the grandson of a Cappadocian captive, became a temporal prince of the Goths.]

[Footnote 62: Ammianus (xxxi. 3) and Jornandes (de Rebus Geticis, c. 24) describe the subversion of the Gothic empire by the Huns.]

[Footnote 62a: The most probable opinion as to the position of this land is that of M. Malte-Brun. He thinks that Caucaland is the territory of the Cacoenses, placed by Ptolemy (l. iii. c. 8) towards the Carpathian Mountains, on the side of the present Transylvania, and therefore the canton of Cacava, to the south of Hermanstadt, the capital of the principality. Caucaland it is evident, is the Gothic form of these different names. St. Martin, iv 103—M.]

After Valens had terminated the Gothic war with some appearance of glory and success, he made a progress through his dominions of Asia, and at length fixed his residence in the capital of Syria. The five years [63] which he spent at Antioch was employed to watch, from a secure distance, the hostile designs of the Persian monarch; to check the depredations of the Saracens and Isaurians; [64] to enforce, by arguments more prevalent than those of reason and eloquence, the belief of the Arian theology; and to satisfy his anxious suspicions by the promiscuous execution of the innocent and the guilty. But the attention of the emperor was most seriously engaged, by the important intelligence which he received from the civil and military officers who were intrusted with the defence of the Danube. He was informed, that the North was agitated by a furious tempest; that the irruption of the Huns, an unknown and monstrous race of savages, had subverted the power of the Goths; and that the suppliant multitudes of that warlike nation, whose pride was now humbled in the dust, covered a space of many miles along the banks of the river. With outstretched arms, and pathetic lamentations, they loudly deplored their past misfortunes and their present danger; acknowledged that their only hope of safety was in the clemency of the Roman government; and most solemnly protested, that if the gracious liberality of the emperor would permit them to cultivate the waste lands of Thrace, they should ever hold themselves bound, by the strongest obligations of duty and gratitude, to obey the laws, and to guard the limits, of the republic. These assurances were confirmed by the ambassadors of the Goths, [64a] who impatiently expected from the mouth of Valens an answer that must finally determine the fate of their unhappy countrymen. The emperor of the East was no longer guided by the wisdom and authority of his elder brother, whose death happened towards the end of the preceding year; and as the distressful situation of the Goths required an instant and peremptory decision, he was deprived of the favorite resources of feeble and timid minds, who consider the use of dilatory and ambiguous measures as the most admirable efforts of consummate prudence. As long as the same passions and interests subsist among mankind, the questions of war and peace, of justice and policy, which were debated in the councils of antiquity, will frequently present themselves as the subject of modern deliberation. But the most experienced statesman of Europe has never been summoned to consider the propriety, or the danger, of admitting, or rejecting, an innumerable multitude of Barbarians, who are driven by despair and hunger to solicit a settlement on the territories of a civilized nation. When that important proposition, so essentially connected with the public safety, was referred to the ministers of Valens, they were perplexed and divided; but they soon acquiesced in the flattering sentiment which seemed the most favorable to the pride, the indolence, and the avarice of their sovereign. The slaves, who were decorated with the titles of praefects and generals, dissembled or disregarded the terrors of this national emigration; so extremely different from the partial and accidental colonies, which had been received on the extreme limits of the empire. But they applauded the liberality of fortune, which had conducted, from the most distant countries of the globe, a numerous and invincible army of strangers, to defend the throne of Valens; who might now add to the royal treasures the immense sums of gold supplied by the provincials to compensate their annual proportion of recruits. The prayers of the Goths were granted, and their service was accepted by the Imperial court: and orders were immediately despatched to the civil and military governors of the Thracian diocese, to make the necessary preparations for the passage and subsistence of a great people, till a proper and sufficient territory could be allotted for their future residence. The liberality of the emperor was accompanied, however, with two harsh and rigorous conditions, which prudence might justify on the side of the Romans; but which distress alone could extort from the indignant Goths. Before they passed the Danube, they were required to deliver their arms: and it was insisted, that their children should be taken from them, and dispersed through the provinces of Asia; where they might be civilized by the arts of education, and serve as hostages to secure the fidelity of their parents.

[Footnote 63: The Chronology of Ammianus is obscure and imperfect. Tillemont has labored to clear and settle the annals of Valens.]

[Footnote 64: Zosimus, l. iv. p. 223. Sozomen, l. vi. c. 38. The Isaurians, each winter, infested the roads of Asia Minor, as far as the neighborhood of Constantinople. Basil, Epist. cel. apud Tillemont, Hist. des Empereurs, tom. v. p. 106.]

[Footnote 64a: Sozomen and Philostorgius say that the bishop Ulphilas was one of these ambassadors—M.]

During the suspense of a doubtful and distant negotiation, the impatient Goths made some rash attempts to pass the Danube, without the permission of the government, whose protection they had implored. Their motions were strictly observed by the vigilance of the troops which were stationed along the river and their foremost detachments were defeated with considerable slaughter; yet such were the timid councils of the reign of Valens, that the brave officers who had served their country in the execution of their duty, were punished by the loss of their employments, and narrowly escaped the loss of their heads. The Imperial mandate was at length received for transporting over the Danube the whole body of the Gothic nation; [65] but the execution of this order was a task of labor and difficulty. The stream of the Danube, which in those parts is above a mile broad, [66] had been swelled by incessant rains; and in this tumultuous passage, many were swept away, and drowned, by the rapid violence of the current. A large fleet of vessels, of boats, and of canoes, was provided; many days and nights they passed and repassed with indefatigable toil; and the most strenuous diligence was exerted by the officers of Valens, that not a single Barbarian, of those who were reserved to subvert the foundations of Rome, should be left on the opposite shore. It was thought expedient that an accurate account should be taken of their numbers; but the persons who were employed soon desisted, with amazement and dismay, from the prosecution of the endless and impracticable task: [67] and the principal historian of the age most seriously affirms, that the prodigious armies of Darius and Xerxes, which had so long been considered as the fables of vain and credulous antiquity, were now justified, in the eyes of mankind, by the evidence of fact and experience. A probable testimony has fixed the number of the Gothic warriors at two hundred thousand men: and if we can venture to add the just proportion of women, of children, and of slaves, the whole mass of people which composed this formidable emigration, must have amounted to near a million of persons, of both sexes, and of all ages. The children of the Goths, those at least of a distinguished rank, were separated from the multitude. They were conducted, without delay, to the distant seats assigned for their residence and education; and as the numerous train of hostages or captives passed through the cities, their gay and splendid apparel, their robust and martial figure, excited the surprise and envy of the Provincials. [67a] But the stipulation, the most offensive to the Goths, and the most important to the Romans, was shamefully eluded. The Barbarians, who considered their arms as the ensigns of honor and the pledges of safety, were disposed to offer a price, which the lust or avarice of the Imperial officers was easily tempted to accept. To preserve their arms, the haughty warriors consented, with some reluctance, to prostitute their wives or their daughters; the charms of a beauteous maid, or a comely boy, secured the connivance of the inspectors; who sometimes cast an eye of covetousness on the fringed carpets and linen garments of their new allies, [68] or who sacrificed their duty to the mean consideration of filling their farms with cattle, and their houses with slaves. The Goths, with arms in their hands, were permitted to enter the boats; and when their strength was collected on the other side of the river, the immense camp which was spread over the plains and the hills of the Lower Maesia, assumed a threatening and even hostile aspect. The leaders of the Ostrogoths, Alatheus and Saphrax, the guardians of their infant king, appeared soon afterwards on the Northern banks of the Danube; and immediately despatched their ambassadors to the court of Antioch, to solicit, with the same professions of allegiance and gratitude, the same favor which had been granted to the suppliant Visigoths. The absolute refusal of Valens suspended their progress, and discovered the repentance, the suspicions, and the fears, of the Imperial council.

[Footnote 65: The passage of the Danube is exposed by Ammianus, (xxxi. 3, 4,) Zosimus, (l. iv. p. 223, 224,) Eunapius in Excerpt. Legat. (p. 19, 20,) and Jornandes, (c. 25, 26.) Ammianus declares (c. 5) that he means only, ispas rerum digerere summitates. But he often takes a false measure of their importance; and his superfluous prolixity is disagreeably balanced by his unseasonable brevity.]

[Footnote 66: Chishull, a curious traveller, has remarked the breadth of the Danube, which he passed to the south of Bucharest near the conflux of the Argish, (p. 77.) He admires the beauty and spontaneous plenty of Maesia, or Bulgaria.]

[Footnote 67:
Quem sci scire velit, Libyci velit aequoris idem
Discere quam multae Zephyro turbentur harenae.

Ammianus has inserted, in his prose, these lines of Virgil, (Georgia l. ii. 105,) originally designed by the poet to express the impossibility of numbering the different sorts of vines. See Plin. Hist. Natur l. xiv.]

[Footnote 67a: A very curious, but obscure, passage of Eunapius, appears to me to have been misunderstood by M. Mai, to whom we owe its discovery. The substance is as follows: "The Goths transported over the river their native deities, with their priests of both sexes; but concerning their rites they maintained a deep and 'adamantine silence.' To the Romans they pretended to be generally Christians, and placed certain persons to represent bishops in a conspicuous manner on their wagons. There was even among them a sort of what are called monks, persons whom it was not difficult to mimic; it was enough to wear black raiment, to be wicked, and held in respect." (Eunapius hated the "black-robed monks," as appears in another passage, with the cordial detestation of a heathen philosopher.) "Thus, while they faithfully but secretly adhered to their own religion, the Romans were weak enough to suppose them perfect Christians." Mai, 277. Eunapius in Niebuhr, 82—M]

[Footnote 68: Eunapius and Zosimus curiously specify these articles of Gothic wealth and luxury. Yet it must be presumed, that they were the manufactures of the provinces; which the Barbarians had acquired as the spoils of war; or as the gifts, or merchandise, of peace.]

An undisciplined and unsettled nation of Barbarians required the firmest temper, and the most dexterous management. The daily subsistence of near a million of extraordinary subjects could be supplied only by constant and skilful diligence, and might continually be interrupted by mistake or accident. The insolence, or the indignation, of the Goths, if they conceived themselves to be the objects either of fear or of contempt, might urge them to the most desperate extremities; and the fortune of the state seemed to depend on the prudence, as well as the integrity, of the generals of Valens. At this important crisis, the military government of Thrace was exercised by Lupicinus and Maximus, in whose venal minds the slightest hope of private emolument outweighed every consideration of public advantage; and whose guilt was only alleviated by their incapacity of discerning the pernicious effects of their rash and criminal administration.

Instead of obeying the orders of their sovereign, and satisfying, with decent liberality, the demands of the Goths, they levied an ungenerous and oppressive tax on the wants of the hungry Barbarians. The vilest food was sold at an extravagant price; and, in the room of wholesome and substantial provisions, the markets were filled with the flesh of dogs, and of unclean animals, who had died of disease. To obtain the valuable acquisition of a pound of bread, the Goths resigned the possession of an expensive, though serviceable, slave; and a small quantity of meat was greedily purchased with ten pounds of a precious, but useless metal, [69] when their property was exhausted, they continued this necessary traffic by the sale of their sons and daughters; and notwithstanding the love of freedom, which animated every Gothic breast, they submitted to the humiliating maxim, that it was better for their children to be maintained in a servile condition, than to perish in a state of wretched and helpless independence. The most lively resentment is excited by the tyranny of pretended benefactors, who sternly exact the debt of gratitude which they have cancelled by subsequent injuries: a spirit of discontent insensibly arose in the camp of the Barbarians, who pleaded, without success, the merit of their patient and dutiful behavior; and loudly complained of the inhospitable treatment which they had received from their new allies. They beheld around them the wealth and plenty of a fertile province, in the midst of which they suffered the intolerable hardships of artificial famine. But the means of relief, and even of revenge, were in their hands; since the rapaciousness of their tyrants had left to an injured people the possession and the use of arms. The clamors of a multitude, untaught to disguise their sentiments, announced the first symptoms of resistance, and alarmed the timid and guilty minds of Lupicinus and Maximus. Those crafty ministers, who substituted the cunning of temporary expedients to the wise and salutary counsels of general policy, attempted to remove the Goths from their dangerous station on the frontiers of the empire; and to disperse them, in separate quarters of cantonment, through the interior provinces. As they were conscious how ill they had deserved the respect, or confidence, of the Barbarians, they diligently collected, from every side, a military force, that might urge the tardy and reluctant march of a people, who had not yet renounced the title, or the duties, of Roman subjects. But the generals of Valens, while their attention was solely directed to the discontented Visigoths, imprudently disarmed the ships and the fortifications which constituted the defence of the Danube. The fatal oversight was observed, and improved, by Alatheus and Saphrax, who anxiously watched the favorable moment of escaping from the pursuit of the Huns. By the help of such rafts and vessels as could be hastily procured, the leaders of the Ostrogoths transported, without opposition, their king and their army; and boldly fixed a hostile and independent camp on the territories of the empire. [70]

[Footnote 69: Decem libras; the word silver must be understood. Jornandes betrays the passions and prejudices of a Goth. The servile Geeks, Eunapius and Zosimus, disguise the Roman oppression, and execrate the perfidy of the Barbarians. Ammianus, a patriot historian, slightly, and reluctantly, touches on the odious subject. Jerom, who wrote almost on the spot, is fair, though concise. Per avaritaim aximi ducis, ad rebellionem fame coacti sunt, (in Chron.) Note: A new passage from the history of Eunapius is nearer to the truth. 'It appeared to our commanders a legitimate source of gain to be bribed by the Barbarians: Edit. Niebuhr, p. 82—M.]

[Footnote 70: Ammianus, xxxi. 4, 5.]

Under the name of Judges, Alavivus and Fritigern were the leaders of the Visigoths in peace and war; and the authority which they derived from their birth was ratified by the free consent of the nation. In a season of tranquility, their power might have been equal, as well as their rank; but, as soon as their countrymen were exasperated by hunger and oppression, the superior abilities of Fritigern assumed the military command, which he was qualified to exercise for the public welfare. He restrained the impatient spirit of the Visigoths till the injuries and the insults of their tyrants should justify their resistance in the opinion of mankind: but he was not disposed to sacrifice any solid advantages for the empty praise of justice and moderation. Sensible of the benefits which would result from the union of the Gothic powers under the same standard, he secretly cultivated the friendship of the Ostrogoths; and while he professed an implicit obedience to the orders of the Roman generals, he proceeded by slow marches towards Marcianopolis, the capital of the Lower Maesia, about seventy miles from the banks of the Danube. On that fatal spot, the flames of discord and mutual hatred burst forth into a dreadful conflagration. Lupicinus had invited the Gothic chiefs to a splendid entertainment; and their martial train remained under arms at the entrance of the palace. But the gates of the city were strictly guarded, and the Barbarians were sternly excluded from the use of a plentiful market, to which they asserted their equal claim of subjects and allies. Their humble prayers were rejected with insolence and derision; and as their patience was now exhausted, the townsmen, the soldiers, and the Goths, were soon involved in a conflict of passionate altercation and angry reproaches. A blow was imprudently given; a sword was hastily drawn; and the first blood that was spilt in this accidental quarrel, became the signal of a long and destructive war. In the midst of noise and brutal intemperance, Lupicinus was informed, by a secret messenger, that many of his soldiers were slain, and despoiled of their arms; and as he was already inflamed by wine, and oppressed by sleep he issued a rash command, that their death should be revenged by the massacre of the guards of Fritigern and Alavivus.

The clamorous shouts and dying groans apprised Fritigern of his extreme danger; and, as he possessed the calm and intrepid spirit of a hero, he saw that he was lost if he allowed a moment of deliberation to the man who had so deeply injured him. "A trifling dispute," said the Gothic leader, with a firm but gentle tone of voice, "appears to have arisen between the two nations; but it may be productive of the most dangerous consequences, unless the tumult is immediately pacified by the assurance of our safety, and the authority of our presence." At these words, Fritigern and his companions drew their swords, opened their passage through the unresisting crowd, which filled the palace, the streets, and the gates, of Marcianopolis, and, mounting their horses, hastily vanished from the eyes of the astonished Romans. The generals of the Goths were saluted by the fierce and joyful acclamations of the camp; war was instantly resolved, and the resolution was executed without delay: the banners of the nation were displayed according to the custom of their ancestors; and the air resounded with the harsh and mournful music of the Barbarian trumpet. [71] The weak and guilty Lupicinus, who had dared to provoke, who had neglected to destroy, and who still presumed to despise, his formidable enemy, marched against the Goths, at the head of such a military force as could be collected on this sudden emergency. The Barbarians expected his approach about nine miles from Marcianopolis; and on this occasion the talents of the general were found to be of more prevailing efficacy than the weapons and discipline of the troops. The valor of the Goths was so ably directed by the genius of Fritigern, that they broke, by a close and vigorous attack, the ranks of the Roman legions. Lupicinus left his arms and standards, his tribunes and his bravest soldiers, on the field of battle; and their useless courage served only to protect the ignominious flight of their leader. "That successful day put an end to the distress of the Barbarians, and the security of the Romans: from that day, the Goths, renouncing the precarious condition of strangers and exiles, assumed the character of citizens and masters, claimed an absolute dominion over the possessors of land, and held, in their own right, the northern provinces of the empire, which are bounded by the Danube." Such are the words of the Gothic historian, [72] who celebrates, with rude eloquence, the glory of his countrymen. But the dominion of the Barbarians was exercised only for the purposes of rapine and destruction. As they had been deprived, by the ministers of the emperor, of the common benefits of nature, and the fair intercourse of social life, they retaliated the injustice on the subjects of the empire; and the crimes of Lupicinus were expiated by the ruin of the peaceful husbandmen of Thrace, the conflagration of their villages, and the massacre, or captivity, of their innocent families. The report of the Gothic victory was soon diffused over the adjacent country; and while it filled the minds of the Romans with terror and dismay, their own hasty imprudence contributed to increase the forces of Fritigern, and the calamities of the province. Some time before the great emigration, a numerous body of Goths, under the command of Suerid and Colias, had been received into the protection and service of the empire. [73] They were encamped under the walls of Hadrianople; but the ministers of Valens were anxious to remove them beyond the Hellespont, at a distance from the dangerous temptation which might so easily be communicated by the neighborhood, and the success, of their countrymen. The respectful submission with which they yielded to the order of their march, might be considered as a proof of their fidelity; and their moderate request of a sufficient allowance of provisions, and of a delay of only two days was expressed in the most dutiful terms. But the first magistrate of Hadrianople, incensed by some disorders which had been committed at his country-house, refused this indulgence; and arming against them the inhabitants and manufacturers of a populous city, he urged, with hostile threats, their instant departure. The Barbarians stood silent and amazed, till they were exasperated by the insulting clamors, and missile weapons, of the populace: but when patience or contempt was fatigued, they crushed the undisciplined multitude, inflicted many a shameful wound on the backs of their flying enemies, and despoiled them of the splendid armor, [74] which they were unworthy to bear. The resemblance of their sufferings and their actions soon united this victorious detachment to the nation of the Visigoths; the troops of Colias and Suerid expected the approach of the great Fritigern, ranged themselves under his standard, and signalized their ardor in the siege of Hadrianople. But the resistance of the garrison informed the Barbarians, that in the attack of regular fortifications, the efforts of unskillful courage are seldom effectual. Their general acknowledged his error, raised the siege, declared that "he was at peace with stone walls," [75] and revenged his disappointment on the adjacent country. He accepted, with pleasure, the useful reenforcement of hardy workmen, who labored in the gold mines of Thrace, [76] for the emolument, and under the lash, of an unfeeling master: [77] and these new associates conducted the Barbarians, through the secret paths, to the most sequestered places, which had been chosen to secure the inhabitants, the cattle, and the magazines of corn. With the assistance of such guides, nothing could remain impervious or inaccessible; resistance was fatal; flight was impracticable; and the patient submission of helpless innocence seldom found mercy from the Barbarian conqueror. In the course of these depredations, a great number of the children of the Goths, who had been sold into captivity, were restored to the embraces of their afflicted parents; but these tender interviews, which might have revived and cherished in their minds some sentiments of humanity, tended only to stimulate their native fierceness by the desire of revenge. They listened, with eager attention, to the complaints of their captive children, who had suffered the most cruel indignities from the lustful or angry passions of their masters, and the same cruelties, the same indignities, were severely retaliated on the sons and daughters of the Romans. [78]

[Footnote 71: Vexillis de more sublatis, auditisque trisie sonantibus classicis. Ammian. xxxi. 5. These are the rauca cornua of Claudian, (in Rufin. ii. 57,) the large horns of the Uri, or wild bull; such as have been more recently used by the Swiss Cantons of Uri and Underwald. (Simler de Republica Helvet, l. ii. p. 201, edit. Fuselin. Tigur 1734.) Their military horn is finely, though perhaps casually, introduced in an original narrative of the battle of Nancy, (A.D. 1477.) "Attendant le combat le dit cor fut corne par trois fois, tant que le vent du souffler pouvoit durer: ce qui esbahit fort Monsieur de Bourgoigne; car deja a Morat l'avoit ouy." (See the Pieces Justificatives in the 4to. edition of Philippe de Comines, tom. iii. p. 493.)]

[Footnote 72: Jornandes de Rebus Geticis, c. 26, p. 648, edit. Grot. These splendidi panm (they are comparatively such) are undoubtedly transcribed from the larger histories of Priscus, Ablavius, or Cassiodorus.]

[Footnote 73: Cum populis suis longe ante suscepti. We are ignorant of the precise date and circumstances of their transmigration.]

[Footnote 74: An Imperial manufacture of shields, &c., was established at Hadrianople; and the populace were headed by the Fabricenses, or workmen. (Vales. ad Ammian. xxxi. 6.)]

[Footnote 75: Pacem sibi esse cum parietibus memorans. Ammian. xxxi. 7.]

[Footnote 76: These mines were in the country of the Bessi, in the ridge of mountains, the Rhodope, that runs between Philippi and Philippopolis; two Macedonian cities, which derived their name and origin from the father of Alexander. From the mines of Thrace he annually received the value, not the weight, of a thousand talents, (200,000l.,) a revenue which paid the phalanx, and corrupted the orators of Greece. See Diodor. Siculus, tom. ii. l. xvi. p. 88, edit. Wesseling. Godefroy's Commentary on the Theodosian Code, tom. iii. p. 496. Cellarius, Geograph. Antiq. tom. i. p. 676, 857. D Anville, Geographie Ancienne, tom. i. p. 336.]

[Footnote 77: As those unhappy workmen often ran away, Valens had enacted severe laws to drag them from their hiding-places. Cod. Theodosian, l. x. tit xix leg. 5, 7.]

[Footnote 78: See Ammianus, xxxi. 5, 6. The historian of the Gothic war loses time and space, by an unseasonable recapitulation of the ancient inroads of the Barbarians.]

The imprudence of Valens and his ministers had introduced into the heart of the empire a nation of enemies; but the Visigoths might even yet have been reconciled, by the manly confession of past errors, and the sincere performance of former engagements. These healing and temperate measures seemed to concur with the timorous disposition of the sovereign of the East: but, on this occasion alone, Valens was brave; and his unseasonable bravery was fatal to himself and to his subjects. He declared his intention of marching from Antioch to Constantinople, to subdue this dangerous rebellion; and, as he was not ignorant of the difficulties of the enterprise, he solicited the assistance of his nephew, the emperor Gratian, who commanded all the forces of the West. The veteran troops were hastily recalled from the defence of Armenia; that important frontier was abandoned to the discretion of Sapor; and the immediate conduct of the Gothic war was intrusted, during the absence of Valens, to his lieutenants Trajan and Profuturus, two generals who indulged themselves in a very false and favorable opinion of their own abilities. On their arrival in Thrace, they were joined by Richomer, count of the domestics; and the auxiliaries of the West, that marched under his banner, were composed of the Gallic legions, reduced indeed, by a spirit of desertion, to the vain appearances of strength and numbers. In a council of war, which was influenced by pride, rather than by reason, it was resolved to seek, and to encounter, the Barbarians, who lay encamped in the spacious and fertile meadows, near the most southern of the six mouths of the Danube. [79] Their camp was surrounded by the usual fortification of wagons; [80] and the Barbarians, secure within the vast circle of the enclosure, enjoyed the fruits of their valor, and the spoils of the province. In the midst of riotous intemperance, the watchful Fritigern observed the motions, and penetrated the designs, of the Romans. He perceived, that the numbers of the enemy were continually increasing: and, as he understood their intention of attacking his rear, as soon as the scarcity of forage should oblige him to remove his camp, he recalled to their standard his predatory detachments, which covered the adjacent country. As soon as they descried the flaming beacons, [81] they obeyed, with incredible speed, the signal of their leader: the camp was filled with the martial crowd of Barbarians; their impatient clamors demanded the battle, and their tumultuous zeal was approved and animated by the spirit of their chiefs. The evening was already far advanced; and the two armies prepared themselves for the approaching combat, which was deferred only till the dawn of day.

While the trumpets sounded to arms, the undaunted courage of the Goths was confirmed by the mutual obligation of a solemn oath; and as they advanced to meet the enemy, the rude songs, which celebrated the glory of their forefathers, were mingled with their fierce and dissonant outcries, and opposed to the artificial harmony of the Roman shout. Some military skill was displayed by Fritigern to gain the advantage of a commanding eminence; but the bloody conflict, which began and ended with the light, was maintained on either side, by the personal and obstinate efforts of strength, valor, and agility. The legions of Armenia supported their fame in arms; but they were oppressed by the irresistible weight of the hostile multitude the left wing of the Romans was thrown into disorder and the field was strewed with their mangled carcasses. This partial defeat was balanced, however, by partial success; and when the two armies, at a late hour of the evening, retreated to their respective camps, neither of them could claim the honors, or the effects, of a decisive victory. The real loss was more severely felt by the Romans, in proportion to the smallness of their numbers; but the Goths were so deeply confounded and dismayed by this vigorous, and perhaps unexpected, resistance, that they remained seven days within the circle of their fortifications. Such funeral rites, as the circumstances of time and place would admit, were piously discharged to some officers of distinguished rank; but the indiscriminate vulgar was left unburied on the plain. Their flesh was greedily devoured by the birds of prey, who in that age enjoyed very frequent and delicious feasts; and several years afterwards the white and naked bones, which covered the wide extent of the fields, presented to the eyes of Ammianus a dreadful monument of the battle of Salices. [82]

[Footnote 79: The Itinerary of Antoninus (p. 226, 227, edit. Wesseling) marks the situation of this place about sixty miles north of Tomi, Ovid's exile; and the name of Salices (the willows) expresses the nature of the soil.]

[Footnote 80: This circle of wagons, the Carrago, was the usual fortification of the Barbarians. (Vegetius de Re Militari, l. iii. c. 10. Valesius ad Ammian. xxxi. 7.) The practice and the name were preserved by their descendants as late as the fifteenth century. The Charroy, which surrounded the Ost, is a word familiar to the readers of Froissard, or Comines.]

[Footnote 81: Statim ut accensi malleoli. I have used the literal sense of real torches or beacons; but I almost suspect, that it is only one of those turgid metaphors, those false ornaments, that perpetually disfigure to style of Ammianus.]

[Footnote 82: Indicant nunc usque albentes ossibus campi. Ammian. xxxi. 7. The historian might have viewed these plains, either as a soldier, or as a traveller. But his modesty has suppressed the adventures of his own life subsequent to the Persian wars of Constantius and Julian. We are ignorant of the time when he quitted the service, and retired to Rome, where he appears to have composed his History of his Own Times.]

The progress of the Goths had been checked by the doubtful event of that bloody day; and the Imperial generals, whose army would have been consumed by the repetition of such a contest, embraced the more rational plan of destroying the Barbarians by the wants and pressure of their own multitudes. They prepared to confine the Visigoths in the narrow angle of land between the Danube, the desert of Scythia, and the mountains of Haemus, till their strength and spirit should be insensibly wasted by the inevitable operation of famine. The design was prosecuted with some conduct and success: the

Barbarians had almost exhausted their own magazines, and the harvests of the country; and the diligence of Saturninus, the master-general of the cavalry, was employed to improve the strength, and to contract the extent, of the Roman fortifications. His labors were interrupted by the alarming intelligence, that new swarms of Barbarians had passed the unguarded Danube, either to support the cause, or to imitate the example, of Fritigern. The just apprehension, that he himself might be surrounded, and overwhelmed, by the arms of hostile and unknown nations, compelled Saturninus to relinquish the siege of the Gothic camp; and the indignant Visigoths, breaking from their confinement, satiated their hunger and revenge by the repeated devastation of the fruitful country, which extends above three hundred miles from the banks of the Danube to the straits of the Hellespont. [83] The sagacious Fritigern had successfully appealed to the passions, as well as to the interest, of his Barbarian allies; and the love of rapine, and the hatred of Rome, seconded, or even prevented, the eloquence of his ambassadors. He cemented a strict and useful alliance with the great body of his countrymen, who obeyed Alatheus and Saphrax as the guardians of their infant king: the long animosity of rival tribes was suspended by the sense of their common interest; the independent part of the nation was associated under one standard; and the chiefs of the Ostrogoths appear to have yielded to the superior genius of the general of the Visigoths. He obtained the formidable aid of the Taifalae, [83a] whose military renown was disgraced and polluted by the public infamy of their domestic manners. Every youth, on his entrance into the world, was united by the ties of honorable friendship, and brutal love, to some warrior of the tribe; nor could he hope to be released from this unnatural connection, till he had approved his manhood by slaying, in single combat, a huge bear, or a wild boar of the forest. [84] But the most powerful auxiliaries of the Goths were drawn from the camp of those enemies who had expelled them from their native seats. The loose subordination, and extensive possessions, of the Huns and the Alani, delayed the conquests, and distracted the councils, of that victorious people. Several of the hordes were allured by the liberal promises of Fritigern; and the rapid cavalry of Scythia added weight and energy to the steady and strenuous efforts of the Gothic infantry. The Sarmatians, who could never forgive the successor of Valentinian, enjoyed and increased the general confusion; and a seasonable irruption of the Alemanni, into the provinces of Gaul, engaged the attention, and diverted the forces, of the emperor of the West. [85]

[Footnote 83: Ammian. xxxi. 8.]

[Footnote 83a: The Taifalae, who at this period inhabited the country which now forms the principality of Wallachia, were, in my opinion, the last remains of the great and powerful nation of the Dacians, (Daci or Dahae.) which has given its name to these regions, over which they had ruled so long. The Taifalae passed with the Goths into the territory of the empire. A great number of them entered the Roman service, and were quartered in different provinces. They are mentioned in the Notitia Imperii. There was a considerable body in the country of the Pictavi, now Poithou. They long retained their manners and language, and caused the name of the Theofalgicus pagus to be given to the district they inhabited. Two places in the department of La Vendee, Tiffanges and La Tiffardiere, still preserve evident traces of this denomination. St. Martin, iv. 118—M.]

[Footnote 84: Hanc Taifalorum gentem turpem, et obscenae vitae flagitiis ita accipimus mersam; ut apud eos nefandi concubitus foedere copulentur mares puberes, aetatis viriditatem in eorum pollutis usibus consumpturi. Porro, siqui jam adultus aprum exceperit solus, vel interemit ursum immanem, colluvione liberatur incesti. Ammian. xxxi. 9. —Among the Greeks, likewise, more especially among the Cretans, the holy bands of friendship were confirmed, and sullied, by unnatural love.]

[Footnote 85: Ammian. xxxi. 8, 9. Jerom (tom. i. p. 26) enumerates the nations and marks a calamitous period of twenty years. This epistle to Heliodorus was composed in the year 397, (Tillemont, Mem. Eccles tom xii. p. 645.)]

PART IV

One of the most dangerous inconveniences of the introduction of the Barbarians into the army and the palace, was sensibly felt in their correspondence with their hostile countrymen; to whom they imprudently, or maliciously, revealed the weakness of the Roman empire. A soldier, of the lifeguards of Gratian, was of the nation of the Alemanni, and of the tribe of the Lentienses, who dwelt beyond the Lake of Constance. Some domestic business obliged him to request a leave of absence. In a short visit to his family and friends, he was exposed to their curious inquiries: and the vanity of the loquacious soldier tempted him to display his intimate acquaintance with the secrets of the state, and the designs of his master. The intelligence, that Gratian was preparing to lead the military force of Gaul, and of the West, to the assistance of his uncle Valens, pointed out to the restless spirit of the Alemanni the moment, and the mode, of a successful invasion. The enterprise of some light detachments, who, in the month of February, passed the Rhine upon the ice, was the prelude of a more important war. The boldest hopes of rapine, perhaps of conquest, outweighed the considerations of timid prudence, or national faith. Every forest, and every village, poured forth a band of hardy adventurers; and the great army of the Alemanni, which, on their approach, was estimated at forty thousand men by the fears of the people, was afterwards magnified to the number of seventy thousand by the vain and credulous flattery of the Imperial court. The legions, which had been ordered to march into Pannonia, were immediately recalled, or detained, for the defence of Gaul; the military command was divided between Nanienus and Mellobaudes; and the youthful emperor, though he respected the long experience and sober wisdom of the former, was much more inclined to admire, and to follow, the martial ardor of his colleague; who was allowed to unite the incompatible characters of count of the domestics, and of king of the Franks. His rival Priarius, king of the Alemanni, was guided, or rather impelled, by the same headstrong valor; and as their troops were animated by the spirit of their leaders, they met, they saw, they encountered each other, near the town of Argentaria, or Colmar, [86] in the plains of Alsace. The glory of the day was justly ascribed to the missile weapons, and well-practised evolutions, of the Roman soldiers; the Alemanni, who long maintained their ground, were slaughtered with unrelenting fury; five thousand only of the Barbarians escaped to the woods and mountains; and the glorious death of their king on the field of battle saved him from the reproaches of the people, who are always disposed to accuse the justice, or policy, of an unsuccessful war. After this signal victory, which secured the peace of Gaul, and asserted the honor of the Roman arms, the emperor Gratian appeared to proceed without delay on his Eastern expedition; but as he approached the confines of the Alemanni, he suddenly inclined to the left, surprised them by his unexpected passage of the Rhine, and boldly advanced into the heart of their country. The Barbarians opposed to his progress the obstacles of nature and of courage; and still continued to retreat, from one hill to another, till they were satisfied, by repeated trials, of the power and perseverance of their enemies. Their submission was accepted as a proof, not indeed of their sincere repentance, but of their actual distress; and a select number of their brave and robust youth was exacted from the faithless nation, as the most substantial pledge of their future moderation. The subjects of the empire, who had so often experienced that the Alemanni could neither be subdued by arms, nor restrained by treaties, might not promise themselves any solid or lasting tranquillity: but they discovered, in the virtues of their young sovereign, the prospect of a long and auspicious reign. When the legions climbed the mountains, and scaled the fortifications of the Barbarians, the valor of Gratian was distinguished in the foremost ranks; and the gilt and variegated armor of his guards was pierced and shattered by the blows which they had received in their constant attachment to the person of their sovereign. At the age of nineteen, the son of Valentinian seemed to possess the talents of peace and war; and his personal success against the Alemanni was interpreted as a sure presage of his Gothic triumphs. [87]

[Footnote 86: The field of battle, Argentaria or Argentovaria, is accurately fixed by M. D'Anville (Notice de l'Ancienne Gaule, p. 96—99) at twenty-three Gallic leagues, or thirty-four and a half Roman miles to the south of Strasburg. From its ruins the adjacent town of Colmar has arisen. Note: It is rather Horburg, on the right bank of the River Ill, opposite to Colmar. From Schoepflin, Alsatia Illustrata. St. Martin, iv. 121—M.]

[Footnote 87: The full and impartial narrative of Ammianus (xxxi. 10) may derive some additional light from the Epitome of Victor, the Chronicle of Jerom, and the History of Orosius, (l. vii. c. 33, p. 552, edit. Havercamp.)]

While Gratian deserved and enjoyed the applause of his subjects, the emperor Valens, who, at length, had removed his court and army from Antioch, was received by the people of Constantinople as the author of the public calamity. Before he had reposed himself ten days in the capital, he was urged by the licentious clamors of the Hippodrome to march against the Barbarians, whom he had invited into his dominions; and the citizens, who are always brave at a distance from any real danger, declared, with confidence, that, if they were supplied with arms, they alone would undertake to deliver the province from the ravages of an insulting foe. [88] The vain reproaches of an ignorant multitude hastened the downfall of the Roman empire; they provoked the desperate rashness of Valens; who did not find, either in his reputation or in his mind, any motives to support with firmness the public contempt. He was soon persuaded, by the successful achievements of his lieutenants, to despise the power of the Goths, who, by the diligence of Fritigern, were now collected in the neighborhood of Hadrianople. The march of the Taifalae had been intercepted by the valiant Frigeric: the king of those licentious Barbarians was slain in battle; and the suppliant captives were sent into distant exile to cultivate the lands of Italy, which were assigned for their settlement in the vacant territories of Modena and Parma. [89] The exploits of Sebastian, [90] who was recently engaged in the service of Valens, and promoted to the rank of master-general of the infantry, were still more honorable to himself, and useful to the republic. He obtained the permission of selecting three hundred soldiers from each of the legions; and this separate detachment soon acquired the spirit of discipline, and the exercise of arms, which were almost forgotten under the reign of Valens. By the vigor and conduct of Sebastian, a large body of the Goths were surprised in their camp; and the immense spoil, which was recovered from their hands, filled the city of Hadrianople, and the adjacent plain. The splendid narratives, which the general transmitted of his own exploits, alarmed the Imperial court by the appearance of superior merit; and though he cautiously insisted on the difficulties of the Gothic war, his valor was praised, his advice was rejected; and Valens, who listened with pride and pleasure to the flattering suggestions of the eunuchs of the palace, was impatient to seize the glory of an easy and assured conquest. His army was strengthened by a numerous reenforcement of veterans; and his march from Constantinople to Hadrianople was conducted with so much military skill, that he prevented the activity of the Barbarians, who designed to occupy the intermediate defiles, and to intercept either the troops themselves, or their convoys of provisions. The camp of Valens, which he pitched under the walls of Hadrianople, was fortified, according to the practice of the Romans, with a ditch and rampart; and a most important council was summoned, to decide the fate of the emperor and of the empire. The party of reason and of delay was strenuously maintained by Victor, who had corrected, by the lessons of experience, the native fierceness of the Sarmatian character; while Sebastian, with the flexible and obsequious eloquence of a courtier, represented every precaution, and every measure, that implied a doubt of immediate victory, as unworthy of the courage and majesty of their invincible monarch. The ruin of Valens was precipitated by the deceitful arts of Fritigern, and the prudent admonitions of the emperor of the West. The advantages of negotiating in the midst of war were perfectly understood by the general of the Barbarians; and a Christian ecclesiastic was despatched, as the holy minister of peace, to penetrate, and to perplex, the councils of the enemy. The misfortunes, as well as the provocations, of the Gothic nation, were forcibly and truly described by their ambassador; who protested, in the name of Fritigern, that he was still disposed to lay down his arms, or to employ them only in the defence of the empire; if he could secure for his wandering countrymen a tranquil settlement on the waste lands of Thrace, and a sufficient allowance of corn and cattle. But he added, in a whisper of confidential friendship, that the exasperated Barbarians were averse to these reasonable conditions; and that Fritigern was doubtful whether he could accomplish the conclusion of the treaty, unless he found himself supported by the presence and terrors of an Imperial army. About the same time, Count Richomer returned from the West to announce the defeat and submission of the Alemanni, to inform Valens that his nephew advanced by rapid marches at the head of the veteran and victorious legions of Gaul, and to request, in the name of Gratian and of the republic, that every dangerous and decisive measure might be suspended, till the junction of the two emperors should insure the success of the Gothic war. But the feeble sovereign of the East was actuated only by the fatal illusions of pride and jealousy. He disdained the importunate advice; he rejected the humiliating aid; he secretly compared the ignominious, at least the inglorious, period of his own reign, with the fame of a beardless youth; and Valens rushed into the field, to erect his imaginary trophy, before the diligence of his colleague could usurp any share of the triumphs of the day.

[Footnote 88: Moratus paucissimos dies, seditione popularium levium pulsus Ammian. xxxi. 11. Socrates (l. iv. c. 38) supplies the dates and some circumstances. Note: Compare fragment of Eunapius. Mai, 272, in Niebuhr, p. 77—M]

[Footnote 89: Vivosque omnes circa Mutinam, Regiumque, et Parmam, Italica oppida, rura culturos exterminavit. Ammianus, xxxi. 9. Those cities and districts, about ten years after the colony of the Taifalae, appear in a very desolate state. See Muratori, Dissertazioni sopra le Antichita Italiane, tom. i. Dissertat. xxi. p. 354.]

[Footnote 90: Ammian. xxxi. 11. Zosimus, l. iv. p. 228—230. The latter expatiates on the desultory exploits of Sebastian, and despatches, in a few lines, the important battle of Hadrianople. According to the ecclesiastical critics, who hate Sebastian, the praise of Zosimus is disgrace, (Tillemont, Hist. des Empereurs, tom. v. p. 121.) His prejudice and ignorance undoubtedly render him a very questionable judge of merit.]

On the ninth of August, a day which has deserved to be marked among the most inauspicious of the Roman Calendar, [91] the emperor Valens, leaving, under a strong guard, his baggage and military treasure, marched from Hadrianople to attack the Goths, who were encamped about twelve miles from the city. [92] By some mistake of the orders, or some ignorance of the ground, the right wing, or column of cavalry arrived in sight of the enemy, whilst the left was still at a considerable distance; the soldiers were compelled, in the sultry heat of summer, to precipitate their pace; and the line of battle was formed with tedious confusion and irregular delay. The Gothic cavalry had been detached to forage in the adjacent country; and Fritigern still continued to practise his customary arts. He despatched messengers of peace, made proposals, required hostages, and wasted the hours, till the Romans, exposed without shelter to the burning rays of the sun, were exhausted by thirst, hunger, and intolerable fatigue. The emperor was persuaded to send an ambassador to the Gothic camp; the zeal of Richomer, who alone had courage to accept the dangerous commission, was applauded; and the count of the domestics, adorned with the splendid ensigns of his dignity, had proceeded some way in the space between the two armies, when he was suddenly recalled by the alarm of battle. The hasty and imprudent attack was made by Bacurius the Iberian, who commanded a body of archers and targeteers; and as they advanced with rashness, they retreated with loss and disgrace. In the same moment, the flying squadrons of Alatheus and Saphrax, whose return was anxiously expected by the general of the Goths, descended like a whirlwind from the hills, swept across the plain, and added new terrors to the tumultuous, but irresistible charge of the Barbarian host. The event of the battle of Hadrianople, so fatal to Valens and to the empire, may be described in a few words: the Roman cavalry fled; the infantry was abandoned, surrounded, and cut in pieces. The most skilful evolutions, the firmest courage, are scarcely sufficient to extricate a body of foot, encompassed, on an open plain, by superior numbers of horse; but the troops of Valens, oppressed by the weight of the enemy and their own fears, were crowded into a narrow space, where it was impossible for them to extend their ranks, or even to use, with effect, their swords and javelins. In the midst of tumult, of slaughter, and of dismay, the emperor, deserted by his guards and wounded, as it was supposed, with an arrow, sought protection among the Lancearii and the Mattiarii, who still maintained their ground with some appearance of order and firmness. His faithful generals, Trajan and Victor, who perceived his danger, loudly exclaimed that all was lost, unless the person of the emperor could be saved. Some troops, animated by their exhortation, advanced to his relief: they found only a bloody spot, covered with a heap of broken arms and mangled bodies, without being able to discover their unfortunate prince, either among the living or the dead. Their search could not indeed be successful, if there is any truth in the circumstances with which some historians have related the death of the emperor.

By the care of his attendants, Valens was removed from the field of battle to a neighboring cottage, where they attempted to dress his wound, and to provide for his future safety. But this humble retreat was instantly surrounded by the enemy: they tried to force the door, they were provoked by a discharge of arrows from the roof, till at length, impatient of delay, they set fire to a pile of dry magots, and consumed the cottage with the Roman emperor and his train. Valens perished in the flames; and a youth, who dropped from the window, alone escaped, to attest the melancholy tale, and to inform the Goths of the inestimable prize which they had lost by their own rashness. A great number of brave and distinguished officers perished in the battle of Hadrianople, which equalled in the actual loss, and far surpassed in the fatal consequences, the misfortune which Rome had formerly sustained in the fields of Cannae. [93] Two master-generals of the cavalry and infantry, two great officers of the palace, and thirty-five tribunes, were found among the slain; and the death of Sebastian might satisfy the world, that he was the victim, as well as the author, of the public calamity. Above two thirds of the Roman army were destroyed: and the darkness of the night was esteemed a very favorable circumstance, as it served to conceal the flight of the multitude, and to protect the more orderly retreat of Victor and Richomer, who alone, amidst the general consternation, maintained the advantage of calm courage and regular discipline. [94]

[Footnote 91: Ammianus (xxxi. 12, 13) almost alone describes the councils and actions which were terminated by the fatal battle of Hadrianople. We might censure the vices of his style, the disorder and perplexity of his narrative: but we must now take leave of this impartial historian; and reproach is silenced by our regret for such an irreparable loss.]

[Footnote 92: The difference of the eight miles of Ammianus, and the twelve of Idatius, can only embarrass those critics (Valesius ad loc.,) who suppose a great army to be a mathematical point, without space or dimensions.]

[Footnote 93: Nec ulla annalibus, praeter Cannensem pugnam, ita ad internecionem res legitur gesta. Ammian. xxxi. 13. According to the grave Polybius, no more than 370 horse, and 3,000 foot, escaped from the field of Cannae: 10,000 were made prisoners; and the number of the slain amounted to 5,630 horse, and 70,000 foot, (Polyb. l. iii. p 371, edit. Casaubon, 8vo.) Livy (xxii. 49) is somewhat less bloody: he slaughters only 2,700 horse, and 40,000 foot. The Roman army was supposed to consist of 87,200 effective men, (xxii. 36.)]

[Footnote 94: We have gained some faint light from Jerom, (tom. i. p. 26 and in Chron. p. 188,) Victor, (in Epitome,) Orosius, (l. vii. c. 33, p. 554,) Jornandes, (c. 27,) Zosimus, (l. iv. p. 230,) Socrates, (l. iv. c. 38,) Sozomen, (l. vi. c. 40,) Idatius, (in Chron.) But their united evidence, if weighed against Ammianus alone, is light and unsubstantial.]

While the impressions of grief and terror were still recent in the minds of men, the most celebrated rhetorician of the age composed the funeral oration of a vanquished army, and of an unpopular prince, whose throne was already occupied by a stranger. "There are not wanting," says the candid Libanius, "those who arraign the prudence of the emperor, or who impute the public misfortune to the want of courage and discipline in the troops. For my own part, I reverence the memory of their former exploits: I reverence the glorious death, which they bravely received, standing, and fighting in their ranks: I reverence the field of battle, stained with their blood, and the blood of the Barbarians. Those honorable marks have been already washed away by the rains; but the lofty monuments of their bones, the bones of generals, of centurions, and of valiant warriors, claim a longer period of duration. The king himself fought and fell in the foremost ranks of the battle. His attendants presented him with the fleetest horses of the Imperial stable, that would soon have carried him beyond the pursuit of the enemy. They vainly pressed him to reserve his important life for the future service of the republic. He still declared that he was unworthy to survive so many of the bravest and most faithful of his subjects; and the monarch was nobly buried under a mountain of the slain. Let none, therefore, presume to ascribe the victory of the Barbarians to the fear, the weakness, or the imprudence, of the Roman troops. The chiefs and the soldiers were animated by the virtue of their ancestors, whom they equalled in discipline and the arts of war. Their generous emulation was supported by the love of glory, which prompted them to contend at the same time with heat and thirst, with fire and the sword; and cheerfully to embrace an honorable death, as their refuge against flight and infamy. The indignation of the gods has been the only cause of the success of our enemies." The truth of history may disclaim some parts of this panegyric, which cannot strictly be reconciled with the character of Valens, or the circumstances of the battle: but the fairest commendation is due to the eloquence, and still more to the generosity, of the sophist of Antioch. [95]

[Footnote 95: Libanius de ulciscend. Julian. nece, c. 3, in Fabricius, Bibliot Graec. tom. vii. p. 146—148.]

The pride of the Goths was elated by this memorable victory; but their avarice was disappointed by the mortifying discovery, that the richest part of the Imperial spoil had been within the walls of Hadrianople. They hastened to possess the reward of their valor; but they were encountered by the remains of a vanquished army, with an intrepid resolution, which was the effect of their despair, and the only hope of their safety. The walls of the city, and the ramparts of the adjacent camp, were lined with military engines, that threw stones of an enormous weight; and astonished the ignorant Barbarians by the noise, and velocity, still more than by the real effects, of the discharge. The soldiers, the citizens, the provincials, the domestics of the palace, were united in the danger, and in the defence: the furious assault of the Goths was repulsed; their secret arts of treachery and treason were discovered; and, after an obstinate conflict of many hours, they retired to their tents; convinced, by experience, that it would be far more advisable to observe the treaty, which their sagacious leader had tacitly stipulated with the fortifications of great and populous cities. After the hasty and impolitic massacre of three hundred deserters, an act of justice extremely useful to the discipline of the Roman armies, the Goths indignantly raised the siege of Hadrianople. The scene of war and tumult was instantly converted into a silent solitude: the multitude suddenly disappeared; the secret paths of the woods and mountains were marked with the footsteps of the trembling fugitives, who sought a refuge in the distant cities of Illyricum and Macedonia; and the faithful officers of the household, and the treasury, cautiously proceeded in search of the emperor, of whose death they were still ignorant. The tide of the Gothic inundation rolled from the walls of Hadrianople to the suburbs of Constantinople. The Barbarians were surprised with the splendid appearance of the capital of the East, the height and extent of the walls, the myriads of wealthy and affrighted citizens who crowded the ramparts, and the various prospect of the sea and land. While they gazed with hopeless desire on the inaccessible beauties of Constantinople, a sally was made from one of the gates by a party of Saracens, [96] who had been fortunately engaged in the service of Valens. The cavalry of Scythia was forced to yield to the admirable swiftness and spirit of the Arabian horses: their riders were skilled in the evolutions of irregular war; and the Northern Barbarians were astonished and dismayed, by the inhuman ferocity of the Barbarians of the South.

A Gothic soldier was slain by the dagger of an Arab; and the hairy, naked savage, applying his lips to the wound, expressed a horrid delight, while he sucked the blood of his vanquished enemy. [97] The army of the Goths, laden with the spoils of the wealthy suburbs and the adjacent territory, slowly moved, from the Bosphorus, to the mountains which form the western boundary of Thrace. The important pass of Succi was betrayed by the fear, or the misconduct, of Maurus; and the Barbarians, who no longer had any resistance to apprehend from the scattered and vanquished troops of the East, spread themselves over the face of a fertile and cultivated country, as far as the confines of Italy and the Hadriatic Sea. [98]

[Footnote 96: Valens had gained, or rather purchased, the friendship of the Saracens, whose vexatious inroads were felt on the borders of Phoenicia, Palestine, and Egypt. The Christian faith had been lately introduced among a people, reserved, in a future age, to propagate another religion, (Tillemont, Hist. des Empereurs, tom. v. p. 104, 106, 141. Mem. Eccles. tom. vii. p. 593.)]

[Footnote 97: Crinitus quidam, nudus omnia praeter pubem, subraunum et ugubre strepens. Ammian. xxxi. 16, and Vales. ad loc. The Arabs often fought naked; a custom which may be ascribed to their sultry climate, and ostentatious bravery. The description of this unknown savage is the lively portrait of Derar, a name so dreadful to the Christians of Syria. See Ockley's Hist. of the Saracens, vol. i. p. 72, 84, 87.]

[Footnote 98: The series of events may still be traced in the last pages of Ammianus, (xxxi. 15, 16.) Zosimus, (l. iv. p. 227, 231,) whom we are now reduced to cherish, misplaces the sally of the Arabs before the death of Valens. Eunapius (in Excerpt. Legat. p. 20) praises the fertility of Thrace, Macedonia, &c.]

The Romans, who so coolly, and so concisely, mention the acts of justice which were exercised by the legions, [99] reserve their compassion, and their eloquence, for their own sufferings, when the provinces were invaded, and desolated, by the arms of the successful Barbarians. The simple circumstantial narrative (did such a narrative exist) of the ruin of a single town, of the misfortunes of a single family, [100] might exhibit an interesting and instructive picture of human manners: but the tedious repetition of vague and declamatory complaints would fatigue the attention of the most patient reader. The same censure may be applied, though not perhaps in an equal degree, to the profane, and the ecclesiastical, writers of this unhappy period; that their minds were inflamed by popular and religious animosity; and that the true size and color of every object is falsified by the exaggerations of their corrupt eloquence. The vehement Jerom [101] might justly deplore the calamities inflicted by the Goths, and their barbarous allies, on his native country of Pannonia, and the wide extent of the provinces, from the walls of Constantinople to the foot of the Julian Alps; the rapes, the massacres, the conflagrations; and, above all, the profanation of the churches, that were turned into stables, and the contemptuous treatment of the relics of holy martyrs. But the Saint is surely transported beyond the limits of nature and history, when he affirms, "that, in those desert countries, nothing was left except the sky and the earth; that, after the destruction of the cities, and the extirpation of the human race, the land was overgrown with thick forests and inextricable brambles; and that the universal desolation, announced by the prophet Zephaniah, was accomplished, in the scarcity of the beasts, the birds, and even of the fish." These complaints were pronounced about twenty years after the death of Valens; and the Illyrian provinces, which were constantly exposed to the invasion and passage of the Barbarians, still continued, after a calamitous period of ten centuries, to supply new materials for rapine and destruction. Could it even be supposed, that a large tract of country had been left without cultivation and without inhabitants, the consequences might not have been so fatal to the inferior productions of animated nature. The useful and feeble animals, which are nourished by the hand of man, might suffer and perish, if they were deprived of his protection; but the beasts of the forest, his enemies or his victims, would multiply in the free and undisturbed possession of their solitary domain. The various tribes that people the air, or the waters, are still less connected with the fate of the human species; and it is highly probable that the fish of the Danube would have felt more terror and distress, from the approach of a voracious pike, than from the hostile inroad of a Gothic army.

[Footnote 99: Observe with how much indifference Caesar relates, in the Commentaries of the Gallic war, that he put to death the whole senate of the Veneti, who had yielded to his mercy, (iii. 16;) that he labored to extirpate the whole nation of the Eburones, (vi. 31;) that forty thousand persons were massacred at Bourges by the just revenge of his soldiers, who spared neither age nor sex, (vii. 27,) &c.]

[Footnote 100: Such are the accounts of the sack of Magdeburgh, by the ecclesiastic and the fisherman, which Mr. Harte has transcribed, (Hist. of Gustavus Adolphus, vol. i. p. 313—320,) with some apprehension of violating the dignity of history.]

[Footnote 101: Et vastatis urbibus, hominibusque interfectis, solitudinem et raritatem bestiarum quoque fieri, et volatilium, pisciumque: testis Illyricum est, testis Thracia, testis in quo ortus sum solum, (Pannonia;) ubi praeter coelum et terram, et crescentes vepres, et condensa sylvarum cuncta perierunt. Tom. vii. p. 250, l, Cap. Sophonias and tom. i. p. 26.]

PART V

Whatever may have been the just measure of the calamities of Europe, there was reason to fear that the same calamities would soon extend to the peaceful countries of Asia. The sons of the Goths had been judiciously distributed through the cities of the East; and the arts of education were employed to polish, and subdue, the native fierceness of their temper. In the space of about twelve years, their numbers had continually increased; and the children, who, in the first emigration, were sent over the

Hellespont, had attained, with rapid growth, the strength and spirit of perfect manhood. [102] It was impossible to conceal from their knowledge the events of the Gothic war; and, as those daring youths had not studied the language of dissimulation, they betrayed their wish, their desire, perhaps their intention, to emulate the glorious example of their fathers The danger of the times seemed to justify the jealous suspicions of the provincials; and these suspicions were admitted as unquestionable evidence, that the Goths of Asia had formed a secret and dangerous conspiracy against the public safety. The death of Valens had left the East without a sovereign; and Julius, who filled the important station of master-general of the troops, with a high reputation of diligence and ability, thought it his duty to consult the senate of Constantinople; which he considered, during the vacancy of the throne, as the representative council of the nation. As soon as he had obtained the discretionary power of acting as he should judge most expedient for the good of the republic, he assembled the principal officers, and privately concerted effectual measures for the execution of his bloody design. An order was immediately promulgated, that, on a stated day, the Gothic youth should assemble in the capital cities of their respective provinces; and, as a report was industriously circulated, that they were summoned to receive a liberal gift of lands and money, the pleasing hope allayed the fury of their resentment, and, perhaps, suspended the motions of the conspiracy. On the appointed day, the unarmed crowd of the Gothic youth was carefully collected in the square or Forum; the streets and avenues were occupied by the Roman troops, and the roofs of the houses were covered with archers and slingers. At the same hour, in all the cities of the East, the signal was given of indiscriminate slaughter; and the provinces of Asia were delivered by the cruel prudence of Julius, from a domestic enemy, who, in a few months, might have carried fire and sword from the Hellespont to the Euphrates. [103] The urgent consideration of the public safety may undoubtedly authorize the violation of every positive law. How far that, or any other, consideration may operate to dissolve the natural obligations of humanity and justice, is a doctrine of which I still desire to remain ignorant.

[Footnote 102: Eunapius (in Excerpt. Legat. p. 20) foolishly supposes a praeternatural growth of the young Goths, that he may introduce Cadmus's armed men, who sprang from the dragon's teeth, &c. Such was the Greek eloquence of the times.]

[Footnote 103: Ammianus evidently approves this execution, efficacia velox et salutaris, which concludes his work, (xxxi. 16.) Zosimus, who is curious and copious, (l. iv. p. 233—236,) mistakes the date, and labors to find the reason, why Julius did not consult the emperor Theodosius who had not yet ascended the throne of the East.]

The emperor Gratian was far advanced on his march towards the plains of Hadrianople, when he was informed, at first by the confused voice of fame, and afterwards by the more accurate reports of Victor and Richomer, that his impatient colleague had been slain in battle, and that two thirds of the Roman army were exterminated by the sword of the victorious Goths. Whatever resentment the rash and jealous vanity of his uncle might deserve, the resentment of a generous mind is easily subdued by the softer emotions of grief and compassion; and even the sense of pity was soon lost in the serious and alarming consideration of the state of the republic. Gratian was too late to assist, he was too weak to revenge, his unfortunate colleague; and the valiant and modest youth felt himself unequal to the support of a sinking world. A formidable tempest of the Barbarians of Germany seemed ready to burst over the provinces of Gaul; and the mind of Gratian was oppressed and distracted by the administration of the Western empire. In this important crisis, the government of the East, and the conduct of the Gothic war, required the undivided attention of a hero and a statesman. A subject invested with such ample command would not long have preserved his fidelity to a distant benefactor; and the Imperial council embraced the wise and manly resolution of conferring an obligation, rather than of yielding to an insult. It was the wish of Gratian to bestow the purple as the reward of virtue; but, at the age of nineteen, it is not easy for a prince, educated in the supreme rank, to understand the true characters of his ministers and generals. He attempted to weigh, with an impartial hand, their various merits and defects; and, whilst he checked the rash confidence of ambition, he distrusted the cautious wisdom which despaired of the republic. As each moment of delay diminished something of the power and resources of the future sovereign of the East, the situation of the times would not allow a tedious debate. The choice of Gratian was soon declared in favor of an exile, whose father, only three years before, had suffered, under the sanction of his authority, an unjust and ignominious death. The great Theodosius, a name celebrated in history, and dear to the Catholic church, [104] was summoned to the Imperial court, which had gradually retreated from the confines of Thrace to the more secure station of Sirmium. Five months after the death of Valens, the emperor Gratian produced before the assembled troops his colleague and their master; who, after a modest, perhaps a sincere, resistance, was compelled to accept, amidst the general acclamations, the diadem, the purple, and the equal title of Augustus. [105] The provinces of Thrace, Asia, and Egypt, over which Valens had reigned, were resigned to the administration of the new emperor; but, as he was specially intrusted with the conduct of the Gothic war, the Illyrian praefecture was dismembered; and the two great dioceses of Dacia and Macedonia were added to the dominions of the Eastern empire. [106]

[Footnote 104: A life of Theodosius the Great was composed in the last century, (Paris, 1679, in 4to-1680, 12mo.,) to inflame the mind of the young Dauphin with Catholic zeal. The author, Flechier, afterwards bishop of Nismes, was a celebrated preacher; and his history is adorned, or tainted, with pulpit eloquence; but he takes his learning from Baronius, and his principles from St. Ambrose and St Augustin.]

[Footnote 105: The birth, character, and elevation of Theodosius are marked in Pacatus, (in Panegyr. Vet. xii. 10, 11, 12,) Themistius, (Orat. xiv. p. 182,) (Zosimus, l. iv. p. 231,) Augustin. (de Civitat. Dei. v. 25,) Orosius, (l. vii. c. 34,) Sozomen, (l. vii. c. 2,) Socrates, (l. v. c. 2,) Theodoret, (l. v. c. 5,) Philostorgius, (l. ix. c. 17, with Godefroy, p. 393,) the Epitome of Victor, and the Chronicles of Prosper, Idatius, and Marcellinus, in the Thesaurus Temporum of Scaliger. Note: Add a hostile fragment of Eunapius. Mai, p. 273, in Niebuhr, p 178—M.]

[Footnote 106: Tillemont, Hist. des Empereurs, tom. v. p. 716, &c.]

The same province, and perhaps the same city, [107] which had given to the throne the virtues of Trajan, and the talents of Hadrian, was the orignal seat of another family of Spaniards, who, in a less fortunate age, possessed, near fourscore years, the declining empire of Rome. [108] They emerged from the obscurity of municipal honors by the active spirit of the elder Theodosius, a general whose exploits in Britain and Africa have formed one of the most splendid parts of the annals of Valentinian. The son of that general, who likewise bore the name of Theodosius, was educated, by skilful preceptors, in the liberal studies of youth; but he was instructed in the art of war by the tender care and severe discipline of his father. [109] Under the standard of such a leader, young Theodosius sought glory and knowledge, in the most distant scenes of military action; inured his constitution to the difference of seasons and climates; distinguished his valor by sea and land; and observed the various warfare of the Scots, the Saxons, and the Moors. His own merit, and the recommendation of the conqueror of Africa, soon raised him to a separate command; and, in the station of Duke of Misaea, he vanquished an army of Sarmatians; saved the province; deserved the love of the soldiers; and provoked the envy of the court. [110] His rising fortunes were soon blasted by the disgrace and execution of his illustrious father; and Theodosius obtained, as a favor, the permission of retiring to a private life in his native province of Spain. He displayed a firm and temperate character in the ease with which he adapted himself to this new situation. His time was almost equally divided between the town and country; the spirit, which had animated his public conduct, was shown in the active and affectionate performance of every social duty; and the diligence of the soldier was profitably converted to the improvement of his ample patrimony, [111] which lay between Valladolid and Segovia, in the midst of a fruitful district, still famous for a most exquisite breed of sheep. [112] From the innocent, but humble labors of his farm, Theodosius was transported, in less than four months, to the throne of the Eastern empire; and the whole period of the history of the world will not perhaps afford a similar example, of an elevation at the same time so pure and so honorable. The princes who peaceably inherit the sceptre of their fathers, claim and enjoy a legal right, the more secure as it is absolutely distinct from the merits of their personal characters. The subjects, who, in a monarchy, or a popular state, acquire the possession of supreme power, may have raised themselves, by the superiority either of genius or virtue, above the heads of their equals; but their virtue is seldom exempt from ambition; and the cause of the successful candidate is frequently stained by the guilt of conspiracy, or civil war. Even in those governments which allow the reigning monarch to declare a colleague or a successor, his partial choice, which may be influenced by the blindest passions, is often directed to an unworthy object But the most suspicious malignity cannot ascribe to Theodosius, in his obscure solitude of Caucha, the arts, the desires, or even the hopes, of an ambitious statesman; and the name of the Exile would long since have been forgotten, if his genuine and distinguished virtues had not left a deep impression in the Imperial court. During the season of prosperity, he had been neglected; but, in the public distress, his superior merit was universally felt and acknowledged. What confidence must have been reposed in his integrity, since Gratian could trust, that a pious son would forgive, for the sake of the republic, the murder of his father! What expectations must have been formed of his abilities to encourage the hope, that a single man could save, and restore, the empire of the East! Theodosius was invested with the purple in the thirty-third year of his age. The vulgar gazed with admiration on the manly beauty of his face, and the graceful majesty of his person, which they were pleased to compare with the pictures and medals of the emperor Trajan; whilst intelligent observers discovered, in the qualities of his heart and understanding, a more important resemblance to the best and greatest of the Roman princes.

[Footnote 107: Italica, founded by Scipio Africanus for his wounded veterans of Italy. The ruins still appear, about a league above Seville, but on the opposite bank of the river. See the Hispania Illustrata of Nonius, a short though valuable treatise, c. xvii. p. 64—67.]

[Footnote 108: I agree with Tillemont (Hist. des Empereurs, tom. v. p. 726) in suspecting the royal pedigree, which remained a secret till the promotion of Theodosius. Even after that event, the silence of Pacatus outweighs the venal evidence of Themistius, Victor, and Claudian, who connect the family of Theodosius with the blood of Trajan and Hadrian.]

[Footnote 109: Pacatas compares, and consequently prefers, the youth of Theodosius to the military education of Alexander, Hannibal, and the second Africanus; who, like him, had served under their fathers, (xii. 8.)]

[Footnote 110: Ammianus (xxix. 6) mentions this victory of Theodosius Junior Dux Maesiae, prima etiam tum lanugine juvenis, princeps postea perspectissimus. The same fact is attested by Themistius and Zosimus but Theodoret, (l. v. c. 5,) who adds some curious circumstances, strangely applies it to the time of the interregnum.]

[Footnote 111: Pacatus (in Panegyr. Vet. xii. 9) prefers the rustic life of Theodosius to that of Cincinnatus; the one was the effect of choice, the other of poverty.]

[Footnote 112: M. D'Anville (Geographie Ancienne, tom. i. p. 25) has fixed the situation of Caucha, or Coca, in the old province of Gallicia, where Zosimus and Idatius have placed the birth, or patrimony, of Theodosius.]

It is not without the most sincere regret, that I must now take leave of an accurate and faithful guide, who has composed the history of his own times, without indulging the prejudices and passions, which usually affect the mind of a contemporary. Ammianus Marcellinus, who terminates his useful work with the defeat and death of Valens, recommends the more glorious subject of the ensuing reign to the youthful vigor and eloquence of the rising generation. [113] The rising generation was not disposed to accept his advice or to imitate his example; [114] and, in the study of the reign of Theodosius, we are reduced to illustrate the partial narrative of Zosimus, by the obscure hints of fragments and chronicles, by the figurative style of poetry or panegyric, and by the precarious assistance of the ecclesiastical writers, who, in the heat of religious faction, are apt to despise the profane virtues of sincerity and moderation. Conscious of these disadvantages, which will continue to involve a considerable portion of the decline and fall of the Roman empire, I shall proceed with doubtful and timorous steps. Yet I may boldly pronounce, that the battle of Hadrianople was never revenged by any signal or decisive victory of Theodosius over the Barbarians: and the expressive silence of his venal orators may be confirmed by the observation of the condition and circumstances of the times. The fabric of a mighty state, which has been reared by the labors of successive ages, could not be overturned by the misfortune of a single day, if the fatal power of the imagination did not exaggerate the real measure of the calamity. The loss of forty thousand Romans, who fell in the plains of Hadrianople, might have been soon recruited in the populous provinces of the East, which contained so many millions of inhabitants. The courage of a soldier is found to be the cheapest, and most common, quality of human nature; and sufficient skill to encounter an undisciplined foe might have been speedily taught by the care of the surviving centurions. If the Barbarians were mounted on the horses, and equipped with the armor, of their vanquished enemies, the numerous studs of Cappadocia and Spain would have supplied new squadrons of cavalry; the thirty-four arsenals of the empire were plentifully stored with magazines of offensive and defensive arms: and the wealth of Asia might still have yielded an ample fund for the expenses of the war. But the effects which were produced by the battle of Hadrianople on the minds of the Barbarians and of the Romans, extended the victory of the former, and the defeat of the latter, far beyond the limits of a single day. A Gothic chief was heard to declare, with insolent moderation, that, for his own part, he was fatigued with slaughter: but that he was astonished how a people, who fled before him like a flock of sheep, could still presume to dispute the possession of their treasures and provinces. [115] The same terrors which the name of the Huns had spread among the Gothic tribes, were inspired, by the formidable name of the Goths, among the subjects and soldiers of the Roman empire. [116] If Theodosius, hastily collecting his scattered forces, had led them into the field to encounter a victorious enemy, his army would have been vanquished by their own fears; and his rashness could not have been excused by the chance of success. But the great Theodosius, an epithet which he honorably deserved on this momentous occasion, conducted himself as the firm and faithful guardian of the republic. He fixed his head-quarters at Thessalonica, the capital of the Macedonian diocese; [117] from whence he could watch the irregular motions of the Barbarians, and direct the operations of his lieutenants, from the gates of Constantinople to the shores of the Hadriatic. The fortifications and garrisons of the cities were strengthened; and the troops, among whom a sense of order and discipline was revived, were insensibly emboldened by the confidence of their own safety. From these secure stations, they were encouraged to make frequent sallies on the Barbarians, who infested the adjacent country; and, as they were seldom allowed to engage, without some decisive superiority, either of ground or of numbers, their enterprises were, for the most part, successful; and they were soon convinced, by their own experience, of the possibility of vanquishing their invincible enemies. The detachments of these separate garrisons were generally united into small armies; the same cautious measures were pursued, according to an extensive and well-concerted plan of operations; the events of each day added strength and spirit to the Roman arms; and the artful diligence of the emperor, who circulated the most favorable reports of the success of the war, contributed to subdue the pride of the Barbarians, and to animate the hopes and courage of his subjects. If, instead of this faint and imperfect outline, we could accurately represent the counsels and actions of Theodosius, in four successive campaigns, there is reason to believe, that his consummate skill would deserve the applause of every military reader. The republic had formerly been saved by the delays of Fabius; and, while the splendid trophies of Scipio, in the field of Zama, attract the eyes of posterity, the camps and marches of the dictator among the hills of the Campania, may claim a juster proportion of the solid and independent fame, which the general is not compelled to share, either with fortune or with his troops. Such was likewise the merit of Theodosius; and the infirmities of his body, which most unseasonably languished under a long and dangerous disease, could not oppress the vigor of his mind, or divert his attention from the public service. [118]

[Footnote 113: Let us hear Ammianus himself. Haec, ut miles quondam et Graecus, a principatu Cassaris Nervae exorsus, adusque Valentis inter, pro virium explicavi mensura: opus veritatem professum nun quam, ut arbitror, sciens, silentio ausus corrumpere vel mendacio. Scribant reliqua potiores aetate, doctrinisque florentes. Quos id, si libuerit, aggressuros, procudere linguas ad majores moneo stilos. Ammian. xxxi. 16. The first thirteen books, a superficial epitome of two hundred and fifty-seven years, are now lost: the last eighteen, which contain no more than twenty-five years, still preserve the copious and authentic history of his own times.]

[Footnote 114: Ammianus was the last subject of Rome who composed a profane history in the Latin language. The East, in the next century, produced some rhetorical historians, Zosimus, Olympiedorus, Malchus, Candidus &c. See Vossius de Historicis Graecis, l. ii. c. 18, de Historicis Latinis l. ii. c. 10, &c.]

[Footnote 115: Chrysostom, tom. i. p. 344, edit. Montfaucon. I have verified and examined this passage: but I should never, without the aid of Tillemont, (Hist. des Emp. tom. v. p. 152,) have detected an historical anecdote, in a strange medley of moral and mystic exhortations, addressed, by the preacher of Antioch, to a young widow.]

[Footnote 116: Eunapius, in Excerpt. Legation. p. 21.]

[Footnote 117: See Godefroy's Chronology of the Laws. Codex Theodos tom. l. Prolegomen. p. xcix—civ.]

[Footnote 118: Most writers insist on the illness, and long repose, of Theodosius, at Thessalonica: Zosimus, to diminish his glory; Jornandes, to favor the Goths; and the ecclesiastical writers, to introduce his baptism.]

The deliverance and peace of the Roman provinces [119] was the work of prudence, rather than of valor: the prudence of Theodosius was seconded by fortune: and the emperor never failed to seize, and to improve, every favorable circumstance. As long as the superior genius of Fritigern preserved the union, and directed the motions of the Barbarians, their power was not inadequate to the conquest of a great empire. The death of that hero, the predecessor and master of the renowned Alaric, relieved an impatient multitude from the intolerable yoke of discipline and discretion. The Barbarians, who had been restrained by his authority, abandoned themselves to the dictates of their passions; and their passions were seldom uniform or consistent. An army of conquerors was broken into many disorderly bands of savage robbers; and their blind and irregular fury was not less pernicious to themselves, than to their enemies. Their mischievous disposition was shown in the destruction of every object which they wanted strength to remove, or taste to enjoy; and they often consumed, with improvident rage, the harvests, or the granaries, which soon afterwards became necessary for their own subsistence. A spirit of discord arose among the independent tribes and nations, which had been united only by the bands of a loose and voluntary alliance. The troops of the Huns and the Alani would naturally upbraid the flight of the Goths; who were not disposed to use with moderation the advantages of their fortune; the ancient jealousy of the Ostrogoths and the Visigoths could not long be suspended; and the haughty chiefs still remembered the insults and injuries, which they had reciprocally offered, or sustained, while the nation was seated in the countries beyond the Danube. The progress of domestic faction abated the more diffusive sentiment of national animosity; and the officers of Theodosius were instructed to purchase, with liberal gifts and promises, the retreat or service of the discontented party. The acquisition of Modar, a prince of the royal blood of the Amali, gave a bold and faithful champion to the cause of Rome. The illustrious deserter soon obtained the rank of master-general, with an important command; surprised an army of his countrymen, who were immersed in wine and sleep; and, after a cruel slaughter of the astonished Goths, returned with an immense spoil, and four thousand wagons, to the Imperial camp. [120] In the hands of a skilful politician, the most different means may be successfully applied to the same ends; and the peace of the empire, which had been forwarded by the divisions, was accomplished by the reunion, of the Gothic nation. Athanaric, who had been a patient spectator of these extraordinary events, was at length driven, by the chance of arms, from the dark recesses of the woods of Caucaland. He no longer hesitated to pass the Danube; and a very considerable part of the subjects of Fritigern, who already felt the inconveniences of anarchy, were easily persuaded to acknowledge for their king a Gothic Judge, whose birth they respected, and whose abilities they had frequently experienced. But age had chilled the daring spirit of Athanaric; and, instead of leading his people to the field of battle and victory, he wisely listened to the fair proposal of an honorable and advantageous treaty. Theodosius, who was acquainted with the merit and power of his new ally, condescended to meet him at the distance of several miles from Constantinople; and entertained him in the Imperial city, with the confidence of a friend, and the magnificence of a monarch. "The Barbarian prince observed, with curious attention, the variety of objects which attracted his notice, and at last broke out into a sincere and passionate exclamation of wonder. I now behold (said he) what I never could believe, the glories of this stupendous capital! And as he cast his eyes around, he viewed, and he admired, the commanding situation of the city, the strength and beauty of the walls and public edifices, the capacious harbor, crowded with innumerable vessels, the perpetual concourse of distant nations, and the arms and discipline of the troops. Indeed, (continued Athanaric,) the emperor of the Romans is a god upon earth; and the presumptuous man, who dares to lift his hand against him, is guilty of his own blood." [121] The Gothic king did not long enjoy this splendid and honorable reception; and, as temperance was not the virtue of his nation, it may justly be suspected, that his mortal disease was contracted amidst the pleasures of the Imperial banquets. But the policy of Theodosius derived more solid benefit from the death, than he could have expected from the most faithful services, of his ally. The funeral of Athanaric was performed with solemn rites in the capital of the East; a stately monument was erected to his memory; and his whole army, won by the liberal courtesy, and decent grief, of Theodosius, enlisted under the standard of the Roman empire. [122] The submission of so great a body of the Visigoths was productive of the most salutary consequences; and the mixed influence of force, of reason, and of corruption, became every day more powerful, and more extensive. Each independent chieftain hastened to obtain a separate treaty, from the apprehension that an obstinate delay might expose him, alone and unprotected, to the revenge, or justice, of the conqueror. The general, or rather the final, capitulation of the Goths, may be dated four years, one month, and twenty-five days, after the defeat and death of the emperor Valens. [123]

[Footnote 119: Compare Themistius (Orat, xiv. p. 181) with Zosimus (l. iv. p. 232,) Jornandes, (c. xxvii. p. 649,) and the prolix Commentary of M. de Buat, (Hist. de Peuples, &c., tom. vi. p. 477—552.) The Chronicles of Idatius and Marcellinus allude, in general terms, to magna certamina, magna multaque praelia. The two epithets are not easily reconciled.]

[Footnote 120: Zosimus (l. iv. p. 232) styles him a Scythian, a name which the more recent Greeks seem to have appropriated to the Goths.]

[Footnote 121: The reader will not be displeased to see the original words of Jornandes, or the author whom he transcribed. Regiam urbem ingressus est, miransque, En, inquit, cerno quod saepe incredulus audiebam, famam videlicet tantae urbis. Et huc illuc oculos volvens, nunc situm urbis, commeatumque navium, nunc moenia clara pro spectans, miratur; populosque diversarum gentium, quasi fonte in uno e diversis partibus scaturiente unda, sic quoque militem ordinatum aspiciens; Deus, inquit, sine dubio est terrenus Imperator, et quisquis adversus eum manum moverit, ipse sui sanguinis reus existit Jornandes (c. xxviii. p. 650) proceeds to mention his death and funeral.]

[Footnote 122: Jornandes, c. xxviii. p. 650. Even Zosimus (l. v. p. 246) is compelled to approve the generosity of Theodosius, so honorable to himself, and so beneficial to the public.]

[Footnote 123: The short, but authentic, hints in the Fasti of Idatius (Chron. Scaliger. p. 52) are stained with contemporary passion. The fourteenth oration of Themistius is a compliment to Peace, and the consul Saturninus, (A.D. 383.)]

The provinces of the Danube had been already relieved from the oppressive weight of the Gruthungi, or Ostrogoths, by the voluntary retreat of Alatheus and Saphrax, whose restless spirit had prompted them to seek new scenes of rapine and glory. Their destructive course was pointed towards the West; but we must be satisfied with a very obscure and imperfect knowledge of their various adventures. The Ostrogoths impelled several of the German tribes on the provinces of Gaul; concluded, and soon violated, a treaty with the emperor Gratian; advanced into the unknown countries of the North; and, after an interval of more than four years, returned, with accumulated force, to the banks of the Lower Danube. Their troops were recruited with the fiercest warriors of Germany and Scythia; and the soldiers, or at least the historians, of the empire, no longer recognized the name and countenances of their former enemies. [124] The general who commanded the military and naval powers of the Thracian frontier, soon perceived that his superiority would be disadvantageous to the public service; and that the Barbarians, awed by the presence of his fleet and legions, would probably defer the passage of the river till the approaching winter. The dexterity of the spies, whom he sent into the Gothic camp, allured the Barbarians into a fatal snare. They were persuaded that, by a bold attempt, they might surprise, in the silence and darkness of the night, the sleeping army of the Romans; and the whole multitude was hastily embarked in a fleet of three thousand canoes. [125] The bravest of the Ostrogoths led the van; the main body consisted of the remainder of their subjects and soldiers; and the women and children securely followed in the rear. One of the nights without a moon had been selected for the execution of their design; and they had almost reached the southern bank of the Danube, in the firm confidence that they should find an easy landing and an unguarded camp. But the progress of the Barbarians was suddenly stopped by an unexpected obstacle a triple line of vessels, strongly connected with each other, and which formed an impenetrable chain of two miles and a half along the river. While they struggled to force their way in the unequal conflict, their right flank was overwhelmed by the irresistible attack of a fleet of galleys, which were urged down the stream by the united impulse of oars and of the tide. The weight and velocity of those ships of war broke, and sunk, and dispersed, the rude and feeble canoes of the Barbarians; their valor was ineffectual; and Alatheus, the king, or general, of the Ostrogoths, perished with his bravest troops, either by the sword of the Romans, or in the waves of the Danube. The last division of this unfortunate fleet might regain the opposite shore; but the distress and disorder of the multitude rendered them alike incapable, either of action or counsel; and they soon implored the clemency of the victorious enemy. On this occasion, as well as on many others, it is a difficult task to reconcile the passions and prejudices of the writers of the age of Theodosius. The partial and malignant historian, who misrepresents every action of his reign, affirms, that the emperor did not appear in the field of battle till the Barbarians had been vanquished by the valor and conduct of his lieutenant Promotus. [126] The flattering poet, who celebrated, in the court of Honorius, the glory of the father and of the son, ascribes the victory to the personal prowess of Theodosius; and almost insinuates, that the king of the Ostrogoths was slain by the hand of the emperor. [127] The truth of history might perhaps be found in a just medium between these extreme and contradictory assertions.

[Footnote 124: Zosimus, l. iv. p. 252.]

[Footnote 125: I am justified, by reason and example, in applying this Indian name to the the Barbarians, the single trees hollowed into the shape of a boat. Zosimus, l. iv. p. 253. Ausi Danubium quondam tranare Gruthungi In lintres fregere nemus: ter mille ruebant Per fluvium plenae cuneis immanibus alni. Claudian, in iv. Cols. Hon. 623.]

[Footnote 126: Zosimus, l. iv. p. 252—255. He too frequently betrays his poverty of judgment by disgracing the most serious narratives with trifling and incredible circumstances.]

[Footnote 127:—Odothaei Regis opima Retulit—Ver. 632. The opima were the spoils which a Roman general could only win from the king, or general, of the enemy, whom he had slain with his own hands: and no more than three such examples are celebrated in the victorious ages of Rome.]

The original treaty which fixed the settlement of the Goths, ascertained their privileges, and stipulated their obligations, would illustrate the history of Theodosius and his successors. The series of their history has imperfectly preserved the spirit and substance of this single agreement. [128] The ravages of war and tyranny had provided many large tracts of fertile but uncultivated land for the use of those Barbarians who might not disdain the practice of agriculture. A numerous colony of the Visigoths was seated in Thrace; the remains of the Ostrogoths were planted in Phrygia and Lydia; their immediate wants were supplied by a distribution of corn and cattle; and their future industry was encouraged by an exemption from tribute, during a certain term of years. The Barbarians would have deserved to feel the cruel and perfidious policy of the Imperial court, if they had suffered themselves to be dispersed through the provinces. They required, and they obtained, the sole possession of the villages and districts assigned for their residence; they still cherished and propagated their native manners and language; asserted, in the bosom of despotism, the freedom of their domestic government; and acknowledged the sovereignty of the emperor, without submitting to the inferior jurisdiction of the laws and magistrates of Rome. The hereditary chiefs of the tribes and families were still permitted to command their followers in peace and war; but the royal dignity was abolished; and the generals of the Goths were appointed and removed at the pleasure of the emperor. An army of forty thousand Goths was maintained for the perpetual service of the empire of the East; and those haughty troops, who assumed the title of Foederati, or allies, were distinguished by their gold collars, liberal pay, and licentious privileges. Their native courage was improved by the use of arms and the knowledge of discipline; and, while the republic was guarded, or threatened, by the doubtful sword of the Barbarians, the last sparks of the military flame were finally extinguished in the minds of the Romans. [129] Theodosius had the address to persuade his allies, that the conditions of peace, which had been extorted from him by prudence and necessity, were the voluntary expressions of his sincere friendship for the Gothic nation. [130] A different mode of vindication or apology was opposed to the complaints of the people; who loudly censured these shameful and dangerous concessions. [131] The calamities of the war were painted in the most lively colors; and the first symptoms of the return of order, of plenty, and security, were diligently exaggerated. The advocates of Theodosius could affirm, with some appearance of truth and reason, that it was impossible to extirpate so many warlike tribes, who were rendered desperate by the loss of their native country; and that the exhausted provinces would be revived by a fresh supply of soldiers and husbandmen. The Barbarians still wore an angry and hostile aspect; but the experience of past times might encourage the hope, that they would acquire the habits of industry and obedience; that their manners would be polished by time, education, and the influence of Christianity; and that their posterity would insensibly blend with the great body of the Roman people. [132]

[Footnote 128: See Themistius, Orat. xvi. p. 211. Claudian (in Eutrop. l. ii. 112) mentions the Phrygian colony:—Ostrogothis colitur mistisque Gruthungis Phyrx ager—and then proceeds to name the rivers of Lydia, the Pactolus, and Herreus.]

[Footnote 129: Compare Jornandes, (c. xx. 27,) who marks the condition and number of the Gothic Foederati, with Zosimus, (l. iv. p. 258,) who mentions their golden collars; and Pacatus, (in Panegyr. Vet. xii. 37,) who applauds, with false or foolish joy, their bravery and discipline.]

[Footnote 130: Amator pacis generisque Gothorum, is the praise bestowed by the Gothic historian, (c. xxix.,) who represents his nation as innocent, peaceable men, slow to anger, and patient of injuries. According to Livy, the Romans conquered the world in their own defence.]

[Footnote 131: Besides the partial invectives of Zosimus, (always discontented with the Christian reigns,) see the grave representations which Synesius addresses to the emperor Arcadius, (de Regno, p. 25, 26, edit. Petav.) The philosophic bishop of Cyrene was near enough to judge; and he was sufficiently removed from the temptation of fear or flattery.]

[Footnote 132: Themistius (Orat. xvi. p. 211, 212) composes an elaborate and rational apology, which is not, however, exempt from the puerilities of Greek rhetoric. Orpheus could only charm the wild beasts of Thrace; but Theodosius enchanted the men and women, whose predecessors in the same country had torn Orpheus in pieces, &c.]

Notwithstanding these specious arguments, and these sanguine expectations, it was apparent to every discerning eye, that the Goths would long remain the enemies, and might soon become the conquerors of the Roman empire. Their rude and insolent behavior expressed their contempt of the citizens and provincials, whom they insulted with impunity. [133] To the zeal and valor of the Barbarians Theodosius was indebted for the success of his arms: but their assistance was precarious; and they were sometimes seduced, by a treacherous and inconstant disposition, to abandon his standard, at the moment when their service was the most essential. During the civil war against Maximus, a great number of Gothic deserters retired into the morasses of Macedonia, wasted the adjacent provinces, and obliged the intrepid monarch to expose his person, and exert his power, to suppress the rising flame of rebellion. [134] The public apprehensions were fortified by the strong suspicion, that these tumults were not the effect of accidental passion, but the result of deep and premeditated design. It was generally believed, that the Goths had signed the treaty of peace with a hostile and insidious spirit; and that their chiefs had previously bound themselves, by a solemn and secret oath, never to keep faith with the Romans; to maintain the fairest show of loyalty and friendship, and to watch the favorable moment of rapine, of conquest, and of revenge. But as the minds of the Barbarians were not insensible to the power of gratitude, several of the Gothic leaders sincerely devoted themselves to the service of the empire, or, at least, of the emperor; the whole nation was insensibly divided into two opposite factions, and much sophistry was employed in conversation and dispute, to compare the obligations of their first, and second, engagements. The Goths, who considered themselves as the friends of peace, of justice, and of Rome, were directed by the authority of Fravitta, a valiant and honorable youth, distinguished above the rest of his countrymen by the politeness of his manners, the liberality of his sentiments, and the mild virtues of social life. But the more numerous faction adhered to the fierce and faithless Priulf, [134a] who inflamed the passions, and asserted the independence, of his warlike followers. On one of the solemn festivals, when the chiefs of both parties were invited to the Imperial table, they were insensibly heated by wine, till they forgot the usual restraints of discretion and respect, and betrayed, in the presence of Theodosius, the fatal secret of their domestic disputes. The emperor, who had been the reluctant witness of this extraordinary controversy, dissembled his fears and resentment, and soon dismissed the tumultuous assembly. Fravitta, alarmed and exasperated by the insolence of his rival, whose departure from the palace might have been the signal of a civil war, boldly followed him; and, drawing his sword, laid Priulf dead at his feet. Their companions flew to arms; and the faithful champion of Rome would have been oppressed by superior numbers, if he had not been protected by the seasonable interposition of the Imperial guards. [135] Such were the scenes of Barbaric rage, which disgraced the palace and table of the Roman emperor; and, as the impatient Goths could only be restrained by the firm and temperate character of Theodosius, the public safety seemed to depend on the life and abilities of a single man. [136]

[Footnote 133: Constantinople was deprived half a day of the public allowance of bread, to expiate the murder of a Gothic soldier: was the guilt of the people. Libanius, Orat. xii. p. 394, edit. Morel.]

[Footnote 134: Zosimus, l. iv. p. 267-271. He tells a long and ridiculous story of the adventurous prince, who roved the country with only five horsemen, of a spy whom they detected, whipped, and killed in an old woman's cottage, &c.]

[Footnote 134a: Eunapius—M.]

[Footnote 135: Compare Eunapius (in Excerpt. Legat. p. 21, 22) with Zosimus, (l. iv. p. 279.) The difference of circumstances and names must undoubtedly be applied to the same story. Fravitta, or Travitta, was afterwards consul, (A.D. 401.) and still continued his faithful services to the eldest son of Theodosius. (Tillemont, Hist. des Empereurs, tom. v. p. 467.)]

[Footnote 136: Les Goths ravagerent tout depuis le Danube jusqu'au Bosphore; exterminerent Valens et son armee; et ne repasserent le Danube, que pour abandonner l'affreuse solitude qu'ils avoient faite, (Oeuvres de Montesquieu, tom. iii. p. 479. Considerations sur les Causes de la Grandeur et de la Decadence des Romains, c. xvii.) The president Montesquieu seems ignorant that the Goths, after the defeat of Valens, never abandoned the Roman territory. It is now thirty years, says Claudian, (de Bello Getico, 166, &c., A.D. 404,) Ex quo jam patrios gens haec oblita Triones, Atque Istrum transvecta semel, vestigia fixit Threicio funesta solo—the error is inexcusable; since it disguises the principal and immediate cause of the fall of the Western empire of Rome.]

EDWARD GIBBON – A SHORT BIOGRAPHY

Edward Gibbon was born on 8th May, 1737, the son of Edward and Judith Gibbon at Lime Grove, in the town of Putney, Surrey. He had six siblings, all of whom died in infancy. His grandfather, also named Edward, had lost everything as a result of the South Sea Bubble collapse in 1720, but eventually regained much of his wealth, so that Gibbon's father was able to inherit a substantial estate.

As a youth, Gibbon's health was under constant threat. He described himself as "a puny child, neglected by my Mother, starved by my nurse". At age nine, he was sent to Dr. Woddeson's school at Kingston-upon-Thames, shortly after which his mother died. He was then moved to the Westminster School boarding house, owned by his adored "Aunt Kitty", Catherine Porten.

By 1751, Gibbon's reading was already extensive and certainly pointed toward his future pursuits having covered such works as Laurence Echard's Roman History (1713), William Howell's An Institution of General History (1680–85), and several of the 65 volumes of the acclaimed Universal History from the Earliest Account of Time (1747–1768).

Following a stay at Bath, at age 15, in 1752 to improve his health, Gibbon was sent by his father to Magdalen College, Oxford, where he was enrolled as a gentleman-commoner (a rank of student above commoners i.e. normal students who paid the normal rate for tuition and boarding but below noblemen. They paid double the tuition fee and enjoyed more privileges). He was ill-suited, however, to the college atmosphere and later rued his 14 months there as the "most idle and unprofitable" of his life. Because of his autobiography, it used to be thought that his penchant for "theological controversy" (his aunt's influence) fully bloomed when he came under the spell of the deist or rationalist theologian Conyers Middleton, the author of Free Inquiry into the Miraculous Powers (1749). In that tract, Middleton denied the validity of such powers; Gibbon promptly objected, or so the argument used to run. The product of that disagreement, with some assistance from the work of Catholic Bishop Jacques-Bénigne Bossuet, and that of the Elizabethan Jesuit Robert Parsons, yielded the most memorable event of his time at Oxford: his conversion to Roman Catholicism on 8th June 1753. He was further 'corrupted' by the 'free thinking' deism of the playwright/poet couple David and Lucy Mallet; and finally Gibbon's father, already deeply in despair, had had enough.

However, this story has fallen somewhat into disrepute only being introduced to the final draft of Gibbon's "Memoirs" in 1792–93. There are also other accounts as to why Gibbons may have given a new 'backstory' to his conversion.

Within weeks of his conversion, the Gibbons was removed from Oxford and sent to live under the care and tutelage of Daniel Pavillard, Reformed pastor of Lausanne in Switzerland.

Here he made great friendships with Jacques Georges Deyverdun (the French-language translator of Goethe's The Sorrows of Young Werther), and John Baker Holroyd (later Lord Sheffield).

Just a year and a half later, after his father threatened to disinherit him, on Christmas Day, 1754, he reconverted to Protestantism. "The various articles of the Romish creed," he wrote, "disappeared like a dream".

He remained in Lausanne for five intellectually productive years, a period that greatly enriched Gibbon's already immense aptitude for scholarship and erudition: he read Latin literature; travelled throughout Switzerland studying its cantons' constitutions; and studied the works of Hugo Grotius, Samuel von Pufendorf, John Locke, Pierre Bayle, and Blaise Pascal.

He also met the one love in his life: the daughter of the pastor of Crassy; Suzanne Curchod. As the two developed an ever-closer relationship; Gibbon raised the question of marriage, but ultimately wedlock was out of the question, blocked both by his father's staunch disapproval and Curchod's refusal to leave Switzerland.

Gibbon returned to England in August 1758 to face his father. There was to be no refusal of his wishes. Gibbon put it rather poetically: "I sighed as a lover, I obeyed as a son." He proceeded to cut off all contact with Suzanne, even as she vowed to wait for him.

Upon his return to England, Gibbon published his first book, Essai sur l'Étude de la Littérature in 1761, which produced an initial taste of celebrity and distinguished him, in Paris at least, as a man of letters.

Interestingly to add to his interests and talents he had, from 1759 to 1770, served on active duty and then in reserve with the South Hampshire militia, his deactivation in December 1762 coinciding with the militia's dispersal after the Seven Years' War.

In 1763, he began as many men of privilege of class then did to round out and embellish their education on the Grand Tour, which included a visit to Rome. In his autobiography Gibbon vividly records his rapture when he finally neared "the great object of my pilgrimage": ...at the distance of twenty-five years I can neither forget nor express the strong emotions which agitated my mind as I first approached and entered the eternal City. After a sleepless night, I trod, with a lofty step the ruins of the Forum; each memorable spot where Romulus stood, or Tully spoke, or Caesar fell, was at once present to my eye; and several days of intoxication were lost or enjoyed before I could descend to a cool and minute investigation.

And it was here that Gibbon first conceived the idea of composing a history of the city, later extended to the entire empire, a moment known to history as the Capitoline vision: "It was at Rome, on the 15th of October 1764, as I sat musing amidst the ruins of the Capitol, while the barefooted fryars were singing Vespers in the temple of Jupiter, that the idea of writing the decline and fall of the City first started to my mind".

In June 1765, Gibbon returned to his father's house. He would remain there for the following five years until his father's death. He always considered this span of time as the worst of his life. He busied himself with various writing projects which failed to reach fruition. His first historical narrative, the History of Switzerland, was neither published nor finished. Gibbon had become too self-critical and abandoned the work a mere 60 pages in.

His second work, Memoires Litteraires de la Grande Bretagne, in two volumes, described both the literary and the social conditions of England at the time. When published it failed to gain any traction.

With the death of his father and the settling of the estate Gibbon had enough of a legacy to be free of any financial problems. He moved to Bentinck Street in London and began to live the life that suited him. He joined a number of clubs, including Dr. Johnson's Literary Club. He succeeded Oliver Goldsmith at the Royal Academy as 'professor in ancient history' (honorary but nonetheless prestigious). And he was writing. The work for which he would gain worldwide fame was under way.

But still other interests would divert his attention.

In late 1774, he was initiated a freemason of the Premier Grand Lodge of England. That same year he was returned to Parliament for the seat of Liskeard in Cornwall through the intervention of his relative and patron, Edward Eliot. Gibbon became a typical backbencher, mute and indifferent to his responsibilities, apart from routinely voting for the Whig Administration.

After several rewrites usually brought on by self-doubt and seven years of work the first volume of The History of the Decline and Fall of the Roman Empire, was published on 17th February 1776.

It was an immediate success. Within a year it had gone through three editions and the royalties were very handsome indeed.

Further volumes followed quickly and with the same measure of success; Volumes II and III were published on 1st March 1781, and volume IV was released in June 1784. Volumes V and VI were completed during a second Lausanne sojourn (September 1783 to August 1787) where Gibbon reunited with his friend Deyverdun. By early 1787, he was "straining for the goal" and with great relief the project was finished in June. Gibbon later wrote: "It was on the day, or rather the night, of 27th June 1787, between the hours of eleven and twelve, that I wrote the last lines of the last page in a summer-house in my garden...I will not dissemble the first emotions of joy on the recovery of my freedom, and perhaps the establishment of my fame. But my pride was soon humbled, and a sober melancholy was spread over my mind by the idea that I had taken my everlasting leave of an old and agreeable companion, and that, whatsoever might be the future date of my history, the life of the historian must be short and precarious".

Volumes V, and VI finally reached the press in May 1788, their publication having been delayed since March, so it could coincide with a dinner party on the 8th celebrating Gibbon's 51st birthday.

Praise came from all directions. Leading it were such contemporary luminaries as Adam Smith, Lord Camden, and Horace Walpole. Smith remarked that Gibbon's triumph had positioned him "at the very head of Europe's literary tribe."

In November of that year, he was elected a Fellow of the Royal Society, the main proposer being his good friend Lord Sheffield.

But the high-water mark had been reached and for Gibbon the following years were of sorrow and increasing health problems.

In 1789 he returned to Lausanne only to learn of and be "deeply affected" by the death of Deyverdun, who had willed Gibbon his home, La Grotte. He resided there with little commotion, took in the local society, received a visit from Sheffield in 1791, and "shared the common abhorrence" of the French Revolution.

In a letter to Lord Sheffield on 5th February 1791, Gibbon praised Burke's Reflections on the Revolution in France: "Burke's book is a most admirable medicine against the French disease, which has made too much progress even in this happy country. I admire his eloquence, I approve his politics, I adore his chivalry, and I can even forgive his superstition...The French spread so many lyes about the sentiments of the English nation, that I wish the most considerable men of all parties and descriptions would join in some public act declaring themselves satisfied with, and resolved to support, our present constitution."

In 1793, word came of Lady Sheffield's death; Gibbon immediately left Lausanne and set sail to comfort a grieving but composed Sheffield. But for Gibbon too, time was failing. His health began to fail critically in December, and at the turn of the new year, he was in rapid decline.

Gibbon is believed to have suffered from an extreme case of scrotal swelling, probably a hydrocele testis, a condition in which the scrotum swell with fluid in a compartment overlying either testicle. In an age when close-fitting clothes were fashionable, his condition led to a chronic and disfiguring inflammation that left Gibbon a lonely figure. As his condition worsened, he underwent numerous procedures to alleviate the condition, but with no enduring success. In early January, the last of a series of three operations caused an unremitting peritonitis to set in and spread, from which he died.

Edward Gibbon, the "English giant of the Enlightenment" finally succumbed at 12:45 pm, 16 January 1794 at age 56. He was buried in the Sheffield Mausoleum attached to the north transept of the Church of St Mary and St Andrew, Fletching, East Sussex.

EDWARD GIBBON – A CONCISE BIBLIOGRAPHY

Essai sur l'Étude de la Littérature (1761)
Critical Observations on the Sixth Book of Vergil's 'The Aeneid' (1770)
The History of the Decline and Fall of the Roman Empire (Vol. I, 1776; Vols. II, III, 1781; Vols. IV, V, VI, 1788–1789)
A Vindication of some passages in the fifteenth and sixteenth chapters of the History of the Decline and Fall of the Roman Empire (1779)
Mémoire Justificatif pour servir de Réponse à l'Exposé, etc. de la Cour de France (1779)
Mémoires Littéraires de la Grande-Bretagne. co-author: Georges Deyverdun (2 vols: vol. 1, 1767; vol. 2, 1768)
Miscellaneous Works of Edward Gibbon, Esq., ed. John Lord Sheffield (2 vols., 1796; 5 vols., 1814; 3 vols., 1815) Includes Memoirs of the Life and Writings of Edward Gibbon, Esq.
Autobiographies of Edward Gibbon, ed. John Murray (1896). Edward Gibbon's complete memoirs (six drafts) from the original manuscripts.
The Private Letters of Edward Gibbon, 2 vols., ed. Rowland E. Prothero (1896)
The works of Edward Gibbon (Volume 3, 1906)
Gibbon's Journal to 28 January 1763, ed. D.M. Low (1929)
Le Journal de Gibbon à Lausanne, ed. Georges A. Bonnard (1945)
Miscellanea Gibboniana, eds. G.R. de Beer, L. Junod, G.A. Bonnard (1952)
The Letters of Edward Gibbon, 3 vols., ed. J.E. Norton (1956). vol. 1: 1750–1773; vol. 2: 1774–1784; vol. 3: 1784–1794. cited as 'Norton, Letters'
Gibbon's Journey from Geneva to Rome, ed. G.A. Bonnard (1961) Journal
Edward Gibbon: Memoirs of My Life, ed. G.A. Bonnard (1969; 1966). portions of Edward Gibbon's memoirs arranged chronologically, omitting repetition.
The English Essays of Edward Gibbon, ed. Patricia Craddock (1972)

www.ingramcontent.com/pod-product-compliance
Lightning Source LLC
Chambersburg PA
CBHW050118170426
43197CB00011B/1634